ERYKAH BADU

THE FIRST LADY OF NEO-SOUL

Printed in the United Kingdom by MPG Books, Bodmin

Published by Sanctuary Publishing Limited, Sanctuary House, 45–53 Sinclair Road, London W14 0NS, United Kingdom

www.sanctuarypublishing.com

Photographs courtesy of London Features International, Tim Mosenfelder/CORBIS, LADN/Tina Burch/CORBIS, SYGMA and Big Pictures.

Cover photograph courtesy of Camera Press/PEROU

ISBN: 1-86074-385-4

ERYKAH BADU

THE FIRST LADY OF NEO-SOUL

Joel McIver

Sanctuary

Contents

Dedicated to the memory of 8 August 2002.
We live in hope because of you.

Introduction And Acknowledgements

Depending on when you're reading this, the 21st century is now at least three years old, and it's a strange time for popular music. Almost every strand of it has undergone a shake-up in the last decade or so, with the new faces of rock, dance, metal, punk, funk and even plain old pop being so interchangeable that it's hard to tell where one ends and another begins. The latest genre to shed its skin and acquire a 'neo' prefix is the warmest and sweetest of all – soul – and at the very forefront of this polished new hybrid stands one artist, a Southern beauty with the voice of an angel, the intellect of a professor and the wisdom of someone three times her age.

Welcome to the story of Erykah Badu, which is an unlikely tale of someone who came from unglamorous roots but chose to go back to them, someone who knows full well the inspiring highs and crushing shallows of public opinion and someone who became known not just as an entertainer but as a prophet and innovator. Getting to know the doe-eyed woman behind the music isn't easy: on the one hand, she's never seen a reason to hide anything about her background, but on the other she seems to have an eerie knack for leaving interviewers with the impression that they've heard much but learned little. Perhaps it's her almost supernatural self-confidence – and perhaps it's best that way.

This book explores the background that made Erykah who she is, the events that brought her to the public's attention and the enormous surge of popularity that took her to the very apogee of popular music. In doing so, I believe it also reveals much about our society, our inspirations and ourselves. Keep your mind open, and enjoy the ride.

Doing her justice was no easy task, though – and it would have been an impossible one without the help of a lot of people. Like Erykah herself, those who know her best are warm, generous and pretty damn talented, and I salute them. My unlimited thanks go to the following for their help with this book:

Thor Christensen, music critic at the *Dallas Morning News*, who kindly permitted me to reproduce his articles from the *DMN*.

Chris Bell, recording engineer for many fine artists, including Badu.

Emmanuel Gillespie, who gave Erykah an early break.

Erykah's cousin and collaborator Robert 'Free' Bradford, for his time and efforts.

James at Colon Online (*www.colononline.com*).

Gillian Clayton at the excellent fansite dedicated to Erykah Badu at *www.anieclayton.freeserve.co.uk*.

Vicki Meek, manager of the South Dallas Cultural Center.

Rose Glenn, for her thoughts. Good luck with all your plans – Erykah is privileged to have fans like you.

Thanks as always to: Andy, Daryl, Tim, Jack, Jake and the other inmates at *Record Collector* magazine, Iain, Michelle, Laura and Penny at Sanctuary, John and Jen, Babs, Billy, Dan 'Blades' Travis, David, Arline and Lily, Simone, Woody and Glynis, Johnny, Lucy and Henry, Phil and Kate, Christian and Anita, the Bossmann-Everitt generations, Ben and Lorraine and Quinn 'Soul Boy' Harrington. Love to Robin and Dad – you're both good men.

Love to Emma – what doesn't kill us has certainly made us stronger.

Joel McIver
September 2002

Got a comment? Contact the author at *www.joelmciver.co.uk*.

1 Steeped In Soul

The lights go down, and there is a moment of hushed silence.

The eight shadowy figures on the stage start their song quietly, with drums and organ beginning a gentle groove and ushering in guitar, bass and percussion. It's a funky but subtle jam, with two backing singers picked out by a spotlight at centre stage, and though their voices are flawless it's hard to hear what they're singing, so perfectly do the words complement the music. After a minute, however, they pick it up a little and a chorus starts to stand out: 'Badu...Badu...' they're crooning, and the atmosphere in the auditorium suddenly feels a little more electric. In another minute or two, the crowd are on their feet. Something is about to happen.

Slowly, without any fuss, a figure appears from the shadows at the back of the stage. She's small – hardly more than 150cm (5ft) tall – and with the dimensions of a child, it seems; but she holds herself with absolute assurance. The glowing tip of an incense stick protrudes from beneath her wide-brimmed hat, and as the singer reaches the front of the stage, the audience recognise her face.

There's a white candle in a metal holder, placed on a small table near the microphone. Erykah takes the incense stick from her mouth and touches it to the wick. After a second, the candle bursts into flame.

The show has begun.

There's nothing particularly unusual about the North Park district in Dallas, except perhaps for the fact that it has no park. It's a small neighbourhood, maybe only 400m square (¼ mile square), with one or two shops but no high school, although there is a grade school for young children, and for still younger children there's a 'K through 6' (kindergarten up to sixth grade, for 4- to 11-year-olds). It's a predominantly black community surrounded by white neighbourhoods, a different situation to that of South Dallas, where most of the city's black population lives. Take a walk down any of the streets and the impression you would get might be that North Park isn't a wealthy community, but it isn't a ghetto either. There are few signs of urban decay and you can hear sounds of activity in the houses as you walk past.

There's one old house, set a little way back from the street, with more activity going on than the others. Think of a typical residence in the South – use *Gone With The Wind* as a reference if you like – and then imagine this house, with a big wooden front porch, a yard at the back and the front. It's in moderate condition: not freshly painted, but nor is it dilapidated. As for the atmosphere, it usually possesses an air of peace that befits its owner.

But not today. It's a special occasion and, while the children of the family (of which there are many) are normally told to stay in the room at the back of the house, leaving the front rooms for the older relations, today they seem to be everywhere. Walk a little closer and you'll see that attention is focused on the parlour, where the sounds of a piano can be heard. This isn't music as such – it's more the sounds of someone hitting the keys irregularly and excitedly, hoping for something approaching a tune to emerge as a result. Look closer still, and all is revealed. There's a toddler dressed in a red cowgirl outfit, sitting on a cushion on the piano stool, striking the keyboard and commanding her audience in imperious tones. 'Sing!' she demands. 'Sing, y'all!'

The date is 26 February 1973, and Erica Abie Wright is two years old today. If you don't believe in omens, now might be a good time to start.

Erica's mother, Kolleen Gipson-Wright, and her father, William Wright Jr, moved house often when their children were small, although they always remained within the limits of Dallas. Kolleen was an actress, appearing on stage in local theatres, and was respected for her talents. These were complemented by a self-assurance that had possibly been inherited from her mother, Thelma, who had worked as a school counsellor. Kolleen's profession might not have been the most lucrative in the world – or the most reliable – but it gave her the chance to devote her time between performances to her two daughters, Erica and Koryan (nicknamed Koko), who were born in 1971 and 1974 respectively. (Kolleen later bore a son, Eevin, in 1983.) Unfortunately, her husband William – who everyone referred to as 'Toosie' – was less dependable: it's known that he was often absent and that he spent time in jail for unknown misdemeanours.

In the early to mid-1970s, the demands of Kolleen's job and the uncertainty of Toosie's presence meant that the Wright sisters spent a lot of time at the North Park house belonging to their maternal grandmother, Thelma Gipson. They enjoyed themselves there, within the protective circle of their family, and Thelma – along with Toosie's mother, Viola, with whom she was firm friends – was at pains to ensure that they were shielded from the stress that Toosie's extended absences entailed. 'He wasn't around very much, not nearly as much as he should have been,' Viola later said. 'Much to his regret, and mine, too… [We] tried to keep them busy with constructive things,' she added, 'so they wouldn't miss him so much.' Not that they needed to keep them busy so much: like all children, the two girls ran around the garden, sang songs and played games without an apparent care in the world.

In 1975, however, Toosie decided to make a permanent exit and left his wife and children. Little is known about the circumstances of his departure, although he would resurface over two decades later and bond successfully with his eldest daughter. Although the impact on Kolleen and the other adults of the separation is bound to have been profound, Erica was barely aware of it, it seems. 'I never knew him, and I don't know much about him,' she later told *Vibe* magazine. However, when she herself became a mother a couple of years after that, her attitude towards Toosie's behaviour refocused slightly: 'I haven't had the nerve to ask him why he wasn't around. Until I became a mother I felt nothing, but when I did, I felt it all…all of my mother's anger and disappointment,' she said, making it clear that Kolleen had suffered deeply at the time. Like many children who are too young for a parental separation to make an emotional impact at the time, she had never felt the rejection that her mother had experienced: 'I never understood why she was so mad,' she added. It was with an adult's capable point of view, which can weigh up variables, that she ultimately decided: 'He brought me into this world and I'm grateful for that, but I'm disappointed because he was not a responsible person.'

One welcome consequence of Toosie's departure was the subsequent closeness that developed between Erica and her mother, to the extent that she would later say, 'My mother is my best friend. She's always supported me, been there for me, gave me everything I ever needed, and if it was any different, I would say the same thing.' Some of this may come from the practical advice her mother gave her – ('I always [said], "Pretty is as pretty does,"' said Kolleen. 'What matters is on the inside, not what you look like… After that, she just naturally blossomed into the beauty that she is') – but also from the fact that her mother never shirked from keeping her daughter aware of discipline and the importance of rules. 'My mother used to say I had a smart mouth because I would say everything that I knew. She'd say stuff like, "I'm twenty-five, you're five. I been here longer than you." But I remember getting up in the morning and doing what I needed to do and feeling very responsible for myself.'

Perhaps the most important trait that the young Erica inherited from Kolleen was a desire to perform. This had manifested itself as early as the piano session she led on her second birthday, and would develop with almost prodigious rapidity long before her father left. In line with this was a need to control her life, which was expressed when she refused to settle into nursery school: 'I went from my house, where I was the boss of all my toys and my little sister, to a classroom, where I couldn't boss no one,' she recalled. 'I said, "I need to go somewhere where I am in more control."' It's a measure of the strength of the Wright family circle that they were able to absorb this development (which must have been something of an inconvenience, meaning that Erica had to be looked after in the daytime), and that the child displayed no negative characteristics because of this. In future years, one of the most striking aspects of Erica's world-view would be the security she felt was provided to her by her family and extended relations. Something was done right, it seems, in these formative years.

The combination of the need to perform and the desire for control is not unusual. Psychologically, it make sense for anyone who needs to express themselves for the benefit of others to want that expression to be competent and accurately executed – especially, say, for a theatre actor or live musician, who knows that one performance is all they have. To ensure that the performance is delivered correctly, a degree of self-control is required and, to ensure that the listeners or viewers respond correctly, the performer must know which emotional buttons to press in them. In other words, a good performer will be controlling the audience, which is an unpredictable entity with many possible responses.

Of course, Erica knew none of this as a child. She just knew that she wanted everything to go the way she wanted it – hence her command to sing at her party. Kolleen, an actress, must have noticed this characteristic in her young daughter and seen herself in Erica – but mothers always realise that their children can only be controlled to a finite degree, usually learning to be deeply patient in the process. Erica herself would learn this when it was her own turn to be a mother.

The performing bug had taken hold of Erica by the time she was four years old. Viola (whom the children called 'Ganny') remembered Erica's earliest attempts to convince an audience to watch her: 'A lot of times, she only had one in the audience,' she later commented. 'And that was me! But I had to sit up and take notice.' This implies that the child was both grabbing her attention and entertaining her at the same time, a manifestation of the need to control and the need to perform. Whether acting a part or singing a song, the impulse was the same – even at this early stage – and Erica's desire to be seen and heard took a step to another level when she appeared on-stage alongside her mother at the Dallas Theater Center in 1975. Although details of her role and the play she appeared in are now sketchy, it's something that she and her family still remember with pride, and remains no mean feat, since the venue is a full-sized professional auditorium.

In line with her acting abilities, Erica had started to absorb the music she heard, and to reproduce it herself. Kolleen was a fan of the music of Marvin Gaye, Chaka Khan and Stevie Wonder, and would play their songs for her daughters, both of whom learned to sing and dance along with them. And this was no childish fancy: Erica in particular was quite clear in her head about what her role should be. 'When I was little,' she said, 'I used to stand in front of the mirror and pretend I was a background singer for Chaka Khan' – a surprisingly sophisticated ambition for such a young child. Her favourite artist was and remains Stevie Wonder, whose inspired albums from the 1970s became nothing less than a way of life for her. The music of Gaye, Wonder and Chaka would merge into a kind of sensory life-force, and at times she felt as if the songs were blending into a single, primal sustenance: 'I emulated those people growing up, and I still have a deep connection to them – there are millions and millions of atoms of their music within my music,' she would later muse. But her musical tastes would soon spread further than these three seminal artists. As she later told *Soul Express*, 'My major influences in music are Stevie Wonder, Chaka Khan, Miles Davis, Thelonious Monk, Charlie Parker, a lot of jazz musicians [and] soul musicians, like classic soul, Curtis Mayfield, Marvin Gaye, you know. People like that. People that were able to bring out emotion in people... Bob Marley.'

As music began to fill her life, Erica started to practise singing. Her favourite childhood ballad was the classic 'The Greatest Love Of All', a soaring tune that her family loved and that exercised her youthful vocal cords to the limit. It wasn't long before she found that her vocal skills and passion for music complemented those of her cousin Robert Bradford, who was three years her senior and one of the children who would often come and play with the Wright sisters at Ganny's house. The pair would sing together for the family, and they soon started to try to write songs together as well.

Robert remembers those days well: 'It was a happy time, man. We were just the babies running around, we didn't know whose father was whose and whatnot. I don't know why Toosie left, I think he was just young.' He also recalls that his young cousin would always hold fast to her beliefs, no matter what the issue was – perhaps this was the result of being the product of two generations of strong women. To this day, Erykah remembers her mother's strength, saying that, 'My sister and I became an extension of her power,' and acknowledging the straitened circumstances that her mother had endured throughout her life with the words, 'She didn't fall prey to a lot of the addiction and a lot of the abuse that most of her peers did.'

It's apparent to this day how important a role the women of the Wright family and their extended relatives played in the raising of Erica. She always acknowledges them all whenever she needs to give thanks in public, and has made a point on several occasions of mentioning the female dominance of her childhood. 'There were really no men around in my family. Just uncles, cousins, younger men, but mostly older women,' she said. She has also often spoken of her belief that she has five mothers: 'My mother, her best friend my godmother, my two grandmothers, Mother Nature. You know, it's just me and mothers.' Elsewhere, she elaborated on this by saying that the first mother is her birth mother Kolleen; that the second is her godmother, Gwen Hargrove, her mother's best friend; the third is Thelma, her maternal grandmother, whom Erykah remembers as being a strict but loving woman; the fourth, Viola, who introduced her granddaughters to religion and matters of the spirit, and, last, Mother Nature, who 'taught me how to cry, how to breathe, how to build, how to destroy when necessary, who bakes me with the sun and who makes me all who I am'.

Perhaps the five-mothers theory is best understood by likening each to a strand of Erica's personality. Kolleen obviously provided her daughter with her love of music and her ability to perform. Her godmother, Gwen Hargrove, was also an enormous influence on her, taking the raw need to play to an audience that Kolleen had implanted and developing it: as the goddaughter would later recall it, laughing: 'I grew up with my godmother. She's an artist too, a director, and an actress. Every summer she had a programme where she would put on one-act plays. I was always in them, and I would always get the lead roles – not because I was her goddaughter, but because I was good. The other kids would just look at me like I got special attention, but no, I was just better than them.'

As for Thelma, she provided her granddaughter with a sense of discipline that Kolleen had encouraged but which Toosie was not available to reinforce. Erica later remembered her as, 'Discipline, you know, Grandma's switches – get out of here, don't slam the screen door, eat all your food, say your prayers!' and that at the time she found these rules almost cruel, but she has also said that today she is grateful for having such discipline. Meanwhile, Toosie's mother Ganny would keep the young Erica's religious education flowing, taking the sisters to the Unity Church she attended, reading them Christian stories and asking the girls to commit the books of the Bible to heart. Erica and Koryan became accustomed to staying at Ganny's house at the weekends and attending church: 'I was a nice young lady there,' said Erica, who has often talked about her relationship with religion, and seems to maintain a strong Christian belief – but with modifications from other religions and, indeed, symbols from pagan and other theologies. As she put it in her late 20s, 'These are the dictates of my life: never have barriers, rules nor roles, and face all obstacles, which appear in front of me, overcoming them or perhaps demolishing them. Always with the help of the Lord.'

As upbringings go, Erica's was not a bad one, despite the family's relative poverty and the absence of her father. Asked to recall the primary images of her childhood, she responded in a kind of stream-of-consciousness style with a flow of comforting images: 'Very quiet. Lots of sun, lots of moon. Barefoot... Not rich at all. Kind of poor, but we didn't know that we were poor, because everything had to be very neat, clean, proud. Beautiful! Beautiful life.'

As the years passed, Erica and her sister grew taller, filled out and learned constantly. By the late 1970s Erica was attending grade school (first school), where she immediately put her acting skills to good use. A notable early appearance was in a production of *Annie*, where she took the lead role and adopted the famous orphan's look by wearing a red, jheri-curled wig. Singing the song 'Somebody Snitched On Me' and skipping around the stage, her grandmother Ganny couldn't hold back the tears: 'I just started crying,' she said. 'I thought, her parents don't know what they have! This girl is going places... She is not only talented, but a hard worker.'

During the long, hot summer vacations it was the job of godmother Gwen Hargrove to keep the two sisters occupied, and she accomplished this with ease by enrolling them in the summer recreation programme in South Dallas that was mentioned earlier. She also organised a place for Erica in the choir of the First Baptist Church of Hamilton Park, in which the child would hone her choral skills and learn about co-operating with fellow singers. Many professional singers credit a choir background for much of their ability, and it seems that the career of this particular performer was no exception.

Along with acting at school and in summer productions, singing in the choir and with her sister and cousin Robert, Erica began to expand her interests into the wider cultural life of Dallas. The city was a haven for festivals – a fact accentuated by its large African-American population – and one of the best was an event called the Harambee Festival in South Dallas. It was at one of these events that Erica began to take an interest in African culture and dress herself accordingly, and where the tall headwraps that she would later make her trademark were originated. She later said, 'Growing up in Dallas, we used to have Harambee Festivals every year. So there was this big festival where everyone gathers in the park, and there was a community of people who shared a love of [African] culture, and express it every day.' This developed into a philosophical standpoint: 'The way I dress – I love adorning myself with my culture. And it is not a black and white thing for me, but I am very interested in the black community because there are a lot of professional artists and geniuses who dwell in that community who need to be uplifted in some kind of way... I want to be a different example of what a black woman is, what a black person is. I wear my headwrap because a headwrap is a crown, and I am a queen. A headwrap demands a certain amount of respect – it just does, and I am always headwrapped.'

The performing portfolio of Erica – still a pre-teen – was expanding rapidly and, as 1980 approached, she discovered that she could dance, too. Kolleen, with the encouragement of her friend Gwen Hargrove, enrolled Erica in a youth troupe called Mahogany, run by an instructor called Dr Van Gilbert – a well-known arts worker in the Dallas area. 'That was a very big part of my life, because Dr Gilbert was a very spiritual man,' she remembered. She would also go on to study formal ballet with the Etta Piper Jamison company. Both dance companies rehearsed at the Martin Luther King Jr Recreation Center, and Erica found most of her free time being spent there. 'I never left the building!' she says now. 'I was always there.'

In one sense, the collective growth of Erica's acting, singing and dancing skills was to be expected; after all, her mother was an established performer and she grew up in a protective environment where self-expression was valued. And the expansion of her activities into various arenas never seemed to strike her as unusual or over-diverse: 'I don't separate it. It's all part of me, you know; it's all one thing,' she said later. 'Unconsciously, that's just how I move.'

Inevitably, all this learning would bring her to attempt to write her own material at some stage – and this came in 1978, when she was just seven years old. Surrounded by the everlovin' soul vibes of Mayfield and Wonder, it's little surprise that her first verse began 'Baby, baby, there you are, You're more precious than a star', and was accompanied by a youthful stab at a soulful piano accompaniment. She told *Soul Express*: 'My grandmother bought me a piano, a Taylor piano, and I knew weird chords, because I only played with four fingers, and it was called "Baby, baby", and then you go, "Baby, baby, there you are, you're more precious than a star, oh, baby, please don't go."' But divine intervention in the considerable form of her grandmother Viola stood in the way of this particular precocious ballad: 'And so my grandmother came around the corner, very religious, and said, "No, you are not supposed to sing like that!"... So about a week later the song was totally changed to '"Jesus, Jesus, there you are" to my grandmother's request. So, you know, I had to do a lot of gospel songs when I was younger, but secretly I was singing good love ballads.' Blame the sweet sounds of soul for this. Like it or not, many of the best songs to come from this or any other genre are sexual in theme (or use love as a metaphor for sex). Ganny knew this perfectly well and, aware that in a few years Erica would be singing what she damn well pleased, stepped in to try to keep her granddaughter's mind pure while she still could.

Not that Ganny's intervention dampened her eldest grandchild's enthusiasm. Erica continued to perform to herself in private when she couldn't find an audience, as she told *Vibe* magazine in a key interview in 1997. Asked if she performed whenever guests came to the family home, she replied, 'No, I did that on my own. Like, Look y'all, I can do this! When you put a lot of energy into something, you get the energy back. I've always been the type of person who wanted to get that energy back,' adding a comment about her ability to perform: 'I've never been shy. I'm always really nervous right before I do a show. You know that natural nervousness that comes? That anxiety? But I know that it's going to come off right because I believe in this.' Erica's mini-performances weren't restricted to singing, either: 'I used to pretend I was a horn all the time. That came from listening to Miles Davis and Bird and Al Jarreau with my uncle. Me and my brother and sister used to pretend we were a band. I'd be the horn, and my sister would be the bass. Stevie Wonder is another person I tried to imitate. But I could never get the vibrato in my voice that Stevie Wonder has, no matter how hard I tried.'

Ah yes – the voice. One of the most remarkable features of the young Erica's upbringing was that, while she sang in a choir and learned the piano, she appears never to have taken formal singing lessons. Yet, as anyone who has heard her sing live will attest, she is capable of the most amazing vocal pyrotechnics, with a range originating with a low, sultry murmur, via a whip-strong mid-range to a very high falsetto. Natural talent, it seems, will out.

A remarkable feature of the young Erica's development – in artistic terms, at least – is that she seemed almost to spring from the womb fully formed as a performer. She has always studied to perfect her art, of course, but so many of her capabilities seem to be inherited rather than learned that it must have been tempting for her teachers and family to regard her as a kind of Mozart-esque prodigy. She later confirmed this, remarking, 'I've got tapes from when I was five years old, and I think I sound exactly the same... Nobody taught me. It was just the right situation. Now it's effortless. The Creator does it.' Whether the Almighty gave her these powers at such an early stage depends entirely on your interpretation, of course, but there was definitely something of the divine talent about this particular cherub.

These were great days, which the elder Badu must now remember with the kind of sun-dappled rosiness that we all apply to our early childhoods. In this case, however, those years seem to have been genuinely pleasant ones, despite the family's relative poverty. Robert Bradford recalls those times with genuine happiness: 'Going way back, you know, we were all just kids. Koryan, Erica, myself, my sister Stacy – we all just kinda grew up together and played like any kids do. Ganny, she lives right down the street from my grandmother on my mother's side, literally right down the street. We lived all over Dallas, we were like nomadic, man. But the grandmothers always stayed friends – there's a long friendship between my grandmother, Thelma and Ganny.'

So what was Erica like? 'She was cool, man, a little cutie. Energetic, fun-going. They tell me I was drawing on the walls when I was a kid, and now I'm a visual artist – I've been at art school all my life – and Erica's talent was there too, right from the beginning. Koryan, too, is an exceptional singer.'

And, like any kids, the four cousins would share their adventures: 'Man, some of the most memorable times were when we were up at night,' says Robert. 'You know, everybody used to spend the night, telling scary stories, know what I mean? My uncle Dinky used to have us *petrified* with those nightmare stories. We all told stories. When Erica told stories, she was pretty animated.' This last comment is hardly surprising, of course, with Erica's imagination beginning to run wild as she grew, and this part of her seems to be shared by the other kids, including Bradford. 'Erica and I used to go out on bicycle adventures,' he remembers. 'I had a bike with these big flags on it, and we would go down to the creek at the bottom of the neighbourhood and mark spots with the flags in case we got lost.'

The thought of the two children riding off on their adventures is perhaps an odd one for anyone who doesn't associate inner-city urban life with allowing children this kind of barely limited freedom, but North Park and the other areas of Dallas to which the Wrights moved appear to have been much, much friendlier a quarter of a century ago than they are today. Furthermore, Erica's experience of life in the South – one of the first things that interviewers in New York would pick up on when she moved there in the mid-1990s – appears to have been nothing but positive. Asked what it was like growing up in Texas, she replied, 'You know, it's supposed to be the home of the Ku Klux Klan, the South – but I didn't have a bad experience. I was pretty sheltered from all of that kind of nonsense by music, art, dance and creativity. I only experienced racism once I got into the music business, and I dealt with people not accustomed to spending time with black people that had more money than they did.'

There is truth to this, of course – we've already seen how the Wrights and their extended family placed value on artistic effort and the familial circle to an unusual degree. But more than this, there is something about Dallas – without wishing to portray it falsely or unrealistically – which made it easy for Erica to develop in the way she did. For one thing, its location makes it a cultural melting-pot: 'Not being on the coasts, we don't have a systematic way of doing music,' Erica would later observe. 'We're free to create our own path, which is what makes the art so diverse.' True enough – although the enormous conurbations of New York and Los Angeles (whose opposition would be highlighted permanently by the hip-hop wars of the 1990s) are unique cauldrons of cultural activity, their prominence makes them prey to the grip of controlling entities: look how the West Coast film industry is in thrall to the norms of Hollywood, for instance, and remember how the Big Apple, perhaps the most influential city in the world, is renowned for its sheer business muscle. But Dallas, a relative minnow in global terms, flourishes unhindered, with the result that artists like Erykah Badu can find their own way in their own time.

The pulse of the city is taken every day by the formidable *Dallas Morning News*, a respected, huge-selling newspaper that extends its reach into every nook and cranny of the area. Its music desk is staffed by a reporter called Thor Christensen, whose perspective on Dallas in musical terms – and therefore on the subject of this book – is unique. He retains a balanced view of the city: 'Dallas is part of the south, which means that it's more conservative and more Republican than a lot of other urban areas in the US. I'd say it *is* a bit conservative but not as conservative as a lot of other cities in the south. Dallas would be a lot more hip and liberal than Des Moines, say, just because it's so big.' And Thor knows only too well the breadth of musical activity on hand: 'Dallas is a huge metropolitan area of four to five million people, so there's a lot of different music going on. So when Badu was coming up, I wasn't even aware of her just because there's so many local musicians performing every night.'

He's being modest – to be precise, Dallas is a city that is overflowing with musical, theatrical and otherwise artistic talent to a degree that many far larger Western cities cannot match. Its West End, the primary entertainment district, draws in no fewer than seven million visitors every year, while Fair Park Dallas, a 112-hectare (277-acre) national historic landmark, is home to many cultural locations, including seven museums. Popular attractions for culture vultures include the Dallas Arts District, the Dallas Museum of Art, the Symphony Center, the Dallas Symphony Orchestra and something called the Dallas Underground, a tunnel complex of shops and restaurants some 5km (3 miles) long. It has a darker side, too – one of the most-visited sites in the whole of the South is the Kennedy Museum, located in the former Texas School Book Depository building (now officially renamed the Sixth Floor Museum At Dealy Plaza), from which tourists can view the spot at which the eponymous president unexpectedly met his maker in 1963.

An area that provides much of the city's most cutting-edge cultural activity is Deep Ellum, named after an early 20th-century pronunciation of 'Elm Street'. Christensen describes it as 'a historic nightclub area. Back in the 1920s, people like Blind Lemon Jefferson and Leadbelly performed there. Since the '80s it's become the hip place for up-and-coming musicians.' This 70-hectare (170-acre) district, partially made up of renovated warehouses, lies three blocks east of downtown Dallas and is the place where most ambitious Southern bands find themselves.

And all this without even mentioning the most important aspect of life in Dallas in terms of the development of Erykah Badu, which is that for decades (centuries, even), it has been the home of a huge African-American community, with a corresponding blossoming of black culture. According to the 1990 census, whites make up 55.3 per cent of the population of Dallas; blacks, 29.5 per cent; Hispanics, 20.9 per cent; people of Asian origin, 2.2 per cent; and native Americans, 0.5 per cent. This means that the black population numbers over one million citizens, who are responsible for the creation of Afrocentric installations such as the African-American Museum, the Dallas Black Dance Theatre, the Booker T Washington School for Performing and Visual Arts, the South Dallas Cultural Center and Freedman's Cemetery (a pre-Civil War burial ground).

The history of the black population of Dallas is similar to that of black communities in the other southern States of the US, which is to say that it is inextricably bound up with the grim spectre of slavery. The city was founded comparatively recently – in 1845 – after the Republic of Texas built a road from the state capital in Austin to the town of Dallas, originally a native American settlement. As the city's wealth grew, the residents purchased black slaves, whose share of the total population rose from eight per cent in 1850 to 12 per cent ten years later. An abolitionist movement rapidly grew, however (leading to various legal measures when violence sporadically erupted, including the suspension of civil liberties and military intervention), and the community grew further when it became a Confederate stronghold during the Civil War. When emancipation finally came for the black slaves in June 1865, many freed men and women from throughout the South moved to Texas looking for opportunities, triggering a wave of resentment among many white Americans. This led to the formation of the Ku Klux Klan three years later and, although the foul history of the KKK has little relevance here, the simple fact of its existence continues to throw the issue of race in the South into sharp relief...all of which illustrates the Dallas myth a little more, and, by association, the life of Erykah Badu.

By 1890, Deep Ellum had become a black enclave, with the African-American population a powerful and proactive force for social progression: a black bank, the Penny Savings Bank, opened shortly afterwards; the *Dallas Express* black newspaper was founded in 1893; and in 1905 Bluit Sanatorium became the first black hospital. Although state leaders felt threatened by their emerging political force and introduced a poll tax that limited the African-American voting protocol and segregated public transportation, while accommodation and education were sanctioned by law and practice, the black population never stopped fighting for its place in the community and positive steps continued to be taken.

The Dallas Black (then 'Negro') Chamber of Commerce was founded in 1926 and a decade later the Hall of Negro Life of Texas was built at Fair Park in Dallas. A series of high-profile court cases in the 1950s and 1960s were supported by protests, and the old segregationist attitudes began to recede. By the time the black Dallas politician Joe Lockridge was elected to the state senate in 1966, an African-American middle class had started to develop, and in 1983 Dallas was named 'one of the ten best cities for African-Americans'. And today the city has a black mayor, Ron Kirk, and a black police chief.

So the young Erica's social background was one that aided in her progression from child prodigy to serious artist. But the journey might never have happened without the most crucial influence on her of all – the music that surrounded her. To this day, she carries with her on most occasions a picture of the late Marvin Gaye, who she says commands her respect and gives her strength because he 'spoke from his soul and his mind' – and such a tribute is not made without a serious emotional investment from her.

Although Gaye dabbled throughout his life in R&B and funk, his chosen genre was always soul, where he excelled to the extent that few other artists in the field (Sam Cooke, Otis Redding, Aretha Franklin, James Brown and Curtis Mayfield come to mind) equal him for sheer stature – and Erica herself would, like her hero, come to change the face of popular music in later life. The music Gaye represented must have appealed to Erica for several reasons. First, it's difficult to describe and pigeonhole, partially because it's often simple (and simple music is often the most difficult to explain), but also because of its multifaceted nature. For example, the Detroit sounds of 1960s Tamla Motown were often catchy, pop-driven tunes bursting with friendly hooks and gospel influences, while those from the Memphis-based Stax/Volt axis were grittier and tougher, with a greater focus on horns. The production was usually smoother on songs that emanated from urban areas like Philadelphia, Chicago and New York, which also emphasised the vocal interplay – whereas Motown was a *mélange* of R&B, rock 'n' roll and even country sounds. Southern soul was harder rather than softer than its northern counterpart. All of this meant that there were many strands of soul...with no easily classifiable sound.

As the 1960s ended and Erica's birth approached, the eccentric genius of stars like Sly Stone and James Brown led to a kind of dissolution of the classic soul sound, as these and other artists pushed out the envelope into funk and R&B territory – but the 1970s saw classic soul acts remain public favourites. In fact, in 1971 (just after Erica's arrival), Isaac Hayes became the first black American to receive an Oscar – for his soundtrack to *Shaft*, which also won a Grammy. The timing of Erica's youth is crucial, as by the late 1970s disco had arrived and with it the joyful sounds of Chaka Khan and Chic. The music that Kolleen and Gwen Hargrove played for their children was undergoing a virtual rebirth.

As Erica grew older, she began to appreciate the lyrical significance of soul as well as the easy attraction of its sound. A vehicle for the longings and self-analyses of the black community since the chants of the chain-gangs had fused with gospel and flowed into both blues and jazz, soul had developed since World War II into a highly self-aware, deeply politicised protest avenue for thousands of musicians, and the impact of this would not have been lost on its latest convert. Add this philosophical and spiritual significance to the beauty of the music she heard, and we can begin to understand why soul meant a lot to Erica, who turned nine years old as the organic 1970s became the predatory 1980s.

The importance of the learning Erica experienced in these early years must not be underestimated. The music Kolleen Gipson-Wright and her extended family played and sang for Erica at this time made an impact on her that would endure throughout childhood and into adulthood, and would always be the highest priority in her life, along with her family and friends. Perhaps part of the reason for this is the obvious security Erica felt when in the bosom of the family, which would lead her to associate the soul and jazz she heard with good times and much affection. Another important influencing factor, of course, would be the nature of the music itself – emotional, open and, above all, warm songs in which Marvin Gaye asked what was going on, Curtis Mayfield moved on up and Stevie Wonder asked us if his baby daughter was lovely.

Why Erica also warmed so much to the sometimes frenzied instrumental jazz of Miles Davis and Charlie Parker is less clear, but it's probable that she enjoyed pretending to play the horns, which appealed to her childish instinct to perform. But this too is organic, sweet music, with fascinating twists and turns for a child to follow and a rhythmic pulse that would have taught Erica much about the structure of music.

By the time she was tinkering on her miniature piano, she would have already had a firm idea of how music was made, how to listen to it and how it can lead to fulfilment.

It's tempting to picture the Wright family home from three decades' distance as an idyllic place in which the kids ran happily free and every day was summer. Experience tells us, of course, that this cannot have been the whole picture, with the family living in an impoverished area of a major American city and with a father largely absent – and, even if this were not the case, no family lives life without arguments and material worries. And yet Erica looks back now with immense affection to those times, crediting her grandmothers, mother and siblings with creating a marvellous childhood for her. We should give thanks for this, too, as it's directly due to that warm, sunlit environment that we have her music today. Much credit must go to her mother Kolleen, who must have struggled desperately to keep the family happy after Toosie's departure – no mean feat, even without children to look after. It's important to have a few years of innocence and, with the support of her family, Erica had many years without fear. But, as time passes, children grow up, and with growth comes self-awareness. Always one of the most self-aware people as an adult, Erica would spend the next few years absorbing all sorts of influences – musical, theatrical, social – and was lucky that the people who surrounded her were strong and intelligent enough to keep her protected while she did so.

Times were changing, however, and in the next few years some profound developments would alter the way that Erica saw her world.

2 What's In A Name?

Jump forward to 1982.

The world was a little different by this point. In the Wrights' family circle, the protective family structure was still there: everyone was a little older, but no one seemed to mind too much and the children still played their games as if nothing would ever change. Erica and Koryan were growing rapidly, Kolleen was pregnant with a son, and Robert Bradford had grown into a gangly youth of 14 years old. Every New Year's Eve, he and his sister joined the family, together with their relatives, for a party, where it had become usual for one or both of the Wright daughters to perform an act or sing a song.

On this occasion, Robert came to the party as usual and settled down to watch when Erica and her sister stood up to perform. This time, however, things were not the same as they were before – and the boy's jaw dropped open: for Erica and Koryan were rapping, old-school style, throwing the gestures and giving off a hip-hop flavour and, what's more, as tight as you like. 'They had little routines, like rap routines,' he remembers. 'They were tight, too, *very* tight – and I'm talking back in the day, right at the brink of coming out of childhood.' He marvels as he recalls, 'I was surprised, just because I didn't know they could put it down like that!'

It turns out that the twosome had been paying close attention to more than just the music that was coming from Kolleen's record collection. The American music world had been turned on its head in 1979 by the freak success of The Sugarhill Gang's 'Rapper's Delight', the single that ushered in the first wave of hip-hop. A host of white-gloved, breakdancing crews would follow in their footsteps, and by 1982 the scene was the most powerful musical force in the world, with 'hip-hop' a buzzword and the whole culture – embodying rap, scratching and graffiti – a veritable cultural phenomenon. The two Wright sisters had heard it, enjoyed it and (like everything they had seen and liked) decided to try it out for themselves, with an almost shocking degree of skill for children so young.

Hence Robert Bradford's stunned silence the first time he witnessed his cousins in action. To add to his surprise, there was the fact that he himself had become an adherent to hip-hop, and specifically breakdancing. 'When I was into hip-hop, I was so deep into it I didn't realise Erica was into it too,' he remarks. 'It was a surprise to me that she was putting it down so well.' Surely he must have known that they were preparing an act? 'I never saw them practising this, but I found out that they wrote the raps pretty much equally... We would have these New Year's Eve parties every year, and we would all get together, all of us, with our close friends and relatives and whatnot, and we'd have like a party at one of our friend's houses. We would all do different things, we'd be dancing and stuff... We'd do it every year, and Koryan and Erica would do routines.'

The rap act that the sisters were developing would soon become a way of life for both children, who immersed themselves in hip-hop – as children in black urban communities would be doing worldwide within a couple of years – and their clothes, hair, listening choices and leisure activities all reflected this. Within a year or two, Robert had honed his breakdancing skills to the extent that his crew – who dubbed themselves the Star City Breakers – were performing regularly at organised shows in front of large audiences. These either took the form of breakdancing competitions in which two rival crews would take it in turn to outdo each other's dancing skills, or stage a 'battle', in which microphone skills were the focus and which saw competing MCs improvise rhymes of incredible complexity and speed. Robert recalls that 'Erica was at some of the battles, man, she was there. We'd hang out and break in front of theatres and whatever. One in particular, early on, was at the Enwood Theater, and I definitely remember her being at that one.'

Official recognition of the Star City Breakers' skills came when the sports clothing manufacturer Puma, which, like its competitors, had not been slow to realise the commercial gains to be derived from hip-hop, approached them and offered them sponsorship. The culture of this new music was growing unstoppably, it seems, and to cap it all Erica saw her first concert as hip-hop reached its mid-1980s peak. It was a Run-DMC show, featuring the young Beastie Boys in support – one of the essential tours to witness at that time for young hip-hop fans, and probably one that cemented the idea of becoming a rapper in her mind.

Every rapper needs a name, of course, and by 1984 Erica had chosen one. The newly christened MC Apples (no explanation for this choice of sobriquet has ever been provided, although Robert thinks it might be because she had a clear, attractive complexion) began rapping in earnest. It wasn't long before she had carved out a niche for herself on the Dallas teenage scene, either, securing live slots at local city festivals – all based on the backyard rap routines she and Koryan would devise when they were not at school. Bradford explains: 'She would perform at festivals in the park – like community centre parks – with pretty big audiences. It was something for the people in the neighbourhood to come and check out. I remember one time she did this rap of hers that's kinda famous called "George Of The Jungle".'

Within a matter of months, it seems, the one-time soul child had been swept away by the tidal wave of hip-hop and developed into a fully fledged B-Girl. The importance of The Big Beat (the central anchor of hip-hop) as opposed to The Melody (the life-force of soul) was also sinking in fast. Drum machines were expensive pieces of studio equipment at this stage, and unavailable to the kids. Meanwhile, the art of the human beatbox (the vocal simulation of drumbeats through a microphone held close to the mouth) that Doug E Fresh and his followers were to perfect had not yet fully come to life. To find a rhythm, Erica, Robert and their friends went to perhaps unsociable lengths, as Bradford recalls: 'We used to beat on things like a car or something, that was our thing, on the hood of any car that was there. If there was a car, you just started rocking the beat. This was way before people started beatboxing.'

Beating on cars, rapping at Dallas festivals, breakdancing in free trackwear: the involvement of the Wright and Bradford teenagers in their music was almost total, it appears. This even extended as far as two classic rock 'n' roll clichés – crazy threads and exploitative management. 'Right around that time she became MC Apples,' says Robert, 'I became Bob Rock. Yes, I know it's a totally '80s name... I had the belt and everything. I didn't have big B-Boy rings with my name on them, though, we couldn't splurge money like that.' He's cringing in embarrassment, of course, as he recalls 'the look': 'Clothes were more, uh, *tapered* back then... My breakdancing crew, the Star City Breakers, were getting paid, we had a manager from New York who came down and exploited everyone. Originally there was like five people in the crew, but then members would fall out and be replaced. We were booked all over the place... That's a whole story right there.' But not one that can be told in these pages – although the exploits of the Star City Breakers might well reveal more about the lifestyle of the young Erica. On the other hand, she confessed years later that she had been an obedient child who didn't often date boys and rarely aggravated her family – so she must have avoided most of the temptations of teenagehood. Robert remembers her as an artist rather than a troublemaker: 'She dabbled in visual arts and all the other arts, and ironically enough we all of us did, although when I was doing visual art at high school, we were more interested in breakdancing.'

The arrival in Dallas of hip-hop was not an inevitability, however. Perhaps due to the South's harsher living conditions (compared to the urban centres of the North), or maybe because the South has always traditionally been poorer than its counterpart, or possibly again because of the blues that fermented in the deltas and swamps, late 20th-century music in the southern States has always been rock-based. Dallas alone produced a host of white guitar bands in the 1990s, ranging from the mellow acoustic tunes of Deep Blue Something, through the eccentric blues of Reverend Horton Heat to the unsociably metallic grind of Pantera, Drowning Pool, Absu and Speedealer. And 'Southern rock', of course, is a whole genre of its own, with the country-flavoured strains of Lynyrd Skynyrd and the Allman Brothers at its forefront.

Thor Christensen muses that, 'There's lots of blues in Dallas, and lots of R&B, but not really any hip-hop. The only famous hip-hop people who ever came out of Dallas were the DOC, who was in an early version of NWA and is now a solo artist, and Vanilla Ice, who was a big star in the early 1990s for a while.' But arrive it did and, although hip-hop may not have been a natural import to the streets of Texas, once it established itself in the black communities of Dallas/Fort Worth it was there to stay, and the clubs and bars of hot spots such as Deep Ellum began to reverberate to the sounds of turntables and drum machines rather than to the blues guitars and jazz horns that had previously held sway in the area.

The importance of hip-hop to Erica's development cannot be overstated. Coupled with the musical sweetness of soul, to which she had been listening since she was a baby, the driving beats and lyrical braggadocio of rap gave an edge to her listening tastes that made her something of an all-rounder. The positivity and harmony of soul complemented the swing and impact of hip-hop perfectly – and the whole musical menu was a sum far, far greater than its parts. Let us also not forget to pinpoint Erica's location in time, too – after all, the fact that soul was fragmenting at this time (few soul fans will point to the mid-1980s as the genre's heyday, after all) and that the airwaves were fresh with the sounds of new music from a new style, makes her appearance both timely and prophetic.

Hip-hop would have influenced Erica as profoundly as her earlier soul favourites. Lyrically, musically and philosophically, hip-hop was the polar opposite of the feel-good vibes of the classic sounds of soul, but was also a consciousness-expanding music. Politically astute (or at least politically aware) rappers would bring their expositions on black affairs to the mainstream white audience in the 1980s, just as soul brothers such as Marvin Gaye and Curtis Mayfield had done in the previous decade...but this time the beats were far more aggressive and the artist's stance much more confrontational. The level gaze of the best rappers made them icons to children and teenagers of the right age (a direct result of the music's ghetto origin, where the best rapper was the fastest, funniest and most indefatigable), and Erica and her contemporaries wanted some of that kudos for themselves.

Here, then, was a young woman with much to offer, and one who had both the need to perform and the courage to make it happen. And, far from being 'just a kid', Erica was clearer in her mind and intentions than most of her contemporaries. The first evidence of this came when she was considering her move from middle school to high school, and found herself thinking about her name, her identity and her beliefs. A profound step was about to be taken and, looking back, it can be recognised as one of the first stages in a long journey towards self-actualisation.

At the time, of course, it may have merely appeared precocious: who knows what thoughts would have entered Kolleen Wright's head when her eldest daughter approached her one day and told her that she intended to change her name?

'I was born Erica Abie Wright,' said Erykah later. 'My mother was very proud of that name. So, when I confronted her with "I want to change my name, you know, this ain't my name. This is a slave name," my mother said, "Well, the white man didn't name you that. *I* named you that and I like the name. I think it's a beautiful name."' Kolleen can hardly be blamed: 'Erica' *is* a nice name. What was she to do?

The answer was to ask her daughter to think about her decision – which she duly did. 'So, I thought about it and I said, "Well, there has to be some way for me to find meaning for myself, because I long for that." Instead of changing my name, I found meaning in it. I changed the spelling from E-R-I-C-A to E-R-Y-K-A-H.'

This, of course, begs several questions. First of all, why would she want to change her name? After all, while it's normal for children to dislike their given names, most of them grow out of this sooner or later. However, she did have a point (although perhaps she put it to her mother a little too bluntly) when she talked of 'slave names': the African-American practice of taking names that were European in origin began in the bad old days of mass slavery, when a freed slave would be given (or would choose) a 'white' name in order to begin a new life. Although the American black community is nowadays neither more in favour of nor wholly against this tradition, there has been a growing awareness in recent decades that other options are available and that it is no longer unusual for a black person to reject a European name.

Second, why might Erica – as she put it – be searching for 'meaning in her life'? Other than attributing this to good old-fashioned teenage angst (which, it should not be forgotten, is a real and potentially lasting anguish), we only need to revisit her past to find an explanation. Tough and resourceful as the car-door-beating, stage-grabbing teenager might seem to have become, remember that she was still practically just a young girl. Remember also that she was a girl without a father, and with a mother whose support was unwavering but who physically could not be with her as much as she would have liked, due to the demands of her job. Finally, look at Erica's later assertion that she had no fewer than five mothers: this was clearly no orthodox upbringing, and although she was clearly a happy, much-loved child the advent of self-awareness was bound to happen sooner rather than later.

Third, how did she arrive at 'Erykah' from 'Erica'? This, at least, is relatively easy to explain, as indeed she has many times. 'Kah', it emerged, is a word denoting 'the inner self', which is defined as 'that which can do no wrong'. For a person of sensitivity and spirituality, this makes perfect sense. The added 'y' is a matter of numerology, in which the singer has always been interested and which provides a theme that runs through many of her songs, as will be revealed later. Y is the 25th letter of the alphabet; 25 can be separated into two and five; and the sum of these is seven, which has variously been described as 'the perfect number', 'a number symbolic to God' and 'the divine number'. It is a prime number, indivisible by any other number than one and itself.

Finally, how did the name-change affect her? The answer, it would seem, is that it made her who she really is – her own person. The symbolism of the event is obvious. She had both changed and retained her name; she had invested in it (and therefore in herself) a spiritual, and even holy, dimension; and she had created a persona of her own – Erykah the singer and performer, as distinct from Erica the teenage girl. Of course, adolescents the world over struggle with issues of identity and self-esteem, but few manage to find as simple and elegant a solution to these perennial subjects. Respect is due to her for her wisdom at such an early stage.

However, the newly renamed Erykah wasn't content merely to exploit the potential of *one* new name. MC Apples had become an in-demand performer, and it was with little surprise but much admiration that her family and friends discovered that she would be appearing live on air at a local radio station, KNON, in recognition of her rhyming skills. The station, an established Dallas broadcaster, was accustomed to playing the popular styles of the day and, since the rapid rise of hip-hop, was seeking accomplished local talent to boost its profile. By this time, the aforementioned Doug E Fresh had pioneered the human beatbox and rap fans across the nation were emulating the style for themselves. A friend, Roy Hargrove (apparently no relation to Erykah's godmother, Gwen) was recruited to back her up at the radio sessions with his beatbox skills, and a live duo was born. Although the radio sessions would not last – because a much more important platform for Erykah's self-expression would soon take their place – they mark an early triumph for the young performer and one that her family and friends remember with great pleasure. As for Roy Hargrove, he went on to become a well-known trumpet player, winning awards for his expertise. He would cross paths with Erykah again, but not for some time and not before her world had changed radically.

In 1985, Erykah turned 14 years old. It was time for her to leave her middle school and select a high school, which would take her through the four years that remained before she would decide whether to attend university. Her choices were many: she had been a talented student in almost all the arts subjects she had ever studied, and a capable (if never brilliant) learner of purer disciplines such as languages and mathematics. Keen to exploit her talents, her mother Kolleen looked at Robert Bradford's choices for an example: the former Bob Rock had excelled at visual arts and was a student at Dallas's premier arts-based high school, the Booker T Washington High School for the Performing and Visual Arts (BTWHS). This school, perhaps just as much as the home environment in which Erykah had grown, learned and finally shed her skin, would be the most profound influence on her young life to date.

Although the concept of progressive education in America might be more typically associated with the urban north rather than the supposedly less advanced south, Dallas has had a history of visionary education authorities: an example of this was a so-called 'super' high school called Skyline High, which opened in 1971. The Skyline curriculum was based on the idea of career strands (rather than isolated subject studies) and attracted students from all ethnic groups around the city, as well as providing adult evening classes. Booker T Washington is not based on the same model, but certain aspects of its ethical approach are the same – it broke relatively new ground when it first opened in the late 1970s at the head of the 'magnet' system (a magnet school is so-called because it attracts students to study there, rather than enforcing a fixed pedagogical regime upon them). Quite simply, the idea is that people go there because it's fun.

Perhaps the best definition of magnet schools comes from BTWHS's own website, which states: 'Magnet schools are based on the premise that all students do not learn in the same ways, that if we find a unifying theme or a different organizational structure for students of similar interest, those students will learn more in all areas. In other words, if a magnet school voluntarily attracts students and teachers, it will succeed because, more than for any other reason, those in attendance want to be there. They will have chosen that school.' Journalist Thor Christensen adds that this school, something of an arts mecca, draws in arts-capable students with great ease: 'Magnet schools are so named because they draw people like a magnet – in other words, if you're artistically inclined, no matter what part of the city you live in, you are drawn to this high school for the performing arts. Roy Hargrove went there, the singer Norah Jones went there... It's a high school right downtown, next to the Symphony Hall.'

Booker T Washington may have a prestigious location (it's on Flora Street, right in the middle of Dallas's arts district), but it's apparent from its unpretentious exterior – the building was erected in 1923 – that what goes on inside its walls is more important than its showy environment. It's neither too big (there are about 700 students there) nor too exclusive – it's a public school in the classic sense, meaning that anyone can attend. It does require an audition from its students, however, which demands both commitment and talent from applicants.

Robert Bradford remembers the powerful attraction of the Arts Magnet (as they called it) with these words: 'I went to a regular high school for a week, and I don't know where I got the idea, but I thought, I cannot do this. So I got up and left the class, then I went down and called my mom – and I guess I must have talked to her already, because she already had an audition set up for me, a late audition.' Despite his impressive dance and musical skills, Bradford had focused on his visual arts abilities for the audition, and took along a portfolio, which impressed the selection panel enough to get him a place.

Kolleen Wright was watching carefully and, as soon as it became clear that her daughters' cousin was flourishing there, she must have begun to consider it for her children. Robert, it seems, had found his niche – and with a vengeance: 'I loved it. It was some of the greatest years of my life,' he recalls. 'The environment, man, it was something I'd never experienced before – it was so open-minded and liberal, and such a great new thing to be introduced to.'

BTWHS organises its teaching schedule into groups called 'clusters' – the theatre cluster for actors, the dance cluster for dancers, the visual arts cluster for painters and sculptors, and so on – and splits its students' daily routine in half, with either the morning or the afternoon devoted to cluster subjects and the other half to 'normal' subjects such as English, history, mathematics and so on. Erykah decided that the school was for her and, once her family had agreed that it was the right place for her to go, she decided to audition not for one but for two clusters – dance and theatre.

Remarkably, Erykah was accepted by the teaching panels for both clusters (a promising early sign). It seems that she was in demand from both departments: 'I got accepted into theater,' she later told *Vibe* magazine, 'but the dance teacher got mad so I was one of the only people who could be in both.' Not that this meant that she would have an easy ride afterwards: 'You have to...maintain a certain grade point average,' she added. But she was happy there, as Robert observed. 'She belonged there, it was like the perfect place. She came in as an underclassman, but she was as excited about going, and she knew I was there. Once you've auditioned for a particular cluster, that's what you concentrate on for your four years. She did modern dance, ballet, tap-dance – they try to introduce you to all the dance forms.'

The four years that Erykah spent at Booker T Washington would be varied not only in terms of the curriculum, but also in the activities the school offered outside class. Erykah would spend two of those years as a member of the Entertainers, the school's musical and theatre group, which was run by a teacher called Nina Johnson. The regime organised by Johnson and the other members of staff was flexible enough to allow such extracurricular activity to flourish – for example, Robert remembers that the academic half of the day could be swapped with the artistic half when necessary. Erykah appreciated this flexibility, recalling that 'The high school...definitely gave me an outlet, because you could feel natural and still fit into the system. That's what we struggle through as artists: to fit into the walk of life like everyone else, to make money and still feel like ourselves.'

Erykah dived deeply into all the school had to offer, but had to work hard at first to keep up, despite her flying colours in both auditions. Her dance teacher, Fern Tresvan-Siebles, had seen some talent in her young pupil and had requested that she focus on dance over theatre, and it's a sign of Tresvan-Siebles' experience (and perhaps of the bond between the student and teacher) that the talent she saw was inherent rather than obvious. 'I wasn't the best dancer,' Erykah said later. 'I was pigeon-toed. But I could *feel* it. And that's what stood out to the teacher... I could close my eyes and feel the music and let my body do what it was supposed to do. Whether it was technically correct or not, it did what it was supposed to do.' And, with the teachers' support, Erykah gradually lost her childish clumsiness and began to develop into a dancer of some note.

As the ballet lessons lent her grace and the arts environment stretched her critical awareness, the another side of Erykah – the brash, bold rapper of MC Apples – blossomed in parallel. As she entered her mid-teens and gained in confidence and fluency, respect started to gather among her friends and fellow students for her rhyme-busting skills, and the nickname 'Apples' became a word uttered in admiration rather than as a joke. Her festival appearances continued, as well as the backyard parties where she had first honed her rhymes, and it was slowly becoming clear that a rather unusual talent was growing. Her family, Robert Bradford among them, have all said that they weren't surprised by her later success, and that they had a strong inkling even at this stage that the world would hear from Erykah Wright sooner or later.

But what none of them knew – Erykah least of all – was that she and popular music were on something of a collision course. We've already seen that the classic soul of the 1960s had become diverted (and some might say diluted) by the parallel schools of pop, funk, R&B and even rock by the end of the 1970s. However, by the mid- to late 1980s the fragmenting process had been taken to another level entirely, thanks to the combination of the march of technology (in particular, studio recording equipment) and the rise of hip-hop, which made pilfering samples an everyday event and the crossover of genres an almost-expected development.

The 1980s weren't a great decade if the original sounds of soul were your preferred listening. Classic soul artists were either languishing in the trough of public indifference, with acts such as the Temptations and James Brown mere shadows of their former selves, or (like Marvin Gaye, who departed this world tragically young in 1984) no longer active. Soul had been robbed of its power by upstarts such as Prince, or was reduced to second-league muzak at the hands of reduced artists such as Luther Vandross. A series of accidents also slowed down the soul heartbeat, with Teddy Pendergrass confined to a wheelchair after a car crash in 1982, while Curtis Mayfield would be left quadraplegic after an on-stage accident eight years later. Elsewhere, white artists had invaded soul's home turf and blanded it into unrecognisability – Philadelphia duo Daryl Hall and John Oates were a notable example.

Where black music was at its most vital in the West was undoubtedly in the field of hip-hop, which (as we've seen) was as great an influence on the young Erykah/MC Apples as soul had been. The combination of the two, fortunately, can be electric, and as she turned 16 in 1987, the sounds of the new rap school – Schooly D, Ice-T, the fledgling NWA featuring Dr Dre and Ice Cube, Public Enemy and KRS-One among them – would have been prominent among the vintage vibes of Stevie Wonder and Chaka Khan that she listened to in earnest in her spare time between all the rehearsals.

Meanwhile, the years flew by – as they do when we're young and busy – and the sum of Erykah's knowledge grew rapidly, thanks to her studies. Much of her development can be attributed to the organic, respectful education she received at the hands of the teachers at BTWHS, and many of the qualities she would discuss in her later work – respect, self-awareness and modesty among them – were emphasised in the very essence of the school's approach. The founders of the school laid down a set of goals when they established the curriculum three decades ago, prominent among which were: 'To attract artistically gifted students from the Dallas community at large'; 'To educate the whole child by fostering the development of perception, conceptualization, sensitivity, and creativity' and 'To provide an educational atmosphere which is conductive to the development and nurturing of creative artistic talent'. Add to this the lack of 'jock and cheerleader culture' – the school proudly maintains no football or basketball teams – and it's clear that, as far as urban educations go, this one was rather special. It's little wonder that the school has received various awards: it became a prototype for subsequent American magnet schools and was named a Mentor School by the Texas Education Agency in 1994.

Despite the importance of these years on Erykah, there isn't much more to report about her time at Booker T Washington High School. She was a fiery but obedient student with a seemingly inexhaustible supply of energy, it seems – Robert Bradford recalls her being very certain of her path in life, and very sure about what she would and would not do. For example, it appears that she never dabbled, as so many adolescents do, in alcohol – 'drinking wasn't for her,' recalls Bradford – and never felt the need to rebel in any obvious way. All of this would seem to add up to a contented, mentally stimulated teenager with a clear mind and a straight path ahead of her – a status that few can claim at the same age.

Erykah graduated from Booker T Washington High School in 1989, when she was 18 years old. The time had come to take another important step, but she would never forget her high school, or the people she had met there, mentioning the school and its influence on her in later interviews with evident pride. Her next move was college, but finding the right one wouldn't be easy at first: while her grade point average on leaving school was better than average it wasn't scintillating, which meant that she had to forgo her first choice. 'I wanted to go to Howard University initially,' she said, 'but my GPA wasn't good enough to get in. So I said OK, I'll just go wherever.'

Her choice was Grambling State University in Louisiana, where she would pursue Theatre Studies with the help of her family and scholarships. Founded in 1901, this college is traditionally an education provider to African-Americans (although the ethnic mix of its students is more varied nowadays) and is proud of its history, as its official anthem proclaims – 'Old Grambling, dear Grambling, We love thee, dear old Grambling, We're loyal to thee, our dear old School, We'll fight for thee for evermore'. Despite this slightly pompous bit of puffery, the college is a relaxed, almost rural place, situated in the small country town of Grambling between two highways and surrounded by countryside – and Erykah loved it from the moment of her arrival in autumn of 1989.

'I had the time of my life,' she said later. 'It was so fun to me, just to be there in a melting-pot with people from all over the United States. To be on this small campus in this wooded area between [the towns of] Shreveport and Monroe – it was a wonderful thing to be there.' It's possible that Erykah found the quiet, academic environment of Grambling State a welcome change from the urban streets of Dallas and the almost ceaseless performance culture of Booker T Washington High, although she certainly applied all her energy to her studies, as she had to everything she had attempted in the past. 'I gave my all to theater,' she said. 'Except I was late all the time! Late for everything. I learned so much there that had nothing to do with scholastics.'

The extracurricular subjects Erykah learned about would appear to explore just about every part of her life. For one thing, she was always full of enthusiasm and was always keen to try new approaches. She later recalled a college roommate called Fred, a good friend who would always try to stem her endless flow of suggestions: 'He would say, "We don't want no more ideas,"' she said. Unsurprisingly, this endless flow of activity also extended to the stage – the head of speech and theatre at Grambling was Allen Williams, who remembered her with these words: 'Erykah always seemed to be on-stage, though she was a sensitive and humane person. She didn't enjoy doing manual labour like sweeping the floors, but she loved performing. She was a fiery little character.'

Two crucial developments occurred while Erykah attended Grambling, and each in its own way was a part of her self-development as a thinker and as a person. The first was her discovery of, and involvement in, the beliefs of the Five Percenters, an African-American school of thought derived from, and interwoven with, the theology of the Nation of Islam, the Muslims whose political activism has underscored the social progress of America's black communities since the early years of the 20th century. As the child of an educated, spiritual family whose environment was no stranger to political and religious thought, it was perhaps inevitable that Erykah should encounter the NOI at some point and immerse herself in their arguments. Not that she accepted their teachings blindly or without consideration, but she would certainly continue to use elements of their thought in her later work.

The Five Percenters believe that five per cent of the world's population has achieved a significant degree of self-awareness. Erykah later explained in *Vibe* that '[It is] five percent in the sense that five percent of the people in the world have knowledge of self, and understand like we understand. Ten percent profit off of that information and just preach it to gain fame for themselves. Eighty-five percent follow, or don't know, or don't care. So that's the percentage part. I thought that was a smart philosophy.' As (in some ways) it is, although as she also wisely said, 'I'm not a part of the organization, because I don't think any one organization can define your relationship with the Creator.'

The history of the Five Percenters is relatively simple: the group was founded in 1964 by Clarence 13X (born Clarence Smith in 1929), a Nation of Islam minister who had spent 17 years in the NOI under the guidance of Malcolm X at Temple Number 7 in Harlem. His inspiration was the lessons of the senior NOI minister Elijah Muhammad, to whose work Clarence added. He then founded the 'Allah School in Mecca' in 1967 – a building in Harlem that remains the Five Percenters' headquarters – but was assassinated by unknown killers two years later. However, he had been allowed sufficient time to establish a firm foundation for his church, which gave itself the official title of the Nation of Gods and Earths (men are Gods, women are Earths) and which had attracted thousands of adherents to itself by the time Erykah Wright came to it two decades later.

However, the Five Percenters' theology is anything but simple, and in fact might be regarded as somewhat arcane. The major difference between the beliefs of Elijah Muhammad and the Nation of Islam, and those of Clarence X, is that the former believe that NOI founder Wallace Fard is the personification of God, while the Five Percenters view the black race as a kind of collective deity once it has achieved the crucial step of attaining mastery of self. The Five Percenters also use something called the Supreme Alphabet and Supreme Mathematics, a system devised by Clarence X in which each letter or number is a concept, and is accompanied by a recitable parable. For example, A stands for Allah, B is Be or Born, C is See and so on, while N stands for Now and Nation, and is accompanied by the words, 'Now is the time for the black man to wake up and come into the realization of Islam, which is the true and righteous self, which is his true Nature and his true Nation.' Users refer to this system as 'dropping science' or 'sciencing out', and the appeal of this practice to a trained rapper does not need to be overemphasised, of course. Add the use of icons such as a crescent and the number seven in Five Percenter symbology and the result is a fully fledged belief system.

How seriously does Erykah take the Five Percenters? Apparently, she has some sympathy towards their beliefs but does not subscribe fully to the way they approach life. This is also true of Rastafarianism, which she supports in part, but not enough to warrant her converting to it formally. Journalist Greg Tate once asked Erykah about the appearance of Five Percenter symbols such as gods, earths and mathematics in her work. She replied, 'I'm talking about the teachings of Clarence X. When I was at Grambling State, it was a big fad. Everybody had these books with a seven and a crescent on them. In high school, I learned a lot about myself. Anything that was about me, I wanted to know. Like, what is that? I want to see that. Seeking the knowledge, I acquired it... I memorized and understood all the information and I use it every day, just like I use Christian proverbs and text, Islamic proverbs and text, and Buddhist proverbs and text. Anything I can use to learn about me.'

The second, and more profound, change in the development of the eldest Wright daughter was her decision to change her name once again – and this time there were no half-measures or adaptations. The change came from her love of jazz, and specifically of a two-syllable word that she would use ad lib to improvise the songs she performed as part of her theatre classes or among friends. The nonsense word 'badu' was evocative enough to denote percussion, or the horn she had so loved to emulate as a child, and became the staple of her scat. 'My last name came from my singing style, which is derived from scat music... When I started singing, that was the scat, the only one that I knew. And that was what I would do every night, and I was known as Erykah Badu,' she recalled. She added in an interview with MTV that '"badu" is paying homage to scat music, bebop music. "Badu" is one of the things I'm always singing in music... I had a whole song just singing that.'

Some kind of fortune was smiling on Erykah when she chose this name (perhaps even the god of self-mastery that Clarence X had visualised?), for it later emerged that 'badu' is a word in its own right, with a semantic function and thus no mere nonsense word. Coincidentally, 'badu' is Arabic (ancestral language of the NOI and its subgroups), and means 'to manifest light and truth'. This fact Erykah would learn from none other than her errant father Toosie, who wrote to her at around this time and ended his letter with the commendation, 'Good choice, kid'. The interplay of fate and coincidence is just too obvious to be ignored – interpret it your own way. Erykah Badu certainly did just that, and the name was hers for ever.

It must have been quite an experience for Erykah to have her father contact her after such a prolonged absence. Among the emotions she must have felt would have been the realisation of just how far she had come since those early days when he was still a part of the Wright family – after all, in spiritual and material terms, she had taken control of her own life long ago. She might also have resented his appearance, having adapted her life successfully to fill the gap he left and having become accustomed to the fact that her life simply did not have a father in it.

Similarly, it must have been strange for Toosie (who does not enter this story after this point, other than as a credit in a sleevenote), to witness the career of his eldest daughter. Although he has never been interviewed to my knowledge, making it impossible to know exactly what he thinks or feels about Erykah, errant fathers tend to feel a mixture of guilt, pride, humility and sadness when they see their offspring excel. He feels guilt because he was not physically present to assist when necessary through what must have been a long haul, especially if fatherless; pride, as a parent, seeing his child outgrow her environment due to talent or hard work; humility, because the child's success is a metaphor for how she obviously does not need him and sadness, because (for whatever reason) he missed out on the joy of contact with his own creation.

Toosie's endorsement of Erykah's new surname, Badu, says much about him. After all, only a man of some education or spiritual awareness would know about the semantic roots of an Arabic verb, and only a man of some strength would congratulate his child on her decision to cast aside the name that originally came from him. It may be that we will never know more about Erykah's father than this, but perhaps that is only the way it should be. Far from exposing her family to a showbiz industry that she herself acknowledges to be the province of hustlers and liars, Badu has drawn a veil across them...and we should let that barrier remain intact.

The newly christened Badu was now wholly her own woman, and the names she had chosen for herself seem to be completely appropriate. Her family and friends rapidly got used to the idea that she had renamed herself, and the transition appears to have gone smoothly. Overnight, Erykah Wright became Erykah Badu, and there was no turning back. The die was cast.

3 Free-Falling

As most people know, a college education isn't just about academia. A typical student will also learn a lot more about themselves and the world they live in – and Erykah Badu was no exception. The habitual performer, it turned out, was also no shrinking violet when it came to partying – and partying hard, as Robert Bradford remembers. 'While she was at Grambling, I went to art school in Chicago. She came up a couple of times to stay with me. I'd go and pick her up from the train or the bus station and I'd meet her downtown in my friend's car. She would stay with me for those one or two days. Man, we kicked it. We would go out to clubs, parties, she'd just hang out.'

Erykah had also joined the Grambling Performing Arts Society, which toured periodically through the South and as far north as Chicago, although Robert never managed to get the time to see one of her shows. Most of their circle had moved away to college, and meetings tended only to occur during vacations. The four years Badu would spend in Louisiana changed her in many ways – the name-change and her discovery of Five Percenter ideology were just two important examples – and her family and friends would notice this when they met up every few months. Perhaps the side of her character that developed the most in these years was her spiritual side: always fascinated by the interwoven symbols of fate and religion that surrounded her, the teenage churchgoer was evolving into a woman situated at the confluence of a multitude of beliefs, respecting all but wholly endorsing none.

When she was later asked about her spiritual beliefs, Erykah included Rastafarianism, Christianity, Buddhism and Islam (and its Five Percenter teachings) in her answer. She went on to define her 'power' as supported by three intangible gifts: knowledge, wisdom and understanding. 'I would say that knowledge is knowing how a thing works; the wisdom is knowing how to use it and understanding is basically knowing what you're doing with it,' she explained. 'That's power to me.' Good old-fashioned astrology had a part to play, too: 'I'm a Pisces to the letter. Secretive, creative, but unable to explain where the creativity comes from.'

Erykah's refusal to bond completely with one religion is both crucial and revealing: 'No one religion can define my relationship with the Creator... My religion, if I have one, is probably the arts. I think the Creator loves that we understand to get a foundation and then to build from there. I don't stifle my creativity or my will to learn.' However, her positive identification of a 'Creator' puts her more in line with a Christian/Islamic axis than with religions that lack the concept of one central deity: 'I just loved art,' she said. 'I didn't realise it then, but now I know that the Creator gave me this gift, and that's what I do... I do the Creator's work best through my art. And it feels very natural for me.' Perhaps she put it most clearly when she explained that, 'Personally, I don't choose any particular religion, symbol, or teachings to define me. That's between the most high and me...but I do learn a lot from each thing, because everything is necessary. We're all here for a reason.'

Many interviewers would choose to focus on this side of her personality. She told the *Sydney Morning Herald* that her use of the red, green and gold colours of Rastafarianism is just a part of her multifaceted religious stance: 'I have just been through a plethora of different philosophies, and what they are are philosophies which all helped to make me who I am.' She also told *Soul Express* that 'I'm a Pisces, so that may have something to do with [my art]... I was blessed with the light of creativity. So it's very effortless, you know, I don't give it a lot of thought. I just kind of dance and move, or sing, or write, and it just comes. I have to share all the time, because I know it's a gift, and I know it's not me by myself. I'm just standing there and it's happening most of the time.'

She appears to view herself merely as a conduit for divine inspiration, telling *Vibe* that 'I know it's not me doing it all', and that this has been the situation for many years: 'I've had a conscience since I was about three or four years old. We all have consciences. That's all we've got. I knew right from wrong at five years old. I could look at people, like, oh, she ain't gonna make it, there's no way. I could just feel it.' This was one of the first interviews in which she explained the broader parameters of her world-view to a journalist, and those parameters are far-reaching: 'I know the weight of physical things, and I understand the weight of the celestial plane as well,' she mused. 'We are on Earth to experience the consequences of our choices. And what I choose to do, I know is going to come back, because it has time and time again since I was a child.' The idea of development and of moving from one spiritual plane to another (and ultimately to a kind of nirvana, perhaps?) was becoming clear: 'If you don't have a desire for knowledge or going to the next level, those things that are no good for you will keep lingering around... If you don't learn from the same mistakes that you keep repeating over and over and over, you'll be looking ass-out all the time.'

When her career took off some eight years after she enrolled at Grambling, many of Erykah's most avid fans were very taken with the sincerity and plurality of her beliefs, but many accused her of being a sham, or merely that her collection of symbols wasn't particularly meaningful. She showed surprising depth by accepting their criticism, explaining that, 'Sometimes it seems like the more your light shines, the more people wanna condemn you. It's frustrating but you have to keep on. You're born with a conscience, worrying about what others will think...but I understand what I'm trying to say. I never underestimate the audience's ability to feel me. I never meant to share as a ploy, to be seen as some great mystic.' She even returned fire with a sense of humour: 'On stage I'll say, hey, hey, I know y'all don't want to hear this shit,' she chuckled. 'Then I step up on my soapbox.' And if all this is starting to sound a little pompous, be reassured that Erykah has never lost sight of the fact that she is at heart an entertainer, as she told the South African *Sunday Times*: 'If it's entertaining, that is a blessing. I know that part of my purpose is to make people feel good.'

There is something ultra-inclusionist, almost magpie-like, in the way that Erykah has selected the spiritual symbols she uses in her work. At heart a Christian, she uses several images from Ancient Egyptian theology in her artwork and clothing and also dips into the rich stock of Islam and Rastafarianism for colours and metaphors. It's not clear how much of this polytheistic approach goes beyond surface symbols, of course – just because she places an Egyptian ankh (cross) on her arm doesn't mean she worships Ra, for example – and her often-stated belief in a 'Creator' seems to step beyond established religion into a purer, more personal relationship with God that requires no doctrine.

Through all this, whether her spiritual message is appreciated or derided, Erykah Badu has maintained a rock-solid centre of confidence. That she has managed to do so is a mystery to many, but it appears to rest on her unshakeable conviction that her work and career is following a divine path set out for her, which neither she nor anyone else can hinder or deflect. She told British DJ Trevor Nelson that, 'I think everything is divine, I think it's all pretty much laid out. I'm going to have a plan, because sometimes I find that I *am* a plan and it all lays itself out pretty smoothly. I just kinda do what I feel is right. You know, creatively, artistically.' With this in mind, it's little surprise that her confidence is hard to rock, even when the tribulations of life are at her doorstep, and it is very possibly the driving force behind her later rise to the top of public life and her extended stay there. After all, the snide words of a few writers don't really amount to much when compared with the full force of divine support.

While Erykah was studying at her theatrical modules in Louisiana, Robert Bradford – whose involvement in the story of Erykah was approaching its pivotal moment – had almost completed his visual arts course in Chicago. Three years older than his cousin, by 1991 he was almost ready to graduate. However, another project had taken the most important place in his life – the band he had developed along with a college friend, Julian Akins (who used the *nom de rap* Judge Mental), which was called Kinetic Order. His old-school sobriquet of 'Bob Rock' had long been replaced by 'Free' or 'Rob Free', a nickname he had acquired while at college – for no clearly defined reason, he says. Judge Mental was a force to be reckoned with at that time, he recalls. 'We were all in the Superman Freestyle MC battle at the New York Music Seminar, the last year they had it. I was eliminated in the first round, and another friend of ours associated with Kinetic Order was eliminated in the second round, but Julian won it. He teaches art in Brooklyn now.'

Like the long-gone Star City Breakers before them, Kinetic Order went a surprisingly long way towards mainstream success, and even signed both a production deal and a record deal, the latter with the Chameleon label (a part of the Elektra empire). Had Chameleon not gone under in the early 1990s – leaving all its artists high and dry – Kinetic Order might have gone much further: 'Chameleon went defunct, and so all the artists on the label who hadn't finished their projects either got dropped or sent on to other labels,' Free remembers, although there is no regret in his voice, for he has moved on to better things. 'I had signed a production deal in Chicago, and they were gonna form a new label and sign us to it – but Judge and I fell out about a year later, due to creative differences.'

Bradford retains fond memories of Akins, however – including a classic case of the rapper being unintentionally provoked by Erykah when she was visiting the Kinetic Order duo while they were at art college. 'Jules went to pick her up and we were in the car going back to my place,' recalls Bradford, laughing. 'And she wanted to drop this new rhyme to me so she started beating on the window. Cos that's what we do, know what I mean?' Badu had reverted to the old car-park habit of using any convenient metallic surface as a beatbox, but Akins was unaware of this practice, and was a little distressed to find his co-rapper's diminutive cousin apparently beating the hell out of his precious vehicle. 'Julian didn't know what was going on – he bugged out! He's like, what's up?' laughs Bradford now.

The combination of plentiful theatrical and musical performances on campus at Grambling, tours through the southern States, visits to the big city to party with Rob Free, stays at home that featured big family-and-friends get-togethers and the general positive experience (personally, politically and socially) that the years 1989 to 1993 provided, all meant that they were some of the best years of Erykah's life. Academically, however, Erykah failed to achieve the one thing she had expected to get from Grambling – a degree. The Wright family were surprised, to say the least, when she announced in the summer of 1993 that she would not be sitting her final exams, and to this day it isn't exactly clear why she didn't qualify. She later provided a variety of reasons, including, 'I was there for four years, but I didn't graduate because I was tired of studying... Academics had never been interesting to me', and that (to her) a degree was just 'a piece of paper'.

Her mother, Kolleen, later said about her daughter's decision that, 'I thought she should have gone ahead to pursue her degree, but I also knew there was something stronger driving her to her goal.' Perceptively, she added that, 'She always knew exactly where she was going and how to get there.' And Erykah was grateful for her mother's understanding, explaining, 'She realized she just had to let me grow and watch me do what I had to do.'

Looking back, it seems that Erykah's decision to leave Grambling without a degree was the right one, although it must have seemed like a dangerous choice to make at the time. After all, she had no way of knowing that she would find success as a solo artist, and the thought of having spent all that time at college with no tangible result to show for it must have been nerve-racking. But ultimately she was proven right. When she succeeded in getting a teaching job a little later, she did so without the benefit of a degree, for example – the skills she could demonstrate as an actor, singer and dancer must have been more than enough for her to get the job.

What Erykah had to do, it seemed, was to take her now-honed acting skills to another level, and she wasted no time on her return to Dallas in doing so, joining the respected Soul Nation theatre company, which later became the troupe-in-residence at the city's African American Museum of Art and Culture after changing its name to Soul Rep. The group, which specialises in plays written from an African-American perspective, was co-founded by a friend of hers called Tisha Crear, and became known in the Texas area for both its acute choice of material and the quality of its productions. Performances were held in respected venues such as Undermain Theater and the Carpenter Theater, situated at the Irving Arts Center. After she joined the company in 1994, shortly after her return to Dallas from Grambling, Soul Nation would feature performances from Erykah for the next two years or so, and if you were in the audience for one of her shows, you witnessed a rare sight – that of the 23-year-old Badu, a fully fledged actor and singer, giving her all in a local environment, before the music industry took her to its bosom.

Perhaps it's just as well that acting was Erykah's chief priority at this stage. The commercial forms of both soul and R&B were in a slightly shaky condition in America in 1994, and the winds of change that had transformed almost all forms of popular music since the early 1990s had not yet settled to allow solid talent to come through. At this time a particularly watered-down form of R&B was very popular, spearheaded by inoffensive but bland vocal groups like Boyz II Men, and had more or less taken the place of classic soul in commercial terms, although relatively underground bands like The Roots (whose début album, *Organix*, had appeared the previous year) were beginning to emerge. There was still some hope for R&B – acts like TLC had injected some edge into the syrupy mainstream – but any genuine barrier-breaking was taking place at club level rather than on a commercial plane.

Conversely, pure hip-hop had rarely been healthier. The buzz-phrase in 1994 was very much 'G-Funk', a genuinely exciting rebranding of the old beats-and-rhymes idiom that had been kickstarted by two 1992 albums – Dr Dre's *The Chronic* and Ice Cube's *The Predator*. Both albums had (coincidentally in the case of the former, intentionally with the latter) nailed the American black community's mood just after the LA riots of April 1992, and a whole wave of sonically mellow, dope-and-guns-inspired albums had risen in their wake. Brand new and massively successful acts such as Snoop Dogg, Bone Thugs-N-Harmony, the Wu-Tang Clan, Warren G, Cypress Hill, Tupac Shakur and the Notorious BIG had brought these retro-flavoured tones to the charts, and it's fair to say that, had Erykah Badu attempted to make her way into the music business just as this enormous tidal wave of beats was cascading onto the airwaves, her subtle, less-is-more vibe might have been swamped entirely and left stillborn.

At this point in her career, therefore, it was fortunate that acting was at the top of Erykah's agenda rather than music, although she still sang as part of her productions, participated in the occasional rap session and was fully immersed in the music she had loved since childhood.

But it wasn't until 1994 that the roles were reversed and the musical side of her skills came to prominence. This happened when Robert Free asked her if she would be interested in making music with him – and it was to the benefit of both parties that she agreed. On her part, joining forces with such an accomplished performer and writer (remember, the ascent of Kinetic Order had only been halted by record company fortunes rather than any lack of drive or talent) was a genuine, strengthening challenge, while it turns out that Robert had been through a fairly traumatic time himself. After the demise of Kinetic Order, the musician's Chicago apartment had been robbed, and a load of valuable recording equipment stolen: 'Kinetic Order had a bunch of equipment, and we were brand new and thought we were big shots – overexposed ourselves and somebody got us. But they didn't get everything: when I got back to Dallas, we had what I had left after Chicago. So what was left over was mostly what me and Erykah used.'

The formation of the duo was not, it seemed, a conscious decision made at one particular moment. Free wanted to keep working on the music that he had developed so much in Chicago, while Erykah knew that this was an opportunity to be creative with her cousin and welcomed it. 'It wasn't like we decided to start a band,' says Free now. 'We just kept working, and we stayed cooped up in a room at my grandmother's house in North Park.' Once again, without the co-operation of the Wrights' extended family no music might have been made, and the generosity of Mema (as everyone called Robert's grandmother) made it possible for the duo to work together.

The roots of preparation for the project went back some way: Free had thought of working with his cousin (whose MCing and singing he had always admired) while he was still in Chicago. 'We'd talked about doing some things, and I was working on tracks as I was preparing to move back to Dallas. I was sending her tracks, which were like hip-hop-based tracks, but I knew she was going to be singing as opposed to MCing, and I was approaching the tracks with that in mind.' Putting the basic songs together was no easy task, given Bradford's straitened circumstances after the theft of Kinetic Order's equipment. 'The songs were just an ASR-10 sampler and a keyboard. At that time I was living with one of my friends – we'd been evicted from our place in Chicago – so we just scrounged around as we prepared to make our next move.'

However, on his return to the family home in Dallas, Free's semi-professional experience was invaluable for steering the advancement of the group, which began composing, recording and performing almost immediately. A name was no problem – 'Erykah Free' was the obvious choice, and one that felt right from the very beginning. Initial progress was rapid: 'We recorded and we did a lot of performing. We developed the group, we decided on a name. I was programming the tracks and writing the tracks, she was writing the lyrics, sometimes we would both write the lyrics, and I was also an MC. So I was a performer as well as a producer,' Bradford recalls.

The music that appeared from the Erykah Free collaboration was an imaginative mix of hip-hop, R&B and soul, with both members' love of all three genres coming to the fore. Two of their earliest compositions were songs called 'On & On' and 'Apple Tree', with the latter inspired by grandmother Viola Wilson's advice to 'pick your friends like picking fruit'. However, Mrs Wilson – whose house had also been given over to Erykah Free at weekends, leading her to say that, 'If anyone came over, I had to entertain on the porch' – was less than impressed with either song when Erykah and Robert gave her a preview. Her reaction to 'Apple Tree' was, 'Uh-uh, that ain't goin' nowhere', while she privately didn't think that 'On & On' would do well, either. She later admitted, with a chuckle, 'I'm glad I didn't say that to her, because I was wrong.'

Familial disapproval notwithstanding, Erykah Free had a full set of songs written, recorded and rehearsed by early 1994, and started looking for a suitable live venue for a performance. The plan was that both Badu and Bradford would rap over a DAT (digital audio tape) of the keyboard and percussion parts of the songs, with the player and PA system the only necessary equipment. This meant that their concert could be staged practically anywhere. Both performers delved deep into their Dallas contacts for an opportunity, and it wasn't long before the perfect chance to prove their skills came along.

The gig came along as the result of Erykah's parallel career as a teacher, which was one of the many jobs she had taken in Dallas to earn a living after returning from college in Grambling. Her CV at this stage resembled that of most ex-college students – moving from one part-time unskilled job to another, she paid for her living costs and those of Erykah Free by waitressing and taking jobs as a summer-school teacher.

One of Erykah's first jobs was a waitressing slot at a Dallas club in the Oak Cliff area called Steve Harvey's Comedy House, home of the now-successful American comedian. She sold tickets, distributed drinks to the customers and, when she had a moment, watched Harvey run through his act from the side of the stage. A crucial moment came one night when (apparently at his call) she ran on-stage to join him in his routine, a move that the audience loved and the comedian himself thought added to his performance considerably. 'It was hilarious to him, and I kept doing it,' Erykah later remembered. 'He'd call me up on stage with him. I was Lucy and he was Ricky.'

The experience of being wanted to perform alongside such an established name – and not only to match up to his talent, but to be recalled night after night – strengthened Erykah's confidence and made her feel respected 'and that's what I needed', she later said. She spent the rest of her time at the Comedy House booking talent and helping with stage management (for which her Theatre Studies college skills must have been invaluable) until the club closed its doors when Harvey moved to Los Angeles to create a TV show for Warner Brothers.

Perhaps slightly disheartened by the closure of the club – but simultaneously heartened by the rapid progress of Erykah Free – Erykah took another waitressing job at Grinders Coffee House on Lower Greenville Avenue, a popular café situated off a main street in Dallas's downtown area. Robert Bradford remembers Grinders as a good place to drop in: 'Grinders was the last place she worked at before she signed her deal – and a lot of people remember that for some reason, even though it's not even there any more! It was a cool spot to go to. It had a patio on the side, it didn't face the main street. Lower Greenville Avenue is a real popular strip. She worked days – I think she liked it there.'

While holding down the waitressing job at Grinders, Erykah also worked part-time as a teacher of dance and acting at Dallas's prestigious arts venue, the South Dallas Cultural Center (SDCC). This £1 million

($1.5 million) building is situated at 3400 South Fitzhugh and is among the biggest and best-equipped arts organisations in the southern States, boasting a 1,670sq m (18,000sq ft) arena, a 100-seat theatre, various art galleries and dance studios, a digital recording suite and spaces for ceramics, printmaking and photography. Its mission statement was, and remains, 'to develop a multi-purpose arts facility in South Dallas to serve the African American artistic community', which it fulfils with a constant programme of exhibition and education. In the summer of 1994 Erykah played a part in the latter by leading classes of children through various acting and dance curricula – a part she was easily qualified to play by now. A Dallas management consultant called Bernestine Singley, who is a long-time friend of the Wright family, was quoted a couple of years later on her memories of seeing Erykah teach an acting improvisation group: 'She was amazingly good,' she said. 'All by herself, she mesmerised 50 little children in that room.'

It seems that Erykah was incredibly busy at this time: juggling jobs as both a waitress and teacher as well as recording with a band is no easy task, and one that left her exhausted, as she later mentioned when discussing the work of the British soul singer Omar: 'He is one of my favourite artists ever. I was already working on [Erykah Free] when I heard him, but he had a continued influence on me. I had three jobs at the time: I was working as a teacher, a waitress and performing. So I was listening to him in my off time, not so much as an artist but as medicine.'

Despite the rigours of her lifestyle, Erykah was utterly devoted to her work with Robert Bradford, and the pressure of securing a live outlet was growing. Enter a Dallas artist called Emmanuel Gillespie, a fellow teacher at the SDCC at this time. Speaking today from his Reciprocity arts venue, Emmanuel remembers how he first met Erykah: 'We came together when we were both doing classes at the South Dallas Cultural Center – we were teaching summer programs. I'm a visual artist, so I was teaching painting and mural classes to students and Erykah was doing theatre or dance. The students were children of all ages – we had 3-year-olds to 12-year-olds.'

As well as being an artist and teacher, Gillespie had been nursing for some time the idea that Dallas needed a music and arts space that would be both easy to access for performers and non-exclusive for audiences. As luck would have it, he was looking for the right act to do a show at a space he had recently located that he thought would be appropriate. 'I had a space, a gallery,' he remembers. 'There was a gallery at the South Dallas Cultural Center, but I wanted to create a separate space for artists to go to. I had this in mind and I threw it at Erykah to see what she thought.'

Needless to say, Erykah was delighted by the idea of a more underground arts space than the excellent (but official) facilities of the SDCC, and was immediately keen not only that Gillespie should proceed with his plans but that Erykah Free should be the act to open it. Emmanuel recalls, 'She told me she had this music and she wanted me to hear the way she sounded.' An audition was duly arranged – and he was struck speechless by Erykah's voice. 'When I heard her,' he remembers, 'I thought – this is it. This is what I'm looking for.'

Robert Free remembers Gillespie's music-gallery project with enthusiasm: 'In 1994 Erykah would have been teaching at the SDCC and coming home in the evening and recording with me,' he says. It turns out that he and Gillespie had been acquaintances at school. 'Emmanuel was a senior, one or two grades above me, and I knew him from arts. We were the first act to perform at his gallery space, which became a regular performance venue on Saturday nights. Everybody called it the Gallery. It was downtown, at the back end of Deep Ellum. It was a small space with a glass front, like a little studio – it was a cool place to hang out and it got real popular.'

The first Erykah Free concert was a resounding success, with the small space packed with listeners and both performers on top form. The pair had rehearsed their act to perfection and the combination of new venue and new act made the atmosphere electric. The Gallery show was the green light for dozens of other Dallas bands to come out of the woodwork: 'We were like the hosts,' recalls Free. 'After the initial one, it became a venue for other local acts to perform. We performed the first two weeks together and then it was like improv, we'd be there hanging out and maybe we'd do some freestyle. It was a good time.'

Gillespie remembers his venue with fondness. 'After that first Erykah Free show, it caught on, and right from day one you had all these different artists, from hip-hop to dance, coming there every Saturday night. It became known quite quickly and lasted at least two years.' The Gallery only ceased operations when Erykah moved away from Dallas and Emmanuel's own career took off, but he retained his original impulse to open up the arts to everyone, and later founded another venue. Today his Reciprocity building is still run with the same spirit. Was he surprised by Erykah's subsequent success? 'No. I just thought, here's this person with all this energy and always doing something. I always told her she would do it.' What was she like as a colleague? 'She was happy and she was an artist. She enjoyed teaching, I know that.'

And this was no easy teaching job, Gillespie recalls. 'We worked with a lot of at-risk kids, because South Dallas is a kind of at-risk community.' He muses that, 'She was just enjoying *being*, you know? My daughter was one of her students – she was just three at the time – and she used to call her "Sister Ra-Ra". I don't know why. The kids loved her, you know.' Bradford confirms the 'Sister Ra-Ra' story: 'She used the name Ra-Ra to rap with for a while, too.'

It seems that people simply liked Erykah Badu for her unpretentious nature, her devotion to her art and her uncomplicated confidence. One of the legacies of her sojourn at the South Dallas Cultural Center is her enduring friendship with the singer N'Dambi, a South Dallas resident who met Erykah while auditioning for a part in a play to be held at the SDCC. At the time, N'Dambi had just adopted her African name (which means 'most beautiful'), but most people still knew her by her given name, Chonita Gilbert. The two became firm friends and performed both separately and as a duo at the Gallery and other venues. Common ground was soon established when Gilbert revealed that she had grown up playing the piano and that one of her earliest memories was of being reprimanded for singing Millie Jackson's '(If Loving You Is Wrong) I Don't Want To Be Right' in the family bathroom. (She is also just a year older than Erykah.) After they had discussed their plans at length – Erykah dreaming of a future for Erykah Free, N'Dambi yearning for a solo career as a singer – they made a pact that if one of them secured a recording contract she would help the other to launch her career. Some years later, Erykah would take pains to fulfil her part of the bargain, and more.

By this stage Erykah was a consummate actor and singer, with little difference in her degree of mastery over both disciplines. 1994 was a crucial year, however, as Robert Bradford estimates that it was at about this time that she made a firm mental commitment to music over the theatre. 'Just like I made a conscious decision that music was gonna be my career,' he states, 'I think Erykah decided that music was gonna be the thing that she was gonna put her all into.' Erykah Free had developed from a backroom band with only a keyboard and beatbox in its arsenal to a much more fully fledged entity, it seems. 'Everything seemed to be pretty serious, it wasn't like we weren't treating it as if it wasn't gonna be big,' the rapper recalls. 'Maybe not as big as her solo career later became, but definitely not something that we were just gonna tinker around with. We definitely approached it with some commitment.'

In retrospect, this development appears to have been the only choice for Erykah. By this time she had spent many years of her young life acquiring and refining her performance skills, and without them she might as well not exist. When *HipOnline* asked her what music meant to her, she replied with the utmost gravitas that, 'I don't think I would really be much without it, without it coming through me. It's my means of communication, my means of growth, my means of transportation from one point in my life to another. It's how I express myself. What singing means to me? I never did consider myself a singer, I just let people watch me feel music and how it comes through me.'

As a statement of a performer's essential function, this can hardly be bettered, but Erykah went even further when she likened the stage to nourishment: 'I'm a starving artist; I'm hungry for the stage. All the time I want to perform. I never get tired of it. It's not just my job, it's my life. Anyone who lets me go up there, I'll go. I think if I was not able to sing and perform for people, I would die. I would probably physically become ill having to hold in all of the love and sorrow and excitement and happiness and sexuality.'

It wouldn't be long before the name of Erykah Free would hit the local music industry, as their reputation had now extended beyond the Dallas city limits and as far as Houston, where a production company called Galaxy Nine had its ears to the ground. This organisation was the vehicle for producer and songwriter Jaborn Jamal, who liked what he heard. 'They were pretty happening,' said Jamal later. 'We went to see them in the hip-hop clubs and the next thing I knew I was in the studio with them.' Once he had had the chance to check out the remarkable vocal and MCing abilities of the duo, he had little doubt as to their potential: 'I knew that they were the move. I was really happy to work with them because Erykah had the most developed voice I had heard thus far.' A production deal was negotiated, and two songs – the aforementioned 'Appletree', and another called 'No Love' – were scheduled for recording.

The recruitment of a name producer to the Erykah Free cause was reason for celebration. It has become an accepted tradition that the support of a decent studio name can lead directly to the appearance of a record deal, from a company which is reassured by his or her presence that there is some genuine quality in the new act. Progress indeed – but ironically it would be the film world, not the music world, that gave Erykah Free their next break. Through her contacts in the Dallas theatre scene, Erykah managed to secure a cameo role in the trailer for a new movie, *The Boulevard*, in 1995. The film is a grim action thriller revolving around a scenario in which a prostitute, played by Rae Dawn Chong, is at the centre of a good-cop versus bad-pimp conflict. It's not a great movie, and its critical and commercial performance reflected this – but its content was hardly relevant to Erykah, whose brief part in the trailer took no more than a couple of hours to complete.

After the shooting of the trailer was complete, Erykah went to a 'wrap party' (the post-production celebration) and met a businessman called Tim Grace, who introduced himself as head of the film production company Legacy, based in neighbouring Fort Worth. Falling into conversation, Erykah casually mentioned that she was the singer in a band, and Grace asked to hear her sing. Reportedly, Erykah burst into song then and there, impressing the film-maker enough for him to offer Erykah Free a management deal on the spot – an unusual offer given the rather impromptu circumstances, perhaps, but one which boded very well for the future, as well as attesting to the remarkable power of Erykah's voice.

The meeting was perfectly timed: Erykah Free's profile and activities had grown to the extent that Free and Erykah could barely handle the recording, booking, transport and marketing duties of the band, as well as lacking the legal and insider knowledge that a competent manager provides. After a lengthy discussion, both Robert Bradford and Erykah were convinced that Grace would make a decent manager: 'He was a real cool guy – he seemed to know what he was doing,' says Free. 'He had the right idea, and he got us gigs, he kept us doing it.' A lawyer, Ward White, whom the duo knew, became their attorney and negotiated the management deal – although there was a slight division over this issue. Says Free, 'I never signed a contract with Tim Grace. I was cautious – *real* cautious – because the management situation I had come out of in Chicago had made me a little leery. Erykah signed. We talked about it. I said, I don't know, we need to be cautious, but she had signed separately.' It doesn't seem to have been a cause of friction between the two artists, but it is indicative of the frame of mind of the two cousins at this point (Erykah perhaps more instinctual, Robert more calculating). How much pressure (if any) Grace placed on both members to sign up for his skills is unknown, as he remains out of the public eye, although he did go on to negotiate later contracts for both artists in due course.

Perhaps Robert's excessive caution was justified given his previous experiences at the hands of the industry, as his career had been thwarted not once but twice by industry forces – once when his record label was pulled out from under him, and again when the production company in Chicago had promised (but failed) to sign his band Kinetic Order to a new label. But in this case it was unnecessary: Tim Grace acquitted himself admirably, it seems, and pushed the Galaxy Nine relationship along while maintaining a healthy live schedule for the band.

And so Erykah Free took an important step, to a level on which they could compete professionally with the many other bands that are ready to sign a deal but are waiting for the right offer to come along. After all, Erykah and Rob were now accomplished musicians and performers, with expert representation and enough industry expertise to spot the right opportunity when it came along. Nowadays, Rob talks with humble amusement about those days of innocence: he knows that Erykah Free were a force to be reckoned with, even if the intervening years have given him enough extra experience to know how young and unschooled they really were, despite the high quality of their work.

They knew enough to recognise a trustworthy manager, however, and Grace – a shining example among a breed of generally unreliable professionals – remains involved with Erykah Badu to this day. As for their music, its evident quality belied the duo's relative youth and reiterates yet again the importance of the years they spent honing their act at club level. Emmanuel Gillespie did more than he knew when he gave them the chance to perform at the Gallery.

The Erykah Free of this time was a different beast from that of previous months: with a manager, a producer and an original portfolio, it seemed that the duo could only go from strength to strength. And so they would, but perhaps not in the way that the two cousins would have imagined.

4 From Motown To New York

At this point Erykah was still not devoted solely to music. As her subsequent career would demonstrate, she has never let go of her acting abilities – and why should she? After all, she herself would argue that her theatre and musical skills are not separate, but one complete side of her character. Even in 1995, when Erykah Free had begun to make serious progress, she was still allocating a significant portion of her time to performing with Soul Nation, and received local critical plaudits for her role in a play called *Love Awaits*, a production by writer Courtney Long. Interestingly, her mother Kolleen Gipson-Wright was also among the cast, although no record exists of how the mother and daughter responded to each other's presence on stage. Soul Nation founder Tisha Crear said after the run that, 'Erykah's improvisational skills are probably the sharpest thing she's got going on. She knows how to work with an audience', an early revelation that would appear to hold more than a grain of truth, given her later predilections for chopping and changing her live shows.

However, more effort was required to keep Erykah Free moving onward and upward, and the duo spent a lot of time preparing for the recording of a professional demo that they could use to sell themselves to a record company. Mid-1995 saw them enter the studio, with Jamal Jaborn at the helm, to produce a 19-song demo CD that was referred to from then on as the *Funky Cousins* demo. More than merely a backroom recording, this collection was a perfect combination of the cousins' passions for soul, R&B and hip-hop, with Jaborn's sympathetic, warm production adding a sweetness to the sound which a self-produced demo might have lacked. Erykah in particular was delighted with the results, to the extent that she decided there and then that it would hardly need to be improved upon, should the requirement to do so ever arise.

Ever the consummate artists, Robert and Erykah applied their visual-artist skills to the recording and produced a whole press kit including photos. The *Funky Cousins* package was an entire concept, their product seemed to say, and both artists and manager were confident that it would be warmly received by the industry and media. Robert remembers the day the final product was complete: 'The demo that we had produced, apart from two of the songs that were done with other producers, was pretty much written and produced by me and Erykah. We had a whole press kit and it was all packaged up. It was a really interesting demo – it has 'On & On', 'Appletree', 'Ye Yo', 'No Love' and 'My Life' on it. We also had photos.'

Good as the demo was, Erykah Free's job now was to get as much live exposure as possible to prepare for the influx of A&R people, whom they would need to impress in order to attract a record deal. They had successfully completed several circuits of the local club scene by late 1995 and were beginning to find the small venues less of a challenge. Luckily for them, their manager Tim Grace was proving to be a powerful ally and had hooked them up with some prestigious support slots when nationally successful acts came through Dallas.

Robert and Erykah were delighted – and possibly a little intimidated – to find themselves on the same bill, at major Texas venues, as A Tribe Called Quest and Naughty By Nature, but they knew they could rise to the occasion and were happy to see their reputation begin to spread. 'We seemed to spawn a buzz,' recalled Badu some years later. 'The rap acts would come in from New York, and their A&R people and their managers would be there, too. And they'd see us and say, who is this? That's sly!' Not that this was any real surprise to the pair: Erykah's liquid, passion-filled vocals had long been the toast of local audiences and Rob knew that both his raps and his backing tracks were funky and innovative.

People were starting to take serious notice of Erykah Free. More astute music fans in the area had noted that they seemed able to please audiences of many types, whether the hardcore hip-hop crowd or the more relaxed, coffee-table audience that followed mellower acts such as

The Roots. This was a direct result of Free's perceptive decision to combine his own beats and raps with Erykah's almost supernatural vocals – a style that few mainstream artists were using, but one for which there was clearly an audience. The nearest a successful act was to using this approach might be Bone Thugs-N-Harmony, whose fusion of soul vocals and gangsta rap had made them superstars – but their music was too electronic and not organic enough to be compared meaningfully with that of Erykah Free.

In retrospect, it's a highly attractive blend of styles, and there's little wonder that critics would struggle to pigeon-hole Erykah's later work. What pleased many listeners was Erykah's ability to bust a rhyme alongside Free and then soar into an acrobatic melody, making the transition without apparent effort. The great thing about this approach was its pan-demographic nature: whether the listener was young, old, black or white, it appealed in some way or other.

Things were moving fast – almost too fast, perhaps. After all, Erykah Free was still a young band with some live experience but relatively little industry expertise, even given Bradford's previous successes with Kinetic Order. More support slots came along – this time with Arrested Development, who in 1995 were touring in support of their *Zingalamaduni* album of the previous year and who, as it turned out, were in something of a commercial decline. However, their fanbase in the South was loyal, and the show (at which Erykah Free had one of their first chances to play before an audience fully tuned into Afrocentric issues) was a big step forward in the life of the young band.

Conversely, their opening slot for Wu-Tang Clan rapper Method Man was akin to riding the crest of a wave. The New Jersey MC had just released his début album, *Tical*, on Def Jam, and would experience an enormous hit some months later thanks to a chartbusting duet with Mary J Blige titled 'I'll Be There For You'/'You're All I Need To Get By'. The word was that Method Man – and the Clan of which he was a member – were the new driving force in US hip-hop, and the experience of playing with him would be something that Robert and Erykah would never forget.

A key moment came when the twosome secured a spot at a show with hardcore rappers Mobb Deep. In 1995 the duo of Queensbridge,

New York-born rappers, Prodigy and Havoc, were taking their *The Infamous* album on the road, fuelled by the chart success of its lead single, 'Shook Ones, Part 2'. The rough beats and dark textures of their music were the product of life in the ghetto and (a parallel with Erykah and Robert) an art-school background – the two had met at the Big Apple's prestigious Graphic Arts High School in Manhattan. The synergy of the two bands was immediate, and Robert remembers *this* show (above, perhaps, all others) as being the spark that lit the touch-paper: 'We had done a lot of performances and gotten a nice little buzz going, and – from my recollection – the explosion happened when we did a show in Austin with Mobb Deep, and their manager, Tammy, was overwhelmed by what we were doing, and especially by Erykah.'

This was a crucial moment. Managers are known for the web of contacts they spin to stay aware of each other's business dealings, and the fact that an associate of an act as currently hot as Mobb Deep was impressed enough with Erykah Free to start making some phone calls was a cause for celebration. 'Tammy went back to New York,' remembers Robert, 'where she had a business relationship with Kedar Massenburg – and that's when the ball really got rolling.'

Enter Kedar Massenburg, who – along with Free, Jaborn and Grace – was, and remains, one of the most influential people in the story of Erykah Badu's career. Massenburg is a music-industry executive with experience of many sides of the industry, including artist management, label management and production, and has been attracting attention as a hot young innovator in American music since the early 1990s. At this time, in 1995, he was focusing his attention on two specific areas – the management of a 21-year-old soul singer called D'Angelo (who would also have a prominent role to play in Erykah's progress to stardom) and the opening of a new division of Universal, the giant music, film and media corporation. A busy man with a board of directors to impress, and a name to make, Massenburg was understandably keen to demonstrate his skill at locating new talent – fortunately for him, he has been described as having 'great ears and great eyes'; in other words, as being able to recognise potential and mould a visual image that fits it perfectly.

The label he was building was Kedar Entertainment, which was attracting a lot of attention due to his reputation as a master of 'set-up'; that is, the building of anticipation among radio, retail, media and fans for the release of an album – and keeping the attention focused on the act as it climbs. He once said, 'I would rather release one record a year that has been properly set up, than three or four albums that haven't... Too often record labels put out an album that hasn't been set up and then blame the artist when it doesn't sell well.' This approach has met approval in high places, with industry figures such as Universal chairman Doug Morris remarking that, 'Kedar has demonstrated that he can be ahead of the curve and find acts that will become successful. He isn't a fad chaser.' And also not a man easily fooled by appearances, for Erykah later recalled that when she first met him she was hardly looking her most rock-star-like: 'I was wearing long braids, no shoes, jeans and a T-shirt. Whatever, it didn't matter to me.'

Clearly Kedar was a man who could do much for the career of Erykah Free, who were overjoyed to find in 1995 that he wanted them to support D'Angelo in Dallas. At the time this singer (born Michael D'Angelo Archer in 1974) was riding a wave of enormous critical praise: he had released his *Brown Sugar* album to great acclaim in July that year and had been favourably compared with Marvin Gaye, Stevie Wonder, Prince and Al Green for his retro-flavoured soul, the sensuous flavour of his music (he remains one of America's main black heartthrobs) and his remarkable voice. A show with him represented a boost to the cousins' career, even without Kedar's managerial interest, and the duo knew that the show would be a pivotal one.

As usual, they played their standard polished set, with 'On & On' an obvious highlight and Erykah's vocals as accomplished as the smooth tones of D'Angelo himself. Massenburg came to see them after the concert and complimented them on their performance; his interest had clearly been aroused and the pair went home jubilant. Sure enough, shortly afterwards he contacted Erykah and told her that he was interested in signing her up to Universal through Kedar Entertainment.

Good news, then? Of course, but there was one slight hitch. Massenburg was only interested in signing Erykah as a solo artist, not

Erykah Free as a band. He explained that this meant that there would categorically be no place for Robert Bradford in the deal.

Erykah and Robert had been close friends for decades and, like the soulmates they were, they sat down together and talked. From the outset, one thing was clear: Robert was unequivocally delighted for his younger cousin. He told her to go ahead and accept Kedar's offer: 'In my heart, I always wanted to be a solo artist,' Erykah said later. 'I don't know how that made Free feel, truly. I probably will never know. But, as my cousin and my friend, he was strong for me. So I owe him a lot for that. He made it be comfortable for me to go forth and go where I wanted. As much as I love him, and as much as he loves me, we knew that it was time to go and be Erykah Badu, and do my thing.'

With the potentially tricky issue of splitting Erykah Free resolved, thanks to Robert's support and sensitivity, Erykah was free to consider Massenburg's offer from an objective point of view. Signing a contract in the music industry is never a simple matter, with basic 'meat-and-potatoes' contracts sent out, examined, revised and returned, and with lawyers on both sides ensuring that their clients' interests are served and protected. However, Erykah was fortunate enough to have Ward White on hand (again) as the band's attorney (he was beginning to assume some managerial duties, as well). Together they considered the Kedar Entertainment deal, compared it to other offers – which had begun to appear once word spread that Massenburg was interested – and came to a decision.

Badu knew even at this stage that the figures were not the most important part of the deal, whereas the record company's attitude was, and Kedar would be the man she would trust to take her career to the next stage. 'I had several offers, but I went with him because he was young, black, very smart, and he had a vision,' she said. 'None of the other labels had a vision. I was afraid I'd get lost in the shuffle of a bigger label.' The label was also prepared to allow her plenty of artistic autonomy, as she told *Soul Express*: 'I can do pretty much what I want to do with the music. They trust me, you know... I also get a lot of help, too, you know, a lot of suggestions, a lot of input creatively. Businesswise, they all help me. But the final decision is mine.'

A milestone in Erykah's life had been reached – the deal was signed, the record company backup was in place and a career strategy could be mapped out. It had been a long journey since the days of Booker T Washington or the South Dallas Cultural Center, it felt, but Erykah's belief that she would somehow succeed had never once left her. 'I had to wait for the right time,' she said much later, 'and although I've been creating all my life, I never stopped believing one time that there would be success for me. You know, I always knew that. I knew it so much that I didn't pay bills. I would tell the bill collector, "Well, when I get a record deal, I'll pay!" I always believed it and knew it, and I know that's why it is.'

Perhaps she had never quite known in which avenue her eventual success would lie, however, as she revealed, 'You know, I was a dancer, and then I was an actor, and I was a poet, and then I was a painter, or a sculptor – it changed a lot. I changed an awful lot, but once I see those people in the audience and get that feedback and know that they're really feeling what I'm feeling, I know I got to be here'. Music is the discipline that nourishes her most of all: 'This is what I need to be doing. That's why this is my first priority at this time in my life. I love to act, I love to do many things, but it isn't as important.'

Although Erykah knew that that moment was right to create her own solo work, leaving Robert Bradford behind was no easy task. For her early solo shows she would light a large white candle on the stage and explain that it represented a reminder of her plans to reunite the group, and a symbol of her respect for her cousin. In her later career a candle would be present at all of her concerts, but to begin with it functioned both as a shrine and a tribute to the lost genius of Erykah Free.

Bradford, meanwhile, was moving on with his own project, and has gone on to become a successful producer, musician and songwriter in his own right. 'We were both very creative kids,' he says now. 'But she had her path and I had my path.' The split of Erykah Free wasn't particularly traumatic in the end, he feels, although there was a difficult moment when he was depicted as being annoyed about the issue in an interview. A national hip-hop magazine printed a feature in which he was quoted as saying, 'I was pissed, to say the least. I feel like anybody in my situation would be. We talked. It was heated, you know what I'm saying?' He says now that this was a simple misquote.

'I remember that interview,' he says firmly, 'and it was a misquote. They asked me, were you upset about not getting signed, and I was telling them well, you ask *any* artist that question and they're gonna say, I would have loved to have had the opportunity to sign a deal. But it wasn't like I was pouting and crying. I was still doing my thing. I was still pushing forward and ultimately wound up signing another deal with Elektra Records. I was really happy for Erykah.'

Badu saw the interview and approached him to discuss it. 'She mentioned it to me, we talked about it for a little while,' Free recalls. 'She asked me about it and I told her about it. She was like, yeah, I understand. She was like, don't worry, because you're gonna produce on the record, you're gonna write, we're always gonna work together.'

This particular hurdle behind her, Erykah could now focus on her impending career as a Universal artist, which would be handled as a signing to the classic Motown label. In early 1996, she made the decision to move from Dallas to New York, where Massenburg could begin the 'set-up' process, get her name known and begin to build expectations for an as-yet-unrecorded album. The relocation was a crucial one for psychological as well as practical reasons. As we have seen, the Wright family circle is a very protective one and, given the safety of Erykah's Dallas background, it's not too much to state that she needed to escape the nest (so to speak) to achieve her fullest potential on her own. While Dallas always gave her a sense of security, it also constrained her in some ways. *Dallas Morning News* writer Thor Christensen remarked that, 'Erykah has always been very open about how important her mom and her grandmother are to who she is, and keeping her young ego in check and keeping her sense of who she is in place, and if she's living in New York that's something she can't have as easily – a sense of family and a sense of place.'

What the move to New York gave Erykah was the chance to develop as a truly independent entity; without the easy option of a loving welcome in the arms of her family, she had to work to make the uncaring audiences of New York love her. These were the conditions under which she would make herself known (no easy trial) and, furthermore, she made her choice to step away from home with full self-awareness. As she later said, 'Even though music is my hustle, and I'm a businesswoman, I know the industry is not trying to pacify my spirit. I have to do that.'

Once installed in her New York apartment, over 2,000km (1,500 miles) from Dallas, it became clear to Erykah how far from home she really was. Luckily for her, she had the considerable muscle of Kedar Entertainment on her side, and little time to become introspective. Massenburg had planned a stringent schedule of marketing and performances to initiate the 'set-up' of the Badu name, and her job was to rise to this challenge.

One of her early engagements was a four-night run at the Soul Café, a soul-food restaurant in Manhattan owned by the American actor Malik Yoba, star of the police drama *New York Undercover*. As legend has it, she was something of an instant success, and by the summer of 1996 word had begun to spread that a serenely composed Southern belle with the voice of an angel was knocking them dead in Manhattan. As she later recalled, 'I put my little tape in the tape recorder and sang "On & On", just to test the waters, and the audience loved it.' The travel-light, sing-loud approach that Kedar had cooked up worked like a dream, and soon Erykah was performing regular slots at other sophisticated New York venues such as Brooklyn's Crash House, Two Steps Down, the Brooklyn Moon and a venue called the Nuyorican Poets Café. The urban audiences loved her voice, her songs and her remarkable 60cm (2ft) headwrap, which she had adopted as a trademark and which was compared affectionately to a creation of Dr Seuss. They also adored her easy manner of singing over DAT or cassette-tape backing tracks from the *Funky Cousins* demo and other recordings, which meant that she didn't need a band at that stage.

Massenburg seized the opportunity to capitalise on Erykah's sudden underground popularity, and his publicity team sent out no fewer than 10,000 sampler cassettes of Badu songs to their contacts in the industry, while vinyl-only pressings of the demo version of 'On & On' (which are now worth a hefty figure) went to radio stations and clubs. The buzz began to build and journalists' attention began to turn to this hot new act. When radio programmers began adding 'On & On' to their playlists, the rise in interest grew and became a flood of calls to Kedar Entertainment requesting an interview. The first stage of Massenburg's vision had fallen into place, within a matter of months of their first meeting.

It's interesting to speculate what might have transpired if Erykah had not signed with Massenburg, and instead opted to go with a different record label. She said later that Kedar's vision had been what drew her to him, and this would appear to lie at the heart of her success. Massenburg had an acute awareness of where she would fit into the market, who would be buying her product, who would be attending her concerts and who would respond with most positivity to her spiritual message. However, another A&R executive might have lacked this perception, and tried to mould Erykah into a big-smiling teen pop act or – a terrible thought – an R&B vixen in thigh boots. He would have found this hard to do (it's difficult to imagine Erykah agreeing to pretend to be something she is not), but the process might have hindered her career and ended up stopping her going as far as she could.

The beauty of the Massenburg deal lay in the fact that Erykah was given enough autonomy as a new artist on a new label division to make her own choices, while her work was backed up by the enormous muscle of Universal and associated with the top-line brand of Motown (which boasts a pedigree unlike any other in soul and R&B). A smaller independent label might have given her the desired autonomy, but lacked serious marketing and distribution power. A straight deal with a big label might have left Erykah swallowed up among the hundreds of other artists on its roster. Signing the deal with Massenburg was, it seems, a smart move.

One of the first writers to publish a feature about Erykah was Miles Marshall Lewis of *One World* magazine, who later recalled his early experiences with her: 'My first encounter with Erykah Badu was in Fort Greene, Brooklyn, during the spring of 1996,' he said. 'My best friend's room-mate was a longtime Dallas buddy of hers, sister to her future back-up singer, the honey-Afroed N'Dambi... I can testify that her high headwraps and incense affinity existed to Brooklyn from Texas, no tacked-on trappings of artifice. No different, really, than a half-dozen other sisters I knew in the community rocking theirs the same way.'

Lewis went on to recall how Badu made an instant splash on the New York club scene: 'The local embrace of Erykah Badu was immediate. Before radio programmers added…"On & On" to their playlists, she was a big hit. At the time, her acceptance by the mainstream seemed questionable, indeed doubtful. Sharing her *mélange* of Yoruba/Five Percent Nation/Islamic theology, wearing sky-high gelees (headwraps), speaking the peace-and-blessings parlance of bohemian Brook-non, we loved her ankhtified ass. She was our little secret.'

Erykah wouldn't remain a secret for long. Kedar broadened his offensive by envisioning a high-profile collaboration to showcase Erykah's talents, and who better to choose than his own protégé, D'Angelo, whose love of classic soul matched Badu's. The idea was that a collaboration would be a valuable boost to both artists' careers, and that a cover version of a known tune would be a suitable vehicle. The question was: which song to choose?

The answer came when a spot on a film soundtrack needed to be filled. In early 1996, production finished on an American movie called *High School High*, a fairly forgettable comedy in which the recent spate of teen films was parodied. Its soundtrack was a different story, however, featuring a solid cast of black soul and hip-hop artists, including Sean 'Puffy' Combs, The Roots, Lil' Kim, Faith Evans (ex-wife of the soon-to-be-assassinated rapper Biggie Smalls), KRS-One, Rakim, A Tribe Called Quest and Wu-Tang Clan members Cappadonna, The RZA, U-God and Method Man. Kedar was one of the executive producers, and the song he, D'Angelo and Erykah chose to record was the classic Marvin Gaye/Tammi Terrell duet 'Your Precious Love'. This light-hearted, swinging slice of classic soul was an excellent choice of song – both singers were free to play within its mid-paced, gentle structure and improvise at will – and the result, which appeared on the album in September 1996, was one of the soundtrack's high points.

Badu acquitted herself gracefully in the recording of the song. She begins with a slow, bluesy croon ad-libbed over the classic 1960s Motown opening, and goes on to deliver her lines with aplomb, never overstated and with evident passion. Her voice evinces a little more vibrato than her later work – perhaps a sign that she had yet to settle into her own style – and together with D'Angelo's laid-back, Marvin-alike tones, makes the record a success. It emerged that the recording took place on Gaye's birthday – 2 April – an obvious omen by anyone's standards.

The recording was an inspired choice. At this time, D'Angelo was extremely popular: his début album *Brown Sugar* was still riding high in the charts and selling well, and for the first time the phrase 'neo-soul' was being used in music circles – a genre that would rise and rise from this moment on. 'My goal is to take the sound of black music to another level,' said the Virginia-born performer. 'To me, soul music is black music and that's what I'm making – soul music. Yet, I refuse to put any limits on what goes into soul, because it can include rock guitars or gospel harmony, rap beats or live jazz bass. Soul music is limitless and that's the way I view my music.' The parallels with Erykah Badu's multifaceted background as a singer and MC are apparent – another reason for the appropriateness of the collaboration. Of Erykah, D'Angelo perceptively remarked that, 'She's got an old soul, and it's been around. It drips off her lyrics. She reflects what's going on now.' He was right, too, for Badu has always seemed to emanate wisdom beyond her years, perhaps because of her grandmothers' importance in her upbringing.

So 1996 had been a pretty good year for Erykah Badu. To recap: she had signed a record deal; she had moved to New York, one of the world's great artistic centres; she had been welcomed with love and respect by audiences and press there and she had recorded with a bona fide superstar. But it would get better. In late 1996 (history does not record the date, but for once it doesn't matter), Erykah was browsing through a music magazine in which she had been interviewed when a picture caught her eye. It was a picture of a rapper, a handsome young black man with attractive, broad features and a slightly eccentric hairstyle. His name, the caption said, was Andre 3000, and he was one of a hip-hop duo called OutKast.

The journalist Jancee Dunn later asked Erykah one simple question: 'Did you fall in love with him the very first time you saw him?' The singer laughed and said, 'Well, not the very first time. I saw him in a magazine, and he saw me in that same magazine. And we felt the same way a few miles away.'

Andre Lauren Benjamin was born in Georgia in May 1975, and was just 21 when he and Erykah met that autumn. The two hit it off from the moment they met, enjoying their common Southern background and their love of classic music. His band, OutKast, had been voted Best New Rap Group of the Year at the 1995 Source Awards on the strength of their quite stunning *Southernplayalisticadillacmuzik* album of the previous year, and its successor, *ATLiens*, was due for release in August 1996. As a rising star pairing off with a hot, new up-and-coming act, the Dre/Erykah partnership was one that the soul community embraced, following the showbiz rule that a celebrity coupling is worth more in gossip value than either of its component parts. It was true love, it seemed, with Badu proclaiming Dre 'a cool guy...one of my best friends'.

The love affair was perfect, according to all the obvious parameters. OutKast – which consists of Dre plus his friend Antwan Patton (Big Boi) – are an unpredictable act who combine psychedelia, funk, vintage soul and gangsta-rap influences to form a unique act in popular music, while the likes of Erykah Badu had quite simply never been seen before. Like Erykah, OutKast had seen success come quickly and at a young age: their grasp of Southern hip-hop had taken the genre in an entirely unexpected direction with their very first single, 'Player's Ball', and (also like Erykah) had taken their songwriting skills to the very best in the black music industry, the Organized Noize production team and the LaFace record label.

While love blossomed, Kedar Massenburg was waiting in the wings with a keen eye on his new signing. The master of set-up had precisely calculated his next move and, with critical expectation around the Badu camp starting to come to the boil, he knew what that move should be. In late 1996 he met with Erykah and Tim Grace – the latter was sharing managerial duties with attorney Ward White by this stage – and suggested the recording of a début album. Fortunately, the *Funky Cousins* demo contained over an album's worth of material and the production of an album would not include much composition. Badu and Grace agreed enthusiastically, and sessions were booked at New York's Battery Studios, a prestigious recording complex situated on West 25th Street in the Chelsea district. The studios have been used by a mighty host of internationally famous artists such as Prince, Stevie Wonder, Britney Spears, Cypress Hill, Isaac Hill, the Spice Girls, Paul Simon, Buddy Guy, the Wu-Tang Clan and a long list of hip-hop and soul acts – no small challenge for an artist whose sole big-studio experience extended as far as cutting one song for a movie soundtrack. But, as we have seen, it takes a lot to discourage Erykah Badu, and she approached this milestone with her head held high and a prayer to the Creator who had brought her so far.

The moment had come. All the backyard raps, the childhood songs, the teenage shows and the acting and singing Erykah had worked on for two decades were about to come to fruition. The Wright family sent their best wishes, Robert Free flew up to New York to offer assistance and a host of producers (including The Roots) began to assemble under the watchful eye of Kedar Massenburg, whose job it was to make the project roll smoothly and within financial limits.

Recording a début album is a unique experience for all artists. First, they are laying down for posterity emotions and words that they have honed for a long period, perhaps many years. Yet the paradox is that, while the material has so often been worked and reworked to perfection, when they come to record at a professional level they are so often novices at the actual art of recording. Erykah had worked with D'Angelo already and produced a competent, inventive piece of work, but to be placed in a leading position on her own project was an entirely different experience, and one that would obviously need to come in on time and on budget.

Fortunately for Erykah, she was allocated a respectable recording budget by Massenburg's team, allowing her to use expert players, top-line session musicians and ancillary staff who would work according to her specifications; that is, warmly and humanly rather than in a clinical or work-to-rule manner. She also had the bonus of the presence of The Roots, who would go on to play a major role in her career and whose values reflect her own. In their world, real instruments and warm atmospheres are as important as technical wizardry and digital clarity – a best-of-both-worlds approach that suits Badu's mind-set perfectly.

The last few days before the studio sessions flew swiftly by – and Erykah readied herself for the performance of a lifetime.

5 The Cult Of Baduizm

In early 1997 Erykah entered Battery Studios to begin recording. She and Massenburg had – with the help of Robert Bradford – dissected the arrangements of the songs on the *Funky Cousins* demo in order to reassemble them in the studio to a commercial level of professionalism. But, as Free recalls, the presence of Kedar plus a bunch of high-profile producers hadn't swayed her respect for the Erykah Free work: 'When Erykah signed her deal with Universal, she was so passionate about the demo that she didn't want to change anything,' he remembers. 'She fought all the way to keep her first album as much true to the demo as possible.' And there is good reason for this: *Funky Cousins* producer Jaborn Jamal was no novice, after all, and much praise had been laid on the demo for its sophisticated sound.

The logistics of the recording seem to have been relatively simple, except for the multiple-producer concept that Massenburg and Badu had chosen: the songs and arrangements were largely already in place (although one or two improvised songs made it to the final cut, as we shall see) and the overall aim was simply to recreate those structures in a professional environment. The cream of the soul session talent had been summoned by Massenburg to record the album, including drummer Ahmir '?uestlove' Thompson of The Roots and bassist Ron Carter, but just as crucial to the album's overall sound were the keyboard and drum programmers, who set up the studio machines to replicate the percussion and atmospheres from the Erykah Free demo. Erykah herself played a major role in all aspects of the recording, including programming and co-production, as well as providing the obvious lead and backing vocals.

Her relationship with Kedar is obviously one that permits her much autonomy and, knowing what we do about her background, this must be welcome.

The goings-on behind studio doors remain more or less secret, but let us make no mistake: the album that this remarkable pool of talent created isn't far short of a masterpiece.

It begins with a simple little song called 'Rimshot (Intro)'. This is a sweet combination of Erykah's gentle, semi-scatted line of 'Rimshot, hey, diggy diggy, a rimshot, hey, come on' and a restrained bassline and percussion. It lasts barely two minutes and is an uncomplicated warning to the listener that this record will be understated rather than overplayed: nowhere does Erykah allow herself to spiral into high registers or improvise away from the simple lyrics. On this album Badu took the trouble to list in the sleevenotes the people who had inspired each individual song: in this case she name-checks her sister Koryan ('Koko') and her brother Eevin. When 'Rimshot' comes to a sudden end, the song that follows it is punctuated by the tiniest of silences, leading more than a few listeners to conclude that the two songs are joined together somehow, part of a suite or a pair: and the second song has passed into popular legend with such speed that its status certainly warrants some kind of extended introduction. 'Rimshot' can therefore be seen both as an introduction to the album and to Erykah's best-known song to date, 'On & On'.

As signature songs go, 'On & On' is a classic. Based on a simple, addictive three-note bass riff and so subtly concocted that at times the song feels almost empty, atmosphere is the song's key quality. Of all Erykah's work, it's this song that has inspired the most debate, due both to the semi-mystical imagery found in its lyrics and the sheer, unclassifiable hookiness of the song's refrain – 'On and on, and on and on, my cipher keeps movin' like a rolling stone'. It would go on to appear on innumerable compilations and would be the song that made Badu's name on its release as the album's pre-release single in early 1997. Erykah credited the song as being inspired by some fairly elevated entities – 'the Gods and the Earths' – but, while many listeners assumed she meant this at face value, we of course know better and can recall her devotion to Five Percenter symbols. Gods and Earths are men and women, and some of the credit for this can be laid at the door of producer Jaborn Jamal, whose contribution to the *Funky Cousins* demo extended as far as co-writing this song.

Jamal was later interviewed about this song, and explained that, 'For a lot of people, everyday life is a struggle, and 'On & On' is intended to be a positive message, as I see it, especially for black people, to let them know that even though there is a struggle, you have to keep moving on and on. You got to keep your head up.' The cyclical theme is more cosmic than political, however, as Erykah once stated: 'When I was little, I used to listen to Marvin Gaye and Chaka Khan, Stevie Wonder and Diana Ross, Smokey Robinson and Patti LaBelle. And I perfectly know that my inspiration comes directly from the thousands of millions of microscopic atoms of memory that my favorite singers instilled in me.' Warming to her somewhat obscure theme, she added, 'Just like I know that music is a process of continuous rebirth, that has to do with the soul and with breathing. Indeed, they are the architects which allow you to build a harmonic construction built on "empty space", that each one of us has available.' As for the 'cipher' that the chorus mentions, she remarked that 'When I say [that] I was talking about my cipher as a sphere or a perfect completion, 360 degrees. My cipher is myself.'

Over the course of the next year or so, literally hundreds of print, radio and TV journalists would quiz Erykah about the meaning of the obscurer sections of 'On & On', and it is little surprise, therefore, that she chose to vary her explanations, to the point where it's hard to ascertain exactly what they meant because she explained them in so many different ways. However, this may well be a deliberate ploy on her part. She once said, 'I like to leave the interpretation of the lyrics up to the listeners,' as a song of this scope (its theme is more or less infinite in breadth, it appears) can only mean what the listener wishes it to hear. But one symbol that was more or less clarified over the course of time was the line, 'I was born under water with three dollars and six dimes, Yeah, you may laugh, cause you did not do your math', which Erykah explained on several occasions as denoting the 360 degrees (3 x 100, plus 6 x 10) of a circle – a clear symbol of the unceasing nature of life and death.

Heavy going? Certainly – but Erykah herself always retained a sense of humour and simplicity when discussing her work, defining 'On & On' as 'the teaching of everyday life and karma through mathematics', adding that, 'The song keeps dropping different jewels of information and belief that I've compiled during my life.' As we've seen, Badu's interest in and application of various symbols is not selective: in early interviews she even showed journalists the large silver ankh (Egyptian cross) she wears on her finger, and invoked ancient Egyptian icons, too: 'The ankh comes from *Khemet*, an ancient word for Egypt,' she said, 'which means "land of burnt people", people who were touched by the sun and given melanin.'

Erykah told Greg Tate at *Vibe* that, 'The vocal style was inspired by the beats. The lyrics were inspired by the gods and the earths, the mathematics and the science I was learning at the time. Not arithmetic, but the physics of life' (an instance where she did *not* mention the Five Percenter definition of gods and earths, perhaps not wishing to be seen as endorsing a particular belief or stance). Let us also not forget that the writing of this song occurred as far back as 1994 or 1995, when Badu's education on Five Percenter matters had yet to mature.

She maintained her practical approach, however. 'I had four minutes to get all of that into one song – everything that I had ever wanted to say about the good things that happened and the knowledge I had acquired up to that point. When I wrote that song, I was looking for a melody and words with the right syllables to fit into that melody. That song basically wrote itself. I just had to do a little fine tuning.'

The search for meaning has always been a major theme of Erykah's interviews, with reporters fascinated by the apparent depths of obscurity that lie beneath her self-contained, almost deliberately calm exterior – and this is strange, given that she is neither a religious/spiritual zealot nor given to penning impenetrable lyrics. Perhaps writers are intimidated by her dress – the headwraps she wore constantly at that stage add at least 30cm (1ft) to her height – or by the aura of confidence she exudes. Add to this the fact that she disclaims her gift, putting it down to divine inspiration ('Well, music makes you hungry, and I had to get the music out of me. I'm just a path for letting the music out. I don't know if it's righteousness or spiritualism... Music shouldn't be abusive, but resourceful. It was something that was given to me, but it is not to keep'), and the enigma of Erykah Badu seems complete to many, who fail to realise that she is as human as the rest of us.

Badu's most famous – and most-repeated – quote about 'On & On' (and her music in general) was the observation that, 'Music is a rebirth process and I am a midwife helping to bring it into the world', a statement that struck some as egotistical (does she regard herself as someone special, then?), naïve or simply pretentious. But most people who heard her say this regarded her in awe: as a kind of spiritual earth mother or divine conduit. Little wonder that the song remains something of a milestone in her career – and that the 'earth mother' tag would stick to Badu as long as it did, even when it became obvious that there were other equally important parts of her personality to be explored.

In contrast to the reflective vibe of 'On & On', the next song, 'Appletree', was much more upbeat. A more hip-hop-driven, beat-heavy song, it is a story told by Erykah in which she relates the advice given to her by her grandmother, Viola Wilson ('Ganny'), who told her to pick friends as she would fruit from a tree. Punctuating the lines with the scat 'ooh wee ooh wee ooh', Badu pokes gentle fun at herself ('I was hangin' out wit some of my "artsy" friends') and ruminates on the sensible principle that she lives by: 'I don't walk around trying to be what I'm not, I don't waste my time trying to get what you got'. Together with the very mellow birdsong and keyboard noodling, the song is both relaxing and inspiring – and something of a break after the universal head-scratching of 'On & On'. The song is credited as 'created by Erykah Badu and Robert Bradford for Erykah Free': the duo is dormant, it seems, rather than extinct, and resurrects itself periodically for co-compositions such as this one.

Of 'Appletree', Erykah explained: 'My grandmother Ganny was the one who said, "always pick your friends like you pick your fruit". She told me, "you don't want to lean up against no rotten tree. Your friends are seasonal. If you're not getting along with Coretta the same time every year then y'all ain't right for each other right then. You just get what you get and then go on to the next one. If it's not good for you in that season then don't even try it in that cycle. The universe is going to give gifts."'

Ganny had been a veritable fount of philosophical information, it seems. Badu went on to say: 'She taught me to learn cycles, which is mathematics. You just have to learn to survive different cycles. Then the natural order of things will come to you. Go with the wind instead of going against it, and you'll get a lot further.' Not that this is always easy to interpret: 'But if my wind is blowing this way and another person's opinion is flowing another way, when I go against them, it might seem like I'm going against the wind, but I'm not. I'm just going my way and not the way they want me to go.'

But it's not Erykah's style to wax lyrical about gods, earths and the universal dialectic for ever – so the next song is the excellent 'Otherside Of The Game', a contemplative paean to the plight of a woman who lives in constant fear that her drug-dealing boyfriend will be arrested and her life shattered. Badu neither paints too dramatic a picture nor overdoes the heartfelt empathy – traps that a lesser singer might not have avoided – and the result is both sensitive and affecting. 'Whatcha gonna do when they come for you?' is the first line of the softly sung chorus, rendered crystal-clear by the production from The Roots and Richard Nichols. 'The seed has grown, I can't make it on my own', croons the singer, revealing that the character is newly pregnant. This song's strength lies in the way that there is no solution at its end: the narrator remains trapped in this nightmare situation and Erykah draws no conclusions. The situation is real, insoluble and ever-present, Badu is saying...and the focus is the here and now, not the outcome. 'Otherside Of The Game' is one of three songs recorded at studios in Philadelphia, and for which the mixing alone took place at Battery in New York.

In terms of full songs (not short snippets) the album is almost halfway through at this point and, as Erykah herself would probably prefer it, the record is one of two halves. The first has been, by anyone's standards, pretty profound – and it's at this point that a more light-hearted Badu emerges, although she never lapses into shallowness or filler. Although the next track is 'Sometimes (Mix 9)', a 44-second bit of whimsy that hints at the fuller version later on, the next real song is 'Next Lifetime', a mellow, bitter-sweet rumination on hope for the next incarnation of life. On this song Erykah may appear to be sad – she's pondering how a potential soulmate is unavailable for love because she herself is already attached – but in fact she's optimistic, promising to meet him the next time the karmic wheel revolves. The song is credited as 'inspired by a threat from Kedar' (although it has never been revealed what this was – a promise from the producer to haunt her next life if the album is not completed on time, perhaps?), and remains one of the finest songs Erykah has ever written. A high point of this slow, extended song (it lasts over six minutes) is the inclusion of whale calls and the surge of waves in the background.

Another song fragment follows, and is the most easygoing piece on the record. Titled 'Afro (Freestyle Skit)', it's a two-minute piece of improvised music in which Erykah alternately advises an unknown listener to 'pick your Afro (or it will be high on one side)' and complains that a lover has promised to take her to a Wu-Tang Clan concert but has failed to deliver on this promise. It begins with Badu's drawled, bluesy vocals, and after she asks 'What y'all waiting for?' a group of horns join in. A simple, blues-based jam, it is the most amusing and simultaneously the most throw-away song on the album, but one that proves Erykah's sense of humour (for anyone still cowed by 'On & On' and 'Otherside Of The Game').

A co-write between Badu and the producer, 'Madi' Madukwu Chinwah, the next song is 'Certainly', a strongly jazz-influenced song in which Erykah complains that her life has been remoulded by a new love without her permission. Apparently both a dig at control freaks and a nod to the unshakeable power of romantic love, the song is a Badu classic, although its simple, sideways message has usually been overshadowed by the blockbuster songs earlier on the album. 'I was not looking for no love affair', warns Erykah, although it is clear by the end of the song that the narrator is deeply involved in one. The song is 'inspired by Bless', although this has not been clarified.

The next song is a cover. Erykah would always be fascinated by reworking other artists' songs, whether as part of her live set or in the studio, and this was one of her earliest attempts to do so. Her cover of Atlantic Starr's 'Touch A Four Leaf Clover' – retitled '4 Leaf Clover' – is a funky, harmony-laden take on the 1983 classic. The choice of song represents her roots perfectly, as this song would have been one of the first 1980s soul songs she heard as a child after disco had finally trailed away. 'Inspired by my mother Kolleen and Atlantic Starr' accompanies the song credits in the sleevenotes – the tune must have been a favourite of her mother's, along with the classic vintage soul and R&B songs that had influenced Erykah so profoundly. It's another Erykah Free production, too, and remains the song that comes from the deepest parts of the Wright family heart.

But it's time to refocus a little: '4 Leaf Clover' is also the last truly dynamic song on the album. Yes, the record as a whole is a classic – the first five or six songs give it that status alone, and there isn't a truly substandard song anywhere on it. Unfortunately, the enormous impact of those early compositions (especially in 'On & On') was obviously difficult to maintain, and Erykah simply fails to match that initial impetus. The next song is 'No Love', a song appropriately 'inspired by imbalance created by confusion' and, while it's excellently produced (as every other song on the album is), it doesn't stick in the listener's mind, musically or lyrically. The crackling-vinyl sound added to the intro is unnecessary (Erykah's influences are genuine enough without needing to labour the point) and her theme – a vague lament from an abandoned or jilted lover – is just too unfocused to seem important.

A similar lack of genius is evident on 'Drama', inspired by 'my godmother Gwen', on which Erykah departs from her usual sensible stance by making one critical error. Where normally she teaches by example – using spiritual metaphors in 'On & On', describing (and not judging) a grim situation in 'Otherside Of The Game' – this time she steps onto a platform and exhorts her listeners to act. There's little chance to absorb and listen: this song is a list of orders to get out there and start worshipping. 'Listen people listen, Lift up your hearts to God!', commands Badu, which feels like a let-down after her earlier passive acceptance of all religious approaches…and five minutes of sentiments such as 'teach your children wisdom' is just too much. The problem is simple: Badu has set up a liberal, all-are-welcome approach on the first half of the album, but then reneges on herself by slipping into straight preaching on this song. It just doesn't work. The last songs redeem themselves slightly – the full version of 'Sometimes' is excellent, while the versions of 'Certainly' (the 'Flipped It' edit) and 'Rimshot (Outro)' (a lovely a cappella kiss-off) are welcome, but the record is flawed.

And there it is: Erykah Badu's first album, which had now been allocated a release date (11 February 1997) and which would be preceded by the release of the 'On & On' single. Perhaps the judgment that the album has some less-than-great songs is a little harsh by normal standards: after all, for a 25-year-old artist to have written and recorded a set of songs as amazing as this is not usual. However, we are not discussing a 'normal' artist here. As we have seen, Badu was the product of a fertile artistic background and had established herself at an early stage as something of a prodigy.

Erykah chose to call her creation by a simple title, one that would both elevate her to spiritual heights and force anyone who read it to ask questions. Its name was *Baduizm*.

As with the symbology of 'On & On', Erykah would be asked constantly what her album title actually meant. On the British music TV show *Later With Jools Holland*, for example, she told the host that 'izm' is hip-hop speak for marijuana. Elsewhere, however, she omitted any reference to dope and stated simply that it stood for a set of beliefs revolving around herself. In other places still, she hinted that 'baduizm' was a term encompassing the parts of organised religion she had appropriated to create her own system. Thor Christensen at the *Dallas Morning News* observed that she probably has different interpretations of what her album and song titles mean depending on her mood, and that each explanation she made contained similarities with all the others. He was also among the first journalists to interview her: 'We hooked up about a month or two before the release of *Baduizm*, she had moved to New York and I knew she was from Dallas, so I did a story. She wasn't really into explaining the lyrics of "On & On", she wanted to keep that a little bit vague.'

Not that Erykah was vague about much else, answering Thor's questions in depth and with honesty. 'When I write all of my songs, the music is the ocean in which all of the lyrics and melodies float,' she said when asked about her songwriting. 'I feel the music and then a melody comes, and a lot of times I try to find words whose syllables fit the melody. And then I listen back and I've created something that I didn't even know happened. So a lot of songs just write themselves.' Her days as a rapper still informed her work as a singer, too, she said. 'I still write about the same things I was rhyming about in my rap songs – the same sort of [lyrics] Brand Nubian or A Tribe Called Quest would rap about. I still write about what's going on in [African-American] culture, about the system of beliefs that we have.'

At this early stage Badu was keen to express her feelings about the industry into which she had just stepped. 'One thing Badu says she can't believe these days is the shoddy state of R&B radio,' wrote Christensen. '"It's all about money," [said Erykah], "it's the same five songs being played all day long. People want to hear different things that have a soul, things with jazz and hip-hop influences, but the industry and the programmers underestimate the audience, so everything sounds monotonous," she says. "But I think music is about to go through a rebirth and become more versatile, and I want to be one of the midwives in the rebirthing process. I used to want to be a superstar. But now I want to be a super-healer, because this industry definitely needs healing."'

Promo copies of the album were pressed and distributed to the press at around the time of the release of 'On & On', and writers and broadcasters were intrigued by the mass of dedications that the booklet contained. Erykah had made a point of mentioning all of her dearest family and friends in the CD booklet, beginning with the words, 'This one's for you FREE'. Tim Grace, Ward White and Kedar Massenburg ('my real peace brother') are mentioned early on, while Kolleen, Ganny, Thelma Gipson, Gwen Hargrove, Koryan and Eevin all receive dedications. One of the most interesting lines may surprise some people: 'To my father, William Wright Jr (Toosie). I love you anyway, Father. Yes I do.' She then lists a whole paragraph of family members new and old, before concluding that, 'Everybody, our family bond is tight. We have a history.'

The rest of the dedications, which combined make up an entire page of small print, are in honour of studio staff and label personnel but their conclusion is most telling: 'Much respect & appreciation to the East,

West, North & South, the Heavens, the Abyss & the Atmosphere, Twa Ntr.' Add to this, 'And last but not least, bless Ji Jaja, words words words' and the seeds of Erykah's reputation as a religious obscurist (which, while not entirely unearned, was far from the whole truth) were fully sown.

Like the sleevenotes, the album artwork was also a complete concept. The cover shot was a half-body picture of Erykah taken side-on, with her head bowed, hand on the back of her neck and a dun-coloured headwrap obscuring her features. Why she chose to hide her face on her album cover became a point for discussion: the under-tray picture depicted her hiding her head underneath a pillow, although the fold-out sleeve does include shots of her lying down, looking over her shoulder and adopting a Christ-like pose in a garden. The fact that the album does not reveal its creator on its surface, but reveals her face on closer examination, is appropriate, though Badu has never said if this was intentional.

The album complete, a release schedule confirmed and distribution poised to execute, Badu's work seemed to be done for the moment...but the truth was otherwise. Talented – even unique – she may be, but in the eyes of the public (and of Universal, Kedar Entertainment's parent company) she was just another new artist, who needed to be marketed extensively if she was to have a chance of standing out from the thousands of new acts that appear every year in America and the wider world. An interview programme commenced, but this was manageable at first. It was the release of the 'On & On' single that changed Erykah's world and the world of all those connected to her.

Put simply, 'On & On' was a massive hit. To Erykah's surprise, the song went to Number One on the *Billboard* R&B Singles chart for two weeks and remained on the *Billboard* R&B Singles Airplay chart for four weeks – an exceptional performance for a début release, and especially so given that Badu represented a completely new style. Proof that interviewers found her entirely unlike the singers of the day came when they could find no contemporary reference points for Erykah (new acts are always compared to existing hitmakers in order to assign a category to a new face), opting instead to ask her about the similarities in her singing style with that of none other than Billie Holiday. This was an immediate point in Erykah's favour: the comparisons (which soon became incessant) with Lady Day gave her an air of vintage gravitas that a successful modern R&B act like, say, Destiny's Child, could not hope to emulate.

This aura of seriousness actually intimidated quite a few people, strange as it may seem. The fact that this tiny black girl from the South could radiate such absolute self-assurance, especially when she was as new to the music scene as Erykah, was difficult to accept for many interviewers. Traditionally, new artists who have been blessed with some degree of early success either indulge in shameless praise of other artists or take the opportunity to cast aspersions on them. Both are highly marketable approaches. Erykah Badu did neither, apart from nodding in quiet respect to those artists whose work she enjoyed.

Her air of calm possession aside, people feared Erykah because she was so overtly spiritual. Her religious stance was so hard to pin down (thanks to the multitude of icons from different beliefs that she discussed) that many listeners began to regard her as some kind of focus point of spiritual energy; an undefined, unlimited messenger who could neither be categorised nor combated. The way she spoke to reporters with a calm, unafraid gaze and clear, even tones added to her super-controlled air, too. And, although she laughed, smiled and otherwise displayed human touches, this didn't make her seem any less other-worldly. All of which is, as we've seen, far from reality: Erykah is as real and as vulnerable as the rest of us. She may have a spiritual side, which most of us lack, but she had served her time on the way up and, after all, goddesses never have to serve coffee for a living...

Both Erykah and Jaborn Jamal were delighted but modest about the performance of their co-creation, 'On & On'. 'I didn't know it was going to be Number One,' said Badu, 'but all the elements were there: the music was slammin', the beat was good, the rhythm was good, and the voice had developed a lot, because I didn't even consider myself a singer.' The more seasoned Jamal was more contemplative, taking the broader view: 'We had a few tracks that were laid back in a style that nobody was really dealing with at the time,' he mused. '"On & On" had a unique thing about it. I was talking to Erykah the other day, and we were discussing how at first we really didn't know that the song would go on to become what it has – but we had a feeling.'

The Holiday questions kept coming – not without reason – and Badu found herself in the strange position of repeatedly praising an artist whose style she admired but had never tried to copy. 'Billie Holiday was a woman who had so much to give and opened herself up to listeners and to the world,' she said, adding that, 'She could reach down into a person's deepest soul and pull it out with the slightest inclination of a note. If they say I'm doing that – then cool.' She was at pains to inform her interviewers that the comparisons were nothing new: 'People have always told me that I sound like Billie, that my phrasing is reminiscent of hers. It's the highest compliment. But it's not something I try to do.' She told *Soul Express* that, 'People have told me that my voice reminds them of Billie Holiday. I can see that, I can feel that. I think it's more the timbre, or maybe the emotion than the sound. I don't think that we sound that much alike,' she said for the hundredth time, before shifting the subject: 'Really, I heard Diana Ross' *interpretation* of Billie Holiday before I heard Billie Holiday, and that's what I love mostly about Billie Holiday, the memory that I have of her is Diana Ross' version of her music. That touched me, that movie *Lady Sings The Blues* had a big effect on my life, and I guess it's very obvious in my music.'

It carried on. She told the South African *Sunday Times* that, 'I first heard her music in a movie called *Lady Sings The Blues* with Diana Ross. I just remember being romanticised by her character. I was so impressed by her freedom of spirit,' and *Vibe* magazine that, 'She was a singer who was able to reach the back of the room with a slight inflection of her voice. If I'm doing that, cool. That's good. I invite an energy into my music and into my cipher that can help me get my point across.'

It got to the point where journalists began asking Erykah how it felt to be asked so many questions about sounding like Billie Holiday. Badu told *Interview* magazine, perhaps not entirely truthfully, that, 'I thought the Billie Holiday comparison was beautiful,' because Holiday was 'a wonderful, creative, helpful spirit. She's someone who wanted to help others by sharing her emotion. That's what I do, too, so I think that's a great comparison.'

'On & On' remains the song for which Erykah is best known. The reasons for this are many. It's probably to do with the cosmic scale of the lyrics, the simplicity of the music and that unforgettable hook – but more important than any of these was the fact that the song seemed to capture a moment in popular music. A song as impressive as this – unaffected, honest, unselfish – had not been heard for some time in the mainstream, and against the slickly produced, multi-layered chart hits of the time it seemed to stand out in stark contrast, a black or white filigree stamped firmly into the shifting greys of radio programming. Its inclusive religious imagery – the gods, the earths, the 360-degree cipher and so on – was also all things to all men, neither classifiable nor describable. 'Most intellects do not believe in God,' the song repeats, 'but they fear us just the same.' What the hell? thought many listeners. Is this woman an evangelist or a puritan? A prophet or a shrewd business operator?

All of these, as it turned out, and before long a video scriptwriter to boot. The release of 'On & On' was accompanied by a video clip, which Erykah had scripted and co-directed with video director Paul Hunter, taking as her inspiration the setting of the movie *The Color Purple*. The video makes an immediate impact when it shows Badu tumbling gracelessly into a pool of mud and making no effort to get out despite the filth that surrounds her – but singing to camera with a strange, unsmiling dignity that is universes away from the 'grins and pirouettes' of the usual video routines. The fact that Badu chose to take such a prominent role in her very first video says much about her ambition and her talent: following in the footsteps of black musicians before her such as Quincy Jones, Queen Latifah and Ice Cube, she had diversified her activities within a very short space of time.

'I love directing,' she told CNN, 'because we live in the video age now. When I'm writing a song now, after the song has come to life with the music and everything... [The] next thing that comes to life is a vision – how you want people to see you.' The wider picture, it seems, is that her desire to create goes far beyond mere performance: 'As an artist, I also take on the role as director for the videos that I appear in, because it's important that my vision is shown in its entirety. I enjoy doing that; it's fun to me. I love it. It's like painting a picture. You don't know exactly how it's going to come out – you know what you have in mind, a rough blueprint in your mind – but you don't know how it's going to come out. Only the artist knows when it's ready.'

On 11 February 1997, it appeared that this artist knew her creation was ready – and *Baduizm* was released. Like a mother, she defended her creation with a fierce pride from the moment it was born, and when *Vibe* magazine asked her why she thought her album was a success, she replied, 'I'm lucky. Being righteous is popular this year,' which the writer thought was 'sarcastic but on the money'. Indeed – the record is instructive, logical and emotional all at once, and can even take the more committed listener on a journey to heightened self-awareness: all of which can be described as 'righteous'. Impressed by this perspicacity, the feature went on to proclaim that, 'Just when we thought couldn't nobody be a black woman in pop music without being a breast-baring pop tart, a put-it-on-the-glass video ho, or a gold-digging hoochie mama, here comes Badu… Celebrating serial motherhood, Mississippi mud baths, *The Color Purple*, shotgun shacks, and sky-high African-village-woman geles, this earth goddess goes on and on in a voice part Ella, part sassy Sarah, part Billie, part Nina, and yet all Badu.'

The issue of sexuality was an immediate feature of all descriptions of Erykah. Like most branches of popular music, hip-hop, soul and R&B had for many years been the province of many an Amazonian pop queen with hiked-up cleavage and racehorse thighs. Not that this was wrong – sex is an important and attractive part of popular culture, and a cause for celebration as long as there's no exploitation – but it had perhaps become a little tedious. Erykah had sex appeal in abundance, of course, but signalled it in an entirely different manner. As *Spin* magazine stated, 'Erykah Badu redefines the word diva… She's replaced attitude with sass, and her sex appeal lies within her own private sensuality.' Absolutely correct, and few female singers can emit as much sensuality as Badu does, with her open, confident stare, her liquid eyes, flawless features and compact, perfectly formed body. I'm sure you get the picture. As did thousands of awed fans.

Quite aside from the music and Erykah's unique appearance, the impact of *Baduizm* was felt on political, spiritual and literary levels. One reason for its success could be that it was simply too full of meaning to be ignored or dismissed, irrespective of the listener's taste for the sounds it contained. Like some kind of bizarre, thousand-leaved tree glowing with a million crystals, the album took root in the public psyche and grew, evolving into a world all of its own. The listener could play it again and again and pick up new gems of information each time. And yet its core features were so simple: love, honesty and spirituality are valued above material gain ('Otherside Of The Game'); the great themes of life are the most significant ('On & On', 'No Love'); the sum of humanity is more than its component parts ('Appletree') and so on.

This brings us to an important point, which is simply that the album, despite its polished sounds and up-to-the-minute imagery ('You said you'd take me to see Wu-Tang!' keens Badu on 'Afro (Freestyle Skit)'), sounds old. Not old as in tired, but as in *wise* – as if Erykah has tapped into some primeval energy source to bring simple, unforgettable sounds to the studio. No wonder the critics could only compare her to Billie Holiday. Quite simply, the themes of the record can be viewed as a return to the old values of classic soul and gospel, which, as we've seen, had been diluted and forcibly blended with other genres by the late 1990s. By worshipping at the altar of classic artists such as Marvin Gaye and Stevie Wonder, Erykah had brought their spirits to bear on her work and produced an album that sounded vintage and polished all at the same time.

For Badu herself, the journey had been a crucial one. She revealed that, 'While writing and creating this music, I continued to build myself as a person, as a woman and as an African-American. I wanted to share these experiences with everyone.' Like some kind of mystical shaman who inhales a rainforest hallucinogen to rise to another plane and bring back stories of another, higher world, Erykah had created a key to a frame of mind. '*Baduizm* is an experience, an emotion, a feeling,' she explained. 'Badu is my name, "izm" is what you smoke, it gets you high. "Baduizm" is designed to get you high through pure music, energy and soul.' Some listeners thought that she had created a religion – but they were wrong. The truth was more far-reaching: '*Baduizm* is not a religion, it is an expression or an extension of the way I feel and the things that I love,' she said. 'While writing and creating this music, I burned candles and lit incense as I continued to build myself as a person.'

The public bought into this wholesale. Not only did *Baduizm* sell well, it sold a million copies within two months of its release and went to sell over two million worldwide. More than this, it broke a record by entering the US *Billboard* Albums chart at Number Two – the highest chart position ever for a début release from a female singer. Pundits scratched their heads in disbelief at the record's phenomenal success, but none of them managed to capture its appeal in prose. Perhaps this is because it is only with the passing of time that its impact can be appreciated or, more plausibly, that it appeared on the cusp of a swing in the American public's musical tastes, and both ushered in and spearheaded a brand new genre of music which only became apparent much later.

For the first time, aficionados of urban music (the blanket term that magazines such as *Vibe* had laid over R&B, hip-hop and other black-oriented popular sounds) were beginning to use the word 'neo-soul' to describe the kind of new music artists such as Erykah Badu were producing. The term would not be widely accepted until several months after the success of *Baduizm*, which was the spark that ignited the air of expectation after the rise of artists such as Maxwell, D'Angelo and even the British singer Seal, who has been labelled by many commentators with slightly implausible sobriquets such as 'the Godfather of Neo-Soul'. What these men (and at this stage, they were mostly men, with the notable exception of Me'Shell NdegéOcello) had in common was their allegiance to old-school soul sounds, messages of love and other emotions in their songs, a degree of romance and gentleness absent from most hip-hop, a certain intellectual edge and a raw sexuality taken directly from the old masters of soul. When female artists entered the field, the concept of neo-soul would truly begin to flourish, but at this stage it remained a buzz-phrase used by a coterie of journalists and not an idea that had been embraced by the wider public. But the clock was ticking…

Few artists have experienced this degree of success, even across years of work, let alone within months of landing a record deal. Remember that only six months before this Badu was trying to create a buzz for herself in the coffee bars of New York, with no band and just a DAT player. But her closest associates didn't seem to be surprised by anything that had happened to her, perhaps sharing her calm sense that her destiny was mapped out for her already. Robert Bradford was interviewed at this time, and said, 'A few years ago, we'd ride around, and Erykah would go, "It's going to happen". Like she knew.' He still says today that, 'I wasn't at all surprised by the amount of success she's had. I recognised something special the first time we started working together. It was meant to be. *Everything* that happened was meant to be.'

Erykah herself told MTV a month after *Baduizm* hit the charts that, 'I was very happy [when it was a hit]. But I wasn't surprised, because I planned it, you know. You never expect for your music not to do well.' This betrays a faith that is rare indeed, but she later revealed to writer Gary Graff, who asked her, 'What was the experience of *Baduizm*'s success like for you?', that, 'Oh, it was a big ego boost. As a child, I always knew that I was different from everybody, and I'm sure most artists will tell you that, because it's a true story. You're different. You know people don't accept you. You don't really fit in too much, and you know there's something wonderful if you continue to be an individual.'

Individuality, the trait that gave Badu her strength, was something she yearned for on others' behalf: 'I think the world has lost so much respect for the individual; there's a lot of individuals walking around, but they don't know that they're individuals because the world doesn't want to let them be.' Time and time again she returned to her home life, emphasising the lineage that had made her what she was. 'Some people are just stronger, especially when you have a mother, a grandmother, other people in your life that encourage you. That's my blessing that I had that. A lot of people don't.'

Erykah's self-awareness helped her endure the gruelling round of publicity that the success of *Baduizm* inevitably generated. Asked by the South African *Mail & Guardian* how it was that she had so much artistic freedom on *Baduizm*, she hammered home the idea that a successful artist needs a vision (the part of Kedar Massenburg's approach that had so impressed her a couple of years before): 'It's unusual for a new artist who does not write [to have so much freedom], but if you're a writer you have a vision. So for artists, who also write, it's not unusual. In the music business you have artists, and self-contained artists. Self-contained artists are artists who are left alone in the studio, like a painter, and left to be.'

This self-contained element she was referring to also included her visual appearance, which many journalists picked up on immediately. *Interview* magazine asked her, 'A lot of articles interpret your personal fashion sense as some kind of majestic Afrocentric statement. Do you think that's a bit overblown, or did you mean it to be taken as a political thing?' She replied, 'Well, if you look at all of the cultures in America, this is a great opportunity for us to really get acquainted with the rest of the world. America is the only place you can do that, but we don't have sense enough to take advantage of that. We would rather separate.' The political message beneath her choice of clothing was something that she would have to spell out again and again – and her self-definition as an African-American is manifested in this way and many others. 'It's not wrong for us to be together, it's wrong for us to put down each other and depreciate each other's values,' she insisted with obvious passion. 'Black people have been depreciated a lot here in America; that's a true thing. And I meet a lot of white people that tell me, well, that was my uncle or my grandfather, and that doesn't have anything to do with me. No, it doesn't have anything to do with you, but since it's still going on, somebody should take responsibility. I've got a record deal so I've got some money, but that doesn't mean I'm just supposed to ignore the other people who are poor as shit.'

The debate over Badu's look would continue far beyond its logical sell-by date, but most people genuinely liked her and her work, it seemed…nowhere more so than in her home town of Dallas, where her international success had made her an instant celebrity. Dallas writer Thor Christensen reports that, 'People are thrilled here, not only because she's so successful but because she's such an innovator. There are a lot of bands that have made it out of Dallas – everybody from Pantera to LeAnn Rimes, the Dixie Chicks, Edie Brickell – but in a sense Erykah is more innovative than any of them. She's the most groundbreaking artist to have come out of Dallas and made a huge impact.' Was he surprised by the speed of her success? 'I was,' admits the journalist, 'because having covered popular music for 17 years now, I know that things that are innovative have high odds against them of ever becoming a hit, because of the nature of the business. The business wants stuff that is familiar, and when "On & On" came out it sounded like nothing else on the radio. I was really surprised, but really delighted.'

Erykah's success was replicated overseas, and specifically in Britain, where the A&R manager of Universal's UK division, Dean Gillard, was quoted as being 'confident that Badu [would] break in the UK'. He said, 'She's created her own vibe already. We've never had such a buzz on an artist before they've even had a record out. At the Brit Awards, I think I promised more people CDs than we have in the country.' *Baduizm*, which had suffered from a rash of bootlegging in the UK because of its later release date there (it appeared on 7 April, which allowed US copies to be brought in and copied illegally), was specially imported into the country ahead of schedule to counter the black market. The very fact that such a market existed was ample proof of the anticipation she was generating, helped along by features in fashionable press titles such as *The Face*. It was suggested that her UK fanbase was large because jazz had always been a part of popular British music, and with good reason – after all, acid jazz had been an enormous commercial force in the first half of the 1990s and jazz-influenced drum 'n' bass acts like Goldie and Roni Size were at their commercial peak at this time.

Of course, one of the most interesting aspects of this theory is the apparent postulation that Erykah Badu is a jazz singer. While this is partially true (all those comparisons with Billie Holiday came from music journalists, who at least allegedly know what they're talking about), it's far from the whole truth. It should, however, be remembered that much of the most memorable singing on *Baduizm* doesn't feature Erykah's formidable MC skills or her classic soul side; it's more or less jazz all the way. Not classic, Ella Fitzgerald-style jazz, of course, but recognisably inflected towards the vintage sound enough that many audiences – British or otherwise – categorised her alongside the other female stars of the great American jazz tradition. Only time, and live performances, would reveal the full Badu skill-set.

At the height of all this excitement Erykah remained happy but composed, telling the UK *Observer* that her recorded persona was only part of the whole Badu experience: 'Performing – that's the most important thing. I think that's what helped me sell records [in Britain]. People always want to know, is this real? What is she talking about? Who is she? But once you see, you understand,' she said. 'There are no gimmicks, just me, a microphone, three backing singers, just giving energy and getting energy back. It's beautiful. It's tribal.' Setting up her live shows with these provocative words was a bold move, but no mere bravado: Badu had years of experience, as we've seen, as a member of a duo or as a solo artist, and knew well the value of a less-is-more live approach. Not that an enormous live ensemble would have been the ideal setting for her subtle, crooning voice; in fact, the fewer accompanists she has, the more striking her voice would become. Look at the success of Erykah Free for evidence of this.

This less-is-more approach runs through the whole of *Baduizm* (listen to the simple bass and drums of 'On & On' and the way that all the backing vocals are murmured, actually almost whispered, for evidence of this), and is a reflection of the way Erykah thinks and speaks. Her thoughts on hundreds of subjects were elicited and analysed almost unceasingly over the next few years, and in almost every instance she articulated with extreme clarity her stance regarding the issue that was at hand.

Few artists can speak as well as Badu outside their chosen medium – in her case we can attribute her acting training, perhaps, to her success as a speaker, whether on a spiritual issue (which is often inevitably cluttered with abstract symbols and ideas) or more mundane topics. Of course, this ability to wax lyrical – coupled with a drive to express opinions – can be slightly intimidating to some. She has never held back on her opinions, but on the other hand she has rarely spoken out without rational thought beforehand.

Erykah's words on the subject of live performances were timely, as it happened, as Tim Grace and Kedar Massenburg had just helped her complete the planning of a US tour. The album was recorded and the people loved it...and now came the moment to expose her live side. This was the aspect of Badu's character that had been growing for years. Remember the backyard performances at Ganny's, the car-thumping rap battles at Dallas theatres, the Soul Nation plays, the Gallery jams and the big-time support slots with Mobb Deep, A Tribe Called Quest and

D'Angelo? Now came the opportunity for Erykah to take what she had learned from all those experiences and distil it down into one show. Her *own* show.

It was time to take *Baduizm* to the people, where it would receive its first real test. Now was the time to perform, in all senses.

6 Stranger In A Strange Land

As 'On & On' remained healthily close to the top of radio programmers' playlists and its video was fast becoming a music-TV staple, the concept of a live tour being a tool to promote Erykah's work seemed almost invalid. *Baduizm*, too, showed little sign of ever leaving the upper echelons of both the pop and R&B albums chart, so Badu approached the dates with less pressure on her than most new acts experience. When it came to live work, she had paid her dues with Erykah Free and solo in New York – and was therefore lucky enough to have a fairly well-honed live act as a result.

The 13-date US tour started on 8 April at the 930 Club in Washington, DC and rolled to a halt three weeks later at the 1st Avenue venue in Minneapolis, taking in New Orleans, Houston, the home straits of Dallas, Las Vegas, San Diego, Los Angeles, San Francisco, Portland and Seattle on the way. Rehearsing a set with a new live band – which had been recruited with the help of Massenburg and Grace, and which included her South Dallas Cultural Center friend N'Dambi – Erykah prepared a full set and settled into the touring routine.

The first few dates revealed a part of Erykah Badu that few had expected – her nervous side. Those early shows saw her perform in an almost introverted manner, as if she had yet to relax into her on-stage role: she stood still at the microphone for much of the set, as if to reassure herself that it would go smoothly as long as she didn't make any sudden moves. This wouldn't last, of course, and after a while she loosened up and injected an air of dynamism into her act, but those who witnessed her first concerts were struck by her almost passive performance.

Not that everyone interpreted this negatively. One reporter said that 'On stage, she stood motionless as an icon, held in place by deep feeling. This was new. Most rhythm singers contort their bodies to demonstrate spirit possession; in Badu's case, spirit possession riveted her to the spot. Paralyzed her. And so she raised her soprano high up, screaming in exorcism, invoking the spirit call in "Certainly" and "Appletree"... [She] never digressed, didn't change the tempo, didn't put aside her shoulder sack or – until the last songs of her set – doff her little green jacket. This was hardly Sade.'

Thor Christensen was another witness to these early performances and, while he was never dismissive of Erykah's formidable talents, he made it clear in the *Dallas Morning News* that she would need to refine her stagecraft a little: 'Even though she's a rookie, Ms Badu hit the pop charts looking like a fully formed star...[but] don't notify the Hollywood Walk of Fame just yet. As dazzling as Ms Badu's talents are, her concert Sunday night at Caravan of Dreams showed she still has some growing to do.' Her problem, he thought, was that she was just too static: 'She was a bit too statuesque at times. Standing mostly still with her eyes closed, she came off as aloof until midway through her 60-minute show, when she loosened up and began to groove during a version of Chaka Khan's "Stay" and her own "Sometimes".'

Christensen's conclusions were positive, however. 'She'll need to hone her stage persona, but for an artist on her first national tour, Ms Badu sang like a seasoned vet. Though she doesn't have a powerhouse voice à la Whitney Houston, she created vocal fireworks with her subtle mix of jazz, '70s-era soul and gospel.' He added that, 'She blended her voice magnificently with backing singers Joyce Strong, Karen Cox and Chonita Gilbert, especially during "Otherside Of The Game", her moving tale of a woman who tries to justify dating a drug dealer.'

The only truly disappointing moment came when Erykah reversed her shy stance and approached a couple of songs with far too much gusto: 'But while she's garnered a lot of ink for her melancholy Holiday-styled singing, she tore into Chaka Khan's "Stay" as if she'd stopped studying *Lady Sings The Blues* and started watching *What's Love Got To Do With It* instead.'

Thor laughs when he remembers writing these words. 'When she started she was so laid back… [Part] of it is the whole vibe she projects, of an almost Zen-like confidence, which is a great part of her appeal. Many of her fans love it, and a lot of critics focus on it – but in the beginning that approach didn't make her an incredible show-person.' Has she managed to overcome this tendency since then, does he think? 'I think she's got a *lot* more interesting to watch – she's become a lot more aware of how to put on a show and the importance of showmanship. She's become a better performer because of that.'

He's right. It didn't take long for Erykah to loosen up and start enjoying her performances, and within a matter of months she was developing a multifaceted, innovative act including spoken-word segments, abstract dance and both musical and lyrical improvisations, in which she would scat or rap. Her commitment to her show was unflagging, it seemed, as she told *Vibe*. 'When I do a show, I stay until the chairs are on the tables and I sign autographs for every single person, up to the person who's behind the bar,' she said. 'I guess it's the Creator's force that gives me that extra burst of energy. I never get tired of writing inspirational words.' And she rarely settled down with a fixed show for too long, keeping the set-list and the jams fluid and funky. As she told writer Gail Smith, 'I change my show all the time to keep me and the band interested in what we're doing – and even with that, we'll change when we get to the place, depending on where the people are. Next time I have to have something for [those who were disappointed] and they'll really love it.'

Needless to say, all this outpouring of energy would take its toll, leaving her drained after each show, but Erykah's training and professional experience sustained her through the process. She knew the tricks of staying fit for the concerts, revealing to *Soul Express* that her voice usually remains in good shape: 'Maybe because of my diet… I'm a vegan-vegetarian, so that means I don't eat meat, or sugar, or eggs or dairy or any preservatives, if I can help it. And while I'm on stage I drink tea, and I sing all the time. It's like any other muscle – you exercise it a lot, and it just gets better and better. When I lay off a while, you'd be able to tell it was rough.' She had also begun to incorporate a solo spot during which she played an acoustic guitar: 'My guitar tuning is just regular major seven, and I just taught myself how to play, so I can't read a bit of music,' she said. 'I totally don't understand the theory of music. If you try to explain it to me theory-wise, I just kind of freeze up and it frightens me. But just to feel it, you know, feel the chords, feel the notes... I think my songs are more primal wills and sighs and moans than notes.'

Audiences loved Erykah's shows, both before and after she found her true performing self. According to one of her biggest fans, Rose Glenn, who has met her backstage on numerous occasions, Erykah's claim that she stays until the last autograph is signed is accurate. Glenn, who had become acquainted with Erykah's mother Kolleen before getting to know Erykah herself, recalls that after Badu's concerts there is usually an informal gathering of her friends and fans whom she has got to know personally. 'Usually when I go backstage I would see people who are familiar with who I am...and people who she knew and were in Erykah's life at some point, such as former teachers, and so on.' In Rose's experience, Badu is a caring individual who respects the people who buy her music and holds them in genuine affection: 'Erykah is very appreciative of all of the love and support that we've given her. She never takes her fans for granted. She is the bright light that outshines the darkness.'

Furthermore, Erykah gets a lot of her energy from the crowd. Glenn remembers that, 'In one interview that she did on MTV, the VJ asked her what she would want the audience to get out of her music. She said, "I would want them to feel better, I would want them to feel different from how they were feeling before. If it could help, then that's a job done".' Rose also reports that, 'About her fans, she says, "My fans have given me a lot of love, a lot of support and I don't take it for granted not one bit, and I appreciate it".' It's a mutually supportive situation all round: 'It is always a pleasure to see Erykah,' she concludes. 'When I see her she is always happy to see me, just as I'm always happy to see her. I let her know that I am in the crowd showing her love and support.'

The thousands of fans who had not been able to attend the April 1997 shows – most of which had rapidly sold out – were able to content themselves with the release of a second single, 'Otherside Of The Game'. A slower, more pensive song than the funk-edged 'On & On', it was an astute choice of single, reflecting Erykah's awareness of the sadness of modern life and impressing many listeners with the subtle, almost murmured chorus from the backing singers.

More impressive still was the accompanying video, which Erykah had scripted and directed. '"Otherside" was the first one I directed by myself,' she said. 'It was a lot of hard work, and I was learning as I went. It was a wonderful experience. It teaches you how to be a good leader and how to be patient.' The clip was full of direct references to the insoluble problems that the couple in the song face (the drug-dealing man trying to protect his understandably insecure partner), yet without going overboard with imagery or tone.

The same was true of the album's third single, released as the summer of 1997 approached. Where 'On & On' had been cosmic and 'Otherside Of The Game' sad, 'Next Lifetime' was bitter-sweet and optimistic at the same time. In the song, Erykah regrets that she cannot build a relationship with another man 'when I'm already someone's girl', but that they will meet in the next life. The video, however, takes in much more than this, choosing to depict in its four minutes different stages in the evolution of African-Americans. The first scenes are set in 17th-century Africa, where Erykah is a tribeswoman living in a village before the arrival of the colonists and their slave ships. The later part of the video is set in 1960s America, amid social strife and the struggle for black emancipation, while the final scenes take place in a future utopia. Erykah also directed this clip (with the assistance of Troy Montgomery-Smith) and her central point is simple and devastating: that the grand struggles of life, such as the fight for freedom, are as enduring as love itself.

The video was even more popular than the *Color Purple*-influenced 'On & On', and inspired the questions of many an interviewer. Erykah told MTV, 'I would have directed the first one if I could. Everything that I need to be conveyed, I can give the direction for – you know, without stepping on anybody's toes – because I'm the director.' *Vibe* asked her what the concept for the video was, to which she explained, 'That's just something in my head I came up with. My friend Jennifer, who helped me with my last video, said you ought to do it life to life, and you'll have a different guise in each lifetime. You'll be a G. And I said, how am I gonna be a G and still be righteous?' she recalled, laughing. 'So, the video starts out in Africa, in the 1600s or maybe earlier. This guy is following me around an African village, and he's checking me out, but I'm happy with my husband. Then it goes to the next lifetime, I'm passing out flyers in the street in 1961, and the same guy is following me around at a rally. Then we go to this shack to register these old people to vote and the Klan comes and burns down the shack.'

Depressing stuff, but (as with most things that Badu does) the wheel comes round again. 'The next lifetime is 3037, which is very similar to the year 1600 because that's the year we went back to our natural ways. Everything is much greener. Chlorophyll is the national drink. We're all healthy and we're beautiful. So we've got three lifetimes in three verses. And we made it work.' With a touch of annoyance, Erykah revealed that she had her fair share of pessimists in her life – presumably at the show-business end: 'I don't like people who say, no-no Erykah. I don't like nobody trying to kill your ideas 'cause they doubt themselves. That's tired to me.'

It's an excellent video. The concept of the three time-periods is clearly something that Erykah is having a lot of fun with as the clip progresses, with her early tribeswoman role the most obviously convincing. It must have been a relief for her to be able to express in images the idea behind the song, which is that love endures beyond death and that the universal balance will take care of everything in the end. The video was so successful that it was incorporated into a study module at a Californian high school in Napa called New Technology High. The course schedule promises to examine the clip as follows: '"Next Lifetime" shows Erykah Badu in three time periods, two historical (in Africa and the US) and one imagined (in the future). There are a number of historical images in the first two periods. Besides singing about love, is Badu (who was co-director) making other statements? About history? About struggles? About morality? About the role of women?' Valid questions all, and very probably ones which the video's creator would have wished it to inspire.

And so Erykah made her mark as a singles artist – a mark that would not be easily erased or forgotten. But her album was also still making waves and, as the impact of *Baduizm* spread, the ripples affected many of its creators. Ahmir '?uestlove' Thompson of The Roots, whose contribution to the record had been so crucial, revealed to *Kronick* magazine that a moment of tension had passed between Badu and himself over a misquote. The issue revolved around the bluesy fragment 'Afro (Freestyle Skit)', in which Erykah had famously crooned about busting up a lover's pager after he failed to take her to see the Wu-Tang Clan.

The *Kronick* writer asked, 'What was the real inspiration behind "Pick Yo Afro"?', to which Ahmir responded, 'It's funny you say that, because [Erykah] and I got in a little tassle yesterday because *Source* did an article, and they were askin' about how songs get written. And I was basically explaining that primarily when any song gets written it's always with The Roots in mind, of course. Like, you don't wanna make no badass joint and give it [away].' The drummer was clearly a little regretful as he related how his words had been twisted, intentionally or innocently: 'Then [the *Source* writer] said, "Well what songs have you done for other people?", because she didn't know. And I said we did Erykah, Jungle Brothers, etc, etc, etc. So the article says, "If we yay it, then we work on it. If we nay it, then it becomes 'Otherside Of The Game' for Erykah Badu."' He concluded: 'Erykah took that offensively, meaning that it wasn't something that we created together. 'Cause she made that song just like it was a collaborative effort. So she's a little hurt because it sounded like I said it was a Roots throwaway.' Luckily, the rift was healed before it developed – another instance of the press putting barriers between Erykah and her people, just as she and Robert Bradford had been forced to resolve the earlier situation caused by a misquote.

After the tour finished, Badu-mania remained healthy and her success began to reflect positively on her associates. One of those to take a step upwards was N'Dambi, who was preparing for the release of a solo album, *Little Lost Girls Blues*. Interviewers picked up on her recent gig in Erykah's band, but she was quick to dispel the notion that her skills were confined to this: 'Getting my foot in the door at the radio stations, and places like that, I definitely have to say I'm a background singer with Erykah Badu,' she pointed out. 'But when I perform, I don't open the show by saying I'm Erykah Badu's back-up singer.'

As N'Dambi made her way upwards and the music-buying public's attention began to refocus on other Erykah Badu-like soul queens, the academics stepped forward to begin their analysis. One such was better informed than most – writer Lisa Jones, the author of a book called *Bullet-Proof Diva*. Jones said, '[Erykah is] a powerful woman to do the type of music she does while projecting an image that shows it's been fought for… Little steps over time prepared the mainstream for Erykah. She represents something different from the cookie-cutter R&B-ingénue made-for-video girl who's mostly body and not much talent mould.' Lisa was one of the few analysts of this trend in music who were able to spot the artists who had paved the way for Erykah – other, less profound thinkers imagined that Erykah had emerged single-handedly bearing the flag of neo-soul. Crediting established female artists such as Tracy Chapman and Me'Shell NdegéOcello with opening the doors for Badu, Jones also pointed out (with some perspicacity) that these women had to achieve credibility with both feminist and mainstream audiences – no mean feat.

Others noticed the freshness of Erykah's approach. *Vibe* magazine breathed a sigh of relief, still bruised from the recent death of Biggie Smalls (aka the Notorious BIG) on 9 March 1997: 'After a year in which the overriding message of black pop culture has been, Get On, Get Paid, and Get Shot, maybe we deserved a break from Murder, Inc. And so, in spite of our sins, the ancestors sent Badu and her 'Izm to help us break out of our genocidal consumptive patterns – and perhaps send a message to the industry that we're down for more in our music than murder, pornography, and prostitution.'

In many ways, the calming messages of *Baduizm* were the polar opposite of the tragic events that had ravaged the hip-hop world in previous months. The recent murders of rappers Tupac Shakur and Biggie Smalls had been the final development in a confrontation between East and West Coast record labels (Sean 'Puffy' Combs's Bad Boy empire and Marion 'Suge' Knight's Death Row label, respectively), which had been allowed to progress far further than it should have done. The feud itself had been simmering since the early to mid-1990s, and just as important as the deaths of the two rappers (whose killers have never been identified) was the fact that hip-hop fans had become accustomed to hip-hop culture being one of aggression, threats and fear, with quarrels and arguments between rappers both public and private. In this context, *Baduizm* was like some sort of healing elixir, asking its listeners for love and harmony rather than anger and retribution.

The writer Greg Tate asked Badu if she ever examined other artists' career paths as examples of what to do and what not to do, to which she responded, 'No, because I think if you're an artist, you're still a human being. Our lives are kind of magnified because it seems like fun to other people. Is it fun to me to have my life magnified? Yes, because this is the energy I want to give back. I love it. I really do. Fortunately, I haven't been a victim of negative energy.' She also revealed that the other soul sisters – such as Mary J Blige – to whose ranks she now belonged, were friends, not competitors: 'I love Mary. I tell her I support her no matter what other people might say. I was in London right before she got there and bought her a ring when she got there, just as a sister thing, you know.'

Very soon after the success of *Baduizm* and Erykah's rise to public awareness, the press began to enquire of her whether she was in competition or otherwise in confrontation with other female artists of the moment. This would become a regular theme of her interviews for some time, although very little reason seems to exist for it: Badu has always spoken graciously and positively about her fellow artists. Maybe her honesty and refusal to stand aside from discussing any issue made a few reporters keen to see if she had a negative side, but they found little success trying to uncover one. Not only did Erykah refuse to rise to the bait, she knew perfectly well what game they were playing. 'I think a great deal of my following was journalists, media, and people in the culture who had positions that influenced the numbers, the masses,' she said some time after her initial rise to fame. It seems clear that she was also focused on the broader picture – the idea that the attention of the press and public will inevitably wax and wane as a matter of course. 'With the kind of energy I think I'm bringing, it doesn't need any votes,' she said. 'I gotta just keep bringing it and do it the best way I can. I can't worry about it, really. The more I'm understanding, the more I see that you have to command the attention of people in order to get the message to 'em.'

Rather than emphasise simple similarities between her music and that of other artists, Erykah usually managed to refocus the interviewers' questions on common themes that existed between them, such as when *Vibe* asked her, 'Artists such as yourself, D'Angelo, Me'Shell NdegéOcello and Maxwell have all brought live bands and performance back into black popular music. Do you feel a kinship with them?' She responded with words wiser than her age: 'I don't think we sound anything alike. We just vibrate on the same level. We're all about the same age and we come from the '70s soul feel. That's just what we understand as music, and we're just now coming to light in the business.' Their success, she maintained, came from the music's genuineness. 'The formula is feel it. And people feel it, because people are real. I don't underestimate my audience. I treat them like intelligent people who can understand what I'm saying.'

Although Erykah chose not to aim barbs at individual artists, she never shied away from commenting on the shallowness of the showbiz industry – especially when it came to the issue of image. 'I think I represent an image that is not focused on by the music business,' she pondered, quite rightly positing that she didn't resemble any previous formula. 'They probably didn't think it would sell, because the music business and music are two different things. One is motivated by money and one is motivated by truth. The truth doesn't sell a lot of times. Lies sell.' However, she also knows perfectly well that her livelihood and her platform is due to the same, falsehood-peddling industry: 'Money – if that's your motivation you gotta do what you gotta do. If healing people is your motivation, you may not sell a lot of records. But what if you got both of them as your motivation? That's my point – they're equal. It goes together. You gotta understand what you're getting into all the time. Not be so spiritually guided that you're blind. Not be so monetarily guided that you're blind. This is real, man. This is life. It's not some Piscean dream.'

As Badu always focused on spiritual and political matters in her interviews, it's no surprise that one or two writers started to ask her about the more mundane things in life – such as how she regarded the root of all evil, money. 'We have to realize that having a Lexus is not succeeding in life. That's just success on the physical level. I want nice things; I deserve nice things. But I'm balanced. I still ride the subway trains.' Clothes, too, were often a feature of these conversations: 'Even though the headwrap means a great deal, the power is in the brain...' – a logical conclusion for someone schooled in the beneath-the-circuit-board analysis of the Five Percenters. But Erykah knew the power of visual attraction, too: 'As women we use our beauty as much as we can, because that's magnetic, and it's what people are attracted to. But we know that it's not between your legs, it's between your ears. So, it's important to keep the communication going, and playing dumb is a part of intelligence too.'

A picture of Erykah was emerging, based on an ever-growing number of features and interviews, gracing practically all areas of print and broadcast media, of an entirely new kind of artist. To the public, Badu was still an enigma, even though she spoke so openly and extensively on a variety of subjects. Many observers found her self-assurance and spiritual approach almost intimidating – it did, after all, break with the tradition that pop performers (of either sex) should be young, vacuous and gullible, only gaining worldly experience as the years passed. Here, it seems, was a young woman with the understanding of a person far beyond her years.

Add to this descriptions of Erykah's background in which her mother Kolleen was quoted as saying, 'Whenever anyone sends out positive messages about love, life and spirituality, these statements are powerful in and of themselves. These words affect people positively; that's power,' and it's little wonder that a zealous Badu fanbase began to grow and that other, more cautious, listeners treated her with a wariness bordering on suspicion. But the people who knew Erykah best – her family and friends – knew that she was just Erykah, the girl who had served coffee at Grinders and taught the kids in South Dallas, not a witch-doctor or a messiah. Still, she herself knew that one day there would be ridicule aimed at her, and with an acute awareness of the wheel of showbiz fortune, told her loved ones that a downturn in her popularity was a distinct possibility. 'When [the people] become more familiar with you, they tend to forget about you,' she warned.

Not that this hindered her keenness to discuss spiritual matters when asked to do so. Asked by *HipOnline* to explain her use of Egyptian words and symbols, she said, 'I'm a Pisces, and I'm very interested in metaphysics, science, spirituality, and the occult, or anything like that. I'm not satisfied with the explanations I get from TV or from school... [There] is so much more to the universe and to us. So I just studied, and memorized. I might go out and look for information like that.' And her fans, it appeared, aided her in her learning: 'Sometimes people will give me books, more so now than before. You know, being in the entertainment business, people will think they know you and what you're interested in. I've gotten so many books and paintings and cards with ankhs, candles, and incense that I'll have enough to read until at least a hundred. I'm interested in it, and I feel that it's good to share information.'

Ankhs (Egyptian crosses) are a favourite symbol of Erykah's, as she explained: 'The ankh is a divine cipher for life and represents a perfect 360 degrees, indicating that physical life is not the end of the cosmic cycle... The top of the ankh represents the womb of life, the feminine principle of who we are. The horizontal part is fashioned like the fallopian tubes, with each side representing an egg, a child, a renewal. Finally, the base of the ankh is characteristic of the male principle, which fertilizes the tubes and produces renewed life in the womb.' Not that the ankh represents the whole of her belief... When asked, 'According to spirituality, are you getting inspired by a certain religion?' she responded, 'Uh, all of them. Just existence, period. I know that they are all one and the same. Personally, I don't choose any particular religion or symbol or group of words or teachings to define me. That's between me and the most high. You know, my higher self. The Creator.' Not that she is unwilling to learn from all available sources: 'But I do learn a lot from each thing, because everything is necessary. We're all here for a reason, not just to group up with your own group.' A small revelation came when she informed the reporter that, 'I'll have more information next album on that.'

With all this – and more – coming off the page every time Erykah was interviewed, were some people actually scared of her? Thor Christensen thinks that would be going too far: 'As much as she comes off as a philosopher, she still has a down-to-earth nature. I don't get the feeling that she takes all the adulation too seriously. She's got a sense of humour about her lyrics.' In person, she is a far cry from the solemn, unsmiling figure who stares out of her publicity shots, he says. 'The times I've interviewed her I've been extremely impressed by how bold and confident she is. She's very easy to interview, she's very laid back, she doesn't come across as a big star, she wants you to know that she's down-to-earth Erykah. She's happy to answer all your questions.' In his experience, Erykah is informed and intelligent ('I think she's a very savvy businesswoman – more power to her. So many musicians, especially in R&B and rap, get ripped off by the record companies, but she seems to have a very firm understanding of the business side of music'), but not at all self-important. And yet she has been portrayed, with some justification, almost as a preacher or prophet, which has made her seem a little other-worldly to some.

Divinely guided or not, Erykah Badu was extremely big news for the rest of 1997, and proved it by pulling off a record-breaking haul of five nominations at the 1997 *Soul Train* Lady of Soul Awards, held in Los Angeles. *Baduizm* was nominated for the cumbersomely titled Best R&B/Soul Album (Solo Category) award, 'On & On' received a mighty three nominations – including R&B/Soul Song of the Year – and 'Next Lifetime' was nominated for Best Music Video. She also received an honourable mention in the Best R&B/Soul or Rap New Artist category. Of these, she was awarded all but the Best Music Video prize – so it was a moment to cherish, indeed. Her presence at the ceremony was a genuine step upwards, as she was asked to co-host the event along with her idol Chaka Khan, and luminaries also present included Janet Jackson (who received the Lena Horne Award for Outstanding Career Achievement) and Queen Latifah (who picked up the Aretha Franklin Award as Entertainer of the Year). The show was broadcast at prime time and represents the moment when Erykah became first known to most of America – a pivotal event.

Yet awards and their attendant ceremonies have never been very important to Badu. Yes, many artists claim not to be interested in this kind of industry recognition...but most are being a little dishonest, as is well-known. In Erykah's case, however, her lack of interest in these phenomena appears to be genuine: what was most important to her as the year progressed was the impact of *Baduizm* on her life and the lives of her family, and her developing relationship with Dre. Proof of this came later in the year when she appeared in a brief cameo role in an ABC soap opera entitled *One Life To Live* – a small event compared to the release of a platinum-selling, record-breaking début album, perhaps, but important to Erykah simply because it pleased her grandmother. *One Life To Live*, it transpired, was Ganny's preferred daytime TV show: 'I did *One Life To Live* because that is my grandmother's favorite soap opera,' explained Badu, 'and I only did it because she'd be able to see me on it. When you get a chance to involve other people in your own blessings, that's the best thing, to me.'

With her typical self-assurance, Erykah told the press of a simple premise that allows her to keep her centre in a spiralling wave of publicity: 'No matter what is going on in your life, sisters,' she remarked, 'take your bubble bath. We all have to remember that if you don't take care of yourself, no one will.' She also revealed some of the secrets of her own routine. 'I like to take a salt bath before I appear in public, to create my own sense of calm,' she said. 'And I start and end each day with a glass of hot lemon water. It flushes out all the impurities and toxins and keeps you healthy.' This combination of proactive advice and unpretentious spiritual musings made Erykah the perfect choice for more or less any magazine and newspaper, and she soon found herself on the cover of the influential *Blues & Soul* magazine, as well as being interviewed by *Vibe*, *Spin*, *Time*, *The Source* and *Rolling Stone*.

Her already-healthy public profile was augmented further when she was asked to perform on the Smokin' Grooves tour, a Pepsi-sponsored rolling festival that was scheduled to cross America in the summer of 1997. East Coast hip-hop crew Cypress Hill were the headliners, while support slots were filled by Erykah, Foxy Brown, the unique George Clinton And The P-Funk All-Stars and Badu's old *compadres* The Roots, while certain shows also featured the talents of The Pharcyde, the Brand New Heavies and OutKast – probably the first time that Erykah and Dre had performed on the same bill. An eclectic line-up, then, covering almost all aspects of late 1990s American black music, with the soul and jazz influences of Badu and The Roots complementing the purer hip-hop of Cypress Hill and OutKast and the funk of George Clinton; and a pioneering concept, too, getting into its stride well before later big-budget hip-hop shows such as the Dr Dre/Eminem/Snoop Dogg Up In Smoke tour became an accepted institution.

However, inspired as the idea behind the tour was, reviews were mixed, and Erykah bore the brunt of many of them. It seems that those who dismissed her spiritual messages as fake had begun to express their scepticism: a part of Erykah's Smokin' Grooves show featured her singing 'Teach!' and explaining Khemetic imagery (the ankhs and other Egypt-derived symbols) to the audience – some of whom found it a little too 'New Age earth goddess' for comfort. The fact that she started her set with the question 'How many degrees are there in a circle?' (a precursor to 'On & On', of course), and lighting a sandalwood incense stick, merely added to the soul-hippy image her critics were beginning to assign to her. One reviewer wrote of the Wantagh, New York show that, although her talent was undoubted ('Like most of the other acts on the bill, Ms Badu was a little of something new and a little of something old. Scatting, rapping, crooning and emoting like a combination of just about any singer who has been associated with the word "diva" in the last 60 years, she made the word a compliment again'), the set design did her no favours ('her giant ankh…looked from a distance like a toilet seat with the cover up'), and that she was perhaps a little insensitive to the feelings of her fellow performers ('Though she knew the night would reach its peak with the landing of George Clinton's mother ship, she still sang the lyric from "On & On", her hit that warns dreamers "The mother ship can't save you".').

At around this time a prominent American music magazine, evidently unhappy with what it perceived as her need to educate, labelled Erykah 'the biggest contrivance since the Spice Girls'. While this is nonsense (for we've examined her personal history, analysed her personal beliefs and the conclusion any rational person would reach is that she believes what she says), it's interesting evidence of a phenomenon that has always dogged Badu since those early days – the existence of a group of sceptics as vocal as her supporters. What do we learn from this? Simply that her message is too strong to be ignored: love it or loathe it, it inspires strong debate either way. As she would like it, listeners will make up their own minds.

The incessant Billie Holiday comparisons had slowed down at last, but that didn't stop interviewers likening her voice to others. Journalist

Dalton Higgins made the perceptive observation that Erykah sounds like the house singer Nicolette, who guested so memorably on Massive Attack's 1994 album *Protection* before launching a solo career. Erykah was less than convinced, however, when he informed her that he thought she sounded like DeBarge singer Bunny DeBarge: 'I ain't never heard that one before,' she responded, before firmly closing the subject with the words, 'By the end of the tour the comparisons will be null and void. I'm Erykah Badu and these are my isms. You know, I invite the energies of any one or being that wants to come into the cipher and help me do my job, but the media tend to go way overboard. I don't respect that.'

Moving on to the subject of racial politics, Erykah talked with some passion about the importance of self-awareness. 'If you're black,' she said, 'it's a requirement that you're conscious of your history and self – it gives you a security and a foundation to build on… As human beings, yes, we're all equal – but we're different. What's good for some people is not necessarily good for black people, and the opposite holds true.' This led to a discussion of the Nation of Islam: 'I wake up every Sunday morning to Brother Farrakhan because I learn much from him,' she observed. 'I appreciate him deeply and I appreciate the brothers in the struggle. As blacks we are gods and goddesses, because we were made in the creator's image.' However, she stopped her flow of thought to interject some realism. 'But not everybody looks at life like I do. Some people live for self. Some live for a Lexus. A Lexus will not take you where you need to go inside.'

Interestingly, the interview ended with Badu asking the interviewer not to mistake her as just another R&B songstress, but to recognise that she is an MC at heart: 'People gotta recognize that my foundation is hip-hop. That's what I know, feel and live. Hip-hop culture is who I am and I'm an MC before I am anything else.' Clearly Erykah's self-identification as a rapper as well as a soul singer and jazz scatter is important to her, and informs her drive to perform accordingly.

After only a few short months, Erykah Badu had been grilled, analysed and picked apart in print by hundreds of journalists from dozens of countries. Her face had appeared on countless pages and various labels had been placed on her, from 'soul diva' to 'jazz singer' to 'blues rapper'.

But one of the most common attempts to categorise her involved the term 'earth mother' – a favourite expression for writers who had been impressed with her calm and spirituality (as well as being a snide expression for those not taken with those same qualities). This term gained a particular resonance in the late spring of 1997, when she made an important discovery...

Erykah was pregnant – and in many ways the everlasting circle to which she often referred was now complete.

7 Many Births

The word 'neo-soul' was now becoming popular. *Baduizm* had made an impression on so many people – fans, press, commentators, musicians – that a word to describe it simply had to be coined, and this one would do as well as any other. But, as Erykah repeatedly explained throughout (and the burden was made no easier by the fact that she was now carrying a child), the movement was far from being her sole creation.

She was right. Some five years after *Baduizm*, neo-soul seems like an established concept, but back in the late 1990s it was new and fragile. Many observers sniggered at its classical pretensions and pointed out (with some justification) that because soul represents human suffering and pride it is ageless and omnipresent, and therefore cannot be new, old or otherwise. Nonetheless, the phrase grew in popularity and by the start of 1998 it was ubiquitous.

Basically, the term was invented because a whole new wave of vocal artists (with Badu merely as their latest proponent) had emerged into the limelight since the early 1990s, all of whom had in common the fact that they were consummate singers and arrangers, upheld the values of classic soul (spirituality, sexuality, honesty, political activism) and brought strong hip-hop, jazz and even rock influences to the table. Bubble-gum lyrics (think Britney Spears) were discouraged, although most neo-soul artists did maintain a strong sense of humour, and 'real' instrumentation was used as much as computer technology. Some pointed at the British artist Seal (whose commercial peak had occurred in around 1991–2) as the instigator of the new movement, but more 'manufactured' acts like Mint Condition and Tony Toni Tone also played a part in its foundation –

note that slick R&B acts such as Boyz II Men were not regarded as neo-soul, as they were just too smooth. Organic rawness was also a part of neo-soul's attraction, and this came to the fore when D'Angelo and Maxwell released successful albums in the mid-1990s.

For some reason it was primarily male artists who kick-started the new sound, but it was females who took it from them and made it what it is today. As we have seen, D'Angelo was a real catalyst in the development of neo-soul – his début album from 1995 was likened (somewhat hysterically, perhaps) to the best work of Marvin Gaye, Sly Stone, Stevie Wonder and Jimi Hendrix – but the commercial and critical praise that was heaped on him was soon regarded as minor compared to that received by the wave of female singers who followed in his wake. Tony Rich and Maxwell were also artists to be reckoned with, but by the time their work had become established, the second generation of women had appeared and made them seem like bit-players.

Erykah didn't like being labelled; 'I don't want to have no flags on me or have any symbols represent me,' she told *Time* magazine. 'I represent *me*.' Yes, indeed, but the press weren't having any of that, and a neo-soul artist she became, until she could prove them otherwise.

A slightly odd facet of neo-soul – and one that probably says more about the society we live in than the nature of the music – was that men were seen as sex gods (D'Angelo, in particular, had a gift for getting women swooning in the aisles) but that women were regarded as earth mothers. (The link with the Five Percenters' gods/earths terminology may be more than coincidental.) Perhaps these profound themes made the lyrics of neo-soul recognisable as belonging to the genre – the ideas of self-expression, struggle and self-actualisation are all part of the intellectual remit of neo-soul (just as they were of classic soul) and made the usual high-charting pop acts of the day seem rather insubstantial.

Musically, neo-soul is a broad church, but – as the underrated rock performer Lenny Kravitz had been preaching since the late 1980s – real instruments contain more substance than electronic ones, and their use was prevalent. D'Angelo famously said, 'I want to take hip-hop and funk and make it new again. I want to take it back to basics. I'm tired of all the synthetic stuff' – words that could have served as some kind of neo-soul manifesto. Another example of this came about ten months before the release of *Baduizm*, when a hip-hop act named The Fugees released their début album, *The Score*. A landmark release, it was much more beats-driven than the Badu album, but many of both records' core aspects were identical: Fugees singer Lauryn Hill (who would go on to become as successful as Badu in future years) said of her record that, 'It was very important to me that the music be very raw...and there be a lot of live instrumentation.' Add to this the jazz tradition of scatting and live improvisation that artists such as Erykah employed frequently, and the picture is complete – neo-soul is sensual, accomplished, gritty and beautiful all at the same time. No wonder America's music buyers flocked to get copies of *Baduizm*.

As Lauryn Hill and later singers Macy Gray, Jill Scott and Angie Stone arrived at the neo-soul podium alongside Erykah Badu, she welcomed them up, saying, 'We're all friends, inside the music and outside the music. I mean, we don't sound anything alike, we don't approach our music anything alike, but we come from the same genuine place. We want our music to be real and we don't want to compromise our art.' Generous words: but she is no fool, and knew the music she had pioneered would not be fashionable forever. What's more, 1997 had been such a bizarrely successful year for her that she knew a backlash must inevitably come.

But not yet. More awards awaited her, including two MTV Video Music Awards nominations for Best Female Video and Best R&B Video. The ceremony took place in September 1997 and was followed shortly by the release of the soundtrack to the movie *Eve's Bayou*, which contained a song Badu had co-written with none other than Curtis Mayfield, entitled 'A Child With The Blues (Izm Mix)'. The film, directed by Kasi Lemmons (who was also an actor, notably in *Gridlock'd* and *The Silence Of The Lambs*), was a success and was compared favourably to period black films such as *The Color Purple*. Its soundtrack was clearly a weighty affair and Erykah's profile was boosted significantly by her appearance on it – although the lasting legacy of the *Eve's Bayou* material was her joy at working with the living legend Mayfield, at the time returning slowly to music after the 1990 accident that had left him paralysed, and just two years away from a tragically early death.

A second collaboration with the voice-of-the-moment D'Angelo came when Erykah was asked to appear in the video for his 'Lady' single. Badu was by turns serious-faced and light-hearted, alternating between shots featuring the male singer – and for some time people who weren't familiar with her solo work thought of her as 'the woman in the D'Angelo video'. Not that this did her any harm, but they were in for a shock when the news came that, a mere nine months after the release of *Baduizm*, a new Erykah Badu album was scheduled to appear. But what was even more unsettling – in marketing terms, at least – was that it would be a live album, the province of the classic male soul artists and (more latterly) the standard mid-career move taken by white rock dinosaurs such as Queen and Iron Maiden.

It soon emerged that Kedar Massenburg had applied some lateral thinking to the challenge of keeping Erykah's name afloat in the public consciousness, after the enormous impact of *Baduizm* had threatened to overexpose her. They needed a shock move, and a live album hot on the heels of its parent record would, they judged, do the trick perfectly. Their concept was proven right when eyebrows went up everywhere after the news broke. A live album, when *Baduizm* still had so much commercial power? Pundits predicted that the new record would damage sales of its predecessor, and according to conventional wisdom they were right (after all, the days when artists such as Cliff Richard could release three chart-topping albums a year were long gone).

The album, simply titled *Live*, was scheduled for release on 18 November 1997, more or less the date that Erykah was predicted to give birth. Basically a one-hour live show plus a studio track, the record was designed to give the listener the full flavour of the Badu live experience, but also to reveal a little more about her than even the keenest listener to *Baduizm* could have learned; that is, how she improvises live, how she turns her show into a learning experience, and what her influences are. Unlike most live albums, *Live* provides the listener with plenty of new material. No mere in-concert rehash of her studio songs, the record contains three covers – Chaka Khan's 'Stay', Roy Ayers' 'Searching' and an intricate medley of Heatwave's 'Boogie Nights', Tom Browne's 'Funkin' For Jamaica' and the Mary Jane Girls' 'All Night Long'. There are also two brand new songs – 'Ye Yo' and 'Tyrone' – the latter of which was released as a single shortly before the album's release, and to great acclaim. What's great about the established songs from *Baduizm* is that Erykah and her band have taken the trouble to recreate them in new forms on *Live*, improvising wildly at points, with Badu herself interjecting skits and spontaneous reworkings of the familiar arrangements.

The show was recorded on 1 October 1997 at Sony Studios in New York and benefits from the responsive, excited audience that gathered for the session. Like *Baduizm*, *Live* begins with 'Rimshot (Intro)' – and it's a welcome, understated opening to the concert – but the beginning has been reworked to include the instantly recognisable opening bars of Miles Davis's 'So What', a bass-and-horns figure that jazz fans worldwide instantly know as a sign that pure cool is on the way. This gives way to the slow-building tension of 'Other Side Of The Game' (*sic – Baduizm* spells it 'Otherside'), with its beautiful opening statement of 'What you gonna do when they come for you?' intoned softly by Badu's backing singers. The two songs make up a subtle intro – there are no opening pyrotechnics here – and the audience is palpably enjoying itself, with cheers and shouted encouragement.

It's with 'On & On', of course, that the show (and record) really takes off. Erykah's famous repeated second-verse shout of 'You feel that?' is responded to with enthusiasm, and the impression is that some kind of devotional, almost churchlike experience is under way. This is reinforced when the fourth track (titled 'Reprise') is made up entirely of Erykah speaking to her listeners over a muted jam on the basic chords of the songs. But she's a teacher, not a preacher, and explains carefully what the ankh on her wrist represents with the instructions, 'This is a womb…sisters, place your hands on your wombs. This is the male part…brothers, place your hands on your…', but is interrupted by a gale of appreciative laughter, which she herself laughs along with. It's a veritable lesson in symbology, with Erykah asking the crowd, 'How many degrees are there in a circle?' and repeating the question until the answer is shouted loud enough. She then explains what her cipher is, embarking on a fairly complex description of the oneness of the atoms of the human body with the axis of the earth.

She knows not to keep talking too long, however – after all, this recording is intended for an album, which people will listen to time and again – and drops into 'Apple Tree' (*sic* – *Baduizm* spells it 'Appletree') with a slick reworking of the melody, with the band still pushing along the chords of 'On & On'. The second line sees a tempo- and key-jump and both singer and band settle into a faster, funkier version of the song than the one from *Baduizm*. It's evidently an audience favourite, with the bass guitar triads keeping it driving forward.

As with *Baduizm*, *Live* has its flaws – and 'Ye Yo' is the first of these. After explaining that the song's title means 'mother' in Swahili and dedicating the song to her soon-to-be-born son, Erykah settles into the song, a very mellow, understated song. So mellow and understated, in fact, that it becomes fairly boring very quickly – and especially so given the contrast with its predecessor, 'Apple Tree', and the song that follows it, Roy Ayers' 'Searching'. Strangely, Badu seems to be having some problems with the melody, straining perceptibly to stay on top of the jumps from interval to interval – something that a studio overdub might have remedied, although that would have been a little dishonest, perhaps.

The three covers are next, sandwiching Erykah's own 'Certainly'. The Ayers song is a cool, rim-shot-driven piece led by the backing singers and emphasising the sweet partnership of organ and bass – Erykah's vocal is either absent or undetectably low in the mix for almost three minutes, before spiralling into some improvisation and giving way to guitar and organ solos. 'Boogie Nights' is a slowed-down, stripped-down version of the original and segues neatly into 'All Night' and, while neither track truly surpasses the originals, they're a funky addition to the show and something of a departure from Erykah's own, more profound compositions. 'Certainly' begins with some improvised piano before dropping into the sinewy bass line that props up the song: in fact, at the beginning there is very little other than the vocal and bass, a masterstroke of economy that keeps the tension tight and allows Erykah to introduce flattened blues notes with the tiniest amount of variation.

A high point comes with Chaka Khan's 'Stay', on which Erykah and her backing singers can truly let go and stretch themselves for the first time in the show. Decorated with the wah-wah guitar that made Khan's original so disco-fied, the song seems to fill the players with renewed vigour – as if they feel that now is their chance to let loose. Erykah's voice in particular is remarkable, hitting a fantastically high peak during improvised sections. From then on, the concert is electric – after teasing the crowd with a few lines from 'Next Lifetime (Interlude)', Erykah informs them that she isn't ready to sing the song yet, and that she is going to do a brand new song instead – a song she wrote on-stage in London with her band during a sound-check, and which would be released as her next single.

The song would become acknowledged as Erykah's second-best-known signature tune (after 'On & On'). Entitled 'Tyrone', it is the sound of Erykah embracing tough-sista values and striking out at a useless lover and his loser friends, one of whom is Tyrone. 'Every time I ask for you for some cash,' she complains, 'you just ask me for some ass.' These lines are received with a scream of appreciation by the audience members, who are clearly enjoying every line, and it's at this point that the crowd is most involved with its idol. The show ends with a 12-minute jammed version of 'Next Lifetime', which at one point sees the musicians, Erykah and her backing singers descend into a maelstrom of scatted improvisation, and at another is based on a call-and-response dialogue between Badu and alternate singers. The song dies down with an a cappella section in which all the vocalists entreat the audience, 'Dry your eyes, Please don't cry', and ends with a glissando-driven flourish.

What is most striking about the album (and is probably the reason that Massenburg and Badu thought a live album would be a good idea) is the passion that runs through it. Erykah's less-is-more approach made every note worth listening to and every word a lesson, and the strength of the emotion behind the songs lends them a crystalline, glimmering air that is another level up from the smoothly organic sounds of *Baduizm*. The musicians that appear on the record are all masters of their craft, but also trained – as their classic soul background dictates – to play with a razor-sharp economy that makes the gaps between the sounds as crucial a part of the whole experience as the music itself.

It's quite a show, and one that should probably have ended there, but the studio version of 'Tyrone' is added onto the end, complete with vintage vinyl crackles during the intro. Not that it's a bad song – it's one of the best that Erykah has ever written, and went on to be one of the most commercially successful – but this version is much drier than the live epic we have witnessed some 15 minutes beforehand. However, Erykah was presumably obliged to include it on the record if it was on the point of being released as a single, and it remains a clever song to cherish. Remarkably, the album was recorded with a mere three-piece band, consisting of Hubert Eaves IV (bass), Charles Bell (drums) and Norman Hurt (keyboard) – the trio that had backed her on the recently completed Smokin' Grooves jaunt – plus Erykah's three backing singers, despite the full sound of the record. Hurt and Badu produced the album, while Massenburg took on the role of executive producer, with Erykah also filling in as his associate.

Live looked great, it has to be said. The album was housed in a sleeve bearing an image of Erykah gazing at the camera and covering her breast, with a pair of swallow-tail butterfly wings emerging from her back, with a similar image on the rear of the inlay sleeve. More stark were the portraits of Badu with her fully pregnant stomach emerging from beneath her dress: the tray picture was her stomach alone, with the song titles written on it in a flourishing hand. Two pages of text from the *Vibe* writer Karen R Good set the scene, revealing, among other facts, that Erykah had endured late pregnancy pains on-stage but had not sat down; that she had drunk tea during 'On & On' right where the song mentions the act; that she had begun the show two hours late, arriving with the regal words 'I apologize for my tardiness'; and that she intended to call her child Fly if a girl and Seven if a boy. Erykah herself added a column thanking her sister Koryan for her love and sisterhood, as well as a page of thanks to her family and friends – and finally there's a small paragraph for Dre, in which Erykah calls him her 'beloved reflection & divine lover Andre' and says, 'You my nigga fo' life'. The album is 'Dedicated to my new baby (Fly – Seven)'.

Reviews of the album were mostly positive, with many writers glad that Erykah had not simply produced an identikit *Baduizm*-with-audience and had deemed her audience worthy of a high-quality product. Many did wonder if she might not be running the risk of overexposing herself, however, with two albums in the charts at the same time, but this ultimately didn't seem to be the case, largely because Kedar had timed the release perfectly. Had the live album appeared too early, the Badu presence might indeed have been too much for the average soul consumer to handle; conversely, another six months and fans would have been disappointed by what they might regard as less than a 'real' second album.

'Tyrone' was the song that would emerge as the album's standout track, and the best song that Erykah had written at this time. Of course, interviewers were almost unanimously keen to enquire exactly who this Tyrone was, to the point where Badu issued a blanket statement whenever the subject was raised, saying, 'Let me clear this up. The song is not about "Tyrone". The song is about my old man, and he needs to call Tyrone who's a friend he spends too much time with. Most people are saying Tyrone this, Tyrone that. Actually Tyrone is the one that needs to come help him get his stuff.' The provenance of the song was a classic Erykah move: '"Tyrone" was a joke. I made it up on stage in London,' she remarked. 'I freestyled it. That's what we do in hip-hop – we just make things up sometimes.' Interestingly, while Western audiences would find the song's sassy, go-girl mock-bitchiness hilarious and respond with shouts of appreciation, Erykah later revealed after a Far Eastern tour that Japanese crowds took it seriously. 'It isn't funny to them,' she said, explaining to one reporter that in that country even minor relationship conflict is cause for shame.

Badu fan and chronicler of her career Thor Christensen wrote an accurate review of *Live* in the *Dallas Morning News*, saying on 16 November that, 'Like most concert albums, it's a hit-and-miss effort that will appeal more to diehard fans who've seen her live than to the casual listener. Ms Badu can be a superb vocalist, and tunes such as "Other Side Of The Game" show her maturing into a master improviser as she scat-sings into gospel, jazz and soul.' But he had one or two criticisms to make, adding, 'Except for "Tyrone", the album never comes close to matching the hypnotic groove of *Baduizm*. The bulk of *Live* can be summed with that old cliche: "Guess you had to be there".' He had a fair point – live albums almost never match up to the studio records from which they draw or the actual experience of witnessing the artist in the flesh – and his observation that Erykah's business savvy was reflected in the choice of a live album was a good one, too: 'Released just eight months after she put out her multimillion-selling debut…the live disc is a clear-cut case of striking while your iron is red-hot – and, of course, while the Christmas-buying frenzy is in full swing… Does a brand new artist like Ms Badu have anything to gain with a live disc – something usually reserved for veteran artists, often just to fulfil contract obligations? And as a young live performer, is she really good enough to merit one?' Good questions all, and ones that he thought *Live* left unanswered.

Appropriate or otherwise, *Live* sold well to the public keen for more Erykah output and 'Tyrone' topped the *Billboard* R&B Singles Airplay chart in the US for six weeks. The album itself entered the main pop charts at Number One. Clearly the concept was both well judged and well executed, and Badu could be satisfied that another step had been taken.

Not that she would have spent much time thinking about chart performance at this stage, for at 2:07pm on the very same day that *Live* appeared, a more lasting event occurred – the birth of her baby son, whom she named Seven Sirius as planned (7 is, Erykah explained, 'a divine number which cannot be divided'). The arrival of the two Badu creations on the same day says much for their mother's belief in the symmetry of the universe and the ceaseless nature of the everlasting circle, of course…and especially so given that he was born two weeks early. The birth took place at Erykah's home with Dre, Erykah's mother and her sisters all present – the baby weighed in at 2.92kg (6lb 7oz).

As with all births, Seven's arrival was a momentous event. It turned out that her mother Kolleen never thought her eldest daughter would choose to have children, adding that Erykah had always been 'a bit of a loner' and that she was not sure she would ever 'have the time or capacity to share herself'. Now that a baby was present, however, Kolleen said that Seven 'has made a difference…and she makes a beautiful little mother'. Not that her first words were meant to sound harsh: as we've seen, Badu was always a headstrong, driven woman with little time to waste, and perhaps her mother construed this as a need to push her own way forward, alone if necessary. The same interview saw the two women reveal a little about their relationship, with Badu pointing out that 'she and her mother did not always agree in years past', but that, 'We're really good friends now. I see her as a person, not only as a mother. I empathize and understand – and "innerstand", even.' Kolleen then asked the interviewer, 'Did she really say that?... Well, that's nice to know. That makes it all worthwhile.'

Family friend Tisha Crear was present at the birth too and described it as a deeply spiritual event, saying, 'It was a calm, peaceful environment. We just chanted and prayed that baby into the world.' *Live* was playing as Seven emerged, a presence that might well have soothed his entry into the world. 'He was very familiar with that music,' Erykah explained, 'because I was on tour my whole pregnancy.' Of special interest to the baby was 'Ye Yo', which Badu had made her child's prenatal lullaby: 'That was the song I sang to him in the womb... He was very still when I sang, and he'd start kicking when the music stopped.'

The impact on Erykah herself was immediate. She reported that, 'I always see mothers with children, and I can really feel the bond now. Just seeing isn't enough. I'm a breast-feeding mom, and it's just a really deep connection. You feel a creation of you. First I was an apartment, now I'm a restaurant. It's an experience.' More than this, of course, was the change in world-view that becoming a parent brings. Asked two years after the birth if she saw the world differently as a mother, Erykah replied: 'Oh, yeah, I see the world differently now. Actually, when I first had the baby, I was breast-feeding him for two years straight. So we were together for two years of his life, every single day, all hours of the day. So I was two people, and I eventually morphed back into one.'

But Seven had begun to make his own way at an early stage, it seemed. 'Now he's like a part of me. He's very independent as a result of it, and I was worried about the opposite. I was very worried that he was going to be so attached, since we were together every day, but I guess it made him feel comfortable, you know, "She's around all the time, she's here for me." It made me feel like a very responsible person. You know, tidy, you know, and now my health is better, because I'm now responsible for someone's whole reason for being. That helped.'

Later still Erykah could reflect on how her whole life had changed from having a child. 'Motherhood gave me a lot of patience, and it is a humbling experience, because this whole new life comes into the world and instinctively knows so much more than you do,' she told CNN. 'Having Seven in my life didn't change my songwriting, but it taught me how to pace myself as an artist. Raising him and writing songs comes from the same place in my soul. It was a really wonderful example to me to get back to my innocence as well, because the child doesn't worry about how you feel, or how it looks or how it smells. He just lives and is peaceful and is kind for no reason at all – that is what love is, and I learned a great lesson in love from my son.'

The link between the love for a child and the creation of music was not lost on her, either – as she told *Soul Express*. 'I found out an important lesson. I found out that giving that kind of love and energy to my music comes from the same exact place it comes to give my son the creative energy he needs, so I have to pace it. You know, it takes a longer time to create music or anything else creative now.' Asked if she wanted her son to be a musician, she adamantly responded, 'Not really. I want him to be what he wants to be. I want him to have a free mind. I don't want to control him. Even though I'm a control freak over my life. But not his. That's his life, you know. My own life, things around me I like to control, not his life.' Not that her input would be half-hearted, of course. 'I just want him to know the difference between right and wrong. He doesn't really have any rules. The rules are, "Do what Mummy says do!" I like changes so much that it's very difficult to enforce some rules. So I want him to be a sweet person, a loving person, you know, to be considerate about people's feelings, and most of all, not to expect anything from life.'

And so Erykah's life changed to another level. She was often asked how she managed to be a mother to a newborn child and still continue to record and perform – and these questions came more and more often when she announced that she had been signed up to act in a major new film. But her answer was simple: she regarded the two jobs as one occupation, and explained that Seven accompanied her everywhere and that while he was a small child she would arrange home-schooling for him. However, she planned for him to attend regular school when the time came.

Along with caring for Seven, the rest of 1997 was taken up with filming scenes for Erykah's first film, a major-studio production that was shrouded in secrecy due to its eagerly awaited status. Most of the shoots took place in Chicago, and little is known of what went on on set – but it can be assumed that Badu, a consummate actress, enjoyed bringing these dormant acting capabilities to the role – a role that would suit her perfectly.

While the rumours gathered and she wound up her involvement, invitations began flooding into Kedar Entertainment from the American Music Awards committee, who were planning their yearly ceremony (or, as it was portentously dubbed, 'the 25th Annual American Music Awards Telecast') for January 1998. Erykah's nominations, it transpired, were to be Favorite New Soul/R&B Artist, Favorite Female Soul/R&B Artist and Favorite Soul/R&B Album. The list of nominees for these and other awards read like a wish list of the great and the good of American urban music, including Kenneth 'Babyface' Edmonds, Boyz II Men, Bone Thugs-N-Harmony, Mary J Blige, Mariah Carey, the Will Smith-led soundtrack for *Men In Black* and – somewhat incongruously – the Spice Girls, whose impact in the US had been unexpectedly huge in late 1996 and the whole of 1997.

Erykah won the Favorite New Soul/R&B Artist award, to her delight and that of Kedar and Tim Grace. The victory was all the more prestigious because it came amid a hip-hop-dominated ceremony: Bone Thugs-N-Harmony had also had a successful evening and reinforced this by thanking the late NWA rapper and Ruthless Records founder Eazy-E (a namesake of Erykah's, as it happened – his given name was Eric Wright), who had died from AIDS-related complications just 18 months before. Elsewhere, the Wu-Tang Clan made the 1997 American Awards more focused on hip-hop by telling reporters that negative media reports had put rappers' lives in danger, and that the press should think about the image they were projecting about hip-hop. All this furrowed a few brows, and few headlines concentrated on the quiet brilliance of Erykah Badu.

But the awards weren't about to stop there, even if the pomp and circumstance of these events went somewhat incongruously with Erykah's less-than-ostentatious demeanour. The most prestigious recognition of all (in American music terms) came in February 1998, when she scooped two Grammys for *Baduizm*, which levelled the competition in the Best Female R&B Vocal Performance and Best R&B Album categories. She was also nominated for Best New Artist and Best R&B Song – not the last time that critics would settle on the R&B category for her, in the absence of any other clearly defined genre. The ceremony, held at New York City's Radio City Music Hall, was a significant one – the institution was celebrating its 40th anniversary – and was made notable by the press's descriptions of the awards as a largely 'black' event, a label borne out in part by wins from R Kelly (three awards, including Best Male R&B Vocal Performance for the nauseating 'I Believe I Can Fly'), Sean 'Puffy' Combs (a remarkable seven nominations and two wins, including Best Rap Performance By A Duo Or Group for 'I'll Be Missing You'), Will Smith and Erykah herself. Smith, in particular, gave his appearance – a performance of 'Men In Black' – a touch of credibility by dedicating the song to the late rappers Tupac Shakur and Biggie Smalls.

Perhaps the biggest shock of the evening came during a speech by Erykah, when the erratic Wu-Tang Clan rapper Ol' Dirty Bastard (serving time in jail at the time of writing) walked up to her, kissed her on the cheek and, taking her microphone, launched into an impromptu speech. The object of his rant appeared to be Sean 'Puffy' Combs, whom he thought should not have won Best Rap Performance. As he was politely escorted away, he shouted, 'Puffy is OK, but Wu-Tang is the best!' although he later apologised profusely for his disruption.

This occasion aside, 1998 started peacefully for Erykah, who was settling into the dual role of pop star (a status she had enjoyed for barely a year) and mother (an even more recent development). On 18 January, however, she travelled to Dallas to receive an important honour: the city had decided to name that date 'Erykah Badu Day' – a sure sign that the great and the good of the metropolis had noticed her success and wanted some it of it for the town that had equipped her for it. A presentation was made at the end of a concert held at the Morton H Meyerson Symphony Center, in which a 318-strong black choir sang gospel songs for the Black Academy of Arts & Letters' annual tribute to the Rev Martin Luther King Jr. The show finished with Erykah's acceptance of a large bunch of red roses, and commentators noticed that the orange chiffon stole and green headwrap she wore made her look almost regal. 'Peace and blessing!' she told the crowd. 'Peace and love. I really appreciate it.'

The *Dallas Morning News* interviewed her some weeks later, revealing that she had in fact decided to return to Dallas from New York to raise her child in the vicinity of her family. This was an obvious decision, in retrospect – after all, she had spent approximately a year and a half in the big city, and had launched her career successfully. Now that it was in motion, why not return home and continue from there? The newspaper reported that her house, into which she had only moved at the start of the year, was 'a spacious, comfortable but by no means palatial house in one of Dallas' older neighborhoods' with 'neighbors [who] are kindly folk, but they don't really know who she is, which gives her privacy'. Erykah welcomed the *DMN* writer into her home, explaining that the neighbours are 'mostly older white people… I wanted to give this one lady my CD, but she said, "Oh, honey, I don't even have a machine to play it on!"'

Badu and the reporter took a peek at the sleeping Seven, who was asleep in 'a handmade, pyramid-shaped cradle crafted with the Egyptian ankh motif', and the singer explained that, while she would put her career aside if necessary in order to devote her time to him, 'I think I can handle both', especially with the help of her mother, who travels with her. As for Dre, Erykah mused that, 'We just connected, like "There you are!" I kind of created him in my mind and he created me in his… We've been real good friends ever since. And we plan to be friends forever. I do see a long future with him.'

Shortly after this a journalist called Pam Easton at the Associated Press wrote an interesting feature in which a teacher at Booker T Washington High School recalled Erykah's prowess. Rosann Cox was her name, and she had been Badu's dance instructor: 'We knew that she had wonderful talent when she was here,' she remembered. 'She had started on rap verses before rap verses were big.' True enough on both counts, of course – Erykah had impressed teachers in two different clusters with her audition, remember, and, as for her rapping skills, years of practise had honed those before she was even in her mid-teens.

Cox continued: '[Erykah had] a spirit about her… [She] would have succeeded whether she had us or not. When you looked at Erykah there was a light behind her eyes and a real special aura about her. You knew destiny was going to do something wonderful for her.' Easton also tracked down a DJ called Lenny Love, who commented that Badu has created her own niche. He remarked, 'If you notice, she brings a different vibe to the industry... She brings a breath of fresh air. She loves to collaborate and she has a certain field that only she can fill.'

The comments made by the people in Erykah's orbit tell us much about her, of course (and the effect she has on people), but what is more interesting is the depth of interest that had been stirred up in her activities – enough for articles solely containing other people's observations to be written. People were keen, even, to read opinions of Erykah, if her own words could not be heard – Baduizm, it seemed, had taken a firm hold. This was taken to an extreme when Erykah and Dre were included in a list of the ten 'hottest celebrity couples' featured in *Ebony* magazine in February 1998, alongside couples such as NBA star Grant Hill and singer Tamia, actors Angela Bassett and Courtney B Vance, and actor Debbi Morgan and photographer Donn Thompson. The magazine gushed, 'Badu, 26, a native of Dallas, says she met Benjamin, 23, who lives in Atlanta, about a year and a half ago. She acknowledges that she made the first move, but it obviously was a mutual attraction. After exchanging telephone numbers, Badu says the two have talked every single day. And more.' For the benefit of the celebrity-hungry reader, the article went on: '[Badu] says there are no marriage plans at this time, that she and Benjamin (both fruit and vegetables-only vegetarians) simply plan to grow together, be friends and be happy.'

Amid all the harmless publicity, Erykah, Dre and Seven appeared to be growing happily and healthily together. Occasionally the topic of conversation was bleak, of course: interviewers were interested to hear Badu's take on the recent shock waves that had rocked the hip-hop community, with *Vibe* magazine asking her, 'What are your feelings about the murders of Biggie Smalls and Tupac Shakur?' The gravity of the subject obviously weighed Erykah down, as she replied 'in a quiet and weary voice', 'I'm just tired, you know? Maybe I expect too much, I don't know. I know the reality of the situation, and no one thing is going to change a whole nation, but I thought that was over. I know that negativity is always going to be around, but the government is killing us... I'm angry at the school system, because we should have more information. I'm angry with the churches. I'm angry that the people who have the power to give information don't tell us anything.' More specifically, she mused, 'I knew Biggie. He was cool to me. But sometimes, you speak things into existence. I know I do. I said I was going to get a record deal, and grow a seed, and continue to pursue positive images and make a change. Biggie said he was ready to die.'

Moving on to more general themes of responsibility, she observed: 'I feel sad for us and hip-hop. I'm a Pisces. I feel responsible for everybody and everything. Then again, I feel lost sometimes, because that's the way it's supposed to be, I guess... Yeah, we have to survive, but there's so much more we need to know and don't. And we think we're supposed to react because of our emotions.'

As for herself, she explained that 'Sometimes, if you're poor you're put in a situation I fortunately wasn't put into. We were poor, but I had the kind of surroundings that made a difference. Ghettos are the same all over the world. They might look a little different, but they've all got the same mentality. I looked around and I didn't want to be there. I didn't want to be on welfare. I'd rather be a derelict on the street than to answer to the government all the time. I'd never let anyone infiltrate my dreams. If I couldn't create, I wouldn't be in this business. Even if I didn't have a deal, I'd still be doing it.'

Brave words...but no more than we have come to expect from Erykah by this stage of the game. Moreover, she said them at a time when the critical backlash she had sensed might come had finally begun to reveal itself. No, the critics didn't stop liking her music – *Baduizm* and *Live* were still spinning at the top of most playlists. No, they hadn't got bored with her – Kedar Massenburg had gauged Erykah's exposure to a fine degree, and he knew exactly how much to give.

Erykah's career had, it must be said, been a remarkable ride to date. In the space of a few short months she had been elevated from New York supper-club singer to one of the world's biggest female artists, with a critical reputation unlike any other, thanks to the almost unearthly qualities of *Baduizm*. Both she and Kedar Massenburg had made some exquisitely gauged decisions, which had helped her along her way. For example, the timing of *Baduizm* and the recruitment of The Roots to help her record it were both examples of Badu and Massenburg's keen eye on the market; an album that would rock the music-buying public to its base was released at exactly the right time, having been put together by exactly the right people for the musical climate.

Another example is the marketing of Erykah's image. Her look, as we know, is entirely her own creation, with her Afrocentric style going back as far as her teenage years; and, as for her spiritual beliefs, they go back even further than that. But Kedar's genius lay in his refusal to try and tamper with the way Erykah looked. He allowed her to disseminate her image and her words in exactly the way she wished, and to an enormously successful response from a public sick of seeing plastic Day-Glo pop chicks come and go.

One of Massenburg's earliest activities on Erykah's behalf was his distribution of the 'On & On' promo tape. This was an inspired move, for one simple reason – it is not a song that grabs the listener immediately. It's a subtle, reedy song and takes a little patience to get into, with at least three or four listens necessary to appreciate it fully. In point of fact, 'Appletree' is much catchier and would have been a more logical choice of single, but the duo stuck to their instincts and went with the song that would become the album's flagship anthem. Massenburg knew that the song was no instant hit and made a point of sending out the demos to allow the press to listen to it a few times – another example of his famous 'set-up' in action.

However, no artist's career is flawless. Erykah was about to discover this to her cost. The critics who turned on her were not music critics. They were film reviewers, and they had just witnessed Badu's feature-film acting début. The movie she had made in late 1997 had been shown in American cinemas on 6 February, and the response had been almost universally negative. At last, it seemed that Erykah had made her first mistake. The name of this false move? *Blues Brothers 2000.*

8 Escaping The Blues

Movie pundits worldwide tend to react with a mixture of approval and despair when asked to give an opinion on the first *Blues Brothers* film, a John Landis-directed comedy from 1980. Combining a classic soul soundtrack with a knowingly gratuitous number of car chases and collisions, the film was excellent entertainment on many levels: the eponymous duo Jake and Elwood Blues, played by John Belushi and Dan Aykroyd, took on their 'mission from God' (the reunification of their old blues band in order to raise money to save an orphanage) with great charisma and wit. Add to this a surreally taut plot (none other than Carrie Fisher – *Star Wars'* Princess Leia – stalks the brothers with murderous intent throughout the movie) and cameo roles from stars such as Ray Charles, and it's little wonder that the result was a critical and commercial success.

Conversely, the huge success of the movie also made it slightly irritating, leading pub bores to recite lines from it and giving blues obsessives a platform for endless comment. Ultimately the film took on a life of its own, inspiring tribute bands, *Blues Brothers*-branded memorabilia and becoming a student-house staple. This is why movie commentators react with such a mixture of emotions when confronted with the *BB* phenomenon – and why Erykah Badu's announcement that she had taken a role in its sequel was not immediately welcomed in all quarters.

Nobody was particularly surprised by Erykah's move into acting, least of all those who knew her from her college days. After all, she had already starred in her own video clips and – although few remembered it – the trailer for *The Boulevard*, four years (and a lifetime, it seemed) before. But for the wider audience, who may not have been familiar with Badu's musical career, she was an unknown quantity.

The plot of *Blues Brothers 2000* was broadly similar to that of its predecessor. Set (as in life) 18 years after the first film, the movie begins with the release from prison of Elwood Blues and wastes no time in telling us that his brother, Jake Blues, is dead (actor Belushi had died in 1982 of a drugs overdose), that the orphanage is no more and that the only popular music available is mindless machine-made wallpaper far removed from the earthy sounds celebrated by the Brothers. With the changed world an alien place to the older Ellwood, he decides to reform the band once again and goes about re-recruiting the members plus a ten-year-old orphan, Buster, and an obvious Belushi substitute, Mighty Mack (played with quiet assurance by the formidable John Goodman). One or two 1990s touches are present in the form of the Russian Mafia and a group of neo-Nazi skinheads – both of whom have a serious bone to pick with the band – and the only way, it seems, that the Brothers can redeem themselves (the FBI are also after them, believing that the orphan has been kidnapped by the band) is to win a 'Battle of the Bands' competition at the Plantation Club, the Louisiana mansion of Voodoo Queen Mousette (Erykah). The band they must beat in the face-off is an intimidating group called the Louisiana Gator Boys, made up of Eric Clapton, Bo Diddley, Dr John, Steve Winwood, Wilson Pickett and other blues luminaries. Musical stars who appear along the way include James Brown and Aretha Franklin (who provides 'Respect', just as she did in the first movie).

So far, so obvious Blues Brothers. Unfortunately, reviews were mixed, at best, with many critics regarding the movie as a lame rehash of the stunning original. Perhaps writer Anthony Leong put it best when he wrote '*Blues Brothers 2000*, the follow-up to the 1980 musical-comedy *Blues Brothers*, is true to the spirit of the original movie...only without the inspiration, originality, spectacle, or humor.' The scale was also less impressive, he noted: '*BB2000* also lacks the epic scope of the original, to the point of appearing incomplete – sure, we get to see a one-hundred police car pile-up, but the flabby climax of *BB2000* pales in comparison to the journey that Jake and Elwood took eighteen years prior, which included one of the greatest car chases in movie history and ended with hundreds of National Guardsmen and law enforcement officers storming the office building where the money for the orphanage was delivered.'

Mediascreen also reached a thumbs-down verdict on the grounds that the director had lost his touch, observing that, 'Without a doubt, *Blues Brothers 2000* is one of the most ill-conceived sequels ever made. John Landis, who hasn't made a consistently funny movie since 1983's *Trading Places*, directs with his typically-leaden camera, and the results are often painful to watch: not just because Landis has lost his flair for comic timing and clever camera composition, but also because the air of desperation is so thick it chokes everyone involved in the production.'

Most reviews ranged from grudging disappointment to outright derision, but hardly any of them had anything to say about Erykah's performance, which had been a solid attempt at a somewhat stereotypical role. The high points of her act came when she cast spells on the Blues Brothers, commanding them to play reggae, when she turned Aykroyd and Goodman into zombies and when the Russian Mafia and the skinheads were magically turned into rats at her command. But the part wasn't particularly demanding, and she filled its requirements so easily that the reviewers felt little need to mention her presence at all.

An inauspicious acting début, then, and one that would have served little purpose other than to familiarise Erykah with the protocol of shooting a feature-length film and got her onto a few casting agents' lists. Luckily, she herself had not been in the direct line of fire of any of the critics, simply because she dispatched her role with consummate ease and didn't contribute to the reviewers' main objection – that the film was a mere rehash of the original.

So why was the film so poor? Perhaps the simplest reason for its dismal reception was the absence of Belushi, whose presence in the first movie had given it a certain dark swagger. Maybe the movie-going audience in 1998 was unlikely to appreciate a movie of this type with as much innocence as that of 1980. It's possible that the simple, good-time *Blues Brothers* recipe was good for one shot only. Not only this, but many observers predicted disaster for the sequel as soon as it was announced, which means that it was doomed from the outset. The movie remains a last-resort rental option, and its relevance here ends with the footnote that Badu would doubtless have learned to choose her acting roles more carefully in future.

Time was passing, however, and no sooner was the *Blues Brothers 2000* débâcle behind Erykah than she was booked to tour with the Lilith Fair package, a women-only festival organised by Canadian singer-songwriter Sarah McLachlan and scheduled to take in 57 dates and feature more than 150 artists. A direct opposite to the usual American festival bills (traditionally ruled by heavy rock and metal, with the Warped, Family Values and Ozzfest events all rolling at the time), the concept behind Lilith Fair, now in its second year, was simple: to present female artists in their own chosen context. On its launch many critics were openly snide about the idea of a women-only festival – comments that McLachlan turned aside with her simple claim that she 'wanted concert-goers to appreciate the artistry of this touring bill of female artists, and to leave questions of its social impact for the history books'. Its title, explained the singer, was a biblical reference to Lilith, the original companion to Adam in the Old Testament's Garden of Eden. Lilith was a powerful, threatening woman who was replaced by the more subservient Eve – and a potent figurehead for a tour of this nature.

The tour was an undoubted success, despite the brown-rice catcalls of the nay-sayers. One particular date – the show in Portland, Oregon, held on 19 June 1998 – featured as its five main acts Sarah McLachlan, Natalie Merchant, the Indigo Girls, Erykah Badu and Sinéad O'Connor. Reviewers noted the common themes behind each woman's music – spirituality, contemplation and inner harmony – and wisely pointed out that the way to assess a festival of this kind was to approach it as you would a Dixieland or bluegrass event; that is, to accept that the artists on the bill were performing one common style of music, which could be named 'feminine folk-pop', for example. This would deflect a major criticism of the event raised by several commentators – that the music on the bill (apart from Badu and the occasional hip-hop artist such as Missy Elliott) was largely homogeneous, with most of the acts producing melodic, acoustic pop and folk. The idea was to focus on social and personal challenges using images that are central to women's lives, avoiding the pomp and circumstance of rock, and eschewing instrumental technicality in favour of harmonic interplay. Yes, it does sound rather earnest – and yet it worked. Reviewers heaped praise on the event almost unequivocally.

Erykah's slot on the festival was short and to the point. Making the maximum visual impact with a stage set including the by-now-trademark candles, incense and 60cm (2ft) tall wooden ankh, plus a vibrant outfit of headwrap and stacked shoes, her set was a mixture of spiritual preaching and her mellow singing. As her appearance was confined to 45 minutes or so, she omitted the lengthier spoken-word sections that she had showcased on *Live*, favouring instead shorter invocations explaining the symbology of 'On & On' in more succinct terms than usual. The audiences loved her, and Lilith Fair has gone down in her personal history as one of the more successful vehicles for her unique message.

Lilith Fair coincided with the rise in prominence of a group of musicians who referred to themselves as the Soulquarians. Focused on the newly christened neo-soul talents of D'Angelo, producer Jay Dee, Mos Def, Ahmir '?uestlove' Thompson, Q-Tip, Bilal, Common and Erykah herself, they were based in Philadelphia (but in actuality almost constantly travelling across America) and most were, it seemed, Aquarians. They first came to the public's attention through interviews with new artist Bilal (whose demo had landed in Badu's hands at some point in the process of deal-hunting), and Erykah, who explained that it had come about through a chance meeting: 'One day we were all in a room together for a photo shoot... I'm the first lady because I'm the only woman in the crew. They call me Mama. The Soulquarians is about good music and bringing forth good energy through music – no matter what the subject matter. We love and appreciate music.' Bilal explained that the Philly connection was a big part of the Soulquarians' commonality: 'It's like a collective. A group of cats that know each other, are musicians and work together on each other's projects... You got a lotta people that play music and instruments moving to Philadelphia which is cool.' The musician would go on to tour with Erykah, explaining that she, 'brought everybody to her own world. She made music captivating again.'

Wise words: once again Erykah's music was in demand for soundtrack use, and in June 1998 her song 'Ye Yo' appeared in *Hav Plenty*, an independent movie exploring the trials of young love within America's black middle class. An indie success without making many major headlines, the film was symptomatic of the second wave of black film that had proliferated since the mid-1990s after the popularity of gangsta movies like *Boyz N The Hood* and *New Jack City* (both 1991) and harmless hood comedies like *Friday* (1995) had shown that white audiences would pay to see black films. And it was important for Badu, both politically and commercially, to be down with this new wave of films, no matter how financially insignificant they might seem. Like Quincy Jones, Ice Cube, Queen Latifah, Chris Rock and Snoop Dogg before her, Erykah was showing signs that she might well join the élite ranks of black performers who could be involved in music, film and business activities rather then sticking to one field – no matter that her one feature-length acting role to date had hardly set the movie world alight.

The American establishment was still worshipping at the altar of *Baduizm*, it emerged, as the summer of 1998 wore on; in June she received the NAACP Image Awards for Outstanding Female Recording Artist and Outstanding New Recording Artist to add to her existing two *Soul Train* Lady of Soul Awards. Add to this the fact that 'Apple Tree', released almost a year before, was still enjoying heavy radio rotation, and the Badu star was showing no sign of falling. She herself provided an insight into the reasons for her continuing success by explaining to the MTV Radio Network that, 'I like interacting with people... [Most] of the fans who come to my show, by the time it's over, have looked into my eyes and I've looked into theirs at least once. We just all relate, but it's not a superstar–fan relationship. It's more, yeah, I understand what you're saying, girl. Yeah, I've been through all that. It's a family thing, and I love it.'

In the following month Erykah was interviewed by *Ebony* magazine, who expanded on their previous 'hottest celebrity couples' theme by going to her home and speaking to her as she nursed the now nine-month-old Seven. 'I feel more responsible and more in order,' she said of how her life had changed since her son's arrival. 'At first I was really nervous because I've never been a mom before and I was worried... I've always been confident in my career and very confident in my talent because I knew where it came from. It's plentiful. But I was insecure about being a mom and sometimes about relationships and about people, period.' An interesting revelation – after all, Badu had always exuded near-total confidence, as anyone who has seen her perform or appear on TV will confirm. It seems that, like all of us, her almost superhuman surface hides a very human range of insecurities...and relationships are near the top of that list, as *Ebony* surmised when Erykah told them that 'Tyrone' – also a huge radio hit at the time – was specifically *not* directed at Andre Benjamin. She said, 'I love him dearly' and, when asked about marriage, 'We'll see about that. Right now we're still dating... We'll know when the time is right.'

Despite the arrival of Seven, Dre was still living in Atlanta – but Erykah insisted that the long-distance relationship had always been a good system throughout their 18-month partnership to date: 'It works for us,' she said. 'It works really good for us. That's how it has always been and we don't have anything to compare it to. Maybe that's what has made the relationship last this long because we don't have to be up in each other's face all the time. Distance brings enchantment to the view.' As for future education plans for Seven, Erykah said: 'He'll be well-traveled, but I think he may be home-schooled... I think his Dad wants him to be home-schooled and kept in a one-on-one atmosphere. We want to make sure that he has the healthiest diet and atmosphere to grow up in – but not sheltered. We want to give him the hard truths at the beginning of life so he won't have to be like me and his Daddy, unlearning a bunch of shit, a bunch of crap that messed us up as human beings.' It would be interesting to know exactly what she was referring to – but we can probably assume that the departure of Erykah's father Toosie at an early age may be among the 'bunch of crap' . The solution, according to Badu, seems to be to give Seven the 'straight truth', as she explained: 'That way he can go ahead and start being the beautiful person that he is. It takes us too long to be the beautiful person we are because we have so much junk to undo.'

It was at this point that Erykah made a promise that has become famous – that she would try to have six more babies. 'That's right, six more babies in five years,' she told the interviewer. 'Time passes so fast. I just follow and have faith. I know that I make the right decisions.' It appears that she was speaking in earnest – although no more babies have appeared in the interim.

She also spent some time discussing monetary issues, and was apparently keen to demonstrate that her intuition extends as far as taking care of business: 'I learned that in order to be a successful entertainer, you have to be a really good businesswoman,' she said. 'Because you can just be at home singing, but if you're in show business, your show has to be tight and your business has to be tight... I've got money stashed everywhere.' She had plenty of advice for young artists on the point of entering the music industry, too: 'You can't get so wrapped up in your business that you lose your creativity, or too wrapped up in the creativity that you don't pay attention to what's going on right in front of your eyes,' she emphasised. 'You have to keep up with the people who work for you and with you. I just want to say to other artists who are in situations where they think they have a boss or something like that: *they* are the boss. *They* are the talent. It takes a lot of people to put an artist's package together, but the artist is the focus and the center. Don't let anyone infiltrate your dreams.'

Although she had been surprised by the speed of her success ('I thought I would be really respected, but never like this. I didn't know it would happen so fast, but I knew it would eventually happen'), Erykah manages to stay afloat because, 'I just take me with me wherever I go. It's good to have real good people and energy around you to make sure that you stay grounded, and to make sure that they keep your ego up, and to stay confident and keep your creative juices flowing.' This individual approach extends as far as image ('I've always been an outcast as far as style. I never followed anybody else, but nobody ever followed me either because it was not their idea of style'), and even the headwrap ('I didn't create the headwrap or the style, I just manifest it').

Badu stated that a new album was in progress, and that she intended to re-enter the studio in August 1998: 'I've already started writing the album,' she added. 'The formula I used for the first album was as I got music I wrote, and as I felt lyrics I wrote them.' However, the music industry had taken a lot from her, and she felt the need to rest a little first. 'I love every aspect of this business,' she explained, 'but sometimes you get tired. The spirit never gets tired, but the body does. It bothers me when I don't have enough energy to give to every single thing. Right now I'm at the point where I need to go and put a battery in my back and recharge.' Fair enough – after all, she was at the hub of a whole network of people who depended on her. 'It sounds crazy and maybe a little selfish and spoiled, but it bothers me that so many people want so many things from me at this time... I'm trying to be Mommie, CEO, friend, lover, daughter. It's difficult, but it can be done. Just remember that you're writing this script and you need to write whatever your need – write yourself some time off.'

Like N'Dambi before her, Erykah's backing singer Yahzara launched a solo career at this time, releasing a solo album despite a flood of Badu comparisons from lazy interviewers. She explained that she had first met Erykah, 'through her music director, Eugene Young. He and I were in a group together a while ago. He called me one summer and told me that somebody had dropped out and she was looking for another background singer. I jumped on the first plane with the little bit of money that I had in my pocket and went to try out.' Asked how she handled the inevitable comparisons, she responded: 'I try to fight the whole thing tooth and nail. I have been hearing that before I even met or knew her. I mean, it was inspiring when I first heard her because we were on the same vibe. It was somebody else out there that wasn't afraid to be herself.' Although her career has to date failed to take off, Yahzara remains a talented artist doing what she does best, although the millstone of coming to fame on the back of Badu may be a difficult one for her to shake off.

As for Erykah, it seemed that the industry would never stop trying to give her awards. Just as she had garnered two *Soul Train* Lady of Soul Awards, the main *Soul Train* event (for Ladies or otherwise) was about to bestow her with wreaths. In August she attended the event, held at the Shrine Auditorium in Los Angeles, where she walked away with no fewer than four awards – for Best Female R&B/Soul Single ('On & On'), Best Female R&B/Soul Album, Best R&B/Soul or Rap Album (both *Baduizm*), and R&B/Soul or Rap New Artist. Other winnings went to

Dru Hill, Usher, Biggie Smalls, Puff Daddy (who scooped the Sammy Davis Jr Award For Entertainer of the Year) and Whitney Houston, who received the clumsily titled Quincy Jones Award for Outstanding Career Achievement in the Field of Entertainment. A stellar cast indeed, but one among which Erykah's own star shone brightly.

All this adulation was followed by a surprise announcement from Badu, but one which should been obvious given her comments about fatigue in *Ebony* the previous month. Her intention, she stated, was to take a break from the industry in order to spend time with her son. Few people disagreed with her decision: after all, in the space of a short year and a half she had released two albums, toured both solo and on the Lilith Fair package, borne a child and acted in a major film. All this, plus the constant grind of giving many hundreds of interviews and flying through most of the Western world's major cities, had left her almost completely drained, and still with a new baby to look after who knew only that he needed to be fed and changed. Time, it seemed, to seek the family bosom.

A couple of months of blissful silence from the Badu front ensued, but it soon emerged that she had not departed the music world entirely: OutKast's third album, *Aquemini*, appeared on 29 September 1998 and featured her vocal talents on the song 'Liberation', an extended jam which contrasted nicely with laid back songs like 'Rosa Parks' (named after the well-known activist – and the cause of a later lawsuit by Parks) and 'Synthesizer', which featured P-Funk godfather George Clinton. Although some fans found the guest spots pointless (Badu and Clinton complemented their songs rather than improving on them, it must be said) and the record over-long in parts, it was generally viewed as a success. In interviews, Dre made much of the inspiration he had gained from the birth of Seven: 'After Seven came,' he said, 'something just zapped me. It just came out of nowhere. I started getting all these ideas, all this inspiration on how the music should sound, how the music should feel. It was like somebody put a battery in me.' In fact, Seven himself appeared on *Aquemini*, contributing some baby noises against a backbeat: perhaps the youngest artist ever to appear on a major record, alongside Stevie Wonder's baby daughter Aisha on 'Isn't She Lovely'.

Erykah also appeared at this time on a superb record by Busta Rhymes called 'Just One'. Like OutKast before him and Nelly after him, Rhymes (whose real name is Trevor Smith) had come to prominence thanks to the slightly psychedelic edge to his raps, and this song was no exception, beginning with a nursery-rhyme-like promise from both singers that they going to 'have some fun'. Erykah's role on this record was to complement Busta's raw baritone with sweetly scatted accompaniments and to provide some layered backing vocals – tasks that she pulls off with ease. She even adds some snatches of 'Apple Tree'-like scat at the end. It's a great record, and one on which the two voices suit each other perfectly.

With a break from the business ahead of her, a healthy baby to nurture and two successful collaborations keeping Erykah's radio and TV profile high, the end of 1998 should have been some of the best months of her career...but an unexpected calamity lay around the corner. It was with genuine shock that Badu's fans and associates learned late in the year that she and Dre had broken off their relationship, suddenly and with little warning. Why would this happen, so soon after Erykah had given out all those glowing reports of their love for each other? She has never fully explained the reasons for this, and nor has Andre – and perhaps it's better that way. The closest Erykah has ever come to revealing the causes of the split was to *Interview* magazine more than two years later, when she said: 'Love...is a big part of our existence here on earth, the personal relationship we have with the person that we love, with the person that we make love to, with the person that we share our lives with. We expect a lot of things back from our loved one, and the lesson is to accept and not expect.' Vague words, perhaps, but they indicate that by this stage she had learned and grown from the pain of the experience of breaking from the man she had called 'my nigga for life' in the sleevenotes of *Baduizm*.

The split must have been traumatic, of course. Andre was the man Erykah had publicly thought would be around for a long time to come, and the father of her child. It's unlikely that Erykah will ever disclose what happened between them, but it seems certain that the love they thought they had was not destined to survive their growth into full adulthood. The lyrics of OutKast's later single, 'Ms Jackson', may hold an answer: Dre rapped, 'Me and your daughter, Got a special thang goin on, You say it's puppy love, We say it's full grown, Hope that we feel this, Feel this way forever', which is perhaps a sign that someone on Erykah's side (such as her mother Kolleen) had not accepted that the bond was an adult one, or an admission on Dre's part that maybe the pair might not be able to 'feel this way forever'. Whatever the circumstances, the breakup was a sad one, and inevitably both Erykah and Kolleen must have been reminded of Erykah's parents' separation all those years before. This might explain Erykah's later insistence that Dre would still be very much a part of Seven's life – with all the fatherly responsibilities that this entailed. Dre, too, was adamant that the child would grow up surrounded by love from his father.

And yet some good would come out of all this anguish. In late 1998 Erykah made a third guest appearance in as many months, and the song she created was a marvel. It would be hailed as a high point in her career, and one that would remind her that the public held her in high esteem, *Blues Brothers* or no *Blues Brothers*. And, to make this step, Badu was given the unexpected help of some old friends – The Roots. The result of the collaboration would be some of the sweetest music heard as the dying century came to a close...and the sound of Erykah's soul, so recently damaged, making its first steps towards recovery.

By now, the show is in full swing.

The white candle by Erykah's side has burned halfway down, and the light smoke that it creates has combined with the heady scents of incense and marijuana that are filling the air above the crowd and the stage. The words that Badu has used to explain the candle ritual – 'I light my candle on-stage... I create my calm where I am. I close my eyes, open them again, and I'm OK. It's what helps me create my peace of mind' – seem to make absolute sense now that she and her band are communicating their message.

But she's not done yet. The flame is still burning strongly, and the words that she needs us to hear are still unspoken.

Erykah opens her mouth to sing once again.

9 She Got Us

The song that Erykah Badu recorded with The Roots was four and a half minutes of classic, mellow hip-hop called 'You Got Me', and appeared in January 1999 to instant acclaim. A slow, heartbreaking lament featuring Erykah's understated tones on an unforgettable hook plus a background of soft strings, it appeared to be a fully formed chart smash on its appearance, but in fact it had endured its fair share of birthing pains, which were due to the slight tension between some of the performers involved in its creation.

First, the female raps on the song – which, complementing the high-speed efforts of Roots rapper Black Thought, are one of the song's definite highlights – were created by the well-known performer Eve, who recorded her vocals but did not appear in the video for the song. Erykah, however, *did* appear in the promo clip – and many viewers assumed that the raps, as well as the chorus melody, were the work of Badu. 'They say it was a miscommunication,' Eve fumed at the time, 'but it was politics and bull,' explaining that The Roots had apparently asked her to appear in the video but not told her where the shoot was taking place. 'At first I was mad,' said the rapper. 'Erykah can rap but give me some credit.' Despite the brief spat, it seems that any feud was rapidly resolved.

More lasting confusion was caused by The Roots' decision to record the original vocal with an up-and-coming new singer called Jill Scott (who would go on to play a prominent role in the establishment of neo-soul) but then re-record her part using Erykah. Roots drummer Ahmir Thompson saw Scott perform live and, excited by the possibilities of her excellent, expressive voice, invited her to do the vocal on 'You Got Me'.

Although her recording was flawless, Badu was still asked to redo it. Thompson later recalled, 'When Erykah heard Jill's version, she was like, why ya'll want me? That sister is bad. But we needed that record to perform a function, and it did.' Presumably the 'function' he was referring to was to get the record into the charts, due to Erykah's status being hotter than the less recognisable Jill Scott's.

Scott heard that the re-recording had happened, and (presumably unnerved by the possible disappearance of her big break) gave Thompson a phone call. 'I was calling Ahmir like, hel-lo? Are you using me or what?' she later explained. But the band repaid the debt by inviting her to support them on tour – no mean offer, especially as the song made them big names overnight and crowds flocked to see them. 'I gave them something, and they gave me something in return,' said Scott. 'They took me on tour, and I got to know what true work ethic for an artist means. Being able to experience that meant a lot to me.'

What Scott learned on that tour would have stood her in good stead for the rest of her career. Life on the road is an eye-opening experience for even the hardest-working musician, with the task of juggling the requirements of promoters, roadies, management, record label, musicians, sound and lighting personnel, transport and admin staff a near-impossible job. Add to this the pressure of being forced to deliver at high quality every night, plus the hours of press interviews that take place in the daytime, and it's clear how much there is to learn. And all this while being a new artist whose record may not sell much and for whom obscurity may well beckon sooner rather than later...

Thanks to her stint on 'You Got Me' and subsequent live shows, Jill Scott can be credited as the first female artist to emerge in Erykah Badu's wake who could seriously claim to have challenged her superiority at the top of the neo-soul tree, although her début album, *Who Is Jill Scott?*, would not appear until July 2000. Born in a poor area of north Philadelphia (she described it as 'a neighborhood of poor folk, some have given up, some haven't'), she spent her childhood and teenage years learning from her family and school the performing skills that would take her out of the city. The parallels with Erykah's early life are obvious – and in fact Scott, too, credits her mother as the primary influence on her world-view.

However, her break came through poetry and acting rather than music, which is how Ahmir Thompson discovered her. He invited her to The Roots' studio, where she composed the 'You Got Me' hook and lyrics – and once the (albeit re-recorded) song had been released and been awarded a Grammy, her path seemed clear. Securing a record deal with Sony later in 1999, she recorded and released the acclaimed *Who Is Jill Scott?* album, which soul fans old and new – including Erykah Badu – loved. Erykah herself said to *Soul Express*, 'Jill Scott? That's my girl. I went to her show. I was on the front row. Cried with everybody else, you know. Beautiful voice, beautiful singer. From Philadelphia, a lot of Philadelphia sound, Philadelphia style.'

As Erykah had been plagued with Billie Holiday comparisons, so Scott was compared endlessly with Erykah. Asked by *B&N* how she felt about this, Jill replied rationally: 'In the beginning, I was upset because I felt those were just lazy ears and that they hadn't listened to me at all. They just heard something that sounded similar and figured that we were the same. Automatically, as a black artist, you are clumped together without even getting the chance to show yourself.' Furthermore, she was likened to the veteran performer Betty Carter, but this troubled her less: 'The difference there is that Betty Carter was doing her thing for umpteen years. Erykah Badu has one album. Say you had two young composers and people said one sounded just like the other. I don't think that would be a compliment. But if they said one of the composers sounded like Mozart – Mozart's music has lasted for centuries.'

Meanwhile, the true story of the 'You Got Me' politics was explained by Jill as follows: 'The Roots and I are both from Philadelphia. They saw me at a poetry reading and asked if I would write something,' she explained, taking care to make the stages of the process as clear as possible. 'So I met with the guys and played them the melody to "You Got Me". I had been thinking about how it is when you're in a relationship and your partner is far away doing his thing. For a woman it's one thing, but a man is going to have his worries, too. I just wanted to dispel those fears.' Unsurprisingly, it seems that industry machinations lay at the heart of the re-recording issue: 'The Roots' record label didn't know who Jill Scott was. It was like, who is Jill Scott? And I've heard that so many times throughout the course of my life as a poet, as a singer, as a student, and as a woman.'

It seems that both Badu and Scott were winners – Erykah took the credit for the performance without making much effort other than visiting a studio, while Jill was recognised as a strong new talent and got on a major tour as a result. In any case, the mutual nature of the recording was part and parcel of the neo-soul approach, as Badu explained to MTV as 'You Got Me' straddled the charts and radio: 'In the underground circuit,' she explained, 'what we do as hip-hop artists is that we keep each other going by supporting the DJs. Because the DJs spin the records, and The Roots were one of the best underground hip-hop acts to mix DJs with live music.'

When the Grammys came round in February 1999, Erykah was pleasantly surprised to find herself nominated for two awards – Best Female R&B Vocal Performance for 'Tyrone' and Best R&B Album for *Live*...and all without being a genuine R&B artist, as the term had come to be defined. R&B, as late 1990s culture had it, focused on Destiny's Child-like choreography and vocals with over-heavy vibrato, or slick Boyz II Men-style vocal histrionics. Erykah's plentiful soul, jazz and hip-hop influences were clearly not abundant enough for the Grammys board to notice. In any case, as neo-soul flourished and the boundaries of music began to blur as the millennium approached, magazines such as *Vibe* were starting to use the aforementioned term 'urban music', an advisedly non-partisan term that encompassed more or less anything that was black and contemporary.

Disposable Heroes Of Hiphoprisy frontman Michael Franti was interviewed at this time and had some well-thought-out points to make about R&B and Erykah's role in it: 'I love Erykah Badu,' he said. 'She's great, because I really think she puts a consciousness in her music which has been missing for a very long time – especially from R&B.' He explained that 'R&B has just become like these empty love songs, and songs about sex and whatever – which is fine, because there's a place for that – but she also puts in what I consider to be soul music, which is asking questions of the soul in the same way that Marvin Gaye or Sly Stone or Stevie Wonder has done in the past. She's great.'

And yet Badu continues to confound categorisation. Even bling-bling culture – trashy, superficial adulation of accessories, largely among young black women with an income – took her to heart in early 1999 when the Brooklyn-based Miksu Cosmetics company launched a range of music-inspired products (eye-shadow, lipstick, blusher and nail varnish) with street-savvy titles such as Busta Wine, Jiggy, Hype Platinum and Badu Blue. The last of these was allegedly chosen by Erykah herself, signalling perhaps that she will find her own way however she wishes, and however people wish to categorise her.

In stark contrast to this razor-sharp endorsement of urban chic came Badu's involvement in the world of reggae, and specifically her slot at the Seventh Annual Bob Marley Caribbean Festival, which took place on 13 February 1999 at Miami Bicentennial Park. The drive behind the show was fund-raising for an organisation called the Food for Life Network, with tickets costing $25 (£15) plus four cans of food. Badu's support slot took place before the headliners, Stephen and Ziggy Marley, who also enjoyed a guest appearance from Jimmy Cliff and the Ghetto Youth Crew. The concert tied in with a tribute album to Marley called *Chant Down Babylon*, for which she recorded a cover version of 'No More Trouble' – her voice lends itself to the mellow preaching style of the song, which is a highlight of the record.

Erykah told MTV Radio that she hadn't known how to react when she was initially approached for the project, largely it seems because she was stepping into unknown territory. 'You just kind of wait and see what happens,' she said. 'I was very happy with [Stephen Marley's] production, and the background singers, which were [Bob Marley's] original ones [The I-Threes], and my vocals. I was happy with it, 'cause it was real. All the notes ain't right, but the spirit was.' And she was in illustrious company, for the record also included Marley covers by Lauryn Hill, Queen Latifah, Toots Hibbert and the Wailers, Jimmy Cliff, Chrissie Hynde and the Marley family, as well as a massed rendition by all the artists of 'One Love'.

The Marley connection was the perfect way forward for Erykah Badu in many respects. As she'd been endlessly described as 'Afrocentric' and 'Nefertitian', her gravitation towards the Caribbean music scene came as no surprise, especially when she began talking in interviews about her great love for reggae and her wider appreciation of Rastafarian culture, even using terms like 'Jah-love' to describe the vibe she felt at concerts. She told the Jamaican magazine *Rootz & Kulcha* that she had felt a connection with Bob Marley since her childhood and that she found reggae the only music that had 'spiritual vibes and words that can be used as healing medicine as well as entertainment'. The interviewer asked her a key question at one point regarding her identity in terms of reggae: 'You may not call yourself a Rasta, but what do you think about the Rastafari culture and way of life?' She responded, 'Oh, that's my favorite question. Rastafari knows who God is and who he or she is, so he or she has no worries. Rasta is the people and represents the people.'

Erykah clearly knew her stuff, adding that the Rasta's vow to the Creator not to put a razor to the body is a necessary show of willpower on their part, and that, 'The principle of Rastafari is to live a clean life, knowing that love is the antidote.' She talked a little about her upbringing, remarking that growing up in what she called 'the dirty South', such principles were not part of her background but that she shares these same principles internally. Other points that she made included the observation that the music industry is biased against women (but that 'I've never had a problem and sometimes it's easier [being a woman]'); that there is a lot of negative energy in the music business, but she hasn't encountered anything that she can't handle and that, although she doesn't really have a plan of her own, she sees herself as just a part of the Creator's plan and that his divine work cannot be stopped, so she doesn't have a problem working in the music industry. Furthermore, she identified Stephen Marley as her favourite reggae singer, stating that he has an 'impeccable spirit' and that, along with his 'effortless passion', there is just something about him that grabs her. She reportedly added that she and Marley had recorded a song together at the Island House Studio on Hope Road in Kingston, Jamaica, which would appear on her next album.

The 'break' that Erykah had promised herself back in August 1998 wasn't turning out to be a particularly relaxed one, after all, as music-related incidents and events just kept on coming up. For example, the ongoing categorisation of her music moved to another level when the music channel VH1 voted her into its 100 Greatest Women of Rock 'n' Roll list: surreally, Badu charted at Number 100, indicating that whoever selected her might not have been wholly convinced of her 'rock 'n' roll' status. The conversation among the selectors must have been worth hearing; after all, here was a soul singer who used the occasional rock guitar, but indulged in a lot of jazz scatting and some hip-hop rhymes. The decision must have been a tough one.

The industry continued to celebrate Erykah (the 1999 *Soul Train* Awards threw a nomination her way for Best R&B/Soul Album of the Year for *Live*) but she had other plans afoot, including an appearance on a Marvin Gaye tribute album called *Marvin Is 60*, released in June 1999. Her contribution was her by-now-slightly-dated D'Angelo collaboration of 'Your Precious Love', and was the most well-known cover on the record. The other 11 tracks were taken by worthy (but lesser-known) artists such as Brian McKnight, Montell Jordan and Kenny Lattimore. Her dedication to the cause of classic soul was appreciated at high levels, it seems, with the singing legend Roberta Flack remarking at around this time that, 'I love the fact that [Badu's] voice is unique...a very wonderful way to express herself without doing what someone else has done.'

Her work didn't stop at national level, though. Dallas was calling for her attentions again, and in June she performed twice in the city as part of the Freedman Memorial celebrations, a city-wide festival that commemorates the dedication of the eponymous memorial, a symbol marking where freed slaves settled around Dallas after the American Civil War. Her commitment was to sing at the opening ceremony on 19 June and then provide a free full-length concert at the Martin Luther King Amphitheater in South Dallas – no mean offer from an artist with so many projects to honour.

The strength of Erykah Badu's fanbase in her home town has been one of the most gratifying aspects of her rise to fame: international artists often lose sight of their roots, or cover them up in an attempt to seem more genuine or true to their scene. This has never been Erykah's way: the higher she has risen, the more she has extolled the simple virtues of family union and the recognition that where you come from is irrevocably part of what you are. Add to this the fact that, in hip-hop circles, the grittier an artist's background is, the more authentic his or her image becomes, and Erykah might easily have portrayed her upbringing as a scene from ghetto hell. In fact, she was supported by family and attended a prestigious school (albeit without much money available to do so) – and she has never pretended differently. Perhaps it's for this very reason that Dallas still loves her.

The theme of home-town pride continued with her next project, another Roots collaboration, which led to a hit single nationwide in late July. Roots rapper Rahzel the Godfather of Noyze was recording for a solo album, *Make The Music 2000*, as far back as winter 1998 and had asked her to travel to Electric Lady Studios in New York to help out: 'Raz got on the mic and started the music,' Badu wrote in the single's sleevenotes. 'I just said the first thing that came out my lips. And before you know it, the concept for "Southern Gul" was born.' One of the most confessional pieces that Erykah has ever produced, 'Southern Gul' (note the authentic Texan pronunciation) focused on her 'Dallas-grown childhood' as she put it, and featured her own cover art on the sleeve – her smiling mouth decorated with four gold teeth bearing the letters B, A, D and U. Credited to both artists (more precisely, as 'Erykah Badu featuring Rahzel') the song was scheduled to appear on albums by both performers, although ultimately it was not included on Erykah's still-unrecorded second studio record.

Fans of both singers loved the song, with its infectious chorus of 'Big D, little A, double L, A-S'. 'We freestyled the whole thing,' Badu told the *Dallas Morning News*. 'He just started beat-boxing, and I just started making stuff up on the spot.' The concept, she told the paper, was to scat and sing about anything Southern that came into her mind (fried tofu was one Southern icon, dominoes were another), leading to a flavour that Rahzel evoked in the sleevenotes with the words, 'This track contains no instruments, no samples, nothing but pure vocals with that dirty South flow provided by Erykah Badu'. Funnily enough, the single had started life merely as a between-song fragment like those so often found on hip-hop albums: 'It was originally just supposed to be an interlude on Rahzel's album,' she told Thor Christensen, 'but...it got on the radio and people were saying, here's Erykah Badu's new single. We don't know how it got out to radio, but everybody was liking it, so we just took advantage of it. We all agreed that we could put it on my next album, too.'

Christensen reflected on Erykah's pride in her roots and how it had come across in interview: 'She talked a little bit about how being from the South and from Dallas has informed her and her sense of style. She's definitely proud of being from the South – she said that the laid-back pace of Dallas is very conducive to her way of performing and writing her style of music. Obviously if she grew up in LA or Chicago or New York, where things move a little bit faster…being here where things are a bit slower has been an important part of her style.' Erykah herself talked about the song in almost abstract terms with *Soul Express*: 'The song "Southern Gul" pretty much describes the background. It says I'm from the South, I'm a Southern girl, home of the burning church, don't know much about the world, home of the pocket stones. Pocket stones is crack cocaine, like in my neighbourhood, that's what they sell, crack, you know. Home of the booty songs. Home of the finger waves that last all night long. It's like a hair-do, where you like conk your hair. Home of the dominoes. It's a game that everybody plays all night. Home of the gold teeth, you know, that's the South, it's like our jewellery.'

Erykah's relationship with her home town and the South in general has always been a double-sided one. She has talked at length about the reduced pressure of life there in comparison to the more frenzied pace of events in Los Angeles or New York, but rarely about the flip side of that fact – which is that, in more conservative areas, change happens slowly (if at all) and people are less willing to accept new ideas. However, as she came from a major city with a thriving musical and otherwise cultural scene, she may not have encountered too much of this. In addition, the lack of an established hip-hop underground in Dallas, as Thor Christensen has also pointed out, may have made it harder for her to find acceptance there, but it also meant that when Erykah Free finally took off, they had a ready-made audience waiting for them in the absence of many other hip-hop acts.

Ultimately, Erykah's love for the South is clear. In the late 1990s the rise of Southern hip-hop (OutKast were another prominent act) was an interesting feature of the spread of the music, which before then had been largely the province of the big coastal cities. In any music scene, it is the more outspoken acts that make the initial headlines: when the second wave of subtler, more introspective artists arrives, they often come from unexpected locations. This was the case with Erykah Badu in particular and hip-hop in general.

After all this talk of a new album, it seemed that Erykah was finally beginning to make concrete plans for recording sessions. However, she appeared reluctant to set firm dates, or even to hint to the press about when any such new album might appear. This is understandable, really. She herself would have been feeling some pressure to deliver her next product, whether from her own creative urge or because her industry allies such as Kedar Massenburg and his team were asking for it. But the question that must have been dogging everyone involved must have been, how on earth could anyone follow up *Baduizm*? After all, an artist's second album is always a difficult one (as they have usually had years to perfect their début, but a follow-up is required at much shorter notice), let alone one that is scheduled to follow a massive hit. Badu was in a strange position as 1999 rolled on: her career had described a roller-coaster ascent of such rapidity in the previous two years that she had never had the luxury of building her profile slowly higher and higher, and now anything short of a massive success would seem like a failure in everyone's eyes. No wonder she was reluctant to commit to a delivery or even a recording date.

Add to this the fact that Erykah's music is no mere machine-generated slush, but organic, crafted soul, and that the songwriting process must necessarily come from the heart and the instincts, and it becomes more and more paramount that the pressure is off. As Badu told *Soul Express*, she is barely in control of the visceral songwriting process: 'There are like 20 million songs within this bed of music, and I have to find the one that fits my voice, a song that fits my voice and the music. You have to have music first most of the time. If not, then it's poetry, you know. So usually I do the music first, or I work with a group of people that create the music and then the words come. They just kind of live there somewhere and I find the melody and the words.' Did her mood – good or bad – influence the process, she was asked? 'It don't matter, but the bad is the best,' she answered. 'The bad is the best time to do anything creative, because you know, it's like rehabilitation. You are motivated. It's like film – best developed in the dark.'

Erykah's songwriting identity was worth holding onto, as well. As PolyGram's Senior Creative Director Nadine Baker put it at the time, 'For the past couple of years urban music has been dominated by producers – the sound of the producer is sometimes more recognizable than the artist. I think one of the great things about Erykah is that she had a successful album without any big-name producers.' Not that the producers would vanish, she added: 'The Puffys and Babyfaces and Jermaine Dupris will still be strong, but I think radio is opening up a bit to include things that are different. That whole "new retro soul" or whatever scene – Maxwell, Erykah, D'Angelo – those acts have strong performance skills and they're more well-rounded, so they're not totally dependent on airplay. So if there's resistance at first because their sound is a bit different, they have the performance skills and the presence to build an audience and eventually force their way onto radio and video.'

Despite the birth pains of the new record, Erykah told Thor Christensen in August 1999 that much progress had been made – in fact, that the album was near completion. 'It's about finished...but I don't know when it'll come out,' she said. 'I'm still making some major decisions as to which songs to use. I have to step my game up, because what I put out last time, you know, other people do that now. So I have to come up with something totally different, as far as rhythmic patterns and melodies and lyrics.' She added that the recording was taking place at her Dallas home studio, 'and that's another reason it takes a little longer, because my son is here,' she said. 'He's not two yet, and most of my creative energy goes to him.' Apparently Seven was 'thinking about' whether to contribute vocals to the album.

23 July 1999 saw the Woodstock '99 event come and go, a huge musical gathering that should by rights have gone down as a memorial to peace, love and global understanding. In the end it became notorious as a virtual disaster, an orgy of destruction and violence that even went as far as the alleged rape of some of the female festival-goers. The Prozac-generation kids weren't ready to pass on the pacific messages of their

forefathers, it seemed, despite the fact that some of the music on offer was decidedly laid back. One such act was The Roots, whose set featured a guest slot from Erykah and was recognised as one of the few high points of a near-total disaster.

Just four days after Woodstock '99 came the release of *On How Life Is*, a much-anticipated album from the new artist Macy Gray, who had been riding high in the charts for several weeks with her excellent, soulful single 'I Try'. Like Badu, Macy had grown up (in her case, in Canton, Ohio) on a steady diet of vintage soul and brand new hip-hop, and had incorporated both influences into her music to bring her alongside Erykah and Jill Scott in the triumvirate of new female neo-soul artists.

Gray's voice (a husky, blues-laden growl) and her sympathetic, soulful arrangements (she was a classically trained pianist) made her sound different enough from the mainstream for critics to flock to her side, and amid all the deserved adulation the reviewers didn't miss out on asking Erykah what she thought of Gray. *HipOnline* told Badu, 'You've been out of the public eye for a couple of years now, and since then you've got people like Macy Gray in your step,' and wondered what her take on the matter was. She replied, as calmly as ever, 'You know, any artist who feels the way I do, I get on their record, too. Let's make it happen. Nothing to prove. I'm only in competition with my last level. It don't have nothing to do with music or anything. And the last level is hard competition, the last place you were.' Warming to her theme, she explained: 'There'll never be another *Baduizm*, another Erykah Badu, another Macy Gray. We were all born, and we all came to the music business with everything we had. Some of us just don't get a chance.'

As for the broader picture of where the neo-soul artists were in relation to the rest of the industry, she mused: 'Now there's a lot of other people like myself, indeed, who are getting heard worldwide. That gives other artists a chance. So we basically represent the artists who are still often unheard. It's a good thing. We're all friends, inside the music and outside the music.' And the common themes that united Erykah and artists like Macy Gray? 'I mean, we don't sound anything alike, we don't approach our music anything alike, but we come from the same genuine place. We want our music to be real and we don't want to compromise our art. Whether we talking about something serious or talking about partying, we don't want to compromise the music at all.'

In fact, the similarities between Gray and Badu are not immediately striking. *On How Life Is* revelled in a far more expansive production than anything the more economical Badu had produced to date (remember that one of the most striking aspects of *Baduizm* at times was its sparse instrumentation) and the 'big singles' from each album – 'On & On' and 'I Try' – were almost radically opposed. Erykah's song was subtle, delicate and used abstract imagery; Macy's was a lavish, anthemic ballad oozing strings and percussion and communicating a simple message of heartbreak. Both were excellent songs, but they had little in common other than that fact. The work of Jill Scott actually has far more in common with Erykah's material but, by the time *Who Is Jill Scott?* appeared, the wheel of fashion had turned once again and neo-soul was no longer a new concept.

Badu and Gray are both strong, autonomy-loving artists whose music may bear the stamp of session musicians but whose own talent drives the work independently. However, where Erykah has always preferred a simpler, straight-ahead jazz or soul vibe, Gray displayed an evident love for Phil Spector-like walls of sound, with a certain over-the-top anthemic approach ('I Try' is a notable example) making her work often unforgettable. The slow-building, flag-waving epic template is not something that Erykah often pursues, however, preferring to nail down a simple groove and lace it with a persistent melody. In this sense, there are few similarities between them.

On the other hand, both women explore spiritual and relationship-based themes in their work and use vintage sounds to express themselves. Both women are lovers of the heartfelt honesty of classic soul, the purity of jazz and the throwaway melodies of pop, and incorporate all these into their work. The similarities are there – but it's more likely that Erykah and Macy were lumped together into the neo-soul category simply because critics didn't know what else to do with them. Generously, while neither woman fully accepted the validity of the neo-soul tag, both acknowledged that the job of categorising their music was something reviewers must inevitably attempt to do for the sake of clarity, but which would be ultimately fruitless because neither artist made any attempt to stay within the boundaries of any one genre. It would be interesting to ask either artist to classify their own music (as their self-perception would be invaluable when trying to understand their music), although the question itself would probably be shunned by both women. After all, no one really likes to be confined within a label – least of all performing artists.

However, the neo-soul tag has remained current and has passed into common usage. Part of this can be attributed to Kedar Massenburg, who first coined the label 'neo-classic soul' to describe the silky tones of his charge D'Angelo. However, the term might have been too grandiose for the record-buying public, whose concept of 'classic' soul might not have tallied with that of the industry. 'Neo-soul' was snappier and just as evocative, with the idea that 'new soul' would be a revisiting of the classic sounds in any case.

It's understandable that Erykah and her contemporaries might not have warmed to the label. After all, we have spent much time examining the hip-hop, jazz, rock and pop elements in her music, and we have seen that soul is just a part of the Badu recipe. In an ideal world, Erykah might be best tagged with the term 'R&B', but in the last decade or so the label has become increasingly synonymous with overproduced acts with little but blandness to offer, so it's perhaps better avoided. Of course, in its classic senses – pre-Motown/Stax black music of the 1950s, or British guitar-based blues – the term would be more relevant, but these definitions of the genre have fallen by the wayside and are not commonly known.

Personally, I like the term 'neo-soul' a lot. It's simple, and it says exactly what the artist's standpoint is. He or she may not be a pure soul artist – Erykah Badu certainly isn't – but to me and those who listen to the music, soul isn't just black voices and Motown horns. It's a state of mind, based on acceptance, political activism, self-worth and the celebration of the important things in life. It's not about smooth tones or saccharine love ballads...and I think Erykah would agree with me.

As Macy rose to the top of the public's awareness and Badu was asked time and again to discuss her apparent 'competition', there were other things on her mind. A new film opportunity had arisen, and she had accepted the offer. With the memory of *Blues Brothers 2000* still fresh, she must have pondered long and hard about whether or not to make a second step into the movie world (especially as Seven was still a babe in arms), but there was something about this project that sounded much more attractive than any simple musical comedy.

This time, there would be no false moves. The film that Erykah had chosen to work on in late 1999 was called *The Cider House Rules* – and this time her judgment was impeccable, for the movie would be a life-changing experience for actor and viewer alike.

10 Sweet Rose

Unaware that the film she was about to participate in would be a critical and commercial success, Erykah explained later that, when her agent handed her a copy of the script for *The Cider House Rules*, she was 'more interested in Seven's education at the time' and that she tried out for the part without much initial enthusiasm. 'I have an agent who saw my videos and thought that I'd be good in movies. She's often sent scripts, and I told her the kinds of roles that I liked. I like period pieces. And she's like, I got a good one for you, and she described it and I went and auditioned for it, not thinking if I was going to do it, whether I got the part or not.'

What swayed the decision for her was one simple fact: neither the director (the renowned Swede Lasse Hallström) nor the crew knew who she was from her music. 'But once I got the role, and I learned that the director didn't know who Erykah Badu was, I felt an ego boost – oh wow, I can act!' she recalled. The situation was the reverse of that in which she had found herself over the last couple of years; no one had any expectations from her, other than that she should measure up to the task ahead of her, and that, in itself, was hugely liberating for her. 'It was wonderful,' she remembered. 'I was new again. I never thought I had an opportunity to walk in and not have people expecting things. I walked in and they didn't know what was gonna happen... Walking on the set, they're like, who is that? We don't keep up with that music. Who is she? She better be good.'

With a second movie part ready to roll, it seemed that her status as performer on many levels was more concrete than before, but she saw little difference between acting and singing, in terms of art: 'I been doing it all my life... [Anything] that had to do with art I been doing all my life,' she explained. 'It was a gift. It's nothing I work real hard at doing. What I work hard at doing is staying on a path of being kind and showing and proving that I'm a good person to society. That's hard. The talent, that's a gift. I just came here like that.'

Filming in Maine, Vermont and Massachusetts took up much of late summer and autumn 1999, with the film more or less split into two parts: an earlier section where the story plays itself out in an old country mansion, and a second half following the film's major character when he travels to an apple orchard to work. Erykah's role was confined to the second section.

The plot is set in the 1940s and runs as follows. The main character, Homer Wells (played by Tobey Maguire), is a young man who has grown up in an institution called St Cloud's, an orphanage in the Maine countryside overseen by the sympathetic Dr Wilbur Larch (Michael Caine). Wells has been trained by Larch as a doctor and assists him both with St Cloud's' official function (to care for unwanted children and deliver babies) and its unofficial but well-known role (performing illegal abortions). Due to moral qualms, Wells refuses to participate in the latter task, despite the reasoning of Larch that such services keep women safe from the backyard abortionists who would otherwise injure them, sometimes fatally.

As Wells approaches manhood, a pivotal point comes when a World War II pilot Wally Worthington (Paul Rudd) and his pregnant girlfriend Candy (Charlize Theron), come to St Cloud's for an abortion. After the procedure Wells impulsively decides to leave with them and see the world beyond the orphanage, although he only makes it as far as the apple orchard and cider brewery owned by Wally's mother. Worthington leaves for the war and in his absence Wells embarks on a love affair with Candy. He also gets to know a group of black fruit pickers who come and go from the orchard as the seasons dictate. Their leader is the cider house foreman Mr Rose (Delroy Lindo), and among them is his daughter Rose Rose (Erykah), a young woman whom Wells discovers – to his horror – has become pregnant by her father. Another member of the fruit pickers is Peaches, played by rapper Heavy D. The rules of the movie's title are those that govern behaviour in the cider house where Wells and the fruit pickers sleep.

The situation is complicated by the news that Wally is about to return from the war a paraplegic and that Wells' love affair with Candy must end. Rose threatens to terminate her pregnancy herself, but Wells – his principles overcome – is able to perform a safe abortion, after which she flees. The end of the film comes when Mr Rose staggers into the orchard and dies (it transpires that his daughter has stabbed him in revenge for what he has done to her). The cripple Wally returns, and Wells leaves the farm and goes back to the orphanage. Larch has died and Wells takes over as the orphanage manager.

It's a moving and sometimes shocking film, and audiences loved it on its release in December 1999. Erykah's co-stars were a prestigious group and, together with the presence of Hallström and scriptwriter John Irving (who had adapted the screenplay from his own 1985 novel), the production was among the most eagerly expected of the year. Irving's involvement with the movie gave it a certain kudos among literati, many of whom had found previous adaptations of his work (including *The World According To Garp* and *The Hotel New Hampshire*) less than universally convincing. Some critics had expected the *Cider House* movie to be too grandiose to work successfully (the original novel was a massive tome with a near-epic scale) and were pleasantly surprised when it turned out to be a well-paced, expertly edited *tour de force*.

Part of the success of the movie was undoubtedly down to Lasse Hallström. Already an acclaimed director (his recent successes had included the quirky-but-charming *What's Eating Gilbert Grape* and *My Life As A Dog*), his eye for detail and a certain flair for panoramas (the Vermont countryside in particular is rendered spectacularly) make the movie eminently watchable. However, he explained that he was not the original choice of director for this long-running project: 'Phillip Borsos was the director who was supposed to do it first,' he said. 'He got sick and couldn't work, and when he realised that, he put me highest on the list.' Borsos had in fact died in 1995, and it was his – and Irving's – desire to have him on the project that had landed the Swede the job: 'John Irving had wanted me, too. I had actually read a very early draft then, which I liked a lot but had problems with. I had a hard time imagining myself traveling all the way to Vermont to tell the writer what I didn't like about his script. I just didn't have the guts.' However, the necessary changes were made, and director and author achieved a good working relationship.

Although Erykah Badu was unknown to Hallström, the director had started his career – bizarrely enough – with a musical act, directing the cult film *ABBA: The Movie* in 1977. 'They had seen my first feature,' he told *The Onion*, 'and as a television producer I had made videos with Benny Andersson, one of the members of the group. He was in a band called Hep Stars. So they hired me to make their videos... [They] were big, but in Sweden they were looked down upon. It was like working for the devil, because they were commercial and had sold out.' As for *The Cider House Rules*, the director explained that some of the difficulties associated with the project had been the sheer size of the original book ('This novel, which is 700 pages long, can't be translated, so [the film] is sort of different from the novel. I shy away from comparing them') and the fact that it is almost made up of two separate movies, the orphanage and orchard sections ('I had a problem reading the script. I got out of the orphanage and to the orchard, but I wanted to go back to the orphanage! But the range the story has is part of the attraction. I wanted to capture those two different emotional worlds').

Hallström's aim, he revealed, had been to keep the emotional aspect of the film from detracting from its realism: 'I didn't want the doctor to dominate the film. He's just a sad story. I wanted to focus on Homer; their relationship is the important story... My goal was to keep it as real as possible. I was watching a sitcom last night, and it was just so broad, not real at all. I really wanted to do the opposite of that. Dealing with so much sentiment, I didn't want to push it too hard. I wanted to keep a balance.' Asked by *Indiewire* what had drawn him to the film (which the interviewer described, mostly accurately, as a 'good old-fashioned, heartwarming epic', he responded, 'It was a movie that I actually turned down eight, nine years ago. I liked the script, but I had reservations. I was fearing collaboration with the writer, John Irving. So I turned it down, and it came back to me two years ago.'

The first script, he revealed, was 'choppy and condensed in a way that didn't have any of the epic scope. I don't think it even had the love story', but that the revised version had contained a scene that attracted him to it once again. 'I think it was just one scene,' he said, 'when the car drives to the orphanage and [the orphan] Curly walks up to this woman and says, "I'm the best one". You get to that moment and feel that there's a movie... It's basically those scenes with Curly that intrigued me. That dialogue hooked me onto that story. I always need a couple of highlights to really spark the passion for a project. I've read so many scripts that focus on story, almost sacrificing character for plot. And this one was an exception. It sort of meandered around the characters. And it had the tone, the particular John Irving tone, mixing the bizarre and the comedic and dramatic.' Hallström likened this particular recipe to *What's Eating Gilbert Grape* and *My Life As A Dog*, both of which had also focused on these three elements and which, together with *Cider House*, made up 'this group of pictures that I'm proud of'.

The Cider House Rules was an almost unqualified success because it evoked a whole range of emotions in the public and the critics. Some dismissed it as a tear-jerker, as if 'tear-jerking' was a shallow or spurious activity, but what these people failed to realise was that the movie had done so without resorting to over-sentimentality. Maguire's blank, almost expressionless exterior is a metaphor for the simple tale-telling of the film – the narrative is straightforward and linear, and neither Irving nor Hallström resorts at any point to manipulating the audience with sudden shocks or unexpected revelations. Yes, Rose's pregnancy by her father comes as something of a blow – but it is revealed with such sensitivity that the viewer can make his or her own decision about how to react to it, rather than being strung along emotionally by an extended build-up.

As well as sad moments (and there are many – the parting of the lovers Homer and Candy; the death of Dr Larch; the pathos of the orphans trying to impress potential adoptive parents), there is plenty of joy. When Homer leaves the orphanage and sees the sea for the first time, it's a happy moment, and when he and Candy are falling in love there is plenty of easy enjoyment in the film. It's also a drama, in the most advised sense. There are few special effects or stunts, and the rises and falls in tension come when relationships grow or are severed. It's a *human* film, which is why so many people related to it. Its moral and political message, toned down from the original text, was very much a secondary function of the movie, but one that many mistook as its most important statement.

The few reviewers who didn't take to *The Cider House Rules* had one point in common, which was that the movie went overboard on sentimentality. This is clearly a subjective point – it's not as if the film descends into Steven Spielberg-esque slushiness, after all – but one that can be understood, given that the film handles so many profound issues, many of which revolve around Erykah's character (a supporting role on paper, but an absolutely central piece of casting in actuality). The director himself had clearly shared some concern that he might overdo the heartstring-tweaking. When one writer told him, 'I was amazed that you avoided falling prey to sentimentality with this film, even when dealing with weighty emotional material,' he responded, 'That makes me very happy and proud to hear. If I managed to do that, I have accomplished something that was important, because that's my deepest fear – to be sentimental and push for emotions. I think I avoid stepping into sentimentality by trying to be as truthful as possible with performances. Just being present emotionally in the scene, truly present emotionally, should be enough to convey what should be conveyed.'

The movie has a limited amount of controversy-attracting content in that it dealt frankly and honestly with the issue of abortion, both in theory (the women who come to St Cloud's for terminations are operated on off-camera and without the viewer learning much about the details) and with more emotional impact (Erykah's character Rose is a fully fledged person, with whom we soon sympathise). Hallström himself was surprised at the impact of the issue on American audiences and critics – as a Swede accustomed to a pro-choice environment in his home country, he had not been expecting reviews to include much discussion of the subject. 'I didn't realize how much of a button that is, coming from Sweden,' he said. 'It's just a natural choice for everyone, to accept the pro-choice standpoint. For me, there was no controversy there. The early scripts had somewhat more emphasis on the message, so I pulled back on that.' However, he accepted that the issue needed to be explored:

'When it comes to the issue of abortion, it's a story that has relevance today. It has to be spelled out today, unfortunately. In those days, it was illegal. Today it's just an inflammatory issue, that is a culture shock for me coming here and realizing how militant this group is. I hope the soft-spoken message here will affect people.'

The director was delighted with the performances he coaxed from his actors. He explained that the idea of recruiting a combination of experienced and new actors to the film had appealed to him: 'I love mixing amateurs and professionals,' he said. 'I love improvising. I love involving actors at all levels – and they have to know that I want to hear their contributions, with dialogue, with story suggestions, with script changes, whatever. I really think that helps. And we have to be in synch – I'd rather have actors inhabit the parts.' As well as the relatively inexperienced Badu and Heavy D (who had previously only played himself in rap videos), he gave scriptwriter Irving a walk-on part as a stationmaster: 'When I see him on TV he seems very imposing – he's this literary giant,' said Hallström of the writer. 'But the producer assured me that he was a nice man, and that really was confirmed.'

The stand-out performances come from Caine, Maguire, Lindo and Badu, with strong support from Theron and Rudd – all of whom shine in vastly different ways. The veteran Caine, of course, emits a marvellously genuine air as the big-hearted but slightly seedy doctor (who is addicted to ether and is not averse to the odd liaison with his nurses, but will move heaven and earth to make his young charges happy, bidding them goodnight with a nightly whisper of 'Good night, you princes of Maine – you kings of New England'). Tobey Maguire, who had distinguished himself in previous roles in *The Ice Storm* and *Pleasantville*, brought his trademark innocent composure to the role of Homer – a kind of youthful serenity that is in stark contrast to the impassivity of Lindo, for example. Referring to Maguire, Lasse Hallström remarked, 'His choices are so low-key... [Another] young actor would want to show off, but he's very brave in trusting the subtle choices. He doesn't fall back on technique or theatrics.'

As for Erykah, her portrayal of the tortured Rose Rose is flawless. A fairly slight character until her pregnancy is revealed towards the end of the film, she is by turns withdrawn, determined and vengeful until the apocalyptic ending, at which she is the only character in the film not to have achieved some kind of peace (Larch dies peacefully; Wells returns to his home; the couple of Worthington and Candy are reunited, albeit with a tragic air; and even Lindo, dying of his wounds, achieves a measure of paradoxical dignity by insisting that his death is reported as a self-inflicted accident). Where the strength of her role lies is in the less-is-more approach she takes: averting her face from the gaze of the camera and keeping her thoughts hidden behind an almost sullen visage, she is impenetrable. Even her running away from the breakfast table during a bout of morning sickness (the none-too-subtle signal given to the audience that she is pregnant) is done without fuss or overacting.

Without a headwrap (fans saw her hair for the first time) and dressed in dun-coloured labourer's clothes, she is miles away from the Nefertiti-style peacock queen that audiences had grown to recognise. 'I felt a little naked,' she told the *Chicago Sun-Times*. 'I was also really chilly.' But the part had been a fascinating experience: 'By taking a movie role, I'm re-creating myself, and I never thought I'd have that opportunity on this planet,' she said, adding that her mentor on the movie had been her on-set father Delroy Lindo, who had told her, 'Whatever it is you're doing, keep doing it. You are an actress.'

The film cost £17 million ($24 million) and recouped this with ease, taking £78 million ($110 million) in its opening weekend in the US and a further £47 million ($67 million) when it opened four months later in the UK. Reviewers were pretty much united that it was an excellent piece of movie-making, with exemplary acting, directing and script, but could not agree about what is said about abortion. *Variety* pointed at its 'controversial pro-choice stance on abortion'; the *Village Voice* remarked that the film 'makes men the arbiters of what happens to a woman's body'; and online critic James Berardinelli concluded that it provided a 'reasonably balanced perspective' on the issue, but other publications saw the subject as secondary to the film's central theme of destiny (Wells cannot escape the orphanage and his moral doubts are soon overcome by events).

The *Chicago Sun-Times* said that the movie was, 'often absorbing or enchanting in its parts. Michael Caine's performance is one of his best, and Charlize Theron is sweet and direct as the girl.' Interestingly, Tobey

Maguire's calm exterior didn't wash well with this paper: 'Maguire is almost maddeningly monotone as Homer (is his performance inspired by Benjamin in *The Graduate*?)' and the reviewer wasn't impressed by Irving's remarkable trick of making the incestuous Mr Rose 'somehow, murkily...not entirely a monster'. The *LA Times* focused more on the broader emotional picture painted by the script: 'The opening sequences at St. Cloud's, with its raft of adorable youngsters and their heart-tugging predicaments, presents a huge potential for sentimentality...but Irving and Hallström move way beyond the seemingly predictable to ponder the way in which everyone must make his or her way through life's constant interplay of choice and fate.' No complaints about the Wells or Rose characters here, though: 'Maguire's combination of ordinary, clean-cut looks and inner resources is just what Homer requires... Lindo suggests the full range of human behavior in his eloquent Mr. Rose, and Rudd is the handsome yet likable and responsible beau ideal... Sterling key support comes from the always notable Alexander, Baker and Nelligan and from newcomer Badu.'

Reviewers were also quick to focus on the film's feel-good ambience, which pervades the sequence of events despite the occasional shocking scenes. The *San Francisco Chronicle* called it a '1940s New England variation on Charles Dickens', pointing out with some justification that it has 'that Dickensian spirit wherein simple acts of kindness can bring an audience close to tears'. The *San Francisco Examiner* was less charitable, however, stating that, 'The film is perfectly nice to begin with and just gets more polite once Homer arrives at the Worthington apple orchard... [Unlike] the movie he's in, he's got a moral center that's not made of chocolate.' However, such snide comments on the film's unashamedly pathos-ridden nature were rare: *The Onion* said that, '*The Cider House Rules* has finally made it to the screen in fine form...[A] beautifully acted, carefully paced story of how we come to accept and live with disappointment and moral ambiguity', with its concluding comment that, 'Every moment in *Cider House* counts: its emotional impact feels hard-won, while its moral universe extends far beyond [a] pro-good/anti-evil stance. A carefully considered labor of love, it's worth every bit of the labor.'

As for Erykah's performance, reviews were almost exclusively positive. The UK *Guardian* allowed itself something of a monologue on Badu alone, observing that 'the 29-year-old gives a convincing performance as an orchard worker who befriends idealistic protagonist Tobey Maguire while carrying a terrible secret. It's a tribute to her MTV image that, while one expects a statuesque figure, she looks suitably waifish as Rose Rose.' Her secret was in her unstudied approach: 'On screen she is a natural performer, at ease sagely reprimanding Maguire, yet elsewhere playfully naïve...as Hollywood emerges from the gangsta-flick of the '90s, producing more aspirational films about black middle-class life, Badu is a likely star in the making.'

Not that the crossover from singer to actor is always so simple. Erykah showed that she had her eyes open about this fact when she told MTV shortly after the film opened: 'But I do [realise] it's a trend...or it's easy for a film company to use a musician in lieu of an actor because of [the musician's] popularity. And not to take anything away from the musicians [who also act], but it does take a little bit away from the actors.' However, she knew that in this instance her involvement was the right thing to do on all levels: 'I feel like my role is justified,' she said. ''Cause I'm an actress and not just a singer. I'm an artist, so anything that has to do with art, I have to do with it because that's just how I live.'

It's undeniably true that the music–film interface has become more and more blurred across the years. Singer/actors such as Frank Sinatra and Elvis Presley had made the transition almost four decades before *The Cider House Rules*, of course, but the trend had never been particularly popular in recent years (with the exception of a few notables such as Madonna), until the wave of black 1990s film had seen hip-hop artists such as Queen Latifah and Ice Cube make débuts on the big screen. The rise of video in the 1980s contributed a lot to the phenomenon, of course, with all manner of pop stars fancying themselves as actors, but so many of the results had been laughable that even in the 1990s Erykah's acting roles caused more than a few raised eyebrows.

The singer-turned-actor trend has been helped, as all trends are, by industry support – and the list of awards that *The Cider House Rules* received is an impressive one indeed. Most notably, Michael Caine won his second Oscar for Best Actor in a Supporting Role: the award was doubly important, as he had been absent from most critics' favourite-actor lists for some years. He had last been acknowledged at this level in 1987, when he won his first Oscar in the same category for *Hannah And Her Sisters* – but had spent much of the following decade in the critical and commercial doldrums. John Irving also scooped an Oscar in the Best Writing: Screenplay Based on Material Previously Produced or Published category. Nominations (not wins) also went to art director David Gropman and set decorator Beth A Rubino for Best Art Direction: Set Decoration in recognition of the dark halls of St Cloud's; Lasse Hallström for Best Director; Lisa Zeno Churgin for Best Editing; Rachel Portman for Best Music: Original Score; and Richard N Gladstein for Best Picture.

Caine was also nominated for a Golden Globe for Best Performance by an Actor in a Supporting Role in a Motion Picture and a Golden Satellite Award for Best Performance by an Actor in a Supporting Role: Drama. He also won a Screen Actors Guild Award for Outstanding Performance by a Male Actor in a Supporting Role. Both Erykah and Charlize Theron were nominated for Golden Satellite Awards for Best Performance by an Actress in a Supporting Role: Drama. Most of the cast, including Erykah, were also nominated for Outstanding Performance by a Cast in a Theatrical Motion Picture.

Did Erykah really care about the awards? Probably not – but her entrance to the movie world had now been successfully managed, after her first step with the *Blues Brothers* sequel had gone so drastically wrong. And the effect was noticeable. Somehow, the way people now looked at her was different since the success of *The Cider House Rules*. There was a new tone to the way people spoke about Erykah: where there had previously been indifference, now there was respect; and where there had previously been respect, now there was awe. Such is the impact of a big movie hit, but the benefits were no less than this unique performer deserved.

At the end of 1999 Erykah spent some time in post-production on the film, working in a studio on voice-overs. The engineer she worked with on the sessions was Chris Bell, who would go on to play a prominent role in her next project – a follow-up album to *Baduizm*. 'I started working with Erykah at the end of 1999,' remembers Bell. 'I was replacing some of her dialogue on the movie *The Cider House Rules*, and we kinda hit it off. My first impressions? I thought she was really cool. She's got a cool vibe about her, which you feel as soon as she walks into the room.'

What Bell witnessed when he first met Erykah Badu was a kind of instinctual warmth, which she reveals to those who deserve it. Badu fan Rose Glenn also detected this part of her character when she met her backstage, and was struck by the time she takes to meet people, her lack of pretension and her simple unhurried air. Bell must have impressed Erykah, because she tends to surround herself with co-workers who are in sympathy with her working methods: he himself is a very laid-back, thoughtful man who takes his time when thinking about his answer to a question, and is calmly honest about what he thinks.

Bell would go on to play a pivotal role in the shaping of her next album, which so many people had been expecting for so long. And as the millennium approached and the more sensitive of her fans started to experience a little *fin du siècle* tension, some felt that all bets were off. There was no way of knowing exactly what Erykah's next move would be.

11 Love Can Make It Better

'Damn, that Badu lady is cool,' was the response of many observers to the news in late November 1999 that Erykah was holding a charity event at New York City's Manhattan's China Club called Café Soul. Why so cool, you ask? Because she had chosen to team up with the original hot-buttered soul man himself, Isaac Hayes, to co-host the event. Hayes, a veteran performer, had been recently elevated to the unlikely position of animated icon to the nu-metal generation due to his show-stealing voice-over role as Chef in the no-brainer cult series *South Park* – not without a few hisses of disapproval from long-standing fans. Although Erykah was taking a step upwards by allying herself with Mr *Shaft*, it should not be ignored that his status among soul-heads was helped along nicely by his association with her.

The concept behind the Café Soul event – which from its very name evokes 1970s club chic, soul food and Bobby Womack – was that the two artists would compère and perform at the event along with hot artists old and new such as TLC, D'Angelo, Chico DeBarge, Maxi Priest, Zhané and Solo. In addition there would be poetry readings from Ras Barka, Juba Dowdell, Tony Medina and a survivor of the reality TV show *Real World* called Kevin Powell. The night was sponsored by Tanqueray gin, who put a cool £14,000 ($20,000) in the pot, and would benefit two charity groups, the Sanctuaries for Families Women's Shelter and the Sheppard Foundation. Hayes had hosted several such events in previous years, all of which had been the toast of the East Coast critics and for which tickets were sold out long in advance. The urban music community would continue to flex its muscle for the good of the community, it seemed, regardless of the wheels of fashion.

In early December a spin-off from the *Chant Down Babylon* Marley tribute album took place in the form of a concert in honour of the late reggae musician, held at the James Bond Beach near Oracabessa on the north coast of Jamaica. The venue was a 15,000-capacity concert hall owned by Island Records founder Chris Blackwell (who had played a pivotal role in bringing Jamaican music to white audiences in the 1970s) and was to host performances from Busta Rhymes, Ben Harper, Lauryn Hill, Erykah, Chrissie Hynde, Jimmy Cliff and many of the artists who had featured on the earlier album. Badu came on to the stage dressed in a long red dress and a green and gold turban, and duetted with Cliff on a version of 'No Woman No Cry', before delivering a solo rendition of 'No More Trouble' and 'Them Belly Full'. Her slot was notable for an impassioned mini-lecture she gave on the subject of the spirituality of the millennium, also labelling Marley's work as 'the living manifestation of the truth of the Creator'.

As the end of the century approached, Erykah spoke more often about the importance of the approaching date, until one or two people began to complain of her overzealousness. Perhaps because the linking of spiritual awareness and cosmic importance to the end of millennia has always been regarded as the province of charlatans and witch-doctors, a definite sub-current of discontent among Erykah's followers could be detected, reinforced by the complaints of a small number of fans who had grown tired of waiting for a new album (it had been almost three years since *Baduizm*) and had started to wonder if the woman they had thought to be a messiah might turn out to be a flash in the pan.

But, as always, Badu explained herself. It turned out that the ups and downs of her personal life (which, as we have seen, was in turmoil) was making her life very difficult. She later explained that the period of 1998 to 2000 was a tough one: 'Saturn's return was very hard,' she said. 'That's the age from 27 to 29 – Saturn's return for most women. That's when you are stuck between being a kid or taking grown-up responsibility. Your youth – I guess in your mind – is leaving you. You on this conveyor belt of life going, no, no. You wanna be a kid, but you don't… I'm out.

I made it. And they say that if you make it, you made. If you don't, the next lifetime. I made it. I made it out.'

She made it out all right. The millennium came and went with little upheaval, life went on as before, with 2000 starting off well for Badu (with yet another Grammy). This time the gong came her way thanks to the enduring success of the remarkable 'You Got Me' (in the Best Rap Performance by a Duo or Group category), which was still flying high even though it had been commercially exposed for several months by this stage. Erykah topped her own stringent clothing standards by arriving at the ceremony not in a designer gown, but dressed in a home-made creation made of green leather squares sewn together with yellow raffia and featuring dried flowers at the seams. Of her extravagant headwrap, she told CNN that it was 'an ego thing' and that it represented 'strength': 'The headwrap is political... This headwrap is a symbol for every group of people who has their own set of rules.' But it wasn't just about power, she added: 'It's beautiful, and I enjoy wearing it, and I enjoy people complimenting me on it.' Her performance with George Benson and Diana Krall was an obvious high point of the show – and much glee was felt among her fans by the fact that neither press nor celeb-ridden audience sounded or looked as interesting as she did.

The following month saw Erykah roll up to the Academy Awards ceremony at the Shrine Auditorium in Los Angeles. *The Cider House Rules* was a clear contender for a victory, with its supporters vindicated and delighted when Michael Caine received his Oscar, and Erykah and Tobey Maguire were even asked to present one of the other awards. The show itself was a fairly dull affair, however, only livened up by some amusing moments such as the piece to camera in which host Tyra Banks interviewed Badu. The image of Banks, a relatively tall woman, struggling to stay in shot with the diminutive singer and her Marge Simpson-like headwrap was one to be cherished. Banks later quipped that Erykah was hiding a stolen Oscar under her hat.

Little wonder Erykah was getting no work done on her new album: she had dozens of public commitments of this type to perform, some more irksome than others. However, she took genuine pleasure in her invitation from the Arts Magnet itself – her old Dallas school, Booker

T Washington High – to place her handprints along Dallas's Walk of Fame at the Lakewood Theater. Three alumni of the school were present for the ceremony: Erykah, the Grammy-winning jazz trumpeter Roy Hargrove (who had helped his schoolmate out on previous recordings) and a visual artist called Chris Arnold. The event attracted corporate sponsorship (and a healthy dash of publicity for the school, no doubt) and was a clear sign of Badu's value both to her city and her Alma Mater.

Awards ceremonies put to one side for the moment, Erykah's fans gave a sigh of relief when they saw her take up her rightful place at the top of the bill at the New Orleans Jazz and Heritage Festival, which was scheduled to run from 28 to 30 April and again from 4 to 7 May. In the previous year she had won awards and received praise as an R&B artist, a soul singer and a hip-hop MC, and this time she had defied categorisation by headlining a jazz bill. On the other hand, the programmers for the Louisiana gig weren't too sure what jazz was, either, it seemed: Badu's co-headliner was none other than Sting, while other acts asked to perform included rocker Lenny Kravitz, gris-gris prophet Dr John, the defiantly funky Meters and gospel and soul performers The Neville Brothers, with only easy-listening pianist Harry Connick Jr a truly recognisable big jazz name.

Music was the name of Erykah's game in summer 2000...with a vengeance. The neo-soul movement she had so memorably 'midwived' was celebrating its newest arrival in July: the dreadlocked soul boy Bilal, newest member of the Soulquarians and much noted for the D'Angelo-like sexuality of his performances. With a single, 'Soul Sista' (a high point of the soundtrack to the recent *Love And Basketball* movie), and his début album *First Born Second* garnering a barrelful of critical plaudits, it seemed that Bilal's time was definitely now. His Soulquarian siblings – including Ahmir '?uestlove' Thompson, Common and Erykah – had contributed to his album, and he was not not slow to pay his respects in interviews. Badu also made a guest appearance at a Burning Spear show on a performance of his classic 'Jah No Dead' – another string to her reggae bow, and an astute choice of duettist, for the singer had just netted his first Grammy win for Reggae Album of the Year, *Calling Rastafari*. Would she ever settle down to work on her own album?

Of course she would – and did so in August 2000, assembling her veteran team at Dallas's Soundlab studio complex and enfolding herself in the warmth and talent of the Soulquarians. Many might have thought that the pressure was on her at this stage, but she later revealed that the opposite was in fact the case: 'There will never be another *Baduizm* – I didn't know it would be that big. I thought I would have a core following, like The Roots and Common and Mos Def. I didn't think that everybody would understand [my music] right away.' The burden of popularity, she explained, had been cleared at the first hurdle. 'With this album, I didn't have any of that in mind. I think I'm over the whole stardom thing. I'm more concerned now with the music being wonderful. And, of course, I never underestimate the audience's ability to get it. They're the ones I do it for.'

Did Erykah feel any pressure to create a masterpiece after the enormous success of *Baduizm*? Quite possibly, although she was always very calm and collected about the new material, never offering it up as any kind of '*Baduizm* Part 2' or a replacement for the original. The problem that she faced, as she and industry observers well knew, was the classic one that awaits all entertainers who rise high and fast: with all eyes on them, they are denied the opportunity to grow in private and can often fall spectacularly from grace. And *Baduizm* had been such a monument, from its title to its contents, that anything that failed to match it would be deemed a failure by the more unthinking sections of Erykah's fanbase.

Engineer Chris Bell, who had recorded *Cider House* overdubs with Erykah, was fascinated by the changes he saw in her when she was in charge of her own project: 'When we started doing the tracking in the studio I saw a different side of her. The film was totally different, there's a producer on the line, she kinda has to do what she's told – but on her album she pretty much takes charge. She knows what she wants, but she has people's input too. She surrounds herself with really talented people.'

Bell saw Erykah try various recording methods until the right way revealed itself: 'I guess a lot of her [previous] music had been sequenced, and so on...but a month later she said, I want to bring in my own band and try doing a live recording. She said, let's try getting all the players in the room at one time and we'll see what magic's gonna happen.' It wasn't long before everyone concerned realised that she had struck gold with this method: 'This worked out really well,' says Bell, whose experience allows him to work in many different ways – the perfect studio foil for Badu. 'It was a multi-room facility and we kinda did a bit of everything.'

Before the fruits of the Soundlab sessions could become known, however, more commercial acclaim thanks to a guest slot would come Erykah's way in the form of a single entitled 'The Light', by Common (real name Rashied Lynn). Both the rapper – an established friend of Erykah's – and Badu herself were surprised by its success: released in October 2000, it later received a Grammy nomination and, like 'You Got Me' before it, would be widely acknowledged as being among some of Badu's most memorable work. Common expressed his shock at its reception in an interview with *Soul Train*: 'Honestly, I didn't know it was gonna be that big,' he said. 'I really just made a song 'cause I felt it, and I was just trying to make a good song more than anything. I didn't know it was gonna be on the radio like a lot and the video would be playing and it would get nominated for a Grammy Award. It was just like one of those songs I felt.' Asked if his aim had been to move his music in a mainstream direction with the single, he responded: 'Nah. I mean, really with this record I was going even *more* out there, like I was even experimenting more, and that's what I strive for. I strive for freedom within the music, you know?'

Interestingly, Common had a lot to say about the collaborations he had done with Erykah and others. 'I work with artists that I feel are creative, artists that are great, you know,' he explained. 'Artists that I respect their music and their message and what they about. That's the artists that I strive to work with.' An example was 'Geto Heaven', which he had recorded with none other than Macy Gray: 'That song...was originally done with D'Angelo and I,' he responded. 'I decided to do a remix, and I asked Macy to come get on it.' His next words were worthy of Erykah herself, so steeped in self-awareness were they: 'Basically, the song is about finding heaven within yourself, so that no matter what situation you in, or environment, just finding that peace of mind and that love for self within yourself and not searching for outer things to try to establish that – that's what the song is about. And it just came together, man. It was a blessing, you know?'

It was clear that Common was – spiritually speaking, at least – something of a match for Erykah. For example, when asked for a fact about his personal life that his fans might not know already, he pondered, 'Well, just that, you know, as much as I'm striving for consciousness and love, I mess up a lot. I fall victim to the same things that y'all fall victim to. I eat, sleep and drink, just like you do. Not that everybody think I'm super-human, but as an artist, man, sometimes people don't look at you as a person, and they don't see sometimes that you hurtin' when they come up to you and ask you for your time or whatever.' But, like Badu, his inner strength was evident: 'You know, as an artist, you know, I chose this profession, so I'm gonna give 'em that love regardless. But I want them to know I'm a person, man. I love like you love, and I go through anger like you go through it and gotta take out the garbage the same way and gotta eat. So that's more than anything – that I'm about elevation.' Like all the best performers, he had an eye for the welfare of the community, too. 'I got this Common Ground Foundation,' he said, 'which is a not-for-profit organization. We're trying to raise money to buy instruments for children. We go out and try to speak to children in schools. We're trying to set up programs eventually where we want to take kids around the world, to be honest, and let them see other parts of the world.'

Common then revealed that he was on the point of doing 'some support dates with Erykah Badu. I'm gonna be doing different little spot dates with me and my band.' Like Erykah, he was in the middle of producing a new album: 'So just be aware that the new album is comin',' he said. 'I ain't gonna say comin' soon, 'cause soon could be next month. But it's gonna take me a little time to work it out, so y'all bear with me. I just wanna take it to another place, and hopefully y'all will dig it, you know?'

In October 2000 Badu fans who had enjoyed her many recent collaborations with other artists but yearned for some original material were rewarded (at last) with the first single from her new album. Titled 'Bag Lady', the song was an instant success, staying at the top of the *Billboard* Hot R&B/Hip-Hop Singles & Tracks chart for a mighty seven weeks – no mean feat in the era of easy-come, quickly-go, one-hit wonders. A mid-tempo, crooned piece of purer hip-hop than she had previously composed, the song was – like the best of her work – a simple metaphor wrapped around an unforgettable groove. The message of the song, encapsulated by the image of a homeless woman dragging around sacks of belongings, was a typical Badu self-awareness call: 'Bag lady,' she murmurs, 'you gone hurt your back,' telling us to leave our useless baggage behind. If it sounds like a hangover from the feel-good pedagogy of *Baduizm*, that's because it dates from the same period: 'I wrote "Bag Lady" right after I finished *Baduizm* and started my live show,' revealed Erykah, adding that she had once been the character in its title. 'I actually started writing it because I was inspired by my own personal growth. You know, I was happy I was able to assess things a little bit better. ' In this sense she was following in the footsteps of many people – artists or otherwise – who find that their work functions as an effective channel for the expression of their personal growth. We change, expand and put the resulting conflict into words or actions to provide closure. If this sounds like therapy-babble to you, then you need to think again.

The conception of the song flowed as if guided by an exterior force, she reasoned: 'It started with a melody I was humming, and usually the words find their place. They're just waitin' to get on a song… [They] just kind of come through me some kind of way. I mean, they can use the album for whatever they need or what they want.' Of the song's message, she explained that she hoped her words would be seen as inspiring: 'Hopefully my music is medicine, some type of antidote for something or some kind of explanation or just to feel good.' Musically, the song was a great introduction to the second phase of her music, and not by accident: the radio and video versions were slightly faster remixes of the original album version.

Erykah told *Jet* magazine that the baggage the song refers to is largely left-over emotion from failed or flawed relationships, although she never explicitly referred to her own recent split with Dre (not a likely inspiration, in any case, as the song had been written so long before): 'The song has a lot to do with…bringing baggage from a relationship situation into the next relationship situation – meaning that you have not forgiven yourself for the last situation. A lot of us carry that baggage... I urge people to pack light. We have a lot of baggage that we have gathered since we were children: the education system and the things that we mislearned, things that really don't have anything to do with us.' Her grasp of the psychology of love seemed to be developed. 'Romantic relationships where we were actually the ones who needed to change, but we always blamed the partner. And we continue to switch partners over and over again wondering why they still won't act right. Ultimately, it's because we have to let go of our own baggage. There are many kinds of bags that we carry.' She elaborated, saying, 'I figured out the reason why I couldn't get though the day as well as I can now was because I had too many things on my mind, on my plate, for one person to have. So I started to eliminate some of the things that were too heavy to carry and unnecessary.' Her plight extended as far as needing to stay with the security of the home. 'I felt very discouraged to go out in public at one time, and the weight was heavy. I wanted to feel light again,' she said. '"Bag Lady" stopped me from thinking that way.'

Although when she wrote 'Bag Lady' Erykah still seemed to be on a high from the success of *Baduizm*, the approaching birth of Seven and the blossoming relationship with Andre, she revealed that the song had come about when things were beginning to weigh her down. 'It was just a point in my life where I felt like, wow, I'm so tired of feeling heavy,' she said. 'I went through my life and thought about it, and took out a few happy things and shared that. As a result, "Bag Lady" was created.' The song came at the end of her creative flow at the time, it seems – 'Then I had writer's block for a little while after "Bag Lady", for about a year or so. I had a son immediately after that, and I couldn't give anything attention but him. I don't know how to separate that creativity; my creativity went into molding his brain, breast-feeding, finding ways to keep myself afloat.'

Erykah faced a particularly perceptive question from the *Interview* magazine reporter who remarked that, 'It's sort of been out of fashion to make socially conscious music, but your first single is about homelessness.' The point he made was dual: why step outside the boundaries of fashion with a crucial comeback release, and why feel the need to educate? Badu missed neither point when she responded succinctly, 'I don't feel like I need to preach to the world or nothing like that. I just feel like I share what I say, and if listeners get it, they get it. And I never underestimate the audience's ability to feel me.' Neither the vagaries of fashion nor the attractions of the soapbox have an unhealthy grasp on her, it appears.

The song's popularity was boosted by its accompanying video, a striking collection of images centring on a colour-coordinated group of women who swagger down urban streets gripping self-help books with whimsical titles such as *Get Over Him Yesterday.* Badu directed it herself, claiming as its inspiration Ntozake Shange's cult book and play *For Colored Girls Who Have Considered Suicide/When The Rainbow Is Enuf: A Choreopoem*. Interestingly, Shange was later asked by a college student at the university where she was lecturing how she felt about Erykah's tribute, and replied, 'I haven't seen the video. I have met her. I admire her, but she should be hearing from somebody really soon.' How to interpret this – as a warning or a well-meaning promise – is a matter open to debate.

The workload attached to video, album and promotion was heavy, but Badu's spirit was light-hearted, as she explained that, 'Every time I would complain [about my many jobs], people would say, well, you said you wanted to do it all. I said, yeah, but...it was a one-woman show this time, but it was great. It was a good experience, and I got it all done, and it went on time.' Indeed it did – and the results not only guaranteed her a chart hit, but the usual run-down of soundtrackers put in requests for its presence on movie compilations. The most notable of these was the Spike Lee film *Bamboozled*, which was released in late September (even ahead of the single's release date) and was thus something of a coup for the film-maker's team. Other artists whose work appeared on the soundtrack included the male vocal quartet Profyle, soul-folkie India Arie and the legendary (but now treading water) Stevie Wonder. More aggressive sounds came courtesy of the ubiquitous Roots, who had gathered in rappers Chuck D (of Public Enemy) and Zack de la Rocha (Rage Against The Machine) on an anti-industry rant called 'Burn Hollywood Burn'.

No piece of fluff like *High School High*, the Lee film was something of a biting satire, although it didn't perform well commercially. The story line revolves with Lee's typical bitter-sweet honesty around an Ivy League-educated black TV writer, who finds little success in his new job at a major network after his version of a *Cosby Show*-like family drama is rejected. In a last-ditch attempt at innovation, he decides to write a minstrel show, with black actors wearing the black make-up. The show is a hit, but the political repercussions of the scheme leave everyone affected profoundly. Badu's presence on the movie's soundtrack did just as much for her profile as a serious political artist as for her work with the Marleys, with 'Bag Lady' rubbing shoulders with wrathful commentaries in song such as the Mau Maus' 'Blak Iz Blak' (the fruits of a collaboration between hip-hoppers Mos Def, Canibus, Charli Baltimore and DJ Scratch). A less oppressive feature of the soundtrack, however, came in the form of the welcome reappearance of Common's 'The Light', with its haunting Badu hook. In historical terms the soundtrack held interest for the appearance of yet another neo-soul rising star – Angie Stone, whose 'Slippery Shoes' would elevate her into the ranks of Erykah, Macy Gray and Jill Scott with apparent ease. And, if it's prestige you need, none other than the sporadically brilliant Prince contributed his psychedelic '2045 Radical Man', one of the few successes of his recent internet-only campaigns.

In November 2000 Erykah conducted a frank interview with *Honey* magazine in which she talked about life post-Andre with an openness that she had not displayed previously. 'My music comes from that same place in my heart where raising Seven comes from, getting over my relationship and loving me again,' she explained. 'I was just tired of carrying a lot of shit... I had to be happy, because I had a kid...but as soon as Seven would go to sleep, that little tear would automatically fall.' The feature was sympathetic and warm, but the writer managed to rouse Erykah's anger when the piece was published by mentioning that Erykah's long dreadlocks weren't real – she'd had extensions woven into her natural hair. When she saw the piece, Badu allegedly telephoned the writer Lola Ogunnaike at home and called her a bitch, although she later apologised for her outburst.

The fake-dreads issue was a shallow one but one that would haunt Erykah for some time, with many interviewers insisting on addressing the matter. She was unashamed of having a hair weave, saying, 'We [as black people] put such an emphasis on our hair... It's like Andre said, everyone with locks ain't for the cause. And everyone with a perm ain't for the fall.' However, when she discovered that fans were having a heated discussion on the matter at her website, it hit home a little harder and she later said, 'It hurt my feelings... Some people really believe in me a lot for being a natural black woman, and they started sending me messages like, why do you wear fake hair? I thought you were real.'

In this case, Erykah's hair became an unexpectedly emotive issue – perhaps because both her fans and her detractors felt that not having real dreads was somehow a betrayal of her 'realness' as a black woman. And, in some ways, this is understandable: Badu's message has always revolved around the concepts of self-worth beneath the surface, of human power and actuality – somehow the idea of part of her body being a cosmetic add-on jars a little. However, people should really have considered the issue and moved on, but many failed to do so and the issue stuck around for quite some time, even becoming the province of expert hairdressers.

One such was Diane Bailey, a Brooklyn-based salon owner who had a sensible answer to the debate, saying that, 'When Erykah Badu had extensions in her hair, I was perfectly fine with it. Because in show business, you're on the road and not able to see a hairdresser every week – you need someone to maintain it, and so on – so having extensions is just something a little extra to make it happen. She's a very hot sista: she's just real clear. She can wear her hair long one minute, and then cut it. And she's like, all of it's me – I bought it, it's mine! Or, if I want to shave it off, it's mine!' The use of artificial extensions is a resource available to anyone, she added, which shouldn't be a cause of stress. 'My thing is this: we have options. We are closer than we've ever been to discovering who we are in a natural state. If adding extensions gets you there, then I'll do it. Some people need extensions, because they just don't have the fullness or the texture, or they may want to add to whatever they already have. They may want to embellish or enhance it. So extensions don't necessarily mean that you're fake or false, it just means that you need some "added help" to get to where you're going. That's how I look at it.' Spiritual issues aside, Erykah uses her extensions just to keep her hair in shape, explaining that, as she wears her headwraps so high, the front of her hair is always breaking off, so she supplements her natural hair with braids.

Erykah herself remarked, 'It's art. Hair is an art form passed down through generations. I don't think it expresses the way I am, as long as anything I wear or do doesn't stop me from being kind or growing. I cover my hair as a statement that hair is not what's important. If people think I'm wrong for wearing [extensions], they'll get over it. As long as they like the songs – that's all I'm concerned about.' This was the core issue, of course, for Badu is a singer and songwriter, not a model, although she knew how much a part image plays in the public awareness. It seemed that the issue irked her at times – she allegedly told one interviewer from *Spin*, 'If you say I've got fake hair, I'm going to kick your ass!... I don't want it to be the focus of who I am', adding that, 'I don't never get a break! They'd recognize me if I had on a damn Ku Klux Klan hood!'

Indeed, Badu went as far as explaining that change (whether in image or, as we would soon see, musically) was an essential part of her approach to her life and work: 'I'm always changing my hair, or something... I heard through the grapevine that sisters are somehow disappointed 'cos I cut my locks, or I shaved my head, or I didn't wear my hair wrap to the left, or to the right. [My show] is about that. It grows and changes with every audience, and every audience is different, and I'm different all the time. Every day. New.' Her last word on the subject came when she pointed out that real or fake hair is hardly the point, since she remains real underneath. 'Most of the people walking around, stuff be fake... Fake hair ain't gonna stop me from being real, and if people don't like it, too damn bad. Like one of my teachers once told me, I'd rather see a man with processed hair and a natural mind than natural hair and processed life and mind.'

None of this affected Erykah's status as a most-wanted performer at events benefiting various political causes, though, and on 16 October 2000 she appeared alongside Macy Gray, Mary J Blige and Kelly Price at the Million Family March in Washington, DC. The event, a Nation of Islam-associated celebration that took place on the fifth anniversary of the original Million Man March, was headed by an 'entertainment committee' including Def Jam founder Russell Simmons, Sean 'Puffy' Combs, Whitney Houston, Bobby Brown, Will Smith and Chris Tucker. The cast of celebrities involved grew even longer when musicians such as Ice Cube, DMX, Eve, Snoop Dogg, Warren G, the Wu-Tang Clan, D'Angelo, Jay-Z, Joe, Common and Jam Master Jay also offered their support. Add to this industry backup from organisations as powerful as Motown Records, Bad Boy Entertainment, J Records, Spike Lee's 40 Acres and a Mule, Def Jam Records and Magic Johnson Enterprises and there was some justification to Simmons' claim that, 'I believe this march will have a dramatic effect on race relations... It's a march about the human family, rising above color and religion, symbols and creed.' Whether his prophecy bears any truth is too early to say, but the broader picture is fascinating: only a decade before, the idea of superstar musicians lending their time (and the cynical showbiz industry investing its money) in an event hosted by the still-left-field Nation of Islam in aid of something as undefined (and philanthropic) as 'improved race relations' would have been a fantasy.

Talking of philanthropy, Erykah took her message to the streets in the most direct way of all when she performed a show in one of America's most feared prisons 11 days after the Million Family March. Inmates at the Rikers Island Correctional Facility in New York City (where the late Tupac Shakur had been incarcerated only four years previously) saw Badu sing and speak at the special event, which was closed to the public and a prestigious part of an ongoing series of appearances by various hip-hop artists at the prison. Badu's press officer at Motown said that Erykah 'was hoping her visit to the facility will send a positive message and help encourage inmates about their options once they are released'.

It was a brave and inspired move. If Erykah wanted people to learn from her messages of hope and self-elevation, where better to speak than before a literally captive audience with a clear motivation to improve their situation? Furthermore, in her position it was a priority to 'keep it real' (as we saw from the dreadlocks issue), an ever-tougher struggle as her wealth and power increased, and nowhere is it more genuine than in the bowels of Rikers Island.

A week later, America was invaded by the pleasant sounds of OutKast once again, who had stepped up their composing efforts a notch and been rewarded for the first time with enormous success. Their new album, *Stankonia*, featured a chart-slaying single in the form of the aforementioned 'Ms Jackson', an enormously catchy song that Andre 3000 later revealed was a direct apology to Erykah's mother Kolleen for causing her daughter so much pain when they'd split up a year before. At first, however, he was less forthcoming, telling one writer that the song was about 'a personal situation that went on between him and his partner' (not mentioning Badu), but it didn't take long for rumours to circulate and he ultimately came out with the truth a little later.

'Ms Jackson' is an excellent song. Clearly influenced by Parliament (the 'woo' backing vocals are pure Clinton) and based on a solid, plodding beat, the song is both emotionally charged and fatalistic, with a clear dash of humour: Andre repeats 'For ever and ever? *Ever* and ever?' as if he can't quite grasp the concept. 'Never meant to make your daughter cry, I apologise a trillion times', he insists, before elaborating that life had started well for the two lovers – 'King meets queen, then the puppy love thing, together dream, 'Bout that crib with the goodyear swing' – and that, even with the love between them gone, Seven would still have a father ('And yes I will be present on the first day of school, and graduation'). It's a sad song, but a positive one, with Dre insisting that in the end all will be well.

Erykah told *Jet* magazine that she loved both the album and the song. 'I am the mother of his first son, so it may have something to do with me,' she said cautiously. 'He wanted to give the world something to think about baby's mama's mother and baby's daddy. We are very proud of him, my whole family. My mom just laughs about "Ms Jackson". She and Dre are really pretty cool; they talk.' What Dre was saying in the song, she explained, was: '"I apologize, my intentions were good. I never meant to make your daughter cry." Nobody wants to do that. He is a very humble, good brother. He is a really good person.' While the sadness may have remained about their breakup, the love between them had stayed too, it seemed. 'It wasn't like one of those breakups where something happens,' Erykah added. 'We're friends still. We just kinda decided that we needed to grow.' Evidence of the continuing bond could be seen in the fact that she had contributed guest vocals to the song 'Humble Mumble', a mellow, P-Funk-alike swing that was a high point of the record.

As the autumn moved on, an announcement of a release date for Erykah's new album was finally made. The record would appear on 20 November and would bear the title of *Mama's Gun*, a name no one understood and about which people immediately started asking questions.

At least *Baduizm* had been a fairly logical concept, but a mama's gun? A mother's gun? What the hell was she talking about?... Erykah must have smiled to herself as she heard the hubbub of questioning voices. The necessary interest had been raised and, especially with the success of the lead-off single 'Bag Lady', the 'set-up' that Kedar Massenburg valued so much was also in place.

But there was a bigger surprise in store for the listeners who (from mid-November) started forming queues for the new album: the new record was to be no mere remake of *Baduizm*. The sparse textures and laid-back atmospheres of the début album were far less in evidence here. The next chapter was about to begin, and this time the Badu cult was wearing a new face. The face of rock.

12 Gunfire

The press were as keen as the fans to hear the latest Badu tunes, and a Motown-organised preview listen was scheduled at the Rihga Royal Hotel in Manhattan. With typical stubborn-headed determination, however, Erykah herself kept the cocktail-sipping hacks waiting for two whole hours before the event could commence, as she herself was stuck in a queue in a record shop, where she was trying to buy a copy of *Stankonia*. 'I wanted the OutKast album and the line was so damn long,' she told the reporters, laughing. 'Really. This is the story of my life.'

The public flocked to buy *Mama's Gun* – which rapidly sold a million units – and were confronted by its cover image, an ice-cool portrait of Erykah staring balefully out of the sleeve and chewing a cocktail stick, Clint Eastwood-style. Turning the case over revealed the equally penetrating question 'What's yo izm?' scrawled on the rear – a fair question, as the complex system of symbols and icons that Erykah had used both in the music and the artwork begged a simple answer.

'I use every aspect of my physical world, my spiritual world, my etherical world to help me every day… [To] ignore it would be crazy,' Badu explained in one of the first interviews for *Mama's Gun*. This included the use of odd words such as 'Hesi' and 'Sumpth' on the lyric sheet, which she explained to *HipOnline* with the words, 'Oh, those are words. Hesi, the word hesi is beside the song "Kiss Me". And what a hesi is in Egypt or Kimet is like an affirmation. Like something you say over and over again. Like if you keep saying "I am brave, I am brave, I am brave," eventually you will become brave, because some people do say that you speak words into existence. And that's what a hesi is, to speak a word or a sentence or a phrase over and over again.' This sentiment tied in logically with the message of the song it accompanied: 'And the song, where I say, "I want somebody to walk up behind me and kiss me on my neck," is a hesi. Because you say it over and over again, and it'll happen. There's a hidden meaning. It's just not that simple.'

It got more complex, with Badu explaining that 'This word, P-T-A-H, that's ptah, body. In Kimet, ptah is a figure who is known as the body. Somebody to walk behind, behind is where all the energy lies…in Egypt, have you seen those Dobermans sitting on each side of them? They're called ampu. The lips of ampu protect and discard all negative energy. So that's the kiss. "Kiss me on my neck." In Kimet, the neck is the throne for the head. "I want somebody to walk behind me and kiss me on my neck," put energy behind me, put me back on my throne, and breathe on my neck.' And all this in just one song: 'Breathe, that's the first action of life. And that's called shu, or ast. It's just a hesi that's saying, "Alright, I've lost my way, and I need to be on my throne again. I need the energy to come in and be behind me." And I didn't want to say that on the song, so I said it in a more understandable way.'

Apart from the imagery on the record, the aspect that intrigued many reporters was the fact that the album boasted a notably more powerful sound than *Baduizm*. The opening song, 'Penitentiary Philosophy', was chock-full of over-driven, layered guitars – the polar opposite of 'On & On', for example – and sounded like Pink Floyd jamming with Jimi Hendrix in his quieter moods. Asked, 'Do you consciously ignore the trends?' by *Interview* magazine, Erykah responded, 'I just do what I do. I guess it goes by your taste and what you like to hear. What I sing is what I like to hear. The kind of music or the kind of arrangements that I do, the kind of musicians I choose, is just what I like to hear', although she did acknowledge the change in direction on this particular song, saying, 'I believe in reinventing myself every time… Power comes with creativity because the innovator is usually the one who is remembered. It took me my whole life to write *Baduizm*. I had less time for this album, but it's a continuation of growth.'

The theme of development was one that Badu warmed to more and more as interviewers brought it up. She reiterated, 'I constantly reinvent myself so my audience can stay focused. I'm seeing that if they really wanna focus on me a lot, then I'm gonna have to give them something to see that takes their mind off…the negative things that come to them.' To CNN she implied that her change was entirely spontaneous, saying, 'I just go with the wind because you get further that way. When it comes into my mind to change and grow, I do. So nobody should ever expect anything from me, because you are gonna be let down every time', but in *Soul Express* she was quoted as explaining that the simple flow of life itself was responsible for her progression: 'You know, everything changes! I was 25 when I did the first one and 30 when I did the second one. I had more gifts musically, creatively, information-wise. I don't think any of us felt the same as we did in 1997, right? I don't know. But I still hold the same theory, you know – I just do what I felt was good.'

There were certain suppositions with which she disagreed strongly. One journalist told her that she believed *Mama's Gun* revealed her inner feelings more than *Baduizm* did, to which she responded, 'No, I disagree with that. No, you just didn't know me then! Because I was giving the inner feelings in the first one, too. It's just the more you know me, the more you can relate to what I'm talking about. No, I don't think so, because that's what music is to me, it's a way to express the way I feel. I feel that I'm not up there singing or doing performing. I feel like I'm interpreting my feelings for the audience, you know. Tomorrow I can feel different.'

After almost four years in the making, it was surreal to learn that Erykah had not managed to deliver a complete product in one way. The track-listing as printed on the sleeve and the actual sequence of the songs did not match, at least on initial print runs; the error was resolved on subsequent pressings of the album. The lyrics themselves were also not finished in time for the CD booklet printer's deadline, and early copies read 'Peace my beloved people, check web site for the rest of these lyrics – ain't finished yet'. Most fans laughed this off as a sign of their idol's slight eccentricity, but for the benefit of those who might not see the funny side, Erykah explained: 'When you get the album, the song list is not going to be in the right order 'cause I had to turn that stuff in way before time and I just kinda guessed an order…and by the time I finished it, I was, like, no, this song should go first, and I switched everything around.' Mastering and other requirements didn't help matters along either, it appeared: 'The reason why it's like that is 'cause I hadn't finished everything,' she added. 'The day before the mastering, I finished the song "Didn't Cha Know". Consequently, "Penitentiary" is first, "Didn't Cha Know" is second, you know, so the last two songs I finished, to me, were the best ones to go up front.' This problem was also sorted out by the time later CD pressings were made, and as the record sold in large quantities very quickly these early copies are now comparatively hard to find.

As an album, *Mama's Gun* is a considered piece of work. It begins with the unexpected rock rush of 'Penitentiary Philosophy', the most upbeat song on the album and the one that caused most surprise among fans expecting a mellow, 'Rimshot'-style jazz opener. Its message was about avoiding deadlines in life, she explained (appropriate, given the last-minute problems detailed above) and was notable for the guitar work by the remarkable session musician Jef Le Johnson. The fact that a year later Erykah would perform this song with none other than Prince – who played Le Johnson's funky guitar line with evident relish – says much about the ice-cool chic of the arrangement. The other musicians who lend their talent to this warm, organic rock vibe were Erykah's old cohort Ahmir '?uestlove' Thompson on drums, renowned session bassist Pino Palladino and the keyboardist James Poyser. 'The music came first, of course,' reported Badu. 'It was a session that Poyser, Ahmir, Pino and I were in. Three peeps and me, we were just clowning around, and we're like, "Hey, let's do this..." and I freestyled the lyrics. The first draft was very close to what you hear now. I knew the reason for the song but I didn't know what it meant yet. I just found that out.'

The song's message became clearer over time, and it was among the most profound statements that Erykah had made to date. It handled nothing less than the freedom of our minds, as she explained: 'We lock ourselves into our own philosophies, our own religions, our own walks of life,' she said, 'and if we fail, we condemn ourselves and then we get sick. I think that if we can find a way to clear our minds and be a little freer and not lock ourselves into things, because I think we're afraid of change...[and] a lot of people have lost respect for the individual...the person who doesn't conform. It's a jail.' Society itself is at fault, it seems: 'It's like, if you don't be this way when you go to work, so and so is gonna talk about you. If I don't do this, someone was like, we live a commercial every day for the world. It's unnecessary. And I'm tired of doing it. So I wanted to write a song about it.'

The next song, 'Didn't Cha Know', is a step down from the technicolor riffs of the opener and is based on the sweet choral vocals of Erykah's backing singer Yahzara and a tight upper-register bass riff. 'Tried to run but I lost my way,' laments Badu on this more introspective song, which focuses on life and its decisions: 'I said ya never know how the cards may lay,' she warns, perhaps a reference to the traumas she had undergone in life and love since her rise to fame.

Conversely, 'My Life' – at a titular level at least as self-regarding as 'Didn't Cha Know' – is much more upbeat, with elements of classic Motown in the piano line that accompanies the vocal throughout, and even Nellee Hooper influences in the strings motif that cuts in later in the song. 'No turnin' back' is the repeated refrain at the song's end, and Erykah seems to be iterating a message of strength throughout, despite lines such as 'Every now and then I wanna to throw my hands up in the sky'.

'On and on and on and on,' begins the next song, to the initial shock of recognition for the listener – before Erykah's gentle exhortation to 'wake the fuck up 'cause it's been too long' makes it clear that '...& On' is a continuation (rather than a repetition) of the famous *Baduizm* theme. 'What good do your words do if they can't understand you?' asks Erykah, making a strangely inverted question, and elaborating with the words 'Don't go talkin' that shit, Badu.' A comment on the critics who constantly ask her about the symbology of her songs, perhaps, or an acceptance that she is alone in her message and cannot easily be understood? Both valid points, of course.

'Cleva', which featured the exquisite talents of Roy Ayers on vibraphone (his scatted singing as he strikes the keys is clearly audible) is the next real high point of *Mama's Gun* after 'Penitentiary Philosophy', and its most obviously jazz-influenced song. Erykah memorably sets up the song by singing, 'This is how I look with no makeup and with no bra, my ninny's hanging down low, got a little pot in my belly now, and now a days my figure ain't so fly' and explained that, 'I want to concentrate more on my inside-pretty than my outside-pretty, because that's gonna go away. But if your inside is beautiful, it never wears away. The light always shows on the outside if you are striving to be good inside.' This classic Badu message is reinforced by the verse's claim that, 'I'm clever when I bust a rhyme, cleva always on ya' mind' – despite her physical failings (which are imaginary – in real life Erykah was as taut as ever), she promises that her mind is as sharp as anyone else's.

This is followed up by a 51-second vocal, flute and percussion jam called 'Hey Sugah', a sweet interlude which dies almost as quickly as it arrives, and ushers in the classic 'Booty', a song in which Erykah alludes to sexual prowess for the first time on record. A funk tune with some soul crooning and a bassline that pushes the stop-start conga-led beat along, its central premise is that Badu is the object of desire by 'ya nigga', but that she doesn't need him: 'You the one with all the money, And he knows my money's funny, But I don't want him', she remarks. Although the song initially seems like the bragging of an old-school MC, its message is actually both enlightened and tender, telling the sister that 'I don't want him, 'Cause of what he doin to you' and finishing off with the invocation that 'I hope you would have done the same thing for me too'.

'Booty' was likened by some to 'Tyrone', with some justification, but Erykah explained: 'Yeah, but [this] ain't no bad-man song… "Booty" is particularly dedicated to those people who are cheaters or those who are untrue, unrealistic. You know, I say in the lyrics, "Your booty might be bigger, but I can still pull yo' nigga, but I don't want him". And I say I don't want him, I don't want him if he ain't made no arrangement with you. And I see so much of that every day, where it's either we're supposed to be monogamous or we're not.' Not that pure fidelity is the only possible way to happiness, Badu reasons; after all, people make their own individual way in relationships. 'I mean, whatever the rules are in your relationship, you should go by that, that's what I'm saying. And I'm not saying it should be either way, but it's gotta be one way or the other. You know, if you make a decision, a pact with someone, your friend, you should say, I'm gonna do this, and you should stick to it.'

More direct references to physical love were contained in 'Kiss Me On My Neck (Hesi)', a song that would become a memorable high point of Badu's subsequent live shows, as she would present her back to the crowd and point to the back of her neck, to the watchers' delight. In the sleevenotes Erykah prefaces the song with a brief paragraph explaining what the Egyptian terms mean and including the line, 'I am a warrior princess from the other SUN'. The groove of the song stays focused throughout, with Erykah's hesi (her repeated mantra) of 'Breathe love in my air, use me, don't abuse me, love me, Cause these herbs are rare', a compelling command.

It's a driven, insistent song and, good as it is, the listener still welcomes the mellow groove of the spectacular 'AD 2000' which follows it. Despite being so easy on the ear, with its keyboard soundscapes and Erykah's delayed, ethereal vocals (which pan from left to right and back in spectral fashion), its message is the toughest of all. The song was inspired by the killing of an African immigrant, Amadou Diallo, at the hands of the New York City police, although she never mentions his name nor the circumstances of the incident other than to mention in abstract terms: 'Say, you won't be name'n no buildings after me, To go down dilapidated'. 'It was such an unsettling time, I felt justified in writing a song,' explained Badu. 'When I sat down to write it, I had no idea what I would say. Now I feel relieved about it every time I sing it. I feel like it's his words, coming through me.' It's a sad, brilliant composition, and among the most memorable on this or any other Badu album.

The most compelling evidence of Erykah's development as a songwriter between 1996 and 2000 lies in the fact that the songs on *Mama's Gun* are unflaggingly good. Although *Baduizm* contained several gems, its second half does not match up to its excellent first five or six songs, and – to my ears at least – loses momentum at that point. The last five songs on *Mama's Gun* are epic, either in scale or in impact: 'Orange Moon', which followed up the remarkable one-two of 'Kiss Me On My Neck' and 'AD 2000', is a seven-minute anthem on which Erykah revisits the calmer vibes of *Baduizm* high points such as 'Otherside Of The Game'. One of the slowest songs she has ever recorded, the pace is almost funereal, but the presence of exquisite backing vocals (N'Dambi adds a touch of excellence) and flute from D'Wayne Kerr make it a soul-jazz essential. The subject matter isn't immediately clear – Erykah sings that 'he said to me how good it is', which may be a reference to Seven, Dre or many other men – but it's a reflective, optimistic song and a definite coup.

Conversely, 'In Love With You' seems almost deliberately fashioned for the three-minute pop single format, although it wasn't released as such. A duet between Badu and Stephen Marley, it's a sparse, echo-laden song driven by a perfectly vibrant plucked Spanish guitar and a bass drone plus finger-snaps. In true Rastafari fashion, the separate singers are labelled 'lion' and 'lioness' in the booklet. Oddly, some reviewers thought that Stephen's vocals were an old recording of his late father's voice and derided the song as tasteless, but the truth is that it is nothing less than a love ballad of great beauty.

The familiar 'Bag Lady' was next, which Erykah revealed was the product of some musical history: a sample from Dr Dre's 'Xxplosive' appeared in the song, which itself had lifted sounds from Isaac Hayes' *Shaft* soundtrack. In context, the song remains a fine listen, but it isn't immediately obvious why it was chosen as the first single to be taken from *Mama's Gun*: an uptempo rocker like 'Penitentiary Philosophy' or even the super-mellow 'AD 2000' would have been more chart-friendly. However, it was a huge hit and set up listeners for the more diverse sounds that were contained in the album, warning them that Badu had taken a change of direction.

The semi-disco strings arrangement of 'Time's A Wastin'' harks directly back to Chic, Chaka Khan and to more recent hip-hop classics such as Soul II Soul's 'Keep On Movin''. It's another great song, and fuelled by an almost palpable sense of urgency, as Badu explained when asked who inspired her to write it: 'I have a brother who's 18 years old, and maybe it was him. He's the closest example of a young man who has idle time and doesn't know exactly what to do with it. Time's a wasting, keep on drifting, ain't no telling where you'll land. Where you running to? Where you running from? Kind of find out what you wanna do.' Warming to her theme, Erykah added, 'You know, it's important. Especially to young brothers. It's almost like a lot of black people in America, a lot of young black men, are born with this cloud over their heads. It's their penitentiary cloud, this philosophy we all have, that it's harder for us. There ain't no heaven, there ain't no hell. It's just weak or strong. Times of weakness, it feels like hell, times when you're strong, it feels like heaven. So you gotta just focus and take out all the demons in your range. There's nothing else you can do, just move forward, and quick.'

The album finishes with Erykah's most grandiose statement to date, a ten-minute, three-part opus called 'Green Eyes', in which she addresses her pain at losing an unnamed lover (we can presume she means Andre from what she later said about the song) for the first time on record. '"Green Eyes" is a song that everybody can probably relate to,' said Erykah. 'It's about when your heart is really broken. We put a lot of emphasis on relationships, to the point where often that's our whole life. But if your relationship ain't going right, your life is kinda wack. You can't fix it with a relationship, and I don't know all the answers or nothing like that, man, but I wrote that song in 1998, and I freestyled the whole song.'

The suite is split into three movements – 'Denial', 'Acceptance?' and 'The Relapse' – with each focusing on a different style of music. The first is pure jazz and, more specifically, pure Billie Holiday jazz: its first two minutes are a deliberately far-off, almost accidentally overheard snatch of piano balladry, with Erykah setting out her stall by intoning, 'My eyes are green, 'Cause I eat a lot of vegetables, It don't have nothing to do with your new friend'. 'Acceptance?' is much calmer and less anguished, with a strolling piano and lyrics of self-awareness the focus; meanwhile, 'The Relapse' ('We are people and we change, so we sometimes might fall back into the heartache,' said Erykah) is faster, higher-pitched and more vague, with Badu concluding that life is made up of pain as much as it is joy.

Reviewers loved the song's scope and asked her many questions about it. Surely writing and singing it was painful, asked one reviewer, to which Badu responded, 'No, because we didn't break up like that – in a way that we didn't agree with. We were just both very young, very much in love. In love enough to say, let's have a kid. Just too young to really decide, to really know what was best for us, for our highest good as a family.' However, it had been written at a time of deep personal turmoil, as she revealed: 'I wrote that song in December 1998 and that was shortly after Dre and I decided to separate. It took such a big toll on my emotions that I had to write about it. And Dre thought it was important that I write about it as well. He said, yeah, you should write about it so other people can feel what we feel and know how that feels, so they won't make the same judgment on themselves. So we thought that it was important as artists that we use our outlet, music, and pray that our freedom of speech and art will aid someone else's growth.' The healing process was done, she maintained: 'You go through all these stages of heartache and getting over it.' Andre had played a role in this, of course – 'The brother helped me through it is as much as he could,' she added. 'But that's something we have to do as adults. We can't make anybody else responsible for our feelings. I hope the song shares that bit of wisdom.'

The completion of the healing process was important to Erykah, and she made sure that interviewers knew about its progress – especially when she was asked about being a single mother. 'We are still together as a family. We are not a functioning couple, but we are a family. So therefore, I am not a single mother. My son has both a father and a mother who are very responsible.' However, she told the *Sydney Morning Herald* on 24 December 2000 that, 'It's a pivotal time in my life now. I'm 29 years old, looking at 30. I have a two-year-old son. I'm a single parent, never bought anything before that cost $100 [£70]. Where else do I go now?', so perhaps some self-definition remained to be completed at that stage. Some pain was still present, it seems: 'Even though we see each other very often, I feel a sense of loss. I went through so many changes, ["Green Eyes"] had to be a suite.'

The album's later pressings finish with a bonus track: the faster, more hip-hop-driven radio mix – the Cheeba Sac Mix – of 'Bag Lady', which was released as a single, although the CD booklet wasn't amended appropriately: 'Hey brothers and sisters there was simply no room on this CD for "Cheeba Sac Mix" – check website' appears before the original-mix lyrics, even after the bonus track has been added to the album. For all intents and purposes, however, it's 'Green Eyes' that closes the album...and in grand style, for the multi-part suite Erykah had devised as a way of expressing her pain was a deserved success.

So Erykah delivered the follow-up to *Baduizm*. As the first and second album of a relatively new artist, they are both immensely worthy of her pride – fully formed classic records that should endure for decades. And yet they are very different to each other: *Baduizm* is the concentrated essence of the messages Erykah had been trying to send for years, as a rapper and in Erykah Free. As she said, she had had her whole life to compose it, which meant that it was impassioned, but also meant that some of the sentiments on there were some years old, and not the words of the adult Erykah, perhaps. Conversely, *Mama's Gun* is a more mature work, the sound of a woman who has endured much and wants to express her pain and her longing in music. It also bears the stamp of many sophisticated minds – The Roots, Poyser, producer Vikter Duplaix and so on – while *Baduizm* was essentially the work of Erykah, Rob Free and (to a certain extent) Jaborn Jamal.

So which is the better album? It depends on your taste. *Baduizm* is much sparser than its successor, with Erykah keeping her cards hidden a little more carefully. She speaks in more abstract terms (it's one of the most symbol-reliant records ever made) and her persona is more confined to one role: that of oracle. On the other hand, *Mama's Gun* is a sprawling, wide-ranging sack of influences, joyously untrammelled and revelling in a looser, more relaxed feel than the début album. The overall vibe of both records shares some common features – spirituality, openness, freedom and so on – and they certainly use vintage influences to the maximum. But *Baduizm* is tight, and *Mama's Gun* is enjoyably loose, with *Live* a stepping-stone curio somewhere in between. Enjoy them both for what they are.

Engineer Chris Bell can provide a unique insight into the way Erykah works in the studio, as no other machine operator was present as constantly as he was, due to the lack of an overall producer (Badu used a series of guest producers and executive-produced herself). Working with her is an experience he enjoyed: 'Oh, it was a great time,' he affirms. 'She's really easy to get along with, and gives good direction. Actually I still have some cool stuff from the *Mama's Gun* sessions.' Is she tough to work with when she's under pressure? 'The label and management people keep tabs on what she's doing, to a point,' he explains, 'but she doesn't really like to be pressured, I don't think. And she takes longer to get things done if they do that to her'.

Bell – who has worked for over ten years with artists as disparate as The Roots, U2, Everclear and Oleander – found an obvious synergy with Erykah's actual recording methods. For starters, the improvisational nature of the jam sessions was always helped along by constantly rolling tape: 'What we would do is we would roll a DAT tape the entire time, and I'd have two-inch analogue 24-track tape ready,' he recalls. 'They'd come up with something, and Erykah would say, let me go home and sleep on this and I'd burn a CD off for her.' Badu would go home and sleep on her work, perhaps playing it for Seven's benefit. 'Then she'd come back and say, I like this section and this section. And then they'd create a song out of the grooves they'd created the previous day and we'd start rolling two-inch tape.'

Although Erykah clearly takes control of her recording – as Bell has explained – she is no control junkie, as is evident from the contributions she invites from the wealth of talent surrounding her. In life, as in art, it seems: 'If it's my life, it's good to be in control of it, and some people even call me a control freak,' she said, 'but I don't see anything freaky about controlling your own destiny, your own path, your own life. It's important.' However, in the case of *Mama's Gun*, the final product took a long time to perfect. 'Oh, man… [Every] song on this album has been recalled at least once or twice, because I decided to fit the music together, like a puzzle,' she explained. 'As a result, some of the songs were taken off the album, and most of the songs were shortened, because we only had 74 minutes to tell the story. We changed the order around several times until I was comfortable, until it was a convincing album to me. The [release date] was set back a couple of times. But I have faith. I know I did a good job. I worked very hard; so did everybody else.'

A *Spin* magazine writer was present at the very last moments of studio activity on *Mama's Gun*, and reported that 'wrapped in wool and smelling of essential oils, she squints at the computer, oblivious to her fatigued management's fidgeting and pacing. "We've got to add more crickets here!" she announces, referring to a break preceding one of the jazzy ballads.' It turned out that the courier had arrived to take the final tapes to be mastered and was waiting outside: 'Oh!' Badu exclaimed. 'I thought we'd missed the deadline and I could keep going! I guess we're done.'

Badu later revealed that the pressure to deliver hadn't bothered her unduly: 'I just didn't pay attention to the deadlines,' she said. 'They'd say, it's time, and I'd go, yeah, OK. Those were the label's dates, not mine.' Motown had originally wanted the album to appear three months earlier, in September, but Erykah wasn't so sure. 'Motown wanted me to make sure I knew the deadline,' she stated. 'But I go by the lifeline. They don't really understand as an artist that you just can't shout on cue. I do it when I feel it.' And yet her relationship with the revitalised soul label has always been a healthy one, even if a touch of commercial pressure has reared its head from time to time.

After mastering, Erykah went straight into a round of press interviews, telling German writer Michael Arens, somewhat breathlessly, that, 'Three days ago I finished the last two songs of the new album and mastered them on the same day. I didn't have time to hear them... [They] went directly from the studio to mastering. And that is hard, of course... I sat for six evenings in Electric Lady Studio with Jimmy the studio cat on the couch and finished all the work.' Some of the final stress, it emerged, had come from that infamous running-order change, but the track-listing needed to be right to set the right tone: 'It took a long time to place the songs in a particular order,' she explained, 'because they needed to communicate a particular mood. And the order of the songs on the album is just as important when you hear it [at home] as it is when you hear it live.'

The final track-listing was the right one, it seemed, and all her angst had been worth it, as she told *Jet*: 'What I am most proud of in this album is its sequence. It took a lot of thought. You can feel the energy of it... The artwork was done before the album was done. As a matter of fact, there was a deadline on the album, and since I don't go by deadline, I go by lifeline, it was not completed until it was completed.' Her fans would accept her apologies, she believed. 'The sequence and all the artwork was finished and turned in, and I just changed it. And I said, hey, just put it on the CD and the next run, we'll change it, and I will put a little apology, but people will understand. I never underestimate people's ability to understand. The lyrics were not completed either. I finished two of the songs the day of mastering. So, the artwork was gone already. So it will be in the next batch or on the website.'

'Second-album' syndrome, the dreaded fate that befalls so many successful début artists, was also a theme of these interviews. VH1 asked her, 'Three years is a while to wait for a follow-up. Why?', to which she responded somewhat tartly, 'If you think this album took me a long time, the first one took me my whole life. There's not really a time on art. The music industry agenda is to sell units and music's agenda is to make people feel good, better, different. So, however long it takes.' British DJ Trevor Nelson remarked that, 'It's always difficult to do a second album – did you feel any pressure?' and Badu agreed. 'Yeah, a little bit, because the label was worried and all that kind of stuff. I just tried not to think about it. But you know, it's always nerve-wracking a little bit, 'cause you kinda know what you wanna do. I don't know, I just never underestimate the audience's ability to dig what I'm doing, 'cause I'm representing them in a lot of senses.' She went on to discuss the art-versus-business contradiction in honest terms, saying that, 'Unfortunately, in the business I'm in, the agenda is to sell units, and a lot of times art doesn't really sell that many. But we have to take our chances. I do the art and they [the record label] have to put it in the best frame. You know, I do what's required from me. But in that I do try to meet the agenda of the business 'cause I'm in it, for me, for a reason. And I try at the same time not to compromise the art too much.'

Others wanted to know which song on *Mama's Gun* was the most personal. Erykah didn't hesitate to answer. 'They all are. Each one I had to take a lot of time on and make sure everything was right on it before I let it go. That's why it took so long... I was producing, as well as writing, as well as singing, and directing the video.' She was also asked if the burden of performing all these tasks had made this album a tougher one to complete than *Baduizm*: '[It was] definitely more complicated,' she reasoned. 'I mean, I was the one calling the shots, but I had a lot of people who were involved with playing music and coming up with ideas, and helping out and adding to the project. All the creativity had to come from me, which was very hard.' Added to this was the fact that Erykah can't read music, which makes the production role a little trickier: 'I don't read music or anything, so when I produce, I go basically by ear,' she admitted. 'So I'm not some super-hot anything.'

The skills that Erykah had gained as a video director and collaborator on other people's records had enabled her to manage the demands of different co-workers and find an acceptable balance, it seems. Co-producing *Mama's Gun* with veterans such as James Poyser and Vikter Duplaix, as well as managing the expertise of guests such as Roy Ayers, must have been something of a juggling feat, but one she had managed to pull off successfully. She explained how she had coped with so many co-workers: 'You shut down, kick everybody out, and make a good record. Everybody believed in me; they don't know what the hell I'm talking about half the time, but they tell me, just do it. They figure "she knows what she's doing" because I'm very confident. It's very hard for me to express my art, music, in words. I can't explain, so I have to just tell people, come back in a week, and you'll see what I'm trying to do, because I don't know the theory of music or anything. I just know how it feels.' In practical terms, this meant being prepared in advance: 'I come ahead of time with the melodies or the guitar line or the chord or the lyrics, and we build it from there. I lay out the fabric, and everybody else is the thread or the yarn or whatever we're going to use to put it together. Sometimes it's staples, sometimes it's raffia. Whatever we use to put it together, they provide me with that – the musicians, the background singers, the producers, the people that are really responsible for this thing. But all of this is my ideas; without them, it's nothing, nothing at all. I will be very honest with you: it's nothing I work real hard at, but it's hard work. Being in the music business, being a recording artist, *that's* what's hard, trying to keep your sanity as a human.'

Erykah had been lucky to work with such a diverse range of talents, she knew, but of them all, the person she had sought out to work with the most was Stephen Marley. 'Steve and I worked together a lot for the food drives that the Marleys have every year, the Marleys' birthday parties,' she said. 'They're like another family for me, an extended family. I mean, I love his voice, and I think it should be heard, basically.' And making this happen can be a strangely soulless affair, as she told the

South African *Sunday Times*: 'Recording in a studio is perfecting a moment in time, but performing is creating a moment. Recording is more like a job. I can listen to it and hear inconsistencies and make corrections. But with performing, I close my eyes and whatever happens is correct – it's right for that moment.' However, while Marley had provided much comfort spiritually, in practical terms it seems that James Poyser helped Erykah the most: 'James is the co-executive producer of the album. When I came to New York, he took care of me immediately. Now he is a good friend of mine. He produced "Otherside Of The Game" on *Baduizm* and played the piano on "Sometimes". At the time, when we began working together in my house in Dallas, he was always very considerate... I could not have made *Mama's Gun* without him. Not possibly.'

Despite the pressure of work and the stresses of the industry, Erykah had still managed to make the sleevenotes of her album spiritual and grateful. She included a poem in the booklet, of which a notable part read, 'Hopefully my music is medicine. Some kind of antidote for something or just to feel good, I love you all, I appreciate you and I do not take you for granted, I know that the music business is to sell units but my agenda will never change, to make you feel better happy sad or whatever you need. My music no longer belongs to me after I put it out. It is now yours, interpret it the way you will.' But this was no passive, do-what-you-will message – it was followed by a tract called 'The Warriors Reminder', which set out her stall with little compromise, including the lines: 'Warriors walk alone, I won't let my focus change. Taking out the demons in my range. That's MAMA'S GUN'. This time around, Erykah had kept her thanks list brief and to the point, too: 'I've shared many significant moments with many folks in this world and I don't take any of them for granted,' she wrote. 'Please keep that will strong everybody.' The album's last words were 'Thank you Seven for being patient with mama. You're a good son, Soldier.'

Erykah gave a revealing interview to the *Dallas Morning News* just as the album was about to be released, explaining the late arrival of the album with these words: 'When an album is alive, then I can put it out... I understand the record label's agenda is to sell units, but at the same time, I cannot compromise the art of the project.' It turned out that the big-hitting producers Babyface and R Kelly had offered to produce songs for the new album, but that Badu had turned them down: 'I respect their music,' she said. 'But it's not necessarily parallel to what I do.' Indeed – she was being modest with those words, as the slick R&B of those particular artists is universes away from her own organic sounds.

The rock approach was intentional, she said, and perhaps inevitable given that Electric Lady Studios (where notables such as Hendrix had recorded) was the environment. 'I caught the spirit of people who rock – and rock well – like Hendrix, like Stevie Wonder, who also played there,' she said. 'I said, let's do some kind of Pink Floyd-ish type music, and we just started jamming and it spun out of that.' She also admitted that she can occasionally overdo the preaching on her songs. 'I know I sound like a big self-help book,' she said.

Some of the success of the music came from the fact that her musicians were also church players, used to performing in an atmosphere of sermonising or prayer: 'The church players, they play it very free, because you don't have any music in front of you – and you are just kind of feeling the spirit of the people, so that's how they play,' she explained later on. 'My musicians have been playing with me from the very beginning. My drummer used to play with D'Angelo, but we all share a common creativity and bond, you know, between us, D'Angelo and The Roots and Common and Mos Def.' Of the obvious neo-soul link, she remarked: 'Besides we are a part of people who feel the same kind of music, you know, we come from different parts of the planet, but we all feel the same. So the band has been with me since I've started. You know, a few people come in and out and in and outside. It's like an eternal gig, an eternal jam session.'

But it was the title of the album that continued to provoke most questions, and Erykah never failed to repeat the evocative line, 'Most of the time, you don't even know your mamma have a gun – and when she pulls it out, and shows it to you, it's something serious', or words to that effect. The metaphor applied to the record, she said: 'Our sons and daughters are going to need something to take with them for protection. So they can put my album in they holster, or on they lap, or on they seat. It would be a better thing to have, you know?' The *Sydney Morning*

Herald wanted to know if the title meant her music was about peace or violence. 'Violence,' she said, before laughing. 'No, I'm only joking... [If] your mama pulled out a gun, mothers are not the kind of people who are just going to pull some kind of shit out for nothing. You pull it out because you mean it, and something serious is about to go down.'

This was the crux of the image, it seemed – the idea that, while others might produce a weapon for effect, a mother will only do it when the threat is real. 'When she pulls it out, she's going to use it; she's not gonna pull it out just to wave it,' warned Badu in yet another interview. 'Mama has more sense than that. What this means is that with everything that goes on in our society – children are dying, parents are killing themselves, people's spirits are just broken – then how about putting *this* in your holster? Stick *this* on your lap while you drive. Put *this* in the seat. Put *this* in the small of your back. *That's* why it's called *Mama's Gun*.' The final message was this: 'My words and my music are my weapon of choice. And as you grow, you need something to go out there with in the world and protect you. I urge folks to use my music and my words as they will, as they should, as they see fit.'

All this talk of weapons is interesting. Erykah had not used any sinister or aggressive imagery on her first record, and fans were taken a little aback by the title of *Mama's Gun*. After all the positivity of the *Baduizm* era, followers might have been expecting something more along the lines of *Mama's Baby* or *Mama's Pillow* – this sudden, unpredicted swing towards the cold image of a gun was not Erykah as they knew her. But she knew exactly what she was doing, and her choice says much about her.

In the three years since *Baduizm*, Erykah had fallen in and out of love and had her life completely reprioritised by the arrival of Seven. She had circumnavigated the globe, performed hundreds of shows, conducted innumerable interviews and appeared before hundreds of thousands, perhaps even millions, of people. She had had no easy ride, and perhaps it was time that she started to show her teeth a little...now she was a mother with a responsibility to protect, and wanted to show the world that she meant business. The mama with a gun could have been one of the matriarchs in her family, or it could well be Erykah herself. Of course, the gun was a symbol for a temper or a fist rather than an actual pistol, but a warning was being made all the same.

The music had been completed. The title had been explained. The picture was complete. But one question remained. Would the world respond to *Mama's Gun* as it had to *Baduizm*?

13 The Smoke Clears

Although Erykah Badu had always placed more faith in her fans and herself than in the reviews of critics, she had also been honest about the fact that a good response to her work gave her an ego boost – a brave admission to make, and not one that many artists would dare to attempt. And she had had her fair share of negativity, from those who found her bold spirituality unconvincing, her music uninspiring, or had simply found her fake dreadlocks wanting. 'Artists always try to impress the journalist or critic,' she told one interviewer. 'But often, the journalist is the artist – so they're gonna write what they want the audience to know. It's a gamble. All we can do is write good music and hope we're judged on that instead of our personal lives.'

This sensible approach had been hinted at in the *Mama's Gun* track '...& On', in which she had parodied some of the criticism that had come her way in the wake of *Baduizm*. She wasn't sure if the press's attitude towards her had changed in the interim. 'I don't know, because I've just come back out. We'll see by the next few interviews. The interviews aren't the public's opinion, but they become just that,' she reasoned. Wise words, and not the first she had expressed on the role of the press. As she so accurately observed, the public often first hears of an artist's work through the interpretation of a critic (who is often no more astute or tasteful than they are), so if the press dislike something or regard it as inferior to what came before, it doesn't matter how often an artists insists that 'reviews don't matter' because, unfortunately, people take them as a valid assessment of quality. The situation is often worsened by the existence of lazy or unprofessional writers (yes, there are a few) who do not take the trouble to review music fully or with due care and respect. This can make the artist's job a tricky one indeed.

Reviews for *Mama's Gun* were mostly positive – it's a finely crafted, inspirational album, after all – but not as awestruck as they had been for *Baduizm*, perhaps an inevitability, given the scene-shaping impact of the earlier record. Some months after its release, *Soul Express* asked if the new record had been as successful as the first: 'It has sold 1.4 million in the US,' she replied. 'So no, it didn't sell as much. This one didn't sell as much as the first two. The first two sold two million apiece, I think, although creatively I feel like this is a better piece of work. I don't know, the music business is very fickle, you never know, but I don't even think about that a lot, the sales.' But this did in fact dent her spirits a little, as she later told the South African *Sunday Times*: 'I worked really hard on *Mama's Gun*. I really felt I had something to prove. And when it came out I was very pleased with my work. But the commercial success in the United States was not as great as I'd expected, and I was down for a little bit and doubted its power... But when I started to tour again and saw all the people show up who knew the words, it was confirmation that the work is not always for commercial success. It's also for spiritual upliftment.'

Spiritual contentment became more and more important to Erykah after the release of her third album. It sold healthily and her fanbase stayed loyal, but her star was no longer in the ascendant of 1997 and 1998, and she was beginning to feel the jibes of the press a little more keenly than before. Asked by *HipOnline* what made her happy and what made her angry, she answered, 'What makes me furious – not just because we're in an interview – but I don't like when writers take your words and put them somewhere else, in the wrong context in their own article about you. Because it's personal, it's *your* personal life, and you're giving your time to help another human being further their career. And they write anything they want about you and I think it's mean. That makes me furious, and I see that happen to other artists, and I'm very sensitive to it.'

Her point about 'other artists' was a perspicacious one: the whole of the neo-soul movement had now grown to be a national force in American music, and the wider critical community had woken up to its strength. As more and more writers decided to take a stance on this slow-burning new music, more and more barbs began to fly – at Macy Gray for her husky 'untrained' voice, at Erykah for her self-confident Afrocentricity and at D'Angelo for his honest sexuality. But Badu retained a lot of human warmth and generosity in the face of this: 'What opens my heart is...oh, so many things, but one in particular is when my son wakes me up in the morning, nudging me and saying, mommy, mommy!' she said. 'That opens my heart. So many other things as well. Good tea. And the kind of warm energy you get from people when they don't expect you to be a superstar for everybody all the time. Where you can just sit down and not sign autographs for everybody. That makes me feel warm, and appreciated, not like I'm some workhorse or something.' Erykah loves her fans – but her fans have to show some affection of their own: 'Some people come up and ask for an autograph and don't even look at me. They're like, here, do it. That don't bother me, but it doesn't open my heart.'

As always, Badu took events into her own hands, launching a series of live shows in the rest of 2000 and the beginning of 2001 and evolving the performance to include a dance routine and a dash of rugged sensuality which audiences loved. Combining her set with *Baduizm* staples such as 'On & On', 'Appletree', 'Certainly' and 'No Love' and tracks drawn from *Mama's Gun*, which included 'My Life', 'Penitentiary Philosophy', 'Didn't Cha Know' and 'In Love with You', her concerts were full of high points. One of these was a section of modern dance accompanied by a solo flute or guitar; another was the aforementioned 'Kiss Me On My Neck', for which she stood with her back to the crowd (a courageous move alone) and exposed her neck, shoulders and back. At around this time she began removing her headwrap halfway through the show – to reveal a completely shaven head: this normally occurred around the time of 'Cleva' and its line 'This is how I look without makeup'. Erykah made a point of removing the headwrap, kissing it reverentially and placing it on her stage table alongside her candle and incense – and don't think that she or anyone else missed the symbolism of the action.

However, Badu stayed down to earth, neither diving into introspection after the relatively modest sales performance of her album nor expanding to fit her exaggerated stage persona. She was managing, it seemed, to retain a grip on reality and could even see herself fitting into the big picture. 'I was this amazing goddess from another planet when I first came around. Everybody was excited,' she told *Rolling Stone*, before alluding to the rise of the other neo-soul artists – 'Since I've been away, there have been about five or six!'

Note the 'since I've been away'. As we've seen, she had hardly been resting on her laurels since the press activity for *Baduizm* had died down, but she was perceptive enough to note that, in the public's eyes, if an artist isn't on TV or on the radio, then for all intents and purposes they are absent – even when their music is being played everywhere. Erykah knew perfectly well that she would have to work hard to make up for the lost ground that had gone (in commercial terms) to Jill Scott and Macy Gray. She might even have doubted that her audience was still there – but, as she said earlier, once she saw that the faithful were still arriving at her shows in their thousands, her faith was restored.

Of her shaved head, she explained to the *New York Times*, 'I wanted to do something brave, to just make way for new things.' She elaborated on this with the words, 'I wanted to be brave personally... Sometimes, we are guards to our own spirits. And I was looking to release my spirit. When you do something brave, that's often where peace comes from. As black women, we put so much emphasis on our hair. I wanted to free myself of all that.'

The rise and fall of all this activity and discussion reminded Erykah of what her life's work really is – the stage. 'I think if I was not able to sing and perform for people, I would die,' she said. 'I'm a starving artist; I'm hungry for the stage.' She explained that the difference between live and studio work is more profound than might be initially presumed: 'I used to feel a little afraid of microphones in the recording studio...because I'm a performer, you know, a stage performer. It was weird and odd, because it didn't sound like I sound now. So I had to learn how to record. It is a totally different thing. Recording in the studio is perfecting a moment, where when you are performing live you are just living a moment.'

This, perhaps more than any of her other explanations of her world-view, encapsulates most clearly the fact that, to Erykah, life is to be lived – fully, and now. Despite her belief in the cosmic wheel of reincarnation, she also places much value on the moment, which (in all its instantly lost glory) is something to be cherished. Apply this approach to the recording studio, where endless takes are required of the same moment, and her distaste for that environment becomes both logical and eminently understandable.

Perhaps her early aversion to the studio environment is linked to her general indifference to the fetishisation of machines that always takes place there. Erykah's official website, for example, is a remarkable piece of work – at the time of writing (summer 2002) it was full of beautifully animated features, including a 'quilt' made up of hundreds of images of fans, and had clearly been created with much thought and skill. And yet she revealed, well after the release of *Mama's Gun*, that she had never visited her own site to see what it is like: 'I've never seen it,' she admitted. 'I don't even have a computer, man! I'm a way behind. It's funny, because in 1997 the web was not booming – websites and all of that. And that's when I went out on the road, and I haven't been home yet, so I'm totally an analogue girl in a digital world, I promise. I don't have an email address yet, but I'm going to get into it. I think I'm going to get one of those pagers, yeah.'

However, the actual ambience of the studio was something Erykah *was* interested in, to an almost religious degree. She revealed that when she is in the Dallas area she records at the Palmyra studio, a venue located 8km (5 miles) into the woods, and which the owner built by hand out of scrap pieces of wood and tin. *Mama's Gun*, however, had been largely committed to tape at New York's Electric Lady Studios, which was previously owned by Jimi Hendrix, and physically as well as spiritually it was the perfect recording spot for Erykah: 'The walls are covered with paintings and collages of Electric Lady-looking stuff,' she explained. 'The booths are the same ones that Jimi, Stevie Wonder, Roy Ayers, and countless other people, a lot of legends, used. D'Angelo had just left the studio.' Of the atmosphere generated by the presence of such greatness, she observed that, 'You feel it. I don't know exactly how to explain it, but you feel the music, and sometimes, when I didn't have an idea, it would come from someplace, and [melodies] would just come out the air.'

A key role on the record had been played by the respected producer Vikter Duplaix, who explained how he had come to begin working with her: 'When we started Erykah's album, we flew to Dallas and literally started working on it in her living room. She had an old, beat-up piano; her son, Seven, had a baby drum set. She was in the process of putting a studio in her home.' But he added that Badu was prone to receiving flashes of inspiration at mundane moments when she was cooking or watching television – when they would quickly commit the results to paper or tape. The results were, as we've seen, inspired, and Erykah was almost beatifically reluctant to attribute either its style or its success to anything other than fate. 'I love that music, and I wouldn't say it was an accident... I would just say it's just natural. That's the way I feel.'

In early 2001 Erykah released a second single from *Mama's Gun* – the excellent 'Didn't Cha Know', which also featured a video of her newly bald head for the first time on sight to the general public. The new round of interviews to promote the song saw a more cautious Badu responding to her interviewers – she said at one point that, 'So many positive things have been said [about me] that I'm waiting for the negative article... Maybe I'm going to have to do something bad now to remain popular.'

She certainly didn't feel the need to do the journalists any favours. Thor Christensen of the *Dallas Morning News* was one of those who felt the edge of her 'erratic' scheduling, waiting four hours for her to arrive at the Palmyra complex in the Texan backwoods. 'Erykah Badu is almost four hours late for her interview, but don't call out the bloodhounds just yet,' he wrote with an ironic tone. 'After all, the Dallas singer has taken almost four years to put out the follow-up to *Baduizm*, the 1997 debut CD that transformed her into the cosmic princess of the neo-soul movement.' Christensen wiled away the time by talking with Chris Bell, who was also awaiting her arrival ('You never know with her,' said the engineer tolerantly) and Ward White IV, who was now working with Erykah under the title of 'manager-attorney' and who recalled with some humour that, 'She drove the record company crazy.'

Thor didn't blame Erykah for being late. He knew what pressures she was under, and she later explained that juggling all her commitments was a mammoth task: 'writing and singing [is] the easy part compared to trying to pull everything together in my life,' she said, 'juggling being the mother of a young son, while producing the album and directing the video and being a famous black star'. Add to this innumerable requests to perform charity work (the day after the interview, she was scheduled to fly to Washington DC to play an AIDS benefit show) and the organising of an imminent US tour, and the Badu workload was heavy indeed at this point. 'People expect a whole hell of a lot from me all the time, and that's hard,' she told him. 'The one thing I don't like is I don't have much privacy… Even when I'm driving on the freeway, people be swerving trying to hand me something – CDs, demos, phone numbers…anything.' At least Seven would never let her down, and seemed to be enjoying his role as celebrity infant: 'He sees a camera and stops and strikes a pose. He knows what's happening,' Erykah said. 'He was born a rock star baby'.

Despite the stresses, Badu was still enjoying the pleasures of fame and fortune, it seemed. She added, 'I love the awards and the props and the love from fans. It feels good. But I'm trying not to get caught up in getting my ego stroked too much.' In fact, her family was as crucial to her mental well-being as they had ever been. 'Dallas is the best place for me, because here I can keep good people around me and keep the focus on doing music that comes from my heart,' she said. 'Whenever I get a little spoiled or get an attitude, my grandma catches me and says hey! You better straighten up. And then I'm over it real quick.'

In December 2000 *Ebony* magazine paid Erykah a rare tribute: they wrote about her beauty. Not traditionally a subject for the glamour pages of the tabloids, Badu was usually respected for spirituality and her lyrical acuity rather than her looks, although she does possess a remarkable face with noble features. The magazine wrote with unexpected poignancy that, 'Slight of body, Badu doesn't overwhelm physically; she envelops. With her mile-high head-wraps and her funky Bohemian style, Badu's botanical beauty is understated but powerful. Some say her beauty radiates from her eyes, but most agree it comes from her aura, her center. She's on Badu time, and only she knows for whom her bell tolls.' It was with clear judgment that the writer added a mention of Erykah's apparently otherworldly self-confidence: 'Badu is taking her time, Badu time. "You have to take care of you and not feel forced," she says. "Because when you start feeling forced to do stuff, that's when it's not fun any more." She believes in taking care of herself. She is a vegetarian who says her beauty secrets are simple – she eats healthy and drinks lots of water to cleanse the skin from the inside out.'

All sectors of society were beginning to take notice of Erykah Badu as 2000 became 2001, it seemed, and it was with a certain sense of balance that she temporarily abandoned her adult audience for a guest spot on that children's institution – *Sesame Street*. Her appearance revolved around a song she sang called 'Friendship' with the puppet characters Elmo, Baby Bear, Zoe and Rosita. In true *Sesame Street* style, the scriptwriters included one or two sly digs at her, which only adults were likely to understand – after she tells the puppets her name, Elmo asks, 'Oh, the "a-jiggy, jiggy, yee-yo-yee-yo, what ya gonna do" Erykah Badu?' Baby Bear also pokes gentle fun at her headwrap, saying, 'But we've never been friends with anyone who...well, who wears what you're wearing on your head.' The song is a mellow, nursery-rhyme-like ballad that includes the lines, 'Doesn't matter what you wear, Or what's in your hair, If you're three furry monsters, Or a brown baby bear, We're all friends' (after which two of the puppets exit and return wearing miniature headwraps themselves) and concludes with the lines, 'Let's be friends, Talking with my friends, Won't you be my friend, Friendship, Talking 'bout friendship'.

Sentimental? Perhaps. But Erykah wouldn't care about that. When your world-view is based on real emotion, an appearance on a TV show as securely cosy as *Sesame Street* makes a lot of sense. Two decades after Erykah and her sister had practised their backyard raps back in Dallas, here she was again, singing a happy, nonsensical song with only peace as its message. Perhaps the wheel had come full circle at last?

14 Milestones

Although more reviewers commented negatively on *Mama's Gun* – and on Erykah Badu's entire stance – than had reacted badly to *Baduizm*, Erykah was starting to relax a little. Her place in the world was more stable now than it had been during those heady days of 1997 – after all, she was approaching 30, her child was growing up healthily, the pain of the split with Dre was passing and (perhaps most importantly), as 2000 passed, she was no longer alone musically. A whole raft of neo-soul queens were selling records, and people were no longer raising their eyebrows in surprise at the sound of the genre. At last, Badu had found her people.

The rise of neo-soul in general can be equated with the rise in 'Philly soul' in particular. Always a hotbed of classic talent, the city of Philadelphia had experienced a rise in the numbers of new soul artists coming out of its clubs and record labels since the mid-1990s, most notably with King Britt's 1998 concept album *When The Funk Hits The Fan* and Lauryn Hill's enormously successful *The Miseducation Of...*, released on the local Ruffhouse label. This was followed up by the rise to prominence of the Soulquarians team, focused on the organic composing and production skills of The Roots: producer/organist James Poyser was tweaking the faders for D'Angelo, Mos Def and Common as well as Badu, and stamping his own identity clearly on the neo-soul scene. In 1999, the Philly International label began releasing material by new artists for the first time in a decade – another sign of the city's creative rebirth. Nor was it confined to soul. Philadelphian hip-hop and house music was also on the rise, building on the 1980s tradition of local rappers such as Cash Money and Schooly D, with a prominent artist, Last Emperor, saying of the surge in Philly-based talent that 'It was always there, but it was untapped.' Even pure pop comes from the city – female artist Pink is a local resident.

Perhaps most relevantly in Badu terms, Jill Scott is also a Philadelphian, and as the year passed it seemed that Badu was constantly being asked about her. Asked by Trevor Nelson, 'What's your relationship with Jill Scott like?', Erykah said, 'I like her style, and her flow. Her perception of me coming first is that I poked a hole in a dam and everybody else got a chance to flow on through.' *HipOnline* asked, 'You don't see any competition between yourself and someone like Jill Scott?', and Badu responded evenly, 'Naw. I mean, we help each other... We talk all the time. I think what makes people think that is because of things people write. It really doesn't have anything to do with the artist. We don't feel like that at all.'

Strong words, although she also revealed that the gossip can be fatiguing at times: 'Sometimes if we're feeling weak at the moment, and I'm reading Jill Scott is like Erykah Badu, or Jill Scott reads that, as humans you feel like, "Awww..." and you get mad at the artist. But you have to remember, it's all a formality. It's just the way the music business is. So we try to encourage one another. "Come on, don't fall into that," you know?'

Of Philadelphia in general, Erykah later said, '[In] Philly they have some kind of real energy that's waiting for you... Pretty much Philadelphia used to run soul music back in the '70s and '80s, so that we didn't have a choice really...it's just a part of our history.' New soul artist Bilal also sees the city as a unique pool of music, saying: 'It has its own particular thing. I can hear something off the bat and be like, oh, that's from Philly. Like when I first heard Erykah Badu's "Otherside Of The Game", I knew that was James Poyser playing keyboards. Or, that's Ahmir on drums. I know Philly.' Asked if The Roots are in charge of the scene, he explained, 'I don't want to say that they can control it in Philly, but they have a large following, and a lot of people who look up to them. They really hit the scene like the Marsalis brothers. When the Marsalis brothers hit the jazz scene, a bunch of young kids wanted to play jazz. That's basically where I came out of. When the Roots started playing instruments, a lot of young kids in Philly said, man, *we* wanna play now. Philly has always been big on the church scene. I met James Poyser in church, because he was a church organist. A lot of church musicians just went hip-hop after they saw the Roots!'

A feature of the neo-soul movement, whether based in Philly or across the nation, is that the artists involved in it are often politically active. Although Badu has rarely expressed a party-political bias (asked by *Soul Express* what she felt about the policies of her fellow Dallas resident George Bush Jr, she said, 'I don't know. No comment'), she made an appearance at a Democratic Convention at around this time alongside Def Jam's Russell Simmons and Common, at which the artists (Simmons in particular) spoke about the importance of being politically active and aware. However, that sole appearance seems to have been her single support of party-aligned politics, although she has often appeared at marches and protests supporting individual cases.

Now resettled in Dallas's Lake Highlands district near White Rock Lake, Erykah was spending a lot of time in early 2001 on having a new house built. It was designed by a local architect, Jamie M Rohe, and was a renovation of a 517 sq m (5,563 sq ft) brick, stone and slate house, originally built in 1949. Building the nest was at the top of her list of priorities at this time, it seemed, after the flurry of activity that had accompanied the release of *Mama's Gun*: she told one interviewer in January that, 'I am dating my music right now. I am in love with my music and my son right now – and myself. I'm kind of moving on through. I am not in a rush to jump right into a relationship... That's not necessary for me to be happy. All I need around me is good people, good friends, good healthy food and my child. That makes me more than happy.'

A milestone was approaching – Erykah would be 30 in February – and she had much to say on the matter. 'When I was 25, I couldn't wait to be 30,' she said. 'I thought, I'm cold now, I'm a be real cold when I'm 30. No matter where you are in life, how much money you have, how much success you have, it's always a scary thing because there's this myth of the unknown. I suspect I won't feel different than I did a day before, but I'm very grateful for all the lessons that I have carried with me to 30. Revolutions around the sun.' Like many people at this time of life, she perceived that her development was about to reverse itself in some ways: 'And I'm growing younger and younger. From 30 on, you kinda regain your innocence it seems like. Thirty's nothing. You ain't did nothing. You seen 30 summers. As far as youth is concerned, it's the same mind really.'

Erykah had survived the roller-coaster ride of becoming a celebrity with her world-view intact, it seemed, and as always she knew where she was in life. Asked by a male interviewer, 'Are you where you expected to be when you were a teen, looking ahead to your far-off thirties?', she answered, 'I just wanted to be here. You a man, that's different. We women raised playing with dolls and playing house and all that. So it's a little scary. Women try to rush to have kids and get married and stuff, because we're competitive people. Because of how society sets it up, or just how nature is.' Not that her coming of age was unimportant. She had been considering life's progress for some time, it seemed: 'It's confusing because you try to be in a certain place by the time you're 30, mentally, spiritually. We're still babies, but you have this grown-up body. You're not mentally, and spiritually where you would imagine a grown-up should be, and are you ever? Are you *ever*?'

A wise question, and one that Erykah might have answered with the oblique observation that, in her case at least, learning was the key to life, and wanting to keep on learning the crux of all progress. She demonstrated this by taking up piano lessons – or at least making enquiries towards setting them up – with the well-known piano teacher Weldon Irvine, who revealed in an interview at this point that Badu and Doug E Fresh were interested in joining his list of celebrity clients, along with Q-Tip of A Tribe Called Quest and Common. Irvine, a veteran composer and artist in his own right (he co-wrote the classic 'To Be Young, Gifted, And Black' with Nina Simone, his songs have been covered by Donny Hathaway, Aretha Franklin, Jamiroquai and Freddie Hubbard among others, and had been sampled by KRS-One and Ice Cube), made the astute remark that, 'As these hip-hoppers get more proficient with jazz, they are going to start making all instrumental songs and improvising on their instruments. That's going to blow a lot of people's minds.'

This comment put in microcosm two neo-soul processes that had been going on for some while. First, the increasing 'realness' (as purists would have it, at least) of much of the genre's new releases was a reflection of the move away from a reliance on studio technology that had been taking place in the 1990s. Artists such as Seal and Lenny Kravitz had been insisting for some years that real instruments and vintage recording hardware makes for better results than computers (without many people taking them seriously, it must be said), but it was only now that these claims were gaining much popular support. And, as musicians and producers turned once again to old-school instruments (and the super-talented session players whose skills were required to play them), Erykah found herself among the wave of musicians who needed to brush up musically – and fast. Hence the piano lessons.

Second, boundaries between genres of popular music were blurring more rapidly in the late 1990s than at any point since the late 1960s. The idea of veteran hip-hopper Doug E Fresh (whose chief claim to fame, remember, had been the invention of the 'human beatbox' technique in the early 1980s) signing up for piano tuition at the hands of a soul legend would have been ludicrous even ten years earlier – he would have been accused of ostentation or even arrogance. Now, however, the fact that soul had merged with hip-hop, which had merged with jazz, which had merged with rock – and so on – made it necessary for him and many others to go back to school, so to speak. It was an exciting time, and one we are all privileged to have witnessed.

Piano lessons aside, after a short break for house-building duties, it was back to work for Erykah Badu, who announced a tour (the Mama's Gun Tour) of the US and Canada for February and March. The tour started on 6 February with a webcast from the Universal Amphitheater in Los Angeles and finished a month later with a triumphant homecoming show at the Bronco Bowl in Dallas – and this time around, there were one or two differences about the shows.

The Mama's Gun Tour was a full-scale rolling affair, with support slots going to neo-soul boys Common, Bilal, Musiq Soulchild and Talib Kweli at different stops of the outing. Most of these had some product available at the time, which made the concerts a must-visit for most fans;

in fact, Common and Erykah's 'The Light' remix was still in heavy radio rotation, which kept the profile of both artists very healthy. Unlike Badu's early live shows, these dates saw Erykah much more animated on-stage and approaching the concerts with an almost religious fervour. Just before the tour commenced, she told *Jet*, 'The Creator has given me a tremendous gift, and I feel that I have a responsibility since I've been given the platform to use my creativity for the Creator. I guess my religion is art because I do the Creator's work through my art.' Obviously thinking of her reputation as a preacher, she reasoned, 'You have to pull the soapbox out sometimes because the Creator doesn't give you a platform to stand on to show off your clothes. I try to find positive ways to do that without making people think that I'm judging, or that I think I know something, because I don't know anything.'

This new devotion showed in the concerts. Thor Christensen at the *Dallas Morning News* thought she was much more collected – especially when she removed her headwrap to reveal her shaven head. 'She was no longer hiding behind a prop,' he explains, 'because in a sense, when you wear a gigantic headdress like that, it is something of a mask. And when you're confident enough to take it off and say OK, here I am, do you still like me without my mask, that is a bold step.' He witnessed her show in Cleveland and wrote that, 'On her first few tours, Erykah Badu played the role of neo-R&B ice queen – a steely-eyed, statuesque performer who kept her emotions wrapped inside her towering headdress. But there's finally a new Badu in town. Forty minutes into the first show of her US tour on Saturday night at the Allen Theater, the Dallas singer unveiled a warmer, wackier and much more engaging persona.' About time too, it seems: 'She's been preaching a message of self-love and individuality since her 1997 debut, *Baduizm*. But on Saturday, she finally seemed to be listening to her own advice,' he added.

The removal of the headwrap was a key moment: 'Fittingly enough, her new character came alive the moment she took off her trademark headdress during "Cleva" to expose – voilà – the baldest scalp this side of Isaac Hayes. After four years of wondering what mysterious 'do lurked beneath her ever-present wrap, fans might have been let down by the sight of a chrome-dome Erykah: imagine staring at an elaborately decorated Christmas present for weeks, only to rip it open and find nothing but a box full of air. But the sold-out crowd of 2,500 greeted the unwrapping ceremony as a moment of celebration. Fans shrieked and cheered and jumped up from their seats – some even sprinted to the stage for a closer look.'

The change in Erykah was more than skin-deep, of course, and he noted that her act had been injected with a dose of unexpected vitality: 'As soon as the head-wrap vanished, so did her inhibitions, and she morphed from subzero Zen hipster into an endearingly madcap performer who cracked jokes, spun witty tales and did whatever she could to get a rise out of the audience.' Christensen also took evident pleasure in relating an incident in which Erykah stopped her band in mid-song, walked over to a mike stand that was blocking her view, threw it to the floor and returned to her position to restart the song. 'She then calmly returned to her perch and restarted the song as if nothing had happened,' he wrote. 'It was a hilarious bit made even better by her actor's sense of perfect timing.' Add to this Erykah's introduction of a complex dance routine to the show ('During... "Orange Moon" she kicked off her four-inch-high [10cm-high] white platform boots and spun ballerina-like up a flight of stairs to a stage riser') and the astounding vocal acrobatics she introduced to some of the songs ('But even more dramatic were the segments where Ms Badu shot unexpectedly into raging vocal crescendos, as she did in "Penitentiary Philosophy"') and it seems almost as if Badu had experienced some kind of rebirth as a performer.

Possibly Erykah was happier with her on-stage technical set-up, which had been revamped recently and may have allowed her to relax a little more. In one of the rare instances of commercial endorsement that she has agreed to, she told Gregory DeTogne (a writer employed by the Shure microphone company, who provided her with monitoring equipment) that 'I started using [Shure's] PSM systems back in '97, out of necessity really. I'm fond of wearing big head-wraps on-stage, as you know, and they cover my ears. The only way I can really hear myself is with in-ear monitors.' In this case she was referring to the company's in-ear monitoring system: 'When I first got my ears, I wasn't used to performing in big spaces,' she said, adding that, 'They all sounded so different acoustically. Once I plugged in with the PSM system, everything was consistent night after night. With my ear molds in, the sound of the music is like every note is right inside of my head. When I used wedges, sometimes I couldn't hear myself, so I would sing louder and still not be able to hear if my pitch was right or not. I like to have control over what comes out of my mouth. That's a lot easier to do when I can hear clearly.' However, the conversation wasn't all dry technicalities. Asked by DeTogne, 'Are you the bridge between all audiences?' (a good question), she responded with imagery she had used many times before: 'Could be. One thing I know is that I am one of the midwives aiding in the rebirth and process of music, and I never underestimate the audience's ability to feel that. Each night, I give them my all, and they give it all back, no matter what happens.'

Unlike many artists, Erykah has never endorsed many commercial products, but those that do get her nod are worth having. She was quoted as saying of a moisturiser called Carol's Daughter's Jamaican Punch Cocoa Butter Body Jam that 'I don't know how they're formulating Carol's Daughter in the lab, but be careful, it's addictive.' As for Shure, her decision to sign an endorsement deal for some of her stage equipment is just the sensible choice – their SM58 mike has long been acknowledged as an industry standard, just as many top guitarists will choose a Gibson or a Fender.

The tour was as rewarding for the artists as it was for the fans. Support artist Musiq Soulchild was ecstatic about getting the opportunity to tour with his idols: 'It's crazy because I'm a fan. And now I'm a peer. For me to work with Erykah Badu, D'Angelo, Common, Mos Def or The Roots it's like, "Yo, I only listen to your records every damn day"... All this stuff is real new. Taking this shit in is real crazy. You're not used to this shit and now it's all you know.' Not that the young artist's plan was to achieve success by working with other names: 'I love collaborating with people, but I want to make a name for myself,' he noted perceptively. 'First time out you really need to establish yourself as an artist... A lot of artists nowadays don't really milk their potentials. Relying on somebody else's star power – that's not cool. Doing it just because you know you'll get props off having somebody dope on your shit – that's wack.'

A brave comment, given the current trend for collaboration at the time (and his membership of the Soulquarian artists' collective), but then Musiq never held back on his opinions. On the subject of the 'neo-soul' label, he was quick to point out that, 'I'm not a fan of that title. How can you call it neo-soul? It's a renaissance. It's a following within tradition, a revolution and a movement that's being cultivated.' Categories notwithstanding, he recognised the power that these artists possessed. 'I give mad respect to D'Angelo, Lauryn Hill and Erykah,' he said. 'We're a minority right now, but in a minute we're about to take things over.'

Roots drummer Ahmir '?uestlove' Thompson was even more vocal than Musiq about Erykah's performance. After the Radio City Music Hall show in New York on Valentine's Day, he told one reporter, 'Just watching her last night has made me wanna step up my game tenfold... Seriously I'm trying to figure out, when was the last time The Roots went on-stage without rehearsal and just winged something so convincingly? I think that one of the hardest things in the world is to go on-stage and not know what you're gonna do,' he mused. Erykah's leadership skills make her unique, he thought: 'I've not seen a female bandleader handle that, not really, and I've seen many a female bandleader: Sheila E, Me'Shell NdegéOcello. That's a hard thing to do. Last night, she truly demonstrated that.'

Quality endures, it seems, and in February 2001 the Grammy selectors nominated Erykah for two awards – in the Best Female R&B Vocal Performance and Best R&B Song categories, both for 'Bag Lady'. The song also received a *Soul Train* nomination for Best Female R&B/Soul Single. The industry were obviously still on her side as a solo artist, although whether the awards committees will ever formally acknowledge the work of the Soulquarians (with whom she was spending much creative time at this juncture) is another matter. The collective performed a show together in February at the Transit Club in Philadelphia to celebrate the birthdays of Ahmir Thompson and James Poyser. Artists included Erykah, Common, Talib Kweli, The Roots, Floetry, Lady Alma and Philly MC Bryan Banks, but the bill was so fluid – with artists constantly putting in cameos on each other's performances – that the event resembled a jam rather than a concert. Erykah's saxophonist, Jacques 'Pepe' Swarzbart, kept the house band together to allow the lead artists to come and go. Thompson said before the show that, 'This event, to me, is the celebration of the cream of the crop that comes from Philadelphia... I feel like Philadelphia is the [leader] when it comes to new soul, or next soul, or neo-soul, or whatever.' Badu herself guested with Common on 'The Light', before performing 'Bag Lady' with a bag hanging on her back, which she later revealed contained an African cloth doll. Her set closed with 'Booty', during which she asked the crowd to give up some birthday vibes by 'screaming for the birth of these two brothers'.

The Soulquarians (sometimes referred to simply by the group name of Soulquarian) are evidently a tightly knit unit. Erykah told VH1 that the idea is to help each other out when necessary: 'I work with every member of Soulquarian,' she explained. 'If someone needs some vocals, they call Erykah. If they need a drummer it's Ahmir. If you need some horns, it's Roy Hargrove. Need someone to put a beat together? That's Jay Dee. Some keys? It's James Poyser. We all just work together well. That's our little crew, and we love it. And there's D'Angelo, of course, when we need vocals, chords, and arranging – and Common with the lyrics.'

Meanwhile, the Mama's Gun Tour was rolling on, with critics noting Erykah's renewed sense of humour during the shows (at one show she saw a front-row guest asleep, told the people next to him to 'wake his ass up' and made him stand throughout the whole of 'Orange Moon') and the strange fact that her lack of hair made her seem more, not less, regal. Writers were not slow to draw the parallel between her bare scalp and the naked emotion of her songs, either, and some found the open honesty of 'Green Eyes' and the spartan angst of 'AD 2000' a profound experience when witnessed live. Backstage reports were interesting, too – Shure writer Gregory DeTogne wrote that, when Erykah's 30th birthday came around, her backing band organised a stripper for her, which she endured with good humour and no little unease: 'It's payback time for Erykah Badu,' he wrote. 'Seated in a big, overstuffed chair and surrounded on all sides by birthday gifts from well-wishers, she is more than mildly embarrassed by the gyrations of a male stripper seductively wriggling out of his clothes in front of her. Nervously casting her big, soulful brown eyes from side to side in an effort to avoid all which is being made obvious, she nonetheless plays the good sport, sheepishly bobbing her head to impromptu striptease music coming from keyboards and congas on the backline.' He also pointed out that, 'Badu's birthday strip-o-gram was arranged as a reprisal for all the times she's done the same for members of her band', and that Erykah had told him that she was enjoying life even more at this stage than after the success of *Baduizm*.

One of the reasons for this may well have been that a relationship was starting between Erykah and her Soulquarian friend Common. In May 2001 rumours of a romance began to fly after Common was seen in New York City's Greenwich Village, apparently shopping for wedding rings. 'We asked him if he needed anything, and we showed him around,' said the rather indiscreet sales staff at one store. 'But he didn't [buy] anything. He didn't say much. He kept it real quiet, he wanted to be incognito.' The gossip really started flying after this, with some magazines even suggesting that Common had already proposed to Badu, that she was pregnant by him and even that Common had changed his mind about marrying her.

Journalist Jancee Dunn put matters to rest by asking Erykah, 'Care to address the rumor that you are pregnant with Common's child?', to which Badu answered, 'He's one of my best friends in the world, and from my planet it's OK for a boy and a girl to be good friends without being in an intimate relationship. It's OK. We're both surprised every time we hear something like that, but we just kind of laugh. Sometimes we want to add to the rumor – we were saying about the pregnant rumor, we were just going to have all the Soulquarians call and say, "No, I'm the daddy!"; "No, I be the pappy"!' However, the rumour mill can be more than merely amusing, she said: 'Those things hurt people, especially when all you do is go to the store and come home every day, and then you read in the paper that you did this or you did that.'

Elsewhere she said, 'We are the best of friends, Rashied Lynn Common is a beautiful person. Sometimes we all laugh, all of us on the whole crew. We get a lot of fun off signs that say "Common heart Erykah" on my wall when I walk into the dressing room. Any news is good, any publicity is good publicity, it doesn't bother us. It don't affect the way I walk through life with him or anyone else. It's a rumor, but that's my boy.'

No one stopped gossiping, of course, but no concrete statement came from either artist for some time and life went on for both of them. 30 May 2001 saw the start of the Soul Beach Music Festival, a five-day, three-stage event in Miami's Orange Bowl that featured as its headliners three neo-soul queens – Angie Stone, Jill Scott and Erykah – and also included Eric Benet, Musiq Soulchild and The Isley Brothers. The event was a great success but was overshadowed by another show at which Badu performed two weeks later: a charity concert organised by Prince at his Paisley Park studios in Minneapolis. The show lasted seven days and was similar in ethos to an event the singer had held the previous year (immodestly titled 'Prince: A Celebration'), designed to celebrate the taking-back of his 'old' name of 'Prince' (he had spent several years trying to convince fans and press to call him The Artist). Fans paid $70 (£50) for a week-long pass, which gave them access to the normally off-limits Paisley Park complex and the chance to listen to his new album, *The Rainbow Children*. The evenings saw concerts featuring Badu, Common, Nikka Costa and Alicia Keys, and celebrations went on late into the night with after-show parties held at a nearby sound stage.

Working with Prince – nothing less than a deity in the eyes of most fans of black music in the late 1980s and most of the 1990s – was a seminal experience for Erykah Badu. 'It was amazing,' she said. 'I went to Paisley Park about three weeks ago and I performed with Prince.' The maestro had even played live with Badu, stepping in as rhythm guitarist for 'Penitentiary Philosophy'. ('I really can't describe it in words,' she added. 'It was amazing.') The final icing on the cake came when Prince and his band, the New Power Generation, played two midweek shows at the Xcel Energy Center in nearby St Paul – and Prince elected to perform a cover of Erykah's 'Didn't Cha Know'. Little wonder that Badu had no words to describe how she felt.

The involvement of Prince in the story of Erykah Badu is fascinating. Although received wisdom has it that his judgment had been slightly off-centre since his music moved away from straight funk-pop tunes to more abstract grooves and eccentric noodling (with predictable commercial consequences) in the mid-1990s, the former Prince Rogers Nelson had always had an eye for a talented co-writer, working with those artists he deemed stood out from the rest of the pack. The fact that he had called in Erykah to perform at his concerts was a compliment like few others. Perhaps more than any tribute (and there had been many recently, including one from crooner extraordinaire Tony Bennett, who had publicly told Badu that Billie Holiday would have enjoyed her work), this was one for Erykah to treasure.

An important question now is this: what can Erykah do in the future? At first sight there seem to be no end of possibilities for her by which she can extend or consolidate her currently global profile. As we've seen, her portfolio of talents is an impressive one, which means that she can choose one of many directions to follow.

Obviously Erykah will continue to make music. But how will her music change as the years pass? Much of the answer depends on how her personal self-development progresses: after all, she is only 31 at the time of writing, and has decades of artistic activity ahead of her if she so chooses. Perhaps some of the answer also depends on how musical tastes evolve; after all, neo-soul is in a state of healthy vibrancy at the moment, but the wheel of fashion turns both unpredictably and erratically, meaning that this year's deeply cool, retro-flavoured sound is tomorrow's unoriginal old hat. However, it's probably safe to assume that she will continue to make heartfelt, soul-influenced music with the emphasis on flavour over technique and emotional content over lyrical cleverness. She will also be an in-demand vocal collaborator for some time to come, as long as the current trend for high-profile duets continues.

Erykah may well also extend her activities in the field of production. Already in possession of some finely honed console-tweaking skills, it's likely that more and more artists will ask her to shape their music as her status as a backroom worker grows to match her role as front-line artist *per se*. With her influences stemming from the opposite worlds of hip-hop (hard-core beats) and soul/jazz (sweetness and atmospherics), she should be able to finesse the work of all sorts of people. Her fans must be eager to hear the results.

Logically, Erykah may also move into the role of record label chief. Many artists sink their financial gains into a personal record label, with Curtis Mayfield and The Rolling Stones right through to Oasis and Limp

Bizkit all memorable examples. What kind of music she might support is open to conjecture, but it's a fair bet that she would focus on developing talent that major labels might not deem commercial enough. Undoubtedly she would have to balance the public's perception of her as a mellow jazz artist with the bands she chose to sign – because the idea of a neo-soul singer recording neo soul acts, for example, might not raise sufficient interest. However, as we have seen, Badu can boast both an astute marketing awareness and a dose of sharp common sense (remember how she said, 'I have money stashed everywhere'?), which would aid her in any business venture she chose to embark upon.

Increasingly, major record labels are using established artists as A&R consultants, too. (This is a role Erykah would be able to fill admirably, for she has a sense for talent. On hearing Jill Scott's demo vocal for 'You Got Me', she had recognised the young singer's skills immediately.) In addition, she has always remained in touch with the underground music scene through her network in Dallas and New York and her feel for tidal changes in the field of popular music. There's no reason why she couldn't apply these facilities in a professional capacity.

Of great interest to many people will be the moves Erykah chooses to make in the arena of acting. After the false start of *Blues Brothers 2000* (after which she still managed to retain her credibility, however), few would have pegged her as the rising young star who would help make *The Cider House Rules* one of the most memorable films of the late 1990s. Her gravitas and her courage took her over that hurdle, however, creating a sensitive, struggling character in Rose Rose and giving many much more experienced actors an object lesson in economy of movement and style.

The key to Erykah's future success or failure hinges on one crucial point – whether she shows that her eye for a decent script is consistently as good as it was when she decided to get involved in *Cider House* (we can forgive her the *Blues Brothers* fiasco as a novice's error). A perfect example of a musician turned actor whose film career started well but went rapidly downhill is ex-NWA rapper Ice Cube, whose filmography includes some excellent movies (*Boyz N The Hood*, *Three Kings*) but who also appeared in some utterly forgettable films (*Ghosts Of Mars*,

Anaconda) through simple misjudgment (for further Cube information, the reader is humbly directed towards my biography, *Ice Cube: Attitude*, also published by Sanctuary). Cube, an intelligent man with his finger firmly on the cultural pulse, has made a few errors of this type, despite his other skills, and Erykah might well do the same unless she has plenty of expert advice and the opportunity to see excellent scripts (not always a given, unfortunately). It's too early to tell if her acting skills will place her in a wide variety of roles – we have only seen her in two movies and some video clips – but it should be remembered that she was a trained actor before she was ever a professional musician, and that in terms of what she can do on screen, we've seen virtually nothing yet. God forbid she ever enters that unholy area of black film – the hood comedy – although judging by her tough-as-nails performance as Queen Mousette in *Blues Brothers 2000*, the sass and anger of a ghetto role would not be beyond her by any means.

Film production, too, might be a possible ancillary career for Badu. Studios often benefit from the clout of having a 'name' producer on board when attracting financial investment, or as a bonus when marketing a movie. Erykah must have by now amassed a contacts list boasting many of the great and the good of Hollywood and the upper echelons of media empires – through Kedar Massenburg alone, many of the doors of Universal (Motown's parent company) stand open for her.

Through those same doors, of course, lies another way: the route to politics. Sounds implausible? Think again. When the major record labels and studios get together, in the boardrooms at the top of the skyscrapers, some of the richest people on earth are assembled – and where there is money, there is power. Where there is power, there are politicians and those who advise them. Not only is Erykah Badu a successful 'face', whose activities are a matter for both the tabloid gossip columns and the stocks prices in *The Wall Street Journal*, but she also has a powerful motivation: she comes from the hood, or as near as can be to it. Remember, Dallas and its North Park district was an impoverished area, and now that one of its residents has made it out, why would she not wish to improve life for her fellow co-residents? And, if so, why not use the platform of politics – still so rarely the province of women or black people

– to make those changes happen? Think about it. After all, she is articulate, energetic and caring – three aspects that make anyone in the public eye very influential indeed.

Let's return to the theatre for a second. As an established actor already, Erykah might well begin writing pieces for the stage and, indeed, she has already scripted and directed many of her own video clips. Why not return to her original arena and create there? After all, her influences are varied – think back to all the visual and musical artists and the films she has mentioned as inspirations to her over the years. Add to this her unique fashion sense (which is normally hailed as striking, although one or two critics have inevitably found it a little strange) and it's clear that she has an eye for adornment, which could presumably translate to the stage. Again, she is trained in theatre studies, even if she chose not to sit her final exams. Put in this context, it seems almost inevitable that a theatre role in some capacity will be hers at some point in the future.

In which case, she could also be an author. The book you are reading will, I'm sure, be only the first in a list of books ultimately to be written about this unique artist. In these pages I have tried to explain the workings of the remarkable mind that lie beneath Erykah Badu's music, and the forces on her life that shaped her, but of course only *she* can tell the whole truth, and one day I hope she does. A full autobiography from Erykah would be a fine read indeed – after all, there is so much to her character that I (or any other biographer) will never be able to unearth. I look forward to the day when we can all hear her own words about her life.

There is one area left unexplored, however: the concept of motherhood. As we've seen, Erykah can be funny and even play the buffoon, to the amusement of her loved ones, but she rarely jokes when she's talking about her life and her plans of how to live it. She said that she wanted six more children – and, of course, we don't know how seriously she meant this, but it sounded fairly prophetic at the time. Hopefully Common shares her ambition, but there is no doubt that it hardly matters who ends up being Badu's life partner. As we saw with Andre and Seven, Erykah's children will be loved and protected (as well as given a hell of an education) by Erykah and their father, perhaps because of her own experience with Toosie, her own father.

Whatever Erykah Badu does with her life – no matter if involves one, two or more of the possibilities listed above – she will live it with passion, honesty and self-awareness, as she has shown all observers with the first three decades of her visit here on the planet. She isn't flawless, of course (she has made errors and suffered the consequences of her actions, as well as enduring heartbreak and hurt, like the rest of us), but she has come through the adversities with her head held high, it seems, and little can divert her from the path that she, or those that determine all our fates, have laid out for her. There are few people like her in the public eye – although there may be many who live their lives away from the limelight who display just as much tenacity and courage – but she represents the best, and most human, qualities in us all. Can you imagine yourself in her position? No...and quite rightly. Erykah exists as a representation of what the human being can achieve in the best and worst of circumstances, and there is much to be learned from her life.

15 On And On

The road goes ever on, as the man said, and in Erykah Badu's case this has been a truism. Early July 2001 saw the second leg of the Mama's Gun Tour kick off in New Orleans, this time with Common (fuelling yet more rumours, of course) and the Jurassic 5 in support. Overseas dates were also scheduled. Despite the considerable live experience Erykah had amassed by this stage (and this was an unusual amount; after all, few new performers manage to release as competent a live album as she had), she still suffered a little from nerves, as she told *Rolling Stone*. 'I get a little nervous before I go on-stage,' she said. 'I just take a couple of breaths, pee and let that adrenaline flow. Sometimes the audience doubts me, sometimes they dote me, sometimes they love me. No matter what anybody else does, it doesn't change my attitude. I am who I am, and I'm gonna do what I'm gonna do.'

On 18 July Erykah squeezed in an appearance on the prestigious *Late Show With David Letterman*, in whose New York studio she gave a lengthy interview amid the pre-show chaos. Of the concerts she was currently performing, she said, 'The show is pretty much spontaneous. My band is very talented, and you get tired of doing the same thing because then it becomes a job. It's a jazz state of mind, but a hip-hop state of mind, too.' Once more she elaborated on the concept behind the *Mama's Gun* title, explaining the shock when a mother produces a weapon: 'I thought of the kind of material that I had, and it was pretty strong, like mamas are,' she said. 'And something that is even stronger is the idea that your mama would have a gun, because they are usually peaceful and nurturing... It makes a statement about where I am musically.' She also talked a little about 'AD 2000' and its subject – she didn't use the actual name 'Amadou Diallo' in the song, she explained, because others had done this already. 'I didn't want to call attention to it because so many people were doing songs to Amadou Diallo... So I'd rather do it as his words, "Say, you won't be name'n no buildings after me, To go down dilapidated".'

Motherhood was still working profound changes in her, despite the fact that Seven was almost four years old and developing an independent spirit. Being a mother had 'taught her patience', said Badu: 'I had the opportunity to give myself to a living being... [Having a son] made me understand how deep [music] was inside of me, because I could not write at the same time I was raising and nurturing him, because it all came from the same place. I wanted all of my art put into molding his mind.' And the ever-present theme of competition with other artists? Erykah took it in her stride, saying of the rise of Macy Gray, Jill Scott and Angie Stone that, 'I was once in their shoes, too. I was once compared to other people... I remember in 1995 there was nothing out like what I was doing, but since then other people have been brave enough to represent the artists that are often unheard. I have a platform to say what I feel, so whether I'm Top 10, Top 50 or no charts at all, I'm going to do it.'

As the Mama's Gun Tour brought Erykah to more and more people, it seemed only appropriate when an announcement came from *Soul Train* that the album had been given the Best R&B/Soul Album of the Year (Solo) prize. Badu would not be available to collect the award in Santa Monica as she would be performing elsewhere that evening, but this was a common occurrence, and plans were made for it to be collected on her behalf. However, some communication breakdown had snarled things up at *Soul Train* and, despite the fact that Erykah's album was listed as the winner on journalists' press releases and announced at the live taping of the show, a crestfallen statement came from the event organisers that a mistake had been made and Jill Scott's *Who Is Jill Scott?* was in fact the winner. The most surreal aspect of the mistake was that printed winners' sheets were handed to reporters as they left the show, all of which stated that Badu had won the award – and which of course then appeared in print the next week.

Writers had a field day at the producers' expense, with comments along the lines of, 'Good thing Erykah wasn't around to pick up the trophy – she'd have to mail it to Jill Scott' seen in various publications. When the show was ultimately broadcast, a voice-over had been introduced to correct the mistake, but the whole incident went down as one of the more hilarious errors in recent showbiz times. And it got even more unlikely when an anonymous source was quoted in the press as saying that the mistake was intentional. This shadowy figure alleged that, because Scott left the ceremony to catch a flight before the category was presented, the organisers opted to give the award to Erykah 'because it [looks bad] for [Scott] to be there all night and then not be around to accept her final award'. Make of this what you will: neither Badu nor Scott had anything to say about the controversial matter, and so the issue went no further.

There was a slight variation from the usual show on 8 August, when the Badu tour went to the DTE Energy Music Theater in Clarkston, Michigan. This concert was billed the 'Marimba Festival' and also featured the talents of Macy Gray, Jill Scott and Zap Mama, who gave the 15,000-plus capacity crowd a show exceeding five hours. The idea was to celebrate sexuality, and Gray introduced the theme in no uncertain manner by announcing at the start of her act, 'Ladies, women, bitches, hos, hoochie mamas...we're here to celebrate one of the most magnificent, most miraculous, things ever created. We want to celebrate the dick!', before leading the women in the venue in a chant of 'Dick, dick, dick!' Eyewitnesses reported that many male members of the audience covered their eyes at this point.

Erykah's performance was more restrained, although she did ask the audience members to scream their names before telling them that, 'You have just witnessed the God in you.' She played for a full two hours with a ten-piece band, all dressed in Cotton Club-style costumes, and kept the sultry jazz quotient high with songs such as 'In Love With You', 'Booty', 'Sometimes' and 'Certainly'. Her strolling, emotional performance combined with Gray's more driven act ('I want to see some asses shaking,' said Macy) and Scott's mellow sounds ('It's been officially a year since *Who Is Jill Scott?* came out,' announced Scott: 'So far, so good') made the festival – which was a pilot event for a possible full-scale tour in 2002 – a resounding success, in the absence of a Lilith Fair or similar female-centred event. Scott's last words from the stage – 'It's sista power up in here…absolutely!' – sum up both the ethos and the impact of the show.

Afterwards Erykah told writer Jancee Dunn that, 'We all friends. Jill Scott, Macy. We gotta be. We give each other advice. I'm the old-head, you know.' At 29? Dunn asked. 'Oh, yeah,' affirmed Badu. 'I've been in the music business longer than Jill and Macy. For the most part, we don't even talk about music. Lauryn [Hill] and I talk about our children and how we do this. When you find somebody as wonderful as Macy or Jill or Lauryn, or my Soulquarian friends – Common or D'Angelo or Mos Def or Ahmir – all these people are my best friends, and I know if something ever happened, they would be here on the next flight. We keep in touch, I mean, daily.'

Badu elaborated on the bonds between the neo-soul singers to a greater degree than she had ever done previously, with these words: 'This may seem strange, but the best way I can describe it, it seems like we are a tribe of lost children who are reunited. Our spirits are shown through our music, and we hear each other. You know, in different tribes, when the slaves were brought over, they had certain drumbeats that were indigenous to each tribe, and it's almost like the music is like that for us.'

Erykah's live confidence had now peaked, leaving her an absolute master of the stage environment, and improvising and adapting as she desired. A show in New York's Central Park was so hot that she was forced to take off her dress and elbow-length gloves, leaving her in a slinky black garment that caused cries of appreciation from the crowd – especially during 'Kiss Me On My Neck'. 'Thank you God for this breeze,' she said, before emitting a sudden shriek, laughing and explaining that 'free living' allows her to scream as she wishes. Her band often improvised, too (some shows included a fragment of India Arie's 'Video'), and a notable feature of the set was a slowed-down, ghost-story rendition of 'Appletree' with its haunting opening lines of 'It was a stormy night, You know the kind when the lightning strikes'. Occasionally Seven would run on-stage to join her for a few moments, and sometimes she would even go so far as to perform a stage-dive and just enjoy crowd-surfing for a while. Clearly her confidence in her act – and also her audience – had developed in giant strides.

Not that all the criticism was positive. The dance moves she had introduced to the show were thought to be a little over-the-top by some reviewers, while others mocked their 'dance-workshop' roots and were openly snide in their write-ups of the concerts. And there's some justification for this: while Erykah is a superb dancer, she can occasionally take herself a little too seriously on-stage and the dance moves she uses can come across as somewhat pretentious at times. However, none of this seems to have bothered Badu herself: her latest tour at the time of writing included a full 10–15 minutes of solo dancing, a part that she excels at and obviously enjoys.

The events of 11 September 2001 must have shocked Erykah as much as the rest of the world's population, although she has never gone on record discussing them. However, the album that appeared just one week later was not overshadowed entirely by the fall of the World Trade Center and stands as a memorable piece of work. The record in question was Macy Gray's second album, *The Id*, which featured Erykah's backing vocals on a song called 'Sweet Baby', the album's first single. Fans' hopes were high for Gray's sophomore release, as her début album, *On How Life Is*, had been an excellent piece of work, selling enormously and standing alongside *Baduizm* and *Who Is Jill Scott?* as the must-have neo-soul records.

Two other soul singers, Angie Stone and Sunshine Anderson (whom Gray manages), appeared on the album, as well as Slick Rick, Mos Def, Billy Preston, Red Hot Chili Peppers guitarist John Frusciante and The Roots' Ahmir Thompson. Asked how she gathered so many guests for the record, Gray responded that, 'It was just artists that I admire. I wanted them on the album so that the album would sound good. I had Erykah Badu on there; it was interesting to see what she came up with. And John Frusciante, he's one of my favourite guitar players. They're all just really great musicians that I wanted to play with.' She also told the *Dallas Morning News* that, 'My dilemma for years was people saying, we wouldn't know what to do with you. It would be too hard to promote. But now with Erykah Badu…it's cool for labels to sign somebody who's different.'

The points that Gray made here are significant. Commercially, the two women are more or less as hot as each other, with both début albums selling massively, and their talents comparably bankable – and yet Gray, whose composing skills are phenomenal, paid tribute to Erykah not only as a desirable guest but as the very first of her kind, someone who opened doors and paved the way for Gray's own success. And Erykah's contribution to 'Sweet Baby' is not immediately obvious (although her vocals are definitely recognisable); Gray could easily have omitted Badu's efforts and kept the song solely 'hers'. It's a potent sign of Erykah's enormous talent that an artist of the calibre of Gray values her contributions, however small.

Neo-soul followers knew that their chosen music had taken root when a compilation of already-classic songs from the genre appeared in October. Titled *Red Star Sounds Volume I: Soul Searching* and released by the new Red Star label (part of the Heineken empire, bizarrely), the album's proceeds went to VH1's music education charity Save The Music. Its 14 tracks were pure soul, with Erykah's 'Today' a high point, as well as India Arie's 'Butterfly', Damian Marley's 'Still Searching' (featuring Stephen Marley and Yami Bolo), Jill Scott's 'A Long Walk (A Touch of Jazz Remix)' and 'Glitches' by Amel Larrieux and The Roots. Related releases included the second long-player from Erykah's long-time backing singer, N'Dambi, whose *Tunin Up And Cosignin* was more of the same jazz-soul fusion that had made her 1999 début, *Little Lost Girls Blues*, a critical, if not commercial, success.

Furthermore, neo-soul (among other musics) was available to be experienced live as well as on record. The cumbersomely titled Coca-Cola Presents The Essence Music Festival took place in November at New Orleans' Louisiana Superdome and artists performed to no fewer than 195,000 people over three nights. A veritable feast of soul, R&B, jazz, blues and reggae, the event featured performances by Erykah, Jill Scott, Destiny's Child, Teena Marie, Kelly Price, Patti LaBelle, The O'Jays, Yolanda Adams, Eric Benet, The Whispers, Bilal, Patti Austin, Steel Pulse, Tower of Power, Brenda Russell, Solomon Burke, The Roots and many more – plus a comedy spot by Steve Harvey, in whose Dallas club Erykah had waitressed six years (and a lifetime) ago.

Just another festival for Erykah, I hear you cry. Yes – but this particular enormo-show was a gig with a difference. Just as we saw earlier how many of the neo-soul artists value political and spiritual awareness as highly as musical skill and lyrical articulation, the festivals at which they appeared incorporated these ideals too. The Essence Festival – which, remember, had the enormous muscle of the biggest soft-drink firm in the world behind it – offered far more than music, and in doing so tells us much about the needs of the market (and how the corporations have assessed those needs for potential profit). In the daytime, gig-goers could attend Essence Empowerment Seminars at the Ernest N Morial Convention Center, which trained them in life skills; they could do a workout with a fitness guru called Donna Richardson; they could discuss matters on a higher literary plane with top-selling American authors such as E Lynn Harris, Michael Baisden, Bebe Moore Campbell, Colin Channer and Pearl Cleage; they could explore matters spiritual under the guidance of luminaries of religious thought such as Bishop T D Jakes, Iyanla Vanzant, Prophetess Juanita Bynam and Dr Therman Evans; or they could expand their minds still further at poetry sessions hosted by Lamar Hill, Taalam Acey, Narubi Seleah and Mariposa. Heavy stuff – but clearly all the work of a team who had sat down to discuss the heart of the festival and come up with the idea that Essence should address visitors' spiritual, dogmatic, literary and physical needs as well as just playing a bit of music.

This may well be the nearest we have come to the philosophical linchpin of neo-soul. The fact that the festival offered all sorts of succour, apart from the merely musical, is a symptom of a change in thinking that has occurred in recent years. As all the old classic soul artists knew, music is about healing and improving the quality of life of the listener, and there is no separating the benefits of musical catharsis from the context in which it is provided. Why not, then, make the listening experience a whole arena of opportunity, including emotional, physical and spiritual training? Sounds like a bunch of hippie platitudes? Possibly – but what the hippies always said was no more than the truth, and hardly more than many enlightened people have said as the years have passed and popular music has evolved.

On a much lighter note, it was at the end of 2001 that the truth behind all those Erykah Badu/Common rumours was finally brought to light. It was Erykah herself who revealed to Skip Cheatham (a DJ at Dallas's K104 station) that, not only were the couple in love as many people had thought, but they were also engaged. 'He asked me to marry him over at my grandmother's house,' Badu admitted, obviously very happy. 'It's lovely.'

Glancing at Common's history, he seems to be a perfect partner for Erykah. He grew up in the south side of Chicago and took his impressions of the streets to some acclaim with a début single in 1992, 'Take It EZ', a call for self-identity released under his first *nom de rap*, Common Sense. It was the high point of a subsequent album, *Can I Borrow A Dollar?*, along with other songs such as 'Breaker 1/9' and 'Soul By The Pound'. The record was less sophisticated than his later work (it appears that he learned a lot in his early 20s, as so many people do) and contained some rather misogynistic undertones, although it also bore evidence to the fact that he was something of a wordsmith.

Common Sense then gained some notoriety after a feud with Ice Cube, who objected to some allegedly anti-West Coast lyrics in one of his songs. Cube recorded a song referring to 'a bitch with no common sense', but victory went to Common (who later shortened his name after losing the rights to it in a court case), who recorded the searing 'I Used To Love HER', a track that accused Cube of having lost his touch since his seminal 1991 début album, *Amerikkka's Most Wanted*. The argument was eventually resolved when the Nation of Islam intervened, afraid that more deaths would occur in the wake of the Shakur/Smalls murders.

Common's *Resurrection* and *One Day It Will All Make Sense* albums continued to evince his rise to lyrical excellence, and he went on to become one of America's more thoughtful performers. A lament for a dead childhood friend called 'Reminding Me (Of Sef)' was also a milestone for him, and his most recent album to date, 2000's *Like Water For Chocolate*, was another inspired work.

Both live and on record, the start of 2002 was a busy time for Erykah. Renowned producer Guru put together an album, *Jazzmatazz Streetsoul*, featuring various neo-soul stars at around this time, explaining to an interviewer how he managed to get so many talents on one record: 'I put together a team, and we scheduled everything', he said. 'It took about ten months to complete the whole thing. But what really made everything come together was my willingness to go to each person's environment – that way they felt more comfortable and gave even more creativity to the project. I went to Dallas to work with Erykah; I went to Philly to work with The Roots; and I went to Virginia to work with the Neptunes to get beats for the Kelis and Macy Gray tracks. With Angie Stone, I sent the track to her while she was on the road. Basically, I lived out of a suitcase.' Erykah's contribution to the album was to produce one of the songs, and she was asked at this time if she enjoyed the role: 'I love it,' she said. 'I love putting the music together. It's like art... I would love to produce Chaka Khan, and N'Dambi – that's one of my sisters... [She] sings background for me, but we grew up like sisters.'

February saw Badu perform more shows in her home town: the first a benefit concert for the Africa-Care Academy, which included Talib Kweli, the ever-present Common and Dead Prez; and the second a jam session at Dallas's Canyon Club, featuring the same artists plus N'Dambi. Of the latter, the ever-attentive Thor Christensen wrote in the *Dallas Morning News* that, 'Ms Badu organized the show as a benefit for the Africa-Care Academy, a private school in Oak Cliff. The Dallas neo-soul queen headlined the jam, and the 14-piece house band included many of her regular musicians. But it wasn't so much The Erykah Show as it was a summit meeting of kindred spirits from the worlds of hip-hop and soul.' High points were N'Dambi's set ('Looking like a 1940s movie star with her black fedora pulled over her eyes, [she] steered the show into pure R&B. Ms Badu's fans already know about N'Dambi's stunning voice...but they probably weren't aware how charismatic she is as a lead singer') and Common, who made an instant impression ('Slinking and bouncing around the stage in his Marvin Gaye-style yellow knit cap, he had all eyes glued upon him – especially during "The Light", his stirring fusion of rap and R&B').

'The Light' was the bridge between the Common and Badu sets, and when it finished the former left the stage, leaving Erykah in charge. That night she was wearing a thigh-length wig, which added an air of urban cool not hindered by a faulty sound system and the loss of a ring, which fell off her finger and vanished (Common, perhaps in an act of bridegroom-to-be valour, stopped the show and demanded that it be returned). Towards the end of her act, Badu indulged in a spot of crowd-surfing. 'Near the end of the set, she snaked through the crowd, climbed atop a table and hurled herself into the crowd,' wrote Christensen, 'surfing across her fans' outstretched hands toward the stage, where Common plucked her from the audience and cradled her in his arms.'

In January and February 2002, the Kraft foods chain issued a charity CD called *Women Of The Times*, which was sold at budget price in a promotion of Kraft products and which raised funds for a charity called the United Negro College Fund. The album was only available in supermarkets (although a mighty 1,650 branches in seven regions – Atlanta, Baltimore, Charlotte, Chicago, Detroit, Memphis and New York – took part, making it relatively easy to track down) and retained a lot of credibility by bearing an official Motown endorsement. In a public statement, Kedar Massenburg said, 'Motown is a hallowed brand name in all of America. Bringing the music of Motown to Black History Month through such a major company as Kraft is a promotion we're proud to be part of.' The album included songs from Sarah Vaughn, India Arie, The Marvelettes, Martha Reeves And The Vandellas, Gladys Knight And The Pips, Patti LaBelle, as well as Erykah's 'Appletree'. Coca-Cola, Heineken, Kraft – clearly neo-soul, black music in general, and popular music right across the spectrum all still offer much potential for opportunity, even among the world's biggest corporations.

In February 2002 Erykah was nominated for a Grammy Award for Best R&B Song ('Didn't Cha Know'). While she didn't win the award this time (although the video of the song was later named Video of the Year by *American Cinematographer* magazine), a possibly more satisfying outcome of her status as Grammy nominee was that in 2001 she was asked to host something called a Grammy Mentor Session in San Francisco, an educational event at which 33 students from the local Civic Arts Education Center and the YMCA learned about career options in music. After question-and-answer sessions with a concert promoter, tour accountant and production manager, Erykah was asked about various subjects and spoke at length about using music as a platform for expression and the therapeutic powers of music. Asked how she broke into the business, she answered, 'I never believed that I wasn't going to make it. Ever.'

Self-belief is a desirable thing, but hard to maintain, as anyone who has struggled to realise an ambition will testify. In this case, Erykah's conviction that she would 'make it' was bolstered by firm facts. Take a look at the evidence. First, she came from a secure family, which urged her to express herself in more or less any way she wanted. Second, her mother was an actor and music ran through the Wright genes, which created an environment in which it was both natural and desirable to perform. Next she attended a prestigious arts school, which put her through a pretty rigorous training schedule in order to hone the skills she would need to make it to the top. Add to this the contacts she would have made in showbiz through Booker T Washington High, and the school's influence was profound.

There's also the very important fact that Erykah had a lot to say. On spiritual matters (remember her involvement with the Five Percenters?), she was bursting with points to be made. Not only did she want to perform, but she felt a conviction to do so that was more than a mundane drive for success or recognition. Erykah's self-awareness makes her a teacher and, somehow or other, those lessons needed to be delivered. Last, she is physically attractive and a graceful, innovative performer.

All this makes her an ideal candidate for success as a musician. But, even with the above advantages, Badu was blessed with one more crucial attitude to help take her to the top – a belief that her path was mapped out for her. She said, 'We are here on earth to experience the consequences of our choices', but she has made the right choices. Whether you believe that fate conspired to help her along the way (the fortuitous meeting with Tim Grace at the *Boulevard* trailer wrap party; the hook-up with Kedar Massenburg, one of thousands of A&R execs who could have signed her up; meeting Andre; meeting Common and so on), or simply that life has been good to her and that she has navigated her way with some perceptiveness, in either case her self-belief has kept her going.

The broader picture – of a woman who took her entire persona and made the world's music fans appreciate it – is an impressive one. How many other artists could have entered the music scene as an outsider (remember that *Baduizm* was a brand new sound in 1997) and made the scene turn to her, rather than adapting herself to fit it? More than this, she has managed to excel musically and as an actor, despite the turmoil that surrounded her – the birth pains of neo-soul, the death throes of gangsta rap, the vagaries of the film industry and the personal strife she has encountered in love and as a mother. So when she talks about self-belief, you know she means what she says.

Badu's career has revolved around dealing with the petty, mundane events of life while holding on to a more serene, overarching spiritual stance, and the logistics of travelling to another continent were all part of this. Just as she had involved herself in Jamaican music, she was booked to play a festival in Africa, and this time as a jazz artist. Late March 2002 saw her travel to South Africa to perform at the North Sea Jazz Festival in Cape Town. Badu performed alongside James Moody, George Duke, Toots Thielemans, Ahmad Jamal, Spyro Gyra and Tower of Power in front of a 22,000-strong audience. Her performance was sound, but she suffered slightly from the fact that she didn't appear until 1am on the last night, by which time many of the crowd were too tired to show much appreciation. Common's guest appearance, plus her by-now-standard stage-dive at the end of the set, revitalised the atmosphere a little, however.

Two months later, Erykah was present at a New York protest which denounced proposed cuts to the city's education budget. Sean Combs (who was now calling himself 'P Diddy'), Erykah, Alicia Keys and Jay-Z spoke at the rally, which made the headlines when Wyclef Jean was arrested for trying to perform (the rally had no performance permit). After the rally Erykah retreated to Dallas, where at the time of writing she is said to be deep in preparation for a new album to appear in 2003.

One question needs to be asked as the story of Badu approaches the present day. How has Erykah affected the world in which she moves? The answer is not simple, and takes in a multitude of levels, but it leads us to a broader understanding of the world of popular music as a result.

First, Badu was among the first of her kind. Female solo artists have always been among the most successful performers in the West, with a long chain of unforgettable singers such as Ella Fitzgerald and Erykah's idol (and millstone) Billie Holiday in the jazz world, through fiery pioneers like Janis Joplin, Diana Ross and Aretha Franklin in the 1960s, punk priestesses like Debbie Harry and Patti Smith a little later, and then earth-straddling pop divas such as Mariah Carey, Whitney Houston and Celine Dion in the last decade or so. The greatness of the pre-1980s figures in this list cannot be denied. But there are few women who have emerged since 1990 who can claim to have brought as much honesty, musicality and simple talent to the musical marketplace as Erykah Badu, with the possible exception of her contemporaries Lauryn Hill, Macy Gray, Jill Scott and Angie Stone. Of these, Badu was the first, although Hill had already achieved a lifetime's worth of recognition with her band, The Fugees.

What this first-off-the-blocks status gives Badu is the aura of a pioneer. As we've seen, she took her vintage Chaka Khan and Stevie Wonder influences and transformed them into a sound that was brand new and ancient at the same time, and it's little wonder that the symbols she required to express the message in the music (the ankh is just one famous example) were so old. The music she makes is pretty much timeless, with few digital effects and very little studio trickery detracting from the simple, organic voices of the instruments and singers.

This has led to a revaluing, a rebirth, of simplicity in music. Look at Dido, for example. Some might say that she is Erykah's polar opposite – making white music for white people – but this is far from true. With vocals, acoustic instruments and studio technology more used for atmospherics than primary sounds (although Dido's dance music background inevitably means that computer-generated beats are usually present), the approach of both artists has much in common. The British hip-hop act Morcheeba are another example of this mellow, back-to-basics stance, with the silky vocals of singer Skye Edwards the main focus.

Erykah Badu must take some of the credit for this rise in simple, emotional pop music. But, as someone famously said, pioneers get all the arrows – and it wasn't long after *Mama's Gun* sold respectably (rather than spectacularly, as its predecessor, *Baduizm*, had done) that the knives began to come out in certain sections of the press. But Erykah took this in her stride – and in this way, too, she has established a kind of template that has left its mark on the music industry. Rather than be an aggressive, take-no-prisoners artist who spits venom in interviews, Badu has always tended to shrug off the antics of the media with an acknowledgement that, while criticism is valid, it is also merely an opinion. This approach is a lesson to us all – not just those among us whose life is lived in the public eye – and its impact is seen more and more among new artists (India Arie is an example) who are simply above this kind of shallowness.

Musically, Erykah emerged from obscurity with a strangely paradoxical approach that was new and untested in 1997 but which is common parlance today. It's also the basis of neo-soul. This duality lies in the fact that Badu's music is simultaneously old- and new-sounding. Her influences are vintage but her recordings are sparkling and modern, with the well-aged sounds of horns and whispered backing vocals harking directly back to vintage Motown, but ensconced in the brightest of digital clarity. Since then, this bipolar approach has become one of the most commercially viable forms of popular music, with artists either replicating it tastefully or self-consciously. Whether this style will fade from popularity in some years remains to be seen but, as things stand at the time of writing, it's a very-much-in-vogue style, which is flourishing, and *Baduizm* helped to establish it. Obviously Erykah was not the first artist to look backwards as well as forwards for her inspiration – longer-established acts such as Jamiroquai, and the majority of their acid-jazz contemporaries, Incognito, Masters at Work and the entire P-Funk-sampling G-Funk network, come to mind – but she was among the first artists to bring it to the forefront of commercial success.

As I write these lines, Erykah has fallen silent and has not made many recent public appearances, apart from an international tour that swept rapidly through Europe in June 2002. Engineer Chris Bell is standing by at his Dallas studio, ready for recording to take place. Strangely enough, the only immediate Badu activity has come from an unexpected source – Erykah's sister Koryan Wright, who has made a few music pages due to the activity of her own band, the tricky-to-pronounce 7onSoff. Musically her direction is a long way from her elder sister's: the band combines influences from Tina Turner, Eddie Van Halen, Jimi Hendrix and P-Funk, and call it 'hood-rock'. Most interestingly, Koryan has renamed herself Nayrok Udab, her first name and 'Badu' reversed, although why she should adopt the name Badu at all (in any form) is something of a mystery. However, her guitarist Whatnott responded to one writer's question – 'Is the band hoping to ride the Badu name into the bigtime?' – with the reasoned response that, 'She's her own woman with her own mind – she's developed her own type of style with music that she loves... [It] doesn't matter who she is, [people are] going to love the music.'

Nayrok herself gives good interviews. She has pointed out that, in her case, her philosophy comes from pain: 'I was in a car accident and broke both my legs,' she told one reporter. 'I just thought God has given me another opportunity to live, so I have to live hard.' This gives her an impetus to perform. 'It just means to me to get on stage and perform – give the audience a great show. At the same time, have a good time and you know, it's not even like a job – it's awesome.' On the subject of Erykah, she said, 'We're total opposites. She's the calm sister with the message, and I'm the wild, vibrant sister that loves to get on stage and let go.' Hence the spelling of her name, for 'Nayrok Udab is the flip side of Koryan Badu,' she said. 'I just didn't start this when Erykah decided to come out.' And she was also at pains to point out that there was no professional rivalry around: 'Of course, everyday sibling rivalry,' she added. 'We're sisters still. But since we'd grown up and had children, we were able to get along a lot better. But when we were little... Oh my goodness.' Good luck to Koryan – if she is anything like her sister, the world needs her. It may be difficult for her to gain acceptance, of course, as one Badu provides enough spiritual assistance for most people, but if she can shake off the inevitable association with Erykah she is sure to find a niche somewhere. Perhaps the world of rock will be her spiritual home – if she ventures into hip-hop or neo-soul territory, she may find that there is little room for her.

Furthermore, Erykah's backing singer Karen Bernod also launched a solo career at this point, as N'Dambi had done before her. Her *Some Othaness For U* album appeared on the Natively Creative Music label, an independent that provided her with much-desired artistic control. 'I've been offered deals, but I didn't want to get mixed up with all the political stuff that goes on with record companies,' said the singer. 'The indie approach offers more autonomy.' With a serious pedigree – as well as working for Erykah, Bernod has backed D'Angelo, Whitney Houston and Mos Def – she may just make a commercial splash. Meanwhile, Dana 'Yahzara' Williams has also released a solo record, *Hear Me* (on Keo Music), another indie item. The singer said, 'My shows are like a funky, juke-joint experience – we go from hot church to [funk] in a heartbeat... I just want to bring grittiness and personality back to music.' Add to the Badu-related clan the industrious Robert 'Free' Bradford – he is now developing a new female artist and looks set to continue his production and A&R career.

In early 2002 Kedar Massenburg brought his unique viewpoint to a discussion of modern black music, and had several excellent points to make about the state of soul. Asked by his interviewer, Gwen Ifill, to define neo-soul as industry panels such as the Grammy selectors saw it, he replied: 'Well, when they classify artists at neo-soul artists, they classify them based on sounds of traditional soul music that you might hear on Motown and might have heard on Philadelphia International coupled with the sonic of hip-hop, as well as more substantive subject matter, more conscious lyrics.' He added that the new wave of artists owe a quantifiable debt to the classic artists. 'These artists that they put in this category are kind of reminiscent of some of the old artists, whether they be jazz greats like Billie Holiday that they might compare Erykah Badu to, or D'Angelo with Marvin Gaye or even India Arie. I mean, that's where you basically get the term from, you know? Neo-classic soul, because it's new soul music today from the classics.'

Where had it come from, his interviewer wanted to know? Massenburg's response was succinct. 'When you look at the real popular hip-hop songs, they're all sampled from old R&B soul music songs...so what happened is that kids got used to hearing these samples or whatever and...wanted to hear the original songs. So hip-hop has helped soul music a lot.' He also knew exactly who his target demographic was for – say – an Erykah Badu release: that is, everyone. 'Say, for example, you put Erykah Badu on and she sounds like Billie Holiday, you bring a CD home and a parent says, "Hey, that sounds like Billie Holiday" until she hears the drums, and then the kid is like, "yeah but you've got drums that sounds like a DMX record". So you combine the two. So I think you have your late teens all the way up to your elderly parents.'

Motown itself was not the label it had once been, claimed the reporter. Kedar concurred, explaining, 'Well, I think when you say that Motown isn't like it was, no label could be like it was because you have too much competition now. With the uprise of a lot of independent labels and a lot of the hip-hop labels, I mean, there's a choice. There wasn't a lot of choices back then when you dealt with popular black music. Berry Gordy was doing what he does best as well as Philadelphia International.' However, he observed (quite accurately) that Motown had needed the fresh approach of artists like Erykah to bring it back to life: 'But when you talk about the revival of Motown, I don't think Motown really ever left. It was just a sleeping giant, and I think we just needed to put some resuscitation to Motown. So the movement helps in terms of letting people know that these are the quality of artists that are on the label, from Brian McKnight, Erykah Badu, India Arie, of course, and a bunch of new artists that's coming out.'

The conversation also covered the function of the term 'neo-soul' as a marketing tool, with Massenburg observing that it's a useful category to have, even if certain artists don't like being categorised into it. Interestingly, another writer, Daniel Gray-Kontar, wrote in 2001 that the lumping-together of Badu, Scott, Gray and the rest of the neo-soul queens is actually a manifestation of prejudice. 'The comparisons between Badu, Scott and others all are slim, really, with their basis in a surface level of typical American racism,' he wrote. 'Really, the only similarities between these vocalists is that they are all black women and all three fall into the relatively gray area of neo-soul vocalists, who have shunned the restrictions of radio-friendly urban contemporary.' When interviewing Erykah, he was told that, 'It's some people's jobs to make those kinds of comparisons… I mean, they get paid to do that. But because Jill [Scott] and I write songs together and share herb secrets with each other, we're able to keep things in perspective. Macy [Gray] and I have a similar relationship.' Both writer and singer had a point.

Erykah has scheduled 'silent' periods before, during which she withdraws to her family and cares for Seven. The last such withdrawal took place in 1999, midway between *Baduizm* and *Mama's Gun*, and she was asked at the time if she ever worried that her creative muse might desert her at these quiet times. 'No, not really,' she said. 'Sometimes you have to get off for a minute in order to see who you really are. And it's OK. You just have to learn really quick and get back to it.'

Since the release of *Mama's Gun*, many interviewers have asked Erykah about her plans for a third studio album. She told *Soul Express* early in 2002 that she had no plans at this stage. 'No, not yet. I think I have a writer's block right now,' she said. 'I'm not really thinking about writing. So I don't know yet where [I'm going]... I've made so many mistakes, you know, I will make so many more, I promise, but you know I'll just have to go with the changes, just go with the wind you know, gotta change.' She had learned much in the last few years, it appears, and had realised how much her development had taken place in the limelight. 'It's always difficult when you choose to grow publicly, and use your platform to show your growth, because you're up against a lot of criticism, but I've got to be brave, you know, and just continue to be honest. I think that's the best way to go for me.'

Although she sounded tired in this interview, she still had some optimism. 'I do see the world changing,' she said. 'In my generation, for example, everybody is becoming more free doing music. And you can follow someone's progression through the music that they listen to or the music that they make, and the music is becoming freer, progressing. You know, it's a hint that we are all growing in some kind of way. We are developing an understanding for some peace inside.' This simple, realistic approach may be the nearest we have yet come to defining the secret of Erykah's success – which rests on her unwillingness to pretend that she is anybody other than her true self. 'I make sure that [people] know I'm from the neighborhood,' she said elsewhere. 'That this is something real, and that I'm not a movie star or any kind of a superstar. I'm me; I'm who I am... And it can happen to anyone who wants it. If you want it, go and get it. Make other people believe it. And don't let anybody infiltrate your dream.'

So who *is* Erykah Badu? Perhaps the only way to find out – other than by listening to her ethereal, almost other-worldly music, of course

– is to read what she herself has to say on the subject of Erykah Badu. For starters, she is an insatiable learner, as she told Gray-Kontar. 'The more I hang around talented musicians, the more I learn. With every project, I'm learning more, and will continue to learn. But I'm never really satisfied. I want to take this music to a place where only God knows.' She's also acutely aware of the balance of things, whether internally or externally. 'I think it comes down to this,' she went on. 'I'm a very spiritual person, and I'm also very much in tune with myself and my surroundings. I always keep those things in mind with whatever I'm doing.' In *Interview* magazine she said that she thought people liked her because 'I'm free. I just do what I want, say what I want, say how I feel, and I don't try to hurt nobody. I just try to make sure that I don't compromise my art in any kind of way, and I think people respect that.'

She is a humble person, it seems. Erykah told the South African *Sunday Times* in April 2002 – the most recent interview to date – that stardom is all relative. 'I think I'm a bigger star at home,' she said. 'Seven travels with me, and we try to keep the same regime. I feed him good food and correct him when he's wrong. So we take home wherever we are. And I try not to feel too guilty about not having a regular home. Because, you know, you can make yourself feel too guilty.' She also knew that she had made mistakes ('It's too soon to say what mistakes I'm making – and I've made a lot of mistakes as a parent. So we'll see, and if I have to change things, I will without hesitation'), but that she had no regrets. 'Looking back, I'm proud to have won awards and got accolades. But there were also moments when songs or shows weren't as well received as I thought they would be. Sometimes I feel sorry for myself for some of the tougher things I've had to encounter in life, but other than that, I wouldn't change a thing. It makes me happy to know I could endure. And it gets easier and easier as you go on.' It seems that she's strong, too – and strength used wisely and carefully is a sign of a character worth respecting.

Erykah is also unpredictable. Few people could have foreseen *Baduizm*. Fewer still could have predicted the swing to rock of *Mama's Gun* or the naked vulnerability of its songs. And no one except Erykah and her closest collaborators can tell what the next album will be like, although Chris Bell has an inkling that it will be a faster one to record than the others. 'I'm hoping to work with her again on her next recordings, but she hasn't been out to do any yet,' he reports. 'But when she was in here she mentioned to me that she's about to do the fastest album she's ever done – like, just come in here and track five songs and get 'em out. I think she's under the gun from the label a little bit. They wanna keep the momentum going.'

She is also a leader and a manager of some considerable skill, it seems. Bell recalls a recent session with Erykah and Common: 'A couple of weeks ago I was working with her on Common's project, she was singing a verse on one of his songs. It's for his album, but when she comes in to do it, he has to leave the room!' Not that she is a control obsessive: 'She just likes to create without anybody around,' observes the engineer. 'The last session was pretty much just me and her, I just run the tape and she has about 20 different ideas for the verse – and they were all good. She does different renditions of the verse and settles on the one she likes best.'

Collaborations are also a distinct possibility. New artist Bilal also hinted that a co-write with Badu might be in the offing, saying that, 'I did a few songs with Erykah Badu but none of them were finished, she didn't have enough time to finish them so they didn't actually make this album' – and Erykah may also have the chance one day to get her dream production job and work with the mighty Chaka Khan (who acknowledged Badu's skills in 2001, saying that 'I have to admire the hootsfah of any artist that wants to cover one of my songs. Mary J Blige and Erykah Badu are the two who have been doing the most covering. They are both good singers.').

Perhaps the most sensible conclusion is that Erykah means something to most people, which would explain her success across such a wide cultural and ethnic demographic. After all, she speaks directly to both men and women. She once said, 'Some would call me a women's liberalist. I mean, I don't think so. I think I'm speaking from a woman's perspective, and I just happen to be a woman. I know more about women's issues than men's issues. And I'm speaking to brothers on [my songs], too. There's a song called "Time's A Wastin'".'

Moreover, she is a black artist who has a global view in racial terms – and a politically outspoken teacher on race issues who nonetheless has never displayed misanthropy to anyone. The following dialogue illustrates this. Asked by *Interview*, 'Do you think it's rare to meet a white person who acknowledges that having lighter skin basically makes life in America easier, and isn't comfortable with that?', her answer expressed perfectly the truth that neither side is completely in the right. 'Yeah, but that's correct,' she replied. 'I mean, you see a bunch of people here in America that have a lot of things, and then a whole bunch of people that have nothing. And it's like, how could you be comfortable with that? However, our society thinks that success means having a car and a lot of money and looking as white as you can or as American as you can. Or if you're white, looking as exotic as you can. We don't have any idea that it's about our hearts and our souls and how we treat the next person.'

Erykah is both a rationalist and an abstract thinker. The *Sydney Morning Herald* asked her in 2000 if she could see an end to racism. Her answer to this somewhat naïve question was placed firmly in reality: 'White kids that I grew up with on my street say stuff to me like, "Erykah, we grew up in the same neighbourhood and you drive a Lexus and I'm walking. Racism is over". No, it's not, it's really not, because every day we experience something new because of the way we look, or something like that.' However, she can philosophise intelligently too. 'Within our own races we distinguish between the "natural" people and the "unnatural" people. But what if none of that really makes a difference? What if we are just black, white, Chinese, African, Native American; what if we're just all here to experience the consequences of our choices and judgments; and what if all this is put in front of us so that we can just all grow as individuals?… You were born by yourself and, when you go to the next level, you're gonna go by yourself.'

There's something pleasingly symmetrical about the life of Erykah Badu, something that harmonises her mind, her music and her environment. As Erykah has grown, the music she moves in has grown too – when *Baduizm* appeared in 1997, she was a young woman with a message in a music scene that could hardly nurture her. By the time *Mama's Gun* appeared three years later, she was older, wiser, tougher, stronger, and a mother to boot – and there was a flourishing neo-soul scene in which she could express herself. Just as she helped create neo-soul, the neo-soul environment supported and nourished her – a balance that she, with her ankhs and hesis and love of universal harmony, would no doubt relish.

Erykah Badu is a messenger, but not from 'the other sun', as *Mama's Gun* had it. She is fully of this earth and, just as this earth sustains those who live on it, her music has the power to sustain its listener. Artists of her vision and her courage do not appear very often – so appreciate her, and give thanks for all that she brings.

The show is over. The last chords die away, the musicians silently leave the stage, and the only person left is Erykah Badu, finishing off that last, long, sweet note, picked out by a spotlight at centre stage. She stops singing, and there is silence.

Bending her head quickly towards the candle burning at her side, she blows out the flame – and all is darkness.

Discography

SOLO ALBUMS

Baduizm (Motown, 1997)
Live (Motown, 1997)
Mama's Gun (Motown, 2000)

SELECTED COMPILATIONS

High School High (Big Beat, 1996)
Eve's Bayou: The Collection (MCA, 1997)
MTV Party To Go '98 (Tommy Boy, 1997)
Blues Brothers 2000 (Universal, 1998)
1998 Grammy Nominees (MCA, 1998)
Hav Plenty (Sony, 1998)
Living The Dream: A Tribute To Martin Luther King (Hip-O Records, 1998)
MTV Jams (Kedar Entertainment, 1998)
BET: Best Of Planet Groove (Noo Trybe, 1999)
Chant Down Babylon (Polygram, 1999)
Marvin Is 60: The Tribute Album (Motown, 1999)
The 24 Hour Woman (WEA Latina, 1999)
The Mix Tape Volume 3 (Loud, 1999)
Jazzmatazz Streetsoul (Virgin, 2000)
Red Star Sounds Volume 1: Soul Searching (Epic, 2001)

Online Resources

Badu's Official Site
www.erykahbadu.com

Badu Gallery
www.geocities.com/neosoulmasters/epg.htm

Badu Home
www.anieclayton.freeserve.co.uk/badu

Badu Fansite
www.geocities.com/erykahbadubaduizm/home.html

Baduteria
www.liquid2k.com/baduteria/news.html

Chris Bell
www.proaudioengineer.com

Dallas Morning News
www.dallasnews.com/

Deep Ellum, Dallas Information
www.ondaweb.com/deep_ellum

Emmanuel Gillespie
www.emmanuelsearthlygoods.com

Kedar Entertainment
www.kedar.com

Neo-Soul
www.neosoul.com

Roy Hargrove
www.royhargrove.com

South Dallas Cultural Center
www.dallasblack.com/channel1/sdcc/index.htm

Index

Stage names are listed as read (for example, *Erykah Badu*, not *Badu, Erykah*), but conventional names (eg *Wright, Erica*) are listed with the surname first.

To the children of Gaza

إلى أطفال غزة

ميزان ما أتقلك هديتلي كتافي
دابت حشيشة قلبي لجلكم دابت
والشعرتين السود يا إما بروسنا شابوا
والشعرتين الشقر يا إما بروسنا دابوا
فارس يا شمعتي سهيل يا مالي
يا مين يجيب الدوا قلت الدوا غالي
فارس يجيب الدوا وسهيل يداويني
لا تحسبون طالت الغربة يا يما ونسيناكوا
صبرت صبر الخشب تحت المناشيري
صبرت لأنو استوي لحم العصافيري
وحياتك تكبر وتجبر والرب يعطيني
جبرة قوية يا اما
وتكيد عدويني
يا ابني

ريم بنا
Rim Banna

Ya Lel Ma Atwalak

This Never Ending Night

This never ending night, all lonely and wandering
My hair has turned to white, my body's ill
Souhail, my little light, and Fares, my precious one!
Some day you'll bring my medicine, I know you will

And I always will remember, like they're wandering beside me
The dearest and beloved ones we were separated from
Stop crying now, my eye, even if it seems forever
I will wander in this night
Till we are home

So sleep and you'll be strong
Sleep on now, my baby boy
Some day you'll take us back again
To where we belong

Palestinian traditional,
English lyrics adapted by Kari Bremnes
based on a translation by Zuhaira Sabbagh.

Contents

Acknowledgements

FROM ERIK

A big thank you goes to my beloved partner Nina Husom, who supported me when I decided to go and throughout my journey, and who has helped me with writing and proof-reading. My children Hilde and Eivind were there for me, as they always have been. They hid their anxieties, which helped me to keep my spirits up. Many thanks to all my friends and acquaintances who sent messages of encouragement and support the whole way.

Thank you to my fellow workers at the Interventional Centre at Rikshospitalet, which is part of Oslo University Hospital. They were there for me when I was in Gaza and afterwards, and they have given me a lot of support and recognition. Thank you to all my colleagues at Oslo University Hospital who support solidarity and healthcare right across the world.

FROM MADS

Heartfelt thanks go to my dear daughters Siri and Anna for all their courageous support and affectionate caring this time – as with all those previous solidarity missions in perilous circumstances. A big thank you is also due to the rest of my family. Thanks for the support and input I have received from close friends and colleagues. Kind thanks to the dependable members of the Palestine Committee in Tromsø.

Thank you to my fellow workers and the head team in the Department of Emergency Medicine at the University Hospital of Northern Norway (UNN) for taking on my work so that I could go on leave, and for the important support work you carried out for Gaza in my absence. Thank you to my bosses, the general manager Knut Schrøder and the hospital CEO Tor Ingebrigtsen, who have managed UNN as a hospital which take on global responsibilities and that has shown long-standing solidarity with the Palestinians.

FROM BOTH

We would both like to thank the NORWAC co-ordinator John Eivind Jensen, the day-to-day management staff at NORWAC and the two teams that relieved us in Gaza in January 2009. Thank you to Ebba Wergeland for her intelligent guidance and solidarity over thirty years. Thanks to the Norwegian Palestine Committee for their support while we were in Gaza. Thanks to the Norwegian Ministry of Foreign Affairs, to the staff and management of the Royal Norwegian Embassy in Cairo and the Representative Office of Norway in Ramallah.

Grateful thanks to the consultants and publishing professionals at Gyldendal Norsk Forlag who have shown patience and optimism towards the project – special thanks to Ane Håbjørg, Jan Swensson, Hans Petter Bakketeig, Veronica Sande, Olav Bakken, Thomas Holter and Geir Mork.

PHOTOGRAPHIC CREDITS

Dagfinn Bjørklid: 154, 217
John Eivind Jensen: 31
Rima Najjar Merriman: 61
Line Monrad-Hansen: maps on page 47
NORWAC: 27, 63, 65, 85, 113, 115, 138, 167, 273
Khalil Hamra/AP: 165
Mohammed Salem/Reuters: 180–1
Majed Hamdam/AP: 207
Ben Curtis/AP: 297
Said Khatib: 307
Anders Vethe: 281
Yanai Yechiel: 301
All other photographs were taken by the authors

Abbreviations

DIME	Dense Inert Metal Explosives. A new type of small bomb with a warhead based on heavy metal alloys, especially tungsten.
ICRC	The International Committee of the Red Cross.
NORWAC	Norwegian Aid Committee. A Norwegian medical aid organization established in 1983.
OCHA	United Nations Office for the Coordination of Humanitarian Affairs.
OCHAopt	United Nations Office for the Coordination of Humanitarian Affairs in the Occupied Palestinian Territory.
PLO	Palestine Liberation Organization.
PRCS	Palestine Red Crescent Society.
UNFPA	United Nations Population Fund.
UNHCR	United Nations High Commissioner for Refugees.
UNICEF	United Nations Children's Fund.
UNRWA	United Nations Relief and Works Agency for Palestine Refugees in the Near East. Established in 1949.

Forewords

Impressions of Gaza by Noam Chomsky – October 2012

Even a single night in jail is enough to give a taste of what it means to be under the total control of some external force. And it hardly takes more than a day in Gaza to begin to appreciate what it must be like to try to survive in the world's largest open-air prison, where a million and a half people, in the most densely populated area of the world, are constantly subject to random and often savage terror and arbitrary punishment, with no purpose other than to humiliate and degrade, and with the further goal of ensuring that Palestinian hopes for a decent future will be crushed and that the overwhelming global support for a diplomatic settlement that will grant these rights will be nullified.

The intensity of this commitment on the part of the Israeli political leadership has been dramatically illustrated just in the past few days, as they warn that they will 'go crazy' if Palestinian rights are given limited recognition at the UN. That is not a new departure. The threat to 'go crazy' ('*nishtagea*') is deeply rooted, back to the Labour governments of the 1950s, along with the related 'Samson Complex': we will bring down the Temple walls if crossed. It was an idle threat then; not today.

The purposeful humiliation is also not new, though it constantly takes new forms. Thirty years ago political leaders, including some of the most noted hawks, submitted to Prime Minister Begin a shocking and detailed account of how settlers regularly abuse Palestinians in the most depraved manner and with total impunity. The prominent military-political analyst Yoram Peri wrote with disgust that the army's task is not to defend the state, but 'to demolish the rights of innocent people just because they are Araboushim ['niggers', 'kikes'] living in territories that God promised to us'.

Gazans have been selected for particularly cruel punishment. It is almost miraculous that people can sustain such an existence. How they do so was described thirty years ago in an eloquent memoir by Raja Shehadeh (*The Third Way: A Journal of Life on the West Bank*, Quartet Books, 1992), based on his work as a lawyer engaged in the hopeless task of trying to protect elementary rights within a legal system designed to ensure failure, and his personal experience as a *Samid*, 'a steadfast one', who watches his home turned into a prison by brutal occupiers and can do nothing but somehow 'endure'.

Since Shehadeh wrote, the situation has become much worse. The Oslo agreements, celebrated with much pomp in 1993, determined that Gaza and the West Bank are a single territorial entity. By then the US and Israel had already initiated their programme of separating them fully from one another, so as to block a diplomatic settlement and punish the Araboushim in both territories.

Punishment of Gazans became still more severe in January 2006, when they committed a major crime: they voted the 'wrong way' in the first free election in the Arab world, electing Hamas. Demonstrating their passionate 'yearning for democracy', the US and Israel, backed by the timid European Union, at once imposed a brutal siege, along with intensive military attacks. The US also turned at once to standard operating procedure when some disobedient population elects the wrong government: prepare a military coup to restore order.

Gazans committed a still greater crime a year later by blocking the coup attempt, leading to a sharp escalation of the siege and military attacks. These culminated in winter 2008–9, with Operation Cast Lead, one of the most cowardly and vicious exercises of military force in recent memory, as a defenceless civilian population, trapped with no way to escape, was subjected to relentless attack by one of the world's most advanced military systems relying on US arms and protected by US diplomacy. An unforgettable eyewitness account of the slaughter – 'infanticide' in their words – is given by the two courageous Norwegian doctors who worked at Gaza's main hospital during the merciless assault, Mads Gilbert and Erik Fosse, in their remarkable book *Eyes in Gaza* (Quartet Books, 2010).

President-elect Obama was unable to say a word, apart from reiterating his heartfelt sympathy for children under attack – in the Israeli town Sderot. The carefully planned assault was brought to an end right before his inauguration, so that he could then say that now is the time to look forward, not backward, the standard refuge of criminals.

Of course, there were pretexts – there always are. The usual one, trotted out when needed, is 'security': in this case, home-made rockets from Gaza. As is commonly the case, the pretext lacked any credibility. In

2008 a truce was established between Israel and Hamas. The Israeli government formally recognizes that Hamas observed it fully. Not a single Hamas rocket was fired until Israel broke the truce under cover of the US election on November 4, 2008, invading Gaza on ludicrous grounds and killing half a dozen Hamas members. The Israeli government was advised by its highest intelligence officials that the truce could be renewed by easing the criminal blockade and ending military attacks. But the government of Ehud Olmert, reputedly a dove, chose to reject these options, preferring to resort to its huge comparative advantage in violence: Operation Cast Lead. The basic facts are reviewed once again by foreign policy analyst Jerome Slater in the current issue of the Harvard-MIT journal *International Security*.

The pattern of bombing under Cast Lead was carefully analysed by the highly informed and internationally respected Gazan human rights advocate Raji Sourani. He points out that the bombing was concentrated in the north, targeting defenceless civilians in the most densely populated areas, with no possible military pretext. The goal, he suggests, may have been to drive the intimidated population to the south, near the Egyptian border. But the *Samidin* stayed put, despite the avalanche of US-Israeli terror.

A further goal might have been to drive them beyond. Back to the earliest days of the Zionist colonization it was argued across much of the spectrum that Arabs have no real reason to be in Palestine; they can be just as happy somewhere else, and should leave – politely 'transferred', the doves suggested. This is surely no small concern in Egypt, and perhaps a reason why Egypt does not open the border freely to civilians or even to desperately needed materials.

Sourani and other knowledgeable sources observe that the discipline of the *Samidin* conceals a powder keg, which might explode any time, unexpectedly, as the first Intifada did in Gaza in 1989 after years of miserable repression that elicited no notice or concern.

Merely to mention one of innumerable cases, shortly before the outbreak of the Intifada a Palestinian girl, Intissar al-Atar, was shot and killed in a schoolyard by a resident of a nearby Jewish settlement. He was one of the several thousand Israeli settlers brought to Gaza in violation of international law and protected by a huge army presence, taking over much of the land and scarce water of the Strip and living 'lavishly in twenty-two settlements in the midst of 1.4 million destitute Palestinians', as the crime is described by Israeli scholar Avi Raz. The murderer of the schoolgirl, Shimon Yifrah, was arrested, but quickly released on bail when the Court determined that 'the offense is not severe enough' to warrant detention. The judge commented that Yifrah only intended to shock the girl by firing his gun at her in a schoolyard, not to kill her, so 'this is not a case of a criminal person who has to be punished, deterred, and taught a lesson by imprisoning him'. Yifrah was given a seven-month suspended sentence, while settlers in the courtroom broke out in song and dance. And the usual silence reigned. After all, it is routine.

And so it is. As Yifrah was freed, the Israeli press reported that an army patrol fired into the yard of a school for boys aged six to twelve in a West Bank refugee camp, wounding five children, allegedly intending only 'to shock them'. There were no charges, and the event again attracted no attention. It was just another episode in the programme of 'illiteracy as punishment', the Israeli press reported, including the closing of schools, use of gas bombs, beating of students with rifle butts, barring of medical aid for victims; and beyond the schools a reign of more severe brutality, becoming even more savage during the Intifada, under the orders of Defence Minister Yitzhak Rabin, another admired dove.

My initial impression, after a visit of several days, was amazement, not only at the ability to go on with life, but also at the vibrancy and vitality among young people, particularly at the university, where I spent much of my time at an international conference. But there too, one can detect signs that the pressure may become too hard to bear. Reports indicate that among young men there is simmering frustration, recognition that under the US-Israeli occupation the future holds nothing for them. There is only so much that caged animals can endure, and there may be an eruption, perhaps taking ugly forms – offering an opportunity for Israeli and western apologists to self-righteously condemn the people who are culturally backward, as Mitt Romney insightfully explained.

Gaza has the look of a typical third world society, with pockets of wealth surrounded by hideous poverty. It is not, however, 'undeveloped'. Rather it is 'de-developed', and very systematically so, to borrow the terms of Sara Roy, the leading academic specialist on Gaza. The Gaza Strip could have become a prosperous Mediterranean region, with rich agriculture and a flourishing fishing industry, marvellous beaches and, as discovered a decade ago, good prospects for extensive natural gas supplies within its territorial waters.

By coincidence or not, that is when Israel intensified its naval blockade, driving fishing boats toward shore, by now to three miles or less.

The favourable prospects were aborted in 1948, when the Strip had to absorb a flood of Palestinian refugees who fled in terror or were forcefully expelled from what became Israel, in some cases expelled months after the formal cease-fire.

In fact, they were being expelled even four years later, as reported in *Ha'aretz* (December 25, 2008), in a thoughtful study by Beni Tziper on the history of Israeli Ashkelon back to the Canaanites. In 1953, he reports, there was a 'cool calculation that it was necessary to cleanse the region of Arabs'. The original name, Majdal, had already been 'Judaized' to today's Ashkelon, regular practice. That was in 1953, when there was no hint of military necessity. Tziper himself was born in 1953, and while walking in the remnants of the old Arab sector, he reflects that 'it is really difficult for me, really difficult, to realize that while my parents were celebrating my birth, other people were being loaded on trucks and expelled from their homes'.

Israel's 1967 conquests and their aftermath administered further blows. Then came the terrible crimes already mentioned, continuing to the present day.

The signs are easy to see, even on a brief visit. Sitting in a hotel near the shore, one can hear the machine gun fire of Israeli gunboats driving fishermen out of Gaza's territorial waters and towards shore, so they are compelled to fish in waters that are heavily polluted because of US-Israeli refusal to allow reconstruction of the sewage and power systems that they destroyed.

The Oslo Accords laid plans for two desalination plants, a necessity in this arid region. One, an advanced facility, was built: in Israel. The second one is in Khan Younis, in the south of Gaza. The engineer in charge of trying to obtain potable water for the population explained that this plant was designed so that it cannot use sea water, but must rely on underground water, a cheaper process, which further degrades the meagre aquifer, guaranteeing severe problems in the future. Even with that, water is severely limited. The United Nations Relief and Works Agency (UNRWA), which cares for refugees (but not other Gazans), recently released a report warning that damage to the aquifer may soon become 'irreversible', and that without remedial action quickly, by 2020 Gaza may not be a 'liveable place'.

Israel permits concrete to enter for UNRWA projects, but not for Gazans engaged in the huge reconstruction needs. The limited heavy equipment mostly lies idle, since Israel does not permit materials for repair. All of this is part of the general programme described by Israeli official Dov Weisglass, an adviser to Prime Minister Ehud Olmert, after Palestinians failed to follow orders in the 2006 elections: 'The idea,' he said, 'is to put the Palestinians on a diet, but not to make them die of hunger'. That would not look good.

And the plan is being scrupulously followed. Sara Roy has provided extensive evidence in her scholarly studies. Recently, after several years of effort, the Israeli human rights organization Gisha succeeded to obtain a court order for the government to release its records detailing plans for the diet, and how they are executed. Israel-based journalist Jonathan Cook summarizes them: 'Health officials provided calculations of the minimum number of calories needed by Gaza's 1.5 million inhabitants to avoid malnutrition. Those figures were then translated into truckloads of food Israel was supposed to allow in each day . . . an average of only 67 trucks – much less than half of the minimum requirement – entered Gaza daily. This compared to more than 400 trucks before the blockade began.' And even this estimate is overly generous, UN relief officials report.

The result of imposing the diet, Middle East scholar Juan Cole observes, is that '[a]bout ten percent of Palestinian children in Gaza under 5 have had their growth stunted by malnutrition . . . in addition, anemia is widespread, affecting over two-thirds of infants, 58.6 percent of schoolchildren, and over a third of pregnant mothers'. The US and Israel want to ensure that nothing more than bare survival is possible.

'What has to be kept in mind,' observes Raji Sourani, 'is that the occupation and the absolute closure is an ongoing attack on the human dignity of the people in Gaza in particular and all Palestinians generally. It is systematic degradation, humiliation, isolation and fragmentation of the Palestinian people.' The conclusion is confirmed by many other sources. In one of the world's leading medical journals, *The Lancet*, a visiting Stanford physician, appalled by what he witnessed, describes Gaza as 'something of a laboratory for observing an absence of dignity', a condition that has 'devastating' effects on physical, mental, and social well-being. 'The constant surveillance from the sky, collective punishment through blockade and isolation, the intrusion into homes and communications, and restrictions on those trying to travel, or marry, or work make it difficult to live a dignified life in Gaza.' The Araboushim must be taught not to raise their heads.

There were hopes that the new Morsi government in Egypt, less in thrall to Israel than the western-backed Mubarak dictatorship, might open the Rafah crossing, the sole access to the outside for trapped Gazans that is not subject to direct Israeli control. There has been slight opening, but not much. Journalist Laila el-Haddad writes that the re-opening under Morsi, 'is simply a return to status quo of years past: only Palestinians carrying an Israeli-approved Gaza ID card can use Rafah Crossing', excluding a great many Palestinians, including el-Haddad's family, where only one spouse has a card.

Furthermore, she continues, 'the crossing does not lead to the West Bank, nor does it allow for the passage of goods, which are restricted to the Israeli-controlled crossings and subject to prohibitions on construction materials and export'. The restricted Rafah crossing does not change the fact that 'Gaza remains under tight maritime and aerial siege, and continues to be closed off to the Palestinians' cultural, economic, and academic capitals in the rest of the [occupied territories], in violation of US-Israeli obligations under the Oslo Accords'.

The effects are painfully evident. In the Khan Younis hospital, the director, who is also chief of surgery, describes with anger and passion how even medicines are lacking for relief of suffering patients, as well as simple surgical equipment, leaving doctors helpless and patients in agony. Personal stories add vivid texture to the general disgust one feels at the obscenity of the harsh occupation. One example is the testimony of a young woman who despaired that her father, who would have been proud that she was the first woman in the refugee camp to gain an advanced degree, had 'passed away after 6 months of fighting cancer aged 60 years. Israeli occupation denied him a permit to go to Israeli hospitals for treatment. I had to suspend my study, work and life and go to set next to his bed. We all sat including my brother the physician and my sister the pharmacist, all powerless and hopeless watching his suffering. He died during the inhumane blockade of Gaza in summer 2006 with very little access to health service. I think feeling powerless and hopeless is the most killing feeling that a human can ever have. It kills the spirit and breaks the heart. You can fight occupation but you cannot fight your feeling of being powerless. You can't even dissolve that feeling.'

Disgust at the obscenity, compounded with guilt: it is within our power to bring the suffering to an end and allow the *Samidin* to enjoy the lives of peace and dignity that they deserve.

Noam Chomsky visited the Gaza Strip on October 25–30, 2012

The Eerie Night by Mads Gilbert

Translator's note: *In November 2012, during what the Israeli Defence Force called Operation Pillar of Defence, Mads Gilbert went back to al-Shifa Hospital, where he worked during the final phase of the attacks. The following report was originally written as 'A Note in the Night' for a mailing list for Norwegian doctors, but was picked up by the Norwegian Broadcasting Corporation (NRK), and published on the NRK website on November 21, 2012.*[1] *A ceasefire, mediated by Egypt, was announced later that day. The attacks killed over 190 in Gaza, and injured over 1490. Of those killed, 48 were children below the age of 18 years, 16 of whom were under 5 years old. Of those wounded, 504 were children under 18 years old, 195 of whom were below the age of 5 years.*[2] *According to the UN, 6 Israelis were killed and 224 injured.*[3] *In the Strip, 298 houses were destroyed or seriously damaged, while over 1,700 sustained minor damage.*[4] *10,473 civilians were displaced to emergency shelters.*[5]

Midnight has passed. No ceasefire yet. Neither is there any rest for men, women or children. I am at al-Shifa Hospital. Gaza is deserted, the streets and markets that usually teem with people and life are empty, almost ghostly. I have never seen Gaza so deserted in the fifteen years I have been working here. The drones buzz above like evil insects, and we know they will be followed by thunderous explosions. The window curtains in the room where I am writing this move with the blasts and I can feel the pressure waves clearly. All the windows are open so that they will not implode, scattering deadly swarms of glass. There are so many deadly swarms here in Gaza. Shrapnel from shells and bombs, swarms of drones, swarms of leaflets dropped from the sky with threatening messages, further terrorizing the civilian population.

It has been a terrible day. It is difficult to describe thirteen bodies torn to pieces, decapitated bodies, torn-off limbs, charred adults and young children: all of these come to al-Shifa. Desperate calls for help, shouts of pain. Mothers collapsing in paralytic despair when their dead children are identified.

We work. Intubating, cutting off clothing, cannulating, trying to understand where the injuries are on those who still show signs of life. Today there were 24 dead and 189 wounded. They don't all come to al-Shifa, but very many of them do. We lost two 'on the table'; splinter injuries to the pulmonary artery and destructive head injuries. A torn-off abdominal vein was salvaged with the help of a skilful vascular surgeon from the group of forty volunteer Palestinian doctors who came from the West Bank yesterday.

We have felt fierce bomb blasts not far from the hospital. Al-Shifa is well organized and relatively calm today, but overcrowded. All elective operations have been suspended, the staff have gone onto emergency shift patterns of 24 hours on and 12–24 hours off, depending on the situation. The hospital has 700 beds, which are full, but 70 beds are kept free the whole time for any further major influxes of patients, as are 6 intensive care beds.

There is a critically low stock of medicines and disposables, enough for several days' influx of patients. Food, power, electricity and water are in short supply due to the prolonged Israeli blockade that has lasted for five long years now.

The latest official figures from Gaza this evening are 850 injured Palestinians, including 455 women, children under the age of 18 and people over the age of 60. 100 Palestinians have been killed, including 46 women, children and elderly. The vast majority of those wounded or killed are civilians, while approximately half are women, children or the elderly: the most vulnerable sections of society.

I have been on a round of the hospital with my old friend and colleague, the surgeon Issam Abu Ajwa. We paid a visit to intensive care: eight patients on ventilators, including four children aged twelve or younger, all with serious head trauma resulting from so-called 'explosive injuries'. Three of them were from the same family, the Abu Zor family, whose house was bombed at about five o' clock this morning. Three members of the family were killed. This had a painful effect on me, and I was almost overwhelmed with despair, but I do as my Palestinian colleagues: I control myself, I stay calm, professional and focused. But all of us in the room there were left shaking.

My colleagues – whom I know well from several years working with them, not least during the Israeli attack of Operation Cast Lead in 2008-2009 – are composed and resolute.

'We are better organized now, more systematic and more capable,' says my colleague Nasser Abu Shaban, one of the hospital managers and a skilled surgeon. 'We have learnt a lot, both in terms of organization and purely technical matters. We'll cope this time too,' he says with a friendly smile.

I don't know how this will go. The losses are not yet as high as in 2008-2009, but the aggression and rhetoric of the Israeli government is at least just as menacing. I sense a murmuring disquiet, the sound of the drones brings back bad memories, a kind of conditioned reflex, we know it will end in fierce explosions, more blood and more suffering. Even just the sleep deprivation and the terrifying sounds of the bombs impacting can be considered torture. It will be yet another uneasy night for the children of Gaza. Over 1 million of the people are 18 or younger, and the average age is 17.6 years among this population of 1.7 million, squeezed together behind walls and barbed wire in an area of 360 square kilometres. A child prison.

Solidarity. New alliances between Palestinians. Large Arab delegations sweep through the hospital with shocked faces while the relentless sound of the falling bombs reminds them of their political responsibility. A family with children comes in during the morning after Israeli jets have bombed and devastated the largest bank in the centre of Gaza City. The father is livid and calls for revenge. The children listen to him, frightened.

Bloody hell, now they're bombing right next to us. Multiple bombs. How can they manage to comfort their children on such a night? I am afraid. Wickedness seems to be winning. I don't know if 'the world' realizes what this prison, with its million inmates, is really like. It's impossible to find shelter, cover, a way out, escape, protection. And, at the same time, the same power that's keeping everyone locked up is bombing the place with one of the world's strongest war machines.

What would have happened if Michelle Obama were here tonight with her two daughters? If she lived in a house in Beit Lahiya on the outskirts of Gaza City, the poor neighbourhood, with no lights, with no security. What if she came running in with one of her beautiful children in her arms, covered with shrapnel, with no way of escaping? Would things have changed then?

I can't understand the behaviour of Norwegian politicians like Prime Minister Jens Stoltenberg, the Foreign Minister Espen Barth Eide or the Minister of Children Inga Marte Thorkildsen, and all the others who spoke so much truth about the fight against terror and political violence just a short while ago. How can they sit there with all their influence and either stay silent or express their understanding for Israel's 'right to self-defence'? Self-defence? They are the ones attacking, just as they've been attacking for the past sixty years. Haven't we learnt that injustice has to be stopped now, in our time, while we know about it and can act; not as an archaeological exercise under the microscope of hindsight, when the cool, historical distance makes our aversion to the offence easier to live with?

Don't send more bandages, doctors, food parcels or meaningless declarations.

Stop the bombing.

Open Gaza.

Stop the occupation of Palestine.

Let the children live in peace.

Let the mothers nurse their babies.

Let the old drink fresh water.

Let the fishermen fish and the farmers gather their harvest.

Let the teachers teach and the children learn.

Let the young travel and discover something other than the siege, the blockade and fear.

Let the long-awaited gentle rest of a soothing night's sleep embrace the people of Gaza like a blanket.

Then they won't need to defend themselves against a superior force. As the Norwegian poet Nordahl Grieg wrote:

> Then the weapons sink
> powerless to the ground!
> By creating human worth,
> we create peace.

Gaza, 00:40 hrs, Wednesday November 21, 2012

Notes to Foreword 2 – The Eerie Night

1 Mads Gilbert, 'Gaza, i nattens uhygge,' NRK, November 21, 2012: http://www.nrk.no/ytring/gaza_-i-nattens-uhygge-1.8404561 (accessed November 22, 2012).

2 Palestinian Health Information Center, 'Monthly report about the Israeli aggression against citizens in Gaza Strip during November,' December 2, 2012.

3 OCHA-oPt, 'Escalation in hostilities Gaza and southern Israel: Situation Report,' November 26, 2012: http://www.ochaopt.org/documents/ochaopt_gaza_sitrep_26_11_2011_english.pdf (accessed December 3, 2012).

4 OCHA-oPt, 'Escalation in hostilities Gaza and southern Israel: Situation Report,' November 22, 2012: http://www.ochaopt.org/documents/ochaopt_gaza_sitrep_26_11_2011_english.pdf (accessed December 3, 2012).

5 OCHA-oPt, 'Escalation in hostilities in Gaza and southern Israel,' November 21, 2012: http://www.ochaopt.org/documents/gaza_escalation_visual_20121221.pdf (accessed December 3, 2012).

Preface

This is the story of Israel's violent attack on Gaza in the winter of 2008-2009 as we experienced it. The extensive Israeli attacks on Palestinian institutions and civilians were probably among the fiercest of all in the recent history of the Palestinians. The attack hit the children of Gaza particularly hard: more than 300 children were killed and over 1,600 injured.

The brutal attack came after more than two years of a comprehensive blockade and impoverishment of the Palestinians in Gaza. Israel had been systematically preventing western health workers and journalists from coming in. We got in to Gaza from Egypt on New Year's Eve 2008, on the fifth day of the attack. We soon discovered that there were only a very few other Europeans there, and no western journalists. Nobody else was able to or wanted to stand up and tell about the Israeli assault. In addition to our work as doctors at al-Shifa Hospital, it was also our job to convey to the world what we were experiencing. We reported on the terrible suffering we saw, on the injuries we were involved in treating and on the crisis caused by the Israeli attacks and the blockade of Gaza. We reported on the Palestinians' heroism, on their humanity, indomitable optimism and will for resistance.

We have both been working with Palestinian colleagues, friends and patients, in occupied Palestine as well as in Lebanon and Egypt, for three decades. We have lived and worked closely together with the Palestinian refugees and the Lebanese population who were hit in Lebanon, and with the population of Palestine. They have allowed us to take part in some of their darkest and most difficult experiences, and we have celebrated festivals and shared happy times with them.

We still believe that it is possible to solve the Palestinian conflict in a peaceful way. A political solution is the only way to lasting peace. In that case, Israel, which currently has full control, must show by their actions that they respect the Palestinians' human rights and national rights, and that they are willing to find a solution based on the UN resolutions on Palestine from 1947 to the present day.

We experienced the attack on Gaza, as doctors and as witnesses, at a hospital. We did not see what was happening elsewhere in Gaza. The brutality of the attacks and the extent to which they were premeditated only became apparent to us afterwards, not least through the documentation that journalists and boards of inquiry have obtained.

Words are powerful. Definitions and terminology influence our understanding of reality. Words and terms that are used in relation to the Middle East conflict have slipped uncritically into everyday speech and into the news, so that a smoke screen is laid down over power relationships and political realities. 'The Palestinian conflict' is used more frequently than 'the Israeli occupation of Palestine', and 'Palestinian territories' is used more often than 'occupied Gaza'. The name of the country where this conflict is taking place *is* Palestine. The state of Israel, the West Bank and Gaza are all to be found in Palestine. This is why we call the West Bank and Gaza 'Palestine' or 'occupied Palestine', not 'the Palestinian territories'.

'Settlement' is often used to describe areas where Israelis have established themselves in Palestine. 'Settlement' gives an impression of a society established in an uninhabited area. When someone takes control of an area with military force, when they chase the original occupants away from their land and homes and drive farmers away in order take possession of the land, then the correct term is 'occupation'. Those who carry out such actions are usually called 'occupiers', and the housing structures that are established there make up a 'colony'. The colonisation of occupied land is against the Geneva Convention. Israeli policy in the West Bank and in Gaza is therefore not one of peaceful settlement, but of brutal occupation and colonisation against international law.

As a result, we describe newly established Israeli communities in occupied areas consistently as 'colonies', and those who live there as 'occupiers'. Because this colonisation of Palestine is based on the Zionist idea of conquering the territory in the Land of Israel – *Eretz Israel* – from the original Palestinian population and establishing a new state there that would only be for Jews, we have used the terms 'Israeli occupiers' and 'Israeli colonies', although those who establish these colonies may belong to other nationalities. Many of the most aggressive and militant occupiers are visiting activists with US citizenship.

The Israeli military forces call themselves the Israeli Defence Forces (IDF). The acts of warfare we write about here are more acts of 'attack' and 'expansion' than they are 'defence'. We have therefore used the more neutral term 'the Israeli military forces'.

The descriptions of those who fight in a conflict also vary depending on the speaker. 'Terrorist' is frequently used in everyday language and actually means 'one who spreads fear'. The Palestinians interpret the blockade, bombing, starvation and daily harassment carried out by Israel as terrorism. Israel calls all Palestinian resistance members, and their families, terrorists. The USA has unilaterally defined a long list of political and humanitarian organisations and individuals as 'terrorists' and 'terror organisations'. They are thereby also defined as criminals and are banned according to American terror legislation. The terror and terrorist terminology used in everyday speech are at best over-simplified and often misleading, and these terms obstruct dialogue and make peace and reconciliation difficult. We have chosen to call Israelis or Egyptians serving in their nations' regular military forces 'soldiers'. We have chosen to call Palestinians who are not part of a state's army, but who carry out armed resistance against the occupation under the direction of known or unknown Palestinian parties and groups, 'combatants'. We have called civilians those who do not take part in the planning or execution of armed action.

The word 'security zone' is also misused; the term gives an impression of zones set up to protect civilians. In occupied Palestine, the establishment by Israel of such 'security zones' on land, in the air and at sea has been a political and military means of denying the Palestinians access to their own land and their own homes and the right to utilise natural resources in their own country. Therefore, we call these areas 'military zones'.

We have described our experiences in Gaza as objectively and accurately as possible. Any mistakes in our account are our responsibility. The book is based on our own notes, diaries, photographs, video recordings and conversations during our time there, and we have subsequently carried out thorough inquiries in the news media and other sources. When our documentary photographs have been treated, we have followed the rules for photo-journalistic use of image processing programs. We have verified names and events as much as has been possible, and we have obtained written permission for the publication of pictures of patients and others at the hospital. Most families strongly urged us to use the pictures. We would like to thank our Palestinian and Norwegian colleagues who have helped us with our work on the book.

We have deep respect for the patients and the families we met, and for the health personnel we worked together with. Thank you for letting us experience your heroism and unshakeable optimism!

Oslo/Tromsø, July 2009

Jumana

MADS GILBERT

At first I didn't realise the background to the case. The little nine month old girl I had been asked to attend to was just an early warning. She was pale and ill-looking after the anaesthetic and was almost unrousable. She was lying on her back, so I gently lifted her chin forwards to keep her airway free. I listened carefully on both sides of her delicate little chest. Good, symmetrical breath sounds. We trundled her on a trolley which was altogether too big, in search of a newly opened intensive care room on the fourth floor. The room was really a post-operative recovery room for adults, but because of the big influx of war-wounded children needing observation after lifesaving surgery and anaesthesia, the hospital management was constantly finding new and improvised solutions to increase the bed capacity.

We eventually found it. The sun was streaming into the six-bedded room. The windows stood open. One of them was broken, and it was icy cold. The staff had evidently had a message about getting ready to receive new patients. They told me clearly that they were not ready yet.

'Please doctor, can you wait?'

Yes, of course we could wait.

I stood beside little Jumana Al-Samouni's trolley. Parts of her tiny little left hand had had to be amputated after the nasty injury she had sustained in the family house. Nobody knew where her mother was, but her father and grandfather must have been killed. There were some Arabic letters written on her chest with a felt pen; the type of injury and priority rating, I assumed. The X-ray picture which lay on the trolley showed that her thumb and second and third fingers had been amputated. The bandage was soaked through with blood, but the bleeding appeared to have stopped.

The little girl had pretty, sharp, almost adult features and strong eyebrows. Her sallow skin colour was suggestive of anaemia following blood loss, or as a result of the undernourishment which so many children in Gaza suffer from. She looked as if she was sleeping peacefully, and her closed eyes had an almost absurdly relaxed appearance. I felt her skin. It felt cool and a little irregular, as if she was chilled. She would certainly have lost heat both during the operation and now as she lay stripped in the chilly room.

That was a problem for all the patients. The hospital had so many broken windows, and the January temperature in Gaza that winter was certainly not showing any signs of tropical heat. The temperature at night was between five and ten degrees, though the sun was warm by day. Al-Shifa Hospital lies only three blocks away from the coast. When you went to see patients in the wards on the third and fourth floors which looked towards the west, you could see the waves breaking on the chalk-white sandy beach. The wind from the sea was chilly, and the scant power supply from the two emergency generators was simply not enough to heat the wards adequately. Only the operating theatres and the intensive care departments seemed to have priority for heating. The rest of the hospital was icy cold.

Most of the patients were equipped with blankets brought to the hospital by their families – often with what little extra food could be obtained – or by Islamic Relief. The relief organisation obviously had stores in Gaza. The blankets were good to have in the cold nights. But Jumana had not got a blanket, either from Islamic Relief or from anybody else. She was all alone, apparently without any family.

While I tried to cover her with the thin hospital sheet, one of the nurses told me that the little girl came from the poor quarter of al-Zaytoun in the south part of Gaza. According to the nurse, the Israelis had bombed the family's house and killed eleven members of the family that morning. Another nurse said that ground forces from an Israeli tank position had forced many of the Samouni family together into one of the family houses overnight, so that the house would be full of people when they bombed it the next morning. The Samouni family is big. Altogether about a hundred of the family members including women, children and the elderly had been herded into a warehouse in al-Zaytoun before they attacked the building.

Could such a well organised and experienced army as Israel's have carried out a comprehensive massacre of defenceless, unarmed Palestinian civilians? An army led by officers who take their orders from the government of a state which describes itself as one of the world's strongest

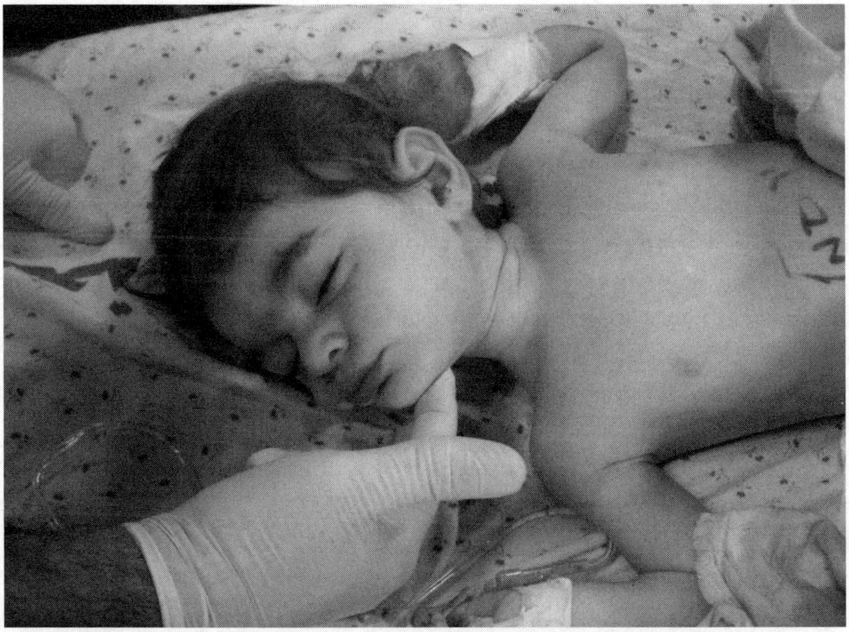

Half of little Jumana's left hand had to be amputated after the attack. Now she was under sedation and sleeping peacefully.

democracies, led by a president who has won the Nobel Peace Prize? It sounded too barbaric. It must have been a misunderstanding, a rumour which had been blown up, a complete exaggeration of the facts. There was a lot of confusion and many rumours circulating in Gaza during these days, and fantasy is often worse than reality. Not in this case.

Unfortunately it turned out to be true. There *was* a massacre. It was no mistake, but evidently a systematically planned and executed Israeli military operation. Soldiers from the Israeli armed forces had carried out the monstrous operation. Our patient, little Jumana, was just one of many victims in the Samouni family that day. More were to follow.

As a defence mechanism we refuse for as long as possible to believe that such things are real. We want the instances of assault, killing, maltreatment and injury to be the result of unfortunate circumstances, a momentary confusion, a miscalculation, a sick mind or horrible misunderstandings. That's not how it was in Gaza.

The appalling details of the massacre of the Samouni family came to light bit by bit. There were a lot of pieces to the jigsaw. We were among the very first outsiders to learn what had happened. I sent out a report as soon as I had a minimum of clear details cross-checked. The Swedish newspaper *Expressen* published a big feature article. The journalist was from Lebanon and recognised the patterns of behaviour of the Israeli army from his own recent history. He was horrified by what he heard. Sabra and Shatila are names which still symbolise the merciless massacres characteristic of the Israeli military forces, names which are branded on the collective memory of all of Arabic birth in the Middle East. The Norwegian newspaper *Aftenposten* also had a small article on its website. Both articles concentrated more on Jumana than on the massacre itself. The world would gradually get to know what had happened.

The nurses wanted me to insert a central venous catheter into Jumana so that we could give fluids to her more easily. She already had a small venous cannula, but they were concerned that it would block. A central venous catheter is a rather longer plastic cannula, which is placed in one of the major blood vessels through an incision in the skin and using a special technique to find the location of the blood vessel, either deep in the chest cavity or in the neck. The advantage is that it makes it easier to give bigger doses of fluid and blood directly into the central circulation. The disadvantages are potential complications from the incision itself, and serious risk of infection. I didn't think she needed a central cannula, because her injuries were moderate and her condition was stable. We discussed the case a little while Jumana gradually wakened up. She looked round without crying and quickly shut her eyes again. Mummy wasn't there. 'I'll come back and see to her later,' I said. 'Take care that she doesn't lie uncovered and get any colder than she is already. Just keep her well covered and check her pulse and respiration.'

'Of course. We'll do our best.'

I saw her again about midnight that evening. She looked like a little doll, lying in a bed that was far too big for her. She was no longer alone; there was an elderly woman dressed in black standing beside the bed. The nurses introduced her as 'a grandmother on the father's side.' First, I examined Jumana. She seemed alert, with normal vital signs of consciousness, breathing and circulation. She looked round the room with a surprised, inquisitive glance. The lady in black was indignant. Just like other relatives I met at al-Shifa Hospital, she wanted to talk about her anger over what had happened.

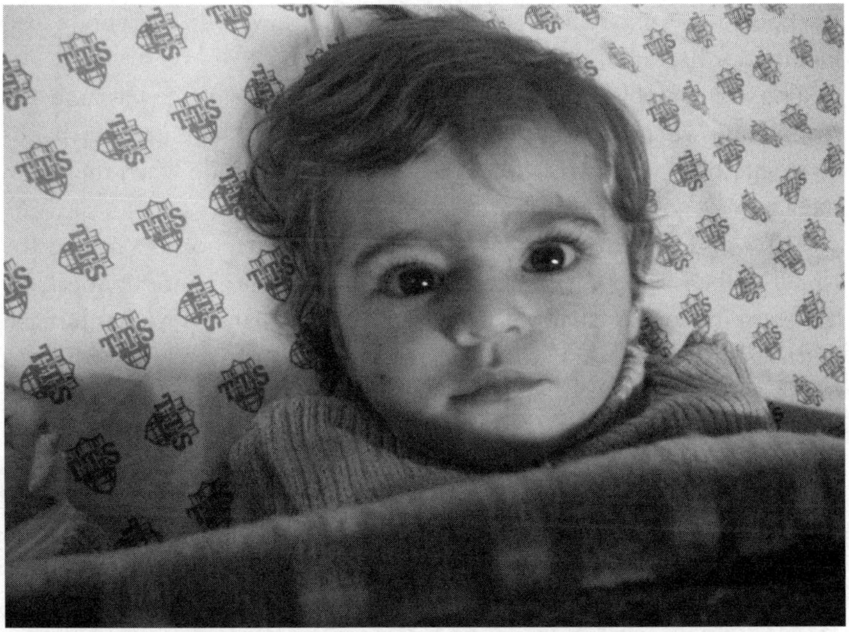

When we reviewed the children post-operatively around midnight, Jumana was awake and watchful.

'Where is Jumana's mother?' she began. 'The child is still being breast-fed. What shall we give her now?'

I obviously had no good answer. 'Tell me what happened,' I asked her.

Through an interpreter, she told me about the massacre. I took notes, and she gave consent right away when I asked for permission to take some pictures.

The family had been herded together in a big house during the day of January 4, nearly a hundred men, women and children of all ages. They had to stay in the house overnight without food or drink, more or less as hostages of the Israeli troops who had taken up position nearby. Early the next morning, the house was bombed by the Israelis. I didn't quite grasp whether it was an air attack by fighter-bombers, helicopters or drones, or whether the house was shot at by tanks. It was undoubtedly such a damaging attack that the house was completely demolished, many people were killed and even more were wounded. Jumana's father, grandfather and grandmother were killed along with many other members of the family, but it was thought that Jumana's mother and uncle had managed to escape. The uncle was captured by the Israelis, but mother just disappeared. Nobody knew where she was now, but everybody was looking for her.

The woman looked straight at me as she spoke. Her voice was high and strong, and when she was telling the worst details, she raised her hands above her head in a sorrowful gesture as Arab women do when they send their cries of anguish up towards heaven and to Allah.

'Why does this happen? Why have we no protection? Why are the Israelis killing us poor, defenceless Palestinians? We are not political, we have nothing to do with it, we are just ordinary civilians. What has Jumana done against them? Are they just evil, these people? Who is going to protect us?'

1

1

Into the Bomb Zone

ERIK FOSSE

Two days before Christmas 2008 a telefax came to NORWAC's office in Oslo. It said that Dr Medhat Abbas was appointed to the post of Director General of the International Co-operation Department Gaza. The letter was signed by Dr Bassem Naim, who was a surgeon and the Health Minister in Gaza. The report explained the division of responsibilities in relation to the serious crisis which was about to develop.

Officially, Bassem Naim was not Health Minister. The internationally recognised government for the self-governing Palestinian Authority sat in Ramallah on the West Bank, and Health Minister Fathi Abu Moghli had his office there. But now it was undoubtedly the Gaza Strip which was the focus of attention, and it was Hamas who were in control there. Bassem Naim was Hamas's Health Minister. NORWAC had been holding a balance between the two governments since 2007.

On Christmas Eve John Eivind Jensen, NORWAC's Palestine co-ordinator, got an e-mail from the health authorities in Gaza. It stated that the stores were completely empty of 105 important drugs and 225 types of essential disposable items. They were lacking practically everything. Since August barely a third of supplies sent from the West Bank had reached Gaza.[1] NORWAC had medical equipment for the hospitals in Gaza that had been stuck in Israel for half a year waiting for permission to get it in to Gaza.

It was a discouraging message to have to pass on to the NORWAC committee just as Christmas was coming in. I wrote: 'The situation is explosive now. We need to discuss how to get ready, whether we should contact the Norwegian authorities, etc. It is very likely that there will be a confrontation in Gaza with numerous casualties.'

The confrontation came.

At half past eleven on the morning of Saturday December 27, Israel

Ready to leave Cairo: Erik Fosse (left), John Eivind Jensen and Mads Gilbert outside the Marriott Hotel in Cairo, December 30, 2008.

began a fierce bombardment of Gaza. More than fifty fighter planes and attack helicopters took part in the attack. More than a hundred bombs were dropped on government offices, police stations and Hamas's headquarters. Somewhere between 225 and 290 Palestinians were killed, and very many were injured on the first day. One of the major targets was the police. All the police stations were bombed. In Gaza City there was an admission ceremony for new police officers that day. More than forty police officers and young police cadets were killed when the station was bombed.[2]

Two hours after the attack started, John Eivind phoned Health Minister Bassem Naim. He was able tell us that patients were streaming into al-Shifa Hospital in Gaza City. Emergency aid was urgently required. John Eivind rang the head of the Norwegian diplomatic office in Ramallah, Ministerial Envoy Tor Wennesland, to inform him of the situation and to say that NORWAC was interested in sending in emergency aid if that was possible.

On Sunday Israel continued the attack with undiminished force. A further twenty-five air attacks raised the casualty toll to 287 killed and 900 wounded.[3] A fighter plane fired a missile into the mosque just across the road from al-Shifa Hospital. The mosque was totally destroyed. Israel also bombed the building complex of al-Saraya, which housed Hamas's government offices and Gaza's main prison. The complex had already been evacuated, and only four people were killed. Meanwhile Hamas was continuing to fire rockets against Israel.

John Eivind Jensen rang me in Oslo on Sunday forenoon.

'Erik, I think I'll go to Cairo tomorrow to see if I can get some supplies into Gaza.'

'Have you been in contact with anyone there?' I asked.

'No, not since yesterday but I'll call Bassem Naim now.'

I could imagine the situation in Gaza. I had been in situations like that several times before. Even if the hospitals were maintaining high standards and had many capable doctors, they would still need more now.

'I may have to go to Gaza,' I said to my partner, Nina Husom.

'That's no surprise,' said Nina quietly. 'But if you must, you must. There goes *this* Christmas.'

Nina had herself worked as a physiotherapist in war zones in Eritrea, and she understood how I felt about it.

I called back to John Eivind.

'I'm coming with you to Cairo. We can get a surgical team together,' I said.

'Yes, and ring Mads Gilbert to ask if the Palestine Committee has anything on the go.'

I phoned Mads in Tromsø that same afternoon. I had known him since the beginning of the 1980s. Mads was a founder member of NORWAC in 1983, and we had worked together in Gaza before. He was an experienced anaesthetist and acute medicine specialist, and he knew Gaza as well as I did.

'Hi Mads, it's all happening again.'

Mads does not take long to move from thought to action. He had already phoned Line Katheeb, the chair of the Palestine Committee, and a number of experienced nurses. He had also phoned the Ambassador in Cairo.

'Nobody is ready. But someone called Vethe at the Embassy in Cairo says that the frontier isn't closed yet.'

I told him about the travel plans.

'I'm coming too. I've booked tickets and cleared it with the family. My daughters Anna and Siri and my son-in-law Torbjørn are celebrating Christmas here in Tromsø. They all support my decision to go,' said Mads. 'But there's a demonstration here in Tromsø tomorrow and I'm due to speak. Can't we wait till Tuesday?'

'No, it's urgent,' I said.

Later on in the afternoon I spoke with John Eivind again.

'Mads has dropped out of the demonstration tomorrow and is coming with us. I've booked tickets,' he said.

John Eivind had also asked Dagfinn Bjørklid, NORWAC's co-ordinator in Beirut, to go to Jerusalem, so that he could get to Erez, the northern border post between Israel and Gaza, at short notice.

'We really don't know how we're going to be able to send supplies in,' he concluded.

It was important to clear NORWAC's emergency aid to Gaza with the official health authorities. John Eivind had sent an e-mail to the Health Minister in Ramallah, Dr Fathi Abu Moghli, to inform him that we were going to Cairo the next day and would try to get into Gaza. That evening I packed a bag with a few clothes, a camera and my mobile phone. While I was throwing them into the bag, I thought about how Mads packs. I reckoned that he would have laid a camera, computer equipment, stethoscopes, pocket torches, a head torch, vital drugs and possibly a few textbooks out on the bed and then packed it all neatly. It struck me how different we were, and that hopefully that was a strength.

At four o'clock on Monday morning I said goodbye to Nina.

'Don't do anything silly,' she said sleepily.

'No, no, I'll be careful and I promise to come back. I have a return ticket in one week.'

I picked up John Eivind on the way to Oslo Gardermoen Airport. Mads had come from Tromsø on Sunday evening and was there to join us. During an intermediate landing in Vienna, we had confirmation from the Foreign Ministry Section for Humanitarian Affairs that 30 million kroner was being granted for emergency aid following Israel's attack on Gaza, and that NORWAC was to get 5 million of this. We informed the Foreign Ministry representative that Hamas's Health Minister in Gaza had given us lists of the emergency drugs required, and that Mads and I would try to travel into Gaza.

At Cairo Airport we were met by a white-haired man in his sixties. He was holding a sign with NORWAC written on it, and he introduced himself as Abdallah, chauffeur at the Norwegian Embassy. He escorted us to the quickest queue at immigration control and then to the embassy car, and drove us to the Marriott Hotel in the centre of Cairo. Outside the entrance stood a big Christmas tree made of cotton wool, sticks and steel wire. Christmas spirits in Cairo.

The weather was like a slightly cool summer day in Norway. We sat by a table under the palm trees and ordered beer.

'I thought it was you sitting there,' said Anders Vethe, smiling. 'Welcome to Cairo.'

'We've had a message from the Foreign Ministry asking us to help you to get into Gaza,' he said. 'We've looked into the matter, and I think we'll almost certainly manage it. We've spoken to Egyptian authorities and there are indications that you can get through.'

All Norwegian ambassadors are dependent on having a good network. Randa Hakim, the Egyptian office manager at the embassy, knew a lot of people throughout Egyptian society. She knew who could fix what.

'We'll drive you to the border,' Vethe continued. Here at the embassy we'll do all we can to get you in and out of Gaza safely.'

John Eivind phoned Tariq Arafat and arranged a meeting for half past seven. Tariq was the son of Fathi Arafat, who founded and led the Palestinian Red Crescent. He was also the nephew of the PLO leader, Yasser Arafat. Tariq was an engineer specialising in medical technology. He was now head of the Palestinian Red Crescent office in Egypt. When I came down into the garden, there sat Tariq and Mai Aref from the information department of the Palestinian Red Crescent (PRCS), smoking hookahs. John Eivind and Mads were also there.

The list we had got from the health authorities in Gaza was very extensive. Tariq phoned several suppliers, and it was very clear that we would have to prioritise what was most important to take in with us.

In the course of the evening Mads picked out the medications he thought were absolutely essential to take with us, mostly anaesthetic drugs and a few antibiotics.

We agreed to travel to the frontier crossing at Rafah the next day and try to get into Gaza. John Eivind would remain in Cairo to act as team co-ordinator and buy in the rest of the supplies on the list. Dagfinn would await developments in Jerusalem.

Waiting for medical supplies in front of the Palestinian Red Crescent Hospital in Heliopolis, Cairo, just before travelling to El Arish.

'We can't hold back a long time waiting for supplies tomorrow. The most important thing is to get on the go early so that we get in,' I said.

'I agree,' said Mads, 'even if we just take some anaesthetic drugs with us.'

On Tuesday morning December 30, the Foreign Ministry reported that Foreign Minister Jonas Gahr Støre was to hold a press conference at ten o'clock, at which he would announce that Norway was sending emergency aid into Gaza that day. The emergency aid was us.

We had planned not to say anything to the press until we had reached Gaza. Now, after the Foreign Minister's press conference, there would be a lot of speculation. I therefore phoned TV2 and told them that Mads and I would try to get over the border. At the press conference, Støre described the humanitarian catastrophe in Gaza and underlined Israel's responsibility to allow help in. He called for an end to the fighting, and confirmed that Norway would work to get aid in.[4]

At the embassy Randa Hakim copied our passports and supplied us with documents in English and Arabic, confirming that we were Norwegian health workers on a humanitarian mission.

The first stop on the journey to Rafah was the Palestinian Red Crescent's hospital in Heliopolis, on the outskirts of Cairo. Tariq Arafat met us outside. He told us that he was in contact with the supplier and believed he would manage to obtain the medicaments on the revised list. But it still wasn't definite. The supplier would be coming in a quarter of an hour.

'We ought to be wearing something which identifies us as health workers,' said Mads. 'We need white coats and if possible a jacket, like the ones the ambulance crews in the Palestinian Red Crescent wear.'

Tariq Arafat directed us to a shop which sold clothes for health workers. It was in the El Korba district of the city. Just round the corner was Sharia Baghdad, or Baghdad Street, where the brothers Yasser and Fathi Arafat had played as youngsters. We each bought a jacket and went back to the Red Crescent Hospital in Heliopolis. The pharmacist was expected in half an hour. Mads and I looked at the time. It usually takes six hours to drive from Cairo to Rafah, and we began to worry that we would be too late in getting to the border.

'Have some tea,' said Tariq.

Late or not, we understood clearly that we would have to take tea with Tariq. This is as important a part of Arabic etiquette as greeting someone or saying 'Goodbye.' Tariq was obliged to invite us to tea, anything else would have been a grave insult, and we were obliged to accept. But both Mads and I were beginning to feel impatient.

After a few years in the Middle East you learn to appreciate the value of this ritual. It is calming, and it reminds you that people are important. We had a high regard for Tariq Arafat, who with his modest but energetic style had been incredibly effective. In the course of a night he had gathered together life-saving medicines for which extensive paperwork is normally required. He was influential, and he was committed to helping people in Gaza. He knew that we would not be working for Fatah or the Red Crescent in Gaza, but in al-Shifa public hospital, which was controlled by Hamas's health authorities. Tariq put help to his fellow countrymen in Gaza before party politics, and that commanded respect. I thought that if all Palestinian leaders had had the same attitude as he had, the current situation in Palestine would have been quite different.

He took out a Red Crescent jacket.

'You can take this one,' he said to Mads. 'This is my jacket.'

New Year's Eve 2008: waiting anxiously on the Egyptian side of the Gaza border, with Fathi Mohamed Abdallah, chauffeur and a capable local guide from the Norwegian Embassy.

With a white coat, an orange jacket and a stethoscope round his neck, Mads really began to look like an emergency medicine doctor, which pleased him. I contented myself with the white coat.

At last the pharmacist arrived with two boxes of medicines, about ten kilos in weight altogether.

'The emergency aid to 1.5 million people in Gaza,' I commented.

I looked at the clock; it was half past one. We were on our way at last, but we still had several hours' journey across the Sinai Desert ahead of us.

The Norwegian Ambassador in Cairo had put a car and driver at our disposal. Hassan Youssef Emara drove while Fathi Mohamed Abdallah reported regularly to the embassy on his mobile phone. Hassan manoeuvred skilfully through the dense Cairo traffic and out onto the highway to Gaza. As I was looking out over the dusty landscape, my phone started to ring. The news that we were trying to get in had reached all the Norwegian media.

'Would you like a Moro chocolate bar?'

Mads opened the carrier bag with water and chocolate which he had bought at a café in the middle of the Sinai desert. He put the bag with the Egyptian equivalent of a Mars bar down between us. Outside the car windows the desert flashed by: the light, almost beige-coloured sand, a scattering of bushes, a few fruit trees – and a few houses here and there. The sun was beating on the car roof, but there was not much warmth in the air.

At ten past three we crossed the enormous bridge over the Suez Canal at El Qantara. Like the canal, the bridge was a gigantic piece of engineering. I looked out of the window. Far down there, seventy metres below us, big boats glided slowly past, red hulls glistening on the calm, blue surface of the water. Life was going on as usual, and we were on our way to hell.

Health Minister Naim phoned to say that we would be met at the other side of the border.

'I don't think we'll get over the border today. I crossed here a year ago, and they close at four o'clock,' said Mads sceptically.

We got there at half past four. Lorries stood lined up in front of the entrance gate to the border post. Hassan manoeuvred the car elegantly past the queue and on to the border post.

Abdallah took our passports and went to speak to the soldiers who stood there. We stayed in the car. At the border there were journalists from many lands. When they saw our white coats, they asked if we were doctors on our way into Gaza.

At last Abdallah came back.

'Nobody here has heard that you are coming,' he said. 'Apparently the security guards who have been requested to let you through have gone for the day.'

Just as Abdallah was trying to phone Randa Hakim at the embassy, there was a loud bang. The blast was so strong that the car moved. Chaos broke out. Everyone ran to their vehicles. Hassan swung the car round, and headed at full speed away from the Gaza border, back through Egypt to the town of El Arish, forty-five kilometres away. The bombs were falling behind us.

El Arish had originally been a little fishing village. During the 1967 war, when Israel occupied Gaza, many Palestinians had fled there. In 2008 there were 120,000 residents in El Arish, of whom 60 per cent were Palestinian. The Egyptian population is mostly Bedouin. The town has gradually become an attractive holiday destination for well-to-do Egyptians, and there are rows of beach hotels along the shore. Hassan drove to one of these, the Swiss Inn Hotel. As Hassan, Abdallah, Mads and I ate dinner in the restaurant, we discussed the news. On Monday, Israeli fighter planes had bombed the laboratory building of the Islamic University, which Israel claimed was being used to store rockets and explosives.[5] They had also bombed a mosque in the refugee camp in Jabaliya. The Red Cross reported that the hospitals in the Gaza Strip were having great problems dealing with all the patients.

'Have you heard about the boat which was attacked by Israeli naval vessels yesterday?' asked Hassan.

'Attacked?' I repeated with disbelief.

We had heard about the *Dignity*, which had set out from Cyprus with aid workers, medical supplies and journalists. The intention was to bring emergency aid to Gaza by sea. But before they got there, they were stopped by an Israeli naval vessel which fired warning machine-gun shots round the boat. Finally they rammed the relatively small yacht three or four times. Fortunately, the *Dignity* did not sink, and managed to reach the Lebanese port of Saida under its own power.[6]

The sun was shining next morning, but there was an icy cold wind from the sea. At eight o'clock we met for breakfast.

'We'll need to get going,' said Mads. He had already checked out ages ago, and he was impatient.

I went to the room to fetch my bag. When I came back to reception, Mads was standing with four men wearing *gellabiya* (the Arab tunic) and *kufiya* (the Arab headscarf). They were doctors and pharmacists from Qatar and Saudi Arabia who had been waiting since Sunday to get into Gaza. They had two complete field hospitals and several trailers loaded with medical equipment, but they couldn't get over the border.

I was struck again by how brutal the blockade was. More than a thousand people had already been injured in the bombing raids. Inside Gaza, just a few kilometres away, they had nothing. In my pocket I had a detailed list of painkillers, lifesaving drugs and equipment which we would try to take in with us. Outside in front of us stood a queue of trailers with medical supplies and doctors who could not get in. Everybody was powerless.

Hassan drove us to the centre of town. We could see that this was a busy place. The trade between Gaza and El Arish had always been important.

After the borders were closed and goods had to be smuggled through tunnels, prices rose. What was an economic catastrophe for the Palestinians in Gaza, was an economic benefit for their relatives in El Arish. During the last days of 2008 the hotel industry also benefited. The beach hotels, which were mostly closed in the winter, got a new clientele of press reporters and aid workers from all over the world who were waiting to get into Gaza.

At nine o'clock we were standing in front of the security chief's office in El Arish. Abdallah disappeared in through the door. After a few minutes he came out again and waved us in. Sitting at the counter was a uniform-clad man with an expressionless face.

'If you're going to sit here and wait for the security chief, you'll need to hand in your mobile phones,' he said without raising an eyelid.

'Absolutely not, we won't sit here and wait, we'll talk with him now.'

'That's not possible, because he's not here.'

'We have an appointment at nine o'clock.'

'Well, he's not here.'

Mads and I looked at each other, and then at Abdallah.

'Does that mean he's coming soon?'

'I don't think so,' said Abdallah.

'Then we'll just leave it and go on to the border now.'

Mads' patience was now stretched to breaking point. But it would take more than that to budge an Egyptian bureaucrat.

'Can you phone Randa Hakim and ask her to call her contacts in the security service as soon as possible? Say that we'll be at the border in half an hour.'

Abdallah had entered the number before I could finish the sentence.

The journey to the border went quickly. I tried to phone Health Minister Bassem Naim for confirmation that someone was waiting for us in Gaza, but I couldn't get through. I also sent a text message, but as there was no certainty that it would get through either, I rang John Eivind Jensen in Cairo. I asked him to contact Bassem Naim and say that we would probably be across the border within an hour. I was worried that we would be waiting on the other side of the border for ages before anyone came to fetch us. The border could be bombed at any time by the Israelis, who were watching over it all the time from the air.

Sinai is completely flat right up to the border crossing at Rafah. The area between El Arish and Rafah is covered with fields and little houses. The morning sun was shining over fields and olive groves. Along the road stood groups of police with weapons, shields and dogs.

'Their job is probably to catch people who try to escape through the tunnels,' Mads explained.

It was like going into a prison. High fences and walls marked the border. Nobody could slip in, and nobody was allowed to slip out.

It was just before half past ten when we came to a stop in front of the border gate. Abdallah disappeared in again with our passports.

We got out of the car. A journalist from the BBC interviewed Mads. The journalist had been trying to get in since Sunday, but without any success. A French journalist interviewed me, but I had little to say except that we were trying to get in. The French journalist had given up and was about to go home.

Abdallah came back with the passports.

'You're getting in,' he said.

Mads gave a shout of joy: 'Yesss!'

We took our passports and hugged Hassan and Abdallah. They seemed worried.

'Take care of yourselves,' said Hassan seriously.

Inside the gate an Egyptian soldier took our passports and told us to follow him. It was about fifty metres of open ground to the main building. Once inside, the baggage was scanned.

Then we were taken through the main building and out onto another area of open ground where four soldiers stood, each with his dog on a metal chain. The dogs stretched their chains and growled, staring angrily at us. We walked forward to a man in a dark grey coat and sunglasses. He looked at our passports.

'What are you doing here?'

'We're going into Gaza to work. We are doctors.'

We were wearing the white coats we had bought in Cairo. Mads had a stethoscope round his neck. Another three men in dark grey greatcoats and sunglasses appeared.

'What are you doing here?' one of them asked.

I realised that things were beginning to turn difficult. Mads took up his mobile phone and rang Randa at the embassy. He explained the situation briefly to her. Then he handed his phone to one of the men with sunglasses.

I don't know what she said, but when he had finished the call, the tone was totally different.

Gaza. Finally through the last check-point at the border crossing in Rafah. In the background, Egyptian soldiers with dogs, behind shields and barbed wire.

Welcome to Gaza! Travelling north to Gaza City in a Palestinian ambulance with a Palestinian ambulance crew, New Year's Eve 2008.

Through the window of the ambulance we could already see extensive damage in Rafah from the Israeli bombing.

Our first experience of the war, New Year's Eve 2008. A doctor killed while working in an ambulance is carried out of the hospital by his family for burial.

'You are welcome to cross the border, but there's a stamp missing in your passports,' he said. 'You'll need to go back and get them stamped.'

We were worried that someone would try to send us back to Egypt, so we put our bags and the boxes of medicines down in the middle of the square, in order to have an excuse for going back if anyone tried to stop us again.

'Can you watch these bags and boxes of medicines for us?' I asked one of the men.

Another one followed us into the office of the chief of the Egyptian border post.

'Wait here,' he said, and took our passports.

After a few minutes he came back with the necessary stamps.

'Welcome, and good luck in Gaza,' he said with a smile.

As we were coming out into the open, several Egyptian soldiers with batons and shields came running out of the barracks on the east side of the square. For a moment I thought that they were going to attack us, but they carried on out through the gate, towards Gaza. The bags and boxes were still in the middle of the square. The first of the men with sunglasses checked that the stamps were in order.

'That's fine,' he said, and waved us through the gateway where the soldiers with shields and batons had run out. They were standing deployed on each side of the twenty metres of no man's land which separated Egypt and Gaza. They were obviously there to prevent Palestinians escaping from Gaza when the gate was opened, but to us it felt like running the gauntlet. We were smiling despite this, glad that we were able to cross the border. Running the gauntlet between soldiers couldn't destroy our morale now.

'Thank you for the help, have a good day,' we said to the ranks of soldiers. Not one of them smiled.

It was half past midday on New Year's Eve when we walked through the gateway into Gaza. It had taken two hours to cross the border.

In Gaza the mood was totally different. Three Palestinian police officers stood assembled informally just inside the gate.

'Welcome to Gaza,' they said, smiling.

The leader of the convoy, Dr Moawya Hassanin, met us. He already knew Mads. One of the police took our passports.

'I'll see to the stamps,' he said. 'Just wait here.'

After a few minutes he came back, holding a telephone.

'The Norwegian Ambassador would like to speak to you,' he said, handing me the phone.

It was Tor Wennesland from the Norwegian Representative Office in Ramallah.

'Good that you managed to come over,' he said. 'Are you coming on further?'

'Yes, we're getting into an ambulance now and we'll report back once we have reached al-Shifa Hospital.'

Settled in the back of the ambulance with the two first aid attendants, Mads and I looked at each other. We were in. In!

'What's the situation like?' I asked the first-aider sitting beside me.

'Bad,' he replied.

'They're bombing all the time. Just wait and see.'

2

2

Prelude

ERIK FOSSE

How did a small humanitarian organisation such as NORWAC (the Norwegian Aid Committee) come to have a role as emissary between Fatah's officially recognised health minister, Fathi Abu Moghli, and Hamas's health minister, Dr Bassem Naim? The story goes right back to 1982.

When Lebanon was attacked by Israel in 1982, the Norwegian Palestine Committee sent a crisis team there. After Israel occupied South Lebanon, we realised that the solidarity organisation could no longer send health workers to the Palestinian refugees there. On advice from the Norwegian Foreign Ministry, the Palestine Committee set up NORWAC as an independent humanitarian organisation. NORWAC soon built up a network of projects in Libya and Palestine and gradually developed into an autonomous humanitarian foundation.[7]

NORWAC was little known in Norway up until the time of the latest war in Gaza. All the projects were financed either by the Foreign Ministry or for short periods by NORAD, the Norwegian Agency for Development Co-operation.

For the first few years, NORWAC worked with various private organisations in Palestine and Lebanon. When the Oslo Accords were signed in 1993, the method of working in Palestine changed. The Accords require Israel to recognise the PLO as a participant in negotiations and as the sole legitimate representative of the Palestinians, and give the PLO the right to set up a system of self-government on the West Bank and in Gaza. In the spring of 1994 the PLO accordingly began to set up government ministries, and on July 1, Yasser Arafat was due to return to Palestine after twenty-seven years in exile. His route took him from Cairo to Gaza, from where he would be flown by helicopter to the town of Jericho, where he was due to meet the Palestinians of the West Bank.

On June 30, 1994, John Eivind Jensen and I were in Gaza to discuss various projects with Riyad Zanoun, who was Minister of Health in the new self-governing Palestinian Authority. Zanoun told us that the Palestinian Red Crescent and the Health Ministry were concerned that there might be an assassination attempt or a bomb in the crowd of people in Jericho. So they had arranged an emergency medical team for Arafat's visit. We asked if they needed a surgical team, and they said yes. The Minister of Health decided that NORWAC should follow with an ambulance in Arafat's motorcade, carrying surgical equipment in case anything happened.

Early the next morning we met in Makassed Hospital in Jerusalem. We were welcomed by the Chief Nursing Officer, who gave us anaesthetic supplies and surgical equipment. Then we set off from Jerusalem in a convoy of ambulances, heading towards Jericho. The convoy stopped. Israeli police said that we would have to wait. We got out of the ambulance. Fifty metres ahead, Israeli occupiers had blocked the road with burning tyres. Their intention was to stop West Bank Palestinians from witnessing Arafat's homecoming. We were kept standing for an hour until the police at last cleared a way past the tyres and we were able to drive slowly through. The occupiers beat on the ambulances and shouted slogans opposing Arafat.

In Jericho the streets were decorated. There were Palestinian flags flying, but the public square where Arafat was due to speak was still empty.

Jericho stands surrounded by hills a short distance north of the Dead Sea, 258 metres below sea level. The temperature in the town that day had risen to forty degrees.

In the ambulance, we had air-conditioning so long as the engine was running. But we were soon hemmed in by a big crowd, and the vehicle was forced to stop. The engine was idling, and was not producing enough power to drive the air-conditioning system. The driver had to stop the engine. The temperature in the ambulance steadily rose to over forty degrees. Among our equipment we had several ice-bags for cooling people who had fainted in the heat. I filled my cap with ice, so at least I kept my head cool.

Arafat arrived, and began talking to the people. There were fewer people there than had been expected. Perhaps the Oslo Accords were not so popular with the majority?

The 'security wall' is situated far inside the West Bank and splits the Palestinian community in two.

The Oslo Accords recognised the PLO and the right of the PLO to set up a self-governing Palestinian Authority, but it gave the Palestinians little else. It did not include any solution to the plight of the Palestinian refugees who came from the part of Palestine which lies within the boundaries of Israel. Nor was there anything about the status of Jerusalem. Probably the greatest weakness of the agreement was that it contained no obligation upon Israel to stop the establishment of new semi-military colonial settlements on the West Bank and in Gaza, despite the fact that this is forbidden under international law. There had been a rapid increase in the settlements on the West Bank and in Gaza in the 1970s and 1980s, and the Likud Party was in favour of annexing the West Bank and the Gaza Strip.

Arafat first set up the headquarters of the Palestinian Authority in Gaza. Later it was moved to the town of Ramallah on the West Bank. The Palestinian Authority took over responsibility for public services which had previously been Israel's responsibility. These included the police authority, and therefore responsibility for Israel's security. As the Palestinian authorities had undertaken to refrain from attacking Israel, the Palestinian police had the task of stopping groups who were continuing to make armed attacks on Israel. Meanwhile, Israel held onto all the colonies in the occupied territories, and the Israelis controlled the borders. They set up checkpoints manned by Israeli soldiers on all the important roads in Gaza and on the West Bank. The Palestinian Authority had control only over a divided Gaza. In 1995 the PLO and Israel signed a new agreement, whereby the Palestinian Authority also got control over most of the towns on the West Bank. But Israel held onto military checkpoints, and controlled all traffic on the West Bank and in Gaza.

The Oslo Accords were difficult to implement. They should have been followed up by negotiations about the status of Jerusalem, about the border between the Palestinian and the Israeli zones and about the rights of all the Palestinians who were driven out in the years from 1947 to 1949, when the state of Israel was being established. The negotiations were also supposed to consider their more than four million descendants who were living in Lebanon, Syria, Egypt and Jordan or on the Gaza Strip or West Bank.[8] According to international law, these people had the right to come back to their homes in Israel, and they may have been entitled to compensation for possessions they had lost. Israel was not willing to give them that. All the while, Israel was continuing to establish new colonies on the occupied West Bank, on the Golan Heights and in East Jerusalem. When the Oslo Accords were signed in 1993, there were 111,600 Israeli occupiers registered in the colonies on the West Bank, in addition to those in Jerusalem. By 2006 the count had more than doubled to 282,400, spread over 121 colonies. In the same period, the number of Israeli occupiers in East Jerusalem increased from 152,800 to 184,000.[9] In the year 2000, Ehud Barak the Israeli Prime Minister and Yasser Arafat of the PLO met at Camp David in Maryland, in a last attempt to implement the Oslo Accords. The talks broke down.

For the Palestinian inhabitants of the West Bank and Gaza, the situation was steadily getting more difficult. They were tied by an agreement to recognise Israel and refrain from hostilities. At the same time, their freedom of movement was being restricted and their land was continuously being taken from them. It came to a head on February 25, 1994, when the American immigrant Baruch Goldstein fired more than a hundred rounds against Palestinians who were assembled for Friday prayers in the Ibrahim Mosque in Hebron (al-Khalil). Thirty Palestinians were killed by the bullets, and more died in the riots which followed.[10] Up until Goldstein's attack, Hamas had been resisting by attacking military units.[11] Unorganised Palestinians threw stones at Israeli soldiers. Following the massacre, a new

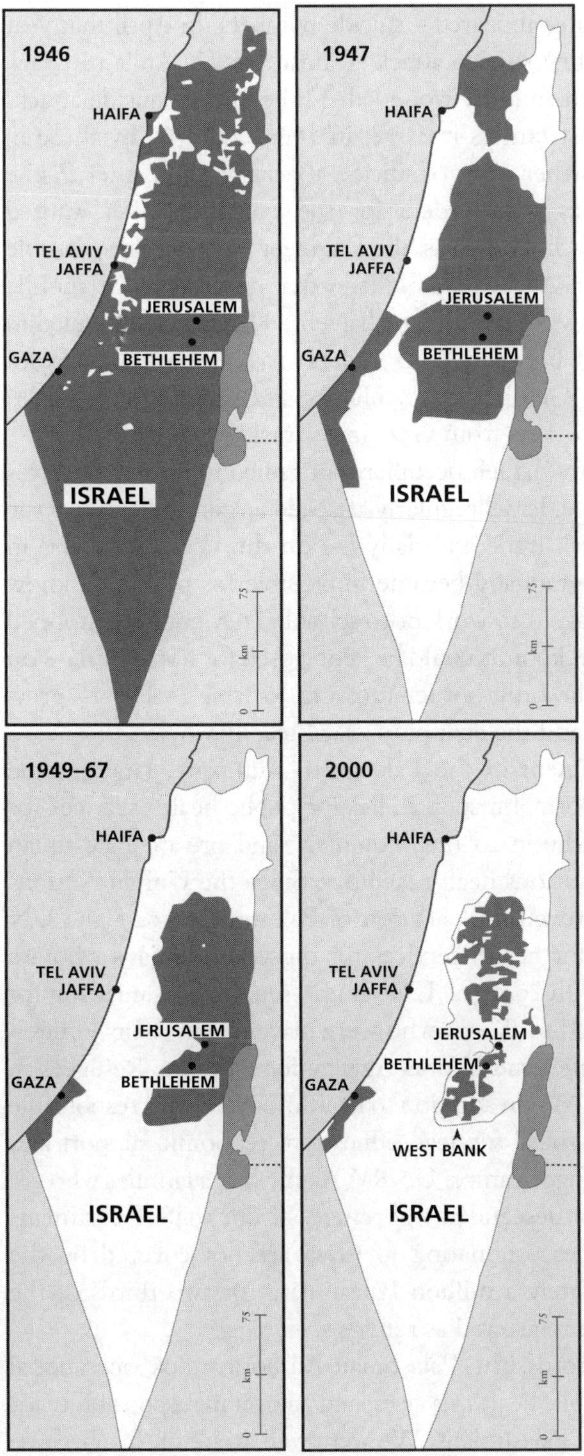

Loss of Palestinian territory between 1946 and 2000. Palestinian land shown by dark shading. The map top right shows the 1947 UN plan for division.

Source: Ann Arbor Quakers, Palestine-Israel Action Group

type of resistance fighting appeared – suicide bombers. In April that year Hamas carried out its first suicide attack, against a bus in Afula in Israel. Eight people were killed and fifty wounded. Three further suicide attacks were carried out against targets in Israel in 1994, followed by three in 1995.[12] There was a further wave of suicide attacks in 1996, after Prime Minister Shimon Peres gave orders for the execution of a wanted Palestinian, Yahya Ayyash, known as 'the Engineer', who was responsible for the suicide attacks. Ayyash was killed after he accepted a mobile telephone full of explosives from an Israeli agent. The assassination led to a widening of the split between PLO and Hamas, and a new wave of violence in Israel.[13] In October 2000, Hamas and other groups began shooting home-made rockets from Gaza into Israel.[14]

On the West Bank the Israeli occupiers continued to help themselves to land. At the same time, Israel regularly attacked targets in Gaza. All the checkpoints made travel, trade and daily life on the West Bank and in Gaza very difficult. It gradually became impossible for people to know whether they would make it to work or to school. They could be stopped at any time, and the checkpoints could be kept closed for hours or days on end. Travel through the only border crossing to Israel – Erez – grew steadily more difficult, and the economy grew steadily worse.

Before the establishment of the Palestinian Authority, Israel as the occupying power had formal responsibility for public health services for the Palestinians. In addition to this, voluntary and private Palestinian organisations built up various health facilities. Since the United Nations General Assembly approved the partition of Palestine in 1947, the UN has had responsibility for health services for those Palestinians who are registered as refugees.[15] In 1949 the UN set up a separate organisation for the Palestinians who had to flee or who were driven from their homes – the United Nations Relief and Works Agency for Palestine Refugees in the Near East (UNRWA).[16] In addition to health, UNRWA is responsible for emergency aid and social services, education, economic support and infrastructure in the refugee camps. UNRWA only helps families who are registered as refugees or descendants of refugees from 1948. Palestinians who come from families originating in Gaza are not covered by the programme. Approximately a million Palestinians, or two thirds of the population of Gaza, are registered as refugees.

Under the Oslo Accords, the Palestinian Authority took operational responsibility for the public health services, and an overall responsibility for all health services to the Palestinians. We were well aware of this, because

Oxygen concentrator: a machine which draws medicinal oxygen from the air. Shown here at al-Shifa Hospital – an important Norwegian Aid Committee project to support the Palestinian hospitals in Gaza.

the Palestinian Red Crescent, which had been central in providing health facilities to the Palestinians, was now playing a lesser role in Palestine.

After the Palestinian Authority was established, it became clear that if the development of a Palestinian state was to have any chance, NORWAC would need to support any project which could strengthen nation-building. One project which would prove to be very important, not least for the situation in Gaza during the 2009 attack, was the oxygen concentrator project. The hospitals on the West Bank and in Gaza were buying all their oxygen in cylinders from Israel. This was expensive and was eating into the meagre health budgets. Gradually, as the boundary crossing at Erez at the northern end of the Gaza Strip came to be closed more and more often, it became difficult to obtain oxygen when needed. Seriously ill patients were not managing to get to hospital and were having to lie in scantily equipped clinics while they waited to get through the checkpoints. It was quite a common occurrence for patients to die while they were waiting for the ambulance to be allowed to carry on to the hospital.

We therefore made an agreement with the Health Minister in Gaza to supply all the major hospitals with oxygen concentrator machines to extract oxygen from the air. A firm in Jerusalem got the contract to obtain and set up the oxygen concentrators, and quite soon all patients had access to oxygen, no matter where they were on the Gaza Strip.

Both Fatah and Hamas have their origins in the Muslim Brotherhood, the resistance movement against British colonialism which was set up in Egypt in 1928. In the 1930s a Palestinian branch of the organisation was established, to fight against the British Mandate Government in Palestine and to protest against the increasing Zionist colonisation. The first leader was Izz ad-Din al-Qassam, and the military arm of Hamas, the Qassam Brigades, are named after him.[17]

Yasser Arafat joined the forces which the Muslim Brotherhood mobilised in Egypt to fight against the Zionist terrorist organisation Haganah in southern Palestine. Arafat was arrested for the first time in 1954, along with members and supporters of the Muslim Brotherhood. That was following an attack by the brotherhood against the Egyptian president, Gamal Abdel Nasser. Khalil al-Wazir, also known as Abu Jihad (father of Jihad), and several of the other founder members of Fatah, had been in the Muslim Brotherhood.[18] During the 1950s and 1960s, Fatah was built up as a national liberation organisation with a vision of a Palestine which would include all faiths. Fatah continued its opposition to Israel after the 1967 war, and gradually took over control of the Palestinian Liberation Organisation, PLO, which had been founded by the Arab countries in 1964. Arafat was elected leader of the PLO in 1969.

Yasser Arafat and the PLO got strong support from the Palestinians for the opposition to Israel throughout the 1970s, but the resistance struggle meant that the leadership had to live in exile. Fatah and the other parties in the PLO could not take part in local or trade union elections in Palestine. The Muslim Brotherhood, on the other hand, which was not involved in any active resistance struggle, was able to operate in the occupied territories with humanitarian and social projects. Apart from the Palestinian Communist Party, there was little competition in the development of institutions in the occupied zones. The communist party and secular organisations had quite strong support on the West Bank, but they were quite small in Gaza, and the Muslim Brotherhood was therefore an important political movement.

Under the leadership of the teacher Ahmed Yassin, the Muslim

Brotherhood built up humanitarian and educational projects for the poorest of the Palestinians. Following the revolution in Iran in 1979 the political aspects of Islamic movements became more significant, which increased support for the Muslim Brotherhood. Yassin and other Palestinian leaders who supported a policy of collaboration with the PLO were later assassinated one after another, with what Israel called justified executions.

With the start of the First *Intifada* in 1987, Hamas was established as a political party, based on the ethical principles of the Muslim Brotherhood. The PLO had been weakened as a result of the Israeli occupation of Lebanon in 1982. Meanwhile the occupation of Gaza and the West Bank was becoming steadily more oppressive. Hamas drew its followers from the same population groups as had supported the Muslim Brotherhood, namely the poor and students. So Hamas's leadership was also dominated by academics.

With the break-up of the Soviet Union in 1989, the nationalist movement and the PLO lost vital political and economic support. Following the Gulf War in 1991, when Yasser Arafat supported Iraq and Saddam Hussein against the USA, the PLO's economic base was further weakened, because Kuwait and Saudi Arabia withdrew their support and expelled Palestinians. The PLO went into secret diplomatic discussions in the 'Oslo channel,' which led on to the Oslo Accords in a situation where the organisation was weak and did not have many choices.

Corruption was widespread in the Palestinian Authority, and criminality increased. Several of the security chiefs enriched themselves at the expense of the community.[19] Criticism of Arafat's leadership grew. The establishment of the Palestinian Authority led to increasing divisions inside Fatah. The Palestinian Authority had no independent economy to support it, there was no taxation income, and it was therefore dependent on direct agreements with donor nations.

In Gaza, moreover, Hamas was becoming more and more prominent through humanitarian work and a growing resistance to Israeli occupation. The humanitarian work was financed with the help of donations from private individuals. It is also claimed that the Syrian branch of the organisation collected money from other lands such as Iran and Syria and smuggled it into Gaza.[20]

When the Camp David negotiations broke down in the summer of 2000, there was already great dissatisfaction among the Palestinians about the outcome of the peace negotiations and the misgovernment of

Palestine. This came to a climax when Ariel Sharon chose to visit Haram al-Sharif, the holy height of the the Temple Mount, outside al-Aqsa mosque in Jerusalem during Friday prayers. The Palestinians were violently provoked, and the Second Intifada broke out. Suicide bombing and the firing of rockets from the Gaza Strip were attributed to Hamas and the Islamic Jihad movement, even though organisations connected with Fatah were also behind them. Anger against Israel's colonialism and ruthless disregard for Palestinian rights was rife throughout the whole Palestinian population, not just the Islamists.

On November 11, 2004, Yasser Arafat became seriously ill while he was under siege in Ramallah. He was flown to Paris for treatment and died there. The cause of death is uncertain. Mahmoud Abbas took over the presidency, but he lacked Arafat's charismatic appeal.

In February 2005, Israel decided that the Israeli colonies in Gaza should be wound up. By September 12 that year, all the colonies were abandoned and ruined, and the Israeli armed forces withdrew from Gaza. They also withdrew from the Philadelphi Corridor, the strip of no man's land along the border between Gaza and Egypt. The corridor was to be controlled by the European Union. The Palestinian Authority had control inside Gaza, but had no control over the borders, airspace or coast. According to international law, the Gaza Strip was therefore still under occupation. Immediately after the signing of the Oslo Accords in 1993, Israel had built a barrier consisting of high fences and sensors right round the Gaza Strip. In the period between 2000 and 2002, the military zone round the barrier was widened by a kilometre and the fences were reinforced.[21] There were only a few border crossing points, and these were carefully controlled. Gaza had become a prison, with Israel controlling all access.

Following the death of Yasser Arafat, a presidential election was held on January 9, 2005. Fatah's leader, Mahmoud Abbas, was elected Palestinian President.

The so-called 'Middle East Quartet', consisting of the United Nations, the European Union, the United States of America and Russia, were dissatisfied with the Palestinian government which had been set up under the Oslo Accords. They therefore demanded that the Palestinians should hold a new election.[22] So on January 25, 2006 the legislative assembly in occupied Palestine conducted another election. The West had sent 600 observers to the election, which was carried out without incident. The election was won by Hamas, with 42.9 per cent of the votes and a clear majority of 74 out of 132 seats in the parliament.[23] Hamas set up a government with Ismail Haniyeh as Prime Minister. The USA and Israel immediately declared that they would not co-operate with a Palestinian government which included Hamas. It was made a condition of any further direct economic aid that Hamas recognise the State of Israel and put an end to all use of violence.[24] Hamas offered to respect agreements which had been entered into. This was an indirect recognition of Israel and of the boundaries from 1967. Hamas also offered a ten year truce (*hudna*). Despite this, the donor nations, including Norway, decided to stop aid to Palestine. This caused big problems both on the West Bank and in Gaza.

For the health sector, this meant that the budgets for salaries and supplies in the public hospitals disappeared overnight. Aid channelled through the United Nations was not stopped. But the whole economic foundation for running the Palestinian Authority disappeared, including the funding for the public health services.

After Hamas's victory in the election, NORWAC was invited to meet the new Minister of Health, Bassem Naim, in Gaza. Bassem Naim met with John Eivind Jensen on April 1, 2006 and told him that the situation had become quite untenable. Patients were dying for lack of drugs and equipment.

On April 9, Hamas's Finance Minister announced that they could no longer afford to pay the salaries of public employees.[25]

This included the employees in the health ministry and the hospitals. The Norwegian Foreign Ministry increased its contributions to the United Nations and urged the other donor countries to do likewise to reduce the effect of the boycott on the civil population. But the United Nations could obviously not instantly take over responsibility for public administration. That would have been to put the Palestinians under external administration.

The European and American boycott functioned as a collective punishment of the Palestinians, because they had given their vote to the 'wrong' party. The political consequences could turn out to be serious, but for those of us who were working in health the most important and immediate problem was the human suffering. When the administration lacked money to equip and run services, the national institutions which the West had spent billions of dollars to build up, began to unravel.

On April 23, 2006 Bassem Naim was the target of an assassination attempt. Armed men stormed his office, and there was an exchange of fire between the attackers and the Hamas security guards. Several people were injured. According to the Israeli newspaper *Ha'aretz*, what lay behind the attack was dissatisfaction with the economic situation and the deficiencies in the health services since Hamas had come to power.

In NORWAC we did not regard this as a political attack, but as a reaction by desperate people and patients' relatives. It underlined the seriousness of the situation and the need to get equipment and medicines to the health services in Gaza. We took this up with the Foreign Ministry, who then allocated resources to Palestine through NORWAC. In May 2006, John Eivind and I had a meeting in Cairo with Bassem Naim and the Mayor of Gaza City, Maged Abu Ramadan, at which we agreed how to channel the support from the Foreign Ministry.

That was to be the start of an extensive collaboration. In the course of two years we transmitted about a hundred million kroner from the Foreign Ministry to the authorities in Palestine. The problem was not just a lack of resources. Getting equipment in over the frontier at Erez became steadily more difficult. In the autumn of 2008 it came to a complete stop, and NORWAC had a lot of supplies in storage in Israel which could not get through to Gaza. The boycott by the Western powers hit hardest at ordinary people, and served as a signal to Israel that a collective punishment of the Palestinians in Gaza had the approval of Europe and the USA.

The list of equipment and materials which could not be brought into Gaza grew longer and longer, and included among other things, cement, ventilation equipment and respirators. Israel claimed that these were materials which could be used to manufacture and fire rockets. As Israel did not recognise the Palestinians' government, it gradually became impossible for the European Union to control the border crossing in Rafah, something which was part of the Oslo Accords. That frontier was therefore closed, which put a stop to all trade and import of goods.

In June 2006, Israel kidnapped sixty leading Hamas politicians on the West Bank, including eight ministers and twenty elected representatives. There was no strong reaction to this incident from the Western powers.[26]

In the spring of 2007, Hamas, Fatah and independent politicians established a coalition government to negotiate with the West and Israel.

One of their objectives was to have the Western boycott lifted. This government had the backing of more than 80 per cent of the Palestinians, but Israel immediately refused to have anything to do with it.[27] The USA also rejected it, even though the government's platform fulfilled all the demands which were made of the Hamas regime. The EU hesitated, but decided in June not to support the coalition government either.

Norway took the view that bilateral collaboration could be started again, since the Mecca Agreement included a recognition of the boundaries from 1967. Apart from Russia, the only other European countries which shared Norway's view were Switzerland and Turkey.[28]

The election which had taken rule away from Fatah changed the balance of power in Palestine. Soon after the election in 2006, the USA began training Fatah fighters to bring down Hamas.[29] By the autumn of 2006 minor skirmishes between Hamas supporters and Fatah supporters were already breaking out on the Gaza Strip. In January 2007 these hostilities flared up and gradually developed into a bigger conflict. Only a small proportion of the population of Gaza took part in the fighting, which was really a conflict between clans but which led to serious consequences.

Fighting continued throughout the spring, and by June 2007 Hamas had full control over Gaza. The conflict had been going on since December 2006, with a few breaks, and between 250 and 300 Palestinians had lost their lives in this tragic civil war.[30] President Abbas immediately dissolved the coalition government, and on June 17, 2007 the independent politician and economist Salam Fayyad set up a government in Ramallah loyal to Fatah.

The EU recognised the new regime in Ramallah right away, and resumed direct support. Norway did likewise. The Palestinians now had two self-governing authorities – one on the West Bank which did not have majority support but which the Western powers recognised, and one in Gaza which had majority support but which the West did not recognise.

For NORWAC, this meant that our official collaborating partner was the Health Minister in Ramallah, Fathi Abu Moghli. In the coalition government, Fatah had had the health minister's post, while Bassem Naim had been Minister for Youth and Sport. After Hamas took control over the Gaza Strip, Naim resumed responsibility for health services in Gaza. NORWAC decided to work with both of them.

In November 2007 I visited the Gaza Strip again with John Eivind. We went first to the Health Ministry and met the new international co-ordinator. The previous co-ordinator, Maged Abu Ramadan, had lost his job, as had most of the other Fatah supporters in the public services. But he was still Mayor of Gaza, so we visited him in the city hall instead.

'The situation is hopeless,' he said.

There were problems with the transmission of funds from Ramallah to Gaza, and the city was unable to maintain public services, including garbage disposal. Gaza was inundated with rubbish.

He was also critical of Hamas firing rockets into Israel, which he considered just made the situation worse.

In February 2008 there was fierce fighting in Gaza. Israel bombed targets in the Gaza Strip, and Hamas fired rockets at Israel. On March 1, 2008, Israel invaded northern Gaza with a force of 2,000 men. In the course of the five days of 'Operation Hot Winter,' 107 Palestinians were killed and 250 wounded, most of them civilians. Twenty-seven of the dead and sixty of the wounded were children.[31]

On June 19, 2008, Israel and Hamas agreed a six-month ceasefire. Hamas did all it could to maintain the truce. Before the truce, various Palestinian groups had been firing between 150 and 250 rockets into Israel every month. In the period from July to October 2008, eleven rockets were fired.

According to Israeli sources, the plan for 'Operation Cast Lead' had already been made when the truce was agreed. The core of the operation would be to bomb and invade the Gaza Strip to destroy the infrastructure and immobilise Hamas.[32] On the very day of the American presidential election, November 4, 2008, Israeli forces went into Gaza near the Palestinian town of Deir al-Balah, which is the administrative centre for the middle section of the Gaza Strip. According to Israel, the objective was to destroy a tunnel which Hamas was allegedly using to kidnap Israeli soldiers from a frontier post 250 metres away. Six members of Hamas were killed in the attack. Israel had broken the fragile truce after just four months.[33] Hamas immediately responded by firing thirty-five rockets into Israel. Hamas proposed a new truce in November, but Israel refused this.[34]

On the morning of December 27, 2008 the new vicious attack on Gaza started.

3

3

Welcome to Gaza

ERIK FOSSE

We sat in the ambulance on the road from the Egyptian border post and turned out onto the road which leads north towards Gaza City, about thirty kilometres away. Over the noise of the engine and the rattling of the bodywork, we could hear a high frequency hum, a bit like the noise of an outboard motor.

'That's an unmanned plane, a drone,' said the leader of the convoy, Dr Moawiya Hassanin from the front seat. 'They are watching over us all the time. You'll get used to them.'

I looked out at the landscape. Gaza is a single long sandy beach with a little strip of land behind it. The Gaza Strip is about 360 square kilometres in area. From the boundary with Israel in the north to the boundary with Egypt in the south is forty-two kilometres. The distance from the Mediterranean Sea in the west to Israel in the east varies from six to twelve kilometres. 1.5 million people live on this small area; over 4,000 people per square kilometre. The Gaza Strip is therefore one of the most densely populated places in the world. Gaza has a very young population, with 56 per cent under the age of eighteen years.[35] The majority of the population is made up of the refugees who came to Gaza between 1947 and 1949 and their descendants. About one million of the inhabitants are registered as refugees with the UN's aid organisation for the Palestinian refugees, UNRWA.[36] There are eight registered refugee camps in the Gaza Strip.

The border crossing at Rafah is the only crossing place between Egypt and the Gaza Strip. At the north end of the Gaza Strip is the border crossing at Erez, which is the only frontier post for people to cross between Israel and Gaza. On Gaza's eastern border with Israel is the border crossing at Karni, which is for transport of goods. In 2006 the border

The streets in Gaza City were empty. Most of the shops were shut. Buildings bombed to the ground.

crossing at Kerem Shalom, between Israel, Egypt and Gaza, was opened for goods traffic.

The landscape of Gaza is flat, characterised by sand and sand dunes out towards the coast, like the terrain we had driven through in Egypt. The sandy beach stretches from Egypt in the south to Israel in the north. Gaza's highest point, Abu Awda, is only 105 metres above sea level. We drove past rows of little fields on either side of the road. Approximately a third of Gaza is cultivated land, dependent on groundwater for irrigation.

According to the UN partition plan of 1947, Gaza was to be a part of the new Arab state in Palestine. But following the war which was waged before and after the establishing of the state of Israel in 1948, Gaza was put under Egyptian rule. Then after the Six-Day War in 1967, Gaza was occupied by Israel. From 1967 until 1987 there was no physical boundary marking between Israel and Gaza. During that period Israel set up twenty-one colonies in the Gaza Strip, and Gaza was under Israeli military rule. The Palestinians gradually lost control of the land. About 10,000 occupiers took possession of 20 per cent of the land ownership, while one and a half million Palestinians shared the rest.

On the little cultivated patches, the Palestinians grew flowers, fruit and vegetables which they exported to Israel. The agricultural production was not big, but it was important. After the insurrection against Israel – the intifada – started in 1987, Israel imposed steadily tightening border controls. But the trade between Israel and Gaza continued and was important for the economy. 70 per cent of the electricity used in Gaza was provided by Israeli power stations, and 30 per cent by Palestinian power stations.[37] Up until the Oslo Accords and the establishment of the self-governing Palestinian Authority in 1993, the public hospitals such as al-Shifa Hospital were run by Israel.

Throughout the 1990s tension increased between the inhabitants of Gaza and the Israeli colonies. Many of the colonies were purely military bases. Agriculture in the Israeli colonies was based on artificial irrigation, which made the water supply for Palestinian agriculture difficult. The colonies were constantly being expanded, with the result that the Palestinian farmers lost important agricultural areas. In 2005 Israel resolved to wind up the colonies in Gaza. On August 17, 2005 the evacuation of the colonies started, and by the end of a week all the Israeli occupiers were out.[38] This meant that the Palestinians regained control of the agricultural areas and the water, but at the same time travel in and out of Gaza became very difficult.

Gaza does have other natural resources; there have been significant gas finds in the adjacent sea-bed.[39]

But there was no sign of enormous riches lying just beyond the sandy beach we were driving past. There was little traffic on the road, and all we saw was an occasional donkey cart. These have always been important for transporting goods. As the lack of motor fuel had become a problem in the past few years, donkeys had become an increasingly common part of the street scene.

The climate in Gaza is mild, with little precipitation. On New Year's Eve in 2008 the trees and the fields were green. It was winter in Gaza. The temperature could drop to less than ten degrees by day, and it might rain. During the summer, when the temperature increases and there is no rain, the landscape dries up. In the last few days of 2008 the sun shone, and the temperature was between fifteen and twenty degrees.

We were on our way to al-Shifa Hospital, in Gaza City. The Gaza Strip is divided into five administrative regions: North Gaza, Gaza City, Deir al-Balah, Khan Younis and Rafah. Altogether there are twenty-seven hospitals in the Gaza Strip. The Health Ministry is responsible for thirteen

The border crossing between Israel and Gaza at Erez. The system is modelled on the methods used to lead cattle to slaughter in the USA.

public hospitals with a total of 1,500 beds. Fourteen of the hospitals, with about 500 beds altogether, are run by voluntary organisations or are private hospitals.[40] Al-Shifa Hospital is a university hospital and has always been the biggest and most important hospital in the Gaza Strip. In 1993 Gaza European Hospital was built in Khan Younis in the south of the Gaza Strip, using European funds. It has 240 beds and is the main hospital for the approximately 400,000 inhabitants of the Khan Younis region.

The Palestinian Red Crescent runs two hospitals in the Gaza Strip: al-Quds Hospital in the centre of Gaza City and a hospital in Khan Younis.[41] Both Mads and I had worked in al-Quds Hospital before.

'Look, that used to be a police station,' said the nurse sitting beside me in the ambulance. 'On Saturday they bombed all the police stations in the Gaza Strip. We picked up people from that building. Most of them had been killed outright.'

'But surely police stations are civilian targets,' I exclaimed.

'Israel claims that they are military targets,' he replied. 'What's more they bombed the Interior Ministry and several other public buildings and mosques.'

I had been to Gaza many times since 1987, but this was the first time I had travelled in via Egypt. The usual route for Europeans is from Israel, through Erez. The frontier there has changed a lot in the twenty years since I crossed the border for the first time.

After the 1967 war the Palestinians could travel into Israel during the daytime. For many of them, commuting daily to work in Israel was the only way they could put bread on the family table. In Israel they were exploited as an underpaid workforce.

Up until 2006 we could see a lot of traffic over the border when we crossed. In the afternoon we would meet queues of Palestinians on their way home from working on building sites or farms in Israel. Many of them were working on land which had belonged to their own families sixty years before. A few were carrying plastic bags with food or clothing which they had been given by their Israeli employers. At the border they were body-searched when they travelled out of Gaza in the morning and searched again when they came back in the evening. The gifts from Israeli employers often disappeared into a rubbish bin on the Israeli side of the border.

The border crossing at Erez became steadily more sophisticated and ingenious throughout the 1990s, with rows of doors and narrow channels in addition to X-ray scanning apparatus. The guards who supervised the border post through surveillance cameras gave orders through loudspeakers telling people what to do. The set-up looked like a sorting system for leading cattle into a slaughterhouse.[42] Palestinian men went through these cattle gates every day on their way to and from work.

When the border control was tightened after the Oslo Accords and the establishment of the self-governing Palestinian Authority in 1993, it took more and more time to cross the border. This meant that the workers had to leave home even earlier to get through. Palestinian family breadwinners were demeaned at the checkpoint every day and spent the whole day getting to and from work. Since summer 2007 the border has been completely closed.

On September 19, 2007 Israel declared that Gaza was a hostile zone, and the import of vehicle fuel and electricity was reduced. In January 2008 Israel closed the border to nearly all traffic, and the import of fuel and electricity stopped completely. People had to buy petrol in cans which were smuggled in from Egypt through the tunnels. The social fabric of Gaza fell apart. Nearly all business activity came to a halt. The smuggling trade and the tunnel system made a few people rich on both

Between six and seven hundred Palestinians queuing outside one of the few bakeries still open in Gaza City. The Israeli blockade caused widespread shortages of grain, flour and electricity.

sides of the border, but most people became poorer. The Palestinians in Gaza began to starve.

On January 21, 2008 Hamas broke through the boundary fence in the south. Several thousand Palestinians streamed over the border into Egypt to buy food and livestock. The Egyptian authorities permitted this, but checked that weapons were not being transported. After twelve days the boundary was closed again.

It was quarter to two on our first day in Gaza.

Mads was talking with the leader of the convoy and the driver. I had travelled to Gaza with Mads once before, in 2002. That year Israel threatened an all-out assault on Palestine and attacked the city and refugee camp of Jenin on the West Bank. Gaza City was exposed to several helicopter attacks and it was on the cards that Israel would invade Gaza also.

At that time the Norwegian Palestine Committee and NORWAC sent a surgical team to Gaza. The team consisted of Mads, myself, theatre nurse Anna Mørseth and nurse Venke Aarethun, who was then Chair of the Palestine Committee. We arrived in Gaza at the beginning of April 2002. The Palestinians had built barricades in the streets of Gaza City – big embankments of sandbags so that they could fight against Israeli tanks. People boarded up their windows.

We discussed what could be done if an attack on Gaza did come.

Since the Oslo Accords, the Palestinians' economy has been totally dependent on financial support from the donor nations in Europe, the USA and Asia, and so the office for international co-operation was one of the most important in the health ministry. We worked with the head of that office, Dr Maged Abu Ramadan, who also was Mayor of Gaza City, to draw up medical emergency plans for Gaza.

As Israeli forces had control both in the air and on the ground, it was important for the emergency health plan to be based on the local population. We arranged to train ordinary Palestinians as first-aiders, in case any of their family were shot. In 2002 we feared an attack, but there was no famine and electricity and water supplies were maintained, even though the situation was difficult.

In 2008 the situation was totally different. The shortage of electricity, fuel and basic foodstuffs made the situation desperate. I had last visited Gaza in September, during Ramadan, the Muslim month of fasting. Trade in Gaza had by then become totally dependent on the smuggling routes through the tunnels. On the street corners in Gaza there were stacks of petrol cans with price labels on them. The smuggling trade had become an established part of the system. In Rafah, where many of the tunnels began, there were improvised stalls all over the place, where you could buy foodstuffs, electrical goods or cigarettes direct from the tunnel.

It was two o'clock on New Year's Eve 2008 when we drove into Gaza City again. There were no cars to be seen. We turned into the streets of the city, between unpainted concrete buildings. Most of the houses were four or five storeys high, with an occasional high-rise block in between them. Facing onto the street were rows of shops. Nearly all of them were closed, and the owners had locked iron shutters in front of the doors. Gaza is usually teeming with life, but now there was no one to be seen.

We came round a street corner and saw a long queue of people. There were men and women and a few young boys.

'They're queuing to buy bread,' said the first-aider beside me.

The Health Minister in Gaza, Dr Bassem Naim, met us in his temporary office as soon as we reached al-Shifa Hospital on the morning of December 31.

'Is that a bread queue?' asked Mads in alarm. 'We haven't seen that in Europe for many a long year.'

'People can stand outside the bakery for five or six hours,' explained the nurse.

We drove on through the city to the entrance to al-Shifa Hospital. On the opposite side of the street lay the remains of a building which was totally destroyed. It was just a heap of concrete and twisted steel.

'Al-Shifa Mosque was bombed on Sunday,' said the nurse.

We turned in through the gateway of the hospital. I gasped. We had driven into a war zone. A crowd of young people stood by the gate, and several men and women sat or stood round about the hospital entrance. There was no lack of people here.

When I had visited al-Shifa Hospital three months earlier, nobody had taken any notice of us when we arrived. This time the people who were standing by the entrance streamed towards us. Then doctors and nurses began to come out of the reception area and flock round us. They asked why we had come.

'We've come here to work,' I said.

'Come here to work? We thought that the West was leaving us alone to die.'

A few of them just stared at us. Many of them held out their hands to touch us. It was an absurd situation.

The driveway into al-Shifa Hospital ends in a roundabout in front of the emergency department and the surgical building, where the ambulances bring patients in. The other departments are further in on the hospital campus. To the right stands a big, unfinished building. That was to be the intensive care and surgical building. The work had been started two years before, but had never been completed, because the Israeli blockade had effectively stopped all building materials from getting in.

To the left of the door stands the administration building, where the Health Minister had moved in temporarily because of the war. We went up the stairs and along the corridor to the director's office. There sat the Deputy Health Minister, Dr Hassan Khalaf, and the director of hospital services for the Gaza Strip, Dr Mohammed Kashif, together with the administrative manager of al-Shifa Hospital, Dr Hussein Ashour. They stood up to greet us.

'Welcome, we've been expecting you,' said Dr Hassan.

In the conference room, behind a swing door, sat the health minister for Gaza, Dr Bassem Naim. He smiled when he saw us.

'Welcome, Dr Erik and Dr Mads. You've come at last. Did you have any problems on the way?'

'No problems,' I replied. 'We were met as arranged.'

'Have you brought any supplies with you?'

We showed him the two small boxes of medicines we had managed to bring with us, and told him that John Eivind was busy gathering more.

'The most important thing is that you are here,' he said. 'How are things with John Eivind?'

'He's doing fine in Cairo, but he would much rather have been here.'

'John Eivind will get here eventually. Israel has bombed the whole of the Gaza Strip, but they are going to lose. They will not succeed in taking control over Gaza. They'll continue the bombing until the new US president is inaugurated, and then they'll stop. Would you like some tea?'

The Health Minister signalled to a man in his twenties. After five minutes we were served small glasses of sweet tea with mint leaves.

The Health Minister spoke into his mobile phone. A TV set in the corner of the room was showing the news on Hamas's own channel, Al Aqsa.

Dr Mohammed sat behind his desk. A window behind him looked out over the entrance drive. Through the window we heard shouts from the square outside. He waved us over to the window. There was a procession of men coming out from the surgical building. They were shouting slogans, and at first we thought that it was a demonstration, until we saw the coffin they were carrying.

'That's one of our colleagues,' said Dr Hassan. 'He was in an ambulance last night when they shot at it. Everybody in it was killed.'

Two men in their fifties came into the office.

'*Al-salaam alaykum*, I am Dr Nasser Abu Shaban, personnel director in the ministry,' said one of them.

'*Wa-alaykum al-salaam*,' replied Mads and I in chorus.

'*Marhaba*, I am Sobhi Skaik, head of the surgical department. It's so good that you are here. We're delighted to have you here in the hospital,' said the other.

We all sat down round the table.

'We would like you to work here at al-Shifa Hospital,' said Dr Naim.

'I thought that Erik could spend some time in the emergency department, and also work in theatre,' said Dr Sobhi.

'Mads can work in the emergency department, in intensive care and in theatre.'

'That's fine by us,' we replied.

'One more thing.' Dr Mohammed broke into the conversation. 'I'd like you to report to me each evening about how you think the hospital is working, so that we can improve things.'

Dr Sobhi continued.

'We've known you a long time and we have confidence in you. You can see things objectively and can think of good ideas for improvement. To be honest with you, we're already worn out. You can't imagine what it was like on the first day of the attack. We don't know if all our emergency plans are working as they should.'

'OK, we can report back, but it will only be at a general level,' we replied.

A man came into the office, and Dr Hassan introduced him to us.

'This is Abu Jafer Besaiso, who works at the hospital as a volunteer. He will look after you for so long as you are our guests.'

We greeted each other warmly.

'Just leave everything to me,' said Abu Jafer. 'I'll try to solve all your problems.'

He went out and came back with two mobile phones.

'Here is a local Jawaal mobile phone for each of you, which you can use in Gaza and which we can use when we want to get in touch with you,' he said.

It had begun to get dark when we came out of the administration building with Dr Sobhi. I was stopped on the stairs by two Palestinians. One of them had a TV camera: 'Are you Dr Erik?'

'Yes,' I replied.

'We film for TV2 in Norway,' he said. 'We've been asked to interview you. Is that OK?'

I was quite unprepared, and it was a few seconds before I understood that Norwegian TV had agreements with Palestinian journalists and cameramen in Gaza.

'I'm on my way to the hospital; can we do it in an hour's time?' I answered.

'That's fine, we'll meet here on the stair in an hour,' he replied.

We carried on down to the square, where we were stopped by another TV team.

'We're from Al Jazeera. Can we interview you?'

'Yes,' said Mads, 'carry on.'

The cameraman set things up, and Mads gave an interview explaining why we had come to Gaza.

The surgical department was in a square building with four storeys. The ambulances stopped at a roundabout in front of the building to deliver patients to the emergency department on the ground floor.

In the emergency department the patients were received and registered. The registration office was a little room with glass windows. Then they were taken in to the right, to the reception room where there were twelve examination trolleys with yellow screens.

In the middle of the room was a table with boxes containing syringes, gloves, bandages and infusion equipment. There was also a little equipment on a shelf above each trolley, and a blood pressure machine on the wall between each trolley. I looked through the scanty equipment on the shelves. I didn't see a single pair of scissors in the whole room, and I

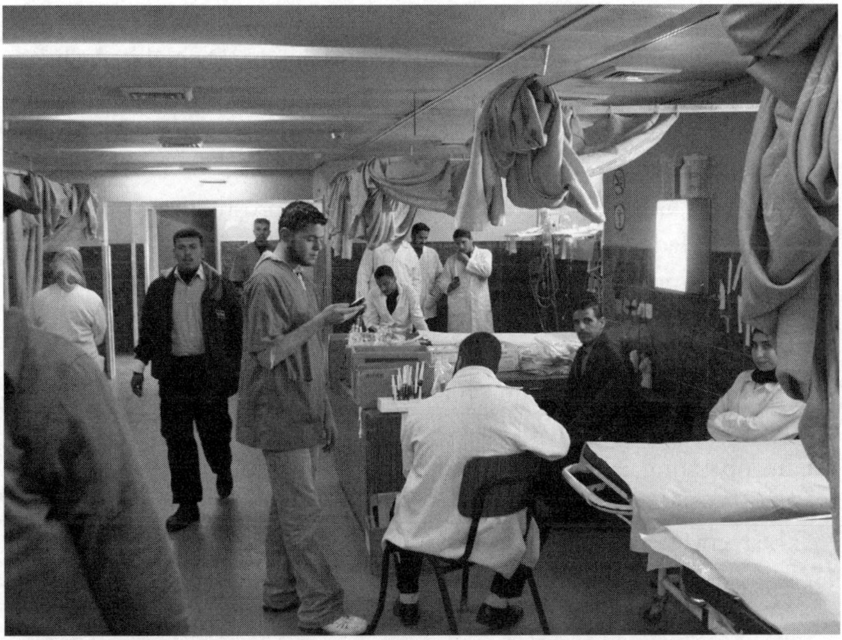

Big supplies of gloves, bandages, plaster, intravenous infusion equipment and cannulae had been set out in the middle of the emergency department, ready for the next wave of casualties.

wondered how they could cut the clothes off patients when things were urgent.

We went on through the examination room out into a corridor at the other end. This led to another area in front of the intensive care department. This space was a continuation of the entrance area and was therefore always full of people.

The door into the intensive care department was always locked. We had to press a bell to get in. The intensive care department was well equipped, with ventilators and monitors beside each bed. The department consisted of one large room, which was clean and tidy and looked just like most other intensive care rooms. The charge-nurse sat at a table in the middle of the room, and there were places for ten patients. Four or five nurses went round among the beds. In a corner of the room there were internal walls, where patients with contagious infections could be isolated.

The X-ray department with three X-ray rooms and a CT (computerised tomographic) scanner was in the basement. On the first floor there were two orthopaedic wards. The smallest rooms had two beds, and the rest had up to eight beds. The head of clinical surgery, Dr Sobhi, and the head of the orthopaedic department, Dr Nabil al-Shawa, both had offices on the first floor. Dr Nabil came out of his office, and smiled when he saw us. Mads knew him from before, and they greeted each other warmly.

'Dr Nabil has medical responsibility for the prosthetics workshop in Gaza,' said Mads. 'That must be a very important institution now with so many amputations.'

On the second floor was the operating suite with six theatres.

The patients were brought up in the lift. Right in front of the lift was an area used for observing patients or inducing anaesthesia. Now they had set up operating lamps and monitoring equipment here, so that they could still operate when all the theatres were busy.

The recovery room, with six beds, was at the end of the operating suite. Here too there were modern monitoring equipment, ventilators and experienced staff.

The children's surgical department and the general surgical department each had a ward on the third floor. In one of the beds lay a man in his twenties holding a TV camera. Both lower limbs had been amputated high in the thigh. When we entered the room, he took up his camera and began to film us.

He was a student and a freelance TV photographer, and had been working for the local TV station when he was struck by an Israeli rocket which tore both legs off him. His colleagues from the TV station had brought him the camera, and he was now filing reports from his bed and filming out of the window.

'We need to document everything that happens. That's the most important thing,' he said, smiling bravely.

There was no way the amputation of both his legs was going to hold him back from doing his job.

Most of the windows in the surgical block which looked out over the main entrance were missing glass, and the rooms were cold.

'The windows were smashed on Sunday when the Israelis bombed the mosque just across the road,' explained Dr Sobhi.

Cold is dangerous for wounded patients who are bleeding, because it reduces the capacity of the blood to clot.

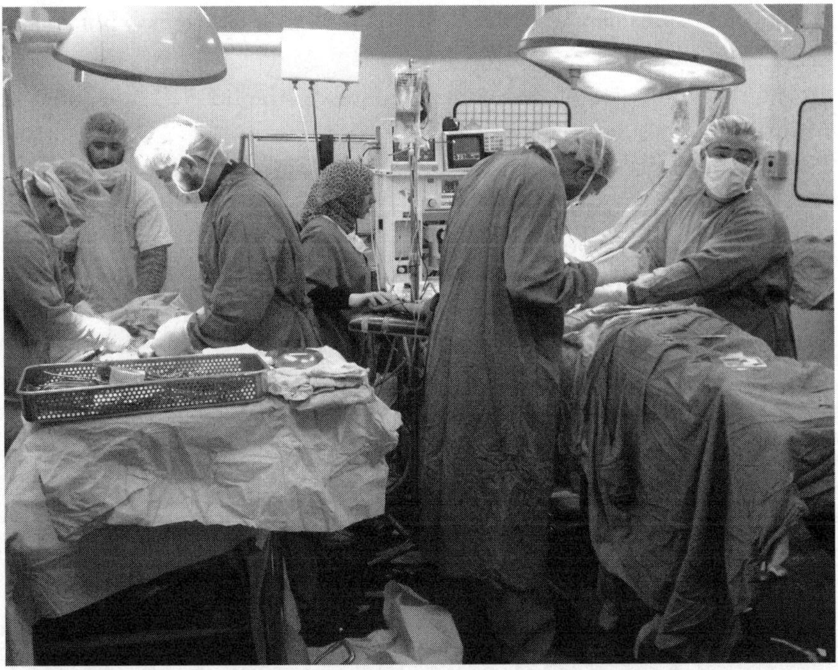

To double the capacity, two casualties were operated upon at the same time in each of the operating theatres.

We went back to the administration building with Dr Sobhi.

Standing outside was the TV team who had come to interview me for TV2. I spoke about the situation in the hospital. Inside the administration building we met our orderly, Abu Jafer, who would look after our accommodation.

'We were thinking of giving you a room here in the hospital,' he said.

Mads and I looked at each other. We would rather not live in the hospital. It would be difficult to relax, because there was so much noise and so many people who would be wanting to get in touch with us.

'Can we live in Marna House?' I asked.

Marna House is a well-known small hotel quite close to al-Shifa Hospital. Abu glanced at Dr Hassan, who said that we could indeed stay at Marna House, if that was what we wanted.

'We'll call for a car.'

'We can just walk,' I quickly pointed out. 'Marna House is surely less than a hundred metres from the hospital entrance.'

'It's a lot safer by car,' said Dr Hassan.

Mads and I exchanged glances. Perhaps Marna House was not such a good idea after all?

We drove the couple of hundred metres to the hotel. The garden in front of the hotel was dark and quiet.

'We're not taking in guests,' replied the man in reception politely.

After a few minutes the manager appeared.

'I can't take any bookings for rooms,' he said outright. 'There are no windows in the rooms, and I can't guarantee safety either for you or for your possessions.'

'What happened?' we asked.

'Israel bombed the house next door, and all the windows in the hotel are broken. You can see for yourselves.'

He took us up the stairs and showed us a room. There was no glass in any of the windows.

'It doesn't bother us that there is no glass.'

'No, but I can't have guests here,' he replied.

It was quite clear that he didn't want us there. I began to think that it had something to do with the fact that we came with our orderly, who was probably a member of Hamas. Perhaps he thought that Mads and I would be an excuse for Israel to bomb the hotel. We thanked him for his help and drove back to al-Shifa.

Mads had an appointment for a live broadcast on Norwegian state broadcaster NRK's nine o'clock news and he was interviewed on the street just in front of the hospital. It felt uncomfortable, because there were no other people around, and the bright lights punctured the darkness of the night with great intensity. A tempting target for a drone with target-seeking rockets, I thought. That was the last time we gave an interview outside the hospital campus.

Abu Jafer did not show his feelings about the fiasco at Marna House, but just asserted that they had a fine, peaceful place for us a little beyond the surgical block. We turned right from the main entrance and followed the road to a white building which housed among other things the internal medicine department. Then we turned right again and down to a corner of the hospital campus, to what was normally the day surgery unit.

The house had everything we needed: kitchen, toilet, a shower and four rooms, three of them with beds. In one room lived a group of Arab doctors who had been there for a while. We were shown to a room with two beds and a monitor over each bed.

'At least we've got monitors,' Mads joked. 'They didn't have these in Marna House.'

'They look after their customers,' I replied. 'You look as if you could have a cardiac arrest at any minute and need one.'

'Speak for yourself,' Mads retorted.

Our man came in with towels and two pairs of light blue pyjamas stamped with the Palestinian national emblem and 'Ministry of Health.' We were also each given our doctor's white coat.

It had been a long New Year's Eve since we had got up in the Swiss Inn Hotel in El Arish. We lay down on the beds. At eleven o'clock one of the neighbours knocked on the door.

'Haniyeh's New Year speech is on TV now.'

We went into the others' room and saw the speech by Hamas's leader in Gaza, Ismail Haniyeh.

We didn't understand very much, but one message was clear: It was important to reach a reconciliation in Palestine.

'We Palestinians have only one problem, and that is Israel.'

After the speech Mads and I went back to our room. There was a bang which shook the whole house. We heard several drones, buzzing above us.

'Happy New Year,' I said.

'We've had fireworks again this New Year,' said Mads. 'Remote-controlled, and all for free.'

We fell asleep to the sound of the Israeli war machine, convinced that we were in the right place at the right time.

4

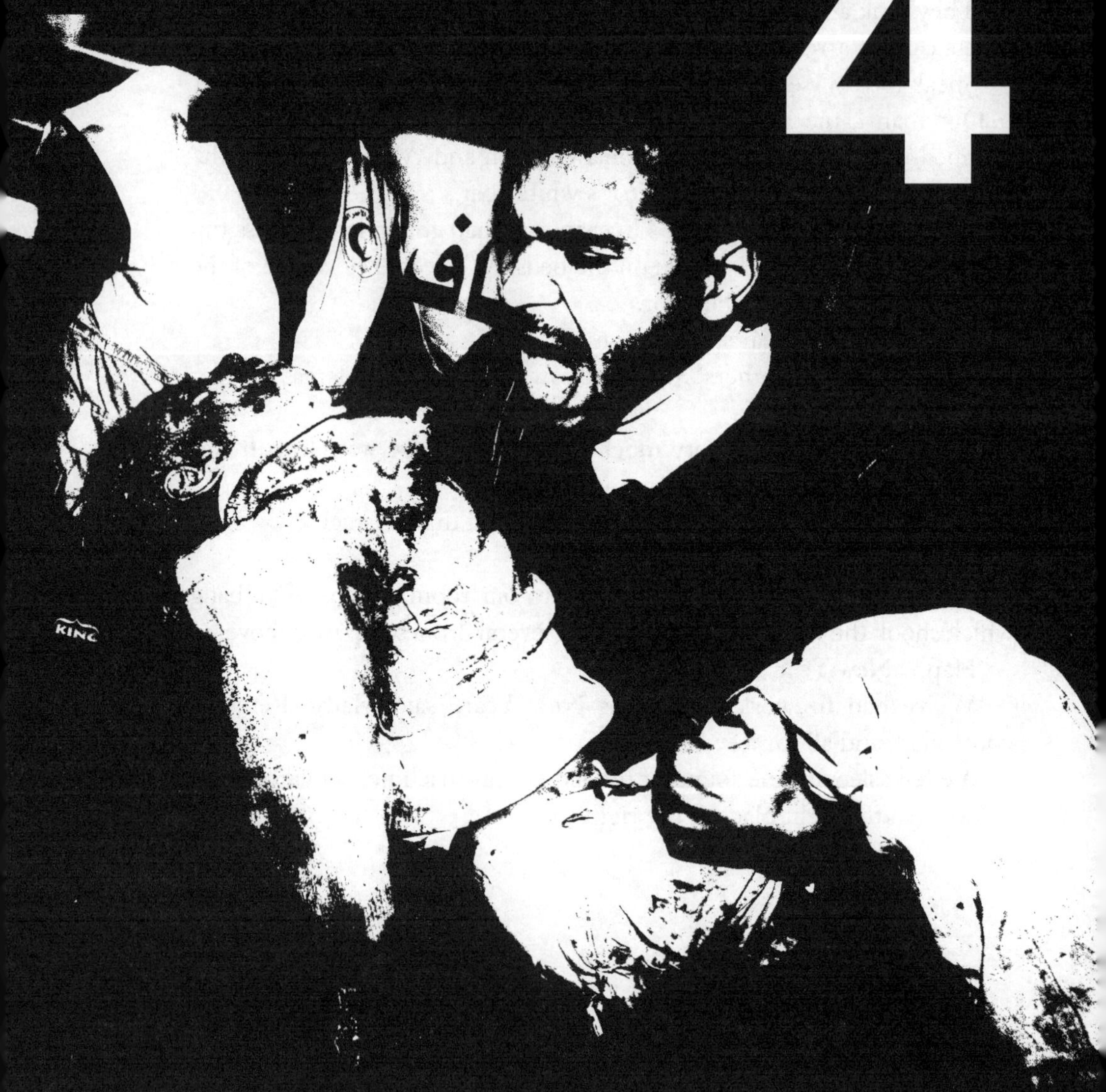

4

It's Raining Death

ERIK FOSSE

I was awakened suddenly by a knock on the door. It was New Year's Day. Mads was standing there, fully dressed.

'They've been bombing heavily during the night.'

I remembered being wakened a couple of times by blasts. We later learned that Israel had bombed the parliament building in the early hours of the morning.

In the room next door there were mattresses on the floor for sitting on, and breakfast was laid out on plates on a rug on the floor. There were hard-boiled eggs, tomatoes, cucumber and a plate of *foul*, a purée made from beans. There was also *kmaj*, the flat pitta bread which is served with all meals.

For almost twenty-four hours now we had heard the noise of the drones circling continuously above us. The frequency of the sound varied as the drones rose up, sank down or turned. It was an irritating noise like an outboard motor, and it took time to get used to it.

The orderly came in to say that we should change rooms. On the other side of the passage there was a much bigger room with its own toilet.

'Yes, this is much better,' said Mads, admiring the little wash-basin and the two beds with sheets and woollen blankets.

'There's a monitor over each bed here too. Perfect for old chaps like us.'

'Where do you want to sleep?' asked Mads.

'Under the window,' said I, as I thought about the splinters of glass which could come flying into the room if the Israeli bombing got too close. We decided to hang a blanket up in front of the window as a shield against flying glass.

Mads was allocated the bed by the door. He began to unpack the gear he had brought with him and laid it out on the bed.

He took out a little LED head-torch.

'Absolutely essential when there's a power cut,' he said.

'I know, but I didn't have a lamp like that to hand,' I said a little enviously.

'That's all right, I've brought two. We anaesthetists are used to looking after the surgeons,' said Mads triumphantly.

Then he took out a stethoscope which he hung round his neck, and a few ampoules of anaesthetic drugs.

'Do you happen to have brought scissors with you too?' I asked.

We both knew from experience that it is very important to have scissors when you are examining and treating emergency patients. It's difficult to undress an unconscious patient, and the only way to do it quickly is to cut the clothes off them.

'We can ask Abu Jafer to buy some for us,' said Mads.

Then we went towards the emergency department, along the outer wall on the north perimeter of the hospital campus. On the other side of the wall we could hear the noise of the traffic blending with the sound of drones and bombs. There was a little group of doctors standing by the department.

'Hi there!' somebody called in Swedish.

A Palestinian aged about forty wearing green theatre clothes came to meet us.

'Hi, Issam, old mate,' said Mads with a broad smile.

Issam Abu Ajwa was a general surgeon. He had worked in Sweden for a year, and he spoke Swedish. Mads knew him well from working with him for several years. Issam was a cheerful fellow, with a ready laugh. We went up to the orthopaedic department, where Dr Issam offered a cigarette according to Palestinian tradition. Mads, who does not usually smoke, took it and stood with Issam by the window. From the window, we could look down towards the entrance and across to the bombed-out al-Shifa mosque.

'How are things, Dr Erik?' Issam asked in Swedish.

There was a roar of bombs falling, followed by the deep, clattering noise of helicopters. An attack was taking place nearby.

At half past eleven the ambulances began to stream in. We ran down to the emergency department. Six or seven patients were coming in at the same time. Most of them were children. In the resuscitation room there was a fourteen-year-old boy with a wound on each side of the back of his head. Several doctors and nurses were working on him. A piece of shrapnel

A friendly meeting with good colleagues at al-Shifa Hospital. From the left: Dr Sobhi Skaik, Dr Abu Hassan Awad, Dr Mads and Dr Issam Abu Ajwa.

had gone right through his head, causing serious brain injury, but the boy was alive. A Palestinian anaesthetist passed an endotracheal tube into his airway and attached it to a bag – a self-expanding plastic balloon – so that they could help him breathe. A nurse inserted two needles into the veins on his arms. It all happened very quickly. It was obvious that they had a lot of experience. The boy was put on a trolley and transferred up to theatre, where the neurosurgeon operated on him. Mads followed the case up. The boy survived.

I went back to the emergency department. Dr Awad Abu Hassan was in charge of this shift. He was an effective leader of his troops.

He gave orders and took decisions on the hoof. Both Dr Awad and Dr Issam were examples of middle-grade doctors in the hospital. They were young consultant doctors who commuted up and down between the emergency department and the theatre, alternating between assessing patients and operating. They were impressively effective in both. They had under their command a group of junior doctors. Above them were the senior-grade doctors who took decisions in the operating theatre.

They helped with particularly difficult operations, did ward rounds and decided which patients could be discharged. I was part of this team of senior doctors.

A little boy of about five with leg injuries lay on a trolley. On another trolley there were two little girls, both with shrapnel wounds on the head. The younger one was only eight months old; the other was two or three years. Their mother was with them. She was crying and was obviously distressed, but was managing to stay composed and quiet. I asked her what had happened.

'The helicopters shot a rocket at one of the houses in the neighbourhood. The children went out of the house to see what had happened. Then they fired another rocket. Three of my children are badly injured,' she told me.

All of the thirteen children who had been playing in that street were injured. That was why so many children had come into the hospital all at once. The three children who had come with their mother were all sent to the operating theatre.

A few minutes later an ambulance stopped outside. The ambulance crew came running in with a young man on a trolley. His relatives were shouting loudly. The man had several small wounds on the right side of his chest, but looked otherwise undistressed. He was breathing and fully conscious. I tried to find a sphygmomanometer to measure his blood pressure. Before I could do that, one of the doctors had produced a thoracic drain, a plastic tube which is put through the chest wall into the thoracic cavity if the lungs are injured or air or blood is leaking out into the chest cavity. Without any form of anaesthetic he made an incision between two ribs and pushed the drain in.

I wouldn't have thought it possible. It is incredibly painful to have anything stuck into the chest cavity without an anaesthetic. But it was all done so quickly that the patient hardly had time to react.

This episode was evidence of one of the problems with the way the Palestinian doctors were working. They had become so used to dealing with massive injuries where treatment had to be started urgently and it was often not possible to do basic investigation. If they had listened to his chest and checked his blood pressure a few times, they would have found that the patient's condition was stable and that there was time therefore to take an X-ray – or at any rate time to inject a local anaesthetic and proceed calmly.

Once the drain had been inserted, the patient was taken at full speed to

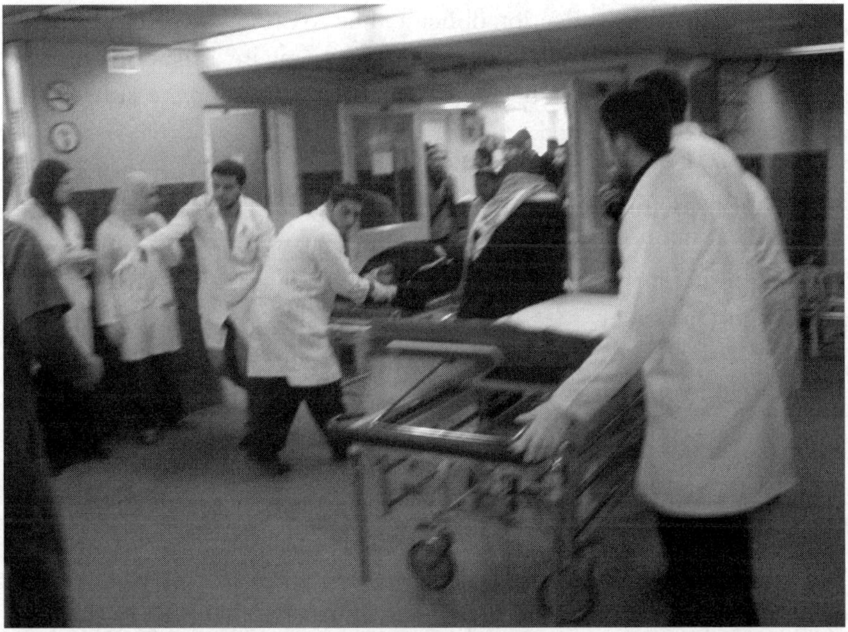

After the Israeli attacks, casualties came streaming in to the emergency department; some in ambulances, some in private cars and some on foot.

the operating theatre without having had his blood pressure measured. Neither air nor blood was coming from the chest drain. An X-ray was taken in the operating theatre. The picture showed that there was no injury to the lung. The wounds on the chest were all superficial. Moreover, the drain had been inserted too low, so that it lay in the abdomen, below the diaphragm, not in the thoracic cavity. He had started off with quite a minor injury, but because the drain had gone into his abdomen he would now have to be kept under observation for twenty-four hours to exclude an injury inside the abdomen.

The situation also illustrated my limitations as a foreign surgeon. Even though I am a specialist in thoracic injuries, these procedures were so drilled that it was difficult to get the doctors to change them in an emergency situation. The Palestinian doctors had learnt, through working with war injuries over many years, that passivity is often fatal when the patient is bleeding. It is important to make decisions and start treatment quickly. The circumstances at al-Shifa Hospital limited the possibilities for making a quick and accurate diagnosis before treatment started. The number of patients coming through the emergency department made even the simplest investigation difficult. The X-ray department was in the basement, and it took time to have a proper X-ray investigation done. So investigations were not done and straightforward cases were either over-treated or wrongly treated.

A total of forty injured patients came into al-Shifa Hospital that day, in small bursts. There were no great problems in carrying out the operations. In the afternoon we did a round of the general surgical wards with Dr Sobhi and Dr Nasser.

Most of the rooms had three beds, with curtains between the beds. We went into one of these rooms. In the bed nearest the window was a young man with several ulcers on his leg. The ulcers were several days old and had begun to heal.

'It looks as if he'll soon be ready for a skin graft,' I commented.

Behind another curtain was a young man in his twenties who evidently was a combatant. He had lost his left arm in the conflicts two years earlier. Now his right leg had been amputated. But he smiled despite this, and said that he was proud to sacrifice a few limbs in the struggle against Israel.

We continued our rounds from room to room. I did not see a single empty bed in the general surgical ward. As we came out of one of the rooms, we were met by a TV crew. They were Palestinian, but had an assignment from the American ABC TV channel. They interviewed both Mads and me.

'There is an enormous need for aid, and it is important that aid workers from all over the world come into Gaza now,' I said.

'Are there any problems with that?' asked the journalist.

'The borders are hermetically sealed, and emergency aid to the civilian population is not getting through. They need food and fuel. In the hospitals the need for medical supplies is almost endless. The international community must press for the borders to be opened,' I replied.

Outside the front of the hospital I was interviewed again by Palestinian journalists for TV2 and for French TV. They asked the same questions. I began to realise the importance of the media, and especially how significant it was that there were no Western journalists on location. I began to understand that Mads and I had another job to do in addition to being doctors. We would have to be reporters. That was a task for which we had not prepared ourselves.

All through the afternoon and evening of New Year's Day there was

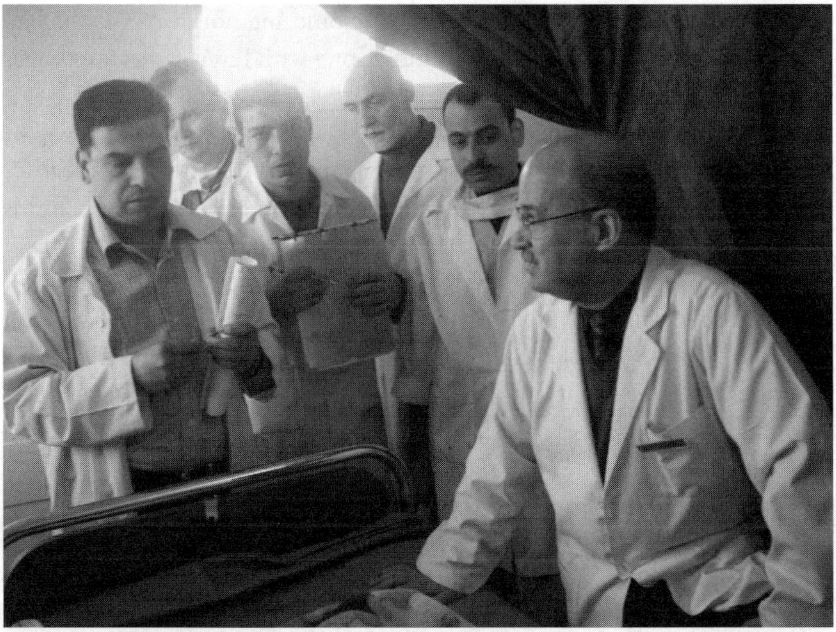

Doctors' rounds in the surgical wards, January 1, 2009 with (from the left): Dr Hamid, Dr Erik, the surgical charge nurse, Dr Nasser, Dr Rami and Dr Skaik.

violent activity by Israeli helicopters and drones. We went to the director's office to report how we thought things were working. We said that we were very impressed by the work of the personnel, but pointed out that there was little equipment with which to investigate the patients. Another challenge was all the relatives who came with the patients and made examination and treatment in the emergency department difficult.

We went in to see the Health Minister, who was sitting in the conference room next door. He told us that the bombing had continued, but that few Hamas fighters had been killed. While we sat there, the news came in that the popular Hamas leader, forty-nine-year-old Nizar Rayyan had been killed. Like most of the leaders, Rayyan was a well educated man, with a doctorate in the history of religion. He had served as a link between the Qassam Brigades and the Hamas leadership. Rayyan was well liked by most of the people, among other reasons because he had refused to flee from his house. The Hamas leaders were threatened at regular intervals by the Israelis, who also dropped leaflets warning that they were going to bomb the houses of ordinary people. Rayyan had appealed to people to do as he did: stay at home and not flee. Now he had paid the price. Israel bombed his home. Along with Rayyan, his four wives and nine children were killed.

We went up to the theatre suite. In the staff-room there were a leather sofa and deep leather chairs where the doctors could relax. A man in his fifties introduced himself as Dr Ahmed Kandil, head of gastro-intestinal surgery.

Dr Ahmed showed us an article he had written for the Egyptian *Scientific Medical Journal*: 'Gunshot Wounds of the Abdomen'.[43] This described the treatment and outcomes in 264 patients with gunshot or shrapnel wounds in the bowel whom he had operated on in the period between 2000 and 2003.

The article demonstrated that al-Shifa Hospital was an academic hospital, but also that war wounds had long been an everyday affair in Gaza. The war in 2009 was just the latest in a long series of attacks. There are not many surgeons who have operated on 264 gunshot wounds of the bowel. Dr Ahmed and his colleagues at al-Shifa Hospital are probably among the most experienced war surgeons in the world.

Al-Shifa Hospital is responsible for the most advanced health services on the Gaza Strip. The hospital has always had prime responsibility for trauma surgery. Since the start of the First Intifada in 1987, the hospital has taken in thousands of patients with serious war wounds and has had comprehensive experience of crises and mass casualties.

As the various departments are situated in their own buildings and are spread over a relatively large campus, the building up of highly specialised services has been difficult. We too became aware of the challenges of the scattered locations. When the beds in the surgical building were full we had to use the beds in the internal medicine department, but they were in a different building. This meant that the doctors had to move around between several buildings to follow up their patients, at the same time as they were taking on new patients.

In these first few days we had not noticed any bed shortage. There was however a shortage of acute medicines. In Egypt, John Eivind was working full out to gather together the medications the Health Ministry had listed before we left home.

On Friday January 2, he phoned from Cairo to say that he was planning to establish a co-ordination office in the Swiss Inn Hotel in El Arish.

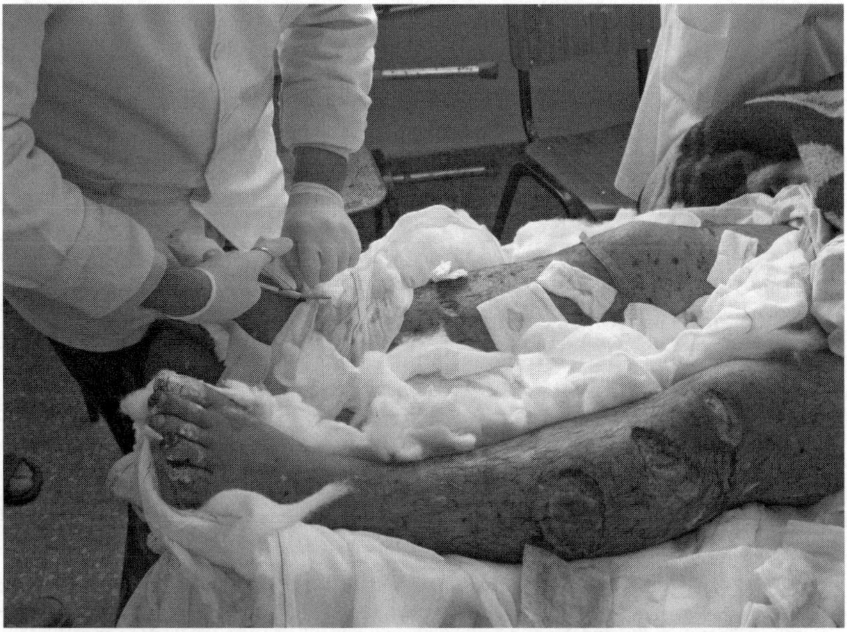

A young Palestinian with extensive shrapnel wounds. War wounds like this need thorough wound care with removal of dead tissue, often several times a day.

'The embassy is lending us a car and driver, and the embassy secretary Anders Vethe will be here for so long as you are in Gaza.'

By doing this John Eivind had set up our evacuation route out of Gaza. He was going to try to send about forty kilos of supplies into Gaza in the course of the forenoon.

The orderly had laid out breakfast for Mads and me on a trolley which stood in the entrance hall of the house where we were living. He slept on the trolley at night, and now it had become a dining table. Apparently he did this so that we would not have to sit on the floor and eat on woollen rugs as the others did.

Breakfast again consisted of *foul*, tomatoes and cucumber, olives, peppers, hard-boiled eggs and a pile of little pitta breads.

'Brilliant,' said Mads. 'I love Palestinian cooking.'

He took an egg in each hand and waved them about.

I sliced open a pitta bread, stuffed it with egg, peppers, tomatoes and cucumber and ate it as a sandwich. Delicious.

I would have to talk with the head of the hospitals in Gaza, Dr Mohammed Kashif, to arrange how we were going to get hold of the medicines if John Eivind managed to get them over the border.

Outside the front of the administration building tubular scaffolding had been rigged up. I asked the workers what it was for.

'It's for Friday prayers,' replied one of the workers.

I had forgotten that it was Friday. Since the mosque across the road had been bombed the previous Sunday, they had moved the prayers in onto the parking place beside al-Shifa Hospital. Here they erected scaffolding and pulled a blue tarpaulin over it. Then they decked the ground with carpets so that they could pray.

Dr Mohammed Kashif was sitting in his office.

'We're due to send some ambulances with patients to Egypt via Rafah today,' he said. 'When they have transferred the patients over into the Egyptian ambulances, they can bring the medicines back.'

He looked stressed, and I was a little unsure whether he fully understood what I was speaking about. There was a lot of work involved in evacuating patients to Egypt. He would need to co-ordinate with the International Red Cross and with the Egyptian hospital in El Arish. Many of the patients who were due to be sent were seriously ill. The medicines we were expecting were largely narcotic substances which we would be using for anaesthesia, and I was concerned that they would go astray. But there was nothing more I could do about that.

Back in the emergency department, Mads was busy intubating a boy, passing a tube down into his airway. The patient had been hit by a mass of shrapnel. He had several wounds on his right leg, a deep gash right behind the crest of his right hip and a wound in his head where a splinter had gone into his brain. Mads secured the tube with a gauze bandage, which was the usual practice at Gaza Hospital. The boy was taken up to theatre.

An ambulance screeched to a halt outside.

The ambulance crew came running in with a new patient, a young boy who was bleeding through his clothes from several small injuries on the right side of his abdomen. He also had a wound on his right forearm, just under the elbow, which was not bleeding.

First he was taken into the emergency department, where he was given a pain-killing drug and one of the nurses put two intravenous needles into his arms. His blood pressure was normal, but they were taking no chances

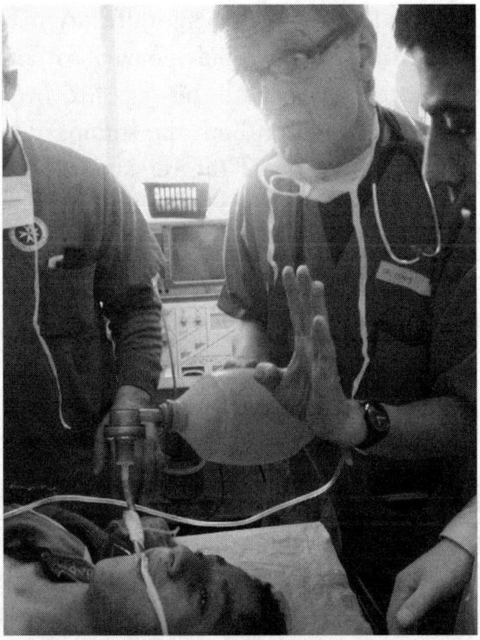

Busy receiving a casualty: a Palestinian boy with life-threatening shrapnel wounds is intubated with an endotracheal tube to keep his airway open, and ventilated with a self-expanding bag.

in emergency and they sent him right up to the theatre suite because they could not exclude intra-abdominal bleeding.

I went up with him. Dr Ahmed Kandil was in theatre. There was no doubt that he was a surgeon of great experience. He examined the wounds on the abdomen and used a pair of scissors to open them up a little. It appeared that none of the wounds had penetrated into the abdominal cavity. An ultrasound scan also showed that there was no bleeding inside the abdomen. All the boy had was a few superficial wounds, so we had not really needed to bring him to theatre. If we had spent a little more time on him in the emergency department, the situation could have been resolved there. Once more, the problem was that it was difficult to distinguish between patients who were stable, with normal blood pressure and respiration, and those who were unstable and obviously bleeding. This was because the situation was changing all the time and lots of people were running in and out of the emergency department.

I was on my way out of theatre again when the lift door opened and Mads came in with a twelve-year-old boy on a trolley. This boy was obviously badly injured, and Mads was having difficulty maintaining his blood pressure, even with intravenous fluids going into both arms. We lifted the sheets which covered him. Both his legs had been blown off. There was soot and signs of burns on both the stumps. They were not bleeding, which is a sign that much of the remaining tissue is dead. I examined his scrotum – it had been torn open, and the one remaining testicle was laid bare. We rolled him round onto his side to assess the injury to his back. I saw that the whole of the anus and lower rectum had gone, along with most of the musculature of the left buttock. The skin was burst, and it looked as if the muscle had been cut away with a knife. In the lower part of his body there were hundreds of little puncture wounds in the skin. I had never seen this type of injury before. It must be a new type of weapon.

Dr Ahmed and I looked at each other. As the boy had low blood pressure he must surely be bleeding inside his abdomen, but the injuries were so extensive that the chance of him surviving was minimal. Nevertheless we asked the nurses to look out instruments to open the abdomen so that we could stop whatever bleeding there might be, while Mads and the anaesthetic team did heart and lung resuscitation.

'Do you know who this is?' Mads whispered to me.

'No.'

'He's the nephew of Dr Issam, the surgeon who speaks Swedish. We can keep going until Dr Issam comes up, so that he can say his farewells.'

Mads and I had discussed Dense Inert Metal Explosive (DIME).[44] DIME is a special explosive which is used in so-called 'small diameter bombs'.[45] These bombs are relatively light, so that they can be carried by smaller aircraft. The unmanned aeroplanes, drones in whose development Israel is a world leader, can easily carry several such bombs. To save weight, they are made of glass fibre. They do not have a metal shell which causes multiple shrapnel wounds, like normal bombs. On the other hand these bombs have wings and an ingenious navigation system consisting of GPS and often video cameras, so that the pilot can steer the bomb right onto the target. The bombs can be designed and manufactured to break through armour plating or to kill people.

The DIME technology has been developed specially to kill or injure people in a restricted area, without harming material or personnel a short distance away from the explosion. This is achieved by combining a strong explosive with small particles of tungsten alloy. When the bomb explodes, the tungsten alloy melts and the victim is struck by a cloud of tungsten dust which tears the body tissue to pieces and causes burns. The bomb is

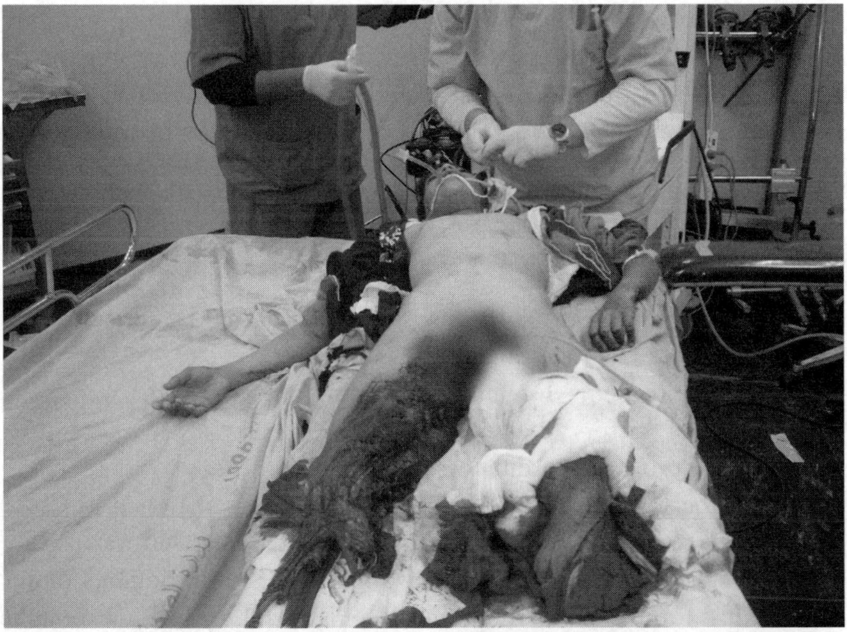

Ahmed (12) was dying when he came to al-Shifa Hospital. Both legs and much of his genitals were blown off by what was probably a DIME bomb.

fired at the ground near the victim, and so the pressure wave comes from below. Anyone standing near the explosion will be blown apart. Adults standing a little distance away sustain injuries mainly to the lower limbs and lower trunk. Studies have shown that tungsten alloy causes cancer in experimental animals. It has therefore been suggested that patients who survive DIME bomb injuries may later develop cancer.[46]

There were claims that Israel used bombs like this during the attack on Lebanon in the summer of 2006. I was there for several weeks while the war was going on, and I spoke with doctors who had treated such injuries. I didn't see any myself, however.

Now I had seen it for myself.

At about one o'clock our orderly came to say that they had an ambulance ready to take us on a tour round Gaza. When we met Bassem Naim on the first day, I had asked him if it was possible for us to see other bits of Gaza. However, Mads had spoken with the Mayor, Maged Abu Ramadan, who advised us not to leave the hospital, because the Israelis shot at ambulances. The level of risk was not clear, but we agreed not to leave al-Shifa.

If we had been journalists, this would have been a golden opportunity to see with our own eyes what was happening in the areas that were being bombed. But we were a surgical team, who had been sent to al-Shifa Hospital to work there. We could certainly let ourselves be interviewed and could talk about the situation in the hospital, but journalism was not our job. We agreed that doctoring was our first priority, and reporting came second.

While I was sitting in the surgeons' staff-room in the theatre suite, two French women and a Palestinian man came in.

'*Bonjour*, we're from Médecins Sans Frontières,' they said.

'Oh, are you doctors?' I asked.

'No, we're project co-ordinators,' they replied.

One of the women and the Palestinian man were stationed in Gaza. The other woman was responsible for the Middle East and was usually based outside Palestine. I asked why Médecins Sans Frontières didn't have health workers in Gaza, and they replied that they had not thought any teams were needed there. They had reassessed the situation now and were deciding to send a surgical team. That was why they were visiting al-Shifa Hospital.

It was apparent that they had problems in recruitment. I began to suspect that it probably was not just Israel's blockade which was preventing health workers from coming in. The Western nations' rejection of the Hamas government appeared to have spread to the major humanitarian organisations. Also, it was difficult to recruit health workers in Europe in the middle of the Christmas holidays.

'I hope you can get a surgical team together,' I said. 'Al-Shifa Hospital needs more Europeans.'

After they had left, I went round the theatre suite. It was quiet there, so I went down to the emergency department. Mads was there, but there were not many patients there either.

'Let's go and see Dr Nabil,' said Mads. 'Remember him? He's head of the orthopaedic department.'

We went to Dr Nabil's rather modest office on the ground floor. Several of the other orthopaedic surgeons were there, and morale was good. We drank tea and chatted.

Later in the evening it was time for our daily meeting with the hospital management.

Dr Sobhi was also there in the manager's office.

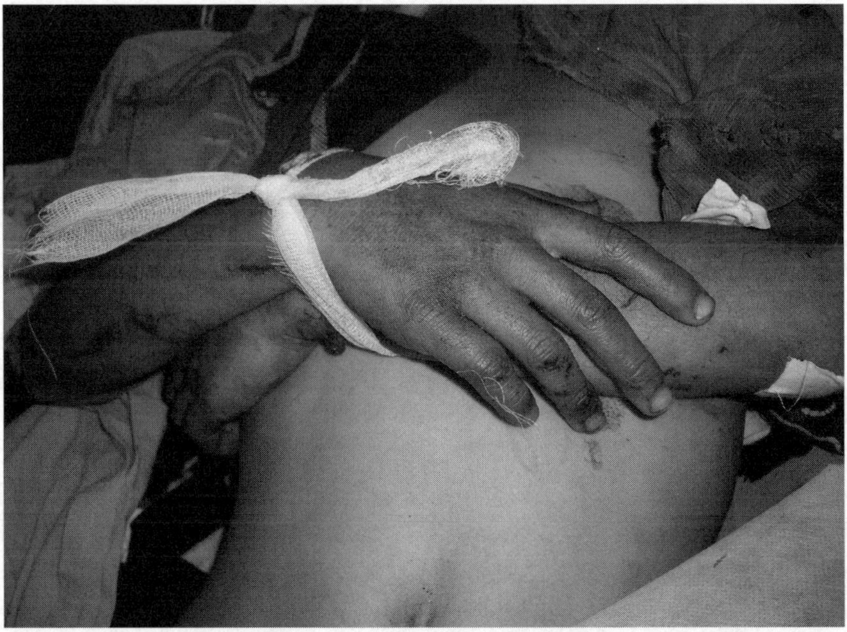

The attempt to resuscitate Ahmed was hopeless. The nurses have tied the twelve-year-old boy's hands according to the Islamic custom for preparing the dead for burial.

'We're worried in case we have another multiple casualty situation like we had on Saturday December 27,' said Dr Mohammed.

'It looks like you're coping fine just now,' I said. 'But I understand that the situation can be different if you get a lot of patients all at once.'

'Erik, we had no control that Saturday,' said Dr Sobhi. 'I'm worried that the same might happen again.'

On Saturday December 27, Dr Sobhi had been working in the emergency department all day, trying to triage and prioritise patients and allocate them throughout the hospital. But it had become chaotic, especially because of all the relatives. We talked about this a little, and it appeared that they had not set aside separate areas for patients with minor injuries and for relatives. All the patients had to be either in the emergency department or in the theatre suite. As the relatives refused to leave the patients, the place soon became jammed full. The relatives were adding to the congestion in the emergency department, or sitting on the stair outside the theatre suite.

As they could not examine patients properly in the emergency

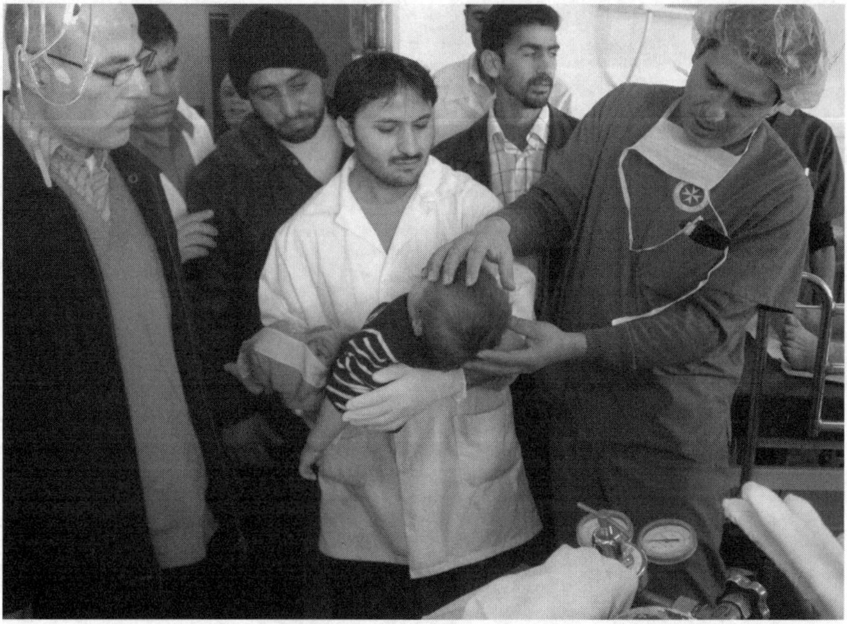

Dr Issam examines one of the many injured children brought to al-Shifa Hospital. The family watch anxiously. There was a shortage of stretchers and beds because of the blockade.

department, they sent all the patients with slightly bigger injuries straight to the theatre suite. This meant that the operating facilities became full and over-stretched, and people were dying in the process.

'Erik, you gave a lecture once about organisation for major incidents. Can you repeat it tomorrow?' asked Dr Sobhi.

'OK, but you'll have to chair the meeting,' I replied. 'We must base it on your experience.'

We agreed to hold the meeting in the administration building at eleven o'clock the next morning.

When we got back to our house, the Health Minister was there. He wanted to discuss the particular injuries we had seen. Mads told him that he had seen such injuries in Gaza both in 2006 and 2008, and had gathered together more information about DIME weapons. He gave us a tutorial on DIME and on what the bombs contained.

I thought about the young boy who had died, and all the other seriously injured patients. It was obvious that we had only seen the beginning.

I began to realise the seriousness of this attack. There was no mercy for anybody in Gaza.

5

5

Who Gets to Live?

ERIK FOSSE

When I awoke on Saturday January 3, Mads was already on his feet.

'You sleep like a log even when the building's shaking,' he said.

'Why not? It's important to be rested,' I replied.

The most important thing was to sleep when we had the chance.

Mads had checked the news.

'There have been demonstrations on the West Bank and in Gaza,' he said. 'I've also spoken with the Norwegian journalists in Israel. They're trying to get in to Gaza, but they're not able to for the time being.'

The orderly served breakfast. We had not noticed the food shortage yet.

The sun was shining outside, but the drones and helicopters were in position. The sound came and went. The drones were there all the time, but the sound of helicopters fluctuated. We heard six bangs in quick succession, then another six bangs a few seconds later.

I had heard this before, in Lebanon. It was a gunboat firing rockets. The first bangs came from the impact, then we heard the sound of them firing from the sea.

We went to the emergency department around nine o'clock and had a chat with the doctors and medical students. There were several female medical students from al-Azhar University working the day shift. Mads had taught there in the autumn of 2008 and knew them.

In the Gaza Strip there are two universities that teach to master's level: the Islamic University of Gaza, which was established in 1978, and al-Azhar University – Gaza, which works in co-operation with al-Azhar University in Egypt.[47] So far, six classes of doctors have graduated from al-Azhar University.

The two universities also symbolise the opposition between Fatah and Hamas. Several of the political leaders of Fatah and Hamas in Gaza teach at the two universities; the Fatah members at al-Azhar University and Hamas members at the Islamic University.

In the struggles between Fatah and Hamas, the Islamic University was stormed by Fatah forces in spring 2007, as they thought that Hamas was hiding weapons in the university buildings. At al-Azhar University in 2008 there were several confrontations between students from the Islamist bloc and the Fatah bloc. On October 14, students from the Islamist bloc destroyed offices in the building and tore down pictures of Yasser Arafat in protest against the expulsion of twelve Islamist students following earlier riots. They also threatened the heads of a number of faculties and occupied the university before being removed by the police.

The Palestinians have a high level of education. Many families survive by sending individual university-educated family members to work outside Palestine and send money home. Over the past few years, however, it had not been so easy to get an education. The blockade of Gaza had hit schools hard and, as early as 2008, UNICEF reported that the schools had a shortage of electricity and heating. Teaching has been sporadic, and many pupils have dropped out of school.

Many Palestinians study abroad, mainly in Egypt and Jordan, but also in Europe and in other Arab countries. When Israel closed the border in June 2007, several hundred Palestinians from Gaza lost the possibility of continuing their studies. On December 29, 2008, the laboratory building at the Islamic University was bombed by Israeli aircraft. Israel claimed that the laboratories were being used to produce bombs.

We ended our discussion with the students. The ministry-appointed director of hospital services Dr Mohammed Kashif, was waiting for us in his office, along with Sobhi Skaik, head of clinical surgery, and Dr Nasser Abu Shaban, the personnel manager. During the night and in the morning, they had summoned all the consultant surgeons to a meeting.

Mads and I had discussed how we should prepare for this meeting. Even if al-Shifa Hospital had had many mass-casualty situations before, the experience of the first day of war on December 27 was unique. As the registration system had broken down, nobody knew how many had been admitted, or how many of them had been operated on. At least 250 people were killed and over 1,000 wounded on that one day, with several hundred seriously injured.

In the days after the first attack, a steady stream of patients came to the hospital, which was really no great challenge for a hospital like al-Shifa.

The hospital management considered this to be the calm before the storm. There would be more incidents with multiple casualties comparable to the first one. The meeting had been called together to prepare the hospital for the next major Israeli attack.

We had taught battlefield surgery and the handling of multiple casualties in Gaza a number of times before, and I was anxious about whether we really had anything further to teach this time. Many of the surgeons and anaesthetists were much more experienced than us. 'Yes, but we know that you also have experience, and everyone at the hospital wants to hear you because they trust you, and because you come from outside,' said Dr Sobhi. We agreed to set in motion a discussion in which we said as little as possible. Dr Sobhi followed us to the tattered auditorium.

Dr Nasser and Dr Sobhi each made a short introduction and welcomed Mads and me. Then I was given the floor. I started by saying a little about who we were and what projects in Gaza NORWAC was involved in. Many in the audience were quite surprised to hear that we had worked for the Palestinians when they were only children. Mads is an anaesthetist and head of the emergency medicine department at the University Hospital of Northern Norway. I have worked with injuries for many years at Ullevål Hospital and for fifteen years as an instructor in battlefield surgery for the Norwegian Defence Medical Service, and I am specialised in heart and lung surgery. We both have experience of working as doctors in war zones across the world.

We quickly moved on to the technical matters at hand: whom should we help, and how can we decide whom to help when time is short and there are few resources?

When many patients arrive at once, they must be treated in the right order. I started by repeating the principles by which patients should be prioritised in a mass-casualty situation or, to give this procedure its technical term, triage. It is impossible to treat everyone when you have mass casualties, so it is important to use resources on those who can be saved. It sounds brutal, but that's the way it is. As I spoke, I wrote up the four categories patients are usually divided into when dealing with mass casualties:

1. Cannot wait
2. Can wait
3. Must wait
4. Expectant (dying)

Around 60 per cent of the patients who come to the hospital after a

A father waits anxiously in the reception at al-Shifa with his two daughters, both with minor injuries. Most of those wounded were young and undernourished. The window in the background was broken in the bombing.

bomb attack usually have minor injuries that do not need extensive treatment. The injuries often amount to several superficial wounds caused by splinters. These are not life-threatening by themselves but are painful and must be cleaned to prevent infections. Even if their wounds are not dangerous, the patients are scared and in need of care, especially when it comes to children. In addition, parents and other relatives must be informed and kept calm.

It is important to separate those who have minor injuries and take them out of the emergency department quickly so that they do not take up space and that, at the same time, they get the care they need. These patients belong to category three and are 'the lucky ones'. We suggested that the best option would be to divert these walking wounded from the emergency department and take them immediately to an area for less serious injuries.

Some patients are in a poor condition due to major bleeding that we cannot control. If these patients come in on a day when there are few other patients, the hospital will use all its resources to try to save them.

But if the hospital has many patients who need operations, it is important to filter out those who are so bad that they have little chance of surviving and not to use resources on them. It does not take much imagination to understand that it is very difficult to decide that a patient who is seriously injured and is dying should not be treated. These patients belong to category four and are 'the unlucky ones'. In peacetime, we do not use this category and instead try to save everyone. It is difficult for doctors to adjust to using this category. This is why it is important to be prepared for this when you visit war zones or are expecting war.

When patients with minor injuries have been sorted out and those we cannot help are being cared for, there remains a group that needs operations, 'the needy ones'. The doctors must prioritise these as well. Some patients must be operated on immediately in order to get through, others can wait.

This prioritisation is crucial when there is a shortage of resources but, at the same time, it is very difficult to do this in a chaotic setting in which there are few opportunities to examine the patients thoroughly.

A number of the doctors said that this had been a problem on the first day of the attacks. There was no place to put all the patients, so far too many people stayed in the emergency department. There were so many patients and relatives that it was almost impossible to work.

In the emergency department, there was always an experienced doctor on hand, who was responsible for prioritising patients and deciding who would be sent to the operating theatre. This doctor had command over the other doctors, the nurses and the volunteers who worked in the emergency department. Dr Sobhi had been in charge of the prioritisation that Saturday and said that he had lost full view of the situation early on. He had concentrated on separating those with minor injuries and getting them out of the hospital as quickly as possible. He had sent all the others to theatre – none of the most seriously injured, who there were not enough resources to save, had been separated out. The final prioritisation had taken place in the corridor of the operating suite, and it had clearly been difficult.

The head of the gastro-intestinal surgery department, consultant surgeon Dr Ahmed Kandil, took the floor. He had been responsible for the prioritisation in the operating suite corridor. The problem was a shortage of surgical resources. They had only six operating theatres, and they lacked equipment. 'If we had had enough equipment, we could have treated everyone,' he said. 'It is difficult to decide that someone will *not* be treated when they are already lying in the operating suite corridor.'

One of the injured belonging to the category of 'the lucky ones'. This girl is covered in dust after the house she was in was bombed, and she only has minor, non-life-threatening wounds.

To increase the capacity of the six theatres, the doctors had begun to operate on two patients in each room. They also operated in the corridor, in an area that was really intended for the observation of patients. The patients had been operated on lying on stretchers under the light of mobile operating lamps.

One of the neurosurgeons, Dr Hamid Abu Ubaid, immediately noted that there was no way they could manage to operate on all the wounded. There was no way to avoid ruthless prioritisation regardless of how much equipment they could get hold of. He also thought it was impossible to increase the operation capacity in the short term. This was backed up by Dr Nasser Abu Shaban. There were no other areas in the hospital that could sensibly be used for operations, so they would have to manage with the space they had. Probably the only thing that could be done in the short term was to bring in more anaesthetic machines and portable lamps, but no one knew where this equipment could be found.

NORWAC had long been trying to resolve the shortage of anaesthetic machines, ventilators and observation monitors at al-Shifa Hospital. We had bought some equipment in the early autumn of 2008, but Israel would not let it over the border. We could have done with that equipment here now, I thought.

Another problem was all the relatives who wanted to be with the patients, and who were now standing in the corridor and on the stairs outside the surgical department. We discussed the possibility of having separate areas where the relatives could stay. It is usual in emergency situations to divide the relatives into groups in the same way as the patients. Ideally, the families of dying patients should have the chance to be with them. Those waiting for an operation to end should have a separate place to wait. The families of those with lighter wounds should be in another place. Maybe the area around the emergency department could be better utilised?

Other doctors took the floor, and the discussion became more vocal. It was clear that everyone had experienced the first day of the attacks as a unique event and needed to talk about it. They were held back a little by having to speak English, and the discussion gradually shifted to Arabic and became quite intense.

We left the meeting and stood outside the hospital for a while. Then an F-16 came tearing by over our heads and something was dropped from it. The others who were standing there said they were leaflets in Arabic appealing to the people to leave their homes. A bomb attack on homes in Gaza City was on the way.

At around half past three, we came back to the emergency department. There we met a group of the doctors who had been at the meeting, who were in full swing reorganising the hospital's ground floor. The group was led by Dr Sobhi. He said that they were going to try to make the improvements we had discussed. Over the course of an hour, they had set up eight stretchers in the hallway outside the intensive care unit. The idea was that we could treat here those with lighter wounds who did not need to be taken to theatre. 'Impressive,' I said. 'Very efficient.'

In this pressured setting, words were translated into deeds in very short order. We were quite proud of what we had taken part in, and we felt that the doctors at the hospital had confidence in us.

Al-Shifa Hospital is structured in a very similar way to other university hospitals in Europe, even if it is small, with about 500 beds. Many of the doctors had been educated in other Arab countries, Europe and the USA. We did not bring any medical expertise they did not already have, so it was important to be modest and to be at their disposition. It was a great advantage that we had worked and given training there before.

That was probably why Dr Mohammed and Dr Sobhi asked us to report to them daily and suggest improvements. With this, we felt that we were being given a task that would be difficult to accomplish well. It takes time to become familiar with all the decision-making processes and procedures. At the same time, the handling of patients and relatives takes not only medical competence but also an understanding of culture and family psychology. Even if we had worked in Gaza previously, we recognised our own limitations.

Dr Mohammed and Dr Sobhi insisted, however, that our comments were important to them. We felt respect for what we understood as a sort of plea for help in a hopeless situation. The difficulty of the situation gradually dawned on us too, and we understood how vulnerable the staff were.

We could not help noticing that many of those who worked in the emergency department and in the other hospital departments went around wearing a small earpiece in one ear. They were listening to local FM radio in order to keep up with *where* in the Gaza Strip was being bombed by Israel. Mads and I had become involved in the war of our own free will and had our homes and our families located safely in Tromsø and Oslo. The Palestinians, on the other hand, lived in constant fear of losing their homes, their families and, not least, their own lives – at the same time as they had to work day and night to save the lives of others.

As time went on, we saw demonstrations that the health workers were exposed to the bombing just as much as everyone else. A colleague came in one day as white as a corpse and said that his house had been bombed. Both Mads and I knew him and had eaten dinner with him and his family at his home on an earlier occasion. Now that home was gone.

'What about the rest of your family?' we asked.

'There was no one home, thank goodness,' he replied.

But one of the doctors from the department of internal medicine was at home when the bomb struck. It killed his pregnant wife and one of his daughters. The doctor himself and his other daughter came in seriously injured.

One of the surgeons, Dr Raid al-Arini, saw his two children brought in to hospital while he was on shift. Their house had been bombed, and both had been seriously injured but luckily survived. Two days later, I met him on the stairs when I was on my rounds, and I asked him about his family.

'They are fine,' Dr Raid replied, but he did not seem happy.

'How are you?' I asked.

'Not so good,' he answered. 'Yesterday they bombed my cousin's house. He was killed, and his brother was injured.'

But Dr Raid carried on working.

While Mads and I knew that we would go back to Norway soon, the Palestinians could not leave Gaza. Even if we gradually became both depressed and angry having seen all the patients – the women and the children – who came in maimed and with their bodies mutilated, our situation was completely different. The Palestinians could not allow themselves to take time off to grieve and feel pain. They had to carry on until it was all over. I think that the most important role Mads and I had was to represent some kind of normality.

The danger in such a hopeless situation is that, at a certain point, it becomes impossible to take in any more suffering. I think this might explain the Palestinians' attitude to pain. The doctors put thoracic drains in patients without anaesthetic, something that patently hurts tremendously. In one room, two orthopaedic surgeons were setting a child's broken arm without any kind of anaesthetic. Mads intervened immediately and gave the child an injection of ketamine.

Even if Mads and I lived under far less pressure, the meaninglessness of the situation changed us too. Young patients were coming in constantly with severe injuries, and we worked on them for hours. Then – just as we thought we had finished – a new load of injured people would arrive. Eventually you can become both dulled and indifferent. Then there is the danger that you can begin to be careless and not to treat every individual patient with the respect and the sympathy to which every person is entitled.

At the same time, it is impossible to avoid being affected emotionally by the situation and starting to identify with your colleagues. We know this from previous wars. This is why it is NORWAC's policy that health workers in an active conflict situation should not work for more than a couple of weeks at the most before they are replaced.

At four o'clock that same day, the mass-casualty situation that the doctors at al-Shifa had feared became a reality: Israeli aircraft bombed al-Maqadma Mosque in the village of Beit Lahiya while 200 Palestinians were gathered in prayer. Twenty-four seriously injured people came in at once. Mads and I hurried back to the emergency department. We peered behind the

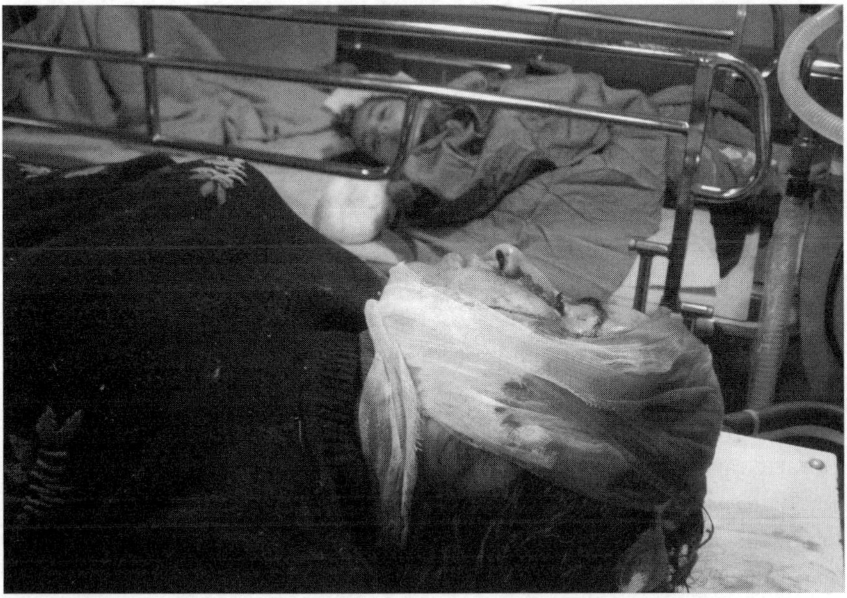

The seriously wounded queued in an empty operating room. Lying on the stretcher in the background are Dr Raid al-Arini's two seriously injured children.

curtains. A man asked us to come and see to a small girl with a head injury. On the stretcher next to hers lay her grandmother. Mads checked the girl who was being treated while I looked at the grandmother. An X-ray picture lay on the stretcher: the image showed fractures in her left thigh bone and calf bone.

The woman was gasping for breath and seemed confused and hazy. Her blood pressure had not been taken, and there were no other doctors nearby. Those who had seen her and sent her for the X-ray were occupied elsewhere. I found a blood pressure monitor and tried to take her pressure but could find no pulse in the artery that goes along the arm. They had carried out an ultrasound scan of her abdomen and had not found any bleeding. There were no signs of chest injuries, but it was clear that the patient was bleeding. Then I realised that her right thigh was much larger than her left – she undoubtedly had a large haemorrhage in her thigh. It was impossible to find out who was responsible for the patient. We wheeled her in to the resuscitation room, but by then she was unconscious. Mads intubated her and I tried to get hold of the equipment to open her groin and apply forceps to the artery. Unfortunately, she had a cardiac arrest before I could get out the equipment.

Episodes such as this demonstrate the chaotic conditions in the emergency department when so many patients arrived. Nobody could have continuous responsibility for individual patients. The surgeon who had seen the patient first had sent for an orthopaedic surgeon who ordered an examination of her leg. When she came back from her X-ray, there were no more doctors to see to her. She was in shock due to severe haemorrhaging when Mads and I found her.

We went back out into the hallway. Just then, an eighteen-year-old boy came in with a small wound on his chest. We turned him round and found a slightly larger opening on his back, on the same side. There was no doubt that a projectile or a splinter had gone straight through his chest. One of the assistant doctors had put in a drain at the base of the thoracic cavity. Neither blood nor air was coming through the drain. The boy had very low blood pressure, and it was clear that he was bleeding somewhere. In such a situation, the location of the haemorrhage must be found urgently. Since both the entrance and exit wounds were towards the top of the chest cage, it was not very likely that there would be any bleeding in the abdomen. To be on the safe side, we carried out an ultrasound scan of the abdominal cavity, which showed no fluid, so the bleeding was not coming from there. There was only the chest cavity left, but there was still not any blood coming from the drain.

Mads gave the boy some anaesthetic, and I made a new opening in the chest just above the first one. I retracted the cut and put my finger into the chest cavity. The lung had fastened itself to the chest wall, so it was difficult to insert a drain to empty the blood. I loosened the lung as far as I could with my finger and inserted another drain, but still only a little blood came out. We had an X-ray taken that showed a lot of blood in the chest cavity. Blood came up when he coughed, so it was certainly a lung injury that needed surgery.

The patient was taken up to theatre, and I operated on him together with the Palestinian thoracic surgeon Dr Abdul Gafar Zaneen. I opened the chest cage on the right side, and we freed the lung. He had probably had a previous lung inflammation with irritation of the pleura, which had caused the lung to stick to the chest wall. In front of and behind the lung there was a lot of blood, which we suctioned out; there was also a large accumulation of blood in the fissure between the upper and lower lobes of the lung. We stitched up the bleeding holes in the lung. He was still bleeding, so we then loosened the lung further in order to see the rearmost part of the cavity. Blood was coming out of the exit wound in the back, probably from the vein

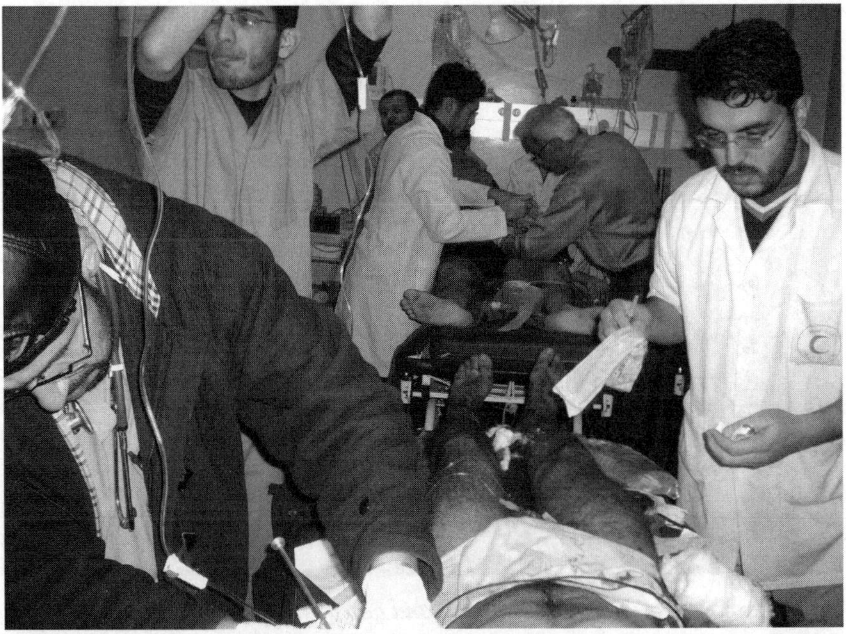

The emergency department and the emergency room are quickly filled with injured people streaming in from the bombing of al-Maqadma Mosque.

between the ribs. I put a stitch around the vein to stop it bleeding, inserted two drains and had him taken to the intensive care unit.

We had spent a couple of hours on this patient alone, who did not really have any extensive injuries but was at the point of bleeding to death. Each single patient needs accurate diagnosis and treatment, and this work takes time.

When I came out of the operating theatre, one of the vascular surgeons, Dr Mohammed al-Dush, asked me if I would help him with a vascular injury. It was yet another young boy with several splinter wounds. The major wound was a large cut in his right upper arm with the artery and vein torn off. There was also a partial tear in one of the three nerves in the arm. Dr Mohammed dissected the blood vessels. The damage to the artery was considerable, and some of it had to be removed. Accordingly, I took out part of the calf vein so that we could use it as an artificial artery between the two ends. When we had finished, the neurosurgeons took over to repair the nerve. I had examined it, and it was only partly torn. He would probably be paralysed in the hand, but there was a good chance that this paralysis could disappear if the neurosurgeons managed to repair

Anxious and confused next of kin and other family members filled the hospital. Often, many members of the same family were injured or killed.

the part of the nerve that had been damaged. I regretted that I had not taken my surgical loupes, which were back at Rikshospitalet in Oslo. It was not possible to procure such luxuries in Gaza.

This was another operation that took several hours. When new patients keep coming in, it is tempting just to tie up the artery and amputate the arm. It is quicker, and then we have space for another patient, so sometimes it is the right thing to do. But it is a serious matter for a teenage boy to loose his right arm, and al-Shifa Hospital had specialists who could carry out most operations to a very high standard. I was continually impressed by how much work was put into saving arms and legs and achieving the best possible result for the patients even in completely chaotic situations where there was terrible pressure to finish quickly.

It was only when we had finished the operation late in the evening that I learned that Israel had begun its ground invasion. A column of tanks had crossed the border at Beit Lahiya in the north of Gaza with support from attack helicopters. Israel reported that they had killed Hamas combatants; Hamas reported that they had killed Israeli soldiers. At the hospital, we had logged thirty-five injured and thirteen dead following the bombing of al-Maqadma Mosque in Beit Lahiya.[48] All the casualties were civilians.

6

6

Powerless Witnesses

MADS GILBERT

It was a long night's journey into the next day and an even longer day's journey into the following night. We were in the intensive care unit until 1.30am on January 4, when Israeli ground forces moved into the Gaza Strip.

The department was full. I was especially busy with two young boys who were fighting for their lives after having received explosive injuries, which was the collective term for surgical injuries inflicted by bombing. One of them, a fifteen-year-old, lay unconscious connected to the ventilator after a fatal splinter injury to the head. His brain had been destroyed and all hope was lost. The boy had no other visible injuries, just this deadly splinter through his head. Both eyes were sealed shut and swollen up with large, pale violet-blue extravasations of blood on his otherwise normal, young face. I had followed him the day after his injury and had some discussions with the other doctors as to whether terminal patients such as him should really cease treatment earlier. It would spare suffering both ethically and in terms of capacity.

'Our culture doesn't allow it. His heart is still beating, and he was given sleeping medicine while we examined and cleaned his head wounds. We don't know whether he will wake up or not, even if the injury to his brain is fatal. And we don't know whether or not he is unconscious as a consequence of his medication. A miracle could still happen.'

I was thinking primarily of the lack of intensive care beds and of the new patients that would need ventilator treatment and intensive care to survive after life-saving operations. The evaluation my colleague made was the same as we make at home with life-threatening cranial injuries when we have reason to suspect that the brain is without blood flow. The situation at al-Shifa, however, was different. The capacity shortage was so severe at times that we could not physically find space for any more intensive care patients. So was it right to continue with this ventilator

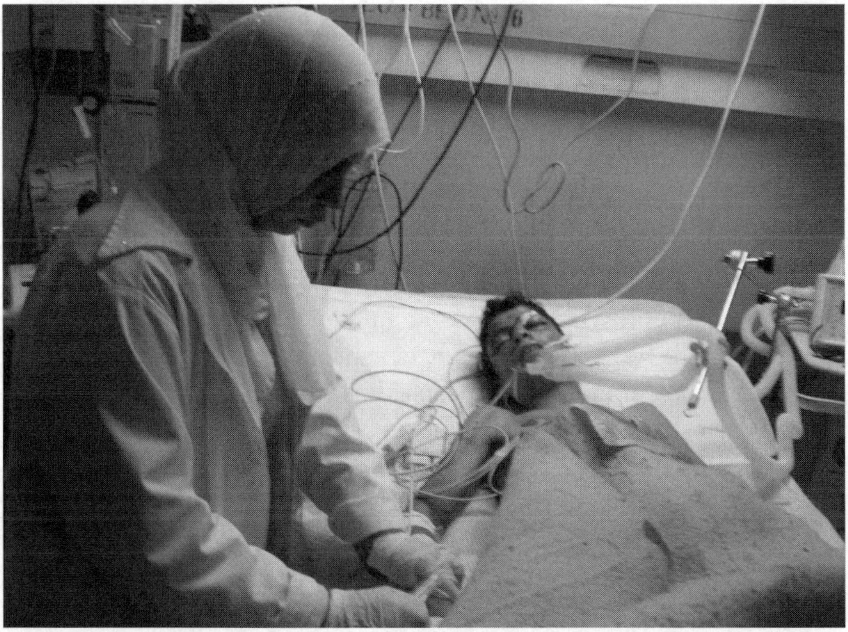

A boy with a fatal splinter injury to the brain. The doctors and nurses in the intensive care unit are highly skilled professionals, but there are shortages of everything as a consequence of the Israeli blockade.

treatment? Should they not move to a more harsh system of prioritisation in intensive care too?

I kept these thoughts to myself. The Palestinians were masters of their own house and had a good grasp of their ethical principles. I also knew from my own experience in intensive care at the University Hospital in Tromsø how emotional it is when we have to decide to stop actively treating people with fatal head injuries, especially when they are young. The balance between hopeful optimism and realistic pessimism is difficult. Patients with these injuries often look normal even if their brains have stopped functioning. Their hearts can keep beating for decades even if they will never wake up again. In our Norwegian medical culture, the legal and clinical criteria of death are linked to the total cessation of brain function, not heart function. For many people, heart activity is the very symbol of life and hope. Most people think that death occurs when the heart stops.

The intensive care unit at al-Shifa had always impressed me. Their therapeutic principles are modern and up-to-date, and their documentation is very good. Even in this disaster setting, they carried out high quality treatment, in spite of the great influx of critically injured patients and the shortage of resources. The blockade of Gaza had left its clear mark on the department. The paint was flaking off the walls, broken windows were not repaired, and a lot of the technical medical equipment was faulty or missing. Things we take for granted in a hospital were impossible to procure. The chemical reagents used to calibrate the vital blood gas machines were missing, and the medical engineers had to use manual methods and improvised solutions in a number of areas. Discipline and working morale were still very high, defiant and restrained.

'We must do our best for our people. It is our duty. We give the victims of the Israeli attacks the best treatment possible even if the conditions are very difficult.'

Another patient lay further towards the middle of the room. He was approximately twelve years old and had terrible injuries in the right side of his body: his right shoulder and upper arm had been almost torn off, his upper arm bone had been crushed and the right side of his head and face had been destroyed.

It was after midnight. He was bleeding profusely everywhere. 'We must operate on him tonight, his arm must be fixed, but he is in a bad way.'

The intensive care nurse looked at me and asked: 'What can we do? We have to do our best, but maybe he will not survive.'

In the distance, the thud of more bombs could be heard. Would this never come to an end? How many others would be torn to pieces tonight?

'Dr Mads, come and have some food with us!'

A large trolley was wheeled into the corridor outside the ICU itself. It was after one o'clock at night on Sunday January 4, and neither the doctors nor the nurses had eaten anything much since lunch, perhaps just a pack of 'high energy biscuits'.[49] On the trolley was what could be found in Gaza now: a stack of not particularly fresh pitta bread, small bowls of sliced tomatoes and snake cucumbers, some olives, spreadable cheese and a plate with a couple of tins of hermetically sealed tuna as today's 'main course', the same as yesterday, and as the day before.

Everything vanished as ten ravenous men finally got a deserved break, and an equally deserved snack. This was really nothing more than 'a snack'. No one was full and the table was soon cleared. Gaza had a shortage of everything, not least food. On December 23, 2008 – just as we began

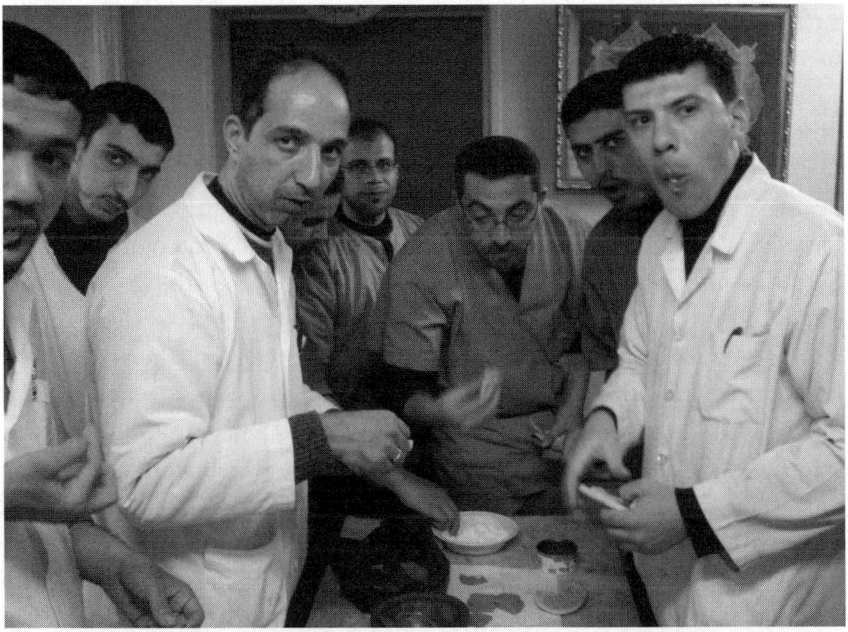

The nightly mealtime in the intensive care unit. Palestinian health workers only slept a few hours a day for several weeks in a row. They shared their small rations like brothers.

our well-fed Christmas celebrations in Norway and the rest of the West – the last mills in Gaza closed because there was no more grain to grind, and there were only 450 tonnes of flour stock, according to the last report of the United Nations Office for the Coordination of Humanitarian Affairs (OCHA).[50] One and half million people need approximately 450 tonnes of flour a day. It is easy to figure out that it was a lean Christmas in Gaza, even for the small Christian minority that makes up about 1 per cent of the population.

The empty food trolley was wheeled away, and the prayer rugs were laid out on the ground, facing towards Mecca. One of the nurses led the prayer time. Beautiful soprano song from the Qur'an filled the room and rose in counterpoint against the ceaseless wheezing and puffing of intensive care machinery and alarms constantly going off. The booming bass sound of the bombs resonated deeply in the distance. I saw the bowed backs, felt the relief of soothing prayer and noticed more intensely than before how the prayer gatherings drew not only them, but also me, into unity and peace around something greater than ourselves. A sacred air filled the room for a moment and muffled the horrible sounds of the profane torrent of bombs.

God save us all, I thought. There are many of us who need protection now. I was exhausted, but I gave one more interview inside the head nurse's office, that I believe was for a French radio station. The office was neat and plain. I emptied my pockets of syringes and ampoules: better to have everything 'freshly loaded' and ready for the next batch of wounded. Syringes and cannulae could be collected on the large trolley just inside the door of the intensive care unit. It was like a small self-service counter with long rows of drawers and boxes. It was tidy now, but when things got going, the 'syringe store' became just as chaotic as the resuscitation room.

As usual, I asked for three capped vials of high-concentration ketamine (50 mg/ml) and filled up several 10 ml syringes, which were clearly and meticulously marked with ink on fabric plasters: 'keta 50 mg/ml'. I did the same with some other medicine that is necessary in order to be able to induce anaesthesia quickly and safely. Battlefield anaesthesia is like battlefield surgery: things are done as quickly, simply and safely as possibly with an absolute minimum of resources.

Resources are strictly rationed in wartime and disaster situations when the influx of the wounded and the dying far exceeds the capacity of the local health services. The focus has to be moved away from giving everything to a single patient and towards the opposite: distributing the limited resources between as many as possible of the patients – or of the wounded – who have a realistic chance of surviving with prompt, life-saving surgery. No more. In order to achieve this, those with minor and non-life-threatening injuries must be filtered out while, at the same time, those with massive, probably fatal injuries, must also be identified. The casualties without hope should receive pain-relieving medication, respect and should have their families near, preferably all in a separated area. This may seem cynical, but it is the only ethically right thing to do in order to save as many as possible of those who can be saved.

The selection of which war casualties should be sent to the first available operating theatre and the decision to give life-saving surgery as quickly as possible involve critical and arduous choices. Critical because prioritising too generously soon leads to the operating suite being inundated with patients and to the system collapsing. Arduous because evaluating the extent of injuries, the bodily responses to the injuries and how realistic the patient's survival chances are from a medical point of view is very complex and difficult. Knowledge of academic theory is not sufficient alone. The doctor who is responsible for this triage process, for the prioritisation of casualties, must have a wide clinical experience and must know what chance the injured patient has of surviving surgical intervention as well as post-operative treatment in intensive care, which is at least just as important.

Giving a patient a general anaesthetic requires two people in order to induce anaesthesia itself and at least one person to tend to the patient during the operation. By choosing more simple forms of anaesthetic, a greater number of patients can be operated on when resources are scarce and there are many patients. The same applies to analgesics. Challenging cultural differences become apparent here as well. We have often found out that pain is a greater part of the bitter realities of life in Arab countries than it is in our 'pain-free' culture. Health workers both in Lebanon and in occupied Palestine use fewer palliative drugs for painful procedures than we do.

Opium-based pain-relieving products such as morphine and codeine are very good painkillers, but they do have adverse side effects for injured patients. Nausea and vomiting combined with weakened breathing are dangerous side effects that can threaten the patient's airway and respiration. Reduced blood pressure is another adverse side effect. These adverse effects are occasionally used as arguments against administering opiates to conscious patients with severe fractures, partial amputations or who need painful life-saving procedures. The alternative is a simple dose of ketamine, which does not have these negative side effects. With a small dose, the patient will stay awake, often slightly euphoric, he or she will not feel pain, will breath clearly and will have an improved blood flow – and will not need advanced observation.

I often gave ketamine as a painkiller to wakeful patients with major, painful injuries. This would not infrequently lead to lively discussions.

'Why are you giving this patient ketamine, Dr Mads? Now we've got a problem. We haven't got any more observation spaces.'

The discussions about analgesics could, like any other discussion – even the most trivial – become loud and intense. I interpreted this as an expression of some of the enormous stress to which we were all subjected. Maybe I should have just accepted the local medical customs?

When choosing between letting patients endure great pain and giving them simple, dependable pain-killing medication that does not require particular monitoring, the traditional practice was to leave them in pain. I could not accept this for the patients for whom I was responsible, not only for reasons of humanity, but also because pain is unphysiological and has a negative effect both on the injured patient's body functions and on his or her general resilience. I also had a clear ethical and moral responsibility for the patients I treated as an anaesthetist, and I emphasised this plainly in my conduct towards my colleagues, both other anaesthetists and surgeons.

It is a demanding exercise to bear in mind local customs and the particular kind of stress that a war situation entails, while at the same time to be open to suggesting improvements and making progress. The mutual trust and respect between us was so well established that we managed the balancing act, but the risk of didactic arrogance and a lack of sensitivity was, naturally, great. Palestinian doctors are proficient, well trained and inquisitive about medical innovations. Still, there is limited space for procedural changes and alterations when bombs are falling and the next group of injured and dead patients may include your own children or spouse. To pick at details in such an extreme situation would, of course, both be meaningless and represent a dangerous distraction from the most important things: tempo, discipline and resolutely prioritised measures to save as many of the acutely injured Palestinians as possible. That our colleagues at al-Shifa and other health establishments in Gaza were still standing at all and carrying out their duties in shifts that stretched around the clock, with minimal opportunities for sleep or rest, was an act of historic heroism, nothing less.

After the late-night snack, I met Erik and his surgeon colleagues. They were making a nocturnal visit to intensive care to see to a recently operated patient. We accompanied them through the large corridor outside, which was almost always full of anxious family members looking for their loved ones, Palestinian TV crews, and visitors on their way to see their relatives. To our great pleasure, we could already see the results of the doctors' meeting on Saturday: half of the corridor had now been organised as another major incident reception area. This is where those with minor injuries would be taken after being filtered in front of the entrance to the emergency department itself. Between ten and fifteen walking wounded could now be examined and completely treated on simple stretchers placed on stretcher supports. The capacity of the emergency department itself could then be screened and prioritised for the seriously injured – those who could not walk.

It was now around half past one, and we staggered down to our sleeping quarters, exhausted, but uplifted by the good procedures we

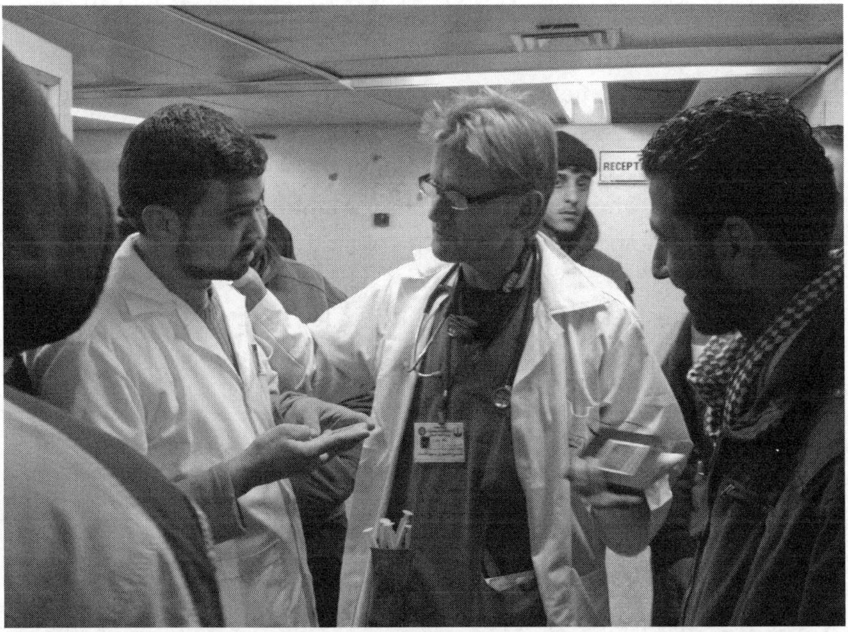

The head nurse Osama always had a full view of the hospital capacity and where patients were being allocated. There was a constant shortage of space for the newly arrived casualties in the operating rooms, in intensive care and in the wards.

had seen and all the warmth we had met in the midst of all the bombing and unpleasantness.

It was a restless night. I slept only sporadically. The bombing thundered closer and closer. There was a ferocious impact not far from the hospital. Both the building and our beds shook. I felt the blast where I lay in my bed, and it rattled the window, which was always open to prevent a deadly shower of glass when there were blasts nearby. Extremely sharp splinters of window glass such as these had already killed one and injured several others in the hospital when the Israelis bombed al-Shifa Mosque across the street.

'Damn, Erik, that was bloody close.'

'Yes, I felt the blast,' Erik mumbled half asleep.

In between the bomb blasts, I became aware of the quiet Gaza night. I thought back to west Beirut in 1982. I remembered the same ominous stillness before the terrible explosions. I was not afraid, but I could picture the injuries and deaths every time I heard the bombs. Did they hit a house? A car? An ambulance? One or more people? What do they look like? What do they feel?

I knew that if anyone had been injured, they would be coming to the hospital soon.

I thought of the pain they must be feeling. The shock when they are hit by the bomb or when their house shakes and is blown to pieces. The worry and the desperation when they search around dark and smoke-filled rooms, perhaps collapsed houses: where are the children? Grand-mother? My husband? Uncle and aunt? Who is alive, who is wounded and who has been killed? Are the ambulances coming? Are more bombs going to come from the sky? Can we escape?

Palestinian families are large, and in Gaza they live close together in cramped homes, piled one floor on top of another as new generations have grown up, settled down and established themselves. The occupation has not exactly allowed for expansion, either for new buildings or more spacious homes. Cramped living conditions and overpopulated residential quarters are the result, especially for the one million Palestinians in Gaza who have refugee status and fewer rights. When Israel chose to drop precision bombs on residential buildings, schools, mosques and streets, they must have known that they were striking civilians. They had confirmation of this when the television pictures a few minutes afterwards showed the injured and killed being taken to Kamal Adwan Hospital to the north, al-Quds Hospital a couple of blocks away from here in Gaza City, Gaza European Hospital to the south or to 'our own' al-Shifa: graphic close-ups of children's faces, dead women, old men with their arms and legs torn off. The Israeli authorities did, after all, see the same television images as the rest of us. How could they allow it? What would they achieve, and what kind of view of humanity had those who let women and children become bombing targets day after day? I pondered this as I fell slowly into a troubled sleep.

There was not much sleep to be had this Sunday night, so it was no loss to start the day at dawn. I gathered my usual equipment from on top of the bed and checked everything was there. I had my notebook with the last day's up-to-date figures from the Health Ministry of those killed and injured. I also had my large pair of scissors that I had ordered especially from the market for cutting open clothes and that became a very popular tool as a replacement for the small scalpel blades they usually used to remove the clothes of the injured. Then I also had my syringes already set

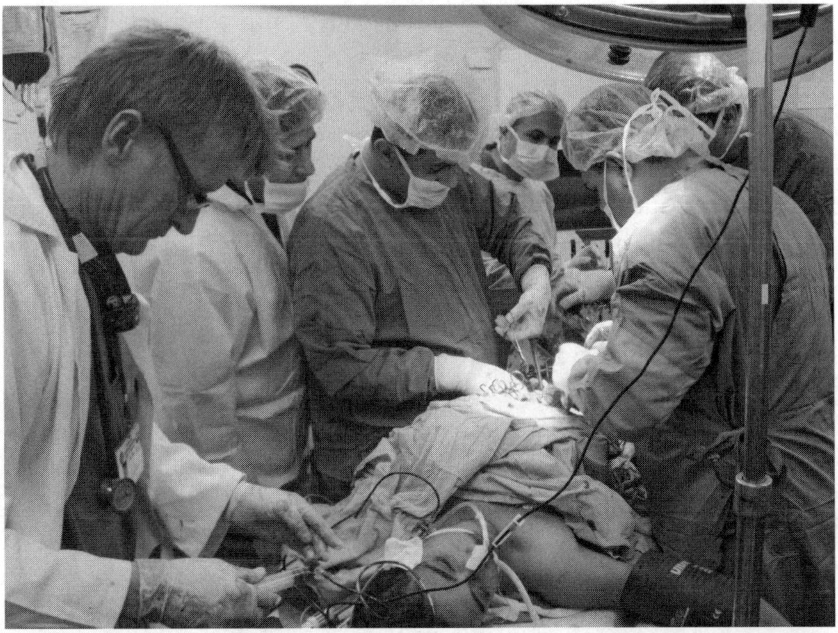

A bomb victim with heavy blood loss undergoing life-saving emergency abdominal surgery as damage limitation. Everyone in the team is suffering from early morning tiredness, but the procedure is flowing well.

up, a couple of intravenous cannulae, a tourniquet, my stethoscope, local and international mobile phones, a plaster roll, a head torch and my Palestinian ID card.

Everything was ready. On with my 'greens', the green operating scrubs, my good hill-walking boots and my winter jacket with decent pockets. It is winter in Gaza too, and the cold quickly crept into the hospital. When the night-time temperature crept down to seven or eight degrees and the cold wind from the Mediterranean pierced us to the bone, the pane-less windows afforded little in the way of shelter either for the patients and their families or for the hospital employees.

The hospital was full of activity. The resuscitation room was occupied by a war casualty with a large abdominal wound. The patient was in shock and was going to be operated on right away. My friends the anaesthetists were in control and greeted me with a devil-may-care smile when I came in.

'Dr Mads, are you already up? Come and help us, we're going to the operating theatre.'

'That's good that you've covered him with a proper woollen blanket so he won't get cold.'

'Yes, we thought we should. You're on about it all the time. But you are quite right, everyone's cold.'

We took the patient quickly to be operated. The gastro-intestinal surgeons were ready, and the abdomen was opened promptly and with precision. Intestinal injuries and lots of bleeding points. The abdomen was packed with gauze to stop the bleeding, and the surgeons started the laborious task of finding their way along the whole small intestine searching for penetrating wounds. If a single hole is overlooked, this will lead to intestinal contents and bacteria leaking into the abdominal cavity after the abdomen is closed. Such a leakage will provoke a life-threatening inflammation of the peritoneum and blood poisoning, which are dreaded complications with a very high fatality rate among wartime casualties with abdominal injuries.

We were all low-voiced and drowsy, but the procedure went well. I carried out the blood transfusion and dealt with the anaesthesia process together with a technician. There was little discussion of the previous day's injuries or thoughts of the coming day's attacks and destruction. Maybe it was better that way. This, too, was a survival mechanism.

After the operation, I went over to the central sterile supplies department, where instruments are washed and sterilised. Everything was in perfect order, and the instruments that were already packed in green paper were put in systematic piles. All of a hospital's functions have to work in harmony to keep it going. The minimal functions must be guaranteed, especially in disaster settings. Teamwork and logistics are crucial.

For the employees, sleep hygiene, food and contact with their own families are decisive for their ability to function over time. The concept of sleep hygiene implies assuring a minimum amount of sleep. Without at least four hours a day of uninterrupted sleep, people's ability to function is soon reduced. Many in Gaza and at al-Shifa Hospital did indeed sleep less than that in periods of this war. The bombing, the destruction and the work to be done could overshadow considerations of sleep. Many slept night after night at the hospital because the journey home was too hazardous. A 'bedside' cup of coffee and a smoke could be had in the improvised dormitory next to the operating theatres. A couple of hours' rest was all they got. More operations were waiting.

An improvised dormitory in the operating room. A cup of strong Arab coffee and a smoke get the next shift going, day and night. The hospital workers had to sleep when they could.

Patients kept coming to the operating suite. The bombing seemed quite close, so I went down to the emergency department. The sound of sirens and another wave of ambulances and private cars streamed towards al-Shifa. Patients were carried in unsystematically and chaotically. They were given their assigned places on the stretchers, and work could begin: securing airways, inserting venous cannulae and taking blood tests are usually the first things to be done, then the injuries are assessed, after which another, more experienced surgeon often arrives. Any external bleeding must be stopped immediately, and the casualty must be kept warm. Many will have a plastic tube inserted between their ribs into the space between the two layers of the pleural sac to relieve it of any blood or air, which often accumulate there in cases of splinter injuries or blast wounds to the thoracic cavity. Thoracic drains such as these are life-savers when there are leakages of air that can lead to the potentially fatal build-up of pressure, or when there is haemorrhaging that can also put strain on the lungs and on large blood vessels in the chest cavity.

Two ambulance workers came running in with an apparently lifeless young boy. He lay on a stretcher. There were no more patient trolleys left, and we had to put the stretcher on the floor. I held my small camera as I filmed his arrival, but I put it down on the floor and took charge of the work. We had obtained permission from the hospital management to take pictures and I would, as far as was practically possible, ask the patient's or family's consent to take photographs.

The boy was unconscious and did not respond at all. At first, I thought he was dead, but all the same I carried out a head tilt/chin lift manoeuvre to open his airway and put my ear right up to his mouth to hear if he was breathing. He was breathing, but only very faintly. I called out several times for a so-called 'bag', a self-inflating plastic balloon. His neck pulse was barely readable. With a face mask and the bag, we managed to get air into him, and we quickly moved into the resuscitation room, where we put a plastic tube into his windpipe (intubation) and took over his breathing. Thoracic drains were immediately put in on both sides, but neither air nor blood came out. The boy had between twenty and thirty small dotted holes in his chest wall. None of them was bleeding. The sound of his breathing was the same on both sides, but he was not responding at all, and his pulse was getting weaker and weaker.

The boy's delicate body had evident blast marks and signs of abdominal bleeding, as well as a head injury. His face was burnt. We examined his chest and abdomen and turned him onto his side, but we could not find anything other than the perforations of his chest wall, the blast marks and the head injury. I felt into one of the perforations with my little finger. The hole did not go all the way through, only to the rib-cage. I took out a small clump from one of the holes. It looked like a piece of popcorn, about the same size as a grain of rice. Not metal, but a greyish, apparently plastic substance. DIME?

The surgeon thought he was dying. I insisted on a reassessment and asked to take him to intensive care. 'No more beds there,' he said.

'But we can't just leave him here, we have to see how things develop, don't you agree?'

'Yes, but where to put him?'

'I can take him to the intensive care unit.'

'OK, try, at least.'

We took him to the ICU.

'But we have no beds free,' the head nurse said harshly when we got there. 'You know that you must reserve the space before you come.'

'But we just have to take him here. He could recover. He has heavy explosive injuries with heavy blast marks to the head, chest and abdomen.

I don't think we can save him, but all the same ... There is nowhere else to take him now.'

'We'll find a bed. Come on!'

A small single room was cleared, and the boy was connected to the monitoring equipment and ventilator. His heart had electrical activity, but otherwise there was no pulse to be found now either in the neck or the groin.

'We've got pulseless electrical activity, we need to give him intravenous volume, I can't feel a pulse.'

His blood pressure was not measurable either.

We started CPR. A nurse carried out the chest compressions, but they were not good enough and his hand position was wrong. This is not unusual in hectic situations, so I gently showed him the landmarks for the hand positions on the chest and demonstrated the proper technique.

Was the pericardium perhaps filled with blood?

I stuck a needle through the diaphragm and into the pericardium. About 8 to 10 ml of blood came out, no more, and hardly enough to explain the lack of a pulse. The ECG signal was changing and flattening. I gestured towards the screen which was showing there was no response to our treatment.

We ended our resuscitation attempts. I crouched down by the bed, took off my gloves and lay my hand on his forehead. He should not leave this world alone. None of my patients should. I felt his skin against mine. It was still warm and smelt of gunpowder residue.

Mahmoud died a few minutes before midday on Sunday January 4. I asked the nurses to call in his family, who we had seen nearby earlier. His brother, Ashraf Mashharawi, who would later turn out to be a local cameraman and TV producer, came in and stood helpless at the foot of the stretcher.

'He is dead,' I said. 'I am terribly sorry. Here is his scarf – to remember him by.'

I carefully put my arm around him.

'He's my little brother. Eleven years old. We sent him and his cousin, Ahmed, who's sixteen, up onto the roof to play. It was safer than playing on the street. So we thought.'

Ashraf cried.

'A bomb came on a small rocket. It was aimed directly at the roof. Mahmoud and Ahmed used the roof so they would be safe: we didn't want them to be in the house or on the street. Al-Wahda Street is in the centre of Gaza City, and it could be dangerous there. We sent them onto the roof to make sure that they wouldn't be injured.'

Tears ran while Ashraf spoke.

His brother Mahmoud reached eleven years, his cousin Ahmed reached sixteen. Typical Gaza boys, they had grown up used to bombs, the blockade and uncertainty, without the external security and protection we take for granted in 2009: human rights, respect, freedom of movement and freedom of expression. Now, they were both dead. Killed by deadly weapons, aimed and fired by a human hand in a distant control room.

Sunday was a terrible day.

On Sunday, Israeli forces killed two young Palestinian boys who were playing on a roof.

On Sunday, Israeli aircraft also bombed the vegetable market in the middle of the busiest shopping area of Gaza City.

On Sunday, we received wave after wave of people frightened to death; some uninjured, some wounded, some dying and some dead – of all ages, with every kind of injury. We saw no soldiers. Only children, women, young men and the elderly. They had one thing in common: they were all Palestinian civilians.

More reports of attacks were coming in the whole time. Many went around listening to the local news in their ear as they worked. Mobile phones received the local FM stations that broadcast live and continuously, like a simple warning and information system.

'They are bombing the vegetable market in Palestine Square. Many killed and injured,' shouted someone by the desk in the emergency department.

The wave of the latest injured was not long in coming. I cannot remember the details, only the feeling of being inundated with dreadful images and sounds. Devastated human bodies were everywhere. On the floor, on stretchers, on tables, in the resuscitation room, behind curtains, and there were walking wounded with bleeding injuries.

A dying pregnant woman. Children with recent amputations. The noise rose and fell like the sound of a numbing cascade of voices and cries, commands, outbursts, despair and moans. In the swarm of desperate activity, it was almost impossible to make out any pattern or organisation. But it was there. Patients were examined, sorted and prioritised. We took the injured that we thought 'salvageable' up to the operating suite, which and openly sympathetic to the Palestinian people – not Hamas – Fox News had a big picture on their website of me at work at al-Shifa with the headline in bold type all over the picture:

THE HAMAS PROPAGANDA DOCTOR.

The situation was intolerable.

'More patients are coming, many more from the vegetable market.'

I felt myself up against a wall. I had to breathe. I went over to the window at the end of the hall. I looked out and saw smoke rising into the air. I heard the bombing. I heard the ambulances. I could not take any more. We must stop this. You all have to hear about it!

I picked up my mobile phone and wrote this text message, without checking it over:

> They bombed the central vegetable market in Gaza City two hours ago. 80 injured, 20 killed, all came here to Shifa. Hades! We are wading in death, blood and amputees. Many children. A pregnant woman. I have never experienced anything so terrible. Now we hear tanks. Pass this on, send it on, shout it out. Anything. DO SOMETHING! DO MORE! We are living in the history books now, all of us! Mads G. 03/01/09 13:50 Gaza City

The words had been written and the appeal had been made, but it still just lay there as mere words in my hand. Who should I send it to? I did not have much time, so I chose the few groups I had made to facilitate quick texting from Gaza. I chose 'Media', 'My kids', and a handful of close names from the address list. Not many. I pressed 'Send', and the remaining radio waves that had not been jammed by Israeli intelligence or bombed by the machinery of war took hold of those words, lifted them on invisible wings and carried them to their destinations. The addressees forwarded the message on to yet more people, who forwarded it to even more.

I had no plan for an SMS campaign. It was just a scream, a cry of distress, an SOS from Gaza to those who could hear. I wrote the wrong date, undeniably because the days ran completely into the nights, and the next day was only an uninterrupted continuation of the previous one. It was not January 3, but January 4, 2009 when I wrote the message.

'I think this is the strongest message I've written since we came here. It's effective, don't you think?'

'Yes,' replied Erik.

'Imagine if there had been the Western media here too. Think about everything that isn't being reported. We cannot leave before someone else can take over reporting.'

Sunday was also a long day's journey towards another restless night. But we had important jobs to do before we turned in. More monitors had to be collected from the cardiac monitoring unit and moved to the emergency department and the resuscitation room. I had discovered that the well-equipped monitoring unit was in the same wing of the hospital in which we were staying. After intense discussions with the internal physicians, we agreed that the terrible standard of electronic patient monitoring in the emergency department and the resuscitation room was unacceptable – if there were any alternatives. It was simple to move four machines from the cardiac monitoring unit to the surgical battlefield to measure blood pressure, ECG, pulse and blood oxygen levels.

After a little more discussion and persuasion, it was agreed that we could upgrade the most important area for patients with four more monitors and upgraded areas for receiving patients. There was a doubling of capacity.

Unfortunately, it all turned out to be needed.

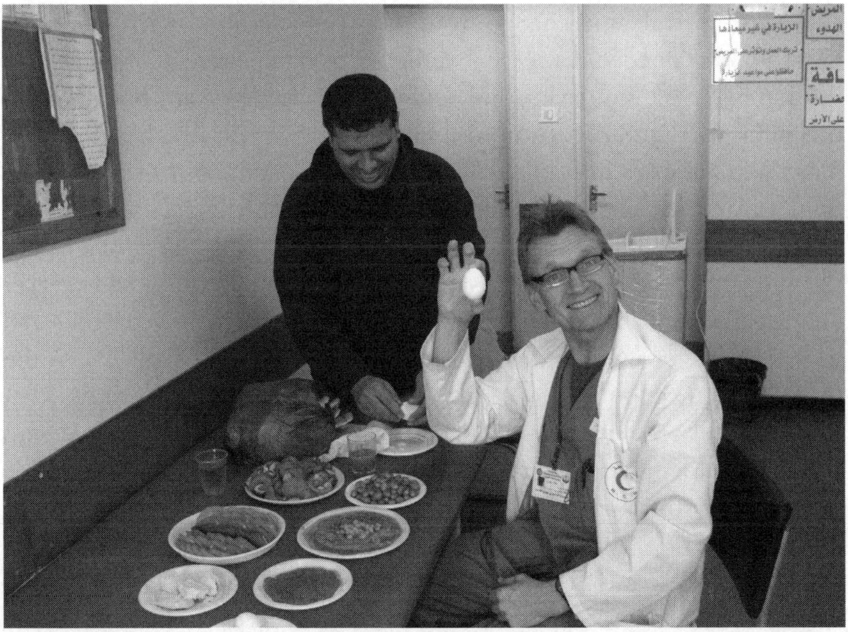

An air of abandon at the breakfast table.
Dr Mads is 'as ready as an egg', as they say in Norway.

and I had certainly done. Seen in this light, we should be well protected against stress, but perhaps we were not so well protected against the massive emotional pressure to which we were all being subjected.

Our shared sense of humour and Erik's warm and resonant laughter helped me through many moments when my ability to cope had been worn thin and despair was about to set in. In spite of the fact that we have extensive experience of war situations and in spite of how well we each know our own reaction patterns and needs, the strain during this war was so heavy and the suffering we saw and experienced was so heart-rending that we were approaching the limits of our own capacity. 'Our room' became a little enclosure where we would let off steam, cry, gather strength, take care of each other and seek repose. Without this close comradeship and the mutual respect we have for each other, we would not have coped as well.

Erik had been shuffling around our small two-person room for a while in his light blue 'Hamas pyjamas', but he had now got dressed in our standard working outfit: green operating scrubs. The pyjamas were comfortable and warm; a welcome change from our green scrubs, which could get both blood-stained and sweaty. Neither of us had packed a lot of clothes, just a pair of jeans, a jacket and some underwear. We are both used to travelling light and do not need much in order to get by. Besides, after many years of work in the field, we know that most things can be got hold of locally, either from the local market or through friends.

There was a lot of work waiting for us every time we got back to our sleeping quarters. Our journals had to be updated; we would answer phone calls that had come in and interview requests on our voice mail and in text messages when the phone-lines were open, or e-mails when the Internet connection was working. I would download and process that day's pictures on the lap-top I had taken with me and write short pieces to accompany them for the small Norwegian press corps on the Israeli side of the border to the north.

Frode Græsvik from TV2, Jon Magnus from the newspaper *VG* and Line Fransson from *Dagbladet* were constantly denied access to Gaza by Israeli authorities as part of a meticulously planned PR strategy to keep Western news media in the dark as far as Gaza was concerned. But should there not then be a limit to the number of times that members of the international press who were not let into Gaza allow themselves to be bussed by Israeli press officers to places just north of the border in Israel where Palestinian rockets had landed, on the whole resulting in holes in the ground?

I felt a great responsibility to share with them what I could in terms of pictures and text, preferably every day, so that they had some material to send home. Altogether, I sent twenty to thirty messages with attachments to various Norwegian press contacts. A drop in the ocean, but authentic 'inside information'. This work took time too. Of course, we never let interviews or other kinds of contact with the media come at the expense of our jobs as doctors or time spent with the patients. Our four hands, two pairs of eyes and fairly wide clinical experience were of course useful and increased the capacity of al-Shifa to a certain extent. It was still only a drop in the ocean. The hospital has over 400 doctors in different specialisations, and they would doubtless have managed their clinical duties, including surgery, anaesthesia and intensive care, without us, even under these extreme circumstances. If we were going to be interviewed at an agreed time – for example live on NRK TV or CNN – then the team around us was informed, and they helped us to keep an eye on the time. Of course, we never interrupted surgery or other procedures in order to

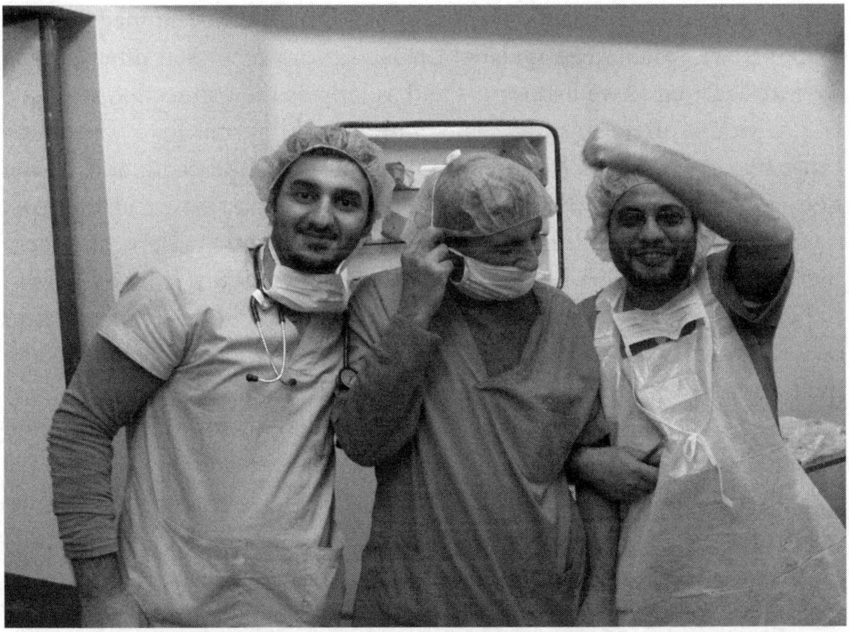

Humour helps to cope with disasters and crisis situations. From left: medical student Mohammed Abu Zanuna, Dr Abdul Gafar Zaneen and Dr Mohammed al-Ronn.

speak with the media, and we never left a patient we were busy treating in order to give interviews. It would have to wait, the mobile would just have to ring, or the television crew would have to film something else until we were ready. We split the interviews between us without any trouble and we were interviewed on a more or less fixed basis by the various television stations. Erik went on CNN most often, I went on the BBC and Press TV most often, while both of us went on the Norwegian TV channels alternately. We gave approximately ten to fifteen interviews daily to every kind of media outlet from all across the world.

We would also eat a little and speak with our Palestinian friends and colleagues who slept in the same wing of the hospital. Through these conversations we were updated on how the attack was developing. The conversations either took place entirely in English or were interpreted by the young man who was our technical support contact and also helped us with our Internet connection and other small practicalities. He would also translate when we were following the news on the television set that was always on at full volume in the 'main dormitory', the room next door where our Arab colleagues stayed. When the Internet connection was working, we would keep updated through Norwegian and international websites as long as we had time – and as long as the connection was up.

We would often go to bed late, and I would get up first. The white cable that gave us our Internet connection was in demand, and I soon figured out that the best slot was between half past five and half past seven. Then I had the Internet to myself while the others slept, and there was often not so much bombing during the small hours. These hours in the early morning gave me the composure to get my thoughts together and put them into words to be sent 'out there' – both to people in the media and to our contacts in Norway.

Ebba Wergeland was indispensable for co-ordinating the distribution of our pictures and information in Norway and for sending us feedback. Ebba is a doctor specialised in occupational medicine and one of the most important figures in the Norwegian solidarity movement for Palestine. She was the co-ordinator of the Norwegian Palestine Committee's surgical crisis team in west Beirut in 1982 and she put in an enormous amount of effort, together with Erik, who was at the time the co-ordinator back home in Norway for the teams that were sent. Ebba has a wide network of contacts in the Arab world and an exceptional overview of the political landscape. Our regular contact with her and with others also gave us continuing evaluation of and feedback on our various media appearances. My two courageous daughters also gave me important feedback on my interviews. They had supported me going from the very first moment and sent a stream of warm and encouraging messages, at the same time as being strongly committed to the passionate solidarity work in Norway. It was very demanding to deliver so many interviews rooted in such different linguistic and cultural backgrounds without having the opportunity to see the footage and to assess our performance.

We had very limited access to television. It was mainly the Arabic channels Al Jazeera, Al Aqsa and Al Arabiya that we saw flicker by in the few places there actually were working TV sets. The feedback we received, especially from Ebba, from Nina – Erik's partner – as well as from my daughters, was therefore important and useful. They helped us to correct ourselves when we inadvertently slipped into sentimentality, when we spoke a little too loudly or became contentious.

'Keep going as you've been doing. Tell them what you've seen and what you're living through. Be concrete; that is the most important thing,' was the advice from Nina and Ebba.

Days and nights were filled with the constant and nerve-racking buzzing of pilotless Israeli aircraft – drones – interrupted only by the excruciating, harrowing sounds of bombs hitting and of violent explosions at varying distances from the hospital. Drones are aircraft without pilots. These 'unmanned aerial vehicles' (UAVs) are fiendish devices in the way they are used over occupied Palestine. They can be used for simple reconnaissance and intelligence or to direct fire. They can also be armed with live weapons such as Hellfire and Spike 'fire-and-forget' guided missiles with special infrared seeker heads. Israel has long been a leader in the development of UAVs and is a large military exporter of these weapons. The Israeli armed forces use drones for reconnaissance and intelligence and as offensive attack weapons. Israeli military industry is constantly developing new types of drones and has just delivered the first in a new generation of drones to the Israeli air force, the Heron UAV. The new mark is called Eitan and is a direct competitor of the US-produced Predator A, also known as the MQ-1. The Shoval weighs 1.2 tons and can stay in the air for forty hours at a time. It can operate right up to 30,000 feet and is equipped with software that allows it to take off, perform its mission and land, all automatically.[53]

Over the years, I have become quite familiar with these pilotless aircraft that circle over Gaza continuously. The local population is used to them, but they get terribly annoyed when they interfere with the TV and mobile signals, especially when this happens during the World Cup, as I experienced in Gaza in July 2006.

The aircraft are remotely controlled by operators, or 'drone pilots', in secure control rooms far inside Israel. From there, they can steer these aircraft wherever they wish. The cameras on the US-made Predator drones are now so good that the operators can tell the difference between men and women on their monitors, according to US military experts who deal with these unmanned death machines. It is absolutely possible for the operator to see if the people on the ground are children: children playing on a roof or playing football in an open space. A definite human responsibility lies with the soldier hunting for his target, aiming and firing his deadly weapon at civilian men, women and children, while he himself sits well protected in his own country, hundreds of kilometres from the 'target'. The soldier piloting the drones from a remote bunker can drive home for dinner at the end of his working day or pick up his children and take them to a football match.

The blood of the dead left lying on the battlefield stains not only the soil, but also the remote control joystick and the hands guiding the remote controls. The distance between the incident, its consequences and the responsibility for it are not diminished even if the murder weapon is no longer physically in the murderer's hand.

The operators are often former fighter pilots and carry out their killing job in well-equipped mobile trailers with air-conditioning or in secure bunkers. The operators of the most common drone, the Predator, see the details of the terrain displayed on a whole wall of monitors, and they 'kill enemies with a couple of keystrokes on the computer'.

'Zero personnel losses' is one of the main arguments made when selling unmanned aircraft. The commercial website 'UAV Forum' uses this argument to explain the strong growth in the production and sale of UAVs, especially to the US armed forces.[54] The same goes for the expanded Israeli production of drones. According to 'UAV Forum', the most important reason why there is a greatly increasing interest in drones among military and political powers in the USA is that the political climate is increasingly setting zero loss of personnel as a condition of involving US military forces in combat. They end their reasoning thus: 'Lessons relearned during the Persian Gulf War [show] that dirty, dangerous, dull missions should best be delegated to unmanned vehicles.'[55]

Even if the physical personnel losses are reduced to zero, the remote manual guidance of killing machines does take its toll on the operators. They often let the drone circle over the target after the attack to survey the damage.

'You do stick around and see the aftermath of what you did, and that does personalise the fight,' explains Colonel Chris Chambliss in an interview. Chambliss is commander of the 432nd Air Expeditionary Wing at Creech Air Force Base in Nevada. 'You have a pretty good optical picture of the individuals on the ground. The images can be pretty graphic, pretty vivid, and those are the things we try to offset. We know that some folks have, in some cases, problems,' he says.[56]

The psychological stress to which the drone operators are subjected is similar to the stress that soldiers on ground operations experience. The US armed forces have therefore brought in chaplains to support the pilots who fly the Predator drones.

'When you come in at 500–600 mph [in a fighter jet], drop a 500-pound bomb and then fly away, you don't see what happens,' says Colonel Albert K. Aimar, commander of the 163rd Reconnaissance Wing at the same airbase. He has a bachelor's degree in psychology. When a Predator fires a missile, however, 'you watch it all the way to impact, and I mean it's very vivid, it's right there and personal. So it does stay in people's minds for a long time.'

How can you 'offset' the effects of moving images showing people torn to pieces, children and innocent people killed? Is it possible to carry out targeted attacks on civilians like these under full visual control without being deeply hurt yourself? Is it possible unless the pilot defines the targets – the 'others' – as different from himself, of lesser value?

It was now half past one on Monday afternoon. A lot had been done at the 'Gaza desk', we had both sent post and given several interviews. The stream of patients was beginning to grow as we entered the emergency department.

'Dr Mads, they need you in the resuscitation room, please. A child.'

The nurse carefully tugged the sleeve of my jacket. It had been a cold morning, and I was frozen after having worked sitting still. It was good to be wrapped up in my outdoor jacket. In the resuscitation room there was

The 'Gaza desk': the little room next to our sleeping quarters was our communications centre. By the light of his head torch, Mads wrote e-mails, listened to news on the Internet and processed photographs.

a little girl with a head injury. She gurgled when she drew breath and was bleeding from the head. I was given a short report: 'It looks like a splinter wound to the head. She's unconscious, but breathing by herself. Breath sounds are good on both sides. Not sure about the kind of weapon, maybe a missile?'

I took over control of her airway, and we examined the child from head to foot, front and back. She had a moderate wound to the head but there was alarmingly little response from her. With head injuries, the patient's level of consciousness is a critical indicator of the seriousness of the wound. Eye response, verbal response and motor response are measured on a numerical scale, and the total score gives the level of consciousness. A measurement like this makes it possible to differentiate between light, moderate and serious head trauma. The deeper the loss of consciousness, the more serious the head injury is.

The little girl just barely grunted, but when we inserted an intravenous cannula and bandaged her head, she blinked her eyes and made appropriate withdrawal movements.

'We don't need to give her a general anaesthetic. She's breathing well and seems to be waking up. Do you agree?' I asked the rest of the team.

'Agreed,' said Dr Rami Suhail al-Sousi, a young, quiet neurosurgeon. 'Let's take her straight for a CT scan, then we'll see the extent of the injury.'[57]

'Yes, let's get going. I'll deal with her airway; we've got to get oxygen. Shall we take her up together?' I asked Dr Rami.

The X-ray examination went quickly. The images just showed a compressed skull fracture and no serious tissue damage to the brain itself or bleeding between the brain and the inside of the skull. Such haemorrhaging can lead to accumulations of blood that take up space and can increase the pressure inside the cranial cavity so much that the soft brain can be destroyed and the blood flow to the brain can be stopped. At that point, the patient will die. Prompt surgery can prevent such fatalities, but it takes good clinical judgement and a good CT diagnosis.

There were a conspicuously high number of children with head injuries, often fatal ones.

One explanation for the fact that a third of the approximately 1,400 killed and 5,400 injured were children is probably that children cannot interpret danger signals the same way that adults can. Children are of a shorter stature than adults and are therefore more vulnerable to weapons with a low-level blast wave and fragmentation profile, such as DIME bombs.

The most important reason for the very high number of casualties and children killed who were under eighteen years of age is, however, the very distinctive demographic situation in Gaza. The median age of the population is just 17.4 years, and 44.4 per cent of the population is in the 0–14 year age group.[58] This makes Gaza a child prison. When the Israeli armed forces elect to bomb this child prison from the sky, there will inevitably be a great many children wounded or killed. The pictures from al-Shifa and the figures from the Health Ministry and the UN confirmed that same thing every single day: children were being killed and seriously injured in vast numbers every day. Nevertheless, Israel showed no sign of easing off the attacks, in spite of the daily documentation of infanticide and of the mutilation of completely innocent children. The drones' sharp eyes showed the Israeli pilots what they were shooting at too, whether they were sitting in a control room, in Apache helicopters or F-16 fighter-bombers.

What about the dead? We owe them one thing alone: the truth.

The little girl was gradually coming round. She looked at me with a surprised and gentle look, unafraid, as if I were a kind relative. I wrapped the blanket round her properly so that she would not be cold. I felt the relief like a wave of joy. The pretty little girl was going to wake up, not die. She was going to see, speak and understand; she was not going to remain unconscious.

All the same, maybe it was not the best fortune she could have had. Maybe death would have been better? I dismissed the thought immediately. Life is always best. That is the way it must be, otherwise we could not endure this.

'No surgery needed. Let's take her to the paediatric ward for further observation.'

The time was now two o'clock, and I felt a certain relief. At least one child would be spared dying from her wounds today.

More and more casualties came to the emergency department. On an orange ambulance stretcher, a man in his thirties lay on his back bleeding, wearing only his underpants, sprayed with blood and with his right leg mutilated and twisted. He was breathing by himself but was not conscious. We took him to the resuscitation room immediately and began work. First clear the airway. I moved his head back, listened to his breathing, put on my stethoscope and heard good breath sounds on both sides over the

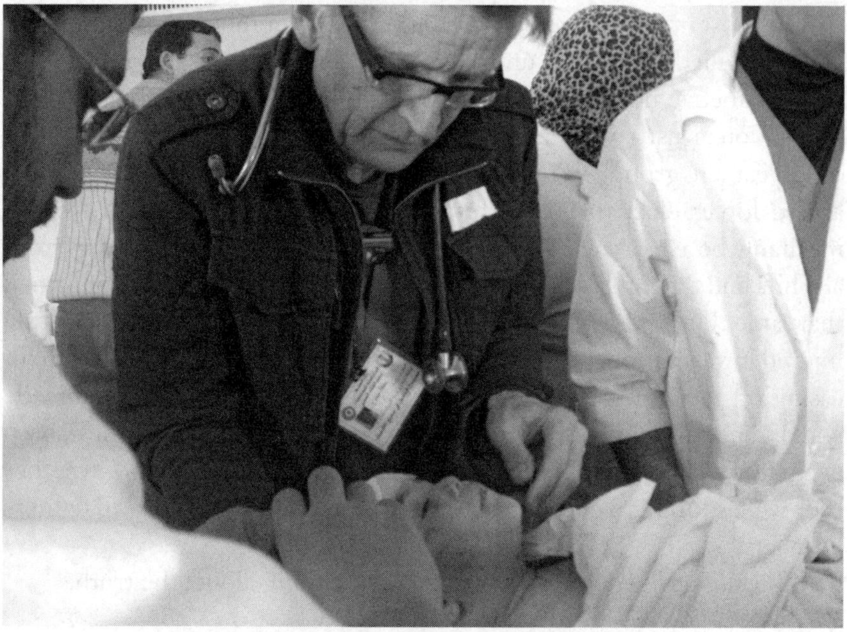

Many wounded children had serious head injuries. The little girl was unconscious but gradually came to and looked around. This is the girl whose photograph is on the front cover.

lungs. If the airways are not open and if there are not good, symmetrical breath sounds on both sides, there might be an airway obstruction or damage to the chest cavity with an accumulation of air or blood, or both. In any case, airway or breathing problems must always be dealt with first, because we are what are called aerobic creatures, completely dependent on a continuous supply of oxygen.[59]

I put an oxygen mask on him and turned up the supply. Like the other hospitals in Gaza, al-Shifa Hospital is equipped with oxygen extractors: dedicated machines that can extract oxygen from atmospheric air. With these, the hospitals in Gaza did not have to be concerned about being dependent on Israel for the importation of oxygen in gas bottles – something that would certainly have been included in the Israeli blockade of Gaza. This was deeply symbolic: when injured Palestinians were given vital oxygen that Palestinian hospitals had produced themselves, despite all the attempts by Israel to suffocate them, it demonstrated the importance of the long-standing medical solidarity campaign.

The man had a brutal amputation wound under his right knee and burn injuries on his left leg. We did not find any other injuries in his head to foot examination. Blood ran from his injured leg, and the bleeding had to be stopped at once. In addition to free airways and good breathing, we are also totally dependent on our red blood cells to transport oxygen from our lungs out to the body's tissue, where the oxygen is freed from the blood cells and becomes available for cellular aerobic metabolism. Every single drop of blood contains the vital haemoglobin, which is red because it has a high iron content. Any blood lost means a reduced capacity to transport oxygen.

'Clamp the femoral artery! Put your clenched fist right on top of it and press hard,' I said. 'Then we can stop the bleeding temporarily while we get ready to pack the wound and stop the bleeding altogether.'

Some rolls of gauze bandages were taken out and we started the task of filling up the hole left by the wound in order to apply counter-pressure to the deepest part of the wound. This is a painful procedure, so I gave an intramuscular dose of ketamine in the patient's thigh before we started. The patient's leg was almost completely torn off across the middle of its lower half. I asked for a knife and a pair of scissors and cut the remaining muscles, nerves and blood vessels to take it off completely. The amputated part was put into a cardboard box. According to Islamic tradition, amputated body parts should be buried, not destroyed as is the practice in the West.

This type of bleeding control is effective and saves the patient major blood loss. It is far better than the old binding method, or the tourniquet, which is unfortunately still used by some. A tourniquet increases bleeding, as well as the fatality rate of such bleeding wounds to the arms or legs, and should be replaced with the simpler and more effective combination of deep packing and elastic bandages. We have introduced a four-stage method for the emergency treatment of haemorrhaging injuries like these: constrict the supplying artery, elevate the bleeding extremity, pack the wound and apply a long elastic bandage. In many places with major and frequent injuries from mines, such as Cambodia and Kurdistan, this method has now been introduced following systematic training. Research we have carried out in war zones and areas with land mines has shown that this simple method can be learnt by everyone, it can stop any limb from bleeding, and it can increase the chances of survival for casualties with bleeding extremity wounds, as with this man.[60]

The packing of the wound went well, but it took some time. We were keeping the bleeding at bay, and the patient was breathing deeply and regularly as he lay there with his torn clothes and amputated foot. What was he doing when he was hit, and what was it that hit him? A DIME bomb?

Eight minutes after we started treating this injury, another amputation wound came into the resuscitation room: a boy, maybe twelve years old. His right leg was almost torn off right up at the hip, and his left foot had also been almost ripped off. He was only breathing weakly, so he was given artificial respiration and oxygen. His life faded away quickly, and we had to give up just nine minutes after he had come in. His young heart stopped. We could not do anything else; his injuries proved fatal.

Both these patients must have been hit by extremely powerful explosives, by so-called DIME explosives. These were the only types of weapon that could be expected to cause injuries like these, and the USA had already let Israel use them in the attack against Lebanon in 2006. I first saw injuries like these in Gaza at al-Shifa in the summer of 2006, during the Israeli attacks code-named 'Operation Summer Rains', and I described them in the Journal of the Norwegian Medical Association.[61]

We took the man with the amputated right leg to the operating suite. He was stable, and the bleeding was all under control, so there was no rush for surgery now. He could have waited until the following day, but who knew what that would bring?

The operating suite was full, and a queue of patients was waiting in the hallway.

I was met by the glance of an elderly man. He looked at me with the same inquiring eyes as the little girl earlier that day. What's happened? Why me?

We spoke to each other, and he told me that he was a farmer, that he had never owned a weapon and had never been politically active. 'So why is this happening to me?'

I had no answer. His left hand was in a bad way and would probably have to be amputated. The operation would have to be carried out in the corridor as a result of the shortage of space inside the theatres.

The operation was carried out a little later. From now on, the old man would have to get by with just one working hand. In Gaza, so they say, you need at least four to get by.

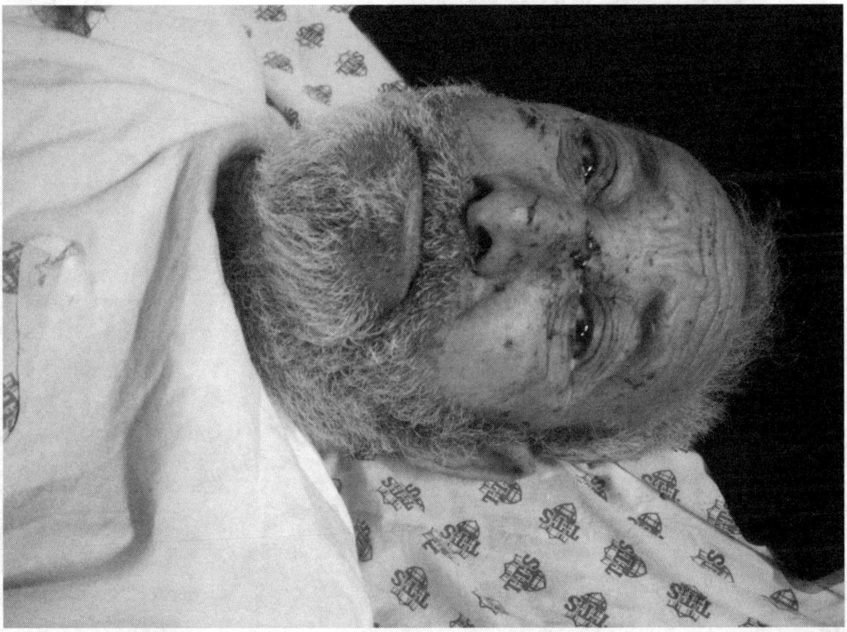

An elderly Palestinian waiting for his left hand to be amputated. 'What have I done wrong?' he asked.

Four patients, all of them civilians, all of them innocent. Their fates are sealed, and perhaps it is fates like these that give meaning to President Peres' statement that the aim of the assault on Gaza was 'to provide a strong blow to the people of Gaza'. The Nobel Peace Prize laureate Peres certainly achieved this.

8

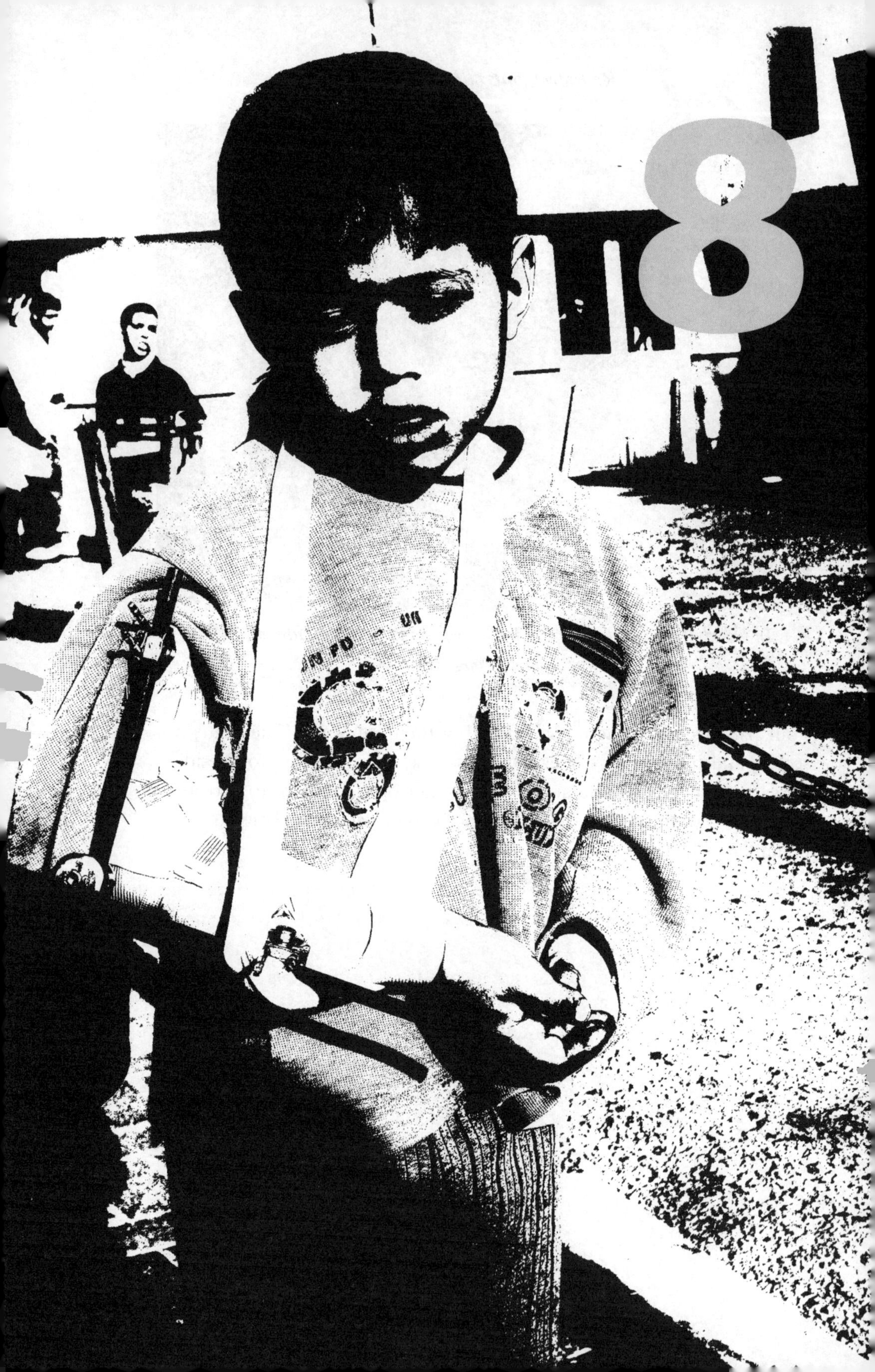

8

'They're Only Hamas Children'

ERIK FOSSE

I was awakened by heavy bombing a couple of times during the night. My bed was against the wall, under the window. The window was always open, despite the cold. It was Tuesday January 6.

The brown and orange rug fluttered whenever bombs landed nearby, but the window held. I was due to be interviewed for the TV2 news channel at seven o'clock Norwegian time. It was now nearly eight o'clock in Gaza, which is one hour ahead of Norway.

Mads was sitting up with his PC, reading e-mails and editing pictures. He was using his head torch, so as not to disturb us others. I could hear him murmuring and swearing as he trawled through the news. There was clearly no good news from Gaza. However, there was a lot about demonstrations and protests against Israel's bombing. At least that was something positive.

The others were asleep. They got up to pray at five o'clock every morning, then went back to bed and slept till half past nine. A few minutes before eight o'clock, the TV2 news channel phoned to ask about the news.

'After four days of the invasion we can hear the Israeli forces getting closer. They appear to be systematically bombing civilian targets. The number of children being injured just goes on rising, and there is a shortage of essential medical supplies. We will soon have no more fuel for the generators, and two specialist hospitals, the eye hospital and the children's hospital, have already had to be closed because of lack of fuel. Al-Shifa Hospital only has enough fuel to keep the generators running for two more days. After that our electricity supply ends,' I explained.

I had heard about the closure of the two hospitals the day before and assumed that the health authorities had closed them to save fuel and to prioritise Al-Shifa Hospital. War-wounded patients now had first priority. Children with chronic illnesses and patients with eye disease would just have to wait. There were now no health services in Gaza for the chronic sick and patients with non-life-threatening illnesses. The services for these patients had been poor for a long time because of the blockade, but when the war was going on they disappeared completely. These were some of the hidden victims of the war.

After the interview I went up to the emergency department. Outside, the sun was shining and the drones were humming. It was still chilly. I heard battle helicopters, but they seemed to be some distance away. There was a group of nurses, doctors and medical students standing in the department.

'*Sabaah al-khayr*, good morning, have you had a quiet night?' I asked.

One of the nurses, Sami Lobad, smiled.

'No, Dr Erik, it's not been so quiet.'

Sami Lobad's mouth began to tremble, and I could see tears in his eyes. They gradually began to run down over his cheeks, while he stood there trying to smile. One of the medical students began crying too. Before we realised it, we were all standing there crying together. Five grown adults: two doctors, two nurses and a medical student. We stood there that morning, weeping.

Seriously injured Palestinians were arriving at the hospital night and day. Children, young, old, women and men. Their houses were disappearing one after another. Their work-places were being flattened. And it just went on and on. It all felt so hopeless. I realised that the hospital personnel were approaching their limits. For ten days now they had been in constant fear of losing their own lives, their families, their homes. The war was getting closer day by day. The explosions sounded a little louder each day. The houses shook more. Attack helicopters and drones were swarming right over us.

Israeli planes had bombed several houses in Gaza City during the night. These were the attacks which had wakened me. The al-Daya family's four-storey house had been hit at six o'clock. The grandfather had gathered all his children and grandchildren there. Thirty members of the family had been killed, most of them children. Many of the survivors came to al-Shifa Hospital for treatment.

We heard more bomb blasts. They were still dropping bombs on the city or a little beyond. After a few minutes an ambulance arrived, bringing a woman with minor injuries. The staff were busy, and they did not need help from me. I went out from the emergency department to check my mobile phone. It was full of text messages from Norwegian media organisations asking for interviews. I tried to ring back, but could not get a connection. On the front steps I met Dr Sobhi, who let me use his

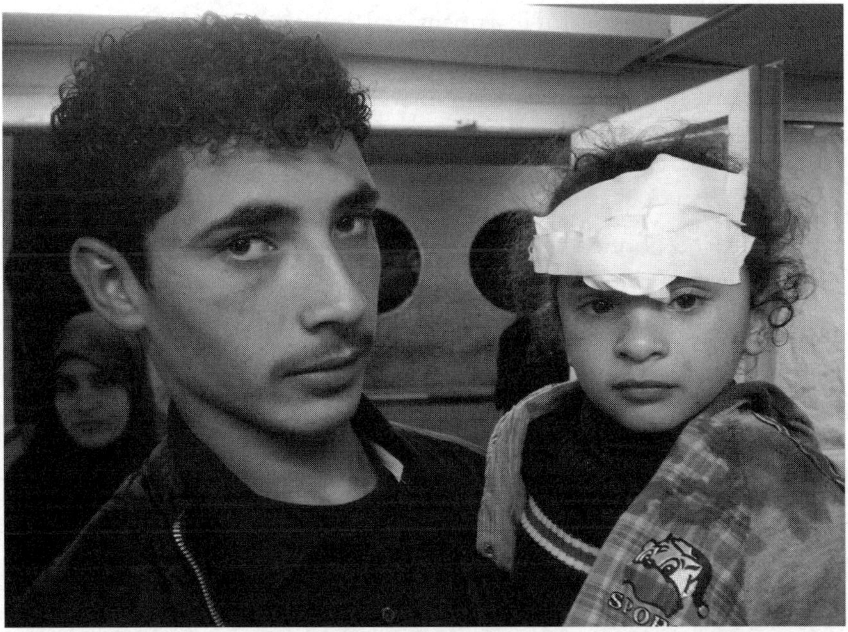

Big brother brings his injured little sister to the hospital. The drones and bomb blasts can be heard all the time.

office. Dr Sobhi understood how important it was for the foreign press to write about what was happening in the Gaza Strip. I could make telephone calls from his office.

'I'll need to go to see if I can find some more bed-spaces,' said Dr Sobhi. 'The hospital is full, and patients are still coming in. We're going to try to evacuate some patients to Egypt today.'

Since Israel had taken control of the road between Gaza City and Rafah two days earlier, convoys of patients had to be arranged by the International Red Cross, who had to ask for permission from Israel. It had become a complicated procedure, with al-Shifa Hospital submitting lists of names and diagnoses to the International Committee of the Red Cross. There also had to be contact with the hospital in El Arish in Egypt. All patients who were evacuated from Gaza were taken to El Arish. From there, many were sent on to other European or Arab countries, or to other hospitals in Egypt. We also sent patients to other hospitals in Gaza City but, because of the difficulties with resources, these were mainly patients with minor injuries.

I leant back in Dr Sobhi's soft leather chair. He had a much bigger office than any head of department at Rikshospitalet in Oslo, and the chair was better than I was used to.

I sent text messages to all the Norwegian and foreign media agencies who had been trying to get in touch with me over the past two days, and gave them Dr Sobhi's telephone number. One after another, they rang back.

John Eivind phoned to tell me that he and anaesthetic nurse Dagfinn Bjørklid were at the border at Rafah.

'I reckon that Dagfinn will be over the border in the course of the next hour.'

'But it can be difficult to get safely to al-Shifa Hospital,' I warned.

We both knew that Israel had set up a road-block near Netzarim on the road between Rafah and Gaza City.[62]

'I've arranged with Dagfinn that if there aren't any ambulances on the other side of the border due to go to al-Shifa, he'll go to the European Hospital in Khan Younis. In that case the plan is to wait till the road is clear.'

I reckoned that Dagfinn would cope, whatever happened. He has had long experience of the Middle East.

'How are plans going for getting Mads and me out?'

The question was unavoidable. Even though Mads and I would have liked to stay, we had decided that we shouldn't remain in the centre of the war for more than one or two weeks. We too were gradually being worn down by the war, all the injuries, the noise, the lack of sleep. After a while we would no longer be any great support to our Palestinian colleagues.

'Johannes Brattebø the orthopaedic surgeon and the Belgian surgeon Najib Ramzi are coming to Cairo tomorrow with Merete Taksdal. Merete will take over from me as co-ordinator here in El Arish after a few days' overlap. We'll try to get the surgeons in sometime on Thursday,' John Eivind told me.

Merete Taksdal is an anaesthetic nurse with long experience of working in war zones. Mads and I had both known her for a long time. We felt reassured by the knowledge that it was she who would be taking over as NORWAC's representative in Egypt while we were in Gaza.

John Eivind had set up the evacuation chain out of Gaza. So long as we had health personnel in Gaza and there was a war going on, we would need to have an office in El Arish able to communicate both with the team in Gaza and with the embassy in Cairo. It was particularly important that the embassy supported us with personnel in El Arish.

By half past eleven I had completed these necessary discussions, and I went to the intensive care ward. I wanted to review carefully a patient from the day before, a young man with a large chest injury. While I was examining him to assess him for an operation, Dr Sobhi came in with four Europeans in Red Cross jackets.

'Meet the surgical team from the International Committee of the Red Cross,' said Dr Sobhi.

I looked up from the patient and saw two men and two women. The team consisted of a Dutch surgeon, an Italian anaesthetist, a Finnish theatre nurse and a Danish intensive care nurse.

'Delighted to see you. We heard that you were on your way.'

'We've been sitting in Jerusalem for a week, waiting for permission to come in through Erez,' said the Dutch surgeon. 'Today we got in at last.'

I was glad to see them. The need was overwhelming. The more Europeans were on site, the sooner the madness would have to stop, I thought. With a lot of international witnesses, the killing of civilians would become a problem for Israel.

A few minutes later the door opened again, this time to admit a large retinue. A photographer dashed forwards to take pictures. I could see that the Deputy Health Minister, Dr Hassan Khalaf, was leading the parade, closely followed by the Director of Hospitals in the ministry, Dr Mohammed Kashif. I realised that this was an important visit. A man came forward and introduced himself as John Ging, leader in Gaza of the UN's aid organisation for the Palestinian refugees (UNRWA).

'What's your assessment of the situation?' he asked politely.

'It's quite hopeless. Israel is attacking civilians, and the hospital is completely full. However, in my opinion the biggest problem is the blockade. People are going hungry in Gaza now, and we lack essential medical supplies. The international community must react. I can't understand how they can go on like this.'

'Yes, I know,' replied Ging, obviously angry and desperate. 'The borders have to be opened and the bombing has to stop.'

In an interview later that day, Ging stated: 'There's nowhere safe in Gaza. Everyone here is terrorised and traumatised.' He added that a million Palestinians were without electricity, and 700,000 are without water.[63]

But the strongest thing was his request to world leaders: 'You are not to sleep, eat or drink until you stop the killing of innocent people in the Gaza Strip.'[64]

I went back to Dr Sobhi's office to take some more phone calls. He was having an anxious discussion with Dr Nasser.

'We'll have to expand our bed capacity,' maintained Dr Sobhi. 'The internal medicine department will have to take in surgical patients.'

'That makes sense, but it will create a logistical problem,' replied Dr Nasser.

The medical department was in a building about fifty metres from the surgical block, and the patients would need to be transported there. The surgeons, who were already overworked, would have to walk some distance to tend their patients. But they had no choice. The bed capacity in the surgical block was stretched to its limit. An even bigger problem was that all the ventilators in the hospital were in use. If we got a lot of patients who could not breathe for themselves after operation, patients would die.

'We're trying to send patients who need ventilation to Egypt, but there's a limit to how many we can send, and the journey is dangerous. Many of the patients are too ill to be transported,' said Dr Nasser.

We heard the sound of a lot of ambulances and cars. The whole of the roundabout in front of the emergency department was full. I went to the department and asked what was up. Israeli tanks had shot at a UN school in the refugee camp at Jabaliya.

The emergency department was full of children on trolleys, with mothers and other family members calling to get medical help for their own. At the same time, the ambulance crews kept coming in with more injured children. They were lifted carefully off the trolleys and laid on the floor. I saw that Mads was already busy with the patients in the resuscitation room.

'Come here, doctor, what should we do?' I heard a woman say.

She pointed to a trolley with a six-year-old boy who had a wound a little behind his ear. He had obviously been X-rayed already, for there was an X-ray film on the trolley. I held the picture up to the light. It showed a fragment of metal in his brain. He had a good pulse and was breathing himself, but he was unconscious. His mother stood watching him with a resigned look. She wasn't crying. One of the volunteers came to fetch him and wheeled him into the lift to take him up to the operating theatre. His mother walked alongside, holding his hand.

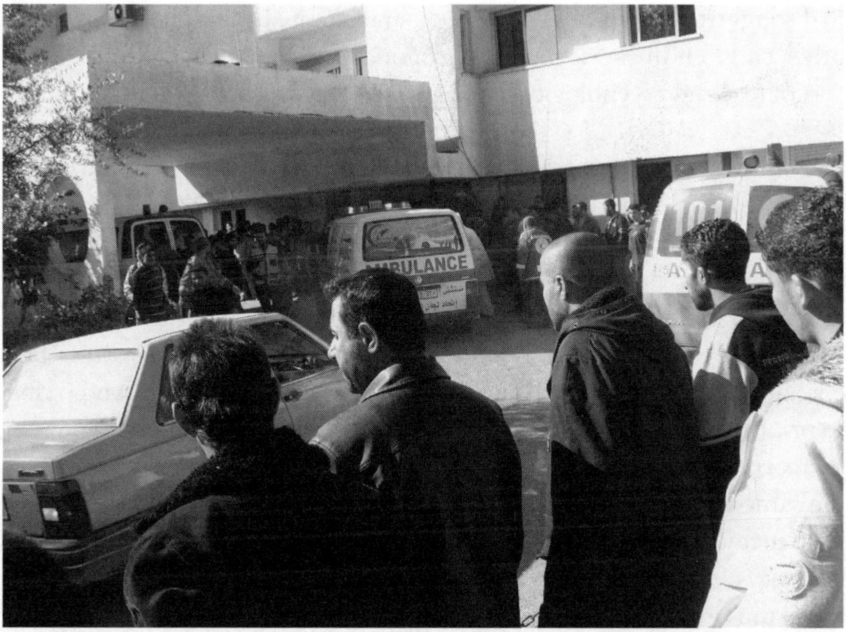

After the bombing of the UN School, injured children came pouring in to al-Shifa Hospital in ambulances and private cars.

I looked round. There were patients lying on the floor around the examination tables. Both the resuscitation rooms were full. There were lines of patients in the corridor between the department and the lift. A doctor was going along the row, examining one after another as they stood leaning against the wall.

An eight-year-old girl wearing a pink jersey and jeans was being treated for a wound on her head. Her mother stood alongside comforting her as the doctor cleaned and bandaged the wound. There was not a single chair to be found for her to sit on while she was being treated.

As two doctors and some volunteers came running through the corridor towards the lift, the girl and her mother were squashed up against the wall.

The doctor who was cleaning her wound also had to squeeze against the wall to let them past. The girl did not make a sound, but just stared straight ahead, wide-eyed. What could she be thinking?

She was probably terrified. She knew that she had survived this attack, but that she could be hit again. There were no safe havens in Gaza. She knew that she could lose her life, or her parents, at any time. The family had sought refuge in the UN school, and she had been playing with the other children in the school playground when the tank shells hit. What sort of fear and psychological damage does that cause to an eight year old?

The lift was taking a steady flow of patients up to the operating theatres. I saw that I could make myself more useful there than in the emergency department. There was no point in trying to take the lift, so I went up the stairs. The staircase was crammed with relatives standing or sitting, all the way up to the second floor. They moved aside as I came running past.

There were operations well under way in several of the theatres. The corridor was packed with trolleys, and Dr Ahmed was going round trying to prioritise the patients. They had already set up operating equipment in the corner of the corridor, where they could operate on four patients at the same time. I helped to operate on a young man with injuries to both legs, including injuries to the blood vessels on one side. He didn't need vascular surgery, however. The orthopaedic surgeon proceeded to screw metal pins into the bone at a right angle on either side of the fracture. The pins were then fastened to a metal rod parallel to the bone, about ten centimetres above the skin. This method of external fixation, which was introduced at the beginning of the 1980s, is perfect for treating fractures caused by shots and splinters, because these fractures are always infected and infection in fractures is dangerous. Infected fractures fail to heal. They must have had a big store of this equipment at al-Shifa Hospital, for they were using up to ten such fixation sets every day.

Chaos reigned in front of the lift on the first floor. Mads came up with two patients. Both were youngsters with serious injuries, and both were unstable.

'Can you look after this patient?' asked Mads. 'I'll need to go to theatre with this one.'

He hurried on with one of the trolleys.

I examined the young boy who lay in front of me. He had been hit on the right lower limb by two pieces of shrapnel and had a deep wound high on the thigh. A fragment had gone right through his right leg. An X-ray showed that large parts of the fibula had gone, but the leg was not bleeding. I felt for the pulses in his feet. They could be felt without difficulty, so we could be confident that there was no damage to the major blood vessels in the leg.

There was a small wound on the right side of his abdomen, just under

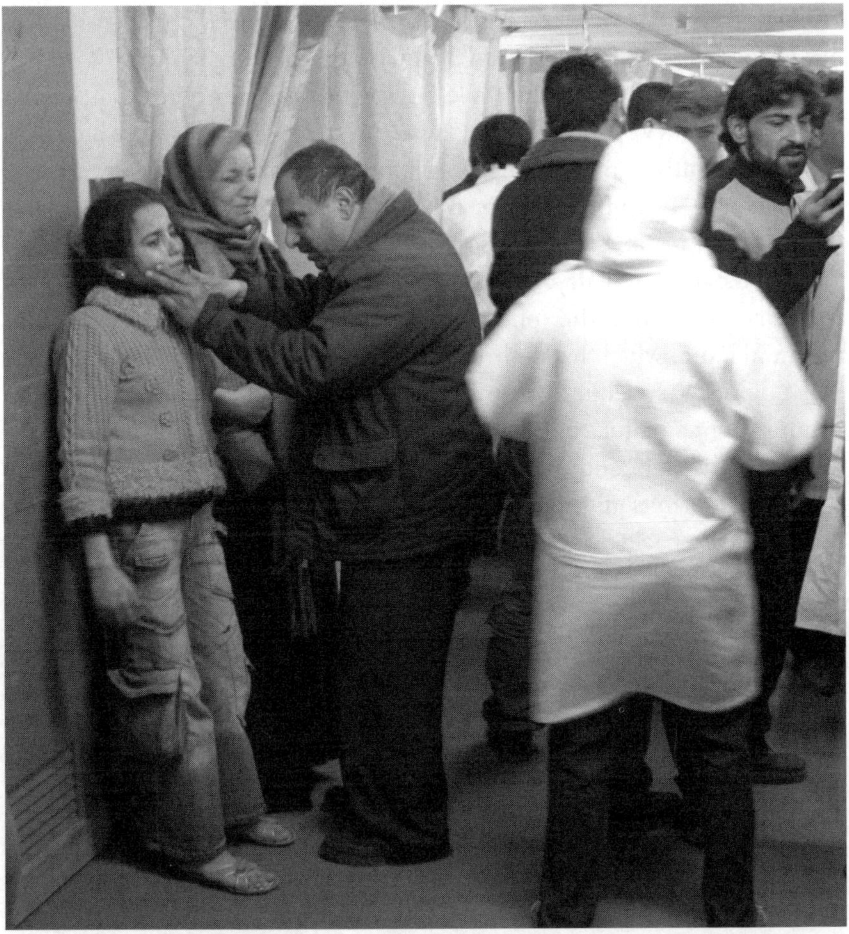

The emergency department was overflowing. This injured girl had to be examined standing against the wall.

the rib margin. I poked my finger into the wound, and it went right through into the abdominal cavity. The wound was just over the position of the liver. I was sure that there was injury to the liver. It was urgent to operate on this boy. One of the junior doctors joined me.

'This boy must be operated on immediately. I'm sure he's got intra-abdominal bleeding.'

'OK,' he said. 'Can we do it together?'

We wheeled him into one of the operating theatres. It was the theatre they occasionally used for heart surgery. Two orthopaedic surgeons came in and began to examine the leg.

'That'll have to wait,' I interrupted. 'He's not bleeding from his leg, but inside his abdomen. We can deal with the fracture later.'

We washed his abdomen while he was being anaesthetised. I opened the abdomen. We immediately saw a big tear in the liver, which was bleeding slightly. I put a compress round it and applied pressure to stop the bleeding. The junior doctor put two big stitches round the tear, and we laid haemostatic compresses on the surface of the wound. They remained completely dry.

We could see that the splinter had gone on through the liver and into the duodenum, which had a three centimetre tear on the anterior surface. Dark blood was welling out through the tear in the bowel. It must be coming from a major vein.

I freed the duodenum and was able to see a tear in the inferior vena cava, which brings all the blood from the lower part of the body back to the heart. We packed a lot of compresses in against the vein and managed to stop the bleeding for the time being.

'OK, now we can repair the hole in the bowel. Then finally we'll sew up the tear in the vena cava. So long as we keep the compresses on the vein, it won't bleed,' I said.

The junior doctor sewed up the tear in the bowel. When he had finished, Dr Abdul Gafar Zaneen the thoracic surgeon, and one of the younger consultants in general surgery, Dr Mohammed al-Ronn, came in to see what we were up to. Dr Mohammed scrubbed up ready to assist.

'You can sew up the vena cava,' I said.

He had not done that before, and I thought that this was a good chance for him to learn the technique. I freed the colon from the abdominal wall so that he could see the whole of the inferior vena cava. Then I took away the compresses and pressed the three centimetre thick vein against the backbone with one hand on either side of the tear to prevent it from bleeding.

'Now you can sew.'

It only took the young surgeon a couple of minutes to close the tear. Now that we had controlled the bleeding inside the abdomen, we let the orthopaedic surgeons set to work on the leg fracture while the two other surgeons closed the abdomen.

I was due to speak to the Danish state broadcaster DR's TV news at half past six, so I hurried downstairs. On the way, I asked Dr Sobhi what had really happened at the school. He told me that Israeli fighter planes had

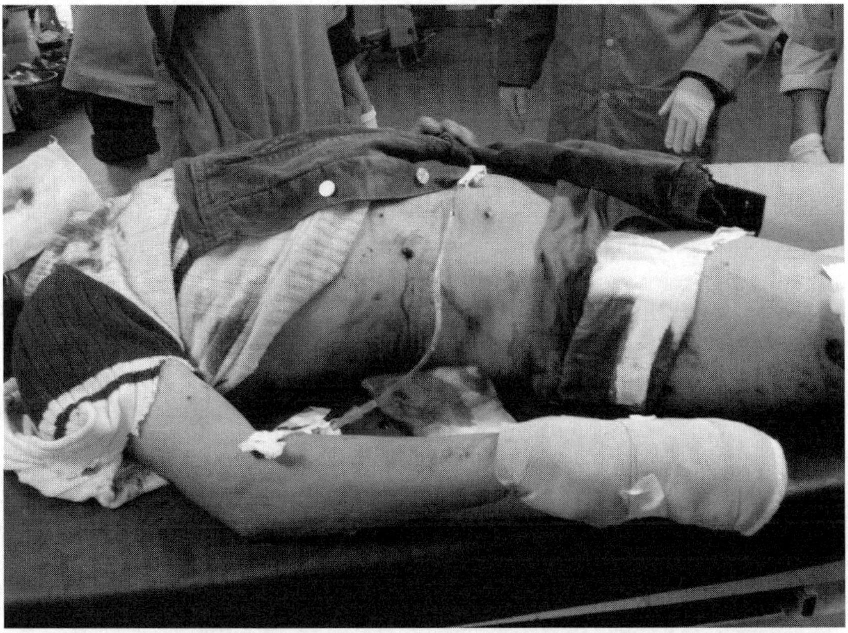

This young Palestinian was hit by numerous splinters and had wounds in his arms, legs and head. The life-threatening injury was in his bowel. The operation took hours.

dropped leaflets over Jabaliya Refugee Camp the day before, stating that they were going to bomb the houses there. A lot of people had therefore taken refuge in al-Fakhoura School, which was clearly marked with the UN emblem. At twelve noon, Israeli tanks had shot at the school and hit a little in front of it where the children were playing.

I went out of the hospital and gave the interview for Danish TV. Then I suddenly thought about Dagfinn Bjørklid. Good God, I had forgotten about Dagfinn! He had been crossing the border that morning, and I did not know how he had got on. When I got back rather breathless to the administration building, I found the hospital manager, Dr Mohammed Kashif.

'Dagfinn got here a good while ago,' Dr Mohammed said reassuringly. 'Dr Mads has been talking to him. Nobody could get hold of you.'

The whole day had gone, and I had exchanged only a couple of words with Mads in the operating theatre. I was incredibly relieved to know that Dagfinn was here.

In front of the hospital stood the satellite van from the Palestinian news agency, Ramattan. Ramattan ran the only satellite van in Gaza and passed news on to news channels throughout the world.[65] They waved me over.

'You're to be interviewed on TV2 News,' they said.

After the interview a young journalist from Al Jazeera came over to me. She had interviewed me the day before.

She wanted to go round the hospital with me. She was accompanied by a young man with a camera and another with a microphone. They set up the camera, and she interviewed me as we walked round – first into the emergency department, where patients were still coming in, though no more from the school. I examined a couple of patients while they filmed. Then we went in, through the resuscitation rooms and the intensive care department, before taking the lift up to the operating theatre along with a patient. I told them about our very competent Palestinian colleagues, and showed them how they were still having to operate on patients outside the operating theatres.

'But the hospital is worn out, and we need more supplies,' I said.

I realised that I was rather tired myself. I glanced down at my stomach and realised that both my shirt and my trousers were heavily stained with blood. I had just given the interviews with Al Jazeera and on Norwegian

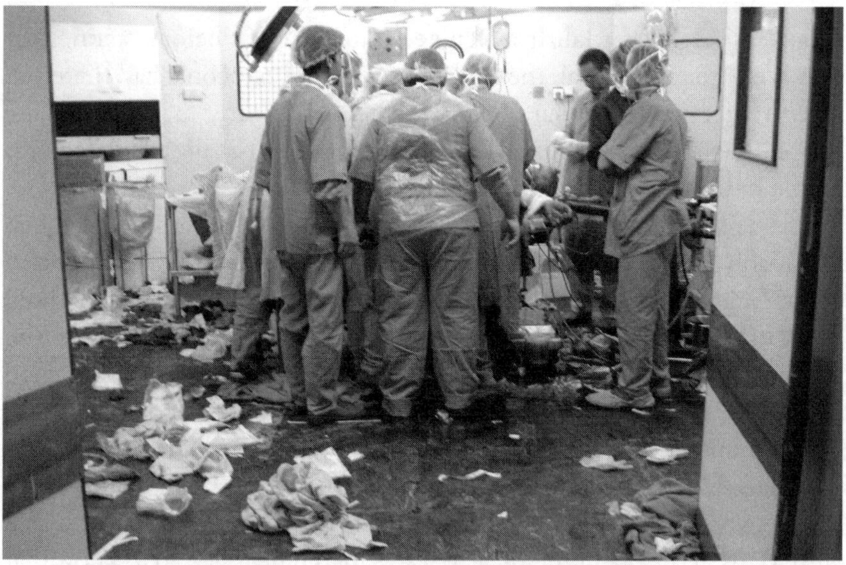

Extensive wound surgery generates a lot of soiled waste. Without effective tidying and cleaning services, the hospital would come to a stop.

and Danish television in this state. In Norway we change out of our green theatre clothes every time we come out of the operating theatre. Here I had to wear the same clothes for days on end, and couldn't even change when I went in and out of theatre.

I went back to our room. Mads and Dagfinn were there. I was glad to see Dagfinn, and we welcomed each other with a hug. Mads had already sent an e-mail to John Eivind to let him know that Dagfinn had arrived safely.

'You'd better take something to eat,' said Mads.

They had been eating rice and chicken and had kept a share for me. I had eaten neither breakfast nor lunch. In all the confusion, I had forgotten that I was hungry.

At ten o'clock I had to go out to the satellite van in front of the emergency department to be interviewed for the nine o'clock news on TV2. Then I went back to our room. I had just realised that another bed had been put into our room so that there was a place for Dagfinn, when the phone rang. It was a journalist from *Der Spiegel* asking for a report on the situation.

'The situation is really terrible. We have been operating on patients all day. Israel has bombed a UN school in Jabaliya Refugee Camp, in the middle of the day while all the children were out playing. You must tell the world that this has to stop. They are killing little children!'

I was becoming overwhelmed by despair.

'Yes, that's exactly what I wanted to ask you about,' she said. 'The UN Secretary-General, Ban Ki-Moon, has condemned the attack on the school, and I have just been interviewing a spokesman from the Israeli armed forces.'

'We took in a lot of children who had been injured in the attack this morning,' I said. 'I don't understand how they could bomb a school full of children.'

'The Israeli spokesman said that rockets had been fired from a location a little in front of the school three days ago,' said the journalist. 'Anywhere that rockets have been fired from loses its immunity, according to the Israeli officer.'

'That may be so, but the people who fired the rockets will almost certainly have moved away three days ago,' I said. 'And there was certainly no need to bomb the school when it was full of children.'

'Yes, but the spokesman from the Israeli Defence Forces said that they were mainly Hamas children,' said the journalist. 'Can you comment on that?'

'What? "Hamas children"? What do you mean?'

I felt violently sad. What sort of a view of human life was this? I had a vision of all the children we had treated in the past week. Children torn apart by target-seeking missiles. Children shot with handguns at close range. The little boy with shrapnel in his head. The girl standing squashed up against the wall while the doctor cleaned the wound on her head.

Israeli tanks had shot at the school playground while it was full of 'Hamas children' running about and playing, able for a short time to forget about the war. I realised that the people who pulled the trigger, the people who sat safely in the tank and shot, no longer saw Palestinians as human beings. All Palestinians were terrorists in their eyes, and the children were defined as 'Hamas children', children that it was all right just to eradicate.

I have forgotten what we spoke about for the rest of the interview. It was now clear to me that this war was no longer only about the Palestinians' rights as an occupied people. It was now about the value of human life.

History shows that dehumanisation is a prerequisite when people set out to do harm against others. When the Europeans colonised America, the Native Americans were portrayed as primitive animals who were standing in the way of civilisation. In the German propaganda of the 1930s, the Jews were referred to as 'vermin' that had to be eradicated. I thought of the film about the hotel owner in Rwanda who saved several Tutsis during the massacre at the beginning of the 1990s. The Hutu militia then referred to the Tutsis as 'cockroaches'. In Gaza the label was 'terrorist' or 'Hamas child'.

Dehumanisation was a prerequisite for attacking civilian targets to the extent that Israel did during the invasion of Gaza.

I thought about Europe's responsibility in this. Had not Europe accepted for a long time that 1.5 million people in Gaza were being branded as terrorists? Because the Palestinians had chosen Hamas in the election, they had all become terrorists not just in Israel's eye but also in the eyes of Europe and the USA. By stopping direct supplies to the self-governing Palestinian Authority in 2006, Europe and the USA had submitted the Palestinians in Gaza to a collective punishment. It was more important for the West to crush Hamas than to nurture and protect the lives of the Palestinian children.

Outside the emergency department, Erik is interviewed through a satellite link by the Palestinian news agency Rammatan, while an ambulance worker listens to the continuous bombing.

Where were the European protests when Israel started the blockade in January 2008? The UN reported regularly on the consequences of the blockade. The whole world knew what was happening.

Many individual people responded, but not the American and European leaders. The former President of the USA, Jimmy Carter, said in a talk at the American University in Cairo on April 17, 2008 that the Palestinians in Gaza were being starved to death, and that they were getting fewer calories per day than people in the poorest parts of Africa.

'It's an atrocity what is being perpetrated as punishment on the people in Gaza. It's a crime... I think it is an abomination that this continues to go on,' proclaimed Jimmy Carter.[66]

The Israeli leaders must have understood that they had the support of the West when they started the overwhelming attack on civilian targets on December 27, 2008. The people in Gaza had already been labelled collectively as terrorists. The distinction between terrorists and civilians had been erased. The systematic bombing of civilian targets and police stations, the murder of political leaders, the destruction of all business

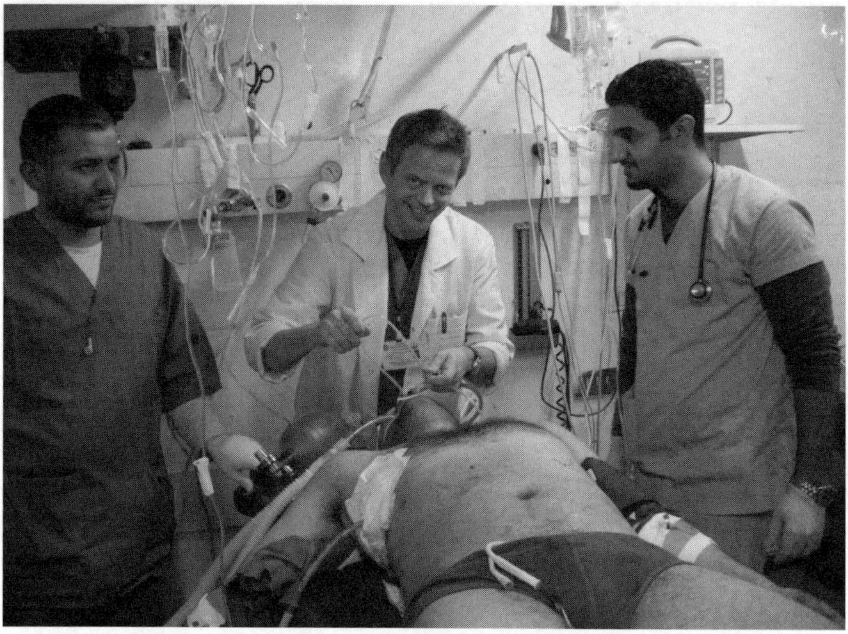

Anaesthetic nurse Dagfinn Bjørklid broke the blockade and arrived at al-Shifa Hospital on January 5. There was work for him in the emergency department straight away.

activity – from fishing boats to factory buildings – all demonstrated that everybody in Gaza was to be hit. The killing of children showed that Israeli leaders and soldiers on the ground no longer regarded the Palestinians as human.

The story of the 'Hamas children' illustrates how useless war is as a means of combating terrorism and violence. If the punishment of terrorists is to have any effect, it has to be the outcome of investigation, trial and proven guilt. Bombing a school playground full of children is not a fight against terrorism.

The attack on Gaza was a humanitarian disaster for the Palestinians, but as I came to understand that Tuesday, it was a moral disaster for Israel.

I went to bed alone in our room. Mads and Dagfinn were both working on overnight in the hospital. My body felt numb. I had experienced unrelenting evil at close quarters.

9

9

Darkness at Noon

MADS GILBERT

It was difficult to get to bed on Tuesday January 6. I was exhausted, sad and full of deep anxiety. The attacks were becoming more violent and the casualty numbers increasing day by day. Where would this end? The memories from west Beirut in the summer of 1982 kept coming back: the claustrophobic feeling of imprisonment, the uncontrollable nature of the Israeli attacks and all the mutilated bodies.

It was worse now. This time, the chances of escaping were next to nil for the Palestinians. No bomb shelters, a much smaller area and a much more vulnerable civilian population. Furthermore, northern Gaza is one of the most densely populated areas in the world, with 6,859 inhabitants per square kilometre: more densely populated than both Hong Kong (6,326/km^2) and Singapore (6,814/km^2).[67] Is it possible to imagine that Singapore, for example, could be surrounded, besieged and starved for two years, then could be bombed mercilessly from land, air and the sea for over three weeks without the world reacting?

I sought shelter in my small hole of an office, where my computer sat on a narrow bench. Most contact was by e-mail; my mobile had completely died now. It happened after I had sent the text about the bombing of the vegetable market; a text which had then clearly spread like wildfire. Israeli intelligence is known as possibly the most technologically advanced in the world. It evidently cost Mossad and Shin Beth – with its motto 'Defender that shall not be seen' – little to monitor all 'traffic' in and out of Gaza on all levels.

The Israeli intelligence organisations are feared. They are seen as particularly ruthless and brutal in their efforts to guarantee not only the security of the Israeli state, but also the Zionistic project, especially Jewish immigration (*Aliyah*) to *Eretz Israel* – 'the Land of Israel'.

We were certainly not all that important, but clearly important enough for them to block my mobile, cut the telephone line between Erik and the

CNN studio in Atlanta when he was going to appear on *Larry King Live*, and for them to start a global smear campaign against us. They also periodically cut the Internet connection to the 'Gaza desk'. We were getting many powerful messages. Colleagues from all over Norway sent emotional declarations of support and warm personal comments. The president of the Norwegian Medical Association gave her strong support. Journalists from home and abroad wanted to set up interviews. Many people I did not know personally wrote of their own desperation and their desire to help. Every time I read these messages, a warm spring of repressed emotions opened up, and the tears flowed. It was good. I felt the same warmth when I read the many appeals to take part in demonstrations, concerts and meetings. It seemed there was a colossal amount of activity at home. I wrote a report for the 'Northern Front' as I had named the small group of Norwegian journalists:

> Vicious attacks from about 12:00. In total, 160 killed in the last 24 hrs (to 18:00), 400 injured according to the Health Ministry in Gaza; 150 injured and 25 dead came to al-Shifa. A school massacre at al-Fakhoura: 43 killed, 100 injured. Another day from hell at al-Shifa too – but worse for the victims. A great number of children, the worst day for women and children up to now. Al-Shifa is at absolute bursting point. Chaotic conditions, 2 operations in each room, in the corridor, everywhere. Amazing rescues: the 10-year-old with liver injuries, quickly and successfully operated on; a boy's leg, which suffered an arterial tear, may yet be saved. But the extent of injuries is horrible, unthinkable. It must be DIME weapons; it cannot be anything else. Bright point: Dagfinn Bjørklid from NORWAC broke the blockade today with the robust support of the Norwegian Ministry of Foreign Affairs, which has set up a forward base in El Arish. He came in this evening with a convoy of ambulances. A significant and incredibly impressive addition to the team. He is an anaesthetic nurse and has been working for NORWAC for a long time, especially in Lebanon. He knows Palestine and Gaza very well. An international Red Cross team came in with two doctors and two nurses, who are also very welcome. This might be a sign that Israel realises that they can no longer keep the world shut out. We will see.
>
> We learn that the Israeli military forces are slowly withdrawing from the Eastern Front and that a ceasefire is in sight in 1-2 days. Everyone is afraid that Israel will do what they usually do: increase the

intensity of the attacks over the last days. I dare not think what that would be like.

Greetings from Erik & Mads, al-Shifa Hospital, Gaza City, Occupied Palestine.

My second e-mail went to Dr Pernille Nylehn, the municipal doctor in Jæren, who had penned such an excellent reply to a message I posted on the Norwegian general practitioners' Internet forum 'Eyr' the day before:

> Thank you, Pernille. It has quietened now. Night is gradually falling on us tonight, almost like a whisper – suddenly without the constant shelling. If only all good forces would gather like a shield over all the trembling, grieving, deathly frightened Palestinians in Gaza and all those torn to pieces, coming round from the simple anaesthetics and crude surgery. May they have just one night without the roaring machines of hell. How can we get the stories from here to be more easily available? I don't know. Maybe the most important thing is for us to say clearly and distinctly how we should *not* treat each other – irrespectively of religion, politics, race and sex, rich or poor. We must lift this above the level of political rhetoric. The people in power are further and further removed from the warm skin of a child waking without legs, or from the uncertain look of a 70-year-old Palestinian farmer with his face full of splinters, whose working hand we have to amputate.
>
> It cannot go on like this. They have to be told what we think. You can speak up, everybody can speak up. And many people are speaking up all over the world now. I believe that this is the most important thing. Everybody must find their way, their voice and their addressee. Everybody must send a message somewhere, so we are not enveloped in darkness.
>
> *'Sov nu barn och sov soldater, vi är vänner och kamrater'* ['Sleep now children, and sleep soldiers, we are friends and comrades'], as Monica Zetterlund sang so beautifully. It is not easy to think like that this evening, but we must move forward. Greetings, Mads.

I have always thought that the events in west Beirut in the summer of 1982 were the worst that I would ever experience. That time I was a young anaesthetist and a member of the Palestine Committee's surgical crisis team, who worked at the provisional underground field hospital at La Houte School, just by the main street in west Beirut, Hamra.

The blood gas machines in the intensive care unit had to be calibrated manually. The Israeli blockade had led to a shortage of vital equipment, reagents and medicine.

Over eleven unbearably warm summer weeks from June 6 to August 21, the then defence minister Ariel Sharon led the Israeli invasion forces up to West Beirut, encircled the city and sealed all main roads in. From the coast, Israeli naval vessels blocked access. Once the city was surrounded, the invasion forces took control of electricity supplies and the waterworks, and effectively stopped all supply lines for energy, food, medicine and aid in the hope that the city's inhabitants would be starved and bombed to submission, to surrender or to insurrection against the PLO leadership and the Lebanese authorities.[68]

That time too, Israel attacked with intense military force. They bombed the besieged city day after day causing enormous destruction and great suffering among civilians. Also in 1982 anything was apparently a legitimate bombing target for the Israeli war machine; there was no regard for the civilian population's right to protection. The conditions were terrible for the Lebanese, but not least for the 175,000 Palestinian refugees in west Beirut who needed acute emergency aid from the UN following the Israeli attacks.[69]

Now, in Gaza, in January 2009, it was as if I were reliving that nightmare.

'This is worse than Beirut in 1982,' I said to a small group of older Palestinian colleagues as we drank one of the day's many cups of coffee as strong as gunpowder.

'Do you think so? Really? Why?'

'Because there are fewer places to find shelter and protection here in Gaza. There is less space and the population is distributed more densely. The civilian population is much younger. We're seeing more injured children here than in Beirut. The Israeli weapons have also evolved a lot over the past twenty-five years. Now they know exactly what they are bombing and where. I cannot see any excuses for them to be hitting so many civilians.'

'You are right, Dr Mads. But how will the world find out about this? In Beirut, at least the world press was there. They are not here now.'

Civilian losses in 1982 were also great. More than 17,000 people were killed, of whom between 10,000 and 12,000 were Lebanese and Palestinian civilians. 368 Israeli soldiers were killed, while it is supposed that 1,400 PLO soldiers fell. In addition, there were the 2,000 to 3,000 Palestinians who were slaughtered by Lebanese Phalangist forces in the refugee camps at Sabra and Shatila between September 16 and September 18, a massacre that took place while Israeli commanders looked on. They did not intervene. On the contrary: from high-rise buildings next to the camps, they could see everything that happened and they intercepted the orders from the Phalangist officers to kill the Palestinians. The Israeli officers sent up two flares a minute all night, while women were being raped and stabbed, whole families were wiped out and excavators prepared mass graves.[70]

Ariel Sharon was removed from office as defence minister after the invasion of Lebanon. This did not happen because of the siege and the reckless and illegal bombing of civilian targets, but for his role in connection with the massacres at Sabra and Shatila which, in itself, would normally be an atrocity great enough to bring down any government.

As a result of the Israeli attack and siege of west Beirut, the PLO leadership left Lebanon by sea, with Arafat at their head, and the Israeli forces withdrew from Beirut but continued to occupy Lebanon to the south and west of the city. On August 21, 350 soldiers from France moved into the city, followed by 800 US marines. Together, they were to oversee the evacuation of the PLO, as a part of the ceasefire agreement entered into between Syria, Israel and the PLO. The siege and bombing

Palestinian civilians with terrible injuries, many of them dying, came to al-Shifa in waves.

of Beirut met with massive international condemnation, including from the USA, which threatened to impose sanctions. The basis for the threat of sanctions was that weapons supplied by the USA had been used by Israel for offensive military purposes, while they were only intended for 'defensive' purposes.

Nothing ever came of the sanctions. The PLO was not significantly weakened and, apart from a temporary reduction in the rocket attacks on Israel from southern Lebanon, the violent military attack was unsuccessful from the Israeli point of view. Sharon stayed on in the government as a minister without portfolio and later became prime minister in 2001. In November 2005, Sharon left the Likud party and founded the Kadima party. He suffered a stroke in January 2006 and retired as prime minister on April 14 that year. In the summer of 2009, Sharon was still in a deep coma at Sheba Medical Center. As recently as in 2008, an opinion poll showed that more than two thirds of Israelis would still have voted for him if he were to wake up.[71]

I kept thinking of my experiences from 1982 while we were working at al-Shifa. Little had changed in twenty-seven years. Was it really possible that the same brutal tactics were being repeated? This merciless siege with the starvation of an entire people, the massive bombing of imprisoned civilians with no chance of fleeing? Did nobody have a good enough memory to say 'We have been through this before. Israel must be stopped now before the same atrocities are repeated'?

As January passed one day at a time, the reality of Gaza became more and more clear: the overwhelming majority of the wounded and killed were civilians. A large number of them were children and young people. The numbers presented by the Health Ministry every day at four o'clock showed unambiguous and alarming tendencies that were in absolute concordance with the impressions we had at al-Shifa. The great majority of the wounded and killed were quite ordinary Palestinians of all ages. Day by day the number of dead children went up, and it went up noticeably more than the number of dead women.

Over our entire stay, we saw a handful of wounded and I saw two fatalities that looked like militia or resistance members, but the rest were civilians.

I had to concentrate hard in order not to lose control when whole families came in to the hospital pale and shocked with their wounded grandparents and children. 'Focus,' I often told myself when the feelings welled up inside me and my throat tightened with grief.

The technique is simple. Focus on saving lives, on the systematic clinical examination of every single patient and then sum up: who needs resuscitation? Who will get by with basic help? Who should be prioritised? Emergency workers are trained to concentrate on the task at hand. Such *perceptual focusing* helps us to put aside disturbing thoughts and distracting feelings that could otherwise overwhelm us, weaken our concentration and reduce the quality of our input.

Of course, these feelings do need to be processed, but that must happen after the job has been done, or in the work-breaks. Any prolonged rejection of your own normal reactions to such extreme situations often leads to chronic and destructive stress reactions and a rigid way of responding that can ultimately make you ill. The most effective way to process sensory impressions and great emotional strain is quite simply to talk openly in the caring companionship of others who have experienced such actions. This, as a rule, is what it takes.

I had a constant and intense feeling of camaraderie with those around me; first and foremost with Erik, but also with our Palestinian colleagues.

Our 'private' lodgings were spartan, but offered some essential calm.

There was a lot of close physical contact. The Palestinians are not afraid of touching each other. All meetings begin with handshakes, and there is often one form or another of physical contact while talking. I often noticed that my Palestinian colleagues would put their arms round our shoulders, they might hold our hands for a long time, and they often sat close to each other. Such contact had a warmth that helped to soften any stress reactions.

Erik and I were also close when we went back to our little two-bed room. We talked through our day informally. We simply shared experiences: our shared desperation over the enormous number of wounded, and our pain over the terrible injuries we saw and treated together with our Palestinian colleagues. We listened to each other, and the balance between our stories gave us each room, both to talk and to let out our frustration, fury and despair.

We cried.

And we laughed. We laughed at ourselves, as we both have a well-developed fondness for self-deprecation, and at episodes the day had brought. Sometimes we almost collapsed in gasps of hysteria about how comical we could appear, not least in our light blue 'Hamas pyjamas'. We needed a daily dose of hysteric laughter. To survive.

That humour is a part of mastering difficult and demanding situations is common knowledge among most groups of emergency workers. Pitch-black humour is a part of the culture in most settings such as this. It can seem offensive, but it is a harmless technique to relieve the most painful of tensions.

I saw the young patient as she was being wheeled on a stretcher through the hospital vestibule towards the lift. She was on her way to theatre. The child lay on her back on the stretcher with her upper body exposed, half-covered by a small quilt. Her uncertain eyes were looking the whole time for familiar faces, but there were none to be seen. She had come in the ambulance alone from her family's house somewhere in the north of Gaza. No one had been able to accompany little Samar, because the Israeli bombing was so intense and there was also an impending danger of attacks on ambulances. It was not clear what had happened, but her family's house had no doubt been shelled that morning. Her mother had supposedly been injured too. Samar was four years old.

The little girl had been through the resuscitation room, where a drainage tube had been put in her right thoracic cavity for relief, a thoracic drain to remove an accumulation of air that could have been caused by the presumed shrapnel injury. A leakage of air in the thoracic cavity between the two layers of the pleural sac can quickly become life-threatening if the wound has caused perforations on the surface of the lung. In that case, with every breath an excess of pressure can build up, pressing on the lung and making it more and more difficult to breathe. After a while, the pressure can become so high in the whole chest cavity that it exceeds the pressure of the veins running through the cavity taking the blood back to the heart. If that happens, the heart stops filling with blood, and circulation stops with fatal consequences, even though the heart can continue to contract for a while yet.

This condition is called *tension pneumothorax*, and it is a deadly result of several kinds of injury to the chest cavity, not least rib fractures, wounds caused by splinters and shots, and injuries caused by a blunt blow to the thoracic cavity. The accumulation of air in the thoracic cavity can be exacerbated if haemorrhaging also takes place there after the injury. A drain can reduce the tension and suck out the build-up of blood so that the lungs can expand freely again.

This treatment is often sufficient to stop the haemorrhage. If a wounded patient has difficulty breathing and signs of injury to the chest cage or

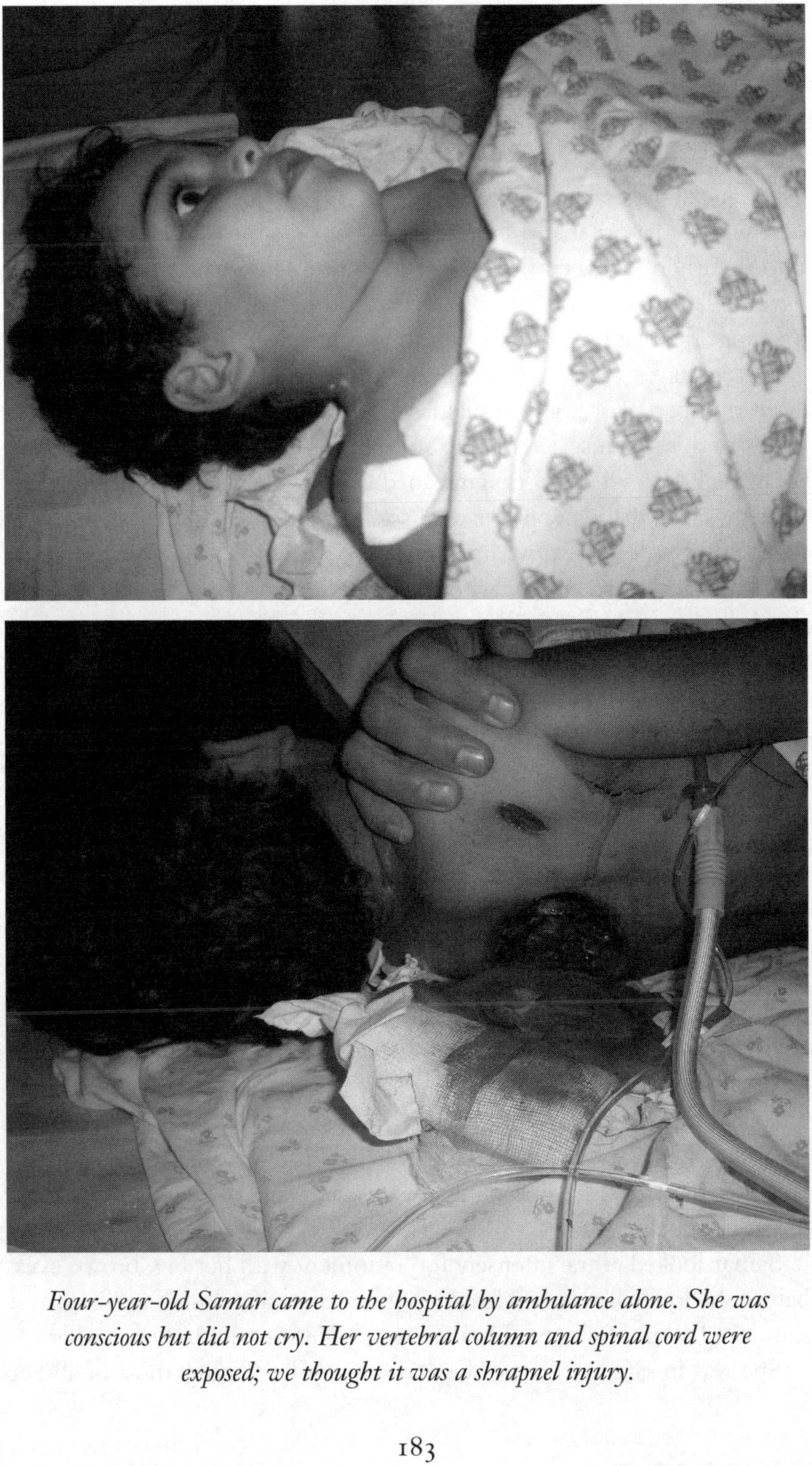

Four-year-old Samar came to the hospital by ambulance alone. She was conscious but did not cry. Her vertebral column and spinal cord were exposed; we thought it was a shrapnel injury.

wounds from splinters, shots or stabs, we quickly suspect this condition and listen especially thoroughly to the patient's breathing with a stethoscope. If the breathing sounds asymmetrical between the two lungs, this suspicion grows.

In such cases, the rapid insertion of a thoracic drain is a lifesaver. In experienced hands, the procedure can be carried out in a few minutes and does not need more than a small incision between the ribs with an opening into the cavity between the inner and outer pleura where air and blood have built up. A plastic tube as thick as a little finger is fed through the opening. It has a hole in its side and is connected to an underwater seal and a vacuum system so that the lung can be cleared of air and fluid. A large number of the war casualties that came to al-Shifa had thoracic drains of this sort inserted on one or both sides, often just out of suspicion of air leakage or haemorrhaging in the chest cavity. This 'play it safe' strategy saved many people, even if some could indeed have been spared this painful procedure if we had had fewer patients and more time.

In addition to treatment with a drainage tube, it was also established that little Samar had an injury on her back. An open wound went in right up to her vertebral column half way up her back. Skin and tissue had been torn away, and we could see parts of the spinal column. She could not move her legs either and appeared to be numb from the waist down. Of course, this suggested that her spinal cord was damaged. She urgently needed neurosurgery to alleviate the problem.

Samar was wide awake and was not crying. She just looked around with a peculiar, surprised expression, as if she were asking us 'What's happened? Where's my mummy?'

When I saw her for the first time outside the lift on her way up to theatre, I was given a short summary of her condition, and the nurse who was with her turned her carefully onto her side so I could see her wound. I shuddered. Is this possible? A four-year-old girl with cross-sectional lesions from an act of war?

'What was the cause of the injury?' I asked.

'We think it's a shrapnel wound. Their house was shelled.'

'Let's move to the operating theatre, but keep her covered so she doesn't get cold.'

Samar looked at me intensely for a moment with her big, brown eyes, before she looked away and fixed her gaze somewhere on the ceiling, as if she were looking for something far away. Without doubt her mother.

She was in safe hands, but she was missing her family, most of all her mother and father. I tried to take in how vulnerable she was, alone without her parents. It was terribly painful.

Samar's assistants wheeled her stretcher into the rickety lift to the operating theatre while I hurried on to the intensive care unit to check some of the patients who had come in that morning.

A demanding challenge of running an intensive care unit is the organisation of the important daily inspection of all the highly specialised machinery. Intensive care represents perhaps the most advanced routines and the most dangerous clinical work we deal with in modern medicine. The preferably temporary life-supporting treatment requires precision instruments and advanced technological knowledge in addition to the specialised medical qualifications that the personnel need. Depending on the extent and seriousness of the illness or the injury, we may need to take over the patient's own bodily functions and replace them with machines that can maintain lung function, kidney function or parts of the heart's functions while the body's own repair processes can slowly regain adequate strength and capacity.

The most frequently used equipment is the modern breathing machine, or ventilator. All the technical components in this must be calibrated and quality-controlled, and critical parts must of course be changed regularly. In Gaza, this is almost impossible as a result of the Israeli blockade, which affects the supply of spare parts and consumable components for the medical equipment in Palestinian hospitals.

Another example is all the essential analysis apparatus that intensive care requires. The most important machine is the 'blood gas machine', which is used to analyse blood samples from ICU patients' arteries. The level of acidity, haemoglobin levels and the partial pressures of oxygen and carbon dioxide in the blood samples are measured. This analysis is crucial for the control of ventilator treatment and for the supply of liquid, oxygen, salts and blood.

Al-Shifa Hospital was now missing the chemical reagents necessary to be able to carry out the automated daily calibrations. The capable medical engineers therefore had to make their daily quality controls and calibrations with elaborate manual methods. The two engineers sat in front of the blood gas machines and went through the time-consuming task. One of them showed me the empty box where the reagents normally lay, and gesticulated wildly.

'They make everything so difficult for us, these Israelis. Why can't we

Large numbers of desperate friends and relatives waiting outside the intensive care unit for news of the casualties.

run our hospitals normally? It is after all humanitarian work we do, we aren't making bombs!'

Darkness at noon. I thought of the title of Arthur Koestler's sombre book while I went on to see the two young boys with facial and head wounds. They lay just on the other side of the blood gas machines, which were almost fully calibrated. Samar was still in the operating theatre.

Both boys had been hit in the head and were on ventilators. One of them had a perforating wound from a splinter or projectile, and his brain had been destroyed. He was not going to survive. The other had a large facial wound but had been awake and was speaking when he arrived at the hospital. His facial bone structure was smashed, but this part of his skull had, at the same time, absorbed a lot of the energy of the shock wave from the explosion. His brain itself was not seriously damaged, as indicated by the fact his ability to speak was not impaired. Both his eyes had been crushed and had to be removed during his operation.

The boy with the destroyed brain did not need anaesthetic; he could no longer feel anything. The other lay in an artificial coma with intravenous anaesthetic agents to soften the pain and allow the ventilator to work without resistance from the boy's own breathing. A large bandage covered both his eyes. He could not see anyway. He was already blind.

Where could I cry out the despair and rage I felt for all this terrible fate we saw at such close quarters? Would the heavens hear? Will the world hear? They know that this is happening, after all. The numbers tick into the West every single afternoon, to the news agencies, to the intelligence services and to the diplomatic missions of the world's most powerful nations, who do not even make an attempt to control the wildness of the Israeli war machine.

Yet another young man with significant head injuries was wheeled past me into the intensive care unit.

'We don't have any more ventilators,' sighed the intensive care nurse. 'We'll have to breathe for him manually for a while. Something will be free soon.'

The time was now 11.53pm. Samar had almost finished in the operating theatre.

The Israelis did not need the seven minutes left over. This eighth day was already the worst so far. Could it get any worse?

10

10

No *Mercy*

MADS GILBERT

It was not easy to get to bed.

I was shaken. The days at al-Shifa Hospital blurred into each other like a long patchwork of faces, looks, mutilated human bodies and surreal sensory impressions. In the background there was the constant, intense whirring of drones. They were like faceless and evil insects, or perhaps predators. The sounds of the bomb blasts and the shells exploding came closer and closer. The artillery fire was also getting stronger, and occasionally we thought we heard the clattering caterpillar tracks of the Israeli tanks. I felt heavy and exhausted. When would this stop? Were they going to bomb al-Shifa? Were we going to be killed too?

My uneasiness was intensified by large amounts of coffee and considerable numbers of cigarettes. I do not normally smoke, but it has regrettably become a bad habit whenever I am in Gaza. As soon as I cross the border into Gaza, I feel a craving to smoke. In Gaza, everyone smokes – in any case the great majority of Palestinian men. Many of my friends among the ambulance guys as well as my good colleagues Khalil Abu Foul, Nafez al-Kirm and Issam Abu Ajwa, my 'Gazan brothers' of many years, smoke heavily. I have known these three young doctors, who were born and grew up in Gaza, since they were newly qualified bachelors. They are now well married and have had *Abu* added to their Arabic names. *Abu* means 'father', and men add *Abu* to their names when they first have children. The name of their first-born is often then included in the father's name, so if a man has a son called Mohammed, the father's name becomes *Abu Mohammed*. Every one of my Gazan brothers has had several delightful children with their hard-working, university-educated wives. I know them and their large families very well. All three of them are proficient doctors and, in spite of their young age, they have very comprehensive experience of working in disasters and mass casualty incidents.

'Gaza is really the perfect place to study trauma surgery and disaster medicine,' as we usually joke when we work together. And we have worked together many times over the years – in mobile field hospitals in the battle zone, at al-Quds and al-Shifa hospitals, during both intifadas. Nafez is an anaesthetist, and the other two are surgeons. Khalil has long held a leading position in the Palestinian Red Crescent, with responsibility for disaster preparedness and ambulance services. Issam has wide clinical experience as a general surgeon, and Nafez dreams of one day being able to embark on proper further anaesthesiology training at a good foreign university hospital. We meet every time I am on an assignment in Gaza. Even if the programme can be tight, they always take the time to invite me to visit them at home with their families to experience generous Palestinian hospitality, with lavish meals and long conversations with their parents, siblings and in-laws. I always bring some small presents, some sweets and some toys for the children – a welcome change from the chronic shortage of everything due to the blockade. To the children I am 'Amu Mads', or Uncle Mads, who comes from a strange, faraway country with snow and tall mountains: a country where there is peace and freedom for everyone, a free country where children can play in thoughtfully provided playgrounds, attend quality-controlled nurseries and go on exciting family holidays wherever they wish with their red Norwegian passports, which ensure free passage and unlimited access right across the world.

Not so in Gaza. The upbringing of Khalil's, Issam's and Nafez' children has been profoundly marked by the constant and deadly presence of the Israeli occupying forces. Throughout their short lives, they have experienced regular attacks from the air and by sea, and at night the deafening, terrifying boom of Israeli F-16s breaking the sound barrier just above their roofs, something they constantly do in order to cause collective sleep deprivation and exhaustion. The siege, military attacks and the chronic condition of the occupation have left a devastating impression on the children, leading to such stress that they become ill.

A close connection has been shown between the number of traumatic experiences and the extent of long-term, chronic stress problems. The children of Gaza are badly affected. Nine out of ten children in Gaza have seen, heard and been close to attacks, death and mutilation. Three out of four children in the six- to eleven-year-old age group have mild to medium chronic stress symptoms, while four out of ten have more serious symptoms.[72] Fear and anxiety are widespread in Gaza, especially among children.[73] Life satisfaction among schoolchildren in occupied Palestine

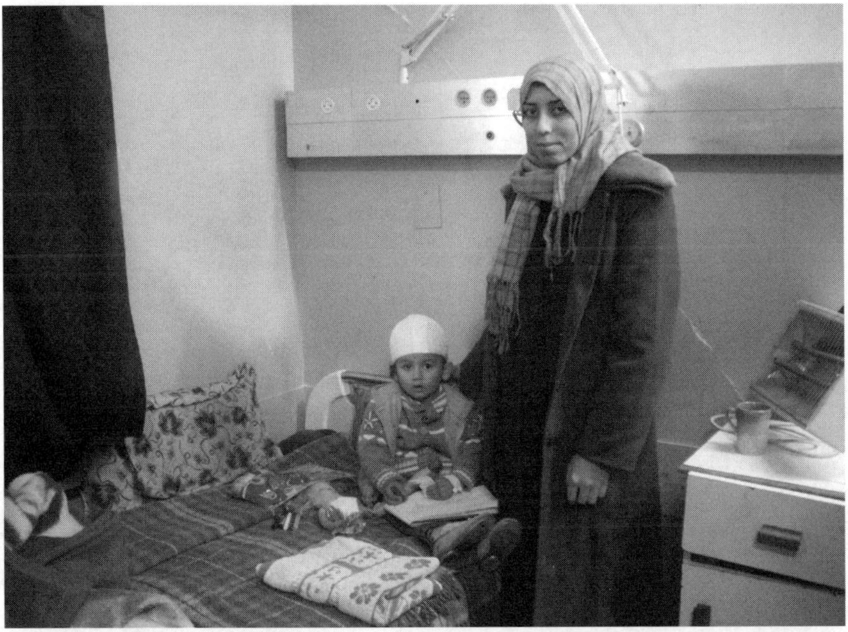

Mother and child together on the ward. For traumatized children, the presence of parents, family and friends is critical for both their physical and psychological survival.

is the lowest in all thirty-five countries investigated.[74]

It is surprising that not *all* children who grow up in the difficult circumstances in Gaza have serious health problems as a result of the long-term psychological stress that such warfare and precariousness inflict, but children also have a great power of resistance to extreme stress and painful life events. These powers of resistance presuppose that children have access to social support structures and to their own coping strategies. Such an ability to absorb and withstand extreme stress without cracking is often called *resilience*. This term comes from metallurgy and refers to the ability of a metal to absorb energy when it is subjected to gradually increasing elastic forces so that it can regain its original form when this stress is unloaded. Resilience represents the maximum energy that can be elastically stored under stress. The body's cartilaginous tissue is an example of a useful biomechanical material or tissue that shares these properties.

Our emotional world is not subject to the laws of metallurgy, but the concept is useful all the same because we have the capacity to absorb and endure even acute stress without losing our original human 'form'.

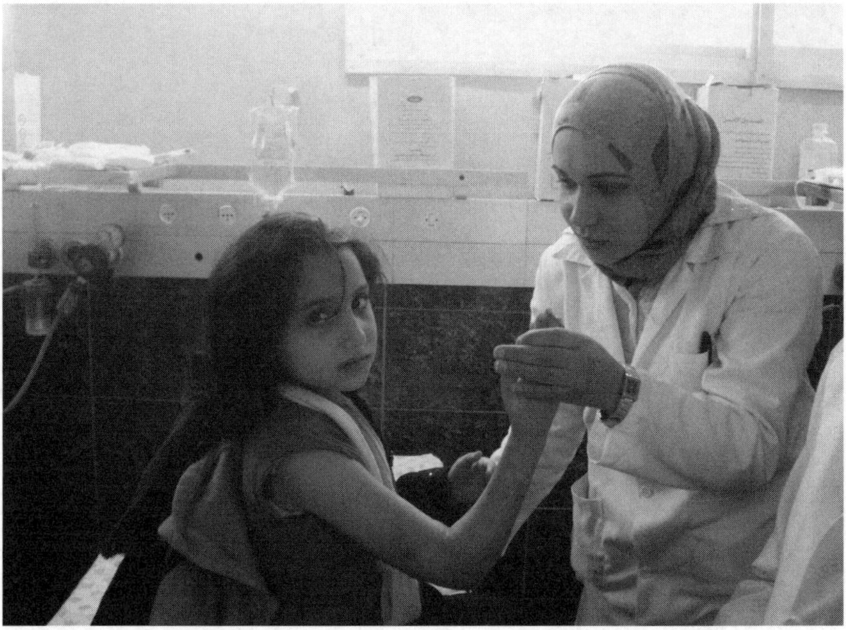

Medical student Jasmine treating a girl with minor injuries.

Anything else would have been unworkable as the human experience implies that we will all suffer painful losses, and many of us undergo extreme stress. If we were to constantly succumb to such stress, our species would be ruined. Coping with stress and being able to absorb even enormous amounts of it are preconditions for survival.

War is an immense strain. Personal control and coping, together with the caring support of social networks, are necessary in order to handle stress on a daily basis as well as massive stress loads. For children, it is important to process an event by retelling it, either verbally in the presence of a good listener or through drawings and play. Children's imagination is also useful for spontaneous processing. Good conversation, respect for each other's feelings and support from their own social networks are coping mechanisms both for children and adults. For children, access to their 'own' adults and to stable adult role-models are critical prerequisites for living through and coping with war or disasters.[75] Caring, affectionate parents and family networks with the capacity to listen to their children and to meet their needs for intimacy and to process events are absolutely essential. When the social structure is itself destroyed, and adults can no longer protect children – let alone retain the capacity to meet their needs for intimacy and sympathetic attention – then the children risk suffering from long-term stress reactions that render them ill. If they survive at all.

In 2005, between 80 and 90 per cent of adult Palestinians in the occupied territories feared daily for their families and their safety. Six out of ten feared they would lose their own homes, while nine out of ten lived in moderate or extreme fear for their future and for the future of their families.[76] Even *before* this most recent Israeli assault on Gaza, the social networks of Gaza and the capacity to cope among Palestinian families were already stretched to absolute breaking point. The new systematic Israeli destruction of civilian residential areas, schools and UN institutions in Gaza, together with the large number of dead and wounded civilians, has further weakened those social networks and drained families' capacity to cope. The extreme levels of stress that have been inflicted on Palestinian children by the acts of warfare themselves then have even greater consequences for their health. The continued blockade of Gaza by Israel and the USA after the attacks only serves to reduce that capacity even further.

The most important measures to strengthen children's resilience in the wake of such violent trauma and loss would be arrangements to strengthen families, whilst building up the attendant civilian infrastructure such as schools, nurseries and food stocks, as well as ensuring their protection. The children's trauma is instead exacerbated and their capability to cope is weakened by the persistent blockade of all of Palestinian civil society.

The Office of Foreign Assets Control (OFAC) is the official US agency tasked with ensuring that the Patriot Act is observed abroad. In practice, they prevent all national and international organisations from co-operating with Palestinian professionals to rebuild civilian structures in Gaza for as long as the education and health services are run by a Hamas government, which the USA defines as a terrorist organisation.[77]

The nine-month-old Jumana, who had to have parts of her hand amputated, lay in a bed that was far too big for her in the second-floor ward at al-Shifa. The woman dressed in black next to her bed had not finished describing the massacres in al-Zaytoun and the terrible fate of the Samouni family. The other thing that outraged her was that the people who were wounded and trapped did not receive any help from those who represent the international community in Gaza. There were several left in the house, some injured, some dying, but the Israelis let neither the International Red Cross nor ambulances with medics get through. The Israeli military forces did not want to have anyone in the

More than 3,000 homes and hundreds of factories, workshops, cow sheds, chicken farms, orange groves, mosques, whole government quarters and prisons were completely destroyed, and 20,000 buildings were partially destroyed. This picture shows the destruction in the centre of Gaza City where both government buildings and homes were hit.

area. The help teams would only manage to get through four days later to save some of the surviving children. Four children sat around their dead relatives and their mother, who had also been killed.[78] The woman told of another family who were said to have been buried alive beneath bulldozers and tanks. First the tank crushed their house, then the Israeli military bulldozer covered the dead with soil. Several other buildings still stand there with the dead inside, she told me through the nurse who translated the stream of Arabic words.

She was furious. Rightfully so, I thought, as I felt how her accusing questions struck me. A feeling of guilt rushed through me. Rationally, I knew that none of this was my fault but, at the same time, I had an intense feeling of how white and European I was. Her justified indignation was addressed at me. Fragments of a quotation from the Swedish author Jan Myrdal flickered through my conscience: 'Europe is stuck in a swamp of pity, incapable of seeing its collective responsibility.'

We were undoubtedly complicit. Sixty years of unjust and bloody occupation. Decades of oppressive contempt and increasing racist violence directed against the Palestinians in the West Bank and in the diaspora, especially in Lebanon, and the endless fatigue of the blockade of Gaza. I had seen so much of this, travelled and learnt about it over almost thirty years. Had I spoken out clearly enough?

One of Norway's most uncompromising friends of Israel, the Norwegian Labour Party politician Haakon Lie, had to reach 103 years old before he agreed that supporting Israel had been at the expense of the Palestinians' right to freedom and to a respectable life. Norwegian social democracy, led by the Labour Party, was a committed pro-Israeli actor and a prominent international supporter, along with the USA, of the Israeli occupation project. The former Labour Party secretary was a fervent friend of Israel and invariably sought out eminent Israeli leaders to show his support.

'I, like other friends of Israel, forgot for far too long that the Palestinians were people too,' he admitted, but not until the autumn of 2008.[79] 'I know what you would like to have an answer for: What about the Palestinians? I will admit that, for many years, they were never in our minds. Our undivided sympathy lay with those who were building a new and better world for the people that had always suffered most,' wrote the Labour Party veteran.[80]

Better late than never, I thought when I saw this in the newspapers just before I left for Gaza to teach medical students at al-Azhar University. But was it really better late than never? Why did Norway not react much sooner and more strongly when the Zionist project and the construction of 'a new and better world' developed into '*Eretz Israel*' – a greater 'Land of Israel' – which meant that even more Palestinians would be driven away.

'They were never in our minds.' It was almost a monstrosity to confess that the Norwegian power structure had 'forgotten' the Palestinians for decade upon decade.

The woman dressed in black looked straight into my eyes and asked me with trembling calm: 'Why? How can this happen without somebody stopping them, stopping the soldiers who are killing us and our children?'

Again I was at a loss for an answer. My despair grew. I stroked Jumana's head, smiled apologetically and left the room with an idiotic 'I'm sorry.'

I had the notion that the story of little Jumana was only the beginning. Over the following days, I would meet many other members of the Samouni family, not least the nine-year-old Amal Atteia al-Samouni and her twenty-two-year-old brother, Faraj al-Samouni.

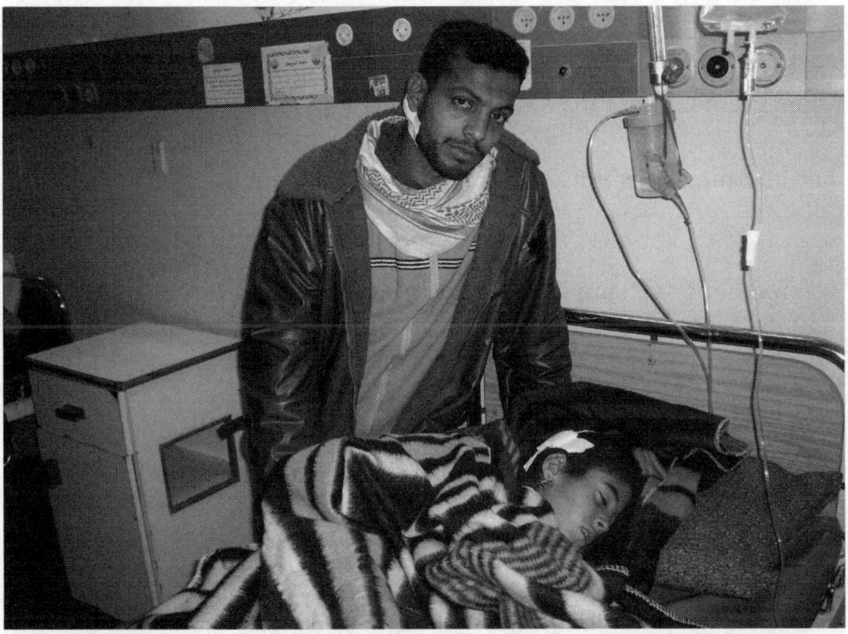

Faraj al-Samouni (22) watches over his little sister Amal Atteia al-Samuni (9), whom he dug out after she had been lying in the ruins of the family home for several days.

On January 5, the morning after Jumana came in, I sent that day's report to the fixed group of Norwegian journalists who were still observing the attacks against Gaza from Israel, on what came to be known as the 'Shameful Heights', directly north of the border with Gaza. Nearly all of the Western correspondents were gathered there and were being made fools of by the excuses the Israelis came up with. The Israeli army's press officers continually used the 'security needs' of the press by way of an excuse for their total censorship. I did my best to supply the Norwegian journalists who were stuck in Israel with first-hand raw material from our experiences at al-Shifa Hospital.

My short reports went to the three Norwegian permanent correspondents – Line Fransson from the newspaper *Dagbladet*, Jon Magnus from *VG* and Fredrik Græsvik from TV2 – with copies to Nina Einem and Nils Mehren, journalists with the state broadcaster NRK from their regional offices for Troms and Finnmark in the north of Norway. Ebba Wergeland and the NORWAC co-ordinator John Eivind Jensen were always on the CC list, so that enquiries from other media outlets looking for pictures and material could be channelled through them. The telephone and e-mail connections were both so unstable that I had to make sure I had several distribution points for the material I sent from the 'Gaza desk', as we jokingly called our little writing table. Many people would eventually get the material.

The morning after the massacre of the Samouni family, I wrote the following group e-mail:

> Another house bombed, the same place where at least eleven members of the Samouni family were massacred yesterday, with only little nine-month-old Jumana surviving. This is a massacre reminiscent of My Lai. I have a great number of sources, but I cannot get to the house where the family was forced together and shelled by Israeli tanks.
>
> Al-Shifa is incredibly worn down. They have shortages of everything: patient trolleys, BP monitors, ventilators, and especially observation monitors. We send patients who have recently been operated on, and who should be in intensive care, straight to the ward. We have to separate injured children and their parents (with heart-rending screams) because there is no space for the parents. Yesterday we did not have enough elastic bandages to control the bleeding of amputees. I even had to carry out more simple amputations to get the bleeding under

control. The heroic Palestinian health workers saved many lives yesterday, without a doubt. Together we managed to bring people in a state of severe blood loss with no measurable blood pressure or pulse back to the operating theatres and managed to carry out life-saving amputations. There are a few bright spots, many lying in the intimacy and companionship here, the warmth between people here in otherwise hellish conditions, but mostly I feel the situation is very bleak right now. I feel that I have seen too much over the past few days – especially yesterday – things I have never seen or come into contact with before. New weapons are being used with terrible consequences.

We collapsed into sleep and uneasy dreams late last night. We are so worn out now that we did not hear much of the bombing, but the attacks on Gaza City are picking up now. The counts of casualties and wounded we send are based on the daily statistics from the health authorities here at al-Shifa. The Health Ministry does its best but it is, of course, impossible to maintain a full overview. The vast majority of the men that come in here are civilians. How can I tell? The few times a fighter comes in, Hamas intelligence naturally comes to identify him. Yesterday it was one hundred per cent civilians.

We have still not seen a single Western journalist here, but a great many proficient Palestinian and Arab journalists.

I am nervous about today. The attacks get fiercer every day: more and more homes, a sharp increase in the number of children killed and wounded – and these complete massacres by ground forces that we are hearing about.

The same day, the Swedish newspaper *Expressen* and the Norwegian *Aftenposten* both published the story I had sent out about little Jumana and the apparent massacre of her family. Little happened. The Israeli forces continued their attacks with undiminished fury.[81] I had not forgotten Jumana, but a lot had happened over the past two days.

I went up the ice-cold stairway to the third floor to do my nightly rounds of the children in the paediatric ward. There I met Dr Hamid Abu Ubaid, the proficient and tireless neurosurgeon who had operated on Samar's back wound and paralysis. He took me into a room with three beds.

'You have to see this patient, Dr Mads,' he said quietly. 'She has just arrived. Hers is another incredible story.'

Wrapped up in several blankets lay nine-year-old Amal Atteia al-

Samouni. She seemed to be sleeping. She was being given intravenous fluids and had a plaster on the right side of her head, but no other visible injuries. A young Palestinian dressed in a brown leather jacket with a fur-lined collar stood by the head of the bed wearing a red *keffiyeh* – or Palestinian scarf, as we call it – loosely around his neck. He looked uninjured, apart from a large plaster on the right side of his neck. The man introduced himself as Faraj al-Samouni; he was twenty-two years old and was Amal's brother. His face was expressionless, almost apathetic, and he looked at me with a dark, almost aggressive gaze.

'His sister has just been dug out of the family's house, which was bombed to pieces,' Dr Hamid said quietly. 'She lay there for four days with no food or water.'

'Is it really possible? What happened?'

'She and her brother are from the Samouni family, the family from al-Zaytoun that you have already heard about.'

I took Faraj by the hand and introduced myself, while Dr Hamid interpreted.

'What happened to your sister?' I asked.

First, he looked at me at length, threw an enquiring look towards my colleague, who nodded at him in encouragement.

'She lay for four days under the collapsed building that the Israelis bombed with my whole family inside.'

His voice was low with an intense, trembling undertone.

'Twenty-nine members of my family were killed, including our father. We don't know how many more are lying in the ruins. The wounded didn't get any help because the Israeli soldiers refused to allow the Red Crescent and Red Cross through. There were over a hundred people gathered in the house when they bombed it.

'But we have already taken in little Jumana al-Samouni – is she also from your family?

'Yes. There are more still. We don't have the full picture. Have you seen anyone from my family?'

I told him briefly about Jumana and her grandmother. He knew about them. He was injured himself but kept looking for the rest of the family. He dug out his sister Amal with his own hands today and got her to the hospital.

'She is completely worn out by thirst, hunger and the cold. Is she going to survive?' he asked me.

I lifted the blanket and quickly examined the little girl's delicate body.

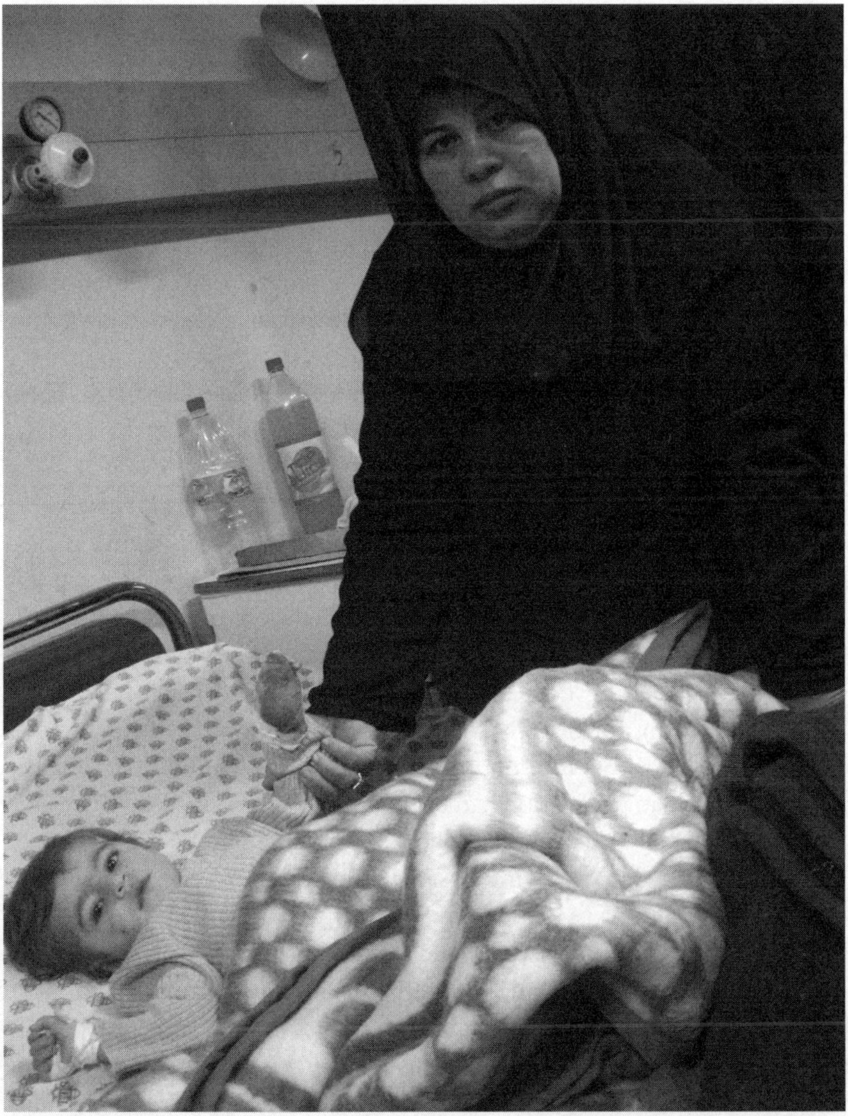

An elder relative tended to Jumana after her operation. 'Why is nobody stopping the Israelis who are killing us and our children?' she asked.

She did not seem to have any serious external physical trauma, but she was cold and suffering from fatigue.

'Does she have any other injuries?' I asked Dr Hamid.

'No, we have not found anything else. But she is exhausted, as you can see.'

'We have to investigate if she has had serious muscle-crush injuries that could cause kidney failure. Let's take the urine myoglobin and blood tests. Is the urine colour normal?'

'As far as I know, the urine's normal, but we'll take the blood tests you suggest. I think she'll come through. We are a strong people.'

They are undoubtedly a strong people. Four days buried alive. Stories like this make headlines round the world after earthquakes. Gaza is not the victim of a natural disaster but of a hundred per cent man-made earthquake; a meticulously planned, brutally executed disaster on a scale undreamed of.

The story of Amal Atteia did not get out of a blacked-out Gaza. Israel wishes to work undisturbed by international opinion.

After my return home to Norway, I found several pictures and interviews with Faraj al-Samouni. In some of the pictures, he is seen taking part in digging out his killed relatives from the ruins. In a television interview outside al-Shifa made on the same day the massacre took place, he tells tearfully of the deaths of his father, his uncle and other family members. He is himself wearing bandages around his head and neck, but he still continued looking for his relatives, right until he dug out his own sister after four days. The international organisations responsible for the Palestinian civilian population had been notified of this misdeed the whole time, as well as of the wounded who needed help, and of the dead – or perhaps living – who were lying buried in the rubble. They tried in vain to get to the spot but were stopped by Israeli fire.

Maybe there were not twenty-nine dead, but thirty-two? Irrespective of the number of killed and injured, the military action against the Samouni family was clearly against the rules of warfare and against international law. I was reminded of the My Lai massacre during the Vietman War, which cost the lives of 347 Vietnamese civilians, mainly women, children and the elderly. Many were also tortured and raped. Were we witnessing similar crimes in Gaza now?

The My Lai massacre was committed on March 16, 1968 by American soldiers from Charlie Company of the 1st Battalion, 20th Infantry Regiment. My Lai became the symbol of American abuse in Vietnam. Lieutenant William Calley was found to be responsible for the massacre and was given a life sentence for murder, but the President ordered him to be released two days later. Calley was then kept under military house arrest for just three and a half years before he was released. He repeatedly put the blame on his superiors. The other soldiers from the company had long since been discharged when the case became public, and of the twenty-six soldiers charged, only Calley was convicted.

The judicial follow-up is referred to as the 'Medina standard', after Captain Ernest Medina, who was the commander of Charlie Company. The standard clarifies the responsibility of superiors for the actions of their subordinates in the military domain.[82] When a commanding officer is informed of human rights violations or war crimes committed by his subordinates, he is personally responsible for those actions unless he actively tries to stop them. War crimes include – but are not limited to – the murder, maltreatment or deportation of civilian inhabitants of an occupied territory.[83] An American officer later said that 'every unit of brigade size has its My Lai hidden some place.' Had Israel got its My Lai?

But *somebody* in Israel reacted to the incidents in al-Zaytoun. The Israeli human rights organisation B'Tselem spoke with little Jumana's nineteen-year-old mother Meysa on January 5, just after she had been made a young widow in an unusually brutal manner.[84]

Meysa told B'Tselem that the nightmare began on Sunday January 4, at around nine o'clock in the morning, when the Israeli soldiers came to the house that her father-in-law, Rashed al-Samouni, owned in al-Zaytoun in the southern suburbs of Gaza City. The house is next to a cement company.

> We were fourteen people in the house, all of us from the al-Samouni family: me, my husband, Tawfiq, 21, our infant, Jumana, nine months old, my father-in-law, Rashed, 41, my mother-in-law, Rabab, 38, and my husband's brothers, Musa, 19, Walid, 17, Halmi, 14, Zeineb, 12, Muhammad, 11, Shaban, 9, Issa, 7, Islam, 12, Israa, 2.
>
> The soldiers came to the house on foot and knocked on the door. We opened and then, threatening us with weapons, they forced us to leave the house. They had bullet-proof vests on and had automatic weapons. Their faces were painted black. We left the house. Walid ran from another door of the house, but the soldiers caught him.
>
> The soldiers led us by foot to the house of my father-in-law's brother, Talal Halmi al-Samouni, 50, about twenty meters away. In the house were already about twenty people, and together we were thirty-five. The soldiers left us, apparently to search my father-in-law's house.

About an hour later, the soldiers came back and ordered us to go with them to the house of Wail al-Samouni, 40. His house is a kind of concrete warehouse, about 200 square meters big, about twenty meters from Talal's house, where we were. We reached Wail's house at 11.00a.m. There were already thirty-five people there, so now we were about seventy in total. We stayed there until the next morning. We didn't have food or drink.

Around six o'clock in the morning (Monday, 5 January), it was quiet in the area. One of the men in the family, Adnan al-Samouni, 20, said that he wanted to go and bring his uncle and family so they could be with us. My father-in law and his nephew, Salah Talal al-Samouni, 30, and his cousin Muhammad Ibrahim al-Samouni, 27, were standing at the door of the house and planned on going together to bring them. The moment they left the house, a missile or shell hit them. Muhammad was killed on the spot and the others were injured from the shrapnel. My husband went over to them to help, and then a shell or missile was fired onto the roof of the warehouse. Based on the intensity of the strike, I think it was a missile from an F-16.

When the missile struck, I lay down with my daughter under me. Everything filled up with smoke and dust, and I heard screams and crying. After the smoke and dust cleared a bit, I looked around and saw 20-30 people who were dead, and about twenty who were wounded. [...]

The persons killed around me were my husband, who was hit in the back, my father-in-law, who was hit in the head and whose brain was on the floor, my mother-in-law Rabab, my father-in-law's brother Talal, and his wife Rhama Muhammad al-Samouni, 45, Talal's son's wife, Maha Muhammad al-Samouni, 19, and her son, Muhammad Hamli al-Samouni, 5 months, whose whole brain was outside his body. Razqa Muhammad al-Samouni, 50, Hanan Khamis al-Samouni, 30, and Hamdi Majid al-Samouni, 22 [were all dead].

My husband's brother, Musa, and I were lightly injured. Musa was injured in the shoulder and my left hand was injured. My daughter [Jumana] was injured in the left hand. Her thumb, second finger, and third finger had been cut off. I took a kerchief and wrapped her hand to stop the bleeding. The wounded who lay on the floor cried for help and couldn't move. The small children and my husband's grandmother, Shifaa al-Samouni, 70, were crying.

About fifteen minutes after the second strike, Musa said that it would be better to escape and go to the house of his uncle, Assad al-Samouni, about twenty meters away. We ran and knocked on the gate, but nobody answered. Musa jumped over the gate [...] opening it and we went inside. We were me, my daughter [Jumana], Musa, and his little sisters Islam, 5, and Isra, 2. There were 40–50 soldiers in the house, and more people were gathered in one of the rooms. There were about thirty people, 7–10 of them men. The men were blindfolded.

One of the soldiers came to me and gave me and my daughter first-aid. He bandaged our hands and checked our pulse. Then the soldiers tied Musa and blindfolded him.

The soldiers told us that they would release us and leave only Musa and his uncle Emad in case Hamas came. I understood that they intended to use them as 'human shields.' They ordered us to leave the house, and we walked along the street about 400–500 meters until we found an ambulance, which took me and my daughter to al-Shifa Hospital. The others from my family continued to walk in the street. Later, some of them also arrived at the hospital.

As far as I know, the dead and wounded who were under the ruins are still there. I didn't see that any of them had been brought to the hospital.

The massacre at al-Zaytoun cost the lives of at least twenty-six members of the Samouni family. There were ten children and seven women among those killed.[85]

The children killed were:
Azza Salah al-Samouni, 3 years
Waleed Rashad al-Samouni, 17 years
Ishaq Ibrahim al-Samouni, 14 years
Ismail Ibrahim al-Samouni, 16 years
Rifka Wael al-Samouni, 8 years
Fares Wael al-Samouni, 12 years
Huda Nael al-Samouni, 17 years
Ahmad Atieh al-Samouni, 14 years
Mu'tassim Mohammed al-Samouni, 6 years
Mohammed Hilmi al-Samouni, 5 years

The women killed were:
Rahma Mohammed al-Samouni, 50 years
Safa' Hilmi al-Samouni, 25 years

Maha Mohammed al-Samouni, 22 years
Rabbab Azzat al-Samouni, 32 years
Laila Nabih al-Samouni, 40 years
Rifqa Mohammed al-Samouni, 50 years
Hanan Khamis al-Samouni, 36 years

The men killed were:
Tallal Hilmi al-Samouni: 55 years
Attieh Hilmi al-Samouni: 25 years
Rashad Hilmi al-Samouni: 42 years
Tawfiq Rashad al-Samouni: 23 years
Mohammed Ibrahim: 26 years
Ziyad Izzat al-Samouni: 28 years
Nidal Ahmad al-Samouni: 30 years
Hamdi Maher al-Samouni: 23 years
Hamdi Mahmoud al-Samouni: 70 years

It was past midnight. There was no rest on the cards for anyone. We left Amal Atteia and her brother Faraj in the room and continued our nightly rounds in the paediatric department into another ward of child war casualties.

In Room 545, there were three adult-sized hospital beds. The beds were divided by blue curtains which were currently lifted up and draped over the curtain rails so that the three little patients and the women who sat with two of them could see each other. Two male nurses were seeing to the bandages on a six-year-old boy who lay furthest towards the window. Essidin Sarzour had two women by his side. In the bed in the middle I recognised four-year-old Samar Abed Rabbo, the girl with the cross-sectional wound and the spine operation, who had just come back from the operating theatre. By the door lay another four-year-old girl, Hamadi Mamluk, who had been hit by a blast in her own home and had injuries to her arms. Her mother sat calmly at the foot of her bed, and they shared a quilt. All the children were awake. Only Samar was all by herself.

The room was filled with a quiet conversation between the three women who sat with their children, and with Samar's quiet, monotonous and uninterrupted whisper 'mama, mama, mama, mama…'. She looked straight at the ceiling while she kept on calling softly and repeatedly for her mother. It shook me to the bone. I went over to her, stroked her cheek and tried to comfort her. The women by the other beds told her in

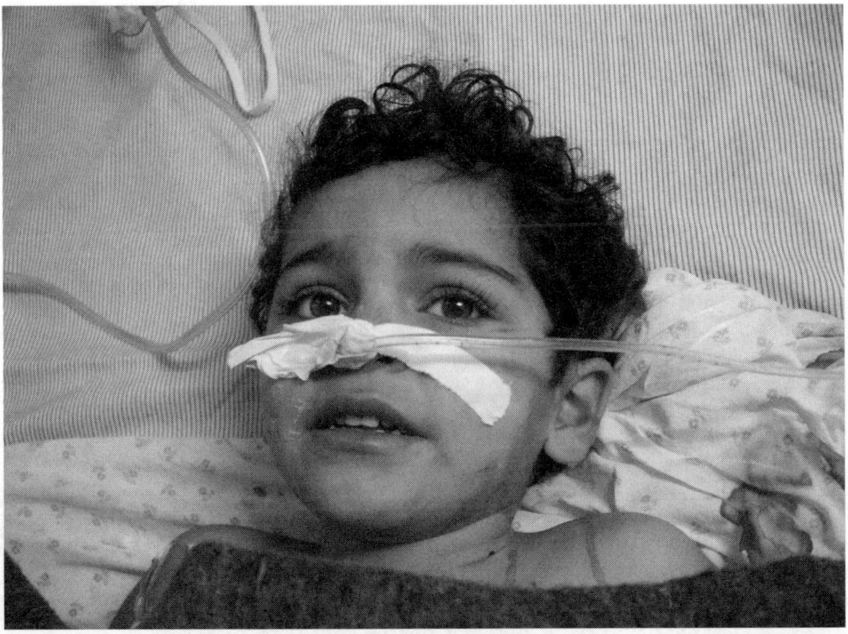

Four-year-old Samar whispered repeatedly 'mama, mama, mama . . .'

a low voice: 'Just stay calm, mummy's coming soon.' Samar had a plastic tube put through her nose during the operation. This tube was intended to drain gastric juice and air from her stomach and the upper parts of her duodenum to stop her from feeling nauseous, vomiting and getting stomach acids down into her lungs. This is a feared and potentially fatal complication after surgery in general and, with Samar's cross-sectional paralysis, the chances of intestinal paralysis and the impaired passage of intestinal contents are greatly increased. Tubes such as these are very uncomfortable to have through the nose, but Samar was surprisingly quiet. The only thing she seemed to be concerned with was 'mama, mama, mama.'

I felt close to tears. What were we going to do? A wounded young child among strangers, who had been through a horrible experience, followed by a dramatic evacuation without her mother, father or other acquaintances, in an ambulance driving at high speed because the enemy forces that had wounded her were prepared to shoot at the ambulance too. And now she lay here, still removed from her nearest and dearest.

The other women evidently understood my worry.

'We'll look after her and comfort her as best we can,' they said.

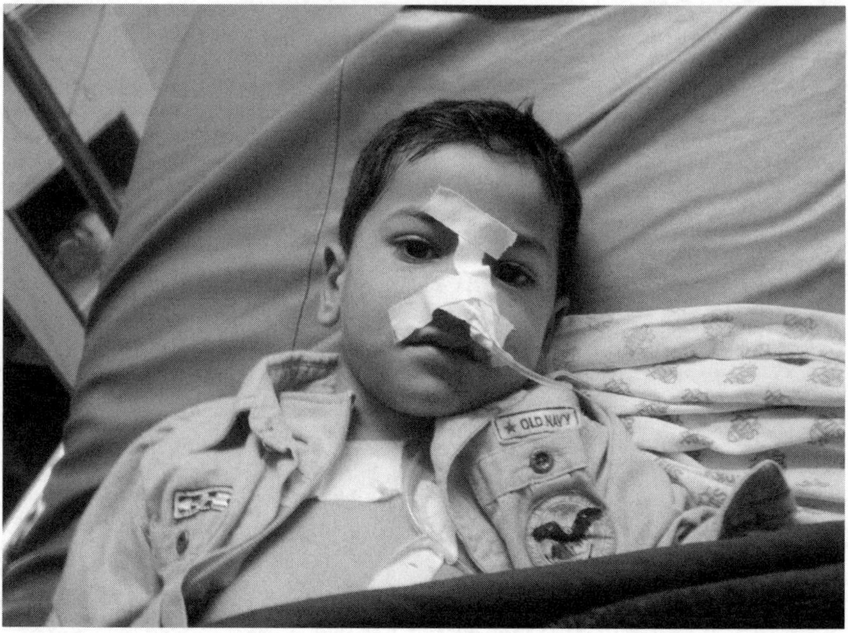

Six-year-old Essidin had been operated on for his shrapnel injuries to the chest and abdominal cavity.

We continued on to the bed by the window. Six-year-old Essidin had been injured the day before when seven Israeli bombs landed outside his house. The boy had received life-threatening shrapnel wounds to the abdomen and the chest and was operated upon as soon as he came to al-Shifa. He also had a substantial stomach probe, as well as a thoracic drain and a large bandage to cover the central incision the surgeons had made when they opened his abdomen in order to stop the life-threatening haemorrhages. The boy's breathing was calm but shallow, due to the painful operation wound. He was wearing a khaki shirt adorned with colourful military emblems – one read 'Old Navy'. His sheet had slid down, and he rested his head on the grey plastic hospital mattress cover. His stomach probe was elaborately plastered with white textile plasters; he would have to struggle to take it out.

Essidin stared at me with a completely motionless gaze. He had beautiful brown eyes, but they were dilated and wore a shocked expression.

'What happened? What am I doing here, and who are you?' his eyes asked silently.

I looked at him for a long time, but the looks we exchanged hardly gave him any good answers. Essidin was not alone. His mother sat by the window, while his grandmother sat on the left side of the bed, between him and Samar. His grandmother was furious. She interrupted my quiet examination of her grandchild and practically shouted at me while she gesticulated with her arms.

'What have we done to deserve this? What is going to happen to us? The blockade has been starving us for years; we have no food to give our own children. We have no food to eat ourselves, to give us the strength we need for the hard life in Gaza. Why should we poor, ordinary people first be starved only to then be bombed? Can you answer this, can you? Why? Why are they hurting our boy and all the other children?'

Her voice rose to a loud, piercing cry. Hamadi, who lay in the bed by the door with her mother sitting up, woke up and began to cry, but her mother joined in vigorously with Samar's grandmother: 'It's terrible. We don't know what to do. Nobody protects us, nobody stops the Israelis.'

The grandmother set her eyes on me and nailed me to the spot with her gaze as she finished: 'I have never been politically active, but I have always supported Fatah. From this day on it will just be Hamas, Hamas, Hamas until the day I die. They are the only ones – the only ones – who defend us, the poor people of Gaza.'

There was not much more to say. We went over to Hamadi, who had several fractures in her right arm, which had been set. Her eleven-year-old sister had been injured in the same attack on their house. She lay down in intensive care with a serious head wound. Their mother had a minor back injury, and their brother was also injured.

'What will we do, where will this end?' she asked me while I studied her daughter's X-ray images, almost as a diversionary manoeuvre.

'I don't know,' I answered. 'I only know that there are many of us who support you, many millions all across the world. At home in Norway there are big demonstrations to support you and, even if you don't hear so much about it here in Gaza, many are trying to stop Israel.'

It sounded like meagre consolation. All three women looked at me with a condescending gaze. It felt in any case like a condescending gaze. I went over to Samar one more time, stroked her hair and gave her a gentle kiss on the forehead.

'I'll come back to you, I promise,' I said.

Dr Hamid translated that. Twice. Samar looked at me slowly with her brown eyes.

Dr Hamid outside Room 545: 'We have no human rights.'

'Mama, mama, mama' was all she answered.

We went out into the corridor. I felt shaken and beaten. Three wounded children. Three more on top of the Samouni children and all the other children. On top of the children killed. On top of all those with more minor injuries, those scared out of their wits, the sleepless, all the ones with cold beds soaked in urine from that night's bed-wetting, all the hungry children. All the parentless children.

'But Dr Hamid, how can this happen? Please tell me,' I asked my colleague, almost imploring him.

He looked slowly at me. His face was drawn with the lack of sleep and far too many operations, but he still had a characteristically gentle expression and a look of unmistakeable warmth.

'You know, Dr Mads. We have no human rights. That's all.'

11

11

The Cowardly War

MADS GILBERT

It was five o'clock in the morning on Friday January 9. Sleep was impossible. I felt that time and space were steadily squeezing in on us. Perhaps the Israeli ground forces would penetrate into the heart of Gaza city today? Right here to al-Shifa, perhaps? Or would there be another attempt to send an ambulance convoy? Perhaps we would be leaving today, with a convoy of Palestinian ambulances to Rafah?

I got up. The little 'office' was filled by the gentle, monotone, singing recitation of the Qur'an by my room-mates next door. They were in the middle of their morning prayers, and I was struck again by how effectively soothing is the recitation of the prayers.

It was in these morning hours that I wrote the article 'Inside Gaza's al-Shifa Hospital' for the British professional journal, *The Lancet*.[86] I had sent editor Richard Horton an e-mail a few days earlier, asking if he would be interested in a report from Gaza. The reply came promptly: 'Just write! We'll take it.'

The problem was not lack of material, but lack of time to write. I had made up my mind that the manuscript would be sent from Gaza, no matter how far I had got with it. Accompanied by the singing of prayers and the noise of bomb blasts, the writing got off to a good start. I still lacked a lot of facts. Erik would gather together as much data as possible about the hospital's capacity and would try to get an overview of surgical activity from the beginning of the war by going through the operation lists.

I concentrated and wrote intently, with a feeling of great awe. *The Lancet* is a prestigious journal which evaluates very critically articles submitted to it. It was obviously impossible for us under present conditions to generate anything approaching that level of scientific scholarship, both because the hospital documentation was affected by war and chaos, and because we ourselves had neither the surplus energy nor the leisure time to do the painstaking work which scholarship requires. But we could obviously give a first-hand eyewitness account to pass on to the readers of *The Lancet* – and to the world – of what we ourselves were experiencing at al-Shifa Hospital. This would be in the form of a 'Special Report', as the column is called. The journal has around 30,000 subscribers, but more than a million people use the website, lancet.com. So an article would reach many people in the international medical community, including in Israel and the USA.

I checked the news and my e-mails. The night's most important events from the outside world were the reports of the big demonstrations throughout Norway and of the Security Council's treatment of Gaza. Seen naively, it could look as if the Security Council was taking a strong line in its resolution. As an irrepressible optimist, I was inspired by the news to send an e-mail to 'The North Flank':

> Al-Shifa, Gaza, 05:30 hrs. Friday January 9
> Thank God! It seems as if we can breathe again! We have just got the news that the Security Council has almost unanimously passed a clear resolution calling for a ceasefire, and that the USA didn't lay down a veto! And that just the day after the huge demonstrations throughout Norway! It's almost unbelievable, and we'll believe it when we see it.
>
> Some of the bomb strikes last night felt as if they were just outside the window, but it quietened down eventually. Now there are just wasps buzzing in the sky.
>
> Will Israel respect the resolution? They can't possibly go on like this.
>
> Perhaps the straw which broke the camel's back was the deadly attack on the UNRWA convoy or the warning shots against the convoy of sixteen ambulances carrying seriously war-wounded patients. The world has seen what the Israeli forces are doing, and the world is pressing their leaders to say 'Stop!' It's too late for those who have been killed and for others who have been torn into pieces, but in time for those who until now haven't known whether they would suffer the same fate.
>
> Oh, may they get to sleep for another hour or two now, all the exhausted, desperate and hungry inhabitants of Gaza. May all the young people in Gaza fall into the deep, warm sleep which is only possible without the noise of bomb blasts and cries of terror. We are holding our breath – again . . .

I let my thoughts turn again to our Palestinian colleagues and their almost unbelievable endurance. What was keeping them going? Where did they get their strength and spirit? Day after day, the thing which impressed us most in al-Shifa was the spirit and dedication of doctors, nurses, volunteers and ambulance crews. Obviously all the individual tragedies affected us too, and the indescribably nasty wounds. But in spite of all the painful impressions, it is the experience of human fortitude which comes first to mind, all the endurance and eager spirit, fellowship and co-operation, among the hundreds of health workers who staffed al-Shifa Hospital day and night, day after day.

In my in-box that morning there was also a message of support from Torunn Janbu, President of the Norwegian Medical Association. She said that she herself had marched in the big demonstration in Oslo the day before. The Medical Association had also encouraged members to take part in the country-wide demonstrations calling for an immediate ceasefire. I replied to her at half past six, describing the situation of our Palestinian colleagues:

> The health workers in al-Shifa Hospital are totally exhausted now. This is the fourteenth day of round-the-clock pressure. They sleep one to three hours in twenty-four, at most. Ash-grey, hungry – there is a serious shortage of food – and struggling continuously to provide space, equipment, help, light, warmth, time and care to the hundreds of casualties coming in – and the many hundreds of despairing relatives who fill up every corner of the hospital. It's like a field hospital now, and everybody has the same anxiety: 'Will the next injured or dying patient be one of my family?'
>
> Yesterday – during the 'ceasefire' – the Israelis bombed the house of a good colleague of mine from the internal medicine department, while he was at home to see to his family and get a little sleep. (They desperately need these three hours with a lull in the bombing to attend to their families, make practical arrangements and so on.) His pregnant wife, who is from Ukraine, was killed along with two of their children. He survived, injured, along with one or two of the children (not one hundred per cent sure about the number of children killed and wounded, will check today).
>
> They deserve a place in history for carrying on with their intensive work to give emergency help to their people. Gaza 2009 will surely come to be written into the history books in letters of blood. In the medical chapter will be the ambulance workers, the nurses, the doctors,

Palestinian doctors, nurses and volunteers ready for their round-the-clock work.

the volunteers (many of them medical students), the hospital workers, the people who look after our vitally important generator (which is stopping more and more often), the lab technicians, yes all the undisputed heroes.

I have never seen so much spirit, courage and human fortitude.

But they can't take much more now. We are all at breaking point.

MADS

al-Shifa Hospital, Gaza, occupied Palestine

The last ten days will stay etched in my memory for all time. Not only the fears of the wounded and dying and all the Palestinian families, not only all the glimpses of human resilience in our dealings with the health workers, not only all we saw of courageous endurance and spirit, but also our own experiences of danger and fear.

One of these experiences was when Israeli forces with heavy weapons forced a convoy of sixteen ambulances to stop and turn back to al-Shifa. The sound of the Israeli machine-guns at Netzarim on Thursday January 8 still echoes in my ears.

The problem with all movement and all evacuation journeys in Gaza was the security situation. The lack of security for all types of emergency and aid operations was an enormous problem for the Palestinians, especially the ambulance staff, for the UN/UNRWA and for the International Red Cross. The Israeli forces were totally unpredictable. They bombed and shot at humanitarian convoys, UN buildings, the UN's food and medicine warehouses, ambulances and places of worship. The problem for humanitarian convoys, whether transporting food or casualties, was emphasised that Friday by the fact that the UN and the International Committee of the Red Cross (ICRC) had suspended all their movements in Gaza. This was an extraordinarily sharp response to the crass Israeli attack the previous day on the ambulance convoy we were in, and to the murderous attacks that same day on the UN's own aid supplies and on the UN aid workers who were bringing these supplies to a civilian population in desperate need.

The well-marked UNRWA lorries which were trying to bring food and other essential supplies from the border crossings at Erez and Karni, were shot at by Israeli forces on the morning of Thursday January 8. Two UN drivers were killed. Both the head of UNRWA, John Ging, and the head of UN humanitarian operations, John Holmes, accused Israeli tank crews of having fired deadly shots against the UN's aid consignments.[87] The convoy had been routinely 'co-ordinated' with the Israeli forces' co-ordination mechanism, according to the proper protocols. This meant that all the GPS positions, the number of vehicles, the identification markings and the route had been submitted through the UN and recognised by the Israeli military authorities. Despite all this they were shot at, with fatal consequences.

Thursday January 8 was a very busy day, and time was pressing as we prepared for departure. Activity reached a peak in the intensive care department. Ambulance personnel worked alongside intensive care nurses and doctors to secure the equipment, documentation, X-ray films and necessary medications for a three- or four-hour ambulance journey. Big groups of anxious relatives waited outside. As we wheeled the patients past on the ambulance trolleys, big family groups assembled round each ambulance to say their goodbyes.

'Doctor, doctor – will it be all right? Will he survive?'

Many of them were crying. This might be the last time they would see their loved one. High in the sky, the drones were watching us. Bomb

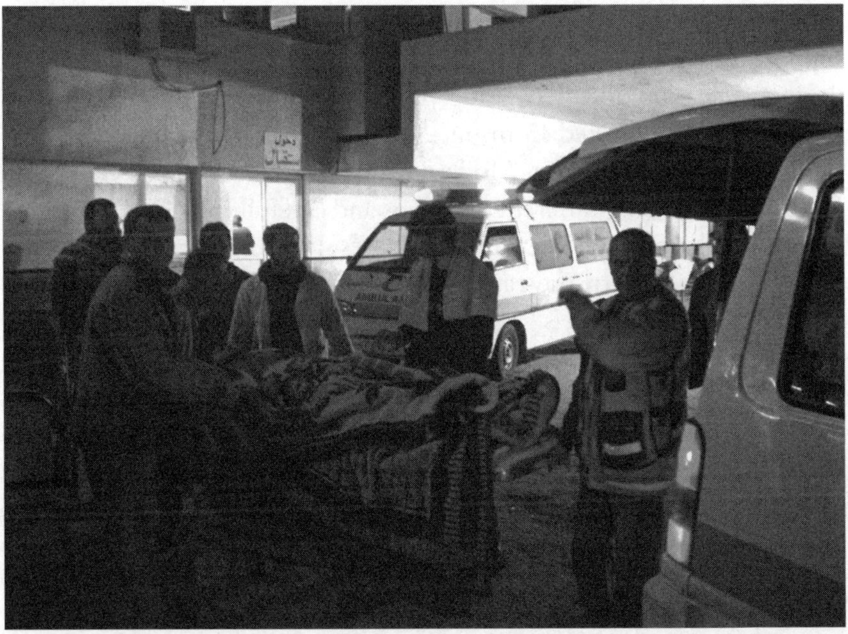

Two ambulance depots and twenty-nine ambulances were destroyed and sixteen health workers, mostly ambulance personnel, were killed by the Israeli forces. More than thirty health workers were injured. Forty health service premises were destroyed or damaged by Israeli attacks.

blasts could be heard in the distance.

'Isn't there a ceasefire now?' I asked.

'That's right, Dr Mads, a ceasefire of the Israeli type. They carry on "light bombing." They call it just a break – a lull – not a ceasefire,' answered intensive care nurse Osama.

I found the patient I was to be responsible for. The crews from four or five of the convoy's ambulances were working with nurses and doctors to get the patients ready for the journey. All the patients were on ventilators, and all were casualties of the war. Patients on mechanical ventilation have an 'artificial airway' which is a plastic tube placed inside their air passage. In this way we can protect the patient's lungs against dangerous, corrosive, acidic reflux which otherwise can leak from the gullet into the air passages. It also makes it possible to control the respiration. The ventilator is really an advanced form of bellows, which can blow air under pressure into the lungs so that the lungs expand and breathe independently of the patient's own ventilatory function. It can also support the patient's own spontaneous breathing by increasing pressure during inhalation and decreasing pressure during exhalation. The gas mixture can be adjusted from pure oxygen to room air, depending on the patient's lung function. Modern ventilators are advanced electronic machines with many different functions and carefully adjusted flow rates during inhalation and exhalation. As a result of the blockade, al-Shifa had only a few top-of-the-range modern ventilators, but quite a lot of probably obsolete models.

My patient was a man in his twenties who had been operated on a couple of days earlier for a severe abdominal injury. He was attached to the ventilator and was in 'deep narcosis' because he also had a chest wound which was being treated with a chest drain. Despite the continuous infusion of substantial doses of sedatives and painkillers, his state of unconsciousness seemed 'light' when I spoke to him and examined his injuries.

I helped to change the bed and to secure the vital tubes and cables which intensive care patients often have a lot of and which have to remain in place during the journey. When I listened to his chest I heard gurgling breath sounds, and proposed that we should suck out the mucus. This procedure consists of feeding down into the airway a thin, sterile plastic catheter connected to a vacuum source, to suck the airway and lungs clean of mucus, blood and other secretions which are blocking the passage of air and can lead to dangerous infections.

'No problem, Dr Mads,' responded the helpful nurse.

We sucked out abundant quantities of sticky mucus mixed with dark, old blood. The patient's breath sounds improved.

'Hurry up there, we need to leave now!' The ambulance worker was impatient. 'The others are waiting. The convoy needs to get going while we still have permission from the Israelis. There's only an hour left!'

We lifted the patient over onto the ambulance trolley, lay the monitoring equipment and the little transport ventilator beside his legs and made him secure. I checked the tubes and connections again. 'The devil is in the details'. Moving intensive care patients who are being ventilated under induced narcosis is an extreme sport. From my long experience as a doctor on ambulance helicopters and ambulance planes in northern Norway, I knew how risky these patient transfers can be – in peacetime – with one or at the most two patients. These patients are totally dependent on us to understand and check their vital functions and to recognise right away any discrepancy or failure in the apparatus which is keeping them alive. Moreover, these are seriously ill or injured patients who need to be given many potentially dangerous drugs. A small false move, failure to spot a tube becoming disconnected, a careless move which entangles a lead and causes it to work loose, batteries running flat, oxygen cylinders running empty – any of these can soon cost the patient's life. Now we were in a war situation, and we would be taking sixteen seriously ill patients on the road south to Rafah and Egypt, a road which was certainly no motorway. Nor was it safe, with Israeli ground forces along the route.

We hurried with the trolley through the main entrance and out to the waiting ambulance. The leader of the convoy was impatient.

'Hurry up, we're already running late,' shouted Dr Walid, an elderly Palestinian colleague with a bright red high-visibility jacket and two hand-held radios which he talked into constantly. 'You're to sit with me, Dr Mads, in the ambulance at the head of the convoy.'

I was accompanied by a young nursing student and the patient's father. A big group of relatives watched us anxiously as we loaded the patient into the ambulance.

'Doctor, how's he doing?' asked a young man.

'He'll pull through all right,' I reassured him.

'Do you have spare equipment in case of problems?' I asked the ambulance driver.

'Yes of course.'

We drove slowly out through the gate and took our place at the front of the column, a couple of hundred metres from the hospital.

While we were waiting for the convoy to start moving, I noticed that the ventilator machine was labouring. At the same time, the blood gas monitor was showing that the oxygen level in the patient's blood was beginning to drop. The red blood corpuscles should normally be 95 per cent saturated with oxygen, but the oxygen saturation had now dropped to 80 per cent. His skin was beginning to turn grey. I listened to his chest through the stethoscope. No breath sounds, no chest movement.

'I need suction. Quickly!' I said firmly. 'And a bag!'

'The bag' is what we call the self-expanding plastic balloon which we use to blow air into a patient when we are not using a mechanical ventilator.

The suction vacuum in the ambulance was feeble and did not supply enough negative pressure to be able to clear the airways. I could not get very far down into the endotracheal tube either, with the thin plastic suction catheter which was connected to the suction machine. The system was blocked.

'Quickly! I need the bag right away!'

He handed me the bag in its plastic wrapping. I had to unpack it before I could attach it to the patient's endotracheal tube. I squeezed it hard to get air into the patient.

'Oh my God, it's leaking,' I said half aloud to myself. 'Split to pieces. Not been checked.'

'Have you another one? Quickly, this one's useless!'

'No, that's the only one,' replied the ambulance man, while my colleague was shouting messages in Arabic into both hand-held radios.

The pulse-rate rose, both the patient's and mine. I looked at the monitor. The oxygen concentration had sunk to 70 per cent, and the pulse rate had risen to over 180 beats per minute. This is the most critical situation we ever have to deal with as anaesthetists: an acutely obstructed airway. This especially applies when the patient is under sedation and receiving intensive care, because we as professionals have decided the treatment. We have taken over responsibility for the patient's vital functions. We hold the patient's life in our hands, or allow him to be dependent on the machines which we have control over. Now I had lost control of the situation. I had not prepared a good enough Plan B, had not checked personally that the back-up arrangements were in place and in working order. I could obviously make excuses for myself on the grounds of being so busy and of not wanting to create bad feeling by double-checking the work of my Palestinian colleagues. They had assured me that they had a bag and the necessary emergency equipment in the ambulance, but I had not checked the equipment myself, and the situation was now critical.

I tried blowing directly into the endotracheal tube. It was blocked solid. Blocked up with dried blood and mucus, I thought. I'll need to change the tube, take out the blocked one right now and put in a new one. 'Laryngoscope!'

I was shouting now. The ambulance-man came back, opened the door and looked questioningly at me. He knew from the tone of my voice that the situation was critical.

'The tube's blocked,' I called. 'I can't get any air into him. I need a new tube and a laryngoscope.'

'No problem, there you are.'

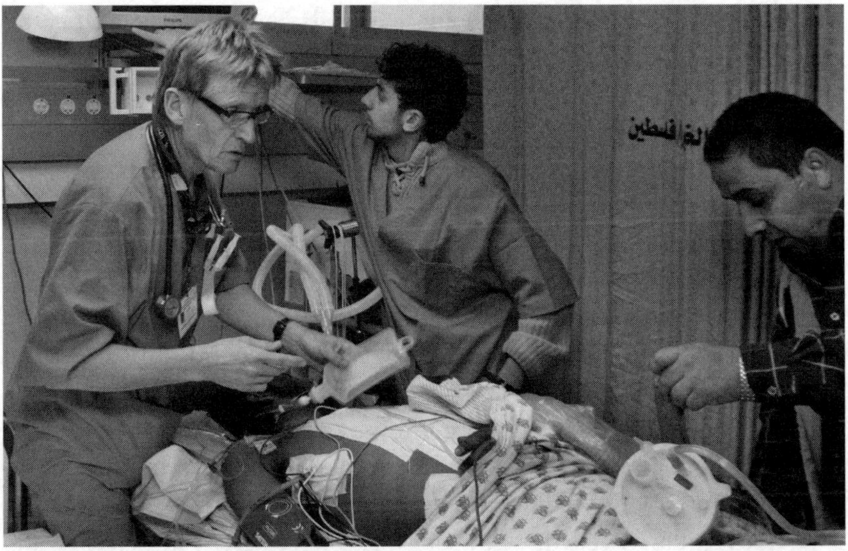

Evacuating patients from the intensive care unit to Egypt. Time was scarce, and vital medical equipment had to be checked before ventilated patients could be moved to the ambulances.

He handed me a black box held shut with little brass catches. I opened it, tore the laryngoscope out and fitted the long, spoon-shaped blade to the handle. The laryngoscope is a special instrument we use to lift the patient's tongue forward, so that we can see into the back of the throat to find the vocal cords and get access to the air passages. At the end of the curved blade there is a little light bulb which casts a strong light down into the throat so that we can see to pass the endotracheal tube accurately, between the vocal cords and on down into the air passage. If it goes down into the gullet instead the patient will choke. The battery for this very specialised light is hidden in the handle.

My hand was shaking as I fixed the blade into the slot on the battery handle. I opened the instrument out, which establishes the electrical contact so that the light comes on.

'There's no light!' I called. I checked that the light bulb was screwed in firmly and that the batteries were set in properly. Still no light.

'D'you have a spare battery?' I pleaded.

'Sorry, doctor.'

Catastrophe was getting closer. In a few more minutes the patient would suffocate. I felt icy cold. Luckily the convoy had not yet started, and we were still standing in a long line of sixteen ambulances. There's only one thing left for it, I thought. The ambulance would have to turn back to the hospital so that we could change the endotracheal tube in the intensive care department.

'Back to the hospital. Right away! Turn round! Fast as you can! He's suffocating!'

I grabbed the driver firmly by the shoulder and looked him straight in the eye as I spoke to him in a quivering voice. He understood the situation and managed to turn the ambulance round. I blew directly into the tube again with the full strength of my lungs. With full sirens and fierce shouting we careered back to al-Shifa. Every second counted. I realised I was getting a little air into him by adjusting the position of the tube. The patient and I both had pulse rates up around 200. His oxygen concentration was still falling, but more slowly.

'Drive right in!' I yelled. The order was unnecessary. The driver swung the ambulance with the tyres squealing, in through the gate and on to the emergency department entrance. I looked at the patient's father with an encouraging glance. As he was being lifted out of the ambulance the patient vomited profusely.

Thank God the tube is in place, I thought. We'll get it sorted out now. Come on. *Yalla, habibi*!

We stormed into intensive care.

'We'll need to change the tube,' I shouted to the nurses. 'Right away!'

In the well-functioning intensive care department, we did this in under a minute. We had the situation under control now.

The tube we took out was choked with dried blood and mucus, leaving an opening no broader than a matchstick. Not enough to let air through.

For the first time during this visit, I was soaked with sweat. I had made a mistake which had almost cost the patient his life. I should have followed my most neurotic check and double-check routines and gone through all the back-up equipment before we started. Oh yes, I could make excuses for myself on the grounds of the war, the cultural differences, language problems, shortage of equipment because of the blockade – all of these things. But I had accepted personal responsibility for the patient and had not quality assured Plan B.

When we finally left al-Shifa, the cortège of well-marked Palestinian ambulances had altogether sixteen severely injured patients.

Right up to the last minute it was uncertain whether the convoy would get past the Israeli lines. The co-ordination mechanism was complex. Palestinian health authorities made contact with the International Committee of the Red Cross, who had contact with special co-ordinators in the Israeli armed forces, who in turn 'recognised' the humanitarian operations in Gaza. When the word finally got through, the patients with all their necessary equipment had to be shifted from their beds onto the ambulance trolleys, wheeled out to the waiting ambulances and installed there.

A big, white-painted Red Cross trailer was the lead vehicle in the convoy. After that came a four-wheel-drive vehicle, also white and flying big Red Cross flags. After the two lead vehicles came sixteen ambulances with clear markings and flashing red lights. Nobody could be in any doubt that this really was the convoy which had been co-ordinated to evacuate the injured south to Rafah.

'Don't take pictures,' said Dr Moawya Hassanin, the convoy leader who was sitting in the front seat beside the driver. We had to be very careful.

'That's fine.'

I was sitting at the head end of the patient with my back to the two people in the front seat, and I had a good view both forwards and backwards of the familiar Gaza landscape.

The convoy drove quickly and with full sirens. It was important to keep following the two white-painted lead vehicles. We quickly came through Gaza City and out onto the coast road. The endless blue Mediterranean shimmered in the sunshine. We felt the fresh sea breeze through the open window, and I thought what a fine place this could have been. Almost paradise. If only there had been peace and freedom. Now we had to go home. Our job was done; a new team was waiting at the border, ready to take over from us. I felt a mixture of relief and despair. We were on our way out now, though the leave-taking had been anything but easy.

We had had an emotional and serious discussion that morning. I had declared to Erik and to Dagfinn that I couldn't bear to leave al-Shifa. I wanted to stay.

'I'll stay till the war is over, I can't just leave now. I've been thinking about it all night.'

The feeling that we were betraying and abandoning our colleagues and our patients was unbearable. I wept in despair.

'The situation can only get worse. They still need us!'

Erik heard me out, listening calmly and attentively. He looked at me carefully.

'We know that's how it has to be, Mads,' he said firmly. 'It's like that. We're becoming so attached to the Palestinians through everything we are going through together and through the whole situation. We're becoming so touched by it all that we forget the distinction between us and them. But this isn't *our* battle, it's the *Palestinians'* battle. We've done our bit, and the agreement was that we would stay until we were relieved. The replacement team has come now. We've overlapped with Dagfinn for several days, and the others are standing ready at the border. We shall move out today, we shall move out together, and there are big tasks awaiting us when we come out. Our task as witnesses, which you yourself put such emphasis on, and our work back home in Norway – that's more important than staying here longer.'

'I know that you are right,' I answered. 'This is what happened in Beirut too, in 1982. I didn't want to come away from there; we almost had to be chased out when the planned period for the team came to an end. We identified so strongly with the Palestinians' situation, and I'm doing that again right now. Of course we must go. I just need help to get rid of the horrible feeling that we're failing them, we're being inadequate, abandoning them when they most need us.'

'We'll do the job here, you can be sure of that,' said Dagfinn. 'I don't have as much experience of dealing with the media as you have, and I don't have the same practice as you two have gained over the first ten days, but I'll do it in my own way.'

'Certainly you'll cope with it, Dagfinn. I have full confidence in you – and in the others who are waiting in Rafah. It's more my own feelings. It's just so hellishly painful to be leaving.'

They let me shed my tears.

'OK, lads. We're leaving. Thanks for being able to listen to me. I needed to get it out! So we start packing, then?'

We laughed a little and went round exchanging warm embraces. I realised how closely the experience of war had bound us together. We knew it was dangerous. We had made our own decision to come to Gaza. We knew that we would carry our experiences, fellowship and friendship with us for the rest of our lives. For better or worse.

The convoy of ambulances had stopped. We were near Netzarim, five kilometres south of Gaza City, where the Israeli forces had driven a

12

12

Dreams in Gaza

ERIK FOSSE

'*Sabaah al-khayr*!'

I was wakened on Friday by one of the doctors who shared our quarters. He was standing in the doorway of our bedroom.

'Have you heard the news?' he whispered. 'The Security Council has passed a resolution calling for a ceasefire and a withdrawal of the Israeli forces.'

The other doctors in the house had got up at five o'clock to pray. I had a vague memory of hearing singing during the night. Usually they prayed in silence, but one of them had a fine voice, and it was good to listen to the prayer when he was leading it. After prayers they had checked the news on the Internet and found out about the Security Council resolution. Usually they went back to bed again after morning prayers. Just like Mads and myself, everybody tried to get some sleep whenever they had the opportunity. I threw the blankets off and went out to the duty room where the lap-top was. I went to the UN's home page: '8 January – The United Nations Security Council tonight overwhelmingly called for an immediate ceasefire in Gaza leading to a full Israeli withdrawal, the unimpeded provision throughout Gaza of food, fuel and medical treatment, and intensified international arrangements to prevent arms and ammunition smuggling.'[92]

Fourteen of the fifteen member states of the Security Council had voted for the resolution, but the USA had abstained.

The proposal in the resolution was a compromise put forward by the United Kingdom. It also contained a call to continue negotiations towards a two-state solution. The proposal took as its starting point the high number of people killed and injured, and the large proportion of women and children in that number. Later, after Mads and I came home to Norway and spoke with Foreign Minister Jonas Gahr Støre, we learned that the reports from 'the two Norwegian doctors in Gaza' had been mentioned in the discussion and had been part of the basis for the decision. The call for an immediate cessation of the attack and opening of the borders was exactly what we had tried to put forward in all the interviews we had given since we came to Gaza. I realised that our contribution had made a difference.

My first reaction was to be glad that the UN had responded at last. But it was altogether too late, and the effectiveness of the statement was uncertain. For three years now, the population of Gaza had been humiliated and collectively punished both by the international community and by Israel. Nearly a thousand Palestinians had already been killed in the first two weeks of the war. It seemed unlikely that Israel would respect the resolution, especially as the USA had abstained. The US Foreign Minister, Condoleezza Rice, wanted to await the outcome of the negotiations in Egypt. That could mean that the USA was prepared to give Israel more time to destroy the Palestinians' will to resist.

This resolution fitted into a long line of resolutions on the Palestinian question, where the USA had either blocked a resolution with a veto or had abstained, thereby weakening its measure of approval.

The President of the UN General Assembly, Nicaraguan politician and priest Miguel d'Escoto Brockmann, spoke sarcastically about the UN Security Council and its ineffectiveness in relation to the war in Gaza: 'I can't stand the smell of formaldehyde. Rigor mortis seems to have taken over, and we are failing the world, we are failing the cause of peace.'[93]

It struck me how distance can lead to dissociation. How easy it is to distance oneself when the victims have a different religion or way of expressing themselves. The labelling of the population of Gaza as religious fanatics and terrorists prevented people in the West from identifying with them and with their suffering. The terrorist label had created a gap between them and us. Every day the war went on, more children's lives were ruined. Either they lost their lives, or they lost arms and legs, or they lost their parents. They were all damaged psychologically by the Armageddon they were living in. Each day of war caused irreparable damage to everybody in Gaza.

While children were dying and being mutilated, American and European politicians were discussing fine detail in the wording of a resolution. It made me sick.

Following the withdrawal of support for Gaza and as a result of the continuing Israeli blockade, Gaza was totally isolated. The UN's responsibility for running schools, clinics and food supplies became more important than ever before. Several of the donor countries increased their contributions to the UN, to compensate for the stopping of direct aid.

The UN's increasing importance to the supply situation in Gaza became a source of conflict between Hamas and the UN. Because the UN had food and other supplies for the families registered as refugees, but not for the families indigenous to Gaza, the Gazan families were hit harder by the boycott than the refugee families. This was seen as very discriminatory. On February 5, 2009, Hamas confiscated the UN's supplies to distribute them to poverty-stricken Gazan families.[94] This led to increasing international criticism of Hamas. The confrontations between Hamas and the UN were used as evidence of Hamas's criminal nature, but for many Palestinians it demonstrated that Hamas was taking responsibility for the population. Other Palestinians claimed that Hamas used the redistribution of food from UNRWA to strengthen themselves and their reputation.

UNRWA's deliveries of aid weakened the effect of the blockade and the collective punishment of the Palestinians. That may be why Israel took the opportunity to attack UN vehicles and then the UN's main food and aid distribution warehouses.

On Friday January 9 we had a demonstration of how tense the situation was between Israel and the UN. The day before, Israeli soldiers had opened fire on a lorry in the north of the Gaza Strip. The lorry had clear UN markings, and it was driving in a convoy which had been guaranteed safe passage by the Israeli authorities. First, the Israeli soldiers shot the driver. Then when the driver's mate tried to pull the driver out of the vehicle, they shot at him too. He was admitted to al-Shifa Hospital the same day with major injuries. The driver died at the scene, the mate survived.

The UN office in Gaza reacted by stopping all transport movements throughout the Gaza Strip, and at the same time calling on Israel to guarantee the safety of all UN employees. The International Committee of the Red Cross joined in the protests after the convoy that Mads and I had been in the day before was stopped when the Israelis fired warning shots at us. By then, several of the Palestinian Red Crescent ambulances had already been shot at. The Red Cross claimed that the Israelis were creating unnecessary hindrances for their aid workers. This was a very

Concerned families waiting outside al-Shifa Hospital for news of their injured relatives. The Samouni family lost a lot of members.

mild protest, given that we had already been admitting patients who had been lying injured among the ruins for up to three days until ambulances could come to rescue them. The Israeli soldiers obstructed the ambulances by shooting at them.[95]

So nobody reckoned that there would be any attempt to evacuate patients from Gaza that Friday.

I continued my reading on the Internet. Immediately after the resolution was passed, Israeli Prime Minister Ehud Olmert declared that Israel did not consider itself bound by the resolution, and that they would continue the attack until the job was done.[96] Olmert boasted that he had persuaded the USA not to vote for the resolution.[97]

In al-Shifa Hospital we experienced nothing to suggest that Israel was letting herself be stopped by the UN resolution; quite the contrary. As I was sitting at the PC, I heard a fierce bombardment close by. Later, I learned that Israel had attacked Beach Camp, which is a refugee camp in the north of Gaza City, not far from al-Shifa Hospital. The camp is on the edge of the beach and was therefore exposed to attack from naval vessels.

Hamas also said that they did not recognise the UN resolution as binding. According to Al Jazeera, sixty rockets were fired from Gaza into Israel that Friday.

One of the other doctors in our residence stopped by the door for a chat.

'What do you think will happen following the Security Council resolution?' I asked.

'Israel will step up the war and hold on for three or four days more,' he replied, shrugging his shoulders. 'Israel doesn't bother about the UN, and they have had a clear signal from the current government in the USA.'

Dagfinn and I went up to the hospital together. The emergency department had taken in ten patients from Beach Camp, but all were being dealt with.

We went up to the second floor. It was half past eight, and Dr Sobhi had not arrived yet. We met Dr Issam. He had been working all night.

Issam, who was generally cheerful and amusing, was now subdued and unshaven. The war was obviously beginning to make its mark. It was a week since we had tried to save his nephew, who had been killed by a bomb from a drone. The war was beginning to wear everybody down, even Dr Issam. He wanted to have a smoke while we waited for Dr Sobhi. We went to a landing which looks out towards the main entrance to the hospital.

There was a bang which shook the whole hospital, and smoke began to rise from a house right across the street from the main gate. I realised that I had just stood and watched a house being bombed. But we hadn't really seen anything, as it all happened so quickly. The building was still standing. Presumably it had been hit by an anti-personnel bomb, which does little damage to buildings.

The ambulance crews from the hospital approached the building cautiously. We heard the drone which had fired the bomb. We all knew that it was circling round, filming. Where we were standing, we had a ringside view of what was happening. I expected another bomb to go off at any moment, and I thought about the ambulance personnel who were going into the building while the drone flew right over them.

Luckily there was no further explosion, and nobody was hurt in this attack.

Dr Sobhi arrived, and we began the daily ward rounds.

The doctors' ward round has two purposes. One is to be sure that every patient is having the best possible treatment, and the other is to make effective use of the resources of the hospital.

There were no computerised patient records at al-Shifa. The notes were handwritten and sparse, but on the patients' charts we could follow the records of their temperature and blood pressure and see which medicines they were being given.

Most of the young consultants were too busy to take part in the ward rounds. As we admitted more than a hundred patients every day and operated on twenty to thirty of them, it was just as important for us to make decisions about discharge and evacuation as it was to advise treatment.

As a result of the bombing, most of the wards had panes missing from the windows. Several of the doctors went around wearing thick winter jackets. Dr Sobhi always wore a white coat. So did I, but I always felt frozen.

There were lots of relatives around. We knew that the families played an integrated role in patient care. Because there was a shortage of nurses, the families had to take part in looking after the patients and preparing food.

We went into a room where there were several children. In one of the beds a twelve-year-old boy was dozing, covered by several blankets. In the bed next to him were two girls lying head to foot.

'These three children are from the same family,' Dr Sobhi explained. 'Hisham, the boy, is twelve years old. The girls in the bed are Zeina who is nine years old and Noor, who is thirteen months. Their house in Jabaliya Refugee Camp was bombed on Tuesday. They were admitted at the same time as their father, who was also injured. Two other siblings were more lightly injured, and one child was killed.'

Dr Spiro leant over Hisham and undid the bandages. 'Hisham was hit in the abdomen by a piece of shrapnel. We operated on him the same day and sewed up several tears in his bowel,' he said.

The wound looked fine.

Dr Sobhi looked at me hesitantly and said: 'We have a particular problem with Hisham. He has epilepsy and is dependent on medicines every day to prevent fits. It's now difficult to get hold of the medicines Hisham needs, and his family are worried about him.'

Hisham's mother helped him to get dressed and wrapped several blankets round him. The room was very cold. There was no glass in any of the windows, and the temperature was not much above ten degrees.

We moved on to the next bed, where the two girls lay. Nine-year-old Zeina was at the foot end. She had a deep cut in her forehead. This had not been stitched, but it was beginning to heal. She lay quite still, but answered when we spoke to her.

In the other end of the bed sat her little sister, Noor. She had wounds both on her head and on her face. She was wearing yellow and white pyjamas which were far too big for her. A big gauze dressing had been placed round her head, with a brown elastic bandage wound round to keep it in place. The bandage stuck up above her head like a crown. Noor sat in bed and yelled. She was still upset by the bombing three days before. Her mother tried to comfort her.

The Palestinian doctors were considerate when they talked with the patients. They introduced themselves to them and explained what they were going to do, before they started to remove bandages or blankets. They had a good rapport with the patients, but it was not easy to console little Noor.

She was cold, she was frightened and she was injured. The Apache helicopter and the drones were thundering outside the open window. The building shook from the bomb blasts in Beach Camp. How does a one-year-old cope with things like that?

Wherever we turned, the story was similar. One of the children of the Samouni family was in the next bed. This young boy had been hit in the right arm and had several fractures. His elbow joint was smashed. His arm was now supported by a frame with metal rods screwed into the bone to stabilise the fractures.

It was mainly children who had been struck by the sophisticated weapons. Children who had legs torn off. Children who didn't understand what was going on. I had never experienced anything like it.

None of the 750,000 children in Gaza had anywhere to flee to. Nowhere was safe. Parents with young children who lived in areas which they thought were targeted for bombing, moved in with relatives who lived in areas of the town which they presumed were safer. These were generally the districts where the better-off Palestinian families lived, and where Hamas had less support than in the poorer parts of the towns and in the refugee camps.

But it gradually became apparent that nowhere was entirely safe. On several occasions we took in children who had been killed or injured while they were playing in these 'safe' areas.

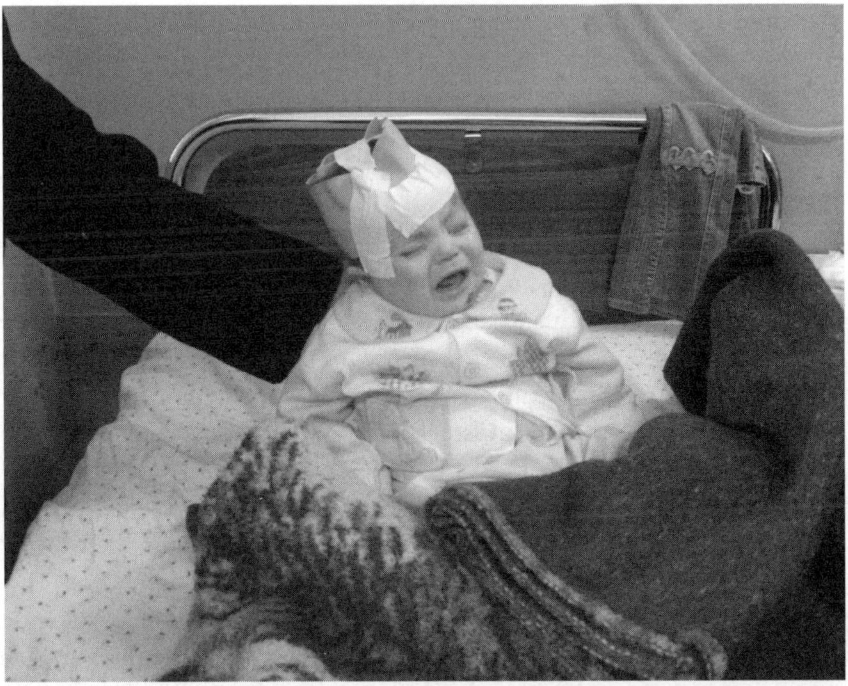

Noor sat in bed screaming. She did not understand what had happened to her.

The nurses on the wards were on duty round the clock.

Children have always been important for the Palestinian leaders, and Yasser Arafat encouraged families to have many children.[98]

Many Palestinians were driven out when the state of Israel was set up in 1948, but many others stayed. The Palestinians who stayed on became Israeli citizens and could vote in elections to the Knesset. Special laws denied them the same rights as Jewish inhabitants in Israel. Nevertheless, the Palestinians were a political force and they could both vote for and be elected to the national assembly. While the birth rate among most of the immigrants followed European patterns in the 1960s and 1970s, the Palestinian women were having many more children. In 2009 the Palestinians in Israel made up 20 per cent of the population. The number of births per woman is 2.75 in Israel, 3.22 on the West Bank and 5.03 in the Gaza Strip. While the rate of population growth in Israel is 1.67 per cent, the Palestinian population is increasing at a rate of 2.18 per cent on the West Bank and 3.35 per cent in Gaza, the fifth highest in the world.[99]

The Hamas leader Nizar Rayyan, who was killed in a bomb attack on January 1, 2009, had encouraged his fifteen-year-old son to be a suicide bomber. The son was killed in a suicide attack against an Israeli colony in October 2001. Rayyan said in an interview for the magazine *The Atlantic* that he would encourage another son to become a suicide bomber. For Rayyan this was a meaningful act because '[Palestine's] our home. It's more dear to me than my kids.'[100]

I am not the only person who has difficulty understanding how a father can be willing to sacrifice his children in a terrorist attack. But I live in a totally different reality, which makes it difficult to put oneself in the Palestinians' desperate situation. They are harassed daily. Land is gradually being annexed from the Palestinians on the West Bank. Slowly but surely, they are being driven out of East Jerusalem. In Gaza they are denied human dignity by a total blockade which causes shortages of everything.

I had been made aware of this reality earlier.

In the spring of 2002 I was in Gaza with Mads and with the nurses Anna Mørseth and Venke Aarethun. The situation was critical. Israel was attacking several places on the West Bank, including the refugee camp in Jenin. There were several helicopter attacks on Gaza, and the Palestinians feared an Israeli invasion. One afternoon we went for a walk round the town. Some young boys were running around, playing some game or other.

Seriously injured, but well treated at al-Shifa. One of the children from the Samouni family, operated with external fixation for a nasty broken arm.

One of the boys ran up to us.

'Boom!' he shouted, and then began to laugh.

'Hi there,' said Mads. 'What game are you playing?'

The boy was about ten years old. He spoke a little English.

'I've got bombs on my body,' he explained, smiling and enthusiastic. 'I run up to Sharon. Boom! Sharon goes to hell, and I go to paradise.'

Then he laughed. The group of children laughed too, before they turned and went their way.

They were playing suicide bombers. What induces children to play at being suicide bombers? What sort of lives do children have who dream of killing themselves? Do they have any other dreams and ambitions?

The children in Gaza are being denied rights, opportunities and a future. Their parents are suffering such humiliation that they are no longer able to care for their children properly. Most of their fathers are unemployed, and their mothers are trying to look after large families. The families have no travel documents. The children are condemned to live in poverty for the rest of their lives. This was as far as their ambitions carried them – to be suicide bombers.

But life is not like that for all children in Gaza.

In September 2008 I visited Gaza with the NORWAC management group. It was Ramadan. Ramadan and the festival of Eid which concludes it are for Muslims what Christmas is for Christians. Our friend Walid Shaqura invited us to *iftar* at his house. *Iftar* is the first meal Muslims eat after sunset when they have been fasting all day. It is really breakfast, though it is eaten in the evening. It is customary to invite friends and relatives to *iftar*. For a whole month, families visit each other and eat together in the evenings.

We found Walid's house in Gaza City and arrived at half past five to be in good time for sunset half an hour later. You mustn't come late for *iftar*. Everybody in the house is hungry, but courtesy requires them to wait for the guests. We were met at the door by Walid and his twelve-year-old son, Mohammed. Walid was forty-eight years old and of middling height, and his hair was beginning to thin.

'*Al-salaam alaykum*, *tafadall* – come in!' said Walid.

We had got to know Walid through his job as general secretary in the Health Ministry. He was out on strike just now, a strike which had its origins in the conflict between Hamas and Fatah. Hamas had full control in all the government ministries in Gaza. However, the Fatah regime on the West Bank had the money, as that was where the direct transmissions of funds from the West were received.

In the late summer of 2008 the Palestinian self-governing authority in Ramallah initiated an unusual form of strike to break Hamas's control of the health services. They called all public employees out on strike. Those who came out on strike still got their pay. Those who refused to come out, lost their pay.

This was hard on the civilian population in Gaza. After a month, all the health personnel were back at their jobs in the hospitals, even though they risked losing their pay. They were not willing to take part in an action whose main effect was to harm the patients. The health authorities in Ramallah would just have to accept that.

But Walid Shaqura was a health administrator, not a doctor. He would not be able to offer any good explanation if he went back to work. So he was still on strike.

The government in Ramallah was continuing to pay all public employees in Gaza, provided they did not work. Hamas gradually took over paying for these positions so that things would get done. The result was that throughout the autumn of 2008 to the spring of 2009, thousands of public

Iftar meal as guests of Walid and Abeer Shaqura in September 2008.

employees were being paid not to work, at the same time as new bureaucrats were being paid by Hamas.

Walid showed us into the living-room, which was comfortably furnished with three sofas and an armchair. There was a young man sitting on one of the sofas.

'Meet Khaled, our eldest daughter's fiancé,' said Walid. 'Jasmin is in the kitchen.'

Jasmin came out from the kitchen, where she was helping her mother, Abeer, to prepare food. She was a good-looking young girl aged about twenty-one. Like the other women in the house, she was wearing a pink shawl over her head.

Jasmin had trained as a secretary at the Islamic University. Now she was engaged to Khaled, and they were planning to get married as soon as better times came. They were obviously in love. Jasmin sat down on the sofa close beside Khaled. He was still a student, continuing to study economics at al-Quds University in Gaza.

We sat down to table at six o'clock. On the table there were traditional Palestinian *meze*, or *muqabbilat*, which are starters consisting of a row of small dishes; there was *hummus* (a kind of dip made from chickpeas), *babaganoush* (a dish made from aubergines and other vegetables), *taboule* (a vegetable salad which includes bulgur wheat, parsley and finely chopped tomato), *falafel*s (deep-fried balls of broad beans and chickpeas) and stacks of the big, round flat-bread, *khobz*.

We made to help ourselves.

'Stop,' said Walid. 'First we must each eat a date. It's the custom at *iftar*.'

Everybody ate a date. Then we got going on the meal. Neither the Israeli blockade nor rising food prices would stop Walid's family from preparing *iftar*.

Abeer and the second eldest daughter, twenty-year-old Nedaa, brought in a big bowl of *sheiriya*, a soup with noodles and minced meat. We ate *khobz* and the various small dishes with it.

Abeer told the children to clear space for the plates of *fatoush*, the salad which is obligatory in Lebanon, Palestine and Jordan during Ramadan.

I asked Nedaa about her career.

She had clear plans. 'I'm studying business administration at al-Azhar University,' she replied.

Walid's son, Mohammed, wanted to be an engineer, while nineteen-year-old Safaa had just begun to study medicine at al-Azhar University.

Walid and Abeer had built up a secure home where all the children had the same ambitions as my children in Norway. They dreamt of a future, despite the Israeli blockade and the crisis between Fatah and Hamas.

The daughters gathered up the soup bowls and brought in the main courses.

There was both *makluba* with meat, tomato and rice cooked in layers, and *mansaf*, which is rice with lamb and almonds.

'Eat up,' Abeer urged us. She was obviously proud of all the lovely food, and with good reason, because it was delicious and we ate far too much. I thought how difficult it must have been to obtain all this food during the blockade.

After dinner Walid brought out an *argeeleh*, an Arab water pipe, which he lit up with tobacco blended with apple and circulated it round the guests.

It is customary for the guests to invite the hosts out after *iftar*.

'Can we invite the whole family out for coffee after dinner?' I asked.

'Yesss!' said the children, as they began to get ready. 'Let's go to the café!'

We all piled into two cars and drove to a café called the Lighthouse, on the edge of the beach looking out towards the Mediterranean Sea. The grown-ups drank coffee and smoked *argeeleh*, the children drank juice.

It was a happy and peaceful Ramadan in Gaza in autumn 2008.

On the street corners outside, people were standing selling black market petrol and food direct from the tunnels. For many families in Gaza, *iftar* was now a lot more sparse than for Walid and his family.

Outside the administration office they were busy setting up the tent for Friday's weekly prayers.

'That must be a tempting target,' I thought.

I went down to Dr Sobhi's office to give interviews on the telephone.

Dr Sobhi came into the office after Friday prayers. I stood up, but he gestured to me to sit down again.

'Just stay seated.'

This was beginning to be a daily ritual. I know that he would allow me to stay sitting at his desk, but I got up whenever he came in, to acknowledge that he was in charge and show that I wasn't taking anything for granted.

Every Friday a temporary prayer tent was erected on the square in front of the emergency department. The hospital's own al-Shifa Mosque had been bombed to pieces on the second day of the attack.

He sat down to read through some documents. Quite soon, Dr Nasser and Dr Spiro arrived. They started discussing the bed shortage.

'The whole of the medical department is full of surgical patients now,' said Dr Sobhi. 'We must move them out of the hospital one way or another. I hope we can evacuate some patients to Egypt tomorrow.'

The assistant brought in plates of rice with a few small pieces of lamb. The meat ration was getting noticeably smaller each day.

'Have lunch with us,' Dr Sobhi invited.

He pushed the few pieces of meat on the plate over towards me. I said that I was full and would just take a little rice, but he wouldn't hear of this.

'You are the guest, you must eat the meat,' he said.

I took one piece of meat and left the rest on the plate. I would soon be leaving Gaza and returning to a country which was overflowing with calories. All our colleagues here must be ravenously hungry, though.

'Mads and I are writing an article for *The Lancet* to tell people about the situation.'

'That's good,' said Dr Sobhi.

'Very good,' said Dr Nasser with interest.

'Is there any overview of how many operations you have done, and what types of injuries have been treated?' I asked.

'We've got the theatre register, which records all the operations,' replied Dr Nasser.

The theatre register is a book where we enter the date, name, diagnosis and operation for every patient. Dr Sobhi phoned his daughter Nashwa and asked her to fetch the theatre register. She was a medical student, working as a volunteer in the emergency department. She appeared with it a few minutes later.

'Yes, here's the list of all the operations that have been done,' said Dr Sobhi.

He turned the pages further. When he came to the date of December 27, there was not a word written.

'That Saturday was a nightmare,' said Dr Nasser. 'We admitted an incredible number of patients, and nobody had time to record anything. I estimate that we carried out at least eighty operations.'

We counted up all the operations. There were 270 operations from December 28 onwards. That is an average of twenty operations per day after the first day, when they estimated a tally of eighty. I took a note of the count. I thought how useful it would have been to have a copy of

Future Palestinian doctors: medical students Nashwa Skaik and Jasmin al-Madhoun from al-Azhar University in Gaza made an important contribution as volunteers at al-Shifa Hospital.

the register, but that was impossible. The theatre suite needed it back immediately.

Dr Sobhi's mobile phone rang.

'That was my wife, Iman,' he said. 'She's a paediatrician and she has finished work now. She's asking if Nashwa would like a lift home.'

'Yes, that would be fine,' said Nashwa.

Nashwa was half way through her studies and appeared to be very able. I reckoned that she could certainly go far as a doctor. But to do that she would have to leave Gaza, at any rate for a while. She would probably travel to Europe for specialist training.

Dr Sobhi's wife arrived a few minutes later. She had the car outside. Nashwa and her mother said goodbye and went home. So normal.

Mads was standing outside the emergency department, talking with Dr Issam. I noticed that Mads had got thinner in the ten days we had been here. He was unshaven, with long stubble. He looked like Dr Issam, who had also grown thinner and had stubble. We'll need to leave soon, I thought. This war is taking its toll on all of us. Mads and I must be relieved by other surgeons and anaesthetists before we have nothing more to give. Dagfinn was here, but as a nurse he couldn't fulfil our role.

Several ambulances arrived a little before seven o'clock.

'Let's go up to theatre,' said Dr Issam.

As usual, we took the stair because the lift was busy. There had been a steady flow of operations all day. A few patients with shrapnel wounds were in the corridor, waiting to be operated.

A young man had been hit by two fragments in the right leg. We immediately set about examining him. One fragment had hit the thigh bone, which was broken at about the middle. The other had struck his leg, but there was no fracture. He also had a big wound in his chest where yet another fragment had gone in. A drain had been inserted into his chest, and his condition was quite stable.

To prepare him for operation on his thigh and his chest we would have to clean the wound on his leg and stop any bleeding. We were concerned that he might bleed under the surgical drapes without us knowing.

The fragment had gone right through his leg, and was stuck fast when we tried to pull it out. I widened the incision to get a better grip. Through the opening we could see into the wound right through the calf muscle. There was no major bleeding and no serious injury. We bandaged the wounds.

Dr Issam and the orthopaedic surgeons began to operate on the fractured femur, screwing in metal pins to mount an external fixation.

Abdul Gafar Zaneen, the thoracic surgeon, came in and invited me to look at the chest wound. We removed the bandages and found a six-centimetre wound which went right into the thoracic cavity. We cleaned it up and removed bits of the rib and dead muscle. I inserted a retractor and pulled the wound open. We saw right in, onto the diaphragm. There was a tear right above the liver. We snipped the ends of the tear to enlarge it, so that we could inspect the liver. There was no injury there. Dr Abdul Gafar sewed up the tear in the diaphragm and closed the musculature and the skin. It was just a small chest wound. The orthopaedic surgeon soon finished the operation on the fractured femur. I looked at the clock. We had taken only forty minutes.

I went out into the corridor. A young man was being wheeled rapidly into the neighbouring theatre. He had a big wound on the inside of his

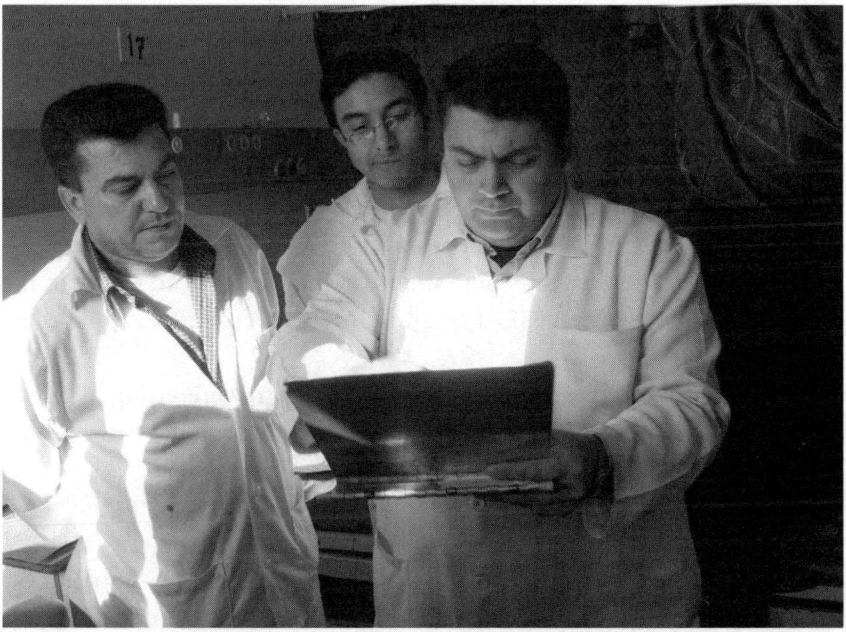

The doctors' rounds were used for deciding which patients could stay, and who had to be evacuated. From the left: charge nurse Yusuf Abu Khalifa, a medical student, Dr Ead Amasi.

left thigh. The vascular surgeon was there already. I looked at the wound; it was big, and the femoral artery had been torn off. Somebody had tied a thin piece of string tightly round the thigh. It was an effective tourniquet, for the wound was not bleeding. We left the tourniquet on while the patient was being anaesthetised and the surgeons were scrubbing up ready to operate. The vascular surgeon didn't need help from me. On the way out of the theatre I met Dr Abdul Gafar.

'Erik, will you come with me to see some patients in intensive care who have chest wounds?'

On the way, we went to the central sterile supplies department. Every big hospital has such a department, where the surgical instruments are washed, packed in boxes or paper and sterilised. A young man stood packing instruments. Abdul Gafar got a pack of instruments. Then we went down together to intensive care to examine a patient with a serious wound in his chest.

We cleaned up the wound, but the patient had low blood pressure and a fever and all the signs of blood poisoning.

'I don't think he'll recover as long as the breastbone is lying exposed and is infected,' I said. 'We can cover it with muscle by freeing muscle from the collar bone and upper arm, but that's a big operation, and there's no certainty that he'll survive.'

'We'll reassess the situation in the morning. We can discuss it then,' said Abdul Gafar.

I thought that we would probably be leaving the next day, and so we would not manage to get this operation done.

Abdul Gafar and I examined another patient, who had an injury to his lung. It was being treated with a chest drain, and everything was in order.

We went back up to theatre. Dr Sobhi and Dr Spiro were sitting in a little office off the corridor with two other surgeons, one of whom was a senior orthopaedic surgeon, Dr Abed Rabbo Abu Hashish.

They were four of the most experienced surgeons in the hospital.

'Hi, Erik, come in and have a seat,' Dr Sobhi called.

'We're talking about how difficult life is here now,' said Dr Sobhi. 'You need to understand, Erik, that none of us are Hamas people. We've all worked as doctors outside Gaza for many years. I worked for three years in Edinburgh and fifteen years in Saudi Arabia. Abed Rabbo lived in Germany for eight years, and Dr Spiro has worked in Ireland for many years. We like Europe, and we have always supported Fatah. But today, during Friday prayers, as we were kneeling under the blue tarpaulin and they were bombing nearby, I thought to myself for the first time: "Just let them drop a bomb now and kill me. My life here in Gaza isn't important any more."'

'Fatah has betrayed us,' said Abed Rabbo in German. 'They're just running Israel's errands. Israel is killing us all.'

'Hamas controls Gaza now, and it is secure,' said Dr Sobhi. 'Erik, you've no idea what it was like here in 2004 and 2005. It was totally lawless. People were exposed to aggravated robberies and didn't dare to go to the police to report it, because then they would be beaten up. It was a dangerous situation. After Hamas won the election and got control, the place became lawful. It's safe for my children to walk in the street now. The crime rate is low. But the West is punishing us. Why couldn't Hamas be given a chance? We could just have voted them out at the next election. The majority voted for them. I could have lived with that.'

That is what the experienced doctors said. It struck me again how little the international reaction to Hamas had been thought through. These doctors did not identify themselves with Hamas socially or culturally,

The village of Abed Rabbo was razed to the ground. Israeli forces used mines to blow up the houses even after they had full control. The blockade hinders rebuilding.

but they were offended by the West's lack of respect for the people's democratic choice.

I felt solidarity with them. We were the same generation of surgeons, and we had all travelled and seen much. We listened to the bomb blasts outside. Every bomb strike tore their lives to pieces a little further. Perhaps it was like that for me too.

I thought that this was probably the last evening we would have together before Mads and I had to leave, and I was touched by the mutual trust and the good friendship we had enjoyed.

13

13

Distress by Design

MADS GILBERT

The Palestinians' freedom of movement and employment opportunities had been progressively constricted for years, before the aggressive blockade of the previous three years made their situation even worse.[101] Soon after Hamas won the election in January 2006, the Israelis and the international community started a punitive campaign not only against Hamas but against the entire population in the occupied territories. Israel blocked all flow of funds, remittance of taxes and passage of donations to the Palestinian self-governing authority. As a consequence of this, 160,000 Palestinian public employees received no salary payments from the beginning of March 2006, and the already badly weakened Palestinian economy collapsed.[102] Between June and August 2007, nearly 75,000 jobs were lost from small businesses which had to close because of the blockade. The unemployment level reached 70 per cent, and 1.1 million of the 1.5 million Palestinians in Gaza became totally dependent on UN aid to survive. In September 2008 a report by the World Bank described the economic situation in Gaza in stark figures: altogether 105,000 Palestinian workers had lost their jobs between 2005 and June 2008, and only 860 still had jobs in the few industrial companies in Gaza which were continuing in business. A massive 98 per cent of industrial enterprises in Gaza had either closed down completely or suspended operation as a result of shortage of raw materials, loss of exports or other insurmountable difficulties created by the blockade.[103]

The economic effects of the Israeli blockade were so damaging to business life and to society that the World Bank considered that even if the blockade was lifted, it was doubtful if the many affected businesses and institutions would be able to recover. According to the World Bank's analysis, the damaging effects of the Israeli blockade on Palestinian productivity, social economy and freedom of movement could scarcely be over-estimated.[104]

The blockade of Gaza compelled the UN to suspend big projects for which some £70 million of finance was already in place. Most of these projects were for the building of schools, houses and sewerage systems. These projects had given employment to 121,000 Palestinians in Gaza. As a result, unemployment and poverty increased even more.

Poverty is severe and widespread in Gaza. Already in 2007, 80 per cent of the inhabitants were having to survive on less than two US dollars per day. In the late autumn of 2008, the World Bank reported that the average family in Gaza now had 40 per cent lower income than before the blockade. In order to survive during this economic crisis, families have had to make big reductions in consumption, and sell their valuables and jewellery. They have had to delay repayments on loans and any new loans have had to be from family and friends, because the cash flow to Palestinian banks is also blocked.

All reserves have been used up, and all solutions tried. When the warehouses are empty and the shops lack nearly everything, from baby food to milk powder, cooking oil and medicines, families often end up having to survive on tea and bread. So long as there is bread to be found.

The blockade has affected all aspects of community life in Gaza. Freedom of movement has been made impossible within the high enclosing walls. The Palestinians are surrounded by continuous, double lines of barbed wire fences enclosing dangerous minefields, with watch-towers placed at carefully planned intervals. People are unable to leave Gaza, either to Israel through the border post at Erez in the north or to Egypt through the southern border post at Rafah. They can only move around in a prison of 360 square kilometres within the Israeli walls. The great majority of Palestinians in Gaza do not have identity cards, valid travel documents, citizenship or a passport. Workers can no longer travel to work in Israel, and fishermen from Gaza risk their lives if they go beyond the new boundary imposed by Israel in 2009, just three nautical miles from the coast. If they do, they will soon be shot at by Israeli naval vessels.

Agriculture and fishing have been important, even if sparse, sources of income, which at the same time have made ongoing contributions to the Palestinian larders in Gaza. 20,000 families in Gaza live off agriculture; this represents 12 per cent of the population.[105] Prior to the year 2000, Gaza had 10,000 people actively engaged in fishing, and the Palestinian fisheries were providing valuable fish protein to a hungry population.[106]

In 2008, fishing accounted for 1.5 per cent of Gaza's economy and

Already in 2008, the fish market in Gaza City had very little to offer, because of the blockade and a dramatic Israeli reduction of Gaza's fishing limits.

agriculture for 8.5 per cent, according to the Ministry of Agriculture in Gaza. Both agriculture and fishing had already declined sharply as a result of the blockade, even before Operation Cast Lead started on December 27, 2008. Gaza had already been brought to its knees economically, and nutrition and health were already failing.

During my two tours of duty in Gaza in 2008, I saw many examples of the pervasive effects the blockade was having on the daily lives of the Palestinians.

'There are hardly any fish to be had, and those we can get hold of are terribly dear,' said Dr Khalil, my good friend for fifteen years, when we visited the fish market in Gaza City one sunny Saturday morning in March 2008. The fish market was right beside the sea, and many exotic sea-food delicacies were on offer. There was a fresh smell of fish and shellfish, but quantities were small and prices were so high that only the most well-off people could afford them.

'They're taking away our food supplies and we're losing the capacity to be self-supporting,' he continued. 'They're increasing restrictions for our fishermen, and there are increasing shortages of fuel and gear.'

'Surely fishing is an important source of protein for the population?'

'Obviously. And we could have developed our fisheries a lot more, if we had had our rightful access to the sea.'

Khalil liked the sea, and he was a good cook.

'Let's buy some fish, and I'll prepare genuine Palestinian seafood for you for dinner this evening.'

'Wonderful! I'll enjoy that. And you shall have cod cooked with the roe and the liver when you come to Tromsø one day. We call it *skreimølja*. Perhaps we should set up some fishery development projects between the twin cities of Tromsø and Gaza? We both have a coast and we could co-operate on fisheries just as we work together on health and ambulance services.'

We grinned. He put his arm round my shoulders.

'One day, Mads, one day when we have got peace and an independent free Palestine, we shall sit together on the white sandy beach down there. We shall look out over the sea, watching the youngsters playing happily without stress, without anxiety, without bombs.'

He looked at me.

'Inshallah,' I replied.

'Inshallah.'

His gaze was steady, and I sensed in his eyes the heavy, exhausting hopelessness I more and more often thought I could see in colleagues and friends after all these years of the increasingly deteriorating situation in Gaza. Increasingly difficult living conditions, increasing concerns for the children and decreasing belief in the future.

We were going on a rare visit to friends in the south of Gaza, but I had insisted on seeing the fish market before we set off.

Pleasure trips are a very welcome diversion for Palestinian families, and the children were excited. We drove southwards along the coast, with the car windows open and a fresh sea breeze filling the car.

'This must be the first time we have gone on a trip together outside Gaza City with the whole family,' I commented to Suzan, Khalil's wife, who was sitting with the children on the back seat.

'You know, Mads, we don't often have the opportunity, with the security situation and the shortage of fuel and our pressure of work.'

She looked at me from behind rather uncommonly large sunglasses. We were on a Sunday outing, we were off duty, the sun was shining, the children were happy and we were on our way to lunch with Aiman and his family in Deir al-Balah, 'Date Grove'. I thought about how in Norway we take all our moments of pleasure, our leisure time, outings, rights and recreation as a matter of course. We take it all for granted.

Fishing has always been a very important activity for the people of the Palestinian 'coastal state' of Gaza. The sea has given rich rewards to the fishing industry and as a source of food for the population. 'Today there are about 3,500 fishermen in Gaza,' as Mohammed Agah, the Fisheries Minister in Gaza, said to the newsletter published by the UN's Office for the Co-ordination of Humanitarian Affairs (OCHA).[107] 'The main obstacle for fishermen before the war was the lack of fuel, but now they are having greater difficulties.'

As Hassan Azman, the head of the Gazan fishing authority, explained in the same publication, since the latest war, the Israelis have even cut down the number of times each boat can go out fishing to ten per month, compared with the previous limit of eighty times per month. A fisherman needs more than this to make a living.

In 2008 the Palestinian fishing fleet in Gaza landed 250 tonnes of fish each month, which amounts to 3,000 tonnes per year. The population of Gaza needs 20,000 tonnes of fish each year to meet its protein requirements. In February 2009, only sixty-five tonnes of fish were landed in Gaza. The people's protein intake is at least 50 per cent less in Gaza than in other Arab countries. The diet is now so deficient that it is threatening children's health and development.[108]

Of the 450 Palestinian fishing boats in Gaza, eighty-five are big vessels. From 1993 to 2000, the Palestinians were able to fish relatively unhindered in the sea off their forty-five kilometre length of coast, but in 2000 the Israelis unilaterally set the fishing boundary at six nautical miles (eleven kilometres) off the coast. Under the Oslo Accords, Gaza's fishing limit should really be twenty nautical miles (thirty-seven kilometres). During Operation Cast Lead, the whole of Gaza's coast was totally blockaded by Israeli naval vessels. After the assaults in January 2009, the Israeli navy took it upon itself to restrict the freedom of movement of the Palestinian fishermen even more, and the boundary was further narrowed. Now, Palestinian fishermen risk deadly fire from Israeli warships if they venture more than three nautical miles (5.6 kilometres) out from their own coast.

The United Nations Convention on the Law of the Sea of 1982 laid an important foundation in international law for the introduction of 200 nautical mile economic zones for coastal states. Within its own economic zone, each coastal state has sovereign rights to use of the resources in the sea and on the sea floor. Coastal states also have additional sovereign right within twelve nautical miles from the coastline. Occupied Palestine is a coastal state, and international law should obviously give Gaza rights to an economic zone of 200 nautical miles and sovereign right over their own territorial waters within twelve nautical miles, not just the three nautical miles which Israel has now implemented unilaterally. Do the Israelis think that there is a special sea law for them, overriding international legal rights? Israel has tried to justify its unilateral constriction of Palestinian territorial waters with its usual 'political security' arguments: 'The sea route could be used to smuggle weapons and ammunition to Gaza.' It is part of the story that the Palestinian Navy does not represent a particularly serious threat to Israel, as it does not exist. But Israel may have other and more important reasons than sardine fishing and weapon smuggling to overturn international law in this area.

In 1999 a British company, the British Gas Group (BGG), discovered big reserves of natural gas under the sea bed between ten and fifteen nautical miles off the coast of Gaza. These newly discovered deposits were named Gaza Marine 1 and 2. The 60 per cent of the field which lay within the area of Palestinian jurisdiction, was estimated to contain about 1.3 trillion (1.3 million billions) of cubic feet of natural gas. This amount of gas is equivalent to 150 million barrels of crude oil, with a value of almost 4,000 million US dollars.[109]

In May 2007 BGG, Israel and the Palestinian self-governing authority very nearly reached a long-term agreement to supply gas from this field to Israel over fifteen years, to a value of almost 4,000 million dollars, but the negotiations failed.[110] Six years earlier, Ariel Sharon had said that they would never buy gas from the Palestinian self-governing authority. The Israeli Supreme Court would also decide the legal status of the territorial waters off Gaza. BGG had already been on the point of signing a gas contract with Egypt instead of with Israel in 2006, but Tony Blair intervened and pushed forward new negotiations with the Israelis. By this agreement, the Palestinian authorities would make a profit of approximately 1,000 million dollars. During the negotiations about an under-sea gas pipeline to the town of Ashkelon in Israel, the Israelis nevertheless put forward a request that the payment to the Palestinians should be in goods and services, not in cash, and that there should be no benefit to Hamas.[111]

Gaza is completely locked in behind Israeli barbed wire, concrete walls, watch-towers and minefields. The border post at Erez is the only place where people can move in and out from Israel.

The end of the road was therefore that the negotiations between BGG and Israel broke down, allegedly because the chief of Mossad, Meir Dagan, and influential Israeli military strategists thought that such an agreement could finance terrorist activity not just in Hamas, but also in al-Qaeda. They described any Palestinian offshore gas installation as 'a magnet for global Jihad.'[112] In December 2007, BGG withdrew from all negotiations with the Israeli government and closed its offices in Israel.[113] The explanation for all that has happened since 2000 may be that the coastal waters off Gaza hide big, profitable gas fields, and may also contain oil.

Several analysts have maintained that Operation Cast Lead was really about Israel's need for energy and her ambitions to take over full control of the Palestinian gas fields. The fields are thought to contain much more than the 1.3 trillion cubic feet of gas which has already been found.[114]

Less than a year after the big gas finds on the Palestinian continental shelf, Israeli warships began attacking Palestinian fishing boats which sailed beyond six nautical miles from Gaza's coast. Since then, fifteen fishermen have been killed and over 200 wounded in attacks by Israeli naval vessels. During and after Operation Cast Lead, more fishermen have been attacked, injured and killed – but now after having passed beyond just three nautical miles. Are Israel and the USA wanting to get their claws on the Palestinian gas reserves? Could Gaza become another Dubai, distributing gas and oil to large parts of the western Arab Peninsula in addition to becoming self-sufficient in energy by building gas-powered electricity generating stations? If the Israelis have geopolitical and energy-political ambitions, it will undoubtedly be strategically important to them to take military control over the Palestinian continental shelf and rob the Palestinian territorial waters. This would clearly be an illegal occupation, this time not of Palestinian land and airspace, but of Palestinian waters.

However, the problem for the Gaza fishermen is not just the constantly narrowing fishing limits. The blockade has also made it impossible to obtain spare parts for the engines, new nets, hooks, gas and gas lanterns for night fishing, and fuel for the boats. In Rafah in the far south of Gaza, fishing has stopped completely because the Israeli armed forces systematically destroyed fishing boats, nets and ropes in the course of the twenty-two days and nights of the attacks. In this way, a hungry population immediately lost an important source of self-sufficiency, income and protein-rich food.

Norway, itself a fishing nation, has not been particularly vociferous in its protests. Norway, as a coastal state, would obviously never allow a foreign power to diminish our sovereign right over our own 200 nautical mile economic zone, move our fishing boundary or take from us our right to the oil and gas reserves on the Norwegian shelf.

'We can't catch healthy big fish within three nautical miles; it's impossible,' says an old Gaza fisherman, Mohammed al-Hisi. 'From April 2009 there will be Egyptian and Israeli fishing boats catching fish beyond three nautical miles, and they will reduce our catches. The sardine season has now started, but we're can't catch sardines either.'

Since the last war, nine Palestinian fishermen have been wounded by shots from Israeli naval vessels.[115]

It's difficult to imagine the claustrophobic feeling which pervades Gaza, unless you have lived there or experienced the situation at close quarters. 1.5 million people who have neither train, plane or bus connections with the world around, and no roads to drive out freely to the neighbouring countries.

Air traffic came to a halt almost before it had started, when the Israelis bombed Gaza's new airport which had been built as a direct result of the Oslo Accords. The brand new airport opened on November 24, 1998 and was named Yasser Arafat International Airport. Both Arafat and President Bill Clinton were present at the opening. The project cost around 600 million dollars, and was financed jointly by Japan, Egypt, Saudi Arabia, Spain and Germany.

The opening of the airport in Gaza and the setting up of Palestine's own airline, Palestinian Airlines, were both seen as important steps on the road towards Palestinian statehood. The richly decorated main terminal building, built as a copy of Casablanca Airport, occupied 4,000 square metres and had 400 employees. The airport was open round the clock, and flight traffic was busy from the very first day. It immediately became important for the significant export of Gaza's fresh flowers and strawberries.

But soon after the start of the Second Intifada, the 'al-Aqsa Intifada', the Israeli authorities closed the airport, and on October 7, 2000 the story of Palestinian air travel came to an end. In 2001 the airport's radar system was destroyed in an Israeli air attack, and in 2002 the runways were torn up by military bulldozers. As late as August 2007, Israeli helicopters bombed the control tower to make quite sure that this delicate symbol of Palestinian statehood had been crushed under the iron heel.

On September 19, 2007, the Israeli Security Cabinet declared Gaza to be a 'hostile entity'. Israel maintained that this definition gave them the right to carry out various punitive measures against the population of Gaza, including restriction of the supplies of electricity and fuel. This was to be their answer to the firing of Qassam rockets from Gaza into Israel. Several Palestinian and Israeli human rights organisations appealed against this decision in the Israeli Supreme Court in October the same year. They argued that the punitive actions and the blockade would lead to widespread damage and loss of human life. The Israeli Supreme Court responded in January 2008 by turning down the appeal, and thereby at the same time gave the green light for the punitive actions against the population of Gaza.

It is difficult to see the blockade as anything other than a brutal and illegal action against a whole people, whose fault – seen through Israeli eyes – was that they didn't accept the continuing Israeli occupation, and that they were so rebellious as to elect leaders and a political party (Hamas) who are committed and ready to continue the struggle against the Israeli occupation.

Another, more cynical purpose probably lies behind the long-standing blockade of Gaza: to put such extreme pressure on the Palestinian people that they come to a point where their own internal disagreements break out into civil war.

But whatever the Israelis' intentions have really been, there is no doubt that the blockade has hit the people of Palestine very hard. The effects on the inhabitants have been ruinous. They have had to survive with less than a quarter of the volume of goods which were imported in December 2005, and sometimes even less. This has led to critical shortages of a long list of goods. Everything from paint and nails to concrete, reinforcing rods, roof gutters, water pipes and window panes has been stopped by the Israelis at the boundary crossings.

Only a few basic 'humanitarian goods' such as some food and some medicines have been brought in through the Israeli barrier posts. No exports have gone out, something which has obviously paralysed the Palestinian economy in Gaza. I saw the disastrous consequences of the blockade during my visits to Gaza in March and October 2008. Poverty was rapidly increasing. My close friends, who belong to the Palestinian middle class and have relatively well paid jobs in the Palestinian Health Service, were also struggling.

'We borrow money, we sell jewellery. Everybody helps each other, both within families and among friends, but the situation is very difficult,' explained another of my closest friends and colleagues, Dr Nafez, in October 2008 when I was last in Gaza.

'We get by. It's worse for the people who are really poor, and for the unemployed. Many of them are living from hand to mouth, and many of them are starving. There's not much food in the market, and the prices keep going up and up. It's almost impossible to get meat. The ration of protein for the population of Gaza is minimal, and you know the consequences of that. Many people are anaemic because they're not getting enough iron in their diet.'

Nafez looked at me and laughed.

'What can we do? We just have to keep up the struggle and survive. Perhaps we'll all end up eating grass? I won't leave Gaza and my family. I can't abandon my people. I was born here, grew up in Beach Camp, and

Gaza lacks everything. The blockade has for years forcibly denied 1.5 million Palestinian men, women and children their most basic human rights.

my whole life is here. I love Gaza, but I hate it that things are so unbearably difficult for us just now. Believe me, Mads – we don't deserve this.'

'Yes, what can we do?' I answered and smiled back. Giving up was not an option for any of us.

Israel has never specified what they will not allow in to Gaza, or what criteria they follow. No one day is like another. This obviously makes planning impossible, not only for those who have built up enterprising local small businesses and agriculture, but also for the whole of the public sector, with its essential functions of securing energy, water and food supplies for 1.5 million people. The public authorities also have responsibility for maintaining the sewerage systems and the rubbish collection, and seeing that education and health services have the supplies they need in order to function. Shortages of fuel and of spare parts hit all these public sectors very quickly.

During my visits to Gaza in 2008, I had long discussions with the Mayor of Gaza City, Dr Maged Abu Ramadan. He is an ophthalmologist, and used to be the international contact person in the Health Ministry when Fatah was in power in Gaza. He now runs a private practice in Gaza City, and has set up laser surgery. Dr Maged is well aware of the many damaging effects the Israeli blockade has had on the daily lives of Palestinians in Gaza. In 2008 he described the blockade as 'very destructive'.

'We have to negotiate about everything. From fuel for the rubbish lorries to free passage for seriously ill patients who have to go to Israel for essential medical treatment. The blockade is strangling Gaza and has made life very difficult for us.'

We drank sweet Palestinian mint tea in one of the few cafés which was open in Gaza City. The café is right opposite the Red Crescent Hospital and is called 'Happyland'.

'But, as you know, we Palestinians have been living in hard times for so long now that we are used to living on the edge.'

The World Food Programme, WFP, had already documented in a comprehensive report in 2003 that food security was seriously threatened in Gaza and on the West Bank. The report emphasised that in order to prevent malnutrition and under-nutrition, access to food would need to be improved by social and economic development and by restoration of damaged infrastructure in the occupied territories.[116]

Since June 2007, raw materials have not been getting into Gaza. Over 90 per cent of businesses have been forced to close. The building industry is totally paralysed. More than 3,500 companies have had to close, and over 75,000 employees have lost their jobs; workers who in turn maintained over half a million of Gaza's other inhabitants.[117] The aid organisations have discovered that the Israeli definition of 'humanitarian supplies' on the whole falls into four groups of goods: food for humans, food for livestock, groceries and medicines.

There was not a lot of food in Gaza.

The blockade had emptied Gaza's natural sources of self-sufficiency, which were already few and sparse. On top of this the UN's food warehouses became empty, all as a result of the blockade.

In our sleeping quarters at al-Shifa, the fridge and the shelf in the little kitchen were almost empty of food. We noticed that our Palestinian hosts could no longer offer up the delicacies to which we as guests were usually treated. The shortage of food was tangible, and even though the hospital's main kitchen did its best, there was less food with every day that passed.

'No more chicken to be had. No bread left in Gaza now. Soon there won't be any more vegetables. Just tomatoes, which are so dear that nobody can afford them.'

Our cook gave an embarrassed smile and stretched out his arms as he showed me that the freezer was empty too.

Palestinian cuisine is tasty, varied and inviting. Food is made up from a wide choice of meat, fish and vegetable dishes well seasoned with all sorts of exotic spices. A guest invited to a meal will enjoy a mouth-watering variety of flavours. Gaza has its own food traditions, worthy of a very ancient culture situated at the meeting point of Asia, Africa, Europe and Arabia. On previous visits, our Palestinian friends had always invited us to share good and plentiful food, no matter what the situation. Things were different now.

I had never been unable to get eggs or chicken meat in Gaza. Our hosts were obviously doing all they could to obtain sufficient and varied food for us, but however hard our hosts tried, the larder was empty and remained empty. For the first few days there was an egg for breakfast and a little cheese, with plenty cucumber and tomato. Now there were just olives.

During our last few days in Gaza we were sustained by emergency rations from the World Food Programme: 'high energy biscuits' in little blue packets were dealt out to the staff in the hospital for breakfast and as an evening meal. There was no more bread; there might be a tomato or a few olives. The only hot meal of the day was lunch. At first this consisted of a little piece of boiled mutton or a chicken thigh and possibly a few vegetables. For the last few days, lunch has just been a plate of boiled rice.

I wondered what the food situation must be like now for the Palestinians in their own homes in Gaza.

'It's very, very difficult. People are unemployed and so they don't have any money. The food shortage is critical. Just look at the prices in the market: Before the war you could get five kilos of tomatoes for one Israeli shekel. Now, one kilo costs five shekels. Nobody can afford that!'

The doctors in the duty room were dejected and despairing, but not so much for their own situation.

'We doctors always get by. But for poor families with children it's hunger, hunger, hunger. People stand in a queue for six hours in the hope of getting a little bread. There's no meat to be had, and even water is beginning to be in short supply. In my house we only have enough water for three more days.'

The Israeli blockade and isolation of Gaza has had particularly serious consequences for the very youngest members of society. The blockade has led to a rapid rise of chronic under-nutrition among children in Gaza. The head of the Ard al-Insan Child Nutrition Centre in Gaza, Dr Adnan al-Wahaidi, has reported an alarming prevalence of under-nutrition among children. The centre only takes in under-nourished children below the age of five. In 2008 they treated almost 8,500 under-nourished infants from northern Gaza, while 8,000 were treated at a similar centre in Rafah in the south. Altogether, almost 17,000 under-nourished children in Gaza were given nutritional supplements and followed up in 2008.[118]

'We receive twenty to twenty-five new referrals every day, and see approximately 350 [under-nourished] a week here at the centre. [...] All of [the 8,400 children we saw here last year and the 8,000 at our centre in Khan Younis] were under five years old, and all of them were under-nourished. Our target group is children suffering second- and third-degree malnutrition,' explains Najah Zuhoud, who runs the nutrition programme at the centre.

'We weigh every child who comes here, and take blood and urine samples. Approximately half the children are mildly malnourished. But 33 per cent are suffering second-degree malnutrition – and the remaining 16 per cent are third-degree malnourished.' The children with second- and third-degree under-nutrition are referred to the nutrition unit. 'We give the children nutritious meals here at the centre, and also train mothers to feed their children a healthy balanced diet. We usually serve the children fresh meat, fruit and vegetables. But this week we cannot serve the children any fruit at all, because of the closure.'

The studies done by Dr al-Wahaidi and his colleagues have shown that there is a big increase in the proportion of children under three years of age who are under-nourished, and the total number of children who are under-nourished is higher than ever, at 10.4 per cent. Ten years ago, the percentage of children who were under-nourished was less than half of that. There has also been a serious increase in growth retardation as a result of chronic under-nutrition.[119]

One of the biggest nutritional problems in Gaza is that there are not enough natural food sources. It is not possible to cultivate the necessary variety of fruit and vegetables which is required to offer children a well balanced diet. Gaza is totally dependent on imported food, but the choice of food on the counter is very limited, especially following the attack. Tens of thousands of families in Gaza have no other means of survival

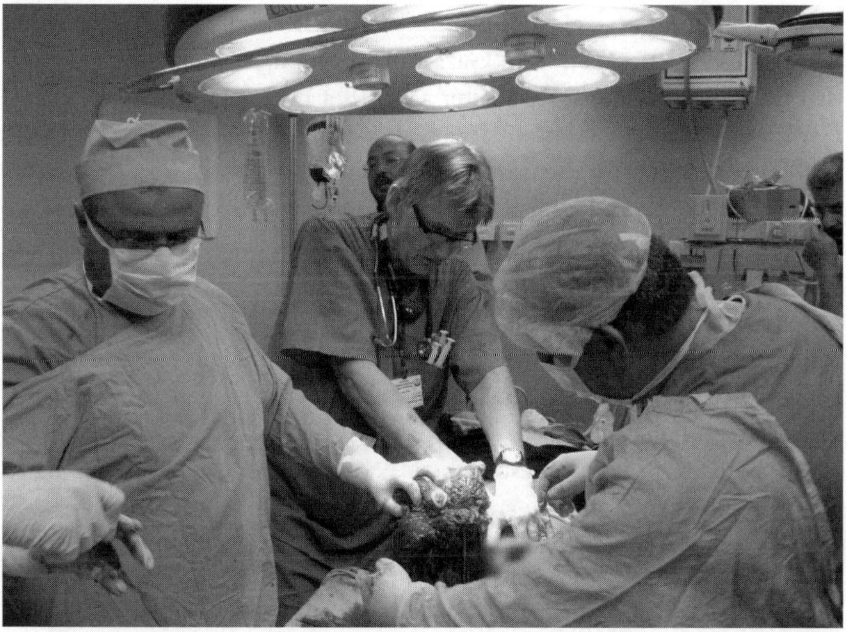

In the first two weeks of the war, more than fifty major amputations were performed at al-Shifa.

than humanitarian aid. 'If the Israeli siege continues, the extra nutrition provided by the centre will not be enough for the children in Gaza. Then both the sickness rate and the mortality rate among children will increase, and we won't be able to keep on top of the situation,' says Dr al-Wahaidi.

Under-nutrition in Gaza is the result not of some unforeseeable natural catastrophe but of a deliberate policy. In the same way as many thousands are being injured and killed by the Israeli military weapons, Palestinians are being injured and killed as a result of the restrictions Israel has inflicted on the civilian population in Gaza. The blockade and all the restrictions of movement have together led to an increasing insecurity of food supply for the great majority of the population in Gaza. In November 2008 the United Nations High Commissioner for Human Rights, the South African judge, Navi Pillay, called for an immediate lifting of the Israeli blockade of Gaza.

'By function of this blockade, 1.5 million Palestinian men, women and children have been forcibly deprived of their most basic human rights for months. This is in direct contravention of international human rights and humanitarian law. It must end now,' she said.[120]

The UN called on Israel to allow immediately the transport in of essential supplies for the population in Gaza, such as food, medicines and fuel, so that the supply of electricity, water and other necessary services could be restored. The High Commissioner also called for free passage for the civilian population for medical, educational and religious purposes.

'Decisive steps must be taken to preserve the dignity and the basic welfare of the civilian population, more than half of which are children,' Pillay added.

'Only a full lifting of the blockade followed by a strong humanitarian response will be adequate to relieve the massive humanitarian suffering evident in Gaza today,' claimed the UN on November 18, 2008, five weeks *before* the bombing of Gaza started.

But both Pillay and the rest of the UN organisation were still talking to deaf ears. By July 2008 the strangulation of Gaza was almost complete. Throughout November the boundary crossings were only open for five days in all. On December 4, 2008 some supplies got through. The food was not put into storage, but went direct to UNRWA's food distribution centres.[121] The following day, the BBC reported that the UN's food warehouses in Gaza were empty. The head of UNRWA, John Ging, confirmed that the population of Gaza was hungry.

'Daily life is a struggle to survive. People were hungry, literally. There was a shortage of everything here, including food, and we actually ran out for a couple of days. The fact that it continues to get worse and worse adds to the despair… so we're searching desperately for reasons to have realistic hope,' he said to the BBC.[122]

We saw several pregnant women with life-threatening and fatal injuries in al-Shifa. The pregnant and the newborn are obviously an especially vulnerable group in times of war. Lack of access to critically important antenatal checks, help at the time of birth and other necessary health services can mean the difference between life and death for the pregnant woman and obviously for the foetus or the newborn infant. The situation was difficult for pregnant women even before Operation Cast Lead started. It could only get worse.

According to the UN Population Fund, UNFPA, there are at all times more than 40,000 pregnant women in Gaza, and 170 women give birth every day.[123] In normal circumstances, about thirty Caesarian sections are performed each day. The Israeli attack made it impossible for most pregnant women to come to hospital, and many had to give birth at home or in the hiding places in which they had sought refuge from the bombing.

Even those who managed to reach the hospital were in danger, because the hospitals were over-populated with war casualties and many labour wards had been converted into surgical units. Stress, trauma and under-nutrition also cause life-threatening complications for Gaza's pregnant women. UNFPA also referred to reports of premature labour and births as a result of shock and trauma from the constant bombing, and of newborn babies becoming hypothermic because of the shortage of electricity and blankets.[124] Nobody knows for sure how many extra stillbirths, abortions and birth complications occurred because of the war.

It is difficult to see the systematic and politically controlled blockade of Gaza as anything other than a conscious attempt to starve out the population of Gaza and force them either to surrender or to overthrow their own politically elected leaders – Hamas. Such a policy would undoubtedly have been called state terrorism if another regime had done this to a whole ethnic group. State terrorism can be defined as terrorism carried out or supported by a government. Like terrorism generally, state terrorism includes deliberate attacks on civilians with the intention of causing fear or humiliation and putting them under compulsion in order to achieve a political or religious goal.[125] The term 'state terrorism' is rather more loosely defined as 1) threatening to use force; 2) a political goal and a wish to change the status quo; 3) spreading fear through spectacular actions; 4) deliberate actions with the purpose of harming civilians. Both the USA and Israel are accused of such state terrorism.[126]

Israeli and US foreign politicians define the debilitating blockade and the direct military attacks on Gaza as 'self-defence', whereas the Palestinian rockets which are fired from Gaza into Israel are defined as 'terrorism' by the same Israel-USA alliance. The Palestinians reply that they are defending themselves as well as they can from the Israeli attacks.

When the BBC interviewed the central Hamas leader and surgeon Mahmoud Zahar in Gaza in the first days of December 2008, he again underlined that 'the prospect of peace is in Israel's hands': 'Peace depends on Israel. If they do what we have already agreed they should do, there will be peace. They must stop all aggression against the Palestinian people and open all the border crossings to Gaza for free passage of commerce.

We have to defend ourselves against the Israeli aggression by all means available to us, as we are accustomed to doing.'

Palestinians see the blockade of Gaza as an act of war with ruinous consequences for all parts of society and all aspects of Palestinian daily life. The Israeli blockade does not hit a single political party or a single armed resistance group, but acts as a collective punishment.

194 nations have ratified the Fourth Geneva Convention of 1949 (GCIV), which includes the protection of civilian populations when they are a defeated 'enemy' or are 'in enemy hands,' as when a foreign power occupies a country. According to the convention, no individual person can be punished or persecuted for an action that he or she has not personally committed.

Israel ratified the convention in December 1949, with minimal reservations. Among other things, they wanted to use the Star of David as a symbol, instead of a red cross.[127] The International Committee of the Red Cross has highlighted that states which are in conflict not uncommonly use humiliating methods to terrorise the civilian population, in order to impede enemy actions. Such inhumane methods strike the guilty and the innocent alike and are contrary to natural justice. Additional Protocol II from 1977 explicitly forbids collective punishment, but few states have ratified the supplementary protocol.[128]

According to international law the blockade of Gaza is a collective punishment, but nobody is prosecuting Israel and its political leaders. The same applies to the establishment of colonies with their own population in occupied territories. The Israeli colonies on the West Bank are also clearly in conflict with the Fourth Geneva Convention.

Israel has broken twenty-eight Security Council resolutions. Such resolutions are binding on all member states. Israel has broken almost a hundred resolutions of the UN's General Assembly. Such resolutions are not binding, but must be regarded as the will of the international community. Israel is also breaking the spectacularly strong verdict of the International Court of Justice (ICJ) in The Hague in 2004. The panel of judges decided on a vote of fourteen against one that the wall Israel has erected right across the whole of the West Bank is contrary to international law. The judges called on the UN General Assembly and the Security Council to find measures 'to bring this illegal situation to an end.'

14

14

Changing the Guard

ERIK FOSSE

Ratatatatatatatata! I recognised the sound of machine guns. It was Saturday January 10 and the first time that I woke to that sound. It rose up above the usual noises of the drones, the helicopters, the gunboat rockets and the bomb blasts. It sounded as if all the instruments of the orchestra were playing the Symphony of Destiny with full force.

We are surrounded, I thought. The war is coming closer. We may not get out until the attack is over. Israeli soldiers might get right up to the hospital.

They were not far away, and yet I felt indifferent.

The Israeli ground invasion had split Gaza in two at Netzarim; nobody could travel between Rafah and Gaza without permission from the Israeli authorities. Mads and I had planned to leave on Thursday January 8. On the morning of Wednesday January 7, I received a telephone call from John Eivind in El Arish, who had been called by Tor Wennesland, the Envoy at the Norwegian Representative Office in Ramallah.

'Wennesland says that Israel is going to let the International Committee of the Red Cross send out a convoy of patients today. Wennesland strongly recommends that you and Mads join this convoy. He has cleared things with the Israeli authorities so that you can get out. I think you should go now, because Dagfinn has got there and the Red Cross team is in position.'

It was clear that John Eivind wished for Mads and I to get out now. I was inclined to follow his counsel even if it was a day earlier than planned. The only concern I had was that Dagfinn had barely spent a day at the hospital and we had not introduced him properly to everyone. He would be the only NORWAC representative at the hospital until the surgical team was in place at the end of the week.

I got hold of Mads and Dagfinn, and we had a meeting in our room.

'John Eivind wants us to leave with a convoy today,' I said.

Dagfinn fell silent. Mads turned pale and serious.

'I'm not going. I can't leave the Palestinians now.'

'Yes, but the Red Cross team has come in now with both a surgeon and an anaesthetist,' I said. 'Besides, there are more teams of doctors on their way.'

'But we know the Red Cross team won't take over our reporting work,' Mads said. 'They aren't going to speak to a single newspaper. What's more we haven't had a reasonable overlap with Dagfinn.'

'No, that's right,' I replied. 'Dagfinn, how would you feel if we left today?'

'I'll manage fine.'

But he did not appear particularly convincing.

'We should have a conference call with John Eivind,' I suggested.

This was a serious situation. I could not leave without Mads.

John Eivind called and insisted that we should leave with that day's convoy. Mads said that it was out of the question for him to leave. The situation reached a deadlock, and I asked John Eivind to call again in half an hour.

In the discussion that followed, Mads said that he did not want to let down the Palestinians. He wanted a longer overlap with Dagfinn, and he would have preferred a NORWAC team of surgeons and anaesthetist to come before we left Gaza. The new team was coming to Egypt on Thursday and would be in Gaza on Saturday at the earliest. I could see that Mads was not going to budge, and I thought that there would surely be more convoys arranged over the coming days, so I supported Mads' wish not to leave on Wednesday, but we agreed to leave with the next convoy. By then Dagfinn would be better known at the hospital, and the new team would be just about to arrive. John Eivind did not like our suggestion, and he thought that I was encroaching on his role as co-ordinator. He was worried about our safety and wanted us to get out, but I had no choice. This was a situation in which Dagfinn, Mads and I had to be in agreement. John Eivind was, however, quite right that he had the responsibility and, formally, it would have been right to abide by his orders.

After our departure was prevented on Thursday, I spoke with Tor Wennesland in Ramallah. On Friday, he presented his own plan to get us out of Gaza.

'I've spoken with the Israeli authorities, and after some discussion, they have agreed to let you come out via Erez and through Israel. They're probably quite eager for you to leave the area.'

'Yes, but how will we get to Erez in one piece?' I asked. 'After all, we'd have to go straight through the front line and the most exposed parts of Gaza. There's no guarantee that we won't be hit by a bomb.'

'I'm getting the UN to transport you out in armoured cars,' replied Wennesland. 'Then we'll have to drive you to Ben Gurion in the Ambassador's car and escort you to your flight.'

'OK, but I think we'll try to leave through Rafah.'

The prospect of leaving via Israel was not an especially attractive one. We had to reckon that Israeli soldiers would go through all the material we had, and we feared that they would confiscate it. After having borne witness to all the outrage and breaches of international law over the last two weeks in Gaza, it was hardly pleasant to have to leave at the mercy of murderers. I quite simply did not want to see a single Israeli soldier for the time being.

I spoke on the telephone with my partner, Nina, and with my children, Hilde and Eivind, on Friday evening and reassured them. They were all worried because we had not been able to get out on Thursday. I told them that we still felt safe at the hospital, and that we would not try to leave unless both the Red Cross and the Norwegian authorities thought it was safe. Deep inside, I knew that nobody was safe anywhere in Gaza, but the risk was probably lowest inside the hospital walls.

At the same time, the situation was beginning to leave its mark on both Mads and me. Mads had not shaved since New Year's Eve and had become visibly thinner. When I saw myself in the mirror, I saw that I had also become thinner. It was easy to get irritable, and we had both been in situations where we had started to whine. There were still moments of humour, but it was becoming more and more morbid. The only things that had not changed were the consideration we showed each other and the fellowship between us. On our way into Gaza, we agreed that we would stick together and support each other no matter what happened. Our safety depended on us keeping this promise.

I understood Mads' feeling that we would be letting down the Palestinians if we left too early, but I did not agree that it was a problem in this particular situation. We had both been through this before and knew this feeling of letting down others. The feeling could stay with us long after we came home, so it was important that we were both entirely convinced that it was no longer necessary for us to be in Gaza. Our Palestinian colleagues were not making it any easier for us. They gave clear signals that they wanted us here; we had become part of the gang. But if more doctors were coming with the same skills we had, there was no more rational reason to stay.

We reached an agreement to leave on Saturday morning. We began to prepare ourselves to go, but the noise level outside the window announced bombing in every part of the city, so it seemed unlikely that we would get to travel that day.

By eight o'clock, it was impossible to sleep through the noise. I peered across the room and saw that Mads was still in bed. Dagfinn had got up and made his bed, with smart folds that would have been the envy of any sergeant. Dagfinn had brought new order to the room, shaped by his military background. Instead of the ridiculous woollen blanket that we had hung in front of the window to catch splinters, Dagfinn had covered the glass with wide adhesive tape.

'Much more effective against splinters,' he remarked.

And much more popular with the others, I thought, now that another woollen blanket was available.

Mads was also just getting up.

'I'll stay here and write the article for *The Lancet*. It would be good if we could send it before we go. After all, that could be today, for all we know.'

'Good idea,' I said. 'I'll get some more data.'

I was impatient to get up to the hospital to find out more about what kinds of injuries had been coming in over the two weeks the war had lasted so far. The young man with the large, open wound, who I had looked at together with the thoracic surgeon Abdul Gafar, was still lying in the intensive care unit. I wondered if Abdul had referred him to the operating theatre so that we could try to cover his breastbone with muscle tissue. If we were going to operate on him, we would have to start soon.

I called Merete Taksdal, the new co-ordinator in El Arish. While we were working at al-Shifa, NORWAC had put together a new team composed of surgeon Johannes Brattebø, neurosurgeon Najib Ramzi and anaesthetist Mohammed Abou Arab.

Merete told me that Johannes and Mohammed had been cleared to come in, but the situation with Najib was still unclear because he had a Belgian passport.

I began my rounds together with Dr Sobhi.

'I have to try to discharge some patients,' he said. 'The hospital is absolutely full, and many more will definitely come today. I have no idea where I'm going to put them.'

He was right. Surgical patients lay everywhere, the medical department was full of injured patients after the bombing and all the ventilators were in use. Something had to be done to make space for the new patients that we knew would come over the course of the day. The hospital management and the International Red Cross would both certainly do everything that lay in their power to evacuate patients to Egypt, even if battles were raging all around the city. Maybe there would be a convoy out of Gaza after all?

We began our rounds. After a few minutes my telephone rang, and I left the patients' room. It was from *Aftenposten*. I understood that there were many journalists in El Arish waiting for us. They had been waiting since Thursday.

'There is fierce fighting here today,' I answered. 'It's impossible to say whether anyone will be able to travel south today.'

'Yes, but if there is an ambulance convoy, will you be coming with it?'

'Yes, I think so.'

It was important to inform the Norwegian authorities, so I called Tor Wennesland in Ramallah and told him that we were going to try to join a convoy if the International Committee of the Red Cross received authorisation to evacuate patients. Wennesland confirmed that he would inform the Israeli authorities that if there was to be any convoy, we would be with it.

After my rounds, I went up to the administration building. At the hospital director's office there were representatives of the International Committee of the Red Cross. They were all busy. Dr Mohammed spoke on the telephone while he went through patient lists together with the Red Cross representatives. When I asked if there was going to be a convoy out, they replied that they had not heard anything from the Israeli army yet.

I went back to the surgical block. Dagfinn was outside the emergency department together with the ambulance personnel. We agreed that he would phone me if he heard there was going to be a convoy of patients.

It was time to find out more about the patients we had treated. The hospital records from the first two weeks of the war were insufficient. We had a good deal of information about the hospital itself, and we had added up how many patients had undergone operations, but I did not know what kinds of injuries and operations each patient had. The operation lists were now back in the operating suite. When we went through them the day before, I had noticed that they wrote the type of operation in English and the patient's name in Arabic, so I went up to theatre to go through the lists once again.

The lists were on the head nurse's desk. I began to count the operations that had been carried out from December 28, 2008. In my notes, I categorised the operations. It took me a couple of hours to interpret the English writing and the dates, which were written in Arabic. I was pleased that I could recognise Arabic numbers and a few characters.

At twelve o'clock I had to interrupt my counting for an interview with the Iranian television channel Press TV. After that, I called Merete Taksdal again to hear how it was going with getting the team across the border. She said that they were in negotiations at the border. The Ambassador reckoned that Johannes and Mohammed would be allowed in, while Najib would probably get in the day after. Merete had been informed that the International Committee of the Red Cross were negotiating to send a convoy out, but she was not aware of the result either.

I finished my tally at half past twelve and came to the following findings:

Operations to treat fractures	43 operations
Amputations	53 operations
Vascular surgery	20 operations
Thoracic surgery	4 operations
Gastric surgery	49 operations
Brain surgery	36 operations
Other procedures	65 operations
Total 28.12.2008–10.01.2009	270 operations

270 operations in fourteen days give an average of twenty operations every day. The number of recorded operations per day ranged from six on December 31 to forty-four on January 4, when the vegetable market was bombed.

On December 27, when the war began, they had not managed to keep records of anything.

Twenty operations a day distributed across six operating theatres was not a large number, but the problem was that the patients came in waves. Forty patients might come at once, and then hours might pass before the next patient. As far as we could tell, 60 per cent of the patients who came to hospital were not operated on but were treated in the emergency department and sent back out. Some patients died in the emergency department before they got to the operating theatre. Approximately one hundred patients were admitted every day with major or minor injuries during the period we were at al-Shifa Hospital.

Mads put the new numbers straight into the article.

In our bedroom, my bag sat on my bed. I had packed everything I had, so it was just a case of picking up my bag if we were told to go.

If we were informed of an evacuation, there would be no time to pack. Israel usually gave convoys a time limit by which they had to get away. In our experience, it could be very short. It was important that we were ready to do our part for the comprehensive task of getting patients out of the hospital and into the ambulances. We would certainly be given responsibility for patients in a critical condition, and it was important not to delay their transport.

I went back up to the director's office.

'Hello Dr Mohammed, is there going to be an evacuation?'

Dr Mohammed looked up from the papers on his desk: 'We have not heard anything yet.'

It was now half past three in the afternoon. The chances of there being a convoy were diminishing all the time. On the stair outside the administration building stood the head of the surgical department at Gaza European Hospital, Dr Elias Arteen, with his suitcase ready.

'So you're going to try again, too?' I asked.

'Hi Erik. Yes, I hope I can get back to my job soon,' he replied.

Dr Elias had been at a meeting in Gaza at the beginning of the week. On Thursday he had joined the convoy to get home to Khan Younis. We had sat in the same ambulance and shared the experience of being forced back by machine gun fire. He had been waiting for two days and was hoping to get out of here this time.

'Elias, NORWAC is sending in a new team today,' I explained. 'There's a surgeon and an anaesthetist, and tomorrow a Belgian neurosurgeon's coming. Is it OK if they go to Gaza European Hospital if the road is blocked?'

'We don't need any foreign surgeons,' he answered. 'We get on average seven or eight patients a day, and we can manage that by ourselves.'

It was clear that he did not want any more doctors at the hospital.

'We wouldn't send them to work at Gaza European,' I said, 'but it would be good if they could stay there until the road is opened, if they can't come further north. Gaza European Hospital is probably the safest place in southern Gaza.'

'Yes, of course they're welcome,' he then said, clearly relieved that they would not be staying.

His reaction was a reflection of a problem that very few international organisations had considered.

The lack of food had now become a problem in the hospitals too. All international aid workers were treated like guests: they had to have a place to live, and they would have the best food. This was another important reason why I thought that Mads and I should leave when replacement surgeons and anaesthetists got to Gaza. There was a very fine line between being helpful and becoming a burden.

We stood on the step and looked out across the hospital grounds. Film photographer Ashraf Mashharawi then came up the stairs. Ashraf was the brother of Mahmoud, who had been killed together with his cousin Ahmed while they played on the roof at Ashraf's house.

'Hello, Dr Erik. I've brought some material for Dr Mads,' Ashraf said in a grave tone. 'Do you know how I can get hold of him?'

I knew that he had brought some small splinters and parts of the guidance system from the bomb that had killed the two boys. He had agreed with Mads that we would take these with us to be analysed by laboratories in Europe. Mads was still writing. It was part of our security arrangements not to show any outsiders whereabouts on the hospital campus we were staying. The situation was awkward; I could not take Ashraf to Mads. I tried to call Mads on his mobile phone, but the network was down.

'I don't know where Mads is right now, he's busy, but I can take the parcel for him.'

'No, I must deliver it in person.'

He tried to ring Mads on his mobile but could not make contact.

'I'll try to find him,' I said.

Dagfinn was outside the emergency department. I asked him to go down to our building and tell Mads that he had to come to the administration building to accept the parcel.

I told Ashraf that Mads would be coming soon, but after twenty minutes there was still no sign of him. There was still no mobile coverage. The Israelis had shut down the network. Ashraf was beginning to become impatient, but he still did not want to give me the parcel.

'Well, I'll go and find him.'

I ran down to our building.

Mads was absorbed. The article had to be finished before we left, and he could not go up to Ashraf.

'He'll just have to wait.'

I had not eaten either breakfast or lunch and realised that I was famished. I peered into the fridge, but it was almost empty. There was a tin of tuna on the bench. I opened it and ate the contents.

I went back up to the administration building. Ashraf was still outside, but Dr Elias Arteen had gone. I began to suspect something was afoot and ran up to ask the director if a convoy was on after all.

'I gave the instruction a while ago,' Dr Mohammed said. 'Where have you been? Israel has given us a short time limit; the convoy must leave in thirty minutes.'

Thirty minutes…? I did not think that would be possible. Outside the office I ran into Ashraf.

'Wait a few minutes, Mads is coming,' I said and ran back down to the house where Mads sat by the computer.

'Mads, we've got to go.'

'Good timing, the article's off now,' said Mads as he clicked on the send button. 'I haven't packed though.'

'You haven't got much time then. Remember that Ashraf is waiting by the stairs outside the director's office,' I said.

I hugged Dagfinn and the others in the building.

'Goodbye.'

'Hope you get over the border safely,' they replied.

I grabbed my bag and ran back to the hospital and into the intensive care unit. The unit head, Khalil al-Nakhal was sitting there dividing the patients to be evacuated between the teams that would be accompanying them. He gave me a sheet of notes.

'This is your patient.'

A nurse came over to me.

'Dr Erik, you're going with me. I've been waiting for you, we need to fetch our patient now.'

'I'll need to bring some medications,' I said and went over to a small table by the entrance to the intensive care room where all the medicines were kept. Last time, my patient had been fully conscious before we left, and he had needed a lot of sedatives on the journey. I wanted to avoid going through such a situation again.

The nurse helped me to fill up some syringes with ketamine and diazepam, diluted in saline solution, so that we could give small doses. I took two sets of syringes with each of these medicines.

'Our patient is coming round. She's by the operating theatre.'

We took the stairs. Outside there was a woman in her thirties wearing a Red Cross vest and a young man with a video camera.

'Are you Dr Erik?' she asked.

'Yes.'

'Great, can you put on this Red Cross badge and go in and operate on a patient while we film you?'

'What? I've got to get a patient out in the ambulance within a quarter of an hour; I can't operate on anyone now.'

'But we need to prove that you are a surgeon so that you can work for us in the ambulance.'

It was clear that the International Committee of the Red Cross was afraid of being suspected of smuggling out people in their ambulances who were not health workers.

'You can film me while we get the patient ready. We've got very little time.'

The situation was absurd.

The patient was a woman in her twenties who had undergone an operation after a splinter had gone through her chest and abdominal cavity. Another splinter had hit her right arm, which was broken. She also had a head injury and was not breathing by herself; she was on a ventilator. A drain had been inserted into her chest cavity and her arm had been operated on the day before.

I greeted her mother, who was next to the bed. 'She was at home in the house when it was bombed,' her mother said. 'How will she be?'

'We're going to get your daughter out of here safely,' I tried to reassure her.

The nurse took out the portable ventilator.

I checked the settings on the ventilator by the bed and saw that she only needed 40 per cent oxygen to maintain a satisfactory blood oxygen saturation level. That suggested that her lungs were functioning quite well, and that there was no major risk that anything would go wrong even if the ventilator should fail on the journey. I adjusted the portable ventilator to the same settings.

The Red Cross team was filming what we were doing the whole time.

The minutes ticked away. I was beginning to worry that we were not going to make it.

We eventually got the patient on to the stretcher, and I checked that everything was working as it should. I swung my bag up onto the stretcher along with the woman's luggage, then we rolled the stretcher over to the lift.

The nurse pressed the lift call button. Nothing happened. The lift was stuck.

He pressed the button several times and kicked the door. The lift was not coming. I began to sweat.

'Let's try the lift in the operating suite corridor,' he said.

We wheeled the patient into the operating suite corridor and ran along to the lift that took patients from the emergency department up to the operating theatre. Outside the lift, there were patients waiting to be operated on. I pushed the stretchers away and pressed the lift button. To my relief, the door opened. We pushed the trolley in and went down to the ground floor.

There was just one ambulance there. The convoy had left. We carefully manoeuvred the patient inside. The nurse sat down by the patient's head, and the mother sat down by the back door; my place was next to the patient, where I could read off the blood oxygen saturation from an indicator, monitor the patient's airway and administer medication via a catheter that went into one of the large veins in the chest.

Dagfinn stood next to the ambulance. We gave each other a hug before I got inside.

'Safe journey,' he said. 'Mads has gone with the convoy, they've just left.'

'Take care of yourself, Dagfinn,' I replied, relieved that Mads had got out but worried for Dagfinn.

We drove out of the gates at full speed and spotted a convoy of twelve vehicles driving slowly down the street. It was clear that the window of time they had been given by the Israelis was shrinking. There was no time to lose now. Our ambulance drove up alongside the convoy and joined as vehicle number two. I assumed that Mads was in the first ambulance. Mads and I had sat in the first two vehicles two days earlier as well.

In the ambulance convoy heading to Rafah four days later, carrying patients seriously wounded in the bombing of the UN school on January 6.

The patient began to struggle, and I gave her a dose of ketamine and diazepam to sedate her. The convoy sped up for the next four to five kilometres. Then we stopped.

We were at Netzarim. Two tanks stood on each side of the road. Their main guns were pointed at us. We stopped at the same place as before and waited. Nobody fired. The first vehicle began to creep forward. We followed them. Nobody fired – yet. The gun turrets on the tanks slowly turned round, following us. Nobody in the ambulance said anything.

The Israelis had demolished the road and made a temporary diversion road out of sand. It had been made very uneven to prevent anyone trying to crash through the roadblock at high speed.

We rolled slowly over the obstacles and back on to the normal road. After a few minutes, the radio crackled. The last ambulance in the convoy had passed the roadblock.

The drivers turned on their red flashing lights and sirens and increased their speed. The patient's mother was next to me. She clung on to her daughter's stretcher. I kept an eye on the oxygen saturation and on the ventilator. The ventilator, which was driven by the pressure from an oxygen bottle, stopped working. We had to perform manual ventilation once again.

The nurse and I took turns to help the patient breathe. We compressed the ventilation bag with one hand and clung on with the other. My phone rang. It was Randa, from the Embassy in Cairo, who needed confirmation that we were on our way. She was clearly in contact with the Egyptian authorities. I confirmed that Mads and I were on our way out.

We eventually slowed down. We had arrived in Rafah. Egypt lay peacefully in the evening light just a few hundred metres away. Between Egypt and us was the 'Philadelphi Corridor', the strip of no-man's land that marked the border.

We drove up to the Palestinian border station. Straight in front of us, to the left of the gate out of Gaza, stood three fully-armed soldiers, each holding an assault rifle.

'Are they going to take us here?' I thought.

But they were not bothered about the ambulances. A Palestinian border soldier opened the side door and asked for the patient's papers. He took the patient's and the mother's passports. I knew that I also needed an exit stamp but, at the same time, I was not especially tempted to wave my Norwegian passport about and signal my intention to leave Gaza, so I kept completely silent.

After a while, the Palestinian soldier came back with the passports, and we were allowed to pass through the gate into the large square in front of the Egyptian border checkpoint. I looked at my watch. It was seven o'clock. We would soon be out of Gaza.

The open square inside the Egyptian border station was full of journalists in addition to the twelve Egyptian ambulances that would carry the patients onward. There were also many soldiers. Altogether there had to be a hundred people there.

I saw Anders Vethe from the Embassy and a man with a beard who I assumed was the Ambassador, Thomas Hauff. It was not possible to communicate with them from where I was, helping the patient to breathe with the ventilation bag. The nurse jumped out through the back door and spoke with the Egyptian ambulance crew. They pulled the stretcher out of the vehicle, and I could hand over the ventilation to them. I got out of the ambulance and gave a report to the Egyptian crew. They were given the sheet of paper that acted as the patient file, and then I was surrounded by reporters. I called to Anders Vethe. He came over and hugged me, clearly relieved, before he called over the Ambassador.

'Now you're here, both of you,' said Hauff. 'That is reassuring!'

I managed to greet Per A. Christiansen from *Aftenposten* before he was pushed aside by journalists from across the world. Three or four microphones were put in front of my face, and they began asking questions in several languages. The ambulance was turning around to head back to Gaza. An Egyptian border guard came over and took me by the arm. He tried to shove me in the ambulance so I would go back with it. I swung the stethoscope and medications in the ambulance and tore myself away.

'I'm not going back,' I shouted.

That did not improve his temper, but there was little he could do. We were completely surrounded by journalists. I gradually cleared a path for myself over into Egyptian territory, and the wall of journalists stopped the soldier getting hold of me.

I eventually caught sight of worldly-wise Mads, who was standing amongst the journalists, being interviewed. I waved to him. He ran towards me, clearly relieved. We threw our arms around each other.

'Erik, I've been so worried. I knew you weren't with us when we left the hospital, and I didn't know if you'd joined us at all.'

'We had a bit of trouble with the lift.'

The square at the Egyptian border station where the patients were transferred was full of members of the international press wanting to interview us.

We stood for some time with our arms around each other while the photographers snapped pictures and the journalists waited.

Next to Mads stood Merete Taksdal and the embassy driver Abdallah who had helped us on the way in. It was wonderful to see them. Standing with them was a man of Arab appearance who I had not seen before.

'This is Dr Najib Ramzi, the neurosurgeon from the NORWAC team; he did not get an entry permit today. But Johannes Brattebø and Mohammed Abou Arab have just crossed into Gaza on a bus together with thirty Egyptian doctors.'

Merete pointed at a bus disappearing through the gates into Gaza.

'Ambassador Hauff has spoken with the Belgian Ambassador, and we reckon that Najib will get across the border tomorrow.'

I greeted Najib. He was not very pleased about having to wait another day, but he was quite confident that he would be allowed in the following day. Both Mohammed Abou Arab and Najib Ramzi had the advantage of speaking Arabic and, furthermore, they knew the culture and picked up on signals in a completely different way from us.

Eventually, the press had almost everything they needed from us. Ambassador Hauff asked for our passports. Hauff, Vethe, Najib, Merete, Mads and I went into the hall in front of passport control. First through some glass doors, behind which were the baggage scanners. They were not staffed, so we carried on into the hall itself. It was large, with plastic chairs along the walls and a desk at the end behind a glass wall, where the passport controllers sat. Hauff, Vethe and Abdallah took the passports into the security chief's small office in the right-hand corner of the hall. Together with us in the large room were approximately twenty doctors from various Arab countries. They were expecting to get across the border the following day. They flocked around Mads, who began to tell them about the situation in Gaza.

I expected that the Ambassador would soon be back with our stamped passports, so I called Nina first to tell her that I was over the border and that we could talk later that evening when we got to the hotel in El Arish. She was relieved. Then I rang my daughter Hilde in Oslo and my son Eivind in Trondheim. They were also clearly relieved.

'We're going to have a press conference in El Arish this evening,' I said. 'I'll call again after that.'

John Eivind had told us that I should call the Office of the Prime Minister, Jens Stoltenberg, as soon as we came into Egypt. They said that Stoltenberg would call back in a few minutes.

At the border station, Mads briefed a large group of Arab doctors on their way to Gaza.

At that very moment, Anders Vethe came out of the security chief's office. He looked concerned.

'What's happened?' I asked.

'They won't let you in,' replied Anders. 'We thought everything was ready. We have been in daily contact with the Egyptians, but they're now asking for someone to call them from the highest authorities in the Egyptian security service and to give them the order to let you in.'

I immediately realised that this was serious and called to Mads, who was with the Arab doctors.

'Mads, you've got to come, we've got a problem.'

We went into the security chief's office with Vethe. It was the same official we had met on our way into Gaza. There were four other men in civilian clothes, probably more security police. Ambassador Hauff asked us to be seated while he continued the negotiations.

Mads and I sat down on a sofa. It was clear that we were in danger. We struck up a conversation with the security officers and began to tell of our work in Gaza. They were friendly and asked if we would like some tea. We asked their names. Mads asked if any of them had a cigarette. We tried to establish as close a rapport with them as we could, so that they would sympathise with us.

The security chief tried to call his superior's office in Cairo but could not get through. He looked up from his desk: 'I see no other possibility than that you go back to Gaza and wait there until tomorrow,' he said. 'Then everything will surely be fine.'

We realised that would be highly dangerous.

'Out of the question,' said Mads. 'We're not going back.'

'We're not leaving the border station,' I said.

I thought of the soldiers I had seen on the Palestinian side of the border.

I looked at Mads. This was a job for the Embassy. We were continuously getting phone calls from the press sitting outside, and we suspected that our mobile phones were being tapped. Maybe they were being traced so that it was possible to find out where we were.

'We can turn off our mobiles and take out the batteries,' suggested Mads.

'Good idea.'

The Prime Minister would have to wait.

Ambassador Hauff took action: 'I'll have to call the diplomatic service emergency line.'

'Call Jonas Gahr Støre,' said Mads. 'Our lives are in danger; you've got to speak to the Foreign Minister.'

Hauff called the emergency line anyway. After a while, State Secretary Raymond Johansen answered. He spoke with Hauff at length, and then he spoke with Mads and me. We told him about the situation in Gaza, as well as about the situation at the border, and that our lives were in danger.

'I have tried to call the leadership of the security service; I spoke with them earlier today,' said Johansen. 'But just now they're in negotiations with Fatah and Hamas and can't be reached. You'll have to keep on negotiating.'

We agreed with Hauff that the Foreign Ministry's emergency office would take over contact with our families and keep them updated into the night if we were arrested or sent back to Gaza.

While we were on the telephone, ten Egyptian soldiers in uniform came in.

'They're here to throw you out,' warned Hauff. 'Go back into the office.'

Mads and I went into the security chief's office and refused to leave it. Hauff, Vethe and Abdallah took up positions outside the door, between us and the soldiers. They continued the negotiations, and our mood turned impetuous.

'I am the Norwegian Ambassador, and I am not leaving this border station without the Norwegian doctors,' said Hauff. 'If they have to stay here tonight, then I'm staying too.'

I began to feel an incredible affection for Hauff at that moment, as he probably saved our lives there and then.

'OK, you don't have to go back to Gaza, but you can't stay in the hall. You'll have to stand out in the square by the entrance,' said the security chief.

'Do you intend to let the Norwegian Ambassador sit outside in front of the border station all night?' I asked. 'What do you think your superior officer will have to say about that?'

It was apparent that both the chief and the other members of the security police felt under pressure and that the situation was uncomfortable. We had a clear impression that they personally felt great sympathy for Mads and me, but they had received orders that we should not be let in to Egypt. The negotiations had now lasted two hours, and it was almost ten o'clock. The security officers wanted to go home, and they had to close the office. The security chief was beginning to get impatient and wanted to reach a solution.

'OK, you can stay inside the building, but you must go on the other side of the baggage scanners,' he said.

'Out of the question,' said Mads. 'It's dangerous there.'

'We'll stay in your office,' I added.

'You know that is an impossible demand,' said Hauff. 'After all, this is a state-owned office and, as foreigners, we can't stay here by ourselves.'

'All right, we can go out of the office, but we're not going to the other side of the scanners. You must guarantee that no soldiers will come during the night and force us to go outdoors,' I said to the security chief.

The security chief was plainly relieved. He was probably only following orders. After having thought it over, he said: 'It's a deal.'

We went out into the hall.

'We can't sit on these plastic chairs all night,' I said. 'This is the Ambassador of Norway; he needs a better chair.'

After a few minutes, they brought some leather armchairs for all six of us. One of the security people fetched a kettle and some tea. Then they also brought a small electric heater.

They shook each of us by the hand.

'Sorry.'

They were relieved that we had reached a compromise. We had not got through passport control, so they had followed their order not to let us in to Egypt. At the same time, we were not sent back unprotected into no man's land or into Gaza.

After having assured themselves that we were relatively comfortable, the security police left the border station. There were only soldiers on duty here at night, and they stayed in another part of the building. We were left to ourselves.

Abdallah, helpful as always, went back to the Egyptian side to buy some provisions. After a while he came back with crisps, cakes, biscuits and mineral water.

Hauff's telephone rang. It was the Prime Minister, Jens Stoltenberg.

Hauff gave me the telephone.

'The Prime Minister wants to speak to you; he's been trying to get hold of you for several hours.'

'Hello.'

'Hello, it's Jens. I'm sitting at home with my parents eating dinner. My sister Camilla is here too, and I said I'd pass on greetings from her and from my father, Thorvald. We're incredibly proud of you.'

'Do return our greetings,' I said.

'On behalf of the government and of the Norwegian people, I thank you for what you and Mads have done in Gaza,' Stoltenberg said. 'We're going to continue to support the work of NORWAC, which we think is important.'

'Thank you,' I said.

I then told him briefly about the situation as I understood it, as I looked across the waiting room to where the Ambassador and the others were sitting around the electric heater.

'Mads is sitting here, would you like to speak with him too?'

I gave the phone to Mads, who also spoke for a while.

We really appreciated that phone call. It began to dawn on us how much attention we had received.

Hauff told us that we had been mentioned in the UN Security Council. Even if we had received a lot of attention from the media, we had not understood the scope of what we had done in Gaza. People right across the world had been following us, and our messages had reached out worldwide.

We put on the kettle to make some tea. Mads and I each had half a bottle of spirits that we had not wanted to drink in Gaza. I discreetly mixed a few drops of cognac into our tea, and then we drank a toast.

We had just finished our toast when two soldiers came in. They suggested that we should move over to a corner of the hall where there were concrete walls on both sides. It was right outside the security chief's office. It was definitely a safer place than the centre of the hall, and we settled in there. After an hour, two journalists came from TV2, Qadafi Zaman and Bjørn Roger Brevik, who had slipped into the border zone.

'We heard that you were stuck at the border,' said Zaman. 'We brought some equipment for you.'

They had borrowed some duvets and pillows at the hotel and had some more crisps and mineral water. It was incredibly thoughtful of them.

'This is turning into a party,' I said.

It was strange that everyone else could get in and out of the border station between Egypt and Gaza, but not us. The soldiers probably wanted us to be as comfortable as possible, since people were let in and out to bring supplies.

When the journalists had left, we wrapped ourselves up in our duvets. I was a little worried for Abdallah, who was in his late sixties. He looked tired, so we wrapped a duvet around him, and he nodded off in his leather chair.

We sat there with the old electric heater in front of our legs.

Mads began to tell jokes. We made sure that there were not any soldiers nearby, and Hauff, who was an experienced bartender, mixed us some drinks.

'Rafah special,' Mads called it, licking his lips in anticipation before having a sip of the orange juice and vodka mix.

We had soon emptied the two half-bottles. The conversation died down, and everyone was half asleep.

Boom!

At three o'clock we were awoken by a ferocious crash. Two large windows in the waiting room shattered.

An Israeli fighter aircraft had broken the sound barrier right above us.

Boom!

Another fighter. The sound barrier was broken again. This time, the ceiling panels fell down all around us.

Everyone was wide awake. What should we do now?

We looked over at the baggage scanners. Where we had been supposed to stay now looked like a battlefield. We exchanged glances, and I knew we were thinking the same thing. If we had been there or out in the square, we would now have been seriously injured. Several soldiers came running.

'Come with us,' they shouted and took us by the arm.

We grabbed our luggage and ran with the soldiers out onto the Egyptian side of the square and ran all the way across to the last gate before Egypt. There they pushed us into a small guard booth with glass windows. There were two officers in the booth. They opened all the windows so they would not shatter and pulled up chairs so that we could sit.

It was a quarter past three. The Israelis had begun a fierce bombardment around the border station. They were mainly bombing in no man's land, but also on the Egyptian side.

The attack lasted several hours. Once more we were surrounded by the noise of aircraft and bombs. Mads and I had become so used to it that we hardly reacted, but we were worn out and happy to be safe. Israel would not bomb the building where we were sitting together with the military commanders of the Egyptian border station.

We wrapped ourselves up in our duvets again and sat close to the Egyptian officers. It steadily grew very cold in the guardhouse, with the windows open, even though we had a small heater. Mads turned on his computer to show pictures from al-Shifa, and they listened to Lars Bremnes singing 'The Vegetable Market'.

The officers took out their packed lunches. They had *khobz* (bread) with *za'tar* (a mixture of wild thyme, sesame seeds and sumach) and cheese, which they toasted on the heater before sharing it with us. At around six o'clock, the bombing subsided. Abdallah and one of the officers went back to the waiting room to fetch the rest of the cakes and sweets we had been given by the TV2 journalists. We had not managed to pick them up when we fled from the bombs.

I handed the officers a soft drink and some cakes and went out to the privates, who were sitting close together around a heater outside the guard booth. I gave them some packets of cakes, chocolate and nuts.

The sun came up, and it was a warm day. At around eight o'clock, the guard changed and a bus came to pick up the soldiers. A new team of guards was in place. After another hour, the security police came to work and escorted us back through the border station. They were clearly relieved to see that we were uninjured.

I became more and more shocked as we walked through the border

We ran for our lives towards the southern border gate.

control building. The ceiling panels had fallen down. Doors had been torn from their hinges. All the windows facing Gaza were shattered. Furniture had been thrown around. Many Israeli bombs had fallen just outside.

We were put in an office, where the lot of us sat half asleep. After a while, Mads and I were fetched by one of the security officers and taken to the desk in the hall. There we finally had our passports stamped. At half past ten we went through the gate into Egypt. The Ambassador's car was waiting.

Hassan was at the wheel.

'Hi Erik and Mads, welcome back to Egypt.'

Merete called the Swiss Inn in El Arish, where all the journalists were waiting for us. She said that there would be a press conference at half past eleven. There was no point postponing it.

Hauff and Vethe would help Najib Ramzi to the border and then travel back to Cairo.

On Sunday January 11, Egypt lodged an official protest with Israel against this bombing. Israel claimed that the tunnels in Rafah were the target.

On Monday afternoon, we finally landed at Oslo Gardermoen Airport, where we were met by our families. Both Nina and Hilde were there to greet me. Both of Mads' daughters, Siri and Anna, were there too, together with his former partner Susanne Engell. Our families were hard pushed to get through all the hullabaloo with the press and the many Palestinian children and adults who had shown up with flowers and placards. The whole experience was incredibly moving, and it was very good to see my family again.

At Gardermoen, we held yet another press conference for the international media. Our task of informing people was not over.

While Mads and I were being received like heroes at Gardermoen, the attack on Gaza continued with undiminished force – now with another Norwegian team in place.

Johannes Brattebø and Mohammed Abou Arab had been taken deep into Gaza in the Red Cross ambulance convoy returning to al-Shifa Hospital. At the hospital, they were met by Dagfinn and Bassem Naim. On Sunday January 11, the second NORWAC team was a complete unit.

The war was escalating day by day. On January 11, thousands of reserve forces were sent in to Gaza. The Israeli forces entered far inside Gaza City. The whole thing came to a head on Thursday January 15 and Friday January 16, with fierce bombing and fighting not far from al-Shifa. The conflict was only becoming more and more brutal. Thousands of Palestinians fled from their homes. Several reports came that soldiers had knowingly shot at civilians inside the city, including those carrying a white flag.[129]

As soon as I heard about this, I called Dagfinn. He told me that the team had moved into the operating suite corridor and would sleep there with the other doctors the next few nights. They lay down mattresses in the anaesthetic department staff-room and slept on the floor. It was no longer safe to stay outside the surgery block.

It was terrifying to hear Israel repeat their message that leading Hamas members were hiding in the basement under the hospital. When Mads and I heard these allegations when we were at al-Shifa Hospital, we were afraid they would be used as a pretext to bomb the hospital. Dagfinn told me that his team had discussed the same issue. Like us, they felt that nobody at the hospital believed the accusations. Everyone thought that it was just scare-mongering Israeli propaganda.

More than seventy targets in Gaza were hit by bombs on the night of

Sunrise in Rafah at last. The guard-house was ice-cold, but the hospitality was warm. From left: Merete Taksdal, Anders Vethe, Thomas Hauff, an Egyptian officer, Mads and Fathi Mohamed Abdallah.

The Egyptian border station had received comprehensive damage from the Israeli attack that night.

January 15. Among the targets hit by white phosphorous shells and set alight was the UNRWA headquarters in Gaza. 700 Palestinians had sought refuge in the headquarters compound, which was also the main food store. Mattresses and rice were destroyed by the fire.[130]

Another target of the white phosphorous shells was al-Quds Hospital, which was founded by Fathi Arafat. The cultural centre that was next to the hospital burned down to the ground. 500 people had sought refuge in this building. A shell also hit the hospital's surgical department but, due to heavy firing in the streets around al-Quds Hospital, they could not evacuate the patients. Fortunately, this shell did not explode.[131] In total, fourteen of the twenty-seven hospitals on the Gaza Strip were damaged by bombs.[132]

On January 16, the bombing of Gaza City continued, and the NORWAC team stayed put in the surgical department. The day after, it seemed as if the soldiers had been withdrawn from the city, but the bombing continued north of Gaza. Among other targets, the UN school in Beit Lahiya was set on fire by Israeli white phosphorous shells. On the night of January 18, Israel declared a unilateral ceasefire.

The team travelled out of Gaza on Tuesday January 20 and arrived in Norway on January 22. The third team, with the two anaesthetic nurses Arve Holm and Kristin Øhren, arrived in Gaza on January 18. From this team, we received the first eyewitness descriptions of the enormous material destruction.

Kristin Øhren had lived in Gaza for many years and speaks fluent Arabic. She established an especially good rapport with the Palestinian women and could report on the very difficult situation the Palestinian women were in:

> I have had the possibility to speak with many women who have either given birth to living children or who have had late-term abortions or stillbirths. Many stories are burned into my memory, but they all have a common denominator of endless despair. There is the woman who gave birth to her seventh child after having lost her home following a bombing in Beit Lahiya. Her family had lost everything, and she did not even have clothes or blankets for the new-born. Her other children were staying in a school building, and she was sick with worry for them.
>
> But there are also the women who had stillbirths in their seventh and eighth months of pregnancy. I will also mention the woman who became pregnant through artificial insemination after seven years of

NORWAC's Team II in place at al-Shifa on January 11, 2009. From left: Dr Mohammed Abou Arab, Nurse Dagfinn Bjørklid, Dr Najib Ramzi and Dr Johannes Brattebø.

marriage. She aborted in her fifth month of pregnancy. These women say themselves that it was fear that caused their stillbirths. Through these women, I also got to hear about the other women who gave birth while the bombs rained down without being able to get to the hospital or to a midwife.

15

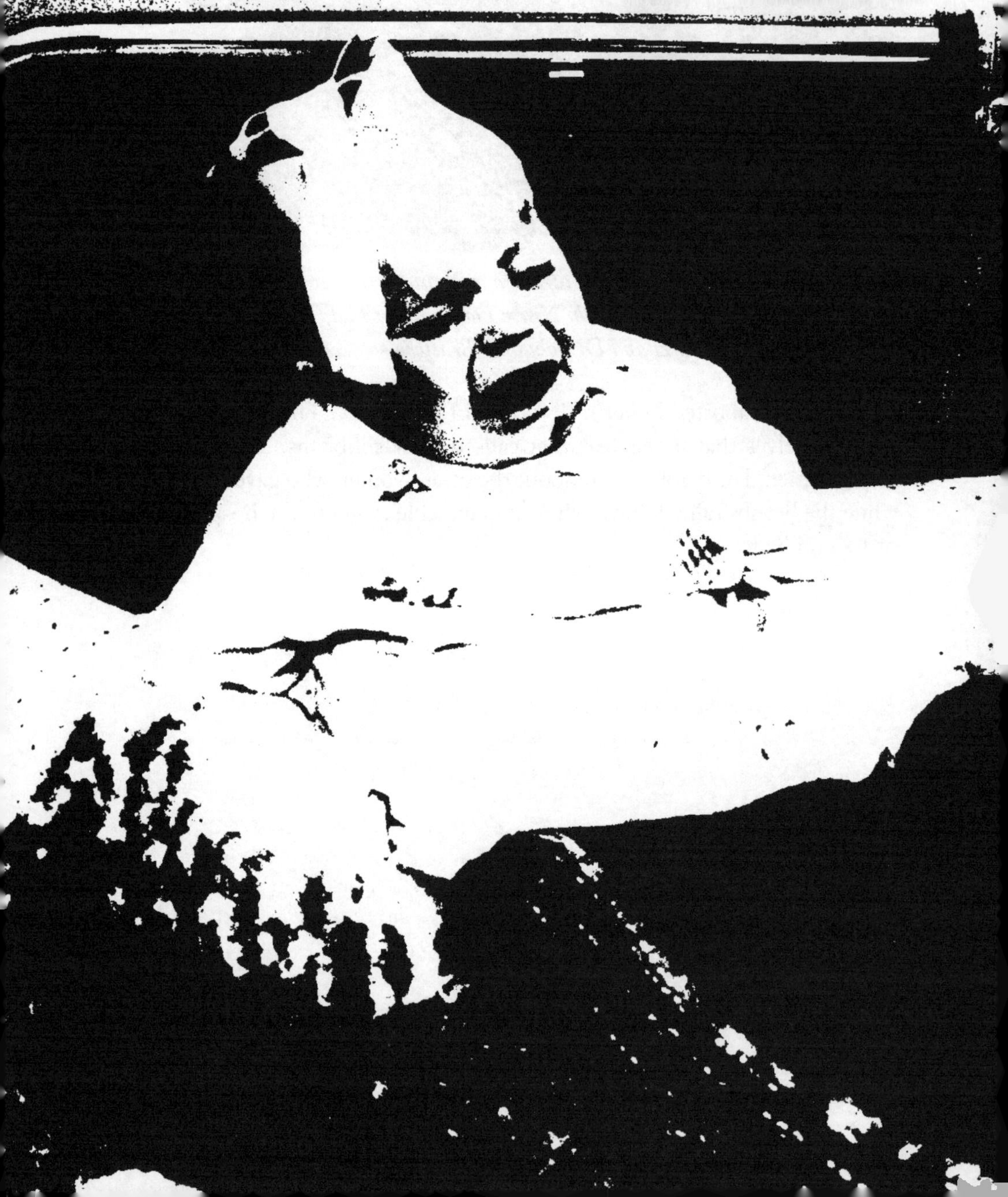

15

War Criminals

MADS GILBERT

'Christian, are you still here? Still not let in?'

He shook his head. Christian Fraser, a British journalist from the BBC, gave a resigned smile. Fraser was one of the few familiar faces among the hoard of international journalists who had shown up at the press conference at the Swiss Inn Hotel in El Arish. It felt unreal to be back in the Egyptian border town, as if we had been away for an eternity. Both Erik and I were still wearing our green scrubs from al-Shifa. I had my stethoscope and head lamp round my neck, and the top pocket on my green smock was full of primed syringes.

Fraser looked at me dejectedly.

'They have really kept the border hermetically sealed. And believe me, I've tried everything to get in. I considered the tunnels, but BBC management said no. Too dangerous.'

'And still no chance of getting in to Gaza?'

'Nope. It doesn't look like the Israelis are planning to open up Gaza for the international press before they've done their 'job' – their dirty job. But we must get an interview with you for BBC TV after the press conference. We can do it on the beach.'

'Of course, but first a bite to eat.'

We were hungry and exhausted after our dramatic departure and almost twenty hours trapped in Egyptian no man's land. I was beginning to trip over my own words. My mouth was as dry as dust.

Christian Fraser took out a microphone and a digital recorder from his car and interviewed me for BBC News. His questions were precise, and he let me finish speaking. It is easy to notice the difference between professional journalists with long foreign experience and all the others. Fraser was a professional, without a doubt.

After waiting for nineteen days, he did eventually get in to Gaza, and was the first Western journalist to do so.[133] He used his time well. Without him, we would never have learnt the truth about what actually happened to the little girl Samar and her family in Abed Rabbo by Jabaliya, just north of Gaza City and barely two kilometres from the border with Israel.

Samar was still paralysed from the waist down when she was evacuated by ambulance from al-Shifa via Rafah to the hospital in El Arish. The hospital had been equipped to accept evacuated war victims from Gaza who needed an intermediate stop there on the long way to hospitals in other Arab countries or in Europe. The city's airport was also important for the comprehensive air bridge that several Arab countries initiated to provide solidarity and support to the Palestinians in Gaza. The Kingdom of Morocco had carried out eighteen sorties with large military Hercules aircraft bringing 250 tonnes of medical equipment, blankets and food.[134] Other Arab countries did the same. The problem was that large quantities of the sorely needed equipment and personnel were accumulating in the dusty city. The city's beach hotels, usually empty in winter, were filled with doctors, pharmacists, logisticians and journalists, and the airport was full of transport aircraft, all because the border with Gaza remained closed. During the waiting period, several international journalists made their way to the hospital in El Arish, where they could at least interview Palestinian war casualties evacuated from Gaza and their families. The patients could tell detailed stories of Israeli warfare and the conditions in Gaza.

Christian Fraser visited Samar at El Arish Hospital a week after she received life-threatening injuries outside the family home. Fraser spoke both with her and with her uncle, Hassan Abed Rabbo, who had accompanied her. Samar had regained her charming smile and the sparkle in her eyes, but she was still paralysed below the waist. The doctors did not think she would recover the use of her legs.

The story of her and her family's fate was told in television reports on the BBC and Al Jazeera.[135] In these reports, her uncle Hassan and her father, Khaled, told quite a different story from the one we had heard at al-Shifa when Samar came to the hospital on January 7. We thought then that she had been hit by shrapnel. The truth was much worse.

Around thirty people had sought shelter from the advancing Israeli army on the ground floor of the family's house when tanks began to shoot at it. They fired first at the second floor, then at the first floor and finally at the ground floor.

'The house began to shake, and we were all scared out of our wits,'

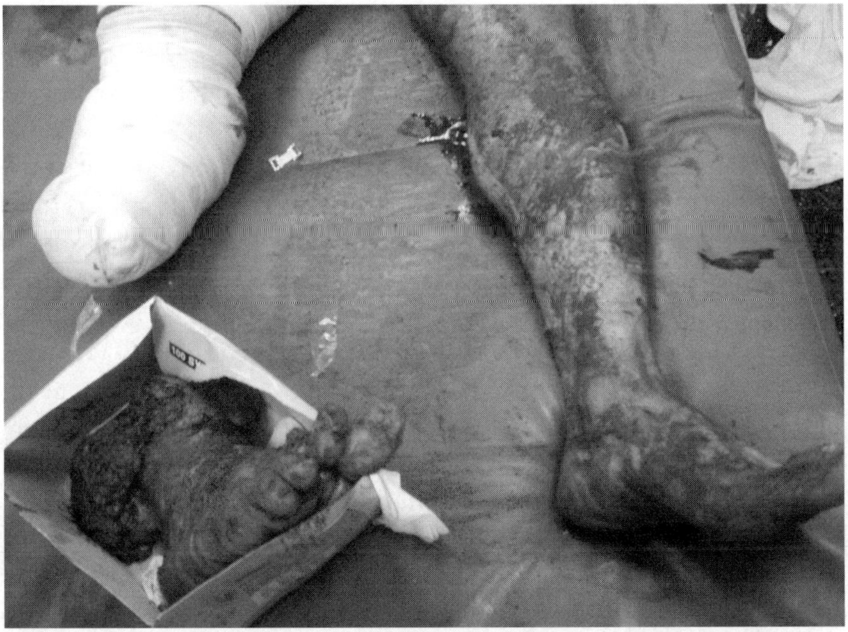

He lost 'only' one foot. The Israeli attacks led to a large number of amputations. According to Islamic custom, lost body parts are taken care of and later buried, even if the patient survives.

Hassan remembered. 'The women and the children were screaming with fear because they thought the house was going to collapse on top of them. Since I can speak Hebrew, I shouted out to the Israelis. The officer replied: "Come out!" The women went out first, with Samar's grandmother waving a white flag.'

Fraser took a picture of Samar in her hospital bed in El Arish and decided to seek out her father in Gaza to get the whole story, so as soon as the Rafah border opened, he and his cameraman went north to the refugee camp in Jabaliya, in the suburbs of Gaza City, and they looked for him in Abed Rabbo. Everything was in ruins following the Israeli attacks. They searched at length, but nobody recognised the little girl in the picture. They were about to give up when they finally found Samar's father. As soon as Khaled Abed Rabbo saw the picture, he recognised his daughter.

'How is she?' was the first thing he asked.[136]

'She can't walk. She's paralysed in both legs,' Fraser answered through an interpreter.

At first, Khaled seemed to take the news calmly, but then he turned away and cried. A Palestinian man held him and comforted him. Khaled then told the BBC crew – with almost unreal composure – what had happened.

'The tank was over here,' he said, pointing, as he stood in front of the completely flattened house.

'It was ten to one in the afternoon. We were told to come out of the house by an officer with a megaphone: my mother, my wife and my three daughters Samar (four years old), Amal (two) and Sohad (seven). We went outside. An Israeli tank was standing there between seven and ten metres away. We saw that there were two soldiers sitting on the tank; one of them was eating chocolate and the other was eating crisps. We were waiting for orders from the soldiers when a third Israeli soldier came out of the tank carrying an M16 rifle, and he started to shoot at the children. All three were hit by the shots. Sohad died instantly. Amal died later from her wounds, and Samar was shot in the back but survived.[137]

'I carried Amal with her intestines hanging out of her front, then I fetched Samar. The Israeli soldiers killed Sohad with more than ten bullets to the chest. My sixty-year-old mother was hit by two bullets, and she was bleeding. We tried to call for an ambulance, but none came. After a while, we decided to leave the house in small groups. When we left, they shot above our heads. While I was carrying my dead children, the Israeli soldiers came out of their tank and laughed at us. At Zimo Square there was a man with a horse and cart who offered to help us, but they shot both him and his horse. He was evacuated to Egypt, but he died later from his injuries.'

An ambulance only came two or three days later to pick up the dead bodies, but the ambulance was also destroyed.

'They were only a few metres away when they shot at us. How could they not see that it was children they were shooting at? They could *see* them,' Samar's uncle Hassan told Fraser.

Samar received medical attention only after several hours. The children's mother was not hit. She carried her one dead child. Samar's grandmother, who had been waving the white flag, was hit in one arm and in the stomach.[138]

Uncle Hassan supports Fatah, not Hamas. Both he and Khaled insisted that there were neither Hamas fighters nor weapons in their house.

I watched the BBC report open-mouthed. Was it possible? I felt completely caught by my own naïveté. Why had I been so sure that Samar had been hit by shrapnel? The answer was simple: I had refused for as long as possible to believe that a modern army under civilian political control and military command would deliberately shoot at civilians, just as I had also self-evidently refused to believe that soldiers from that army would shoot at children. We are supposed to be fooled into thinking that Israel conducts 'humane' warfare, in spite of all the warnings that the opposite was happening. In spite of all my own experience from decades observing Israeli brutality from a front-row seat in Lebanon, the West Bank and Gaza. And in spite of what our colleagues, our patients and their families told us over those twelve days. Everyone said the same thing.

'They're massacring us,' the Palestinians told us.

We had indeed heard accounts of whole families being slaughtered and of brutal attacks on civilians, women and children. These accounts were often connected to patients who came to al-Shifa, such as that of the Samouni family massacre, but we could not verify these reports independently or with any certainty. We could not leave the hospital, and we did not manage to follow up all our patients' stories.

'What they are doing is ethnic cleansing,' the Palestinians told us.

We could still not confirm this assertion unambiguously or with legally valid documentation. We were neither journalists nor legal experts, and the forensic capacity of the Palestinian health services was close to nil. There was no time for autopsies or systematic documentation. There was no police authority intact that could investigate the attacks, injuries and deaths of civilians and, perhaps most importantly of all, there were no Western journalists in Gaza who could go over all the stories with a fine-toothed comb. For weeks, Western journalists walked obediently in single file behind Israeli press officers showing them the holes that the home-made Qassam rockets from Gaza made on well-kept lawns in Sderot and Ashkelon. At the same time, the Palestinian inhabitants driven away from Najd and al-Majdal – as these settlements were called before the Zionists occupied the area – were being massacred in Gaza.

It became apparent afterwards that many of the patients we were involved in treating had been subjected to precisely this kind of systematic violence against large groups of unarmed, unprotected Palestinian civilians. We reported the whole time to the media that 80 to 90 per cent of the dead and the wounded we saw at al-Shifa were civilians, but we still flinched from really taking in the full extent of the systematic and merciless Israeli attacks against civilians.

The testimonies of Israeli soldiers who took part in the ground invasion give an insight into the Israeli way of thinking:

> 'We're going to war,' the Israeli commander told his soldiers. 'We're not doing routine security work or anything like that. I want aggressiveness – if there's someone suspicious on the upper floor of a house, we'll shell it. If we have suspicions about a house, we'll take it down.'
>
> The commander went on: 'There will be no hesitation. If it's us or them, it'll be them. If someone approaches us unarmed, shoot in the air. If he keeps going, that man is dead. Nobody will deliberate – let the mistakes be over their lives, not ours.'[139]

The Israelis were well aware of what they were doing, who they were shooting at, and what they hit. They received intelligence from their own soldiers, from the video cameras mounted in the nose of each missile – which clearly show what kind of targets they are being guided to and then hit – and from their own and US-owned spy satellite data. They also obtained intelligence from all the paid agents they have among the Palestinians, from the pictures continuously scrolling across television screens, especially in the Arab world, from the UN's detailed satellite imagery and damage summaries, from the daily situation reports issued by a number of UN agencies, and from us. They summarised and discussed how the war was progressing on a daily basis, they knew that they were going to hide it, and they knew that they were not going to get rid of Hamas. Neither was that their intention.

Their intention was to punish the whole Palestinian population of Gaza collectively. The punishment was a merciless slaughter of men, women and children, the old and the young, and a comprehensive bombing campaign that would send Gaza decades back into the past. The years of the blockade had hit the civilian population of Gaza not in an accidental or unsystematic manner, but with full intent. The carnage also had little to do with bombs accidentally missing their targets. The children were not killed because it was dark in the night, nor because the wrong co-ordinates had been entered into the GPS guidance system, nor because of a few undisciplined soldiers. The women killed and injured were not really intended to be spared. Like the civilian men, they were all zeroed in on by weapons, drones, helicopters and fighter aircraft because they were *intended* to be killed, injured and terrorised. To the Israeli soldiers, all the Palestinians in Gaza were terrorists, so they were also, in the Israelis' eyes, legitimate targets to be attacked, hurt and killed.[140]

The President of the State of Israel, the Nobel Peace Prize laureate Shimon Peres, would be the one to expose the Israeli political and military objective of Operation Cast Lead most clearly for the whole world.

Four days before the 'operation' was over, Shimon Peres said: 'The implementation of the current operation has gone 90 per cent according to plan.'[141]

In his speech to the lobbying group the American Israel Public Affairs Committee (AIPAC)[142] in Beit Hanassi in Jerusalem on January 14, 2009, while the bombs were still falling on Gaza, he disclosed Israel's actual plan: 'Israel's aim is to provide a strong blow to the people of Gaza so that they lose their appetite for shooting at Israel. That's all.'

According to the plan, the assault on Gaza was supposed to take place in absolute darkness; the world was not supposed to learn of it. The Palestinians in Gaza would be forced so harshly down onto their knees that Israel hoped they would rise up against the Hamas leadership, and that they would be lining up behind white flags – split, subdued, frightened, capitulating, dejected and doomed to defeat. The Palestinians

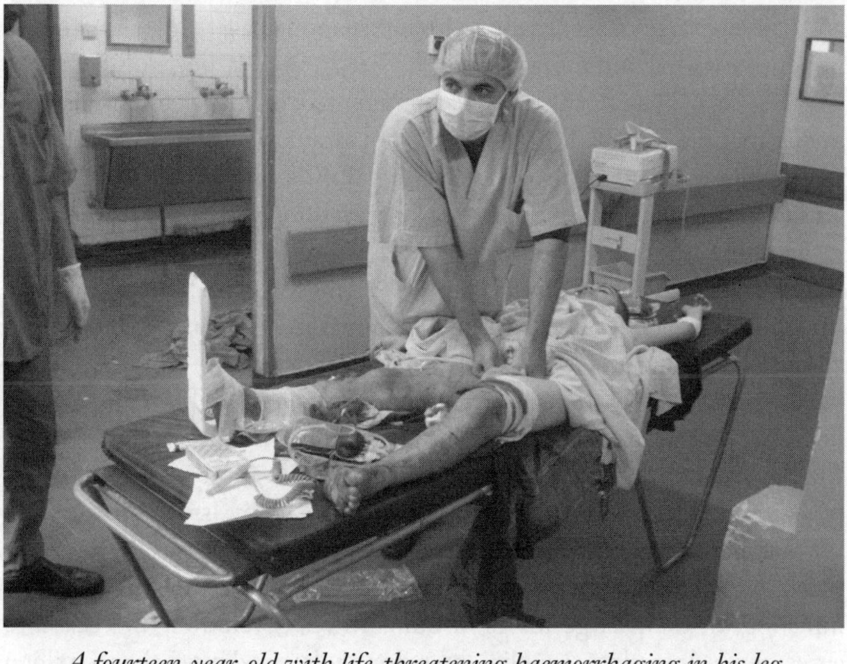

A fourteen-year-old with life-threatening haemorrhaging in his leg waiting for treatment. 'The implementation of the current operation has gone 90 per cent according to plan,' remarked President Shimon Peres.

would be dealt a blow so hard that they would never forget it, a blow that would fill them with such shock and fear that they would never think of defending themselves against Israeli occupation and humiliation again.

The suffering of the Palestinians and the murder of civilians were part of a plan that was implemented with 90 per cent success for the State of Israel. For Samar and her family, the result was a 100 per cent loss. Her two killed siblings and the rest of her family, her home and her village, all shelled to pieces, serve as horrible examples of the 'strong blow' that Israel methodically directed against 'the people of Gaza' over twenty-two days. No Israeli politician, officer or soldier was held responsible, no court martial was established, no war reparations were paid, and no apologies were given by Israel.

Quite the opposite. Up against international criticism and claims of war crimes and aggression against the civilian population, the Israeli Chief of General Staff, Lieutenant General Gabi Ashkenazi initiated an internal inquiry. The investigations were carried out by five military teams led by Israeli officers from the IDF. As early as April 23, 2009, the Chief of General Staff presented the results which, not unexpectedly, suggested that Israeli forces 'acted with restraint in order to avoid harming civilians,' and had 'operated in accordance with international law [and] maintained a high professional and moral level.'[143]

Defence Minister Ehud Barak commented on the self-appraisal by saying that the IDF had shown it was 'not afraid to investigate itself,' and that it had once again proved 'that the IDF is one of the most moral armies in the world.'[144] In other words, everything was fine and well. The EU and the USA made no comment.

Shimon Peres' declaration to the AIPAC meeting was not coincidental: the military attack was very carefully planned, and the aim was to punish all the Palestinians in Gaza. The Israeli military operations in Gaza are an illustration of a new military strategy that they have dubbed the Dahiya doctrine. *Dahiya* means 'suburb' in Arabic, and is used as a collective term for the southern districts of west Beirut, which is seen as Hizbollah's stronghold. These districts were totally destroyed by Israeli air forces in the Second Lebanon War in July 2006. The Israelis' aim was to destroy as much of the infrastructure as possible and to intimidate the inhabitants by inflicting on them large losses of human lives. Even after the ceasefire agreement was in place, Israeli fighter aircraft dropped more than a million cluster bombs over southern Lebanon in order to make those areas uninhabitable as well.

The Dahiya doctrine means striking areas where rockets are fired towards Israel as quickly as possible with overwhelming military force, and carrying out wide-ranging attacks to inflict structural damage and to kill. No distinction is made between civilian and military targets. The argumentation made is that these areas, whether they are villages or urban areas, provide shelter for those who are firing at Israel. Everyone is to be held responsible irrespective of whether they are military or civilian and regardless of age or gender. Israeli military strategists and high-ranking officers believe that the response to rocket threats and attacks from Syria, Lebanon and Gaza should be an immediate and disproportionately forceful attack 'at the heart of the enemy's weakest point'. The objective of weakening the rocket-firing capability of their victims is secondary. The Israeli military strategists claim that such destructive attacks will be remembered by decision makers in their neighbouring countries for many years, thereby increasing the deterrent force of the Israelis.

The doctrine is well documented through declarations from the Israeli top brass. It was publicly mentioned in an interview with the head of the Israeli Northern Command, Major General Gadi Eisenkot, published by the big Israeli tabloid *Yedioth Ahronoth*: 'We will wield disproportionate power against every village from which shots are fired on Israel, and cause immense damage and destruction. From our perspective, these are military bases. This isn't a suggestion. This is a plan that has already been authorised. We won't be deterred by the protests of the world.'[145]

Another military theorist is Colonel Gabriel Siboni, a reserve officer who has previously served as a commander in the Golani Brigade and as chief of staff of an armoured division.[146] In a report from the Institute for National Security Studies (INSS) at Tel Aviv University, he goes even further than Major General Eisenkot to claim that the use of force must also be disproportionate in relation to the *actual threat* the enemy represents. The intention of the military response should be to deal out destructive punishment to such an extent that long and costly reconstruction will also be required.[147]

The aim of the Israeli attack should be to 'send Gaza decades into the past' while, at the same time, attaining 'the maximum number of enemy casualties and keeping Israeli Defence Forces casualties at a minimum,' remarked the commander of the Israeli military forces' Southern Command, Major General Yoav Galant, in a message to the world the day after the assault on Gaza began.[148] The numbers of Palestinian and

Israeli casualties and the destruction of Gaza demonstrated that he and the other Israeli commanders went on to keep the promises they had made.[149]

The report from the Israeli military forces claims that 295 'non-combatant' Palestinians 'died during the operation', of whom ostensibly eighty-nine were under sixteen years of age, and forty-nine were women.[150] No other organisations have numbers close to these official Israeli figures. Confronted with the large discrepancies in the number of civilians killed, the Israeli forces' spokesperson responded that the Palestinians had included naturally occurring deaths in their figures, but he was not able either to present a list of names of the Palestinians killed or to explain which methods they have used to collect these figures.[151]

The Palestinian figures vary somewhat, but the Palestinian Centre for Human Rights (PCHR) stands fast by its numbers: over 1,400 were killed in the period between December 17, 2008 and January 18, 2009. In contrast to the complete lack of documentation from the Israelis, the PCHR has presented an overview of 1,415 casualties with name, age, sex, address and the date and place of both the attack and death.[152] The detailed list shows that almost 85 per cent of those killed were civilians, and that 334 Palestinians were killed on the first day of the attack. The list also includes details on the occupations of the victims, and it differentiates between civilians and militants. Women and children made up 38 per cent of the casualties (319 children and 216 women), 20 per cent were policemen, while just 16.5 per cent of those killed were 'militants' (233). These numbers are close to those in other external reports and to the numbers from the Health Ministry.

The new Israeli deterrence dogma means that the Israeli war machine is using its disproportionately superior fire-power to terrify and threaten those opposed to subjugation and forced obedience, through an asymmetrically violent use of military weapons and other offensive means directed against both civilian and military infrastructure as well as human targets. Both these kinds of action are illegal according to international law. The Israeli armed forces' own experts, however, offer entirely different assessments.

In the months leading up to the attack on Gaza, there were wide-ranging discussions about these questions among the leadership of the Israeli armed forces. They reviewed the legality of attacking government buildings and the police schools in Gaza, where large groups of police

Palestinians at their Friday prayers among the ruins of a mosque in Beit Lahiya in January 2009. Over a hundred mosques in Gaza were wholly or partly destroyed by Israeli bombs.

cadets would be having their graduation ceremony. Both targets were defined as civilian according to international law and should not be attacked. Prior to the attacks, they were nevertheless defined as legitimate targets for the Israeli forces, through a legal indulgence from military legal advisors in the Israeli Military Prosecutor's International Law Department (ILD).[153] Legal experts from this office were present in the operational military command structure throughout the attack against Gaza. They took part in evaluating and approving various tactical military targets that had been selected for bombing as well as other kinds of Israeli attacks. They also approved more incidental targets that came up during the course of the attacks, for example Palestinian rocket launching sites. There is good reason to suppose that the bombing of UN buildings, such as schools and food stores, was thoroughly evaluated with international law in mind, and that it was not down to a misunderstanding. A separate legal addendum to the written orders for Operation Cast Lead recommended that 'to the extent that circumstances allow it, the civilian population proximate to a legitimate target should be warned before the attack,' but the exception to the same rule followed immediately afterwards in the legal experts' instructions: 'It is possible to refrain from this if it might endanger the action or the [Israeli] forces.'[154]

Several Israeli specialists in international law were, however, in strong disagreement with the military commanders and with the assessments made by the military law experts. 'In an organised state, attacking police as soldiers is forbidden,' states law professor Yuval Shani from the Hebrew University of Jerusalem.[155] 'You have to draw a line, attacking people only when they're in active service.'

Professor Orna Ben-Naftali is Law Faculty Dean at the College of Management Academic Studies (COMAS) in Rishon LeZion, in Israel. She is another Israeli legal expert critical of these assessments and believes that international law has gone 'bankrupt', pointing out that the Israeli armed forces used international law to legitimise their use of force during the operations in Gaza. She contends that 'it's possible to raise serious arguments to justify just about any action. The meaning of this is the approval of the use of almost unlimited force, in a way that totally contradicts the basic goal of the humanitarian law [sic].' She continues to argue that legal advice and international humanitarian law, 'instead of limiting suffering, […] provide legitimacy for all uses of force.'[156] She claims that the way international law is employed in the occupied territories, especially in Gaza, facilitates war crimes in which the legal advisors to the Israeli armed forces are complicit.

'It is likely that the legal advice authorises violations [of international law…]. A situation is created where one can relate to most of the men and most of the buildings in Gaza, as legitimate targets. In fact, the law has been stood on its head. It has stopped fulfilling its function so we must admit that it has reached the stage of insolvency before bankruptcy.'[157]

'The [Israeli] response to the Qassam rockets was disproportionate and the soldiers' testimonies only show how brutal it was on the field,' concluded Valentina Azarov, a legal expert with HaMoked, the Centre for the Defence of the Individual.[158] This is one of the twenty to thirty various Israeli organisations that work to systematically unveil and to document violations of the Palestinians' human rights.[159]

It was not just Israeli military legal advisors who tried to give the assault on Gaza legitimacy. Rabbis inside and outside the Israeli armed forces provided soldiers with extreme religious grounds for the attack and for murdering Palestinians. The Israeli army's chief rabbi, Brigadier General Avichai Rontzki, who is himself an occupier in an Israeli colony on the West Bank, organised the production of a controversial religious book that was distributed to soldiers as preparation for Operation Cast Lead.[160]

The book was written by the ultra-nationalist rabbi Shlomo Aviner, who leads the fundamentalist seminary Ateret Cohanim in the Muslim Quarter of Jerusalem and who is seen by many as a spokesman for the most extreme Israeli occupiers on the West Bank. The book was entitled *Go Fight My Fight: A Daily Study Table for the Soldier and Commander in a Time of War*.

The former chief rabbi of the Sephardi Jews, the right-wing Mordechai Eliyahu, recommended the carpet bombing of Gaza in a letter to the then Prime Minister Ehud Olmert in 2007. In Gaza, he wrote, 'the entire populace is [collectively] responsible' for the rocket attacks against Israel.[161] The chief rabbi's religious judgement was clear: there is absolutely no moral obstacle to the indiscriminate killing of civilians during a potential major military offensive against Gaza in order to stop the rocket attacks. In a pamphlet distributed to all the synagogues in the country, he also asserted that Jewish war ethics prescribe that whole cities can be held responsible for the immoral behaviour of individual inhabitants, making reference to the Old Testament story of the massacre in Shechem (present-day Nablus on the West Bank).[162]

Against this backdrop, the Israeli soldiers' own revelations about the injustices inflicted on civilians in Gaza should hardly come as a shock. The soldiers' accounts of the battle actions in Gaza came out during discussions at a military preparatory school shortly after the end of the fighting in Gaza. This school – the Yitzhak Rabin Pre-Military Preparatory Programme, led by a liberal reserve officer, Danny Zamir – has been bringing together young soldiers at Oranim Academic College in Kiryat Tivon for over twenty years. Many of those who have gone through the programme have later reached command positions in combat and elite units of the Israeli armed forces.

On Friday February 13, 2009, Zamir reunited soldiers who had been through the programme to go over and discuss their experiences of service in Gaza. A detailed transcript was published in the school's news bulletin *Briza*, which was then leaked and immediately reproduced in a lengthy article in the Israeli newspaper *Haaretz*.[163] The soldiers tell of the abuse and killing of Palestinian civilians and the destruction of private property. Their testimonies confirm that barely any distinction between civilians and military resistance existed. The troops opened rapid fire on civilians, killing them, children too, as a result of what was described as 'lax rules of engagement.'[164]

In the series of revelations about the Israeli armed forces' moral platform and 'code of conduct', there also came the news of Israeli soldiers who, having finished their mission in Gaza, had customised T-shirts, hooded sweaters and caps made. The caricature drawings and the text show the soldiers' attitudes to Palestinian civilians with graphic clarity.[165] Some show Palestinian women and children behind cross-hairs with captions that cannot be misinterpreted. One T-shirt made for the snipers from the Shaked Battalion, Givati Brigade, includes the text '1 shot 2 kills' in English under a drawing of an evidently pregnant Palestinian woman wearing traditional Arab women's clothing and hijab, positioned in the middle of a sniper rifle's or a gun's cross-hairs.[166] Another motif features a young Palestinian boy holding a rifle, right behind the cross-hairs together with the message 'The smaller, the harder' in Hebrew. The double meaning is intended to illustrate how challenging it is to shoot at children.[167] 'Better use Durex' reads the text on a shirt ordered by infantry snipers, showing a small child killed holding a Palestinian flag in his hand. A teddy bear and a crying mother are shown next to the killed child.

A spokesman for the Israeli armed forces claimed that the T-shirts were printed on the soldiers' private initiative, and the designs 'are not in accordance with IDF values and are simply tasteless. This type of humour is unacceptable and should be condemned.'[168] The proprietor of a shop in Tel Aviv, Haim Yisrael, who produces the special clothing to order for Israeli soldiers, says that they produce around 500 T-shirts with various designs for soldiers every month. Soldiers from all branches order the shirts, and the snipers in particular have a long tradition of requesting provocative patterns with caricatures of what they see as hostile Palestinian targets.[169]

Both the report by Amnesty International and the testimonies of forty Israeli soldiers published by the veterans' organisation Breaking the Silence confirm that Operation Cast Lead was carried out with brutal, widespread and systematic abuses against the Palestinian civilian population and violations of international law.[170]

On my many journeys through Israel and in occupied Palestine, I often get the feeling that the Israelis are living in a different world from the rest of us. Self-legitimising self-defence is ubiquitous. The segregation policy is pursued openly and unabashedly, as if that were the way the world should be. The extensive controls at countless checkpoints; the tall, bare, cruel wall; the wide-ranging militarisation and arming of Israeli

'1 shot 2 kills' and 'The smaller, the harder' – the wording on T-shirts made by Israeli soldiers from a sniper company.

civil society; the existence of two levels of almost all legal rights and the constant expansion of occupied land through numerous new illegal colonies – everything is organised with meticulous precision and an almost unbearable arrogance.

I do not understand how so many people can avoid noticing how fundamentally unjust and inhuman the organisation of their own society is.

Fortunately, however, when the Israelis direct their aggressive rhetoric against anyone who raises critical objections, not everyone takes the bait.[171]

For the first time in Norwegian legal history, political and military leaders were to be reported for 'war crimes and gross violation of international humanitarian law'. On April 22, 2009, lawyers Loai Deeb, Kjell Brygfjeld, Bent Endresen, Pål Hadler, Harald Stabell and Geir Høin filed charges against the leaders of the Israeli government and the Israeli armed forces for war crimes to the new Norwegian public prosecutor for international crimes.[172] The list of the subjects of the complaint was startling: the former Israeli Prime Minister, Ehud Olmert; former Foreign Minister Tzipi Livni; former and current Defence Minister Ehud Barak; the Israeli defence chief Gabi Ashkenazi; the head of ground forces, Major General Avi Mizrahi; the head of naval forces, Admiral Eliezer Marom; the head of air forces, Major General Ido Nehoshtan; the chief of the Israeli war forces' 'Southern Command', General Yoav Galant; the commander of the Givati Brigade, Colonel Ilan Malka; and the commander of the Golani Brigade, Colonel Avi Peled. They were all reported for contravening Sections 102–109 of the Norwegian General Civil Penal Code (2005), read together with Section 5.

The new national prosecuting authority is tasked with preventing Norway from becoming a sanctuary for people who may be suspected of having committed serious crimes abroad, including war crimes. Through its endorsement of the Geneva Convention and other conventions of international law and its ratification of the Rome Statute, Norway has acknowledged its obligation as a state to be pro-active in the prosecution of international crimes and crimes against humanity. Through their action, the five solicitors wanted to trigger this duty and right.

When the complaint was delivered to public prosecutor Siri S. Frigaard in her office, I could see for myself that Norwegian media interest in Gaza had already died down. Only Al Jazeera sent a TV crew to cover the event and the following press conference at which the solicitors outlined the background to the complaint: 'There can be no doubt that all the subjects knew about, had considered the consequences of, and ordered or approved the criminal acts. At the very least, they failed to stop the contraventions when they became aware of them, despite being able to do so.'

The solicitors request that those named in the complaint be arrested if they come to Norway, or that they be investigated and arrested through international police co-operation. The Norwegian Bar Association's human rights committee has supported the complaint.[173] The Norwegian complaint is on a level with a number of legal campaigns by human rights organisations and by other countries. In Israel too, calls have been made for a legal investigation into what happened in Gaza.[174]

A fact-finding committee of leading experts in international law that was appointed by the Arab League concluded that there is proof that Israel committed war crimes and crimes against humanity during the attack on Gaza. The committee also believes that Israel may possibly have committed genocide, which is the most serious violation in international criminal law.[175] The respected Norwegian human rights judge Finn Lynghjem served on the committee, and he sent the report to the Norwegian national prosecuting authority at the start of May in the hope that they would bring charges against the Israeli leaders *in absentia*. It remains to be seen how independent and courageous the Norwegian judicial authorities will be in relation to the serious Israeli violations of international law.[176]

March 7, 2009, and we are in Ramallah on the West Bank.

'Nothing's happening, Dr Mads. Nothing. No reconstruction or repairs. We have no materials, and nothing's getting in to Gaza. The blockade is just as harsh as before.'

The large lobby in the Palestinian Red Crescent's headquarters in al-Birah on the West Bank is full of delegates with typical name badges and conference bags over their shoulders. It is a great contrast with the worn-down – and now bombed-out – Palestinian Red Crescent offices in Gaza, where Dr Khalil Abu Foul has his daily job, and where we usually meet.

'But you got out of Gaza. Did you come with a big delegation?' I asked Dr Khalil.

'Yes, a whole lot. Several of the surgeons from al-Quds Hospital and the Palestinian Red Crescent managers.'

'But not Dr Nafez?'

'No, he's not coming.'

Khalil was pale with dark rings under his eyes. His voice trembled as he spoke. According to the programme, Erik, Khalil and I were each going to hold an introduction speech at this fortieth anniversary event for the Red Crescent.

'I'm looking forward to hearing you,' I said in encouragement.

'The situation is difficult, Mads. Our children are scared and worn out, so is my wife Suzan. It was traumatic for us when they bombed al-Quds Hospital and it started to burn. You know that we had to evacuate all the patients?'

'Yes, I know. Awful! But were Mohammed, Juda and Jamila all there too?'

'We had all our three children there. We had to go to work, so we could not be separated from them. Everyone was evacuated down to the surgical department. We were there for forty-eight hours. I think it was worst for Jamila.'

'So is the black dog back under her bed now?'

'Not yet, but both Suzan and I are afraid it'll come. Jamila says that Amu Mads will kill it.[177] I don't know how much more we can take. We need a break. A break from the blockade, from the shelling and from the uncertainty. We don't have 5,400 injured. We have one and a half million injured. Everyone in Gaza is traumatised.'

He looked at me. His face was expressionless. His eyes filled with tears. Jamila is almost six, Juda is seven, and Mohammed is two and a half; three Palestinian children who, through no fault of their own, have had a childhood full of humiliations, occupation, siege and bombing.

'I don't know if we can manage any more,' said Khalil.

Again, I did not know what to say. He was going back to Gaza. Three days' parole from the prison that is Gaza, then back behind the walls and to the Israeli jailers' unpredictable punitive expeditions. More bomb attacks? Maybe so. Enough food? Maybe. Fresh water? Well, we'll see. Roof gutters? Nope. Window panes? Definitely not. Playgrounds? Forget it! Oxygen masks for children? Maybe. Work? None at all. Electricity? A little, maybe? Reconstruction? None at all. Respect? Never!

The Palestinians of Gaza have been given an absurd sentence. They have not done anything wrong; they have never had and never will have their case heard in any court of law. They have been given a sentence that has no foundation in any legislation, either nationally or internationally. They have no court of appeal and no right to reprieve. They are imprisoned together with their children, their grandchildren and their great-grandchildren. Their prison has, at any time, 40,000 pregnant women. Children born and still to be born will never learn if they are ever going to get out. The jailers are unpredictable and cynical, punishing all the prisoners with scheming malice for deeds that they have absolutely no responsibility for or control over. The awfulness cannot be understood from outside. If anyone had really understood it, it would have been stopped long ago, the prisoners would have been let free and the jailers punished.

Khalil spoke calmly and methodically of the destruction, of the difficulties of procuring new ambulances when the Israelis bombed and destroyed the ones they had, of the trouble finding new solutions when the emergency call centre was bombed. Or when the ambulance crews were injured and killed on their treacherous missions to rescue the wounded and the dying after the bombs had fallen, and to get them to hospital.

I studied him while he spoke. Dignified, controlled and professionally sound. Focused on his managerial role, on coping and control. Palestinian health workers are not in the habit of assuming the role of suffering, helpless victims. They are resolutely determined to manage their jobs by themselves, and they do not expect others to solve their problems. For decades, I have admired their determination and their will to protect and

October 2008: Juda (on the left) and Jamila say goodbye to 'Amu Mads' – Uncle Mads. Their father, Khalil, is deeply concerned for his children and the future.

treat their patients as well as to protect their local communities and the future of the Palestinians.

The assembly listened, just as they also listened to the lecture Erik and I gave. Many of the Palestinian representatives cried when they saw the pictures from Gaza again and heard the stories of individual fates. But why is engagement for the Palestinians so weak at high levels and so strong at the grass roots? Would the international delegates do anything with what they saw testified and documented?

I am filled with deep concern at what is happening. Our platform of universal values is being threatened by the great Western powers and by states that take the law into their own hands, establishing new exceptions to universally accepted norms that we have struggled hard to achieve over the last few centuries. Our societies have slowly evolved away from barbaric medieval methods of punishment and the ranking of human worth, away from the use by authorities of torture, the death penalty, debasement and lawlessness and towards societies of people in which equality and human rights should apply to all. We live 220 years after the

French Revolution, but our experiences in Gaza and other events over the last decade have given me a feeling of historical retrogression.

We are doctors, but we do not want to be only doctors. There is little use in just carrying out one-sided curative medical treatment in the occupied territories and of Palestinian refugees in Lebanon, Syria and Jordan. We must also relate to the political and social realities. Today there are 4.5 million Palestinian refugees or descendents of those who were driven away in 1948, and a third of these still live in refugee camps.[178] The World Health Organisation places great emphasis on social factors as determinants for health. In particular, they have focused on the negative effects on health of low income, insufficient housing, uncertain employment and lack of access to health services.[179] Sixty consecutive years of war and forty years of Israeli occupation have had negative consequences across the board for the state of health and life expectancy of millions of Palestinians.[180]

Between September 2000 and June 2008, Israeli forces killed almost 5,000 Palestinians, mostly civilians. More than 900 of those killed were children. Over 1,000 Israeli military and civilians were killed by Palestinians over the same period. It is only through a deeper understanding of the political and structural circumstances caused by the Israeli occupation that it is possible to carry out directed transformation and medical development work. Perhaps time may be slipping away from us. Perhaps the disaster is already irrevocable for generations. I do not believe so. It is, of course, possible to find political solutions but, in order to do so, Israel will have to change its fixed positions, and the USA must assume another, more independent role in its relations with Israel. The continued occupation, blockade and military attacks are not leading anywhere and only generate more hate and bitterness on the Palestinian and Arab side. If dialogue is to evolve, the truth must come forward. The laborious task of instilling trust requires the culture of a state governed by law in order to find those responsible for all the deaths and injuries, to bring charges and to punish them according to the law.

'If you want to make peace with your enemy, you have to work with your enemy,' as Nelson Mandela said. As long as Hamas remain branded as political lepers and are excluded from all kinds of conversation, the situation will not change. As long as there is not established a truth or reconciliation commission to which both sides can put forward their own cases, reconciliation and understanding will remain an illusion. The State of Israel is a European and American construction. The population of

Gaza, April 2009. The Palestinians stand up to the Israeli blockade and experiment by making building materials from clay and water. This building material is now being used to reconstruct individual homes as well as mosques and clinics.

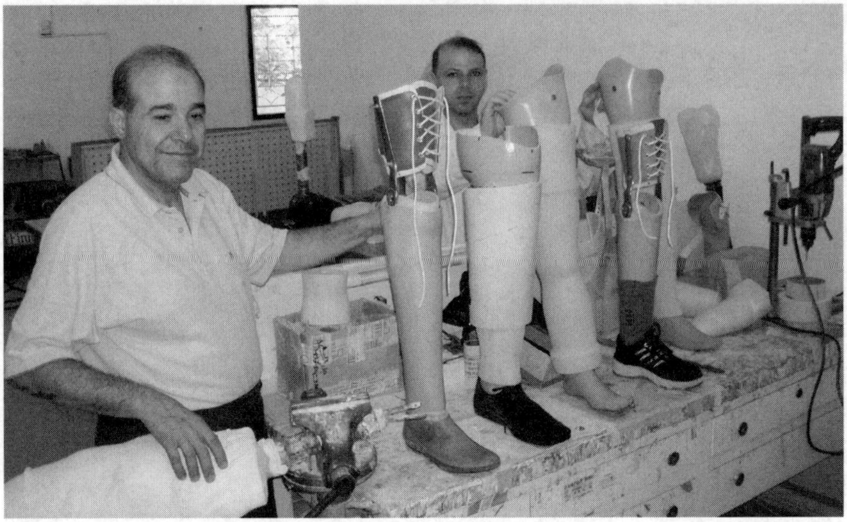

Hazim Shawa, director of Gaza's municipal prosthetics workshop: 'It's not the money that's important, but your solidarity. The light from Norway helps us not to lose hope.'

Gaza and the West Bank are victims of this construction. Instead of supporting an inhuman and heartless blockade and continued isolation, the West should strive for a just, political solution to the conflict. The Palestinians need support in their resistance to occupation. Isolation, condemnation and patronising pity serve only the occupier and will, in time, lead to further tragedies.

There is a lovely pair of home-knitted mittens in the last envelope. I am slowly working my way through all the letters and the parcels with beautiful books, CDs and other greetings that have been piling up in Tromsø while I have been in Gaza. The mittens are beautifully knitted in the colours of the Palestinian flag – red, white, green and black – and each of the mittens has its own pattern. The knitting is even and the pattern is original. In the attached letter, it says: 'I can't go to Gaza to do what you did, but I can knit. These mittens should keep your hands warm.'

I do not know the sender, but the letter was written by a friend: not first and foremost my friend personally, but a friend of the Palestinian people. The lump I feel in my throat is difficult to swallow; I am so moved by all this kindness. We have been met by a warm wave of attention, interest and support since we came home. The invitations to speak about

Gaza have been countless, and it has not been possible to say yes to them all. I am reading through the newspapers from the Christmas period and the first weeks of January and I am again overwhelmed by all the reports of solidarity events that have been held. From the Seamen's Church in Las Palmas right up to arctic Svalbard there have been broad, non-partisan concerts, demonstrations, appeals, exhibitions: a rare and diverse expression of one common feeling – the bombing must stop. Gaza must be opened. The Palestinians must be helped!

The home front has always been the most important. The Norwegian solidarity campaign has a long and bleak history. It has at times been a steep and winding road because Norway was long a bastion of one-sided support for Israel. Slowly and patiently, through an awareness campaign and thousands of meetings large and small, as well as journeys, projects and debates, public opinion has turned, and the reality of the situation faced by the Palestinians has become more clear and urgent. The dam burst, and out flowed the accumulated sympathy and solidarity with a small, courageous population. Tens of thousands stood up and said: 'Enough is enough.'

Everyone can do something; each of us can speak with our own voice. People can write a letter, a poem or a song; read and gather knowledge; travel to occupied Palestine, make friends and learn about Palestinian culture; support a project; establish twinning projects between towns, hospitals or schools; or join a Palestinian solidarity group or association. There are no limits to what an individual can do, or to what we can achieve together. The threads may be thin, but woven they are strong.

'The most important thing isn't the money – it's the solidarity,' says the director of Gaza's municipal prosthetics workshop, Hazim Shawa, every time we come with funds raised in northern Norway. This fund-raising has enabled Palestinians to continue with their local production of prosthetics and other orthopaedic aids in spite of the economic blockade and difficult working conditions.

'You are our universe now,' he adds. 'Everything is dark around us, but we can see the lights from Norway – like stars. Then we know that we are not alone, and that hope is not lost.'

'The Palestinian people's most dangerous enemy is lost hope,' says ophthalmologist Maged Abu Ramadan, a good friend of many years. He has been the Mayor of Gaza City and an important partner of the Mayor of Tromsø, Gaza's twin city.

'If we lose hope, we lose everything. You keep our hope alive,' he reiterates every time we meet.

The collection for the prosthetics workshop was started by an enterprising woman from coastal Norway. When Ingrid Evertsen, from the municipality of Berg on Senja island, heard about the Israeli attacks and destruction of Gaza in July 2006, during 'Operation Summer Rains', she decided to act. In a telephone interview with the NRK local studios in Troms county, I described in desperation the difficult situation at al-Shifa Hospital, the many nasty amputation wounds and the wide-ranging effects of the blockade of Gaza.[181]

'When that Mads shrieks down the phone, then it's serious,' she said and called her many friends among cultural workers in northern Norway. In a short time, she had mobilised a group of stars and started a cultural caravan of locally and nationally known entertainers who played, sang and performed for the benefit of the prosthetics workshop and the population of Gaza. The motto of the fund-raising initiative was a line from the Danish psalmist Thomas Kingo's 'Sorrow and Joy': '*Svakhet skal reises på sundeste ben*' ['Weakness be raised upon limbs that are strong']. By supporting the talented Palestinian prosthetics craftsmen in the workshop in Gaza City, we would support the Palestinians' own self-sufficiency and contribute to the replacement of amputated legs and arms by the Palestinians themselves.

May 2009, the telephone rings.

'Hello, this is from Radio Nea in Selbu [near Trondheim, in central Norway]. Please could we interview you about the collection going on here for the prosthetics workshop in Gaza?'

'Of course,' I reply.

Venke Aarethun, a tireless solidarity activist from Trondheim, chair of the Trondheim-Ramallah Friendship Association and a chair of the Palestine Committee for many years, had just told me about the fund-raising in Selbu. After two large solidarity concerts for Gaza in Trondheim, Inger Granby from Selbu decided that her municipality could do at least as well. She organised a local campaign and solidarity concert that raised all of 150,000 kroner.

The interview is going fine. I think of the delightful mittens in Palestinian colours that I had received when I came home. Maybe we could start a local Palestine craft industry rooted in Selbu's proud tradition of knitted woollen mittens?

Graffiti on a wall in Bethlehem, occupied Palestine, May 2009.

'Yes, bring your mittens and come to Selbu. We can certainly make mittens, hats and scarfs as well, for the benefit of the Palestinians,' is Inger Granby's response to my suggestion when I call to thank her for the effort she and her village put in.

'A new knitting trend,' I laugh. 'The "Gaza-Selbu pattern", almost like the red stocking caps during the war?' Those hats became a symbol of civil resistance to the German occupation.

'Why not?' answers Inger.

In June 2009, I call Suzan and Khalil in Gaza. Suzan speaks in a quiet, intense voice while her children shout 'Amu Mads, Amu Mads' in the background.

'We're still short of most things. The children are better, but they are so scared that the bombing will start again. Are you well in Norway?'

'Yes, we're fine, but we're more concerned about you. We're so worried.'

'We'll manage. If only we can live in peace like other ordinary people. Here comes Khalil.'

His voice is hoarse as he answers my carefully encouraging '*Marhaba, habibi.*'

'The situation is not good. It is tense here in Gaza now. We're expecting more.'

'More?'

'Yes, more bombing and more Israeli attacks. They haven't finished. They want to punish us more.'

I feel no pity, just a burning rage.

'We're coming back, Khalil, if you need us, both Erik and me, and others too. There are many of us now. Don't give up. Things must get better. They *will* get better!'

'Inshallah, Mads.'

'Inshallah, Khalil!'

Afterwords

Breakfast in Gaza by Erik Fosse

The Al Deira Hotel stands right on the edge of the beach, just north of the harbour in Gaza. Early one morning towards the end of February 2010, I was sitting on the terrace eating breakfast, together with my partner Nina Husom and the NRK correspondent, Sidsel Wold. The day was calm and the sun was shining. A fisherman stood in the water, casting his net out into the shallows.

Tatatatataa, a machine gun rattled from the Mediterranean. We could see an Israeli gunboat on the horizon.

'They're shooting at a fishing boat which has gone too far out,' said Sidsel.

We couldn't see the fishing boat; it must have been quite small. There were gunboats patrolling the security zone that Israel had set up, restricting fishing boats from Gaza to three nautical miles from the shore. The Palestinian Centre for Human Rights regularly reports attacks on fishermen. Because of the high unemployment in Gaza, the number of fishermen has increased in the past year. Some fish from land, like those we saw from the hotel, but to catch bigger fish you need to have a boat and go out as far as possible.

In the first four months of 2010 the Palestinian Centre for Human Rights recorded eight instances of Israeli gunboats shooting at fishing boats. Two fishermen were injured in the attacks. Three fishing boats were arrested, and six had their fishing gear confiscated or destroyed.[182]

This was the third time I had visited Gaza since Mads and I had left during the attack in January 2009. The first time was at the end of May 2009, five months after the attack. I had applied for permission to come into Gaza straight after we had come out in January, and I was uncertain whether I would be let back in. The young woman at border control acted correctly and just checked that my permit was in order before waving me through the automatic prison gates and sluices and into Gaza. Sidsel Wold followed me in. On the other side of the border were TV crews from NRK and TV2, but the most important thing for me was that the nurse Dagfinn Bjørklid was there. Dagfinn was NORWAC's co-ordinator in Gaza in the spring of 2009.

Just south of the border crossing at Erez there had been an industrial zone with big buildings. Now all the buildings had gone. It was like driving through a desert landscape.

Sidsel Wold's driver Raed al-Atamna came from the village of Abed Rabbo, just a couple of kilometres from Erez. He wanted to show me the remains of his village. This was the village where Samar Abed Rabbo, her sisters and mother were shot by Israeli soldiers. There was no resistance against the invasion in Abed Rabbo. The Israeli soldiers drove in without a shot being fired. They took over the town, killed or chased away all the inhabitants and blew up all the houses with mines. There was just one house left standing in the whole village, the rest were all ruins. For some reason or another the mine which had been placed in that house had not exploded. The house left standing was Raed al-Atamna's. He pointed into the house, where the mine lay among the remains of the wall which had fallen in. Raed al-Atamna and his family were now living in a few tents right beside the house.

The systematic destruction of factories and dwellings was thoroughly documented by several organizations. The first authoritative report was by the commission of legal experts sent by the Arab League in the spring of 2009. This commission reported 3,000 homes totally destroyed and 11,000 damaged. 215 factories and 700 commercial buildings were severely damaged or destroyed. 28 public buildings and 60 police stations were either partly or totally destroyed. 30 mosques were totally destroyed and 28 damaged. 10 schools were totally destroyed and 168 damaged. 3 university and college buildings were totally destroyed and 14 damaged. 15 hospitals and 43 health centres were damaged or destroyed. 53 UN installations were damaged.[183]

In May 2009, Human Rights Watch published a report on their investigations into 12 particular incidents during the war. The study included 189 buildings, comprising 11 factories, 8 warehouses and 170 dwelling houses which were totally destroyed. According to Human Rights Watch this represented 5 per cent of the total building stock which was destroyed in the war.[184]

On the first anniversary of the invasion, on December 27, 2009, I was back in Gaza for the second time since the war. In the refugee camp in Jabaliya, the anniversary was marked by a big spontaneous demonstration outside the home of the Hamas leader Nizar Rayyan, who had been killed together with his family the day after Mads and I had arrived in Gaza. There was a big crowd there, and we couldn't get through to the house. My partner Nina, and Sidsel Wold, who had come this time too, covered their hair with shawls. The demonstrators, mostly women, were carrying large placards with pictures of family members who had been killed in the war. There were pictures of young men, women and many children. The women carrying the pictures wept loudly.

We went on to al-Fakhoura School in the refugee camp at Jabaliya. I took a picture of the square outside the school where Israeli tanks attacked on Tuesday January 6, 2009, when we had so many children admitted to al-Shifa Hospital. Now I was standing at the scene of the crime. In connection with the anniversary, a big tent had been set up against the wall that goes around the school. On the wall there was a picture painted of the Israeli Prime Minister Ehud Olmert, the Foreign Minister Tzipi Livni and the head of the Israeli army, all with blood dripping from their hands. Beside the picture of those responsible for the killings, there was a picture painted of the school and the square. In the square there were piles of child corpses.

I wondered what it must have been like in the square that sunny Tuesday morning. The shells probably did not all land at once. Did one land first? Did the children try to flee? It must have been chaos. In the pictures a lot of them were lying on top of each other. They must have been standing close together when the shells landed.

In the tent there was also a display of photographs from the attack. The photos showed that the detail in the painting was accurate. There were a lot of other pictures too. The tent was crammed with people. A group of young boys passed in front of me. One of the boys pointed at a picture and said: 'Look, that's my mother and our house.'

It was a picture of a bombed-out house with a woman's corpse lying on the road outside. Several of the boys recognized family members or the remains of their houses.

In the middle of the tent there was a display of flechettes: small metal arrows which fly out of the shells when they explode and inflict multiple injuries on anybody nearby.

While Mads and I were writing this book, several boards of inquiry published reports on their attempts to find out what had really happened on those fateful days between 2008 and 2009. Some of these reports had used Mads and me as sources. The first in-depth report was the 'Report of the Independent Fact-Finding Committee on Gaza', published by the Arab League on April 30, 2009. On May 21, 2009, the WHO published its report on the WHO Specialized Health Mission to the Gaza Strip. The best known report is 'Human Rights in Palestine and Other Occupied Arab Territories', written by the UN Fact-Finding Mission on the Gaza Conflict, led by the South African former Constitutional Court judge, Richard Goldstone. When this report, known as the Goldstone Report, was published on September 15, 2009, I was especially interested in what they wrote about the attack on al-Fakhoura School. We had heard conflicting information about this attack. Some said that the school itself was attacked, others that it was the square outside the school. Nor did we know what type of weapon had been used.

The Goldstone Report said that the school was opened as a shelter on January 5. According to UNRWA, 1368 Palestinians sought refuge in the school. 90 per cent of those seeking refuge came from the area of al-Atatra outside the Jabaliya camp.

One of the witnesses in the Goldstone Report was Mohammed Fuad Abu Askar, who lived quite near al-Fakhoura School. At 01:45 on the morning of January 6, Abu Askar had a telephone message from the Israeli military saying that his house would shortly be bombed from the air. More than forty family members were evacuated in the course of a few minutes. Seven minutes after the telephone call, the house was bombed by an F-16. Abu Askar and his family were then homeless, and they found themselves on the square outside al-Fakhoura School, together with about 150 other people, when it was shot at by tanks at 16:00 on the same day. In the course of two minutes, three mortar bombs landed in the square and one at the home of the al-Deeb family who lived nearby. It was estimated that twenty-four people were killed and at least forty injured by the mortars which hit the square. It was Israeli information which led us to believe that they had bombed the school. Israel claimed that Hamas had shot several mortars from the school, and that they were returning fire. Later, it emerged that there was a Hamas position eighty metres from the school. Israel then changed its explanation to say that they had shot at the square outside the school. In the Goldstone Report there is nothing about rockets having been launched three days earlier, as we were informed that evening.

Mohammed Fuad Abu Askar lost his brother and his two sons Imad and Khaled Abu Askar, thirteen and nineteen years old, who were in the square with him when it was bombed. The Israeli Defence Forces reported that they had killed the two 'Hamas operatives,' Imad and Hassan Abu Askar. The boys' father denied to the Goldstone Commission that his sons had any connection with Hamas. Neither did the Goldstone Commission find any evidence that the thirteen-year-old Imad was a dangerous Hamas terrorist, or that he even had any contact with Hamas. Nor could they trace anyone who had been killed who went by the name Hassan Abu Askar.[185]

Mads and I formed the impression that Israel used Hamas infiltration as an excuse to attack schools and mosques. Every time they bombed such buildings, they justified it by saying that weapons or soldiers were hidden in the building. They also claimed several times that there were Hamas leaders hiding in al-Shifa Hospital.

All the reports published in 2009 supported our assessment that the attack was targeted against civilians, and that Israel's explanations about Hamas positions and depots were in most cases groundless.

When I was in Gaza in May 2009, most of the shops in Gaza City were closed. In December 2009 they were open and there were goods in the market in Jabaliya. At that time Israel was letting only a few goods in. Without the tunnels which had been dug under the Philadelphi Corridor, the strip of land between Egypt and Rafah, the situation would have been precarious, but the building materials which were being smuggled in through the tunnels were still dear.

Raed al-Atamna told us that he couldn't afford to buy building materials from the tunnels, and he invited us to visit Abed Rabbo again. When we visited Abed Rabbo a year after the attack, most of the ruins had been cleared. Raed Al-Atamna had built a house of dried mud, an adobe house, on the site where his family's houses had stood before. The house was better than the tents, but there wasn't room in the adobe house for all of his extended family, and so the tents were still there.

A little further up in the town, two young men were busy breaking up concrete with a sledgehammer to remove the old iron reinforcing rods. A man stood at a simple bench nearby, straightening out the rods with hand tools. Since Israel was still not letting cement or reinforcing rods in, they were making do by re-using them. The expensive cement which was being smuggled in through the tunnels was diluted with old cement which had been broken down.

On December 28, 2009, we visited the tunnels outside Rafah, which were now Gaza's lifeline. We drove to Rafah and turned west. There was a fence along the side of the road. On the other side of the fence were rows of big tents. We came to a gate which was controlled by a Hamas soldier. Behind the gate, there was a parking place and a little shed. This was the Hamas customs office. Duty was paid on all goods coming in through the tunnels. The supervisor in the office told us that there were between five hundred and six hundred tunnels operating and that all goods were checked and taxed. It was forbidden to bring in weapons or explosives.

We drove along a road between the tents. Inside each tent was an entrance down into a tunnel. Entry to the cheapest tunnels was by a vertical shaft some tens of metres deep, with a winch. At the bottom of the shaft there was a horizontal tunnel over to the Egyptian side. The goods were brought through the horizontal tunnel and hoisted up. All types of foodstuffs, building materials, toys and kitchen equipment were pulled through the tunnel and winched up. In one tunnel there was a pipeline for pumping fuel. It was no longer necessary to transport fuel in cans.

As there was competition between the owners of the various tunnels, the prices of groceries had fallen in the course of 2009, but building materials smuggled through the tunnels were still dear.

On the other side of the two-metre-high boundary wall and the Philadelphi Corridor we could see the Egyptian machines driving long steel piles down into the ground to form an underground wall of steel eighteen metres down in the ground, to close the tunnels.

The obvious smuggling and the half-hearted attempts to block the tunnels were difficult to understand. The Egyptian authorities' attempts to halt the tunnel trading seemed half-hearted. If we could see the extent of tents and tunnels on the Gaza side, it must have been easy to locate the tunnel openings on the Egyptian side. Since the war, there have been several reports of both Israeli and Egyptian attacks on the tunnels. In April 2010, Hamas accused Egypt of having pumped poison gas into one of them.[186] That same month, *Haaretz* reported that Egyptian authorities had blasted two tunnels, without anyone being harmed.[187] When I asked my colleagues at al-Shifa about these half-hearted attempts to close the tunnels, they replied that people high up in the Egyptian system earned money from the tunnel trade.

The hospitals in Gaza have been working at full capacity since the invasion. During the first weeks after the war, Israel had allowed some equipment and medical supplies in, but since then the blockade has become progressively more difficult for the hospitals.

In December 2009 I walked with Dr Sobhi Skaik through the emergency department where a year before we had taken in all those injured patients. It was strange to see how peaceful it all was. Behind one of the curtains was a mother with her four-year-old son who had a stomach ache. Behind another curtain, an elderly man lay waiting to be seen by a doctor. The atmosphere was calm. Nobody was running. Nobody was shouting or screaming. But behind the calm facade, the blockade was still creating problems.

In recent years the Palestinians have been self-sufficient in oxygen, thanks to NORWAC's projects to provide oxygen concentrators in all the hospitals in the Gaza Strip and on the West Bank. These concentrators, providing life-saving oxygen, had enabled many severely injured patients to survive in 2009.

Many of the concentrators in Gaza were acquired around the year 2000 or soon after, and they are beginning to fail. In April 2009, the Palestinian Health Ministry and NORWAC sought permission from the Israeli authorities to import seven oxygen concentrators, one to Gaza and six to the West Bank. In addition, NORWAC donated a new CT scanner (an advanced X-ray machine) to al-Shifa Hospital.

In December 2009 the Health Ministry applied to bring in the oxygen concentrator, the CT scanner, two intensive care beds and two sets of intensive care monitoring equipment. Along with this, they applied to import some minor equipment for the other public hospitals in the Gaza Strip. In February 2010 they applied for a prior guarantee to allow them to bring in a MRI machine (a system which takes pictures using magnetic fields) to al-Shifa Hospital.

By June 2010, Israel had still not replied to the applications from the Health Ministry. The Ministry asked the UN for help. The UN added this to a list of other equipment which was not being allowed in. After an appeal from the Norwegian Foreign Ministry, most of the equipment came in at the end of June. But the Palestinian authorities were not allowed to import the vital oxygen concentrators until October 2010, after repeated requests. The concentrators mean that the Palestinian hospitals do not have to buy bottled oxygen from Israel.

The blockade is still in effect, severely reducing the Palestinians' scope of action and creating major class differences. At the same time, several countries are donating large sums to earmarked health projects. In the autumn of 2010, Malaysia made plans to build a ten-storey children's hospital in Gaza, to be called the Malaysian Hospital. Indonesia planned to build a trauma surgery hospital in northern Gaza. The Jordanian organization Emaar planned to build a maternity hospital in central Gaza. There were also plans to build a new hospital in Rafah. These projects are not based on the Palestinian authorities' plans, and they create major challenges for the health authorities in Gaza. Even though the hospitals are donated, they will still eventually have to be run by the local health authorities.

At the same time as these major health projects are being planned, the public hospitals are lacking vital equipment and medicine, which is being stopped at the border. In June 2010, the WHO sent a demand to Israel that the population of Gaza must be allowed to import medical equipment unimpeded, and that health workers be allowed free movement in and out of Gaza. According to the WHO, the blockade of medicine and equipment was causing life-threatening situations, with patients not getting the healthcare they needed.[188]

I crossed back into Gaza in December 2011. So much had happened in the Arab world that year. In one Arab country after another, the population had protested against increasing class divisions and oppression and had demanded more democracy. The uprising started in Tunisia in December 2010 and in January 2011 President Ben Ali had to flee the country. In Egypt, President Mubarak was overthrown a month later. The military took control and arranged elections for a new national assembly in December 2011 and spring 2012. The Islamist and Salafist parties won by a landslide. But even though the Muslim Brotherhood had greater influence, little changed at the border with Gaza. Trade in goods still went through the tunnels. It had become slightly simpler for Palestinians to cross into Egypt, but overall there was strikingly little change from before. The revolutions in the Arab countries diverted attention away from Israel, which continued the blockade. In Gaza, Hamas was being challenged by militant groups, and they responded by increasing their control. Sobhi Skaik explained that life had become normal, but on a different level from before.

When I went through the last turnstile in the border station at Erez for the last time a few days before Christmas in 2011, it was with a lump in my throat.

For a short time after the violent attack in 2009, Gaza was in the world's spotlight. But now they were continuing a lonely struggle.

You Can't Say that You Didn't Know
by Mads Gilbert

We are writing in 2012. The brutal, medieval Israeli siege and blockade of Gaza continues into its sixth year. With growing intensity. The situation is worse than before, according to the UN.[189] Gaza is still one of the world's most densely populated areas, with over 4,500 inhabitants per square kilometre. The UN's assessment of the situation after five years of the blockade is shocking and confirms my own observations from trips to Gaza after Operation Cast Lead.

Every third inhabitant is unemployed, and half of the young people of working age are without a job. Eight out of ten families receive aid and almost half of families live in food insecurity, not knowing how they can manage to get hold of food. In 2011, one lorry-load of goods per day got out of Gaza, which is 3 per cent of Gaza's export volume from the first half of 2007, before the elections. 35 per cent of the arable land has been made inaccessible to Palestinian farmers, leading to an annual loss of at least 75,000 tonnes of agricultural produce. 85 per cent of Gaza's coastal and maritime territories are inaccessible to Gaza's fishermen. Although Gaza and Palestine are a coastal state with the right to an economic zone stretching out 200 nautical miles, Israel has unilaterally cut the fishing limits to three nautical miles. The result for the fishing industry is catastrophic. Barely 380 tonnes of fish were landed in 2011, compared to almost 2,000 tonnes in 2008. For the young population of Gaza, this means a shortage of food, undernourishment and food insecurity.

The blockade also means an energy and electricity crisis: power cuts last up to twelve hours a day. 90 million cubic metres of untreated sewage is pumped out into the Mediterranean every day as a result of a shortage of energy and spare parts for the sewage treatment plants. The sources of drinking water are unsafe. 90 per cent of Gaza's water supplies are unfit for human consumption. Half of Gaza's population has running water for six to eight hours every fourth day, while a third has water for six to eight hours every third day.[190]

The smugglers' tunnels under the Egyptian border are still the umbilical cord for the importation of vital supplies and ordinary consumer goods. Necessary but dangerous jobs in this tunnel industry have cost the lives of at least 172 Palestinians over the last five years, mostly young boys, while 318 have been injured.

Israel continues with the brutal collective punishment of Palestinians for using their ballot papers in legitimate democratic elections. This prolonged and wearing collective punishment is directed at the entire civilian population and civil society in Gaza. The siege and blockade hit the children and young people of Gaza especially hard. Extensive anaemia, undernourishment and stunted height are apparent, but there also less immediately obvious consequences from limited access to a secure education and from a lack of hope for the future. 85 per cent of the schools in Gaza are now forced to teach the children in two shifts because so few of the schools the Israeli forces bombed and destroyed have been rebuilt. All this happens with the constant and solid support of the USA, continuing even after Obama became president.

Since June 2007, Israeli government forces have killed almost 2,300 Palestinians and have wounded over 7,700. Two thirds of these were killed and injured during Operation Cast Lead. Over the same period, 37 Israelis have been killed and 380 wounded in attacks carried out from Gaza, 60 per cent of whom were military personnel. Even though Israeli military forces withdrew at the end of January 2009, the military siege, surveillance and systematic killing of Palestinians in Gaza continues with drones, artillery and individual attacks. So far this year, from January to August 2012, Israeli government forces have killed 47 Palestinians in Gaza and wounded 247. One Israeli has been killed in the same period, and 18 wounded.[191]

I have travelled back to Gaza several times. My last trip was in January 2012 to take part in commemorations marking three years since the attack. The bombed-out areas were still there as sunburnt heaps of concrete rubble, bricks and twisted iron reinforcing rods. In the destroyed parts of Gaza City, Abed Rabbo, the poor quarter of al-Zaytoun, the refugee camp in Jabaliya and other settlements in northern Gaza, little had been restored. The blockade prevents building materials from being imported. Those that are smuggled are too expensive for the poor. Almost 40 per cent of all the buildings in Gaza were completely or partially destroyed during Operation Cast Lead, and 74 per cent of the ruined buildings have not been repaired.[192]

Every time I drove around the poor and bombed-out neighbourhoods of Gaza, I thought about Colonel Gabriel Siboni, an Israeli military analyst. He wrote in 2008 that the intention of the Israeli attacks should be 'to deal out destructive punishment to such an extent that long and costly reconstruction will be required'. I also thought about the Israeli Major General Yoav Galant, who declared the day after the offensive began on 27 December 2008 that the aim of the Israeli bombing was to 'send Gaza decades into the past' (see p. 309).

That is what happened, and that is still the situation now. Gaza really has been sent many decades back into the past while the collective punishment of the people continues.

Little Jumana has grown into a beautiful little girl and was almost four years old when I last met her again in January 2012. This time she was no longer sitting in her mother Meysa's arms, but like a little princess on her throne of a sofa at home with her grandparents where the two of them now live. Jumana's mother became a widow at only nineteen years of age. She survived the Israeli massacre together with her nine-month-old daughter. The massacre cost the lives of her husband and many of her closest relatives (see p. 33 and pp. 203–206).

Now Jumana was both curious and animated. She manipulated the toys she was given with great skill, using the two remaining fingers on her partially amputated left hand. Both she and her mother were dressed smartly and met me with dignified courtesy. Meysa had begun to study and wanted to move on with her life. Her father, Jumana's grandfather, was furious.

'Nothing happens,' he said. 'We are being starved and tortured. The West lets Israel carry on unrestrained. What should we do?'

'Tell the American people that their tax money is killing us,' he said when he heard I was going on another lecture tour to the USA.

The Samouni family and the tens of thousands of Palestinian children who went through the massacre and those three weeks of terror will all carry on living. They need a safe and predictable everyday life, education, food, housing and not least confident adults with jobs, income and self-respect who can make their children believe in a just future. The 800,000 children of Gaza all carry a dream for a better life and a future without the blockade or occupation. Without a future, nobody has the strength to live, and without dignity, respect and freedom there are high chances that the oppressed children of Gaza will become an uncontrolled reservoir for the recruitment of desperate warriors, and not teachers, musicians or farmers.

The destructive Israeli logic based on extreme control and disproportionate retaliation is also evident in Gaza today, more than three years after the attack. Gaza still lies in ruins. Practically none of the bombed and shattered infrastructure, schools, agriculture, fisheries, local industry, sewage and water treatment plants, power supply or waste disposal facilities have been rebuilt. The blockade and continued regular attacks and bombings are an endless collective punishment directed at an unbending population that refuses to give up, refuses to resign itself or surrender to the occupier. The encroachments take place in broad daylight, while Western leaders make mumbled verbal protests or, even worse, express understanding 'that Israel must have control of goods going in and out of Gaza', as the Norwegian Foreign Minister Jonas Gahr Støre said on 16 August 2010 during his visit to Gaza. On the same visit he refused to meet representatives of Gaza's politically elected authorities from Hamas.[193]

The extent and consequences of the collective punishment imposed by Israel, contrary to international law, have been extremely well documented. Read the countless reports from the UN, from Israeli, Palestinian and international human rights organizations. You can read scientific studies documenting systematic undernourishment, stunted growth and long-term psychological damage among the whole population of Gaza, you can go through careful legal arguments and reports on culpable Israeli leaders and officers by respected experts in international law, and you can find facts about much worse events that those we document in this book if you study the UN's comprehensive Goldstone Report. Nonetheless, Israel is allowed to continue its serious, systematic violations of international law and human rights. Nobody is held responsible, no investigations are opened and no Israeli leaders so far have risked being prosecuted and tried for war crimes in Gaza by the International Criminal Court in The Hague. On the contrary, the official Israeli version of the assault on Gaza shows no remorse or admission.[194]

Israel reacted just as violently to the Goldstone Report as to any other scrutiny of the Israeli attack on Gaza. They denied the facts, hurled out serious accusations of anti-Semitism and lies, and resisted any form of further investigation.

'We are going to deploy great diplomatic and political efforts on the international stage to block and contain the perverse and noxious effects of the Goldstone Commission report,' the Israeli Foreign Ministry spokesman Yigal Palmor said when the report was published. 'The goal is to avoid a slippery slope which would lead Israel to the International Criminal Court in The Hague,' an Israeli official said on that same day.[195]

A report by the Israeli human rights organization B'Tselem from 2010 documents how the Israeli legal system seldom or never opens cases against Israeli soldiers who kill, wound or abuse Palestinian civilians.[196] Because the official Israeli policy is to classify what is happening in occupied Palestine as an 'armed conflict' and not an illegal occupation, soldiers and officers are guaranteed immunity. The Israeli Military Police Investigation Unit (MPIU) only opens investigations in exceptional cases in which Palestinian civilians have been killed by Israeli soldiers. The consequence of this is that Israeli soldiers are not held responsible when they kill, wound or abuse Palestinian civilians who are not engaged in armed resistance to the occupation. This is against international law, according to which an occupier is responsible for protecting the civilian population of occupied areas.

Only one single Israeli soldier has been indicted for manslaughter as a result of Operation Cast Lead. The former Israeli soldier was sentenced in 2012 to serving forty-five days in prison on charges in connection with the killing of a Palestinian mother and her daughter, who were shot dead while waving white flags during Operation Cast Lead. The former Israeli soldier agreed to a plea bargain so that he was convicted of shooting without permission, and thereby had the original charge of manslaughter dropped. He shot dead Majda Abu Hajaj (35) and her mother Rayah (64), who were among thirty people, including children, trying to leave a house where they had taken shelter. The group was fired upon and the two women were killed. The killing of Majda and Rayah was mentioned in the Goldstone Report. The Israeli military said when the original indictment came in 2010 that the charge was based on evidence that the former soldier, a marksman, 'deliberately targeted an individual walking with a group of people waving a white flag without being ordered or authorised to do so.'[197]

The sentence is outrageous and racist: twenty-two and a half days in prison for killing one defenceless Palestinian woman is an offence to fundamental human rights, a grave violation of human dignity, global human values and justice. The sentence is in keeping with the general strategy of Israeli vindication: to deny any external investigation and avoid all international courts and judges. Many human rights groups have criticized the Israeli Defence Forces for conducting their own investigations into allegations of wrongdoing.

No national or international courts have opened investigations or proceedings, or indicted culpable Israeli leaders or higher-ranking officers for war crimes committed in Gaza during Operation Cast Lead. What the Goldstone Report describes as serious war crimes and possible crimes against human rights have passed without prosecution. So far, only two Israeli sergeants have been indicted and found guilty by an Israeli military tribunal. They were convicted for having forced a Palestinian boy to open bags that they suspected to be booby traps when they were searching a house in the Tel al-Hawa district of Gaza.[198]

'Why are sanctions and blockades implemented against Iraq, Iran and others who "break international law", but never against Israel? Why are they treated differently? Don't we have human rights?' our Palestinian colleagues ask us when we meet them again at al-Shifa or when I am invited to their homes for *iftar*, the long-awaited evening meal after the day's fasting, after sunset.

'Are we inferior human beings, those of us living under the Israeli occupation?'

Once again I am still at a loss for words.

The result of the destruction and the continued blockade of Gaza is that 1.5 million Palestinians are starving. At the same time, the population and the authorities are denied the opportunity to rebuild their homes, schools, factories, farms and other destroyed infrastructure. Their children are denied a full education and everyone is denied free movement in and out of Gaza. So the destructive collective punishment of Gaza goes on, but with other means than bombs and rocket attacks. An important consequence is that the long-term effects of the strain and trauma of Operation Cast Lead are intensified and exacerbated. One of the most important measures to prevent chronic stress and negative effects on health caused by war trauma is to restore people's safe and normal daily lives as quickly as possible, with work, school and family life. The occupying power, Israel, has absolute responsibility for the Palestinian civilian population's safety and welfare, including in Gaza. The USA, the EU, NATO and unfortunately Norway in practice accept and allow these systematic violations of international law to continue quite openly.

Does it make any difference?

On 11 December 2009, a very important document was released at a seminar in Bethlehem with local and international church leaders. The

'Kairos Palestine Document' was written by a group of theologians, church leaders and engaged individuals from most churches in the region. The document was entitled 'A Moment of Truth'. It was a cry to the international community about what life is like under the Israeli occupation, and at the same time a powerful testament to its authors' faith, hope and will to bring fairness and peaceful co-existence for everyone who lives in the region. The document's authors show clear engagement against the occupation, and they show hope. They challenge everyone, both locally and internationally, to play their part in putting pressure on the Israeli state to stop what they call Israel's policy of repression and disregard of international law.

The document encourages everyone to join in the popular initiatives for economic sanctions and boycotting Israeli. The Kairos Document represents another step on the road towards an effective international boycott, divestment and sanctions (BDS) campaign against the Israeli state.[199] This is the most important resource we now have in the struggle against the apartheid policy Israel carries out – and is allowed to carry out – against the Palestinians, not only in Gaza, but also in Israel and on the West Bank.

Over the last three years, I have been invited to a number of universities in the USA, Canada and the UK to lecture on our experiences in Gaza. On these tours I have given a large number of well-attended lectures and met thousands of engaged people: Muslims, Jews, Christians, socialists, conservatives and other activists. What they have had in common is that they have all in their own countries personally taken the initiative and responsibility to find out about the situation in Gaza and occupied Palestine, and they want to do something concrete to change the current situation. In an ecumenical church meeting under the auspices of the Sabeel Conference in a beautiful Presbyterian church in San Francisco in the spring of 2010, I met several hundred engaged church leaders and activists from many religious communities.[200] They wanted to further the struggle for a fair solution for the Palestinian people. The theme of the conference was experiences and methods in the continuing 'BDS' movement: how to organize a consumer boycott of Israeli goods and services, how to get church communities, universities and various companies to withdraw money and investments from Israel (selling shares in Israeli companies) and how to influence the US and Canadian governments to impose sanctions on Israel.

They had considerable engagement and many initiatives. One talk summed up the experiences of the struggle against apartheid thus: when the large church communities and the sports movement joined the consumer boycott of South African goods, the white minority regime was brought to its knees and apartheid fell.

BDS campaigns yield results, and not only in the USA. The Norwegian campaign to boycott Israel and especially to withdraw Norwegian funds invested in Israeli companies has already won victories. In November 2010, there came an important appeal from a hundred Norwegian academics and cultural figures, encouraging a cultural and academic boycott of Israel.[201] Norwegian trade unions are also active. The Bergen district branch of the Norwegian Confederation of Trade Unions has taken the initiative of starting a 'boycott relay' in the trade union movement.[202] Several Norwegian bishops are said to be contemplating a boycott of Israel.[203] True enough they were strongly reprimanded by the Foreign Minister, Jonas Gahr Støre, who said that 'the church should not get involved in politics'.

Solidarity does make a difference! Actions large and small empower and change political positions. When Berit Slåttum, a friend of Palestine, knitted a pair of mittens in Palestinian colours for me while we were in Gaza, she did not realize that those very mittens would be an important example of practical solidarity. When I came home, I took the mittens to Inger Granby, that warm-hearted local crafts activist from Selbu, near Trondheim. Now she and the skilful weavers of the Selbu Folk Art and Craft Association have further developed the idea into the 'Gaza mittens', beautiful Selbu pattern mittens in the Palestinian flag's colours of red, white, green and black. The 'Gaza mitten' can be bought as a special pack of wool, and anybody who wants to can knit solidarity mittens. 100 kroner from each pack of wool goes straight to the prosthetics workshop in Gaza.[204] Their fundraising for the prosthetics workshop has made it possible, in spite of the blockade, for Palestinian professionals to continue helping those of their own people who have had to have arms and legs amputated following Israeli attacks.

In the struggle for justice for the Palestinians, politicians, the Foreign Ministry and the government can also be influenced and pressured. The government decided to sell all the Norwegian Pension Fund's shares in the Israeli arms manufacturer Elbit Systems, which makes drones and surveillance equipment for the illegal wall on the West Bank. This important divestment came following political and popular pressure. Several other Scandinavian funds have followed suit and sold their shares in Elbit Systems.[205] A similar thing has happened with the large French transportation company Veolia, which entered into a thirty-year contract with Israel to build and operate a new, illegal tram line that would connect illegally built Israeli colonies on the West Bank with Jerusalem. Veolia has been under incredible international pressure and has lost several large contracts as a result of the contract with Israel. Most of all, Israel fears isolation in the West and financial consequences of the boycott movement. And with good reason: if the church communities of the West really take their responsibility seriously, if the sports movement boycotts Israeli teams and meetings and Israel is shut out from, for example, the Olympic movement, and if the big investment funds – such as the Norwegian Oil Fund – no longer find it worth the bother to invest in Israeli companies, then Israel can be forced to make political changes.

After repeated calls from the great majority of Palestinian political parties, Palestinian religious communities, grassroots movements and individual activists, it is high time that we join in carrying out a consumer and arms boycott of Israel, pressuring the government to sell all the Oil Fund's shares in Israeli companies (to the value of 5 billion kroner) and introduce effective political sanctions against the state of Israel.[206]

These are well-proven peaceful, non-violent, legal methods to force the state of Israel to end their occupation, ethnic cleansing, colonial policy and bloody oppression of the whole Palestinian people. It is our duty to get out of our easy chairs and play our part.[207]

Now you know what the lives of Jumana, Amal and all the other children and adults in Gaza are like.

You can't say that you didn't know.

Palestinian Demographic Trends 1973–2007

This table is based on official census data on the Palestinian population. It demonstrates that the population has more than tripled since the 1970s. The Palestinian population is twice as large as the population of Norway, but only half of the Palestinians live in their own country, where they live either as second-rate residents of Israel or under Israeli occupation in the West Bank and in Gaza.

Country	1973	2007	Growth 1973–2007 (%)
West Bank	700,000	2,517,000	260
Gaza	380,000	1,499,000	294
Israel	400,000	1,450,000	263
Occupied Palestine (total)	1,480,000	5,466,000	269
Jordan	950,000	3,102,000	227
Syria	200,000	495,000	148
Lebanon	260,000	463,000	78
Other Arab countries	247,000	733,000	197
Arab countries outside Palestine (total)	1,657,000	4,793,000	189
Rest of the world	32,000	594,000	1,756
Total Palestinian population	**3,169,000**	**10,853,000**	**242**

Source: Peder Martin Lysestøl: *Palestinerne: Historie og frigjøringskamp* [The Palestinians: History and Struggle for Liberation] (p. 262), published by Tidsskriftet Rødt! (2009).

Notes

Notes to Chapter 1 – Into the Bomb Zone

1 Heather Sharp, 'Guide: Gaza under blockade,' BBC: http://news.bbc.co.uk/2/hi/middle_east/7545636.stm (accessed June 4, 2009).

2 Sameh A. Habeeb, 'Massacre in Gaza: 230 Killed,' Countercurrents.org, December 28, 2009: http://www.countercurrents.org/habeeb281208.htm (accessed July 2, 2009).

Kuwait Times, 'Egypt slams Israeli "murder",' December 28, 2008: http://www.kuwaittimes.net/read_news.php?newsid=MTQ0OTIyOTY0 (accessed July 2, 2009).

ReliefWeb, 'Gaza offensive enters second week (28 Dec – 03 Jan),' source: The Palestinian Initiative for the Promotion of Global Dialogue and Democracy, January 3, 2009: http://www.reliefweb.int/rw/rwb.nsf/db900SID/RMOI-7MXMPD?OpenDocument (accessed July 2, 2009).

Palestine News Network, 'Israelis kill 225 Palestinians in Gaza and say this is just the beginning,' December 27, 2008: http://english.pnn.ps/index.php?option=com_content&task=view&id=4297 (accessed July 2, 2009).

3 China View, 'Israel continues airstrikes on Gaza, 271 killed,' December 28, 2008: http://news.xinhuanet.com/english/2008–12/28/content-_10570955.htm (accessed December 28, 2008).

4 Press release from the Norwegian Ministry of Foreign Affairs, December 29, 2008:

> The Government decided today to provide NOK 30 million in immediate humanitarian relief in connection with the assaults in Gaza. 'We are extremely concerned about the precarious humanitarian situation in Gaza,' said Foreign Minister Jonas Gahr Støre.
>
> Many innocent civilians are suffering as a result of the violence in Gaza. The Foreign Minister pointed out how crucial it is to ensure that humanitarian assistance reaches those who need it in Gaza.
>
> 'We presume that Israel will provide the necessary access for humanitarian aid. There is an acute need for medical and surgical equipment at the hospitals in Gaza.
>
> 'We join in a broad international appeal to Israel to help to ensure that humanitarian relief supplies reach those in need,' said Mr Støre.

The Ministry of Foreign Affairs is now allocating funds to several humanitarian organisations providing emergency medical aid and assistance to the wounded and injured in Gaza, and is giving priority to those that are able to ensure the rapid and effective delivery of emergency relief. The funds are being channelled primarily through the World Health Organisation (WHO), the UN Relief and Works Agency for Palestine Refugees in the Near East (UNRWA), the International Red Cross (ICRC) and the Norwegian Aid Committee (NORWAC).

'Norway is following the situation closely and we are ready to provide additional humanitarian funds,' said the Foreign Minister.

During the past few days the Foreign Minister has been in contact with several of his colleagues in the region, with the Palestinian Authority, and with the French EU Presidency.

'I have conveyed Norway's view that the fighting must stop, a new ceasefire must be put in place, and border crossings must be opened to provide access for humanitarian relief supplies,' said Mr Støre. 'Norway is working for and supporting diplomatic initiatives designed for this purpose, such as the efforts being made by Egypt and initiatives taken by the EU.'

5 Yaakov Katz, 'IAF hits Islamic University targets,' *Jerusalem Post*, December 28, 2009: http://www.jpost.com/servlet/Satellite?cid= 1230111723191&pagename=JPost%2FJPArticle%2FShowFull (accessed June 5, 2009).

6 *Die Welt* Online, 'Gaza aid boat reaches Lebanon,' December 30, 2008: http://www.welt.de/english-news/article2951960/Gaza-aid-boat-reaches-Lebanon.html (accessed June 4, 2009).

Notes to Chapter 2 – Prelude

7 Since 1994, NORWAC has had a management committee consisting of Erik Fosse, Synne Holan, John Eivind Jensen and Kjersti Fiveland. Holan is responsible for NORWAC's projects in the Balkans, Fiveland for the projects in Lebanon and Jensen for the projects in Palestine. Erik Fosse has been leader of the organisation from the start. Because of a big increase in the size of projects and financial turnover, the management set up an operational company, NORWAC AS, in 2008. Two new members have been recruitd to the board of NORWAC AS: Tormod Furuset and Berit Jagman. Erik Fosse is director general of NORWAC AS.

8 UNRWA, 'Palestine refugees': http://www.un.org/unrwa/refugees/index.html (accessed July 2, 2009).

9 BBC News, 'Jerusalem: Crucible of the conflict,' December 4, 2001: http:/

/news.bbc.co.uk/1/hi/in_depth/middle_east/2001/israel_and_the_palestinians/ issues/1682594.stm (accessed August 2, 2009).

Palestine Monitor factsheet, 'Israeli settlements,' December 17, 2008: http://www.palestinemonitor.org/spip/spip.php?article7 (accessed August 2, 2009).

10 Israel Ministry of Foreign Affairs, General Yatom press conference, February 27, 1994: http://www.mfa.gov.il/MFA/Archive/Peace+Process/1994/GENERAL+YATOM+PRESS+CONFERENCE+-+27-Feb-94.htm?DisplayMode=print (accessed June 2, 2009).

11 Anti-Defamation League, 'Hamas Fact Sheet,' January 30, 2006: http://www.adl.org/main_israel/hamas_facts.htm (accessed June 5, 2009).

12 List of Hamas suicide attacks: http://en.wikipedia.org/wiki/List_of_Hamas_suicide_attacks (accessed June 5, 2009).

13 Neil MacFarquhar, 'Blow for Blow: Israelis Demolish Bomb-Maker's Family Home,' *New York Times*, March 15, 1996: http://www.nytimes.com/1996/03/15/world/blow-for-blow-israelis-demolish-bomb-maker-s-family-home.html (accessed July 1, 2009).

Alon Ben-Meir, 'The Assassination of Yahya Ayyash: Untimely and Unwise,' Washington Report on Middle East Affairs, March 1996: http://www. wrmea.com/backissues/0296/9602021.html (accessed July 1, 2009).

14 Qassam rocket: http://en.wikipedia.org/wiki/Qassam_rocket (accessed June 5, 2009).

GlobalSecurity.org, 'Hamas rockets': http://www.globalsecurity.org/military/world/para/hamas-qassam.htm (accessed June 5, 2009).

15 UN Resolution 181: http://www.allaboutpalestine.com/un_resolutions.html#ga_res_181 (accessed April 1, 2009).

16 UNRWA Overview: http://www.unrwa.org/etemplate.php?id=85 (accessed April 11, 2010).

UNRWA Programmes: http://www.unrwa.org/etemplate.php?id=18 (accessed April 11, 2010).

17 Jeroen Gunning, *Hamas in Politics: Democracy, Religion, Violence* (London: Hurst and Company, 2007).

18 Alan Hart, *Arafat: Terrorist or Peacemaker?* (London: Sidgwick & Jackson, 1985).

19 *Arab News*, 'Editorial: Corruption in Palestine,' February 6, 2006: http://www.arabnews.com/?page=7&section=08&article=77375&d=6&m=2&y=2006 (accessed July 2, 2009).

20 Matthew Levitt, 'Hamas' hidden economy,' *Los Angeles Times*, July 3, 2007: http://www.latimes.com/news/opinion/la-oe-levitt3jul03,0,4057571.story?coll=la-opinionrightrail (accessed July 2, 2009).

21 Maj. Gen. Doron Almog, 'Lessons of the Gaza Security Fence for the West Bank,' *Jerusalem Issue Brief*, 4(12), December 23, 2004: http://www.jcpa.org/brief/brief004-12.htm (accessed June 5, 2009).

22 As Palestine is not a state, it does not have a formal parliament, but a legislative assembly for the self-governing authority (the Palestinian Legislative Council) with one chamber and 132 members elected from sixteen electoral districts in occupied Palestine.

23 Scott Wilson, 'Hamas Sweeps Palestinian Elections, Complicating Peace Efforts in Mideast,' *Washington Post*, January 27, 2006: http://www.washingtonpost.com/wp-dyn/content/article/2006/01/26/AR2006012600372. html (accessed June 5, 2009).

24 Speech by Commissioner Ferrero-Waldner: Suspension of aid to the Palestinian Authority government, Brussels, April 26, 2006: http://www.europa-eu-un.org/articles/en/article_5930_en.htm (accessed June 5, 2009).

VOA News, 'Mideast Quartet Demands Hamas Give Up Violence, Recognise Israel,' January 30, 2006: http://www.voanews.com/bangla/archive/2006-01/2006-01-30-voa8.cfm?moddate=2006-01-30 (accessed July 2, 2009).

Arjan El Fassed, 'EU and US disrupt Palestinian elections,' Electronic Intifada, January 4, 2006: http://electronicintifada.net/v2/article4374.shtml (accessed July 2, 2009).

25 *Jerusalem Times*, 'This Week in Palestine... Behind the News with Hanna Siniora,' April 9, 2006: http://www.ipcri.org/files/weekpalapril9-06.html (accessed July 30, 2009).

26 Ali Waked, 'Israel detains senior Hamas officials,' Ynetnews, June 29, 2006: http://www.ynet.co.il/english/articles/0,7340,L-3268844,00.html (accessed June 5, 2009).

27 Israel Ministry of Foreign Affairs, 'The State of Israel's policy towards the Palestinian Government,' March 18, 2007: http://www.mfa.gov.il/MFA/Government/Communiques/2007/The+State+of+Israels+policy+towards+the+Palestinian+Government+18-Mar-2007.htm (accessed May 6, 2009).

28 Nina Berglund, 'Top Israeli diplomat shuns Norwegian envoy,' *Aftenposten*, March 20, 2007: http://www.aftenposten.no/english/article1698989.ece (accessed June 5, 2009).

29 Mark Perrey and Alastair Crooke, 'No-goodniks and the Palestinian shootout,' *Asia Times* Online, January 9, 2007: http://www.atimes.com/atimes/Middle_East/IA09Ak03.html (accessed May 24, 2009).

30 Fatah-Hamas conflict: http://en.wikipedia.org/wiki/2006_Palestinian_civil_skirmishes (accessed May 24, 2009).

31 OCHA-oPt, 'Gaza Humanitarian Situation Report: Escalation in Violence, 27 Feb – 3 March 2008': http://www.ochaopt.org/documents/Gaza_Situation_Report_2008_02_30_Final5.pdf (accessed June 20, 2009)

32 Barak Ravid, 'Operation "Cast Lead": Israeli Air Force strike followed months of planning,' *Haaretz*, December 28, 2008: http://www. global research.ca/index.php?context=va&aid=11521 (accessed May 25, 2009).

33 OCHA, 'IDF operation in the Gaza Strip and rocket firing at Israel,' Protection of Civilians Weekly Report, 284, October 29–November 4, 2008: http://www.ochaopt.org/documents/ocha_opt_protection_of_civilians_weekly_2008_11_08_english.pdf (accessed April 11, 2010).

Rory McCarthy, 'Gaza truce broken as Israeli raid kills six Hamas gunmen,' *The Guardian*, November 5, 2008: http://www.guardian.co.uk/world/2008/nov/05/israelandthepalestinians (accessed July 2, 2009).

34 Henry Siegman, 'Israel's Lies,' *London Review of Books*, January 29, 2009: http://www.lrb.co.uk/v31/n02/print/sieg01_.html (June 5, 2009).

Notes to Chapter 3 – Welcome to Gaza

35 Office of the Special Representative of the Secretary-General for Children and Armed Conflict, 'Middle-East: Children demand answers and we must deliver now,' February 6, 2009: http://www.un.org/children/conflict/english/pr/2009-02-05207.html (accessed July 2, 2009).

36 UNRWA, Where UNRWA works: http://www.unrwa.org/etemplate.php?id=41 (accessed April 11, 2010).

37 Tani Goldstein, '"We're supplying electricity to Gaza under Qassam fire,"' Ynetnews, January 21, 2008: http://www.ynet.co.il/english/articles/0,7340,L-3496729,00.html (accessed June 5, 2009).

38 Scott Wilson, 'After 38 Years, Gaza Settlers Gone,' *Washington Post*, August 23, 2005: http://www.washingtonpost.com/wp-dyn/content/article/2005/08/22/AR2005082200114.html (accessed June 5, 2009).

39 Michel Chossudovsky, 'War and Natural Gas: The Israeli Invasion and Gaza's Offshore Gas Fields,' Global Research, January 8, 2009: http://www.globalresearch.ca/index.php?context=va&aid=11680 (accessed July 2, 2009).

40 WHO, 'The health situation in the Gaza Strip: Report by the Secretariat,' January 20, 2009: http://apps.who.int/gb/ebwha/pdf_files/EB124/B124_35-en.pdf (accessed May 24, 2009).

41 ICRC, 'The ICRC in Gaza: Facts and Figures,' February 2, 2009: http://www.icrc.org/web/eng/siteengo.nsf/html/palestine-update-020209! Open Document (accessed May 24, 2009).

42 International Middle East Media Center, ' "Herding cattle" at Erez,' July 1, 2005: http://www.imemc.org/article/12263 (accessed May 20, 2009).

Notes to Chapter 4 – It's Raining Death

43 Ahmed A. Kandil, 'Gunshot wounds of the abdomen,' *Scientific Medical Journal* (Egypt), 17(4), 65–73.
44 GlobalSecurity.org, 'Dense Inert Metal Explosive': http://www.globalsecurity.org/military/systems/munitions/dime.htm (accessed July 2, 2009).
45 GlobalSecurity.org, 'Small Diameter Bomb / Small Smart Bomb': http://www.globalsecurity.org/military/systems/munitions/sdb.htm (accessed July 2, 2009).
46 James Brooks, 'The DIME Bomb: Yet another genotoxic weapon, Part III,' Aljazeerah.info, December 7, 2006: http://www.thetruthseeker.co.uk/article.asp?ID=5648 (accessed July 2, 2009).

Notes to Chapter 5 – Who Gets to Live?

47 Islamic University of Gaza: http://www.iugaza.edu.ps/en/ (accessed June 8, 2009).
International Colleges and Universities – al-Azhar University: http://www.4icu.org/reviews/3566.htm (accessed June 8, 2009).
48 Palestinian Centre for Human Rights, 'The number of Palestinians killed rises to 424, mostly civilians, including 88 children and 19 women,' January 6, 2009: http://euromedrights.net/pages/556/news/focus/68493 (accessed June 5, 2009).

Notes to Chapter 6 – Powerless Witnesses

49 The World Food Programme had distributed 'High Energy Biscuits – Gift from France'. These 100 g packets of high energy biscuits were a considerable boost for the health workers in Gaza. The hospital apportioned the biscuits to its employees as a meagre but welcome alternative to no food at all. The biscuits contain protein and fat as well as a good deal of vitamins and iron, but they did not taste especially good.
50 United Nations Office for the Coordination of Humanitarian Affairs (OCHA). About OCHA: http://ochaonline.un.org/tabid/5838/language/en-US/Default.aspx (accessed April 11, 2010). This important UN body is based in New York and Geneva with thirty regional offices across the world. The regional office for the occupied Palestinian territories (OCHA-oPt) is located in East Jerusalem, but there are field-workers both in Gaza and the West Bank. This arm of the UN gathers comprehensive statistical data and makes useful maps of Palestine. OCHA-oPt released systematic and regular updates on the humanitarian situation in Gaza during the attacks by Israel, see the OCHA-oPt website: http://www.ochaopt.org/ (accessed June 30, 2009).

51 Kjetil Haanes, '"Målet var å skremme oss": Når media vert krigsmål' ['The aim was to scare us': When the media becomes a target of warfare], *Syn og Segn* 1/2009, 4–12.

52 Ibid.

Notes to Chapter 7 – Remote-Controlled Genocide

53 The Strategy Page, 'Israeli Predator Competitor,' March 12, 2007: http://www.strategypage.com/htmw/htairfo/articles/20070312.aspx (accessed June 30, 2009).

54 UAV Forum: http://www.uavforum.com/index.shtml (accessed June 30, 2009).

55 'Vendors': http://www.uavforum.com/vendors/vendors.htm (accessed June 30, 2009).

56 Scott Lindaw, 'UAV operators suffer war stress,' The Associated Press, *Air Force Times*, August 8, 2008: http://www.airforcetimes.com/news/2008/08/ap_remote_stress_080708/ (accessed June 30, 2009).

57 Computed tomography (CT) is a special form of examination carried out in the radiology departments of most hospitals. The technique allows for the detailed survey of thin 'slices' of different kinds of tissue such as brain tissue. It is an invaluable resource for the diagnosis and follow-up of, for example, head injuries. Al-Shifa Hospital had one X-ray laboratory for CT with a modern scanner.

58 CIA, *The World Factbook 2003–2008*, Middle East, Gaza Strip: https://www.cia.gov/library/publications/the-world-factbook/geos/gz.html (accessed April 11, 2010).

59 Aerobic cellular respiration uses oxygen, as opposed to anaerobic respiration, which is without oxygen. Our brain cells can only cope for a few seconds without oxygen before damage occurs.

60 See Hans Husum, Mads Gilbert and Torben Wisborg, *Save Lives, Save Limbs* (Penang, Malaysia: Third World Network, 2000).

Hans Husum, Mads Gilbert, Torben Wisborg, Yang Van Heng and Mudhafar Murad, 'Rural Prehospital Trauma Systems Improve Trauma Outcome in Low-Income Countries: A Prospective Study from North Iraq and Cambodia,' *Journal of Trauma Injury, Infection and Critical Care*, 2003, 54 (6), 1188–1196.

Hans Husum, Mads Gilbert, Torben Wisborg and Johan Pillgram-Larsen, 'Ban the Tourniquet!' letter to the editor, *Journal of Trauma Injury, Infection and Critical Care*, 2004, 56 (1), 214–15.

61 Mads Gilbert, 'Sommerregn i Gaza' [Summer rains in Gaza], *Tidsskrift for Den norske lægeforening*, 16/2006, 2136–9.

Notes to Chapter 8 – 'They're Only Hamas Children'

62 Netzarim is five kilometres south of Gaza City.

63 Aljazeerah.info: Cross-Cultural Understanding, 'Day 11 of Israeli Terrorist Attacks on Gaza, 135 Killed, 400 Injured, 45 Civilians Massacred in UN School, War Crimes Everywhere,' January 6, 2009: http://www.ccun.org/News/2009/January/6%20n/Day%2011%20of%20Israeli%20 Terrorist %20Attacks%20on%20Gaza,%20135%20Killed,%20400%20Injured, %2045%20Civilians%20Massacred%20in%20UN%20School,%20War%20Crimes%20Everywhere.htm (accessed June 5, 2009).

64 Ahmed Burai and Jeffrey Fleishman, 'Israel strikes deeper into Gaza,' *Los Angeles Times*, January 7, 2009: http://articles.latimes.com/2009/jan/07/world/fg-gaza7 (accessed June 5, 2009).

65 Toufic Haddad, 'Ramattan's war: The World's eyes into Gaza,' Electronic Intifada, February 20, 2009: http://electronicintifada.net/v2/article10324.shtml (accessed April 11, 2010).

66 Reuters, 'Carter calls Gaza blockade a "crime and atrocity",' *Haaretz*, April 17, 2008: http://www.haaretz.com/hasen/spages/976086.html (accessed June 5, 2009).

Notes to Chapter 9 – Darkness at Noon

67 UN Office for the Coordination of Humanitarian Affairs (OCHA), Gaza Strip Population Density, January 2009: http://www.ochaopt.org/gaza crisis/admin/output/files/ocha_opt_gaza_crisis_population_dinsety_2009. pdf (accessed June 18, 2009).

List of countries and dependencies by population density: http://en.wikipedia.org/wiki/List_of_countries_by_population_density (accessed June 18, 2009).

68 Seige of Beirut: http://en.wikipedia.org/wiki/Siege_of_Beirut (accessed June 30, 2009).

69 Mahmoud Darwish, *Memory for Forgetfulness: August, Beirut, 1982* (Berkeley, Calif.: University of California Press, 1995).

Yearbook of the United Nations, 1982 (New York: UN Department of Public Information), pp. 549–50.

70 NTB, '20 år siden massakrene i Sabra og Shatila' [20 years since the massacres in Sabra and Shatila], *Dagbladet*, September 16, 2002: http://www.dagbladet.no/nyheter/2002/09/16/348841.html (accessed June 8, 2009).

Ahmad al-Tal, 'The Massacre of Sabra and Chatila in 1982': http://www.jerusalemites.org/crimes/massacres/1.htm (accessed June 30, 2009).

Martin Asser, 'Sabra and Shatila 20 years on,' BBC News, September 14, 2002: http://news.bbc.co.uk/1/hi/world/middle_east/2255902.stm (accessed July 8, 2009).

71 Sheera Frenkel, 'After two years in a coma, Ariel Sharon is now a symbol in the hall of heroes,' *The Times*, January 4, 2008: http://www.timesonline.co.uk/tol/news/world/middle_east/article3129250.ece (accessed June 8, 2009).

Notes to Chapter 10 – No Mercy

72 Abdel Azis Mousa Thabet and Panos Vostanis, 'Post-Traumatic Stress Reactions in Children of War,' *Journal of Child Psychology and Psychiatry*, 40 (1999), 385–91.

73 Rita Giacaman, Rana Khatib, Luay Shabaneh, Asad Ramlawi, Belgacem Sabri, Guido Sabatinelli, Marwan Khawaja and Tony Laurance, 'Health Status and Health Services in the Occupied Palestinian Territory,' *The Lancet*, 373 (2009), 837–49.

74 Rita Giacaman, Harry S. Shannon, Hana Saab, Neil Arya and Will Boyce, 'Individual and Collective Exposure to Political Violence: Palestinian Adolescents Coping with Conflict,' *European Journal of Public Health*, 17 (2007), 361–8.

75 Raija-Leena Punamäki, Samir Qouta, and Eyad El-Sarraj: 'Resiliency Factors Predicting Psychological Adjustment after Political Violence among Palestinian Children,' *International Journal of Behavioral Development*, 25 (2001), 256–67.

Samir Qouta, Raija-Leena Punamäki, and Eyad El-Sarraj: 'Child Development and Family Mental Health in War and Military Violence: The Palestinian Experience', International Journal of Behavioral Development, 32 (2008), 310–21.

76 See Giacaman et al. (note 73 above).

77 The US government monitors the execution of the Patriot Act and the blockade of all individuals and organisations that they have unilaterally branded 'terrorists' or 'terrorist organisations'. Because Hamas is on this list, no US aid organisations, such as Save the Children, can collaborate with Palestinian education authorities in Gaza without risking prosecution and the loss of financial assistance. The same applies to aid for al-Shifa Hospital because it is run by the Health Ministry and the Hamas Health Minister, Dr Naim. See OFAC: 'What You Need to Know about U.S. Sanctions': http://www.treas.gov/offices/enforcement/ofac/programs/terror/terror.pdf (accessed June 9, 2009).

78 Rushdie Aboualaf, 'Gaza survivors' four days without water,' BBC News, January 9, 2009: http://news.bbc.co.uk/2/hi/middle_east/7819261.stm (accessed June 30, 2009).

Jan McGirk, 'Medical Facilities under Intense Pressure in Gaza,' *The Lancet*, 373 (2009), 199.

79 Johannes Morken, 'Vi glemte palestinerne' [We forgot the Palestinians], *Vårt Land*, September 20, 2008: http://www.vl.no/samfunn/article 3798327.ece (accessed June 9, 2009).

80 Thomas Spence, 'Vi glemte palestinerne' [We forgot the Palestinians], *Aftenposten*, September 20, 2008: http://www.aftenposten.no/nyheter/iriks/politikk/article2665128.ece (accessed June 9, 2009).

81 A number of news media reported what happened on January 4 in al-Zaytoun. On January 29, *Aftenposten* published another side of the same story, but with the focus on a different family, the al-Helu family.

82 'My Lai Massacre': http://en.wikipedia.org/wiki/My_Lai_Massacre (accessed June 30, 2009).

83 Nicolas Werth, Karel Bartošek, Jean-Louis Panné, Jean-Louis Margolin, Andrzej Paczkowski and Stéphane Courtois, *The Black Book of Communism: Crimes, Terror, Repression* (Cambridge, Mass.: Harvard University Press, 1999), p. 5.

84 Testimony given by Jumana's mother, Meysa Fawzi al-Samouni, a nineteen-year-old, married housewife and resident of Gaza City, to Iyad Haddad from B'Tselem by telephone on January 7, 2009. See B'Tselem – the Israeli Information Center for Human Rights in the Occupied Territories, 'Testimony: Soldiers killed and injured dozens of persons from a-Samuni family in a-Zeitun neighborhood, Gaza,' January 2009: http://www.btselem.org/english/testimonies/20090104_Soldiers_ kill_and_wound_members_of_a_Samuni_family.asp (accessed June 30, 2009).

In the following text quoted from this testimony, some names have been retransliterated to maintain consistency.

85 A number of Israeli and Palestinian human rights organisations have comprehensive documentation of both the Samouni massacre and the attack on the Abbed Rabbo family. See: http://www.ngo-monitor.org/article.php?operation=print&id=2247 (accessed May 27, 2009), and al-Haq, 'The Plight of Al Samouni Family in Gaza: In Their Own Voices': http://www.alhaq.org/etemplate.php?id=416 (accessed May 27, 2009).

Notes to Chapter 11 – The Cowardly War

86 Mads Gilbert and Erik Fosse, 'Inside Gaza's al-Shifa Hospital,' *The Lancet*, 373 (2009), 200–2.

87 CBC News, 'UN Security Council calls for Gaza ceasefire,' January 8, 2009: http://www.cbc.ca/world/story/2009/01/08/israel-gaza.html (accessed June 30, 2009).

88 UNRWA: United Nations Relief and Works Agency for Palestine Refugees in the Near East. The UN's sixty-year-old organisation for Palestinian refugees. This is the UN's oldest and most permanent refugee organisation, founded in 1949. Official home page: http://www.unrwa.org/ (accessed April 11, 2010).

89 United Nations Department of Public Information, News and Media Division, New York, 'Press Conference on Humanitarian Situation in Gaza,' January 9, 2009: http://www.un.org/News/briefings/docs/2009/090109_Gaza.doc.htm (accessed April 11, 2010).

90 From the UN official website, ibid.:

> He went on to say that the food situation continued to deteriorate, with 80 per cent of the 1.5 million people in need of assistance, the health situation was 'extremely worrying', with access problems for hospital staff, most of Gaza was without power, and solid sewage waste was piling up.
>
> For his part, Mr. Ging told reporters that the intensity of the bombing had remained 'consistent' and 'relentless', which had left the Palestinian population traumatised and sleep-derpived. The noise of the drones was also exacerbating the psychological effects of the fighting. Responding to a question, he said that the development of the next generation of Palestinians was one of UNRWA's top priorities. He was frustrated that some 200,000 children who should be attending school had so far this year been unable to do so because of the fighting.
>
> Moreover, he continued, the deleterious impact of daily violence that overshadowed the lives of young Palestinians needed to be countered. UNRWA 'gave great emphasis' to the development of their mindset, orientation and outlook, and stresssed human rights education. 'Something we all need to realise is that one of the unseen consequences of all this violence is its impact on the mindset and outlook of the kids coming up,' he reiterated.

91 Major Avital Leibovic, IDF spokeswoman: 'Many civilian facilities were turned into military camps for Hamas's needs.' See BBC News – the report about Samar and the killing of her siblings in Khaled Abed Rabbo's family: http://news.bbc.co.uk/2/hi/middle_east/7843430.stm (accessed June 30, 2009).

Notes to Chapter 12 – Dreams in Gaza

92 *UN Daily News*, 'Security Council overwhelmingly calls for immediate Gaza ceasefire,' January 8, 2009: http://www.un.org/news/dh/pdf/english/2009/08012009.pdf (accessed July 2, 2009).

93 Ibid. Matthew Russell Lee, 'From Sulfur to Formaldehyde, Latin Smells at UN as d'Escoto Calls Gaza Meeting,' Inner City Press, January 8, 2009: http://www.innercitypress.com/gaza1formaldehyde010809.html (accessed July 2, 2009).

94 UNRWA, 'UNRWA Suspends Imports into Gaza Following Aid Confiscation,' February 6, 2009: http://unrwa.org/etemplate. php?id=493 (accessed April 11, 2010).

95 'Physicians for Human Rights-Israel Gaza, Update 11 Jan 2009,' Relief Web, January 11, 2009: http://www.reliefweb.int/rw/rwb.nsf/db900sid/RMOI-7N7N8Q?OpenDocument (accessed June 5, 2009).

96 Israel Ministry of Foreign Affairs, 'PM Olmert's reaction to diplomatic developments & UNSC Resolution 1860,' January 9, 2009: http://www.mfa.gov.il/MFA/Government/Communiques/2009/PM_Olmert_UNSC_Res_1860_9-Jan-2009.htm (accessed July 2, 2009).

97 Nathan Guttman, 'Olmert's boast of "Shaming" Rice Provokes Diplomatic Furor,' *Forward*, January 15, 2009: http://www.forward.com/articles/14957/ (accessed June 8, 2009).

98 Sylvana Foa, 'Battle of the Wombs: The Future's Numbers Game,' *Village Voice*, December 3, 2002: http://www.villagevoice.com/2002-12-03/news/battle-of-the-wombs/ (accessed June 5, 2009).

99 CIA, *The World Factbook 2009* (accessed April 11, 2010):
Israel: https://www.cia.gov/library/publications/the-world-factbook/geos/is.html
Gaza Strip: https://www.cia.gov/library/publications/the-world-factbook/geos/gz.html
West Bank: https://www.cia.gov/library/publications/the-world-factbook/geos/we.html

100 James Bennet, 'Beyond Belief,' *The Atlantic*, March 2009: http://www.theatlantic.com/doc/200903/editors-note (accessed July 2, 2009).

Notes to Chapter 13 – Distress by Design

101 European Institute for Research on Mediterranean and Euro-Arab Co-operation, 'Palestinian Workers in Israel,' June 2004: http://www. medea.be/index.html?page=2&lang=en&doc=284 (accessed June 30, 2009).

102 World Bank Group, 'Country Brief: West Bank and Gaza,' September 2008: http://siteresources.worldbank.org/INTWESTBANKGAZA/Resources/WBG-ENG_2008AMpdf.pdf (accessed June 30, 2009).

103 Ibid.

104 Ibid.

105 'Gaza and West Bank,' ICRC Bulletin 27 (2007): http://www.icrc.org/web/eng/siteengo.nsf/htmlall/palestine-news-051107?opendocument (accessed April 11, 2010).

106 IRIN News (OCHA, UN), 'ISRAEL-OPT: Gaza fishing industry reeling,' March 12, 2009: http://www.irinnews.org/Report.aspx?ReportId=83422 (June 30, 2009).

107 Ibid.

108 Ibid.

109 See the BGG website: http://www.bg-group.com/OurBusiness/WhereWeOperate/Pages/pgIsraelandAreasofPalestinianAuthority.aspx (accessed July 28, 2009).

Post, May 30, 2007: http://www.jpost.com/servlet/Satellite?cid= 1180527966693&pagename=JPost%2FJPArticle%2FPrinter (accessed May 16, 2009).

162 'The letter, published in Olam Katan [Small World], a weekly pamphlet to be distributed in synagogues nationwide this Friday, cited the biblical story of the Shechem massacre (Genesis 34) and Maimonides' commentary (Laws of Kings 9:14) on the story as proof texts for his legal decision.'

163 Amos Harel, 'Shooting and crying,' *Haaretz*, April 28, 2009: http://www.haaretz.com/hasen/spages/1072475.html (accessed May 19, 2009).

164 Amos Harel, 'IDF in Gaza: Killing civilians, vandalism, and lax rules of engagement,' *Haaretz*, March 19, 2009: http://www.haaretz.com/hasen/spages/1072040.html (accessed June 30, 2009).

165 Uri Blau, 'Dead Palestinian babies and bombed mosques – IDF fashion 2009,' *Haaretz*, March 20, 2009: http://www.haaretz.com/hasen/spages/1072466.html (accessed May 19, 2009).

166 Ibid.

167 Dominic Waghorn, 'Israeli Army T-Shirts Mock Gaza Killings,' Sky News, March 20, 2009: http://news.sky.com/skynews/Home/World-News/Israeli-Army-T-Shirts-Mock-Killing-Palestinian-Women-And-Children-During-Gaza-Offensive/Article/200903315245946 (accessed May 19, 2009).

168 Ibid.

169 See note 165 above.

170 Amnesty International, 'Israel/Gaza Operation "Cast Lead": 22 Days of Death and Destruction,' July 2009: http://www.amnesty.no/sites/default/files/news_attaches/Gaza%20War%20Report%20Death%20&%20Destruction.pdf (accessed April 11, 2010).

Breaking the Silence, 'Soldiers' Testimonies from Operation Cast Lead, Gaza 2009,' Jerusalem, June 2009: http://www.breakingthesilence.org.il/oferet/ENGLISH_oferet.pdf (accessed July 20, 2009).

171 See Norman G. Finkelstein, *Beyond Chutzpah: On the Misuse of Anti-Semitism and the Abuse of History*, (London and New York: Verso, 2005).

172 Marit Aschehoug, 'Advokater anmelder det israelske lederskap for krigsforbrytelser' [Solicitors report the Israeli leadership for war crimes], *Advokatbladet*, May 11, 2009: http://www.advokatbladet.no/_/Nyhetsarkivet/Saker-fra-nr-5-2009/Israel-anmeldt-av-advokater-2009-5/ (accessed April 11, 2010).

See: Complaint to the National Prosecutor's Office for Combating Organised and Other Serious Crime, dated April 22, 2009, signed by lawyers Bent Endresen, Geir Høin, Pål Hadler, Harald Stabell, Loai Deeb and Kjell M. Brygfjeld: http://www.icawc.net/fonds/complaint.pdf (accessed April 11, 2010).

173 Sissel Henriksen, 'Norge bør ta ut tiltale' [Norway should press charges], *Klassekampen*, May 16, 2009: http://www.klassekampen.no/56056/article/item/null (accessed June 10, 2009).

174 Eyal Benvenisti, 'An obligation to investigate,' *Haaretz*, January 28, 2009: http://www.haaretz.com/hasen/spages/1059435.html (accessed April 11, 2010).

175 'Report of the Independent Fact Finding Committee on Gaza: No Safe Place,' presented to the League of Arab States, April 30, 2009: http://www.arableagueonline.org/las/picture_gallery/reportfullFINAL.pdf (accessed June 10, 2009).

176 Unfortunately, the Norwegian public prosecutor shelved the complaint in November 2009.

177 *Amu* (Arabic): uncle.

178 UNRWA Statistics: http://www.unrwa.org/etemplate.php?id=253 (accessed April 11, 2010).

179 Commission on Social Determinants of Health, World Health Organisation, 2006, WHO/WIP/EQH/OI/2006: http://www.who.int/social_determinants/resources/csdh_brochure.pdf (accessed May 17, 2009).

180 Rita Giacaman, Rana Khatib, Luay Shabaneh, Asad Ramlawi, Belgacem Sabri, Guido Sabatinelli, Marwan Khawaja and Tony Laurance, 'Health Status and Health Services in the Occupied Palestinian Territory,' *The Lancet*, 373 (2009), 837–49.

181 Mads Gilbert, 'Sommerregn i Gaza' [Summer rains in Gaza], *Tidsskrift for Den norske lægeforening*, 16/2006: 2136–9.

Notes to Afterword 1 – Breakfast in Gaza

182 Palestinian Centre for Human Rights, 'Israeli Attacks on Palestinian Fishermen in Gaza,' May 5, 2010: http://www.pchrgaza.org/portal/en/index. php?option=com_content&view=article&id=6671:israeli-attacks-on-palestinian-fishermen-in-gaza-&catid=56:fact-sheets-&Itemid=18 (accessed October 2, 2010).

183 'Report of the Independent Fact Finding Committee on Gaza: No Safe Place,' presented to the League of Arab States, April 30, 2009: http://www.humanityvoice .net/images/no_safe_place.pdf (accessed October 30, 2012).

184 BBC News, 'Human Rights Watch say destruction in Gaza "unlawful",' May 13, 2010: http://news.bbc.co.uk/1/hi/8680769.stm (accessed October 30, 2012).

185 United Nations Fact-Finding Mission on the Gaza Conflict, 'Human Rights in Palestine and Other Occupied Arab Territories,' September 25, 2009: http://www2.ohchr.org/english/bodies/hrcouncil/docs/12session/A-HRC-12-48.pdf (accessed October 30, 2012), p. 151.

Muir Mathieson

1911 – 1975

A LIFE IN FILM MUSIC

First published 2006 by
Scottish Cultural Press
Unit 6, Newbattle Abbey Business Park
Newbattle Road, Dalkeith, EH22 3LJ, Scotland
Tel: +44 (0)131 660 6366 • Fax: +44 (0)870 285 4846
Email: info@scottishbooks.com
www.scottishbooks.com

British Library Cataloguing in Publication Data
A catalogue record for this book is available from the British Library

ISBN-10: 1 898218 11 0
ISBN-13: 978 1 898218 11 1

Printed and bound by Athenæum Press Ltd, Gateshead, Tyne & Wear

Muir Mathieson

1911 – 1975

A Life in Film Music

Biography by

S J Hetherington

Analysis of Film Scores by

Mark Brownrigg

Scottish Cultural Press

www.scottishbooks.com

The Authors

SJ Hetherington is a writer whose previous work includes a biography of Scotland's first woman MP, the Duchess of Atholl (*Katharine Atholl: Against the Tide*). She has lived near Stirling for 25 years, and divides her time between that home and a cottage on the Black Isle.

Dr Mark Brownrigg is a lecturer in the department of Film and Media at the University of Stirling, where he teaches a film music course. His PhD explored the relationship between film music and film genre, and he is currently working on a monograph on John Williams' score for *Close Encounters of the Third Kind*.

CONTENTS

Foreword

by

Miguel Mera

Miguel Mera is a professor at the Royal College of Music
and composes for film, television and theatre

More than any other person, Muir Mathieson was responsible for the naissance and development of British film music from the mid-1930s onwards. Across the Atlantic, the Hollywood film music sound was being perfected by European émigrés such as Max Steiner and Erich Wolfgang Korngold, but in the United Kingdom there was no such distinctive sound. Muir Mathieson brought about a radical transformation and it was his role as leader, guide, advocate, promoter, and visionary that this book celebrates.

Although he was an able and talented composer, Mathieson was not concerned with self-promotion and had a larger, altogether more altruistic plan which was to improve the quality of music in British films, and he persuaded many of the great composers of the day to write music for the moving image. Arthur Bliss, Arnold Bax, Malcolm Arnold, Ralph Vaughan Williams, and William Walton all benefited from Muir's direct encouragement. Not only did Mathieson work with many composers who had little or no experience of writing for movies, helping them to understand the form and function of film music, but he also gave confidence to directors and film producers allowing them to appreciate the importance of music in combination with moving images. Shining through Sheila Hetherington's biography is Mathieson's quiet passion, his charm, his skill as a mentor, and his powers of persuasion. Equally, the book uncovers a fascinating social history that spans pre and post World War II which can be viewed through the prism of the British film industry.

Following the biographical account in the first half of the book, Mark Brownrigg undertakes a number of analyses of selected films on which Mathieson made a significant contribution as music director and/or conductor. The sheer range of projects in which Mathieson was involved is itself a testament to his total immersion in film music and his importance to the British film industry. Indeed, he was the musical linchpin for some of the most influential film scores of the 1940s and 1950s, including *Dangerous Moonlight, Oliver Twist, Brief Encounter,* and *Hamlet* amongst many others. Their success is due as much to his efforts as to those of the respective composers. It is fitting that the book finishes with a reading of Bernard Herrmann's score for *Vertigo* which was recorded respectively in London and Vienna under Mathieson's baton. It is challenging to define what makes a great conductor, even for orchestral musicians. Is it something to do with technique, clarity, personality, confidence, or a combination of all of these? In this book we come a little closer to understanding the elusive and untranslatable quality that Muir Mathieson clearly possessed which allowed him to communicate the spirit of music with an ensemble to an audience.

Acknowledgements

Although Muir's name and work are remembered and celebrated by mature (-ing!) filmgoers, young afficionados are probably quite unaware of his remarkable impact and enduring contribution to the music of cinema. This book is, I hope, a reminder – and a salute.

I have enjoyed the last few years of research and writing, not least because of the people I encountered along the way, who have generously provided memories and comments. Firstly, and above all, I am grateful to Muir's widow, Hermione Mathieson, for her kindness, patience, and unfailing willingness to be interviewed and bombarded with questions: and to her family, Muirne van Wyk, Niall Mathieson and Shuna Randel, for written recollections of their father. I am also grateful to Alison Lang, daughter of John (Dock) Mathieson, for memories of her father and for additional details of family history.

I am much indebted to Bessie Cameron, widow of Ken Cameron, for permission to quote extensively from Ken's personal memoir.

John Huntley provided much valuable material, both in conversation and in writing. After his death, his daughter kindly endorsed John's permission to quote from his books.

I must also thank the following (listed in no particular order). Without their practical help and personal contributions towards an account of Muir Mathieson's life, this book would not have been possible: Ken Scrivener; Edward Williams; Dr Grace Matchett (Royal Scottish Academy of Music and Drama); Catherine Alexander; Angus Cameron (especially for his help in scanning the photographs used in this book); Stephen Peet; James Stevens; John Legard; Peter Clapham (Archivist, Stirling Council); Sean Delaney (British Film Institute); Lillian Gray; Professor John Izod (Film & Media Department, Stirling University); Bob Keen; Leslie Dear; Jane Cameron; Rupert Scrivener; Dr Elspeth King (Curator, Smith Museum, Stirling); Lindy Cameron; Peter Horton (Reference Librarian, Royal College of Music); Sir Denis Forman; Teddy Darvas and Hilary Meech.

Sincere thanks also to Sarah Hepworth (Glasgow School of Art); David Crichton; Donald Coutts; Ken Somerville; Karen McAulay (Royal Scottish Academy of Music and Drama); Ann Dawson, Derek Barnard and Mike Ward, all of Boosey and Hawkes.

Finally, my thanks to John Beaumont; Harry Fairbairn; Vincent Carey; Dick Best; Bobbie Ferranti; J.G. Burton; the staff of Stirling University Library (Grierson Archive) and the staff of the Mitchell Library, Glasgow. Warm thanks to our editor, Avril Gray, and everyone at Scottish Cultural Press.

Mark Brownrigg and I worked separately, but were united in enthusiasm for our subject. I should like to pay my own tribute to him for the insights and analyses that he presents, brilliantly illuminating our understanding of ten selected scores.

– S.J. Hetherington

'Music is and always must be a vital part of our film art. Music can help to humanise the subject and widen its appeal. Music can make a film less intellectual and more emotional. It can influence the reaction of the audience to any given words. It can carry ideas through dissolves and fade-outs. It can prepare the eye through the ear. It can merge unnoticeably from realistic sound into pure music. It can shock. It can startle. It can sympathise. It can sweeten. But for the love of mike never let it be mediocre.'

– Muir Mathieson –

(as quoted in ***British Film Music*** by John Huntley)

Stirling Castle, set on top of The Rock
(photograph by John McPake)

Chapter 1

Sons of the Rock

Stirling is an amazing place for any child with imagination and a sense of history to be born and brought up in. There are cobbled streets and old wynds at the top of the town, a dark dungeon, a medieval tolbooth. One of Scotland's oldest Royal Burghs, it lies at the heart of Scotland and at the centre of Scottish history. It is dominated by an ancient castle with a defensive ditch and drawbridge, set at the top of a 400-foot volcanic core, known locally as The Rock. To the north/east the rock slides gently away, but on the south/west there is a perpendicular drop from the battlements.

From the time of the Picts – and possibly in the Iron Age – there had been a simple settlement and place of refuge on the rock. By the twelfth century there was a fortress, and by the sixteenth century a magnificent Great Hall and Palace had been built, where generations of Stuart Kings and Queens presided over sumptuous stately courts.

Below the castle, the River Forth winds over a flat tidal floodplain. To the east – the direction of flow – the river was too wide to cross, but at Stirling it could be shallow enough to ford on horseback at low tide and was sufficiently narrow to erect a simple wooden footbridge. The highway from the English Border to the north (The King's Highway) passed through the town: in medieval times to hold Stirling Castle was to command control of Scotland.

From time to time, after great and bloody battles, the castle passed from Scottish to English garrisons and back again. Wallace led the Scots to glory beside the wooden bridge, as did Robert the Bruce in the fields at nearby Bannockburn. Mary Queen of Scots was crowned there. Her infant son was baptised within the castle's precincts. Only seven months later, on his mother's abdication, he was crowned King James VI in the parish church. Prince Charles Edward Stuart and his Highland army, returning from their fruitless foray into England, tried to take the castle, but were forced to abandon the attempt and retreated northwards to meet ultimate defeat at Culloden in 1746.

By 1911, when Muir Mathieson was born, the battles and sieges were, of course, long over, though the legends not forgotten. Now it was a douce market town of some 21,000 inhabitants, set amidst beautiful scenery on the northern edge of the Scottish industrial central belt. The castle was now the regimental headquarters of the Argyll and Sutherland Highlanders.

Beyond the town lay the rural villages upon which at that time much of its business depended. To the north and west lay the plain of the Carse of Stirling and the great farming areas, surrounded by a distant arc of mountains – Ben Lomond, Ben Venue, Ben Ledi, Stuc à Chroin and Ben Vorlich. To the east lay the low Ochil Hills, containing small deposits of silver and copper: at their foot the little Hillfoots mill towns, where woollen cloth was spun, woven and exported. To the south there were coal-mines and a string of busy mining villages: much of the central belt of Scotland lies on a rich seam of coal, which at that time supplied fuel for homes and industries. Stirling lay at the centre of this spider's web.

Clan Matheson (in Gaelic, clan *Mathaineach* – Sons of the Bear) originated in the mists of ancient Alba, somewhere in Wester Ross, where for a time they were keepers of the romantic Eilean Donan castle. To be a member of a Scottish clan is to claim distant kinship with all others of the same name, owing a nodding allegiance to the hereditary chief. As was the way of Highland clans in former days, a feud with a neighbouring clan (in this case, the Mackenzies) was conducted over many centuries. As a result, Matheson numbers were diminished, whilst the Mackenzies flourished, as a glance through telephone directories in Scotland, Canada, Australia and New Zealand will demonstrate. Muir was to remark wryly (and with some exaggeration) that most of his clan had been wiped out; and was highly gratified when Matheson of Matheson, Chief of Clan Matheson, attended one of his concerts at the Albert Hall and made himself known to him afterwards.

Muir's father was John George (JG) Mathieson. Son of a large family from Glasgow, he had trained initially as a silver engraver, but was, by the time of Muir's birth, a well-known artist. Muir's mother, Jessie Wordie Davie, was the daughter of a prominent iron founder in Stirling. The foundry had been set up in the middle of the nineteenth century and was sold on to a partnership – Wylie, a millwright; Smith, a moulder; and Davie, a blacksmith – in 1857. On the retirement of these three men, Davie's son took over and was, in time, duly followed by his sons: John and James.

James Davie was Muir's grandfather. Grandpa Davie, as he was known in the family, took over the business on the death of his father in 1885 and brought his own sons into partnership in 1902. They were to be succeeded in due course by his grandsons. Thus five generations of the Davie family were successive owners of a business renowned for excellence and reliability, much of it providing beams and cast columns for the building industry. Amongst many contracts, James Davie and Sons, Ironfounders and Engineers, were engaged to provide a framework for the structure of the Templeton carpet factory in Glasgow and for Singers machine works at Clydebank.

By 1909 the Victorian/Edwardian boom in the building industry was beginning to decline: Grandpa Davie was almost sixty and happy to retire, though he continued to visit the foundry daily until a few days before his death fifteen years later.

Grandpa Davie's gift to his family was not only the substantial foundry business: he had been devoted to music from his earliest days, and played both violin and cornet. He was a member –

sometimes soloist – of Stirling Choral Society and Kirkcaldy Choral Societies' orchestras. At his insistence, each member of the family learnt to play an instrument and 'The Davie Family' frequently performed together at charity concerts. From his photograph, probably taken about the age of sixty-five, one can guess that an evening in his company would be intelligent, entertaining and convivial. He was a kind-faced, twinkling-eyed man, wearing a neat, short beard in the fashion of the time. Sunday suppers at his home were always followed by lively music-making, with every member of the family, and any visitors, taking part. James's legacy to posterity was to provide, in his grandsons, three major British musicians of the twentieth century: Muir Mathieson, his brother Dock and their cousin, the Glasgow-born composer Cedric Thorpe Davie.

Grandpa Davie's daughter Jessie (Jen), Muir's mother, had studied under Maurice Sons at Glasgow Athaeneum. She played piano and violin, and was a magnificent fiddle player. Jen was small and slight, with slightly frizzy golden hair and a strong, determined personality. Oddly foreshadowing Muir's career in film music, she sometimes played the piano accompaniment for silent films at the local cinema. The music was possibly improvised, but more probably followed cue sheets provided by Fox or Edison.

In the earliest days, music had been essential to mask the noise of the primitive projector in some rather dismal hall. Now, as warm, purpose-built picture houses were beginning to appear, it was effectively used to enhance the emotions aroused by whatever was happening on the screen. Pathos, unrequited love, slapstick comedy, fear, and occasionally a much-loved classic 'chase', were all part of the repertoire. Cue sheets specified exact requirements: 1 minute 5 seconds of Beethoven's *Moonlight Sonata* while the titles come up. Play main theme from Debussy's *Claire de Lune* softly for 1 minute 30 seconds during lovers' parting scene. Play theme from *Shenandoah* for 2 minutes 7 seconds under conversation with father as he dies.

In later years, Muir would bring the house down at parties with his own brilliant, hilarious variations and commentary on the silent film theme clichés: Good Guy, Bad Guy, Cops and Robbers, Cowboys, Indians, Hearts and Flowers and so on.

John George (JG) Mathieson and Jen Davie first met as members of the choir of the United Free Church, where Jen's older brother James played the organ. When John began courting Jen, he needed to play an instrument in order to wangle an invitation to the Sunday evening parties. He chose the double bass as the easiest option, or so he thought, and it also seemed to be the perfect instrument to complete Grandpa Davie's little chamber orchestra. His efforts in both directions were rewarded: Jen and John were married in 1909.

After her marriage, Jen taught music at home and was judged to be an excellent teacher, though something of a martinet – 'a wee bit nebbit', as she would be described in Scotland. Muir was born in 1911 and John (or 'Dock' – his own childhood pronunciation of 'Jock' stuck throughout his life) in 1914. Jen was a thrifty woman, probably more because of the ingrained habit of previous generations than of particular necessity. She took motherhood, her children's welfare, their upbringing and diet, seriously. She gave the boys orange juice to drink and kept a stockpot going, making hearty soups and broths. Milky puddings also featured on the menu. Her 'pink shape' (a blancmange) was fondly remembered by both her sons in later years. They would return from school to a substantial home-baked tea, which they much enjoyed, but they always looked forward to days when the adults had kippers for their evening meal, as they would be given the delicious 'brown crispy bits' from the edges.

Jen's passion for fresh hill air led her, at least once, on an unusually energetic expedition. She set off, pushing Muir in his pram, from their home in Stirling up to Sheriffmuir. This entailed a walk of three miles to Bridge of Allan then a steep, uphill push of one and a half miles to reach the top of the escarpment, where the road leads across the hillside for nearly ten miles.

In 1917 the family moved along the road from their first home at 1 Allan Park to 16 Allan Park – a handsome, greystone, nineteenth-century house set in spacious gardens near the centre of the town, not far from Grandpa Davie's house. When his grandchildren were young, the Sunday evening concerts after the evening meal at Grandpa's were preceded by afternoons spent in the manner of Scottish Presbyterian households of the day. The family would sit quietly, perhaps reading or studying, with the blinds partly drawn, showing a proper respect for the Sabbath. Muir and Dock tried to liven the time as far as possible, sometimes in desperation playing a game of guessing whose feet were passing by along the pavement outside.

Jen was ambitious for her sons. As young boys they were sent for elocution lessons, and entered for music and poetry competitions. Both were taught Scottish Country Dancing, which they performed at various Highland Games and festivals. Later in life, during exuberant moments, Muir would gladly execute the sword dance, Dock playing the accompaniment. Like their mother, they were natural performers. There can be no doubt that it was Jen's driving force that guided her sons towards their future careers: everything possible was done to encourage their musical talent. Dock wrote of her later, 'She brought us up with vision, confidence and meticulous attention to every aspect.' He also commented that, for him, life at that time seemed to be a round of school and music, music and school.

As they grew up, the Mathieson boys do not seem to have taken part in the high-spirited indiscretions of their more adventurous fellow students, some of whom secretly gambled for money in their various homes and nonchalantly drove their fathers' cars round the county in style. (One of their contemporaries drove himself to school from Falkirk each day in his own sports car.)

Jen could be strict and demanding. When Muir asked his parents for a pair of rugby boots, he was given one boot, the other being supplied only after his work was deemed to be up to her standard –

sporting activities were not her first priority. Her ambition for her sons produced high achievers. Muir, with his charismatic personality, would become self-confident, success-orientated, adaptable, pragmatic, perhaps even a bit driven. In his working life, he would sometimes be a challenging colleague, but always a loyal friend. Dock was quieter, a little more reflective and relaxed. The brothers, who shared a great sense of humour, always seemed to get on well and to support each other. The intensity of their musical upbringing ensured that they understood each other's moods well. Muir always referred cheerfully to his younger brother as 'Junior', though Dock grew to be taller and more physically solid than his brother. Throughout their lives, Muir may have unintentionally overshadowed Dock, but for his part Dock was content to take life at his own pace.

In the beginning, Jen taught her sons music herself. Dock recalled that at the same time as he began primary school he had

Muir and Dock in the garden, 16 Allan Park, about 1921

been led to the piano and shown where to find middle C. Violin lessons began when he was seven. Meantime, Muir was already accompanying his mother's fiddle performances on the piano. He was also an accomplished performer on the viola and cello. Jen, having had the benefit of studying music at the Athaeneum, ensured that Muir would have the same opportunity. Now, on Fridays after school, Muir was sent off to Glasgow by bus for music lessons – a not inconsiderable undertaking for a small boy in those days. In later life, he would recall with amusement the events of his homeward journey, when the bus would frequently stop to allow men in various states of inebriation to enter or alight.

He could hardly have had a better teacher: Professor Philip Halstead was a highly distinguished piano teacher, who had studied at Leipzig Conservatorium under the Polish composer Leschetizky. In turn, Leschetizky had taught at the Conservatory of St Petersburg before going on to Vienna, where Paderewski became one of his pupils.

> Halstead . . . was considered so highly by the staff there that they nominated him to perform the Mendelsohn D Minor Concerto at the opening concert of the new Leipzig Gewandhaus . . . He maintained an impressive career on the concert platform while teaching at the Academy for nearly fifty years.
>
> – *Royal Scottish Academy of Music and Drama: The first 150 years*

Muir was not a prodigy: his love of music was inborn, but his achievements were the result of an exacting parent, a magnificent teacher and his own hard work. When he was thirteen he formed a children's orchestra – a small group of players, all under the age of sixteen. (It is not difficult to discern Jen's hand in this enterprise.) Muir was the conductor, and the ensemble included ten-year-old Dock, who played the violin and viola. Their concerts were held at the Albert Hall in Stirling, and were occasionally broadcast by the

BBC in Scotland. Both Mathieson boys (perhaps by now regarded as *wünderkinder)* also appeared from time to time on *Uncle Mac's Children's Hour* – a five o'clock radio programme with a devoted Scottish audience.

JG Mathieson's influence on his sons was perhaps less forceful than Jen's, but he had a profound effect on their characters and interests. He was a quiet, gentle man, well-known as an etcher, drypoint artist and painter, one of a small group of artists and engravers working in Stirling at that time. JG particularly admired, and was influenced by, two older members of the group – Sir DY Cameron (1865–1945), etcher and painter in vibrant oils of Scottish landscapes; and Sir Russell Flint (1880–1969), whose paintings, particularly of grouped figures, concentrated on texture and light.

JG owned an art gallery in Murray Place in Stirling. His studio at home was, at that time, in an extension, overlooking a large garden. It was littered with oil paints, copper plates, canvases and also housed the etching press. After his sons had left home, both studio and art gallery were incorporated into the main part of the house. JG taught his sons to sketch and paint, but although Muir had a lot of ability and drew well, he was never likely to make his career as an artist.

During summer holidays, JG rented a cottage in Kippen, a nearby hillside village with a magnificent view across the low-lying carse of Flanders Moss to the Highland hills. There he would leave Jen and the boys to enjoy the summer's freedom, while he returned home to paint from sketches he had made. After all, that was how he earned his living and his Glasgow agent demanded a regular supply. JG's work was much sought after, both in Scotland, where his watercolours were often reproduced on calendars, and abroad. Apart from the annual visits to Kippen, there would be holidays in small Highland places, where they were always welcome visitors, particularly as the Mathieson boys would cheerfully provide the music for a village ceilidh or dance.

Fly-fishing for trout was another of JG's passions. He shared this mystery with his boys, patiently teaching them to tie flies and handle rod and line. He taught them how, with a cunning flick of the wrist, to drop the cast of flies with exact precision onto a chosen eddy in a river or on the dark surface of a loch, and how to play and land a fish. Muir retained his love of angling throughout his life, returning again and again to the Highlands for fishing holidays. One of JG's paintings shows Muir and his wife, fishing together in the wilds of Rannoch Moor, with Hermione on the point of landing a large fish, while Muir's hook sadly dangles, empty.

Muir passed his love of fishing on to his children. His daughter Muirne recalled their introduction to it, when their father spent several weeks teaching them to cast, practising on the lawn at home, before being taken off to fish in earnest. Muir's son Niall, has remarked, 'Dad was always impeccably honest – except maybe when it came to fishing. Poaching was a sport, not a crime. One year we trekked for hours across the moors to a loch near Morar. The fishing was fabulous and we left well rewarded. The following year we stayed with friends in Morar. Dad cheerfully recounted the tale of the previous year's excellent catch – imagine his chagrin when it became evident that the loch was owned by our host!'

Perhaps Muir inherited his father's views on the matter of poaching which, in turn, were firmly endorsed by Lord Bannerman. 'Banny' was a President of the Liberal Party and famous winner of thirty-nine rugby caps for Scotland. His pronouncement on the ethics of fishing was recalled in a book by his old friend Ben Coutts: 'Taking a salmon for the pot is not poaching'. (It should be added, however, that Muir's poaching habit would usually have been in pursuit of brown trout rather than salmon.)

Muirne, who was used to having proper birthday parties, discovered that the treat for her tenth was to be a fishing expedition. Her father had rented a house in Scotland for a month. On that cold, rainy day, the family climbed, wearily and reluctantly, up a rugged path to a lochan in the hills. Muir's own enthusiasm kept them going, despite flagging spirits. On arrival, they ate their sandwiches and dropped their casts disconsolately into the water. 'Within seconds the water was alive and the fish were taking the flies. What a day! Dad went to endless trouble to make sure that I would land all my fish, even when it meant losing one of his own. A birthday I will never forget!'

That summer, whilst out fishing at the far end of a loch, a vicious storm blew up. At the same time the small motor on their boat broke down. With Muir's encouragement, the party, by now cold, drenched and exhausted, was able to row the considerable distance back to the shelter of the boathouse and to the ultimate comfort of hot baths all round.

Like his Davie grandfather, Muir attended the 'School on the Rock' – Stirling High School. This is one of the earliest-known schools in Scotland – or, indeed, anywhere else in Britain. Centuries older than establishments such as Eton or Harrow, its origins were already noted by the middle of the twelfth century. It had been established under ecclesiastical orders by the Bishop of St Andrews, with Scottish disregard for class, so that 'the sons of the nobility, gentry and honest men's bairns' – Sons of The Rock – might study English and the Classics.

The original school buildings were destroyed in a fire in 1406, but by the middle of the sixteenth century the school was housed in a single-storey, thatch-roofed building on Castle Hill, provided by the Town Council. In 1856, a large and handsome new school was built round a great courtyard halfway down the hill, on what had been the Franciscan Greyfriars Yard. In 1889, the local MP, later Prime Minister, Campbell Bannerman, personally donated money for a superb copper-domed observatory to be erected on its roof for the use of scholars and others. A local businessman, Laurence Pullar, provided a telescope – a 12.5 inch Newtonian reflector. This was restored in the 1970s and is used by the Stirling Astronomical Society today. The school buildings have been converted into a hotel and leisure centre and the school itself has moved from The Rock to a site on the flat lands below.

This ancient school was to produce, almost simultaneously, four great luminaries of the new medium of cinema, whose professional lives would be interwoven. The oldest of these, John Grierson, was half a generation older than Muir. Born in 1898, son of a schoolmaster, his home was a few miles from the town and he walked in to the High School each day. During the 1914–18 war he served on minesweepers and afterwards studied philosophy at Glasgow University. John was a splendid personality. His only fault may have been a certain grimness of outlook and perhaps a lack of spontaneous humour. As a Rockefeller research fellow in Chicago in 1924, he studied the politics of Lenin. At the same time he joined a group of amateur film-makers and became fascinated by the medium. Film-making soon turned from a hobby to chosen profession as he came to realise its power to influence the ideas and attitudes of the general public.

In true British style, one of the first films made in UK had been a recording of the Epsom Derby in 1895. By the mid-twenties the British film world was mainly producing B-movies for home audiences and it tended to be run by men whose films reflected their own social backgrounds. The world they presented was a fairly frivolous one, often involving tennis parties, champagne cocktails and fast motor cars. Working class characters appeared from time to time as light relief: deferential, cheerful, comic, without dangerous aspirations – much as black characters in American films were depicted at the time. A man of strict Calvinist upbringing and belief, Grierson despised all that as sheer vacuity. His intention was to make gritty films about the lives of real, hardworking men and women.

On his return to Britain, having persuaded Sir Stephen Tallents of the Treasury into allowing him to make a film for the Empire Marketing Board (EMB), Grierson set about focussing the minds of the public on social issues. His films were not intended to be commercial ventures. He was unashamedly polemical. His aim was similar to that of the Reithian BBC at that time – 'to educate and inform'. It was Grierson who coined the term 'documentary', commenting that it was 'the runaway from the synthetic world of contemporary cinema, but also represented a reaction from the art world of the early and middle 1920s – Bloomsbury, Left Bank, T.S. Eliot, Clive Bell – by people with every reason to know it well' (*The Long View*).

Grierson's two feisty sisters, Ruby and Marion, followed their brother into film-making, each making historic contributions to actuality in film: in particular, Ruby's *Housing Problems* in the mid-thirties caused a public outcry by its stark presentation of the appalling living conditions in many of Britain's cities. Her style of film-making was more intimate and personal than her brother's, which tended to be more clinical and didactic. Ruby was drowned, along with most of the passengers and crew, during the early months of the war, when the *City of Benares* was torpedoed on its voyage to Canada. She was accompanying a group of children, to film their experience of being evacuated to safety.

Drifters (1928) was Grierson's first production for the EMB. The film examined the lives and work of North Sea fishermen. His wartime experience on minesweepers provided him with an understanding of the experience of the crew of a frail little fishing boat facing the merciless onslaught of wind and wave. Writing in a periodical of the day, he commented on the making of the film. 'It is about the sea and fishermen, and there is not a Piccadilly actor in the piece. The men do their own acting and the sea does its – if the result does not bear out the 107th Psalm, it is my fault . . . If you can tell me a story more plainly dramatic than the gathering of the ships for the herring season, the going out, the shooting at evening, the long drift in the night, the hauling of nets by infinite agony of shoulder muscles in the teeth of a storm, the drive home against a head sea . . . if you can tell me a story with better crescendo in energies, images, atmospherics and all that make up the sum and substance of cinema, I promise you I shall make a film of it when I can (*Close-up, vol. v, no. 5, November 1929*).

They that go down to the sea in ships, that do business in great
waters;
These see the works of the Lord, and his wonders in the deep.
For he commandeth, and raiseth the stormy wind, which lifteth
up the waves thereof.
They mount up to the heaven, they go down again to the depths;
their soul is melted because of trouble.
They reel to and fro, and stagger like a drunken man, and are at
their wit's end,
Then they cry unto the Lord in their trouble, and he bringeth
them out of their distresses.
He maketh the storm a calm, so that the waves thereof are still.
Then are they glad because they be quiet. So he bringeth them to
their desired haven.

– FROM PSALM 107 –

The World Premiere of *Drifters* was held in a local cinema in Stirling, especially for the pupils of Stirling High School: Grierson's old school. A former pupil, in conversation with Dr Elspeth King (Curator of the Smith Museum in Stirling), recalled the excitement of the occasion, adding: 'Not many school children can look back on attending a World Premiere!'

On its release, after a more formal premiere in London, the film was well received and was praised as a unique, fresh approach to film-making, but it was not without its critics, some of whom were fairly hostile. It had been made on a shoe-string and Grierson was as yet inexperienced. A review (date unknown) in the *New York Times* complained . . . 'No element of surprise . . . only a feeling of comfortless monotony . . . Its efforts at human interest in showing the men either cooking, eating or idling are far from exciting.' Others, though, understood Grierson's vision and the originality of his approach. As a result, the EMB Film Unit was formally set up, with John Grierson as Films Officer. Dozens of eager young applicants vied with each other to join his team.

When the government axed the EMB as an economy measure during the financial crisis of 1932, Grierson helped to set up the famous General Post Office (GPO) Film Unit to replace it. As the years of economic depression advanced, he concentrated on the realities of British working life. He was a genius and a pioneer, leading the world in the field of documentary films. Grierson produced and inspired. The young directors trained by him, such as Basil Wright, Paul Rotha and John Taylor (who became his brother-in-law) shared Grierson's socialist vision, as did guest directors Robert Flaherty and the Brazilian Alberto Cavalcanti.

Wright's *Song of Ceylon*, made by the GPO unit for the Ceylon Tea Propaganda Board in 1935, is said to be one of the most beautiful, eloquently poetic films ever made. The score was by Walter Leigh. The following year, the classic film *Night Mail* was produced by Grierson and directed by Wright, with urgent narrative poetry by W.H. Auden and score by Benjamin Britten. It followed the journey of a bag of letters being sorted on an overnight mail train from London to Scotland and delivered to various destinations next morning. *Coal Face*, for which Britten again provided the score, was directed about the same time by Cavalcanti and drew uncompromisingly upon the life of a mining community. The American film-maker Robert Flaherty's *Industrial Britain* examined the daily lives of workers and their families in the surroundings of grim steel mills and factories, and of craftsmen and potters at their trade. Grierson and Edgar Anstey edited the film, Flaherty having slightly lost his way, gone over budget and run out of his allocation of film stock.

Flaherty's temporary presence with them in England was a considerable coup for the documentary makers and if from time to time he betrayed slightly prima donna tendencies, these were accepted (as far as possible) with good grace. Flaherty was a legend: as a young mining engineer in Alaska, he dropped into film-making by accident, whilst making a record of the life of the Inuit people. He made only six films, including *Nanook of the North* (his first film) and *Man of Aran*. Each was acknowledged to be magnificent – a classic. Wright reminds us that he was a truly creative artist, not simply a reporter with a camera (*The Long View*).

At last what Grierson referred to as 'the creative treatment of actuality' was beginning to change the expectations of British filmgoers. An entirely new concept of film-making had been introduced. The work of the GPO Film Unit had the accidental effect of helping to bring about a sea-change in the making of feature films. Public taste matured after watching the realism and immediacy of the short films from the Unit. Audiences were no longer satisfied by the trivialities of B-class offerings: now they began to look for something substantial. Producers and directors started to follow the trend in their feature films, though fortunately sentiment, emotion and aesthetism were never abandoned.

In 1936, Grierson adjudicated at an amateur film festival in Glasgow. One of the entries was by students from the Glasgow College of Art. He was so impressed by the innovative quality of their work that he offered apprenticeships to two of them. One of these was Norman McLaren, who, as it happened, had been a Stirling High School scholar and a contemporary of Muir Mathieson's younger brother, Dock. McLaren worked on his first film with Grierson in that same year of 1936, before going to work as a cameraman during the Spanish Civil War. As an artist, his particular interest lay in making animation films. On his return from Spain he began to experiment with new techniques, eventually going to New York to gain more experience. When Grierson became director of the National Film Board of Canada in 1939, McLaren was invited to join him and went on to spend the rest of his life there, becoming one of the most internationally respected film animators of all time. He was highly innovative, at times almost mystical. He might paint straight on to a negative to achieve an effect, or perhaps use stereoscopic effects to reach the result he wanted. In 1952, at the height of the Cold War, he made what was probably his most important film, *Neighbours*, an allegory demonstrating how a major war can develop following a trivial argument between two close friends – on this occasion a dispute over the ownership of a small garden flower. For this film McLaren was given an Academy Award and also won a number of other international prizes.

Basil Wright speaks of McLaren as one of cinema's purest geniuses, describing his 1947 film *L'Aviron* in lyrical terms: 'The prow of a little boat takes us forward and forward and forward forever towards a receding horizon, until our perception of reality is blurred into a waking dream' (*The Long View*).

The youngest of the quartet, Dock Mathieson, trained as a music teacher at the Scottish National Academy of Music, supplemented by violin lessons with Sevcik in Edinburgh, before winning a Caird scholarship to the Royal College of Music. On leaving the college in 1935, he joined the London Symphony Orchestra as leader of the viola section. He later became Assistant Music Master at Sedbergh School and Music Master at West Buckland School in Devon. He career was interrupted by army service in India fom 1941 to 1946. On returning from the war, he joined the film industry as Assistant Music Director, then Musical Director, at Ealing Film Studios. Dock was arranger and conductor of scores for an impressive number of first-class movies. Some of his early work was with the director Charles Crichton on his gently hilarious post-war films, which included *The Lavender Hill Mob* (1951), starring Alex Guinness, the classic comedy *The Titfield Thunderbolt* (1953), as well as McKendrick's much-loved film about the adventures of the crew of a Clyde puffer, *The Maggie* (1954).

These four Sons of the Rock – John Grierson, Norman McLaren, Muir Mathieson and Dock Mathieson – each had a profound and enduring effect on the film industry. Grierson inspired the documentary and fundamentally changed the approach to production and direction. McLaren brought a lyrical and mature quality to animation films, rigorously avoiding the sentimentality of some of Disney's brilliant output. He did not produce cartoons,

Muir Mathieson's parents,
Jen and JG, at Allan Park, Stirling

but short works of self-conscious art. As John Huntley has said, Muir Mathieson blazed a trail of distinction for British film music, so that even American film critics wrote regretfully, 'America has nothing like this'. Dock Mathieson's film career began 13 years after his brother's, but he too made a highly significant contribution to the industry.

Although all four left Stirling forever on leaving school, they retained their personal links and memories. Muir and Dock would often return to visit their parents and to speak – or to conduct concerts – at local events. Norman, who died in Canada in 1987, left a series of his extraordinary *trompe l'oeil* drawings to Stirling University, open to public view as part of the University Art Collection. John Grierson (1898–1972) donated his papers to that university's media archive.

Chapter 2

Korda's Overture

At the age of eighteen, after a rigorous oral and written examination, Muir won a scholarship to the Royal College of Music (RCM) in London. This was perhaps an unusual destination for a Stirling High School pupil in those days. Most boys leaving at eighteen would go on to one of the (then) five Scottish universities, or to a Scottish Art College. If music was to be his choice, then he could attend the renowned Scottish National Academy of Music – now the Royal Scottish Academy of Music and Drama – in Glasgow. Muir's decision to accept a place at the college in London would shape the rest of his life and career. He would never return to Scotland to live, but there could never be any doubt as to his origins. He retained the warm and comforting Scottish cadences of his voice, making no attempt to affect an alien accent.

The RCM had been founded, with a small number of students, by Sir George Grove in 1883. It was situated in a large red building off Exhibition Road in Kensington, London. Sir George was a benevolent Principal, regarding the students as 'his children' and the college as a large family. The college quickly burgeoned in staff and student numbers, its reputation grew, and it swiftly became recognised as one of the world's leading music establishments.

In 1929, the teaching staff included several illustrious composers, amongst them Vaughan Williams as Professor of Composition, John Ireland and Arthur Benjamin. Vaughan Williams, Gustav Holst, Alfred Bliss, Arthur Benjamin and Samuel

Coleridge Taylor had been among the pupils of Grove, Stanford and Parry at the college. Now Vaughan Williams and Arthur Benjamin were handing on their knowledge to a new generation of students. Holst had also taught at the college until illness forced him to resign. Composers – even the greatest – were notoriously underpaid and frequently hard-up. For many of the senior staff, the salary from the RCM, in addition to what they could earn privately from their music, was a life-saver.

Muir entered the College at half-term, on 18 February 1929. Initially, he stayed with a rather 'well-to-do' uncle and aunt in Southgate, an arrangement that he did not greatly appreciate. He felt smothered by their way of life, and by the tedium of his aunt's endless coffee mornings and bridge parties. It seemed to him that London must surely have more to offer an enterprising eighteen-year-old Scotsman. Besides, he exulted in student life and had already found new and interesting companions within the college. He soon discovered something much more to his liking: a small hotel in Lexham Gardens in Kensington, which charged £2 a week for a room and board. He and several other students moved in together, much to the consternation of the elderly residents already established there.

For the first six months at college, Muir studied Piano as his principal subject, with Conducting and Theory in addition. After Christmas he switched to Conducting as his first subject, with Piano as second, and later took Orchestration as an extra study. He was fortunate, studying Conducting under the personal direction of the stylish, ever-elegant Malcolm Sargent, and Piano under the young Australian, Arthur Benjamin.

Another of his tutors was a keen cricket fan and they would sometimes miss a lesson and casually slip off to Lords together for the afternoon. This sense of rather jolly amateurism at the college was observed and criticised by Muir's slightly younger fellow-student, Benjamin Britten. Britten (who also studied under Arthur Benjamin) later complained that Sir Hubert Parry, director of the college from 1894 until 1918, had left a lasting legacy of informality. As a result of this, he thought, it seemed to be regarded as bad form – even perhaps a little *déclassé* – to be an earnest and hardworking student. The attitude of most of his fellow students at the RCM, he later declared, had been 'amateurish and folksy'.

Some years later, Peter Pears apparently shared Britten's opinion to some extent. This judgement may or may not have been justified. Parry had died many years earlier, in 1918, and in any case there was nothing remotely amateurish in his attitude to music. He was a man of great integrity: warm, humorous and, like Britten, politically radical. It may also be fair to add that whilst at college Britten was apparently not an admirer of Vaughan Williams's music, nor of Elgar – or of Brahms, for that matter – and was also critical of the conductors Adrian Boult and Thomas Beecham. (In 1935, he declared Arthur Bliss's clarinet quintet to be 'very unoriginal piffle'.)

As a son of Jen Mathieson, Muir was unlikely to have been an indolent or offhand student, whatever the fashion of the day. Reflecting her own Presbyterian background and times, Jen firmly believed that it was necessary to have a personal goal in life. A sound education laid the foundation. Hard work and self-discipline were essential to its achievement. Muir's musicianship and diligence brought its reward. Just eleven months after entering the College, he won the Katherine Boult scholarship in Conducting, held it until July 1931, and was awarded a Leverhulme Scholarship for the academic year 1932–3.

It is hard to define what qualities distinguish great conductors from competent ones. Personal dynamism may have guided them towards that role. There may be a subconscious wish to be the focus of attention; even, perhaps, an instinctive need to be in control. This is not to imply that conductors are natural showmen, but courage – perhaps even a bit of chutzpah – is necessary. They will, after all, enter an expectant concert hall last, and alone, to become the centre of attention and cynosure of all eyes, every movement and expression closely observed by members of the orchestra and audience alike.

A conductor will have studied musical history. He will be familiar with the technique and range of each of the instruments. He will have learned to follow a score rigorously and to have developed proficiency in baton technique. He will understand how to interpret a composer's directions in terms of sound, texture, rhythm and emotion. But great conductors possess something far beyond workmanlike competence. They have an added dimension that is unfathomable, but immediately recognisable. They possess a rare ability to dissect and reconstruct the sound patterns within the music, eliciting a magnificent response from the orchestra. It might perhaps be called 'soul': a profundity of interpretation and subtlety of phrasing that comes from within, from spirit, instinct and perception; a sense of unity with performers and audience alike; and a boundless joy in making music.

As early as 1931, Muir began to understudy Sir Malcolm Sargent. Rehearsing and performing with live orchestras is an essential part of a student conductor's training, but understudying Sargent was a great honour. The opening night performances of three short College operas – *Alfred and the Cakes*, *Prince Ferelon* and *Catherine Parr* – were conducted by Sir Malcolm, but on the second night conducting was delegated to three students: Geoffrey Corbett, Muir Mathieson and George Weldon. According to the (unpublished) College history, *The First Eighty-Five Years*, Muir and Ivan Clayton conducted two 'rather eviscerated' performances of Verdi's *La Forza del Destino*, supervised by Aylmer Buesst, in July 1932.

Muir also conducted a choir of Welsh miners in London; Winchester Operatic Society in Gilbert and Sullivan (*Pirates*) and, on the cusp of his twentieth/twenty-first year, toured Canada for a few months as conductor to Lady George Cholmondely's ballet company. During their tour the company was entertained to dinner in Ottawa by Lord Tweedsmuir, then Governor General of Canada. Muir, not having as yet acquired an evening dress suit, wore his kilt.

This met with the disapproval of Lord Tweedsmuir's butler and as a result Muir was sent to eat by himself. Had he been aware of it, Tweedsmuir (John Buchan) would certainly have been delighted to welcome this young fellow Scot to his table. Most of the company travelled steerage, but on the return voyage Lady Cholmondely invited Muir to join her on the first-class deck for a glass of champagne to celebrate his twenty-first birthday.

Muir would never be patronised again. Whilst still at college, he had already gained the respect of many in London's musical world. He was very young, but he was becoming celebrated in music circles and was 'taken up' by such people as Lord and Lady Moyne, who took an interest in him, inviting him to houseparties and dances at their home at Felpham. He felt at ease within their social circle, his self-confidence born, not from any sense of superiority, but of genuine knowledge of his own worth.

Over the years, Muir would come to know the great British conductors of the mid-twentieth century well. These were towering, legendary figures, completely different from each other in character – all great men, magnificent conductors, internationally renowned and much loved by the concert-going public. Each had his own loyal following. They were also often autocratic and sometimes temperamental: tantrums were not unusual. Members of the orchestras were genuinely proud to play under these distinguished conductors, but they pounced gleefully upon their foibles and idiosyncracies. Stories, true or apocryphal, reverent or irreverent, abounded.

Sir Henry Wood (1869–1944) was revered for all that he had done to ensure London's position as one of the greatest centres of the musical world, establishing the Promenade Concerts and directing them for half a century. In his day, he was the doyen of conductors, though by now his life and career were drawing to a close. Sir Henry apparently irritated members of the string section by asking each of them to tune their instrument by sounding A to a tuning fork and sounding board in his presence. He would thereupon declare each one to be flat, sharp, or – perhaps – satisfactory. In retaliation, the musicians began to pass the same instrument on to each other for the test. According to the flautist Gerald Jackson (*First Flute*), they would be hugely and secretly delighted when Sir Henry condemned an instrument that he had pronounced to be perfect a few minutes earlier (or vice-versa).

Sir Thomas Beecham (1879–1961) was internationally esteemed. His particular admiration for the music of Delius inspired the love of the public for that composer's work. He was regarded with some amusement as 'a bit of a nabob' and noted for a certain exuberant flamboyance, for a bon mot or the perfect squelch. He could be hilariously lofty – 'There are two golden rules for an orchestra: start together and finish together. The public doesn't give a damn what happens in between' – but his personal generosity enabled the foundation of two great orchestras in London: the London Philharmonic in 1932 and the Royal Philharmonic Orchestra in 1946. Sir Thomas's considerable wealth was derived from Beechams laxative pills, but even that abundant source of income eventually proved insufficient and he became bankrupt on behalf of the post-war Royal Philharmonic, a personal misfortune that was not permitted to overshadow his illustrious musical career.

Sir Adrian Boult (1889–1983) was an avuncular, sympathetic figure whose interpretations of Elgar and Vaughan Williams in particular were without parallel. He also apologetically described himself as having a 'fiendish' temper, though this was mercifully displayed relatively infrequently (*First Flute*). Despite this, he took immense trouble to concern himself over the wellbeing and comfort of his players.

During the war, Sir Adrian and the BBC Symphony Orchestra were evacuated to Bristol and later to Bedford. At this time, he held a senior position within the BBC Home Guard Unit and, rather endearingly, would occasionally conduct them in army drill, his baton temporarily exchanged for a swagger stick: perhaps there were certain similarities between the two roles. As Gerald Jackson also records, BBC Home Guardsmen/orchestral players were not always particularly quick in military uptake. On one occasion, at drill, the company disconcertingly ended up facing a wall, their backs towards the advancing 'enemy'.

The best-beloved conductor of that era was probably Sir John Barbirolli (1899–1970), whose intensity and darkly handsome appearance delighted audiences and orchestral players alike. He occasionally conducted in London, but became conductor of the Scottish National Orchestra and the New York Philharmonic before becoming principal conductor of the Halle Orchestra in Manchester in 1942, building its great international reputation during the following fifteen years.

Sir Malcolm Sargent (1895–1967), was slender, elegant and dashing, though he maintained a constant battle against ill-health. He conducted the BBC Symphony Orchestra for several years and directed the Proms for almost twenty seasons. The public adored him – particularly promenade concert audiences, who loved the wit and grace of his last-night speeches and his immaculate appearance, which included the custom of wearing a white carnation in his buttonhole. Some of the musicians had private reservations. He could be fiery and sarcastic on occasion, and during rehearsal orchestras found his constant interruptions and complaints rather tiresome. Sir Malcolm's (unused) first name was Harold and he became known irreverently as 'Flash Harry'on account of his stylish appearance.

In 1933, the Royal College received a request from the film magnate Alexander Korda for the services of a conductor – someone who could demonstrate to his Musical Director how to beat time in seven for the score of *Catherine the Great*. (Beating time is apparently not as straightforward as it may seem to be.) The composer Edward Williams believes that Korda (never a timid man) approached Sir Malcolm personally, in the hope that he might be persuaded to come himself. Sargent, who in any case would never have condescended to such a thing – the film world being regarded as a rather lowly business at that time – suggested Muir, who was about to graduate after four years' study. His work and personality impressed Korda so greatly that he offered him the post of Assistant Director of Music, at a salary of £4 a week.

Alexander Korda had been born and raised in a village in Hungary (or Austro-Hungary as it then was) in 1893. He was of a Jewish family and his real name was Sandor Kellner. Korda was a name he invented and adopted on behalf of his brothers and himself. From a very early age, Sandor had been smitten by the idea of making films. He left home for work in Budapest, became a journalist and critic at the age of eighteen and soon joined the fast-developing Hungarian film industry.

Film-making had grown steadily during the first two decades of the twentieth century. From the *fin-de-siecle* magic lantern stage, when it was perceived as a pleasant curiosity, it had developed into a major enterprise. Many countries began to produce films – France, Germany, Sweden, Hungary, the Soviet Union, Britain and, above all, Hollywood in California, USA, where film-makers could be certain of space, quality of light and constant sunshine. Money-making was the ultimate object of the new film companies, but out of crude commerce an exciting and highly influential art form was born. During the succeeding century, the output would vary between the frankly ridiculous and the truly sublime, but usually poised somewhere between those extremes. People were now enticed to cinemas to watch flickering images of high drama and low comedy, interspersed with unaccustomed passion. (Unaccustomed in the sense that they were unused to witnessing such scenes in public: for that generation, Fairbanks and Valentino in action were literally eye-openers.)

A fair proportion of these cinema audiences might never have had the opportunity of visiting a theatre and perhaps did not read many books, but in watching films they were fulfilling an atavistic longing to return to the pleasures of story-telling. From the time of the Stone Age, people had found delight in gathering round the flames of a communal fire to listen to tales of adventure and love. Now they found similar delight in gathering together under the subdued glow of a cinema screen and were magically transported into exciting, alien worlds.

Korda began as a member of the crew in Budapest, directing his first film when he was twenty-one. After filming in Paris and Berlin, he was invited to Hollywood in the mid-twenties. This was not a success. The place seemed to Korda to be the end of the world – a tedious journey to a hot and tedious place, lacking, in his view, opportunities for civilized friendships and conversation, and totally without culture. Worse, for a man of some ego, he felt patronised and, according to his nephew Michael, began to suspect that the main reason for his invitation had been because he would bring his beautiful actress wife, Maria, with him. He was, however, very handsomely paid for directing several movies which, though he

Muir and Korda

viewed them as slightly absurd, proved to be financial successes from the point of view of his employers – First National and, later, Fox.

In 1930, Korda divorced Maria, had a huge row with Fox, abandoned both (having either been fired or resigned, depending on one's point of view) and returned to film-making in France. The following year, Paramount offered him a temporary post at their studios in England. He accepted, apparently intending to stay for a short time. But, despite complaining of the weather and the food (a robust goulash was rarely to be found on the menu of London hotels), life in England impressed him. Soon he decided to make it his permanent home and as Nazism began to cast its deepening shadow over Europe he became fiercely loyal and patriotic towards his adopted country.

British film-making was not thriving – second-rate B-movies were still being churned out, but little of major impact was then being produced. Korda's plan now was to build a film industry in Britain that would equal – even surpass – that of Hollywood. His Paramount contract fulfilled, he founded his own company, London Film Productions, with that aim. He was a man of considerable charm, with an equally considerable temperament. His blazing (though short-lived) rows with his brothers Zoltan and Vincent, and with members of his crews, were apparently legendary.

Korda had made his name as a director, but turned to producing when he found that the exhilaration of making financial deals suited him better. In earlier days he had alternated as Director, Producer, Writer and Actor: he knew the business of film-making as few others did. Although London Films would never outdo MGM, Paramount or Universal in terms of output, he set a standard that was perhaps without parallel at that time. He wanted to be the best and in those early years he sometimes was, though it was not always acknowledged.

Zoltan now directed films for his brother, whilst Vincent, an artist, was brought over from Paris as Art Director. When Kurt Schröder, his Musical Director, left London Films in 1934, Korda offered to promote Muir to the post, at a salary of £7 a week. At Muir's age and level of experience, this seemed an amazing proposition. Moreover it was highly flattering. This was heady stuff and, as he said himself, the salary was very tempting. It was the midst of the depression. Unemployment and poverty were eating away the heart of the country and the confidence of its people. Jobs were as hard to find in the field of music as they were in an office or on a factory floor. The security of a fascinating post combined with a generous salary must have seemed a splendid prospect.

Muir had been born just as film music was born. His mother had, in a sense, been one of its midwives. He and the cinema had grown up together: the breakthrough of recorded cinema sound had come into being in the same year as he had entered music college. He could foresee that the film industry – and with it the need for excellent film music – was likely to develop and grow. Without doubt it was a glamorous world, inhabited by rich and famous people, but his reason for finally accepting Korda's offer was that he was convinced that he now had an opportunity to create new music for a new and exciting era. It may not have occurred to him then that he would be committing himself to the film world for the rest of his life.

Some of Muir's colleagues have suggested that he could easily have established himself with outstanding success in other musical fields. He would certainly have cherished the opportunity to undertake more sustained concert work. His first appearance as conductor at a public concert was in October 1943, when he conducted the London Symphony Orchestra at the Cambridge Theatre in London. He went on to conduct almost every British orchestra and many of the world's major orchestras during his lifetime. Fortunately for the film industry, however, he fell in love with the medium and was, in future, to arrange, direct, conduct, and occasionally compose, the music for almost one thousand films between 1934 and 1970. It was almost as if his career had been predetermined from the moment that Jen first set her small son down beside her at the piano.

As films became more sophisticated, it became obvious to many that music was as essential a component to a film as the script and the actors, even if the audience was not consciously aware of it. Indeed, Muir believed that if the music became overtly intrusive, so that audiences found themselves consciously listening to it, there was a failure on the part of everyone involved in the production. In the past, a few scores had been specially commissioned for major productions and in some of the largest city-centre cinemas live orchestras had sometimes been engaged to accompany films. Now, with recorded sound, music would become an integral part of each film. It would be possible to be more subtle, more complex, perhaps more emotionally manipulative, in its use.

The Hollywood practice was to have a resident composer permanently attached to one studio and it was Korda's intention that Muir would both compose and conduct all the music for London Films productions. Muir was quick to disabuse him. In an interview with Leslie Mitchell, reported in *The March of the Movies*, he remarked: '. . . While I believed in my own ability as a conductor, I was well aware of my limitations as a composer.' The twenty-two year old addressed the fiery, forty-year-old film magnate: 'If you will guarantee me first-rate composers for every score, I'll take on the job, but I am not going to write you one note of indifferent music, which is the only kind of music I can write. It is ridiculous that you should pay vast sums of money for the finest of everything in the film and then, when it comes to adding the music, let the whole thing down by getting me or some other "hack" to supply the score.' Korda quickly agreed. Whatever the terms, he wanted the best and he was already aware that the best in his field was young Mathieson. Muir insisted in advance that he should be allowed, at his own discretion, to approach the greatest composers to write his film scores. The contract was signed.

Muir later described that decision as the most important he ever made. His future was sealed, though he might not have been so quick to accept his annual £364 had he realised that Korda himself was in receipt of a salary of £9,000 per annum, with a £3,000 personal allowance, plus £1,500 for each completed film. Presumably both his brothers and the senior technicians were rewarded on a similar scale. He was, moreover, proposing to pay Winston Churchill £10,000 for the completed script of a proposed film about his ancestor, the Duke of Marlborough, and an additional £4,000 a year retainer as Editor, Associate Producer and Advisor.

In the event, Korda's collaboration with Churchill came to a fruitless, though amicable, end. The film was never made. But, happily for both, Korda had bought himself a powerful friend and Churchill had received a handsome and (given his dire financial circumstances at the time) welcome salary for his advice. By contrast, Muir Mathieson was to prove a priceless asset to London Films productions and indeed to the future of cinema. In personal terms, he was about to enter an unknown and, to him, entirely strange, milieu. He had grown up in a quiet, sheltered, Scottish environment, followed by the intensive years at the Royal College of Music, where most of his companions were aspiring young English musicians. Now his colleagues would hail from diverse backgrounds, countries and traditions. He was friendly and outgoing, and he delighted in their company. If to some observers he seemed at times to be a bit clannish, part of a magic inner circle, this was surely because he felt most at ease amongst people whose ways he understood best, rather than a deliberate attempt at exclusivity. The same would be said of Korda, who instinctively surrounded himself with his own countrymen.

Chapter 3

Like Ducks to Water

As Muir observed, writing music to order was neither a new nor a demeaning proposition. Mozart, Beethoven, Bach and countless others had produced much of their music for a specific occasion or purpose, or at the behest of a 'patron'. In some ways it was no different from a commissioned portrait by a fine artist, or, as Muir put it in his interview with Leslie Mitchell, 'The fact that he (Mozart) wrote a better Mass than anyone else enabled him to save enough to write a symphony.'

In Muir's view, writing for film was as valid and creative a pursuit as composing for the concert hall and, moreover, it would reach a vast audience. He would not countenance snobbish complaints that music would be 'churned out like a machine' or that there would be a loss of status in writing for the new medium: rather the reverse. The opportunities were there as never before for first-rate composers. He did not believe that they would be particularly interested in material reward for its own sake, but on the other hand their futures could be secure. Freed from financial anxieties, they could work as they chose and grasp the new chances available to them.

The film historian and archivist, John Huntley, commented in the *Penguin Film Review of 1947*: 'Today the motion-picture industry provides a living for modern composers of serious music. From the studios we may look for music representative of our times as we might have looked at the chorales and preludes of a German organist to discover Bach, the court music files of German principalities to discover Mozart, the opera house in London to discover Handel. Today, we may look for strips of celluloid 35mm wide in large, flat, round tins.'

John Huntley, who had worked at Denham pre-war, played a significant part at post-war Denham. He returned from service with Coastal Command in 1945 and became Muir's technical assistant, working with him on many films, such as *Hamlet* and *Oliver Twist*. He went on to write for screen journals, wrote several books on films and film music, was Head of the Regional Unit of the British Film Institute for a time and set up the Huntley Film Archive in 1985.

In the *Penguin Film Review*, Huntley quotes Muir:

> The first competitor met by film music is usually commentary. We are beginning to learn that the transition from music to speech is of the greatest importance to the flow of the sound-track. The old method of fading music in and out of a commentary is no longer satisfactory. Presumably it is based on the idea that the music could come and go unobserved, but it seems to me that either a sound is audible or it is not. Efforts must be made to create a continuity of commentary and music, whereby the music carries through the ideas suggested by the speech to their logical conclusion.

Although, in the final analysis, it is the film director who dominates, and the film ultimately bears his or her stamp and signature, film-making is the work of a creative team. Each member of a film crew is a specialist who contributes to the excellence, or otherwise, of the final result. Muir maintained that the quality of a film depended equally upon the combination of script-writer, actors, director, editor, art director, cameraman, composer and music director, pointing out that a weakness in any one of these areas would be apparent in the final result. Ken Cameron agreed, stating that ultimately, no matter how perfectly and lovingly a film had been made, there was a further potential hazard: the combined efforts of sound recordist, director, producer or laboratory would not make the slightest difference if a cinema operator was incompetent in using the volume control to set the correct level of sound in a film theatre.

So what exactly was the role of the musical director? His duties were exacting and manifold. Firstly, he would be responsible to the director and producer for the choice of composer (though theoretically the film director would have the final word). He must therefore be *au fait* with the musical styles of a wide range of composers. The film budget was of prime importance and a musical director must start by finding out how much money he was to be allocated. Based on that, he and the screenwriter would decide where, when and with what intention, music would be required.

Now he would consider the names of appropriate composers, discover their possible availability, privately estimate what fee they would be likely to ask for and decide whether or not they could afford them. He would then approach his chosen composer and, if the discussion went well, confirm an agreement. They would watch the film together several times, conferring closely and discussing the director's requirements. While the score was being composed, the musical director would be available to give any help or advice the composer might require. If musicians were to appear on-screen, he would collaborate with the art director over positioning of the orchestra and confer with the chief cameraman to choose the most suitable angles for filming. He would coach apparent 'soloists' (such as Anton Walbrook in *Dangerous Moonlight*), to make their screen performance appear convincing.

When the score became available, he would rehearse it with the orchestra a number of times. If all went well, he would make arrangements for the booking of a suitable hall. There he would conduct the orchestra, with the film running on a large screen in front of him, so that he could record the appropriate piece of music for each sequence. At this point he would depend on the knowledge and experience of both sound recordist and music mixer to ensure that the recordings were perfect. After all that, there would be a lengthy and complicated period of collaboration between himself and the film editor, to fit the music to the film (*The Technique of Film Music*).

Muir would seek out the finest composers and persuade or cajole them into the business of writing music for films. He soon discovered that his gallery of leading composers took to the new medium like proverbial ducks to water. Despite initial individual reservations, he found that they began to understand the particular demands of film composition surprisingly quickly. Suddenly the public was exposed to a great range of new music, some of which was recorded for sale by Columbia, Decca or HMV. Muir believed that filmgoers, many hitherto unused to hearing music by great composers, were enjoying the experience, becoming responsive and knowledgeable, and perhaps now prepared to explore further on their own.

Muir kept a 'casting directory' of composers most suited to particular types of film. Each composer had his/her own distinctive characteristics and these were carefully weighed up before a recommendation was made to the film director. For example, Arnold Bax, whose compositions had a certain dreamy, Debussy-like quality, might be the first choice for a film concerning landscape or the sea. William Alwyn might be invited to score a film in which fantasy or emotional turmoil were paramount requirements. According to John Huntley, two strands of composers were brought into film music by Muir – the first were the great, established concert composers of the day, such as Vaughan Williams, Bax, Bliss, Benjamin, Walton and Arnold. Then came a second group, who came to be known best as film composers. These included John Greenwood, Clifton Parker, Alan Rawsthorne and, probably most of all, Richard Addinsell, who came from a theatre background to become an outstanding film composer.

With Clifton Parker, intent on the screen
(photograph by Ian Jeayes)

Muir himself had a dual role. This was the key to his success – and this success was due to his personality. Firstly, there was his relationship with composers. He was invariably sensitive and sympathetic towards them, welcoming and guiding them into the unfamiliar world of film, and working closely with them. The second aspect of his role was equally crucial: that of dealing with directors, some of whom were not particularly musical, or musically literate. By the time filming had ended and work was beginning on the score, the director was often in a state of emotional tension and exhaustion. It was Muir's duty to soothe and reassure them – yes, the right composer had certainly been chosen, yes, the score would be ready on time, yes, it would be excellent and yes, yes, all would be well.

Although Muir rightly believed in the artistic integrity of his composers, working with them cannot always have been easy.

There were initial and continuing difficulties, but part of Muir's success lay in his ability to talk to composers on their own level. For their part, they respected him, valued his judgement and were excited to find themselves part of a team with an outcome that would bring pleasure to a vast audience. Some critics of the time were, of course, critical. More recently, Norman Lebrecht has suggested that in the particular case of Walton the impetus of hunger had been removed early in his career and with it his potential for a lifetime of superb creativity. Nonetheless, one of Muir's earliest and greatest prizes was to secure the services of William Walton.

Still in his early thirties, Walton had inherited the mantle of Sir Edward Elgar (who had died in 1932) as Britain's greatest living composer. A product of the choir school at Christ Church, Oxford, he had begun to compose music at the age of sixteen. Walton had a pronounced sense of humour and his accompaniment to Edith Sitwell's *Facade,* composed when he was only twenty, had been widely hailed as a hugely witty complement to the extraordinary originality of the recital itself.

Walton wrote his first scores for Muir for the Elizabeth Bergner film *Escape Me Never* in 1934 (David Lean as editor), for *As You Like It* in 1936 and went on to write scores for no fewer than forty films throughout his career. He remarked that while he had struggled to keep body and soul together whilst composing *Belshazzar's Feast,* he had earned more than a whole year's income for ten days' work on the film. In 1941, he scored *The Next of Kin,* in 1942 *Went the Day Well?* and *The First of the Few.* The soaring beauty and dignity of Walton's *Spitfire Fugue* for this film paid tribute to the heroism and sacrifice of young British fighter pilots during the Battle of Britain in the first months of the war. In 1944, Muir invited Walton to write the score for Olivier's *Henry V.* It was, as Olivier declared, an outstanding score, contributing enormously to the success of the film. This was not a war film in 1940s terms, but it was stirringly patriotic. The music alternated between the exquisitely tender *Touch her Soft Lips and Part*, the devout *Non Nobis and Te Deum* and the triumphant climax of the Battle of Agincourt. Disregarding the impact of the Norman Conquest, Shakepeare's ringing lines . . . *This England never did, nor never shall* . . . declaimed by Olivier, sent audiences – already sensing Allied victory – into the night in an uplifted frame of mind.

Walton's film music was admired and acclaimed world-wide. He had reservations of his own, however, deploring the limitations imposed upon his work and outlining some of his difficulties. After viewing the rough-cut with the director and music director, the editor would give him a time-sheet to which music was to be fitted. As with the old cue sheets of the 1920s, a sequence might call for a composition of 1 minute and 23 seconds of music – not a second less, not a second more – to be set against a particular scene. The next sequence might require 2 minutes 45 seconds of completely different tempo and atmosphere for another shot. This was an exacting imposition. Walton pointed out that, whereas a composer had freedom when writing a concerto, a symphony, or an opera, in writing for film he was constrained by the requirements of other people and also by the speed with which he was expected to supply the completed score.

Muir spoke of Walton as one of the greatest names in film throughout the world, which he undoubtedly was. Sadly, his film work ended in 1969. Having been invited by the American production company, United Artists, to write the score for *The Battle of Britain*, starring Olivier, he was humiliated and distressed to find his work rejected in favour of a new score by Ron Goodwin. Goodwin, though an experienced film composer, came from an entirely different musical background from Walton. It is thought that the company had hoped to release a recording of the music and Walton's spare, eloquent score was not long enough to provide a long-playing record. It is also possible that United Artists believed that the music did not provide sufficient impact, which is why they turned to Goodwin.

There was uproar. Olivier refused to allow his own name to be credited on the film unless Walton's score was reinstated. Walton was then unwell, living permanently on Ischia and unable to be present at directors' conferences. In the event, a compromise was reached: music by both composers was used. Walton's sequence for the Battle in the Air was perfect for that section of the film. Sir Malcolm Arnold came to the rescue of his old friend, helpfully reworking Walton's score and conducting the orchestra for the recording.

Walton went on to finish one more film score and wrote several scores for TV programmes during the 1970s 1980s. He also made a personal appearance as King Friedrich of Austria in a programme about Wagner. A recent DVD of *The Battle of Britain*, using Walton's entire score, is now available.

Vaughan Williams, who came to film music with enthusiasm and great distinction late in his life, was as dismayed by the constraints as Walton, and helpfully suggested that it might be better if the music was written first, then the film devised to accompany it. He did, however, willingly concede that composing for film was 'a splendid discipline and I recommend a course of it to all composition teachers whose pupils are apt to be dawdling in their ideas, or whose every bar is sacred and must not be cut or altered.'

Other composers also expressed their tribulations in writing film music. The problems were undoubtedly immense. They were dealing with an entirely unknown medium, asked to conjure up an emotion or evoke a particular sense within the time-limitations of a short film scene, yet the resulting score must be so subtle as to be almost surreptitious. Moreover, they were usually asked to perform this miracle in record time.

Sir Arthur Bliss regretted that the composer's individuality was submerged for the sake of the film – 'Writing for the screen requires a very special technique. The composer has to be a kind of musical epigrammist, compressing the sense of an idea into the shortest possible time and conveying it with the greatest economy and effectiveness.' He did, however, assert that music – whether for film or concert hall – should be judged solely on its merits as music.

Muir had the greatest difficulty in persuading Sir Arnold Bax (Master of the King's Musick) to compose for film, having to seek him out several times at his residential hotel in Shoreham to coax him into doing it. Nevertheless, Bax, a shy and retiring man, produced an imaginative and exciting score for the RAF Unit for the 1942 short film *Malta GC* – a tribute to people of that island for their suffering under intense and relentless bombardment. Muir recorded the score with the RAF Orchestra.

Benjamin Britten had become involved in composing music for film and theatre productions almost from the time he left the RCM. He had been intermittently employed by the young GPO Film Unit since 1935, producing scores for Grierson's short films for a smallish fee. Composing for a feature film aroused ambivalent feelings. He was grateful for the money, but disapproved of the commercialism surrounding the cinema world and was disturbed by his sudden – perhaps, in his view, unwarranted – affluence.

It was Muir's firm view that a fresh score should be developed for every film. He said that, ideally, if you were to shut your eyes and listen to the soundtrack alone, it should make a complete pattern. Deploring the custom of using excerpts from existing music, he maintained that 'contemporary films require contemporary sound'. He might have added that in his view 'English films require English music'.

Chapter 4

Things to Come: A Pinch of Paprika

The year was 1933, and Korda's young assistant musical director was plunged straight into the making of *The Private Life of Don Juan*. He was fired with excitement about his challenging new work, and he learned quickly. The film starred Douglas Fairbanks and Merle Oberon, with Joan Gardner in a supporting role. The two women were fated to become sisters-in-law – married to Korda brothers – for a time. It was essentially a Hungarian film – the Producer/Director was Alexander Korda and the Art Director was Vincent Korda. The writer was Korda's friend from early days in Budapest, Lajos Biro. The score was composed by the Russian Mischa Spoliansky and the German Ernst Toch. No doubt a strong current of volatility, as well as vitality, enlivened the atmosphere throughout the production. The music department, however, worked harmoniously, and Spoliansky became, and remained, a friend of Muir's.

Unfortunately, the film was not a success. This was thought to be mainly due to the appearance of Douglas Fairbanks Snr in the title role. His career had begun in 1917 and he was now no longer the attractive, graceful hero of silent movies. Moreover the voice of this now middle-aged actor, heard on film for the first time, turned out to be a disappointment. Few people wanted to watch a series of beautiful young women being seduced by an ageing man with an unattractive speaking voice. A disillusioned public stayed away and the film did not recover its costs.

If Korda was to succeed in his plan to outdo the Hollywood film industry, he needed to recover his money and make a great deal more – urgently. As it happened, he did so remarkably quickly. According to his nephew, Michael Korda, recalling the story of the making of *The Private Life of Henry VIII* in his family biography, *Charmed Lives,* the reason why *Henry* was chosen was because Korda had engaged Charles Laughton as his next leading man, though with no definite film as yet in mind. The Fairbanks vehicle having failed, he needed a certain box-office success for his next film, whatever it was to be.

Laughton's appearance could hardly be described as an improvement on that of Fairbanks: he famously described his own face as resembling a retreating elephant. He was, however, one of the country's most admired actors, possessing, moreover, a rich, resonant and theatrically-trained voice. Korda was convinced that a film starring Laughton could not fail to attract a large and admiring public. On this occasion he judged correctly.

Henry VIII's private life had long aroused public interest and curiosity. Now it occurred to Korda that Laughton's face and physique resembled that of the king in his corpulent middle years – a fascinating film subject combined with ideal casting. A good script was all that was needed. The rest was history – or rather, it was not, as historical accuracy tended to be cheerfully but charmingly abandoned by the writer (Biro again, with Arthur Wimperis).

The subject of Henry's relations with five of his wives did indeed capture the public's interest, both in Britain and America. The leading man gave a bravura performance, as did the five wives. The cast included Merle Oberon, Laughton's own wife Elsa Lanchester and Robert Donat. *Henry* was an international success, Laughton won an Oscar and Korda was nominated for one. More importantly from his point of view, the grosses brought Korda at last the fortune he needed and craved.

On the back of this success, all three Kordas bought impressive homes in central London. Zoltan and Vincent married the actresses

Joan Gardner and Gertrude Musgrove respectively. Korda was widely feted in public and gratifyingly wooed in the City. Substantial offers of finance were received and some eagerly accepted. At last his cherished dream was about to become reality.

The Fishery, a 170-acre estate in Buckinghamshire, was purchased on behalf of London Films, its out-of-town location chosen to avoid London's then notorious fogs. Extravagantly designed and expensively equipped, Denham Studios opened in May 1936. Korda himself occupied a magnificent, antique-furnished office suite overlooking the river. Swans personally provided by Churchill glided in stately procession across the water.

Unfortunately for everyone, as it turned out, a studio for another mogul was simultaneously under construction. J. Arthur Rank had bought Heatherden Hall, an estate within a few miles of the Fishery, to found Pinewood Studios, which, like Denham, opened in a spirit of optimism during the summer of 1936. With twelve sound stages between them, the English film industry would never be able to sustain both studios. Pinewood (still in use today) outlasted Denham, but in the end both film studios failed financially.

Happily installed at Denham for the time being, Korda's next big project was to be *Things to Come*, based on a recent book by the author H.G. Wells, whom he admired and whose friendship he wished to cultivate. Scenting another blockbuster, Korda invited Wells to prepare a storyline and script. Pleased and flattered, Wells agreed. He was not a particularly modest man and it was his declared intention to make people think. He determined that, from that year of 1936, the film would predict the future of mankind for the next hundred years. The resulting script was full of foreboding. An international war was imminent. This would last for thirty years, causing the ultimate disintegration of society. This disaster would be followed by a pandemic – a walking sickness – which would eliminate most of the earth's population. The remaining earthlings would be forced to live in underground city bunkers. The film ends more hopefully, with two young people leaving Planet

Earth in a space-ship, bound for some new galaxy, to start life again: a latter-day Adam and Eve, perhaps. Despite the accuracy of his predictions regarding the coming of war and the development of spacecraft, Wells's later global disasters have not come to pass. Pessimists might point out that there is still time.

Muir invited Sir Arthur Bliss, one of England's leading composers, to write the score. There was already a personal link between them: Bliss (born in 1891) had also studied at the Royal College, under Stanford. He was a kindly, warm-hearted man and he and his American wife Trudy were to become Muir's close friends. Muir was absorbed in the production throughout the making of the film, collaborating with every department and working particularly closely with the director, William Cameron Menzies, and of course with Bliss himself. Muir himself conducted the score with the London Symphony Orchestra, in the Scala Theatre in Charlotte Street. As he wrote later, this was probably the first time a composer had worked on a film from beginning to end – from initial scripting to final edit.

At last the film was finished and ready for public viewing. Bliss was pleased with his score, which he later reworked as a concert suite. Vincent had created marvellous sets. Menzies's direction was excellent and the special effects were spectacular. Korda, as producer, was perhaps already a little wary. But Wells was ecstatic, pink with pride and pleasure – as well he might be, as he had interfered shockingly with the filming from start to finish. For his part, Muir reflected appreciatively on how much the production had taught him.

The reception for the film was mixed. Grierson, amongst many others, was sceptical: 'Is the human spirit so craven as to endure the destruction of civilisation in the name of whatever patriotism?' Young Alistair Cooke (as yet relatively unknown) was even more critical, roundly condemning both the acting and Wells's psychological approach. *Things to Come* nosedived. British cinema-goers, suffering hardship in the midst of the depression and despondent about the future, were daunted by the prospect of watching H.G. Wells's doom-laden predictions. The war, which had ended only seventeen years earlier, remained a vivid and terrible memory. The Peace Movement held political sway, from the Houses of Parliament to the homes of millions of hard-working Britons and to the debating chambers of Oxford colleges. Most British people were in a mood to close their eyes to the appalling developments in Europe and were largely in favour of disarmament and of appeasement. They chose to watch the Hollywood offerings of the singing and dancing escapism of Astaire and Rogers, the infant charm of Shirley Temple, or the sophisticated light comedy of Hepburn and Grant.

American distributors and audiences (who mattered most financially) largely ignored the Wells film, complaining, as usual, that English accents were hard to understand. *Things to Come* has long been despatched to some cinematic Valhalla, but the score by Bliss, full of magnificent menace, was hailed world-wide as a masterpiece. Decca issued a set of three twelve-inch records of the music, which was regularly played in the concert hall, as it still is sixty years on. Young Mathieson had proved his worth to Korda.

Long before the great output of film music became a fashionable and highly lucrative business, Decca had the vision to provide many contemporary recordings, including, in 1946, Arthur Bliss's score for *Men of Two Worlds*. For this film, Bliss built his score round African music recorded on location – a striking combination of vivid ethnic music and European orchestration. Muir conducted Eileen Joyce and the National Symphony Orchestra in this performance.

In 1935, Muir had his first meeting with a young Hungarian composer, Miklos Rozsa. Rozsa was in a sense a mirror image of Muir, though he was about four years older. They both owed their love of music to their pianist mothers, had chosen music to be their way of life almost from infancy, learning to play piano and violin aged about five, and playing in children's orchestras in their early

Recording soundtrack for *Men of Two Worlds* (1946)
with National Symphony Orchestra, at Kingsway Hall, London.
From left to right: Arthur Bliss, Alexander Korda, Thorold Dickinson, Eileen Joyce (seated at piano), unknown, Muir Mathieson, Paul Robeson, John Hollingsworth

teens. There were, however, contrasts. Whilst Muir had attended the Royal College of Music in London from the age of eighteen, the eighteen-year-old Rozsa had attended the Leipzig Conservatory. This had been founded by Mendelssohn, who had taught at the conservatorium himself, as had Schumann and many of Germany's foremost musicians.

Rozsa had begun to write music as a student, moved to Paris on graduation in 1931 and made his debut as a serious composer in France during that year. He found it very hard to scrape a living. Arthur Honneger came to the rescue, persuading him to write 'silly little pieces' for a French film company under a *nom de plume*. Having acquired the knack, Rozsa decided to try for film work in England and arrived in London in 1935. Korda welcomed this fellow-Hungarian and promptly invited him to write the score for a

London Films production, *Knight Without Armour*, starring Marlene Dietrich and Robert Donat.

It appears that Korda made the invitation to Rozsa off the cuff, without consulting Muir, and in breach of the spirit of Muir's contract. Muir would never have recommended using a composer whom he had not even met. From the outset, it had been agreed that the choice of composer was to be a matter for joint consultation, following initial recommendation by the musical director. This was a fundamental matter for Muir. He guarded his rights closely, believing his selection of the appropriate composer for a film to be one of the most important decisions he would make. Hearing the news from Korda that Rozsa was to score this film may have been hard to swallow, though he apparently accepted it with dignity.

In his memoir, *Double Life*, Rozsa recalls meeting Muir for the first time. After his contract came through, he was told to call on Muir and introduce himself. Rozsa thought the young Scotsman very pleasant, likeable, kind and helpful, though he had the impression that Muir did not particularly like his music, adding wryly that he 'never forgave me for not being British'. Their personal liking for each other was mutual and their friendship lasted for many years. Muir teased Rozsa about his poor English and Rozsa teased Muir about his Scottish accent. For his part, Rozsa greatly appreciated the fact that he was dealing with someone highly experienced in the field of film music, who had studied at the Royal College of Music, in contrast to those who had migrated into film music from a music-hall or dance-band background.

Muir and Miklos were equals in musicianship. Rozsa had a genuine affection for Muir, appreciated his friendship and advice long after he had moved to America, and was amused rather than annoyed by what he felt to be Muir's chauvinism. Rozsa's period of study in Budapest, Leipzig, Berlin and Paris was inevitably more cosmopolitan than Muir's, whose experience had been emphatically and essentially English. Challenged on the subject by Leslie Mitchell in an interview, Muir defended his view:

> Hollywood . . . seems to be sold on the idea that only middle-Europeans are musicians, and it'll take a lot of argument and propaganda to persuade them that they are wrong. So far as their own music is concerned, in my opinion they have produced very little that is worth while. The things at which they excel are in technique and the very lighter type of music. The Hollywood powers-that-be are still demanding second-rate stuff, as a rule. No, there isn't a country anywhere in the world with half as much musical inspiration as there is here. What we've got to do is get that fact recognised.
>
> – *The March of the Movies*

Muir's staunch support for the English idiom may have been influenced by the declared enthusiasm of pre-eminent conductors of the time, Sir Henry Wood and Sir Thomas Beecham. His education at the RCM must also have been, at least in part, responsible for his dedication to it, perhaps by a process of osmosis. An atmosphere of delight in English folk and landscape music pervaded the college. Sir Malcolm Sargent (Muir's tutor) was a devotee of contemporary English music, as was Holst. Vaughan Williams, perhaps the most influential of all as Head of Composition, believed that English composers 'should not try to copy the style of other nations: they should write music particular to their own country and its people, cultivating a sense of music citizenship and incorporating the folk and traditional music of the English countryside'.

Vaughan Williams later studied under Bruch and Ravel, but his early life coincided with a period of rediscovery of English folk music and dance. Cecil Sharp, a teacher of music, devoted his life to collecting long-forgotten songs and tunes and founded the English Folk Song Society in 1898, which the twenty-five year old Williams enthusiastically joined. Today, the Cecil Sharp House in London contains the Vaughan Williams Memorial Library.

Throughout his life Williams went on missions of exploration round the countryside and personally collected eight hundred songs that might otherwise have been lost. His friend, George Butterworth, who had also studied at the RCM under Parry, was equally keen. Before Butterworth's death on the Somme in 1916, he had collected three hundred. Both composers evoke the beauty of the English rural landscape in their rhapsodic music.

Vaughan Williams's influence on Muir was indirect – Muir did not study with him, as he did not take Composition as his principal subject – and later Williams remarked that until he began writing film music, he hardly knew Muir.

The British film industry at that time was dominated, as already noted, by a rich vein of Hungarian emigrées whose dedication, imagination and flair virtually brought the British film industry into being. These included the three Kordas, Emeric Pressburger, Miklos Rozsa, Lajos Biro, Gabriel Pascal, the actor Leslie Howard (born in England of Hungarian parents) and many of the great film technicians of the time. Perhaps most importantly of all, in Korda's view, a Hungarian chef presided over the studio restaurant. ('What distinguishes . . . Hungarian cooking . . . is the love and affection that Hungarians lavish upon it' (*The Life and Death of a Screenwriter*).

Korda viewed life through a spectrum of primary colours and his chosen subjects were almost always great, expensive epics, though they were never as extravagantly produced as those conjured up by Hollywood's Cecil B de Mille. He spent a great deal of money buying up film rights to books that he rarely made into films – and probably never intended to – perhaps simply in order to prevent other people from doing so.

In the decade before the war, however, a series of sometimes memorable, and sometimes better-forgotten, films came from London Film Productions. Among these was an adaptation of *The Scarlet Pimpernel* in 1935. This was based on a piece of hokum written by Baroness Orzsy and featured Leslie Howard in the title role. Merle Oberon played his wife, Lady Blakeney, and Vincent Massey was the vengeful ambassador to the French Republic, a role he conveyed with all the menace that he, alone, was capable. Arthur Benjamin supplied the score, which Muir used with restraint.

It must be admitted that the patriotic overtones of the final scene of the film, in which Sir Percy and Lady Blakeney, escaping from France by sea, view the white cliffs of the English coast, seems almost embarrassing to watch today. For Korda, the theme of the film was perhaps an allegory for the plight of Jewish people now living under the Nazi regime. These were still the early days of the Third Reich, but already their terrible situation was becoming apparent – at least to those who cared to observe.

Other films of this era included *The Ghost Goes West*, *Men are not Gods* (music by another RCM trained composer, Samuel Coleridge Taylor); and a second Wells non-event, *The Man Who Could Work Miracles*. *Sanders of the River* was scored by Spoliansky, and the theme of the boating song from the film captured the public's ear and became extremely popular – so much so that it was apparently adopted as 'folk' music in parts of Africa.

A likeness between Henry VIII and Rembrandt had never previously been discerned or remarked upon, but Korda came to a unilateral decision that Charles Laughton closely resembled both. Money was needed urgently and he decided to produce another Laughton triumph. In 1936, Korda cast Laughton in the role of the great Dutch artist, with the unlikely pairing of Gertrude Lawrence as his unruly second wife. Korda produced and directed the film himself. Despite a magnificent performance by Laughton, wonderful, almost completely authentic sets by Vincent and an excellent score by Geoffrey Toye, the film flopped badly at the box office: the subject did not appeal to the British public.

In 1937, the film *Victoria Regina*, starring Anna Neagle as the eponymus queen, was made. The score, arranged by Muir, was composed by Anthony Collins and included an interpretation of some of the music from that queen's coronation. A string of other films followed, with scores by fine British composers, each orchestrated and conducted by Mathieson. None of these films grossed sufficient money to maintain Denham studios as had been hoped. Film-making in England as a whole was passing through difficult waters in the mid-to-late thirties. This was largely due to the unwillingness of American studios, which largely controlled distribution both here and in the US, to put British films on the circuits – times were hard enough and competition unwelcome. They justified this stance by complaining (probably with some truth) that British films lost money, as audiences failed to materialise.

Production costs at LFP were never stinted in the name of economy, however. London Films began to descend into financial freefall, losing large amounts of money for Korda's long-suffering principal backer, the Prudential Assurance Company. In 1936, the losses already ran at £330,842. By 1938, matters had become so serious, with losses of £2 million and overheads running at over £30,000 weekly, that Korda was forced to resign from chairmanship of the company. 'The Pru', together with the enterprising businessman J. Arthur Rank, took over the studios to try to recoup the losses. Henceforth the company bore the logo D & P (Denham and Pinewood) and, like other producers, Korda would simply have to rent a stage whenever he needed to. Muir remained at Denham, becoming musical director for D & P.

Korda reacted by metaphorically thumbing his nose, forming his own company, Alexander Korda Films, and by hurrying off to France to marry one of his leading ladies, Merle Oberon. His career had suffered a temporary blip, but it was very far from over. Further triumphs and disasters, and the first-ever film knighthood, awaited him.

Chapter 5

Hiawatha, Hermione, Home Life

Meantime, romantically and domestically, Muir's life had taken on a new radiance. In 1933, he met a rising young star of the ballet, Hermione Darnborough. It happened at the Albert Hall on a night when Coleridge Taylor's oratorio *Hiawatha* was being performed. This two-week annual production was celebrated for many years between the wars. It was produced on a scale that could never be dreamed of today. There was a cast of one thousand – eight hundred members of the Royal Choral Society and two hundred ballet dancers. Tickets were in great demand and the audience of up to seven thousand was always in a state of high excitement.

Hermione had danced in *Hiawatha* for several years, first as the child, dancing with Lydia Lopokova, and later with Phyllis Bedells as principal. Now she was taking the principal role of Flora herself. Malcolm Sargent was to conduct this production throughout the run. Sargent was a frail man, who at that time suffered from tuberculosis. One night he was taken ill and could not appear. Hermione (who had already heard much about Muir from members of the Sadlers Wells Opera) remembers:

> I made my entrance and was taken by surprise at finding Muir had taken over the baton, having borrowed his brother Dock's tails. Muir conducted the rest of the run and we saw a lot of each other that summer. Muir had promised to conduct a season of *A Midsummer Night's Dream* for the Oxford

> University Dramatic Society at the beautiful manor of Ovington, Hants, belonging to Sir Samuel and Lady Hoare. The play was given in a floodlit grove in the grounds. Muir suggested that I should dance to the Nocturne of Mendelsohn's music. The cast all stayed with Sir Samuel and Lady Hoare, and while we were rehearsing one had to dress for dinner at night. I had no evening dress with me, but my mother sent me a beautiful pale blue satin one with a rose. Luckily, she knew my size and I have never felt so elegant! I was about eighteen at the time. It was a very jolly time and once, I remember, as we were walking by the stream, watching the trout rise, Muir said, 'If we go on like this, I might ask you to marry me one day.' – A bit condescending, I thought!

Hermione was (and is) charming – thistledown, elegant and full of fun. Muir was good-looking – even a bit dashing, in white tie and tails, on the podium. Although he was not a man of marked physical characteristics, being of medium height, build and colouring, he had considerable presence and an air of confidence. He was also dynamic, full of ideas and, as Hermione has commented, had a knack of making everything interesting and amusing. It is not surprising that the attraction had been immediate and mutual.

William Nelson Darnborough, Hermione's father, was American. Her mother, Frances Erskine Shaw, was part English and part Scottish – a cousin of the Duke of Argyll. Frances's father, the Hon James Erskine Shaw, was an officer in the 14th Hussars and she had been brought up largely in Paris. William and Frances had met in Monte Carlo, where he broke the bank, but she persuaded him to give up gambling when they married and moved to England. Hermione was their younger child. Her older brother, Anthony Darnborough, became a film producer/director, working with Anthony Asquith and Noël Coward, and later with Betty Box.

Hermione was sent to the Lycée Francais in South Kensington, but by the age of thirteen she was already dancing in the Lyceum Pantomime and other Christmas shows. The Lycée did not approve of rehearsal leave, however, and she moved to Roland House School. Here she was trained by Euphan Maclaren, who had danced with the legendary Adeline Genee and Phyllis Bedells. Encouraged by Euphan, Hermione's mother took her to classes in Soho attended by Anton Dolin and by members of Diaghileff's Russian Ballet. Before her seventeenth birthday, Ninette de Valois invited her to join her young company at Sadler's Wells, dancing in ballets and operas both there and at the Old Vic. Alicia Markova and Anton Dolin were the principals. Frederick Ashton did much of the choreography: notably, at that time, his own creation *Les Rendevous* and productions of *Giselle, Casse-Noisette, The Haunted Ballroom, Swan Lake* and others. Hermione danced with the rest of the company in most of the ballets, but she was soon given solo parts, dancing with names such as Robert Helpman and Antony Tudor.

Muir was amazingly fortunate. Hermione, enchantingly beautiful and on the verge of becoming a principal ballerina, was willing to give up her career with Sadler's Wells to marry him. It cannot have been an easy decision to abandon the years of training and discipline and almost certainly a dazzling future, but she was in love: more in love with Muir than with ballet.

On the other hand, Markova chose to sacrifice the possibility of marriage in order to dedicate her entire life to ballet. She left Sadler's Wells to pursue her career elsewhere at almost the same time as Hermione; thus the company lost both its star dancer and a promising young ballerina within one year. From that time, sixteen-year-old Margot Fonteyn began to perform some of the principal roles.

Hermione and Muir were married in Brompton Oratory at Christmas 1935. Hermione was twenty, Muir twenty-four. For some time Muir had been sharing a little mews house in Knaresbrough Place, off Brompton Road, with the film editor (later distinguished director) Charles Crichton, a young woman opera singer, and Muir's close friend, Neville Wynne, known as Pooh. When Muir and Hermione married, both Charles and the young woman offered to move out, but Pooh stayed on. Hermione thinks that this was because he had paid most of the deposit on the house.

> So we started our new life *a trois*. I knew nothing about housekeeping. Dock had to show me how to cook a chop on the gas. We got a French cook/housekeeper, Basthilde, who, we discovered, had previously worked in a brothel. She insisted on going to Soho to shop and would come back in a taxi with a crate of peaches and a large box of anchovies. I also felt it necessary to spend £1 a week on flowers, so Muir's salary of £14 a week didn't go far.

Hermione appeared as a gypsy dancer in the first English film to be made in Technicolor, *Wings of the Morning*, starring Henry Fonda and the French star Annabella She also appeared on stage as a countess in *Balalaika* at the Adelphi, but her career was ending. She had to leave after a few months, as the first of their four children was on the way.

In 1937, the Mathieson family – Hermione, Muir and their baby daughter Muirne – moved from London to a house close to the studios in Denham, where they employed a cook/housekeeper from Devon. (Although Muirne seems to be a combination of Muir and Hermione, this is a happy coincidence. The Gaelic name Muirne, or Morna, means 'beloved'.) Their social group quickly expanded and their home was constantly filled with friends – actors, musicians (including Sir Thomas Beecham), singers, composers, artists and visitors working with Muir.

Muir was a warm and generous host, loved entertaining and took a genuine interest in all that was happening in the lives of his guests. He worked with many celebrities and there was much visiting between homes. Through friendship with the composer

Hermione Darnborough (Mathieson)
in the film, *Wings of the Morning*

Richard Addinsell, they were welcomed into his circle: Noël Coward, author Clemence Dane, actresses Joyce Grenfell and Joyce Carey, film designer Gladys Calthrop and many others. There would be parties, at which Addinsell and Grenfell would play and sing together. Arthur and Trudy Bliss invited them to stay with them in their modern, flat-topped home in Dorset. Through their friendship with Walton, they went to stay at Ashby St Leger, the Lutyens-designed home of Lady Wimborne, where they enjoyed the unaccustomed luxury of an open fire in their bedroom.

Two regular weekend visitors to their home were Muir's agent,

Alan Grogan, a partner in Christopher Mann Ltd., and his wife, Winifred, who came up from Sussex, where they ran a successful farm. The Grogans brought a croquet set, which, according to Hermione, often led to sulks all round.

In a curious little *ronde*, Winifred was Christopher Mann's sister. Christopher (who appears to have represented almost all the major stars of British cinema at the time) was married to the beautiful Australian pianist, Eileen Joyce. Eileen in turn frequently worked with Muir in concerts and films over the years, notably recording the piano scores for *Brief Encounter* and *The Seventh Veil*, in which Muir made a personal appearance as conductor of the orchestra, whilst Ann Todd played the part of the pianist. The composer on this occasion was Ben Frankel. Muir had a very high opinion of Frankel, who, according to a retrospective article by Edmund Tracey (*The Listener*, 27 October 1960), had been 'the golden boy of theatre music during the 1930s and the most accomplished composer of film music in the country during the 40s and 50s'.

In 1937, Muir persuaded his old college tutor, Arthur Benjamin, to write the score for *Wings of the Morning*. Benjamin had already scored two films the previous year and went on to provide the music for a dozen or so more, including *The Conquest of Everest* and *The Scarlet Pimpernel*. William Walton had already provided several scores. Bliss's first contribution had been outstanding. Over next few years, Muir would persuade Arnold Bax, Richard Rodney Bennet, Richard Addinsell, Guy Warrack and later Vaughan Williams – as well as the Europeans Spoliansky, Rozsa and Auric – to write music for the screen.

Naturally, composers were not the only people to benefit from the burgeoning use of film music throughout the thirties. Musicians and technicians now competed for generously paid extra-mural employment. Their normal rates of pay were meagre – two pounds, eight shillings a night for a principal player, about one pound, seventeen shillings and sixpence for members of the orchestra, seventeen shillings and sixpence a night in a theatre pit, plus a small

Muir Mathieson conducts the Royal Philharmonic Orchestra
at 'Filmharmic '70' at Royal Albert Hall, London

fee for rehearsals (*First Flute*). Players were rarely able to find more than one or two bookings a week and many eked out a living for themselves and their families by teaching privately.

Any offers of commission were always refused outright: Muir tried to give work even-handedly to all the big orchestras. Musicians from the London Philharmonic and the Philharmonia got regular work. The soloists of the London Symphony Orchestra formed a recording orchestra – the London Symphonia – which included George Stratton as leader; clarinetist Jack Brymer; Marie, Sidonie and Leon Goosens (harp and oboe), and three generations of flautists, Gordon, Eddie and Anthony Walker.

When Beecham created the post-war Royal Philharmonic Orchestra, Muir was of great help, giving the orchestra studio work at a time when they had lamentably few bookings. Beecham quickly got the measure of the film business and was soon enthusiastically interfering with the music cues arranged by Muir and the film director. After one recording, during which he had exhausted the orchestra by demanding constant repeats, Beecham remarked with satisfaction, 'Absurdly easy business, this film business; absurdly easy!' (*First Flute*).

Whereas today film scores are frequently written with large commercial sales in mind, at that time it was never the deliberate intention to produce concert hall pieces. However, some of the music was so appealing and important that the composer, or Muir, would later adapt it for public performance. In 1938, Muir conducted the Symphonia in a series of concerts of film music for the BBC.

In the beginning, the music department at Denham was housed in a cottage in the spacious grounds of London Film Studios. Here Muir employed a series of young conductors or pianists who would later make their names: John Hollingworth, Marcus Dods, Leo Quayle, Fred Lewis, Lionel Salter and Bill Blezzard. Muir's secretary was 'Dusty' Buck, who travelled to Denham daily from Chichester. Later to become a production manager, Dusty is still fondly remembered by many of Muir's colleagues – she was tremendously efficient, knew 'all the answers' and generally kept everyone and everything in order.

Muir was now working all hours at Denham – in the film world 'overtime' did not exist (particularly under Korda, who would normally begin work about lunchtime and would expect his staff and crews to work – without extra compensation – late into the night). Muir would leave for the studio at 8am to return home tired out and often wringing with sweat from the emotional intensity of conducting for long periods.

The relationship between orchestra and conductor is crucial. Sometimes the chemistry between them is poor, with damaging results in performance. Muir was much respected and very well liked on the floor. He was a perfectionist and could be tough to work with, and it is true that he acquired a reputation for assertiveness. It was also acknowledged that he had good reason: he was, after all, a star. Because he got things right himself, he expected others to do the same. 'If you got it wrong, he told you straight that you'd got it wrong, and in no uncertain terms: but you respected him for it' (John Huntley in conversation).

Not to put too fine a point upon it, Muir seems to have inherited his mother's short fuse. He is said to have shouted at everyone if necessary, including Korda, who was also wont to shout. Korda and Muir seem to have enjoyed something of a love/hate relationship, although 'hate' is too strong a word: they admired, respected and at times infuriated each other. Muir's sense of humour always triumphed in the end. One of his favourite anecdotes, recounted with a broad grin, was of Korda screaming with rage (it is not clear whether at Muir or at someone else), in his strong Hungarian accent: 'You think you know fuck all. You don't know fuck nothing!'

Muir was protective on behalf of others. John Huntley recalled an occasion when Muir reprimanded him on a train returning from Brighton. Huntley, then a very junior member of the team, had had the temerity to address the actress Rosamund John as 'Roz'. Everyone did, but Muir was angry, declaring that it had shown a complete lack of respect. On a later occasion, Muir 'bawled him out' for criticizing the work of an ageing composer as 'dull and boring' in a printed article. Muir complained that Huntley had 'broken an old man's heart' and the confrontation had terrified Huntley at the time, but as he said, Muir's wrath never lasted long – he would return to his habitual good humour very quickly. 'He greeted you next day as ever and never held grudges. He was a dynamic character, full of energy and had great personal charm.'

Muir made no distinction according to rank. His frank manner and habit of expressing himself forthrightly remained the same, whether he was addressing the most junior member of the orchestra, Laurence Olivier or David Lean. The clapper boy, George Bernard Shaw and the dowager Queen were treated as equals. There is no record of his having shouted at Her Majesty, however. Queen Mary visited his recording stage during the making of *The Four Feathers* in 1939 and was apparently delighted to witness the recording of a session of choral singing with tom toms.

Muir was responsible for commissioning, arranging and conducting the music for all the LFP films of the later thirties, and he quickly developed an unerring understanding of when and how music should be introduced within a film. Quite often he recommended that no music at all should be used, preferring to underline the dramatic effect with silence. William Alwyn shared his view that sound could only be effective in contrast to silence, remarking that without periods of silence a film could make little impact.

On first reading the original script, Muir was able to see and hear the finished film. His imagination, artistic sense and emotional intensity (he would sometimes weep when watching poignant scenes) provided the key to his understanding of film. He also loved comedy – so much so that once, when laughing at a Charlie Chaplin film, he literally fell off his seat into the aisle.

Because of the urgency with which a score would be demanded once filming was over, Muir was usually one of the first people to view a completed, or almost-completed, film. Directors – including David Lean, who was as apt to fly off the handle as his friend Muir – watched his reactions eagerly. They earnestly consulted him, knowing that he would immediately grasp whatever they were aiming to achieve. They were particularly gratified if he wept, or laughed uproariously.

In 1947, Muir described his method of working in *The Film 'Hamlet'*, a book which included contributions from writers, actors and technicians who made the film. He would begin from the moment the final shooting script arrived, reading it through and making a note of the scenes that obviously called for particular music and atmosphere. This would be discussed with the chosen composer, with whom he worked closely at every stage. They would first view a roughcut of the entire film together and then analyse it reel by reel. A decision was then made about the form the music should take.

The result of their preliminary work would be discussed with the director and producer. The editor would prepare a time sheet of the music required. The score would arrive (usually quite quickly, as time was a crucial factor at this stage) and Muir and the composer would begin to work on it together. Eventually the film would go 'on the floor', with the music department arranging for playbacks as necessary. When the score was ready in its final form, the music would be recorded in short sessions in a concert hall.

During the 1930s and throughout the war, music sessions were recorded in one of a number of halls in the London area, whichever happened to be available. The Town Halls at Watford and Wembley – particularly Watford – were preferred, as the acoustics were excellent. As always, Muir would conduct, insisting on a prompt start. If, as sometimes happened, some members of the orchestra were late for the 10am call, or wandered in casually, discarding coats, gloves and scarves on the way, he would rap his baton and say, a little testily, 'Gentlemen, you really must arrive on time. One minute now, please!'

Combining music and film exactly in those early days was difficult, but it was generally acknowledged that no one could do it better than Muir. During a recording, Muir was in charge, but his team worked as a unit. The film and disc recording equipment were the overall responsibility of the sound recordist. At the beginning of each session, the music mixer called the shots, placing microphone in various positions throughout the hall. During the session the mixer would have to check that the balance remained constant.

A complete score often took several days to record, depending on the length of music to be used. The film was projected onto a large backing screen within view of conductor, whilst the orchestra played the requisite scraps of score needed for each scene. It was a laborious, not to say boring, process, involving frequent stops to check the balance, to confer, to perfect the timing of union between music and film, followed by endless repetitions, much akin to the process of the making of the film itself. Not unreasonably, members of the orchestra sometimes complained amongst themselves about the tedium of the process.

It must have been an exhausting experience for everyone, especially later, during the war. Some of the sessions lasted from 10am until 10.30 at night and afterwards the weary musicians, carrying their instruments, had to make the journey home to various parts of London by whatever means available, in the uncertain gloom and chill of the blackout.

It would be 1946 before a music stage that could accommodate a large orchestra would be created at Denham by the Rank Organisation. John Huntley, then working as Muir's technical assistant, remembers how the building which used to be Stage One was transformed into a first-class floor, incorporating the most refined and up-to-date sound recording facilities, and was in constant use for both Denham and Pinewood productions.

Discussing the score of *Hamlet*.
Left to right: E. A. Drake (Music Recordist), Muir Mathieson
(after riding accident) William Walton, Laurence Olivier and John Hollingsworth
(photograph by Ian Jeayes)

Muir Mathieson (far right) directing

Magnetic recording began in Europe after the war and spread to America. This was a revelation and a joy, as the quality of sound was greatly superior to photographic recording, virtually eliminating background noise. The composer James Stevens has remarked that, initially at least, Muir seemed a bit uncomfortable with the new technology. It was no longer so easy to control the speed at which the music was played according to the dialogue on screen – slowing it down or speeding it up wherever he thought appropriate – though he quickly adapted to it.

But that would come in 1946. It was still only 1939 and there was much to be achieved. War was inevitable and Britain was ill-prepared for it. The mood of the country had changed, but national self-confidence needed to be boosted. The youth who had entered Korda's service five years earlier was still only twenty-nine, but he had already acquired a world-wide reputation. Muir now had a unique, but important, part to play in the conflict.

Chapter 6

Wartime Film-making

When war began, Korda hurriedly made what was to be his final film in England for the time being – *The Lion has Wings*. Twenty minutes long, this piece of syrupy propaganda starred his new wife, Merle, and the great actor Ralph Richardson, who were required to deliver some painfully sentimental lines. (Merle pleaded for people to fight . . . for 'truth and beauty . . . and kindness'.) The film was, of course, well-intentioned, but the rigorous documentary-maker Harry Watt was not the only critic to find this offering 'bloody ghastly'. Yet perhaps it did strike a patriotic chord for many at a time when an understandably apprehensive population needed reassurance as they geared up for the war to come. The score, arranged and conducted by Muir, was by Richard Addinsell.

By this time Korda had abandoned London and taken a house near Denham for his entire family. The arrangement was not thought to be an entirely happy experience. No doubt the language barrier did not invite an harmonious atmosphere – three English-speaking wives, Merle Oberon, Gertrude Musgrove and Joan Gardner, living with brothers who argued loudly in Hungarian. Vincent, for one, had a poor command of English. Merle quickly made her escape to Hollywood, ostensibly because of her commitments there.

At that time, Hermione Mathieson made a brief return to the stage in *Who's Taking Liberty*, a wartime satire by Pamela Frankau, at the Whitehall Theatre. Muir conducted the music. Gertrude

Musgrove and Joan Gardner were also in the cast, and all of them drove up to London from Denham together each day. Joan and Vincent's nanny came to stay with Hermione and Muir, looking after their little son Michael and the Mathiesons' three-year-old daughter Muirne.

It was evident that film production was going to be greatly curtailed – perhaps even impossible – during the war. In fact, all film-making did come to an end for a time. Alex Korda had already made great plans for future productions. He, his brothers and Muir, with Miklos Rozsa as composer, were in the throes of making a major film loosely based on *The Arabian Nights*, to be called *The Thief of Baghdad*. The script and lyrics were partly written by Sir Robert Vansittart, senior diplomat at the Foreign Office, who, one might have expected, must have had far more urgent matters to attend to at the time. Throughout the previous decade, from his Foreign Office eyrie, Sir Robert had been one of the strongest pillars of the anti-appeasement campaign, maintaining a constant undercover network of information about fascist activities throughout Europe. But 'Van' was also a man of culture, a writer and a poet.

Korda had put Miklos Rozsa under contract to write the score, but Korda's chosen director, a German by the name of Dr Ludwig Berger, insisted on a change: either the music would be written by Oscar Straus, an Austrian light opera composer, or Berger would resign. Under pressure, Korda gave in, meanwhile assuring a deeply offended Rozsa that he would remain under contract and be paid accordingly.

The score, when delivered, proved to be Austrian café music, quite unsuited to a romantic Middle Eastern extravaganza. Rozsa records that Muir complained bitterly. Korda, in a furious temper, sent for Miklos and Muir, and declared that he had learned that they had been making disparaging remarks about Straus's score. Muir was apparently equally enraged, shouting back at Korda that the score was ludicrous and totally impossible. He thereupon left the room abruptly. Korda then spoke soothingly to Miklos and secretly invited him to write some new music, instructing him to tell neither Muir nor Berger. When Berger eventually heard the music (by means of an 'accident' cunningly arranged by Korda), he greatly preferred it to that of Straus and said so. Miklos was restored as sole composer. Straus threatened to sue, but Korda paid him in full and that was the end of the matter. For Muir this was a blessed, and unexpectedly happy, ending.

The film was more than half-finished, but there was now no chance of completing it under wartime conditions at Denham. For Korda, film-making was his life. Moreover, he missed Merle. Reluctantly, he and his brothers, with their wives, children and nannies, packed up in turns and moved to Hollywood. Rozsa joined them shortly afterwards.

Korda's dream of establishing a rival to Hollywood in Britain would remain unfulfilled. The British Government – or at least Korda's old friend Churchill – secretly encouraged the move. Korda's offices were apparently to be used as cover for British agents during the period of American neutrality. It has been rumoured that he became a personal courier of top-level secrets between America and Britain: certainly his close friendship with Van makes this liaison likely. It was also expected that he would produce films aimed both at influencing public opinion in favour of the British cause in America (whose people were at that time still fairly widely isolationist) and at boosting the morale of British people – an undertaking that he willingly fulfilled. His first venture was to be a 'timely' film about Horatio Nelson, starring Olivier and Vivien Leigh. The film would portray English heroism without being overtly propagandist.

By now the team of British film- and music-makers had been severely depleted. Many had been called up for the Services. The three Korda brothers, their wives and families, John Grierson and one of his directors, Stuart Legg, Arthur Benjamin, Benjamin Britten, Peter Pears, Norman McLaren and Miklos Rozsa were all working on the other side of the Atlantic. (Rozsa spent the rest of his life there, composing the music – with varying degrees of success – for dozens of Hollywood films during the following three and a half decades, including *Quo Vadis*, *Ben Hur*, *El Cid* and *Spellbound*.)

At first, despite enormous discomfort and disruption to the lives of families and individuals, a strange and sinister lull occurred. The country was at war. Life was grim. Young men and women were in the services. Those at home were obliged to carry gas masks and identity cards. City children had been separated from their parents and evacuated to places and homes that were strange and sometimes unwelcoming. Lights were dimmed or forbidden, food and fuel were rationed. Barrage balloons dominated skylines. Yet nothing seemed to happen. There was a strange stillness in the air: everyone held their breath, dreading what they knew must come.

A year later, the bombing began in earnest. Most of the original inhabitants of Muir's bachelor flat – their great friends Charles Crichton, his wife Pearl, their son David, and Pooh (Neville Wynne) – moved in with Hermione and Muir, to share a home once again. David and Muirne slept under the dining table during air raids. It was apparently Pooh's responsibility to grow vegetables.

Muir had been called up for war service and was already preparing to go, but the Ministry of Information intervened. Recognising that his film work would be of greater national importance than membership of one of the Services, they asked to have him put in the 'Reserved Occupation' category. This he understood and accepted, but determined to play at least some part, he became an air-raid warden, armed with tin hat and stirrup pump, and was also occasionally on fireguard watch at Denham railway station.

All cinemas and theatres had been closed at the beginning of the war, but within a year the restrictions were eased. Once again people poured into warm picture houses from the cold, darkened streets. By now it was estimated that between half and three-quarters of the population were visiting the cinema on a regular basis. Meantime, Korda made some not-too-blatantly propaganda films in Hollywood and in the next few years he dotted to and fro across the Atlantic with remarkable frequency, given the risks. But for him the return to California was, in a sense, as if an entire decade had slipped away: once again he was overtaken by financial troubles, quarrels with fellow producers, mounting marital disharmony and a general dislike of Hollywood.

When filming was permitted again, the British film industry responded to the country's needs with a magnificent output, though film stock and equipment were in short supply. Muir became busier than at any time in his life. He wrote later, 'I think the war years, which gave us far fewer drawing-room comedies and the eternal-triangle dramas, made for more serious approaches and widened the scope considerably.' (Not all the offerings produced were classic wartime epics, however. Buckles were often swashed with great success during these years. From the mid-1940s Gainsborough turned out period melodramas with exceedingly

Composer William Alwyn, Music Director Muir Mathieson and Sir Michael Balcon explain to the Queen some of the technicalities of recording film music on the set of *The Magic Box* (1951)

unlikely plots. The storylines were pure Heyer or Cartland and the British film-going public adored them – particularly the finale, in which the wicked Margaret Lockwood and/or James Mason were finally foiled or eliminated.)

Men who had learned their craft as pre-war editors or directors of B-movies now came into their own, directing the new films. Many of them were friends of Muir. There was, of course, his particular friend Charles Crichton, who became one of the finest directors of comedy at Ealing Studios. The names of the great directors of that time are still celebrated in the halls of cinematic fame: David Lean, Michael Powell, Emeric Pressburger, Carol Reed and Michael Balcon.

Major films of wartime Britain were soon pouring out from Denham and Elstree; patriotic films, screened for audiences not only in Britain, but also in America, Canada, Australia, New Zealand and India, portraying, in a British, understated, way, tales of heroism, ingenuity and stoicism in the face of Nazi brutality. This was an asset that had never previously been available to a government at war and which, as Churchill remarked, was worth an extra division or two in the field. (Film of the atrocious suffering in the trenches on the Somme, edited to spare people's feelings, had been shown to a deeply shocked public in 1917 and 1918.)

Denham and Gainsborough were now both largely owned by J. Arthur Rank. He, of course, also owned Pinewood, which he had leased to the Government during wartime. In 1944 he would acquire Elstree as well. Like Grierson – though from a very different perspective – Rank had been drawn into film-making because he understood the power of cinema to influence the public at large. Rank was a Methodist and came to the industry in the 1930s believing that he could help to spread the message by setting up a film company. His enthusiasm had grown and over the last year or two he had indulged in a buying spree akin to the winner in the final throes of a game of Monopoly. He owned a chain of cinemas up and down the country and thus controlled a large share of the distribution rights – an asset that had eluded Korda with such unfortunate results.

Rank did not possess Korda's flair or personal charm and was not particularly interested in making films *per se*. For him, it was a business: the film industry was on an equal footing with his flour-milling enterprise. He was a Yorkshireman with a hard-earned personal fortune. This he proceeded to invest in the industry, content on the whole to leave matters of production to his producers and directors – who were, of course, delighted by their new-found freedom. (There may be an analogy here between their situation and that of the editor of a newspaper. A proprietor could interfere disastrously with his newspaper's policy and general line: an enlightened proprietor would deal with business matters and leave the running of the paper to his editor.)

Hitler and Goebbels (who was in charge of the German film industry) were appalled by intelligence reports of the effect of these films on the morale of the British public. As a result, Denham and Beaconsfield were added to the Germans' list of bombing targets. The tunnels leading from Denham's own electricity generating station in the grounds were used as air raid shelters. The studios were never hit, but one intended for Denham, or for the nearby aerodrome, landed in the Mathiesons' garden. Mercifully, it did not explode. Perhaps less mercifully (though all ended well) Muir found another one in a nearby wood and carefully placed it in the boot of his car for personal delivery to the local police station . . .

Work on filming the thriller *Gaslight*, by Thorold Dickinson, had begun in 1939, but it was first screened to wartime audiences in 1940. Muir had again chosen Richard Addinsell to compose the score. Diana Wynyard plays the lead, as an innocent wife whose malevolent husband, Anton Walbrook, planning to fall heir both to her inheritance and to her obliging housemaid, is driving her to the edge of madness by psychological manipulation. Addinsell's score added greatly to the mounting tension. This film was considered by critics of the time to be vastly superior to the Hitchcock version starring Ingrid Bergman, which was produced in Hollywood a few years later. The deepening intensity of unrestrained malice in Anton Walbrook's portrayal is thought to be much more powerful than that of the romantic Frenchman, Charles Boyer. (Comparison today is not possible, as Hitchcock apparently insisted that all copies of the British version be destroyed.)

The 1941 production of *49th Parallel* – a Nazi spy thriller, with Leslie Howard, Raymond Massey and Laurence Olivier, was Vaughan Williams's first film score. Vaughan Williams, who had fought in the First World War, was by now an elderly man, but anxious to do all that he could for the war effort and depressed that he was unable to play an active role. Visiting him at his home, Muir found his revered college tutor driving a salvage collection van round the town. Muir explained the Powell/Pressburger story-line for *49th Parallel,* which was to be financed jointly by the Ministry of Information and by Rank. It was a powerful tale: six members of a Nazi U-boat crew are on the run in northern Canada. During their attempt to escape over the 49th Parallel – the border between Canada and the still-neutral USA – and return to Germany, they encounter a series of Canadians of diverse backgrounds: Eskimos, native Americans, a French-Canadian, a German Hutterite, a Canadian soldier, a reflective, English academic. In each situation the escapees (who will eventually perish one by one) are confronted by a fundamental belief in individual freedom and a contempt and loathing of Nazi philosophy and brutality.

Muir found that no persuasion was necessary. The opportunity to support the cause by composing music for the film delighted the ageing composer and he set to it with a will and with outstanding success: the score and film married beautifully. *49th Parallel* proved an extremely difficult film to make. The cast and crew crossed the hazardous shipping lanes of the Atlantic to film in Canada. Once there, they encountered several disasters, major and minor. However, at least in part due to David Lean's inspired post-production editing, *49th Parallel* became a superb film.

It was at this point that young Edward Williams joined Muir as his assistant. Williams had left Cambridge early, having been sent down due to lack of interest in his studies. He hoped, as he had always done, to carve a career in music. He had had no formal training apart from school music lessons, but nonetheless knew with certainty that music must be his life. Whilst awaiting his call-up papers for the navy, which were expected to come in six months' time, a friend suggested that he should discuss prospects with Muir, who was known to be looking for an assistant. To Edward's delight, Muir immediately took him on. 'Start on Monday', he was told. Williams found Muir kindly and professionally generous. 'He was a very nice man – young and amusing, though perhaps a bit fierce. If he was cross on occasion, it seemed to me that he was cross with *things* rather than people. He never lost his temper with me.'

One morning, whilst working on *49th Parallel*, Muir was conducting a large orchestra, rehearsing the Vaughan Williams score. Edward Williams was standing nearby, observing. Suddenly, Muir thrust the baton into his hand, with the instruction, 'You take over, Edward. I want to go and hear it in the listening box'. Nineteen-year-old Edward, having only conducted a university orchestra once or twice, did his best. He had never been so frightened in his life. It did not make it any easier that the musicians were all old enough to be his grandfather. Afterwards, George Stratton, the leader of the orchestra, congratulated him – 'Well done, lad, you followed us very well!'

A further embarrassment awaited Edward. He had already learned to his cost that moving a music stand personally would cause immense trouble with the musicians' union. So, while waiting for the orchestra to arrive one morning, he spotted a little props man in the studio and asked him to bring in two more stands. He thought the man reacted with some surprise, but dutifully obeyed, carefully placing the additional stands in position. Muir arrived at that point and warmly greeted the 'props' – producer/director Sir Herbert Wilcox.

That year (1941), the film *Dangerous Moonlight* was made, with Anton Walbrook giving a compelling performance as a blinded Polish airman/composer. The score, which included the famous and much-loved *Warsaw Concerto*, was composed by Richard Addinsell and performed off-camera by Louis Kentner. The film was a huge success. Addinsell's composition, although not a concerto in strictly musical terms, was such a resounding success in the concert hall and as a commercial recording (three million copies were sold at the time), that he became extremely wealthy as a result. Not everyone who worked on the score was so fortunate. According to Roy Douglas, the musician who worked until two or three in the mornings, orchestrating the score on behalf of Addinsell, he received no royalties at all for his work (*The Best Years of British Film Music*). It was apparently fairly general practice amongst composers to turn out a melody and hand it over to an orchestrator with explanation as to requirements.

In Which We Serve (1942) was written, produced, directed, scored and narrated by Noël Coward, who also played the leading role – captain of a stricken British destroyer. The success of the film was, as always, due to the combined efforts of many. In effect, Anthony Havelock-Allen produced. David Lean was drafted in as co-director – his first film in that capacity and a brilliant choice. Lord Louis Mountbatten (on whom the leading role was loosely based) advised. Noël composed, with the assistance of a young woman copyist. Muir, of course, was constantly on hand to advise, to provide structure, to arrange and conduct the score. Viewed today, the film has a curiously antiquated veneer, demonstrating the appalling, patronising, British and naval class obsessions of that era, but also portraying great heroism and nobility of spirit. Coward was awarded a special Oscar for the film.

Another major Coward offering was made in 1943 and released in 1944. *This Happy Breed* was based on one of his earlier plays: a series of vignettes covering the life of an ordinary London family, encompassing its complexity of characters; their humour, pathos and stoicism in the face of tragedy. This time David Lean was given full status and one of the most outstanding directorial careers of all time was launched. Lean, Havelock-Allen and Neame formed their own company, Cineguild. Coward was relieved to be free of the responsibility of direction and production, but he again provided the score, which Muir adapted and conducted. The film, made in Technicolor and starring Celia Johnson and Robert Newton, grossed the highest takings of any British film that year.

These were a few of the more outstanding wartime films, but Muir was responsible for commissioning, arranging and conducting the music for almost fifty films during the war. Mores, accents, attitudes, techniques of acting and film-making have changed dramatically in the last sixty years, but to wartime audiences they were heroic and inspiring, and undoubtedly helped stiffen British resolve at a most critical time in the country's history.

Alongside his work on these films, Muir became musical director for the Army, Navy and Air Force film units. These units provided information and education to members of the forces. Crews also covered actions abroad, often working in dangerous combat conditions. Footage was returned to Britain for censorship and editing as speedily as possible. (Film of the Normandy Landings on 6 June 1944 reached Pinewood within seventy-two hours of the action.)

Muir was also in charge of music for the Crown Film Unit. This was a descendant of the GPO Film Unit of the thirties, which had been renamed by the Ministry of Information in 1940. Jack Beddington became head of the film unit, with Ian Dalrymple, a former editor, as producer in charge. A series of magnificent films showing Britain at war was produced, with amazing speed and success, with Montague Slater, John Betjeman and Arnott Robertson providing voice-overs and giving a reassuring sense of authority and stability to the scripts. In addition, short films, usually shown after the newsreel and before the feature film, provided vital information for the public. These were watched by millions of people: reminders to have children immunised against diphtheria, encouragement to dig for victory, how to deal with wounds, what to do in case of incendiary bombs, and films illustrating ways in which careless gossip or chatter could cost the lives of servicemen.

The unit also made specialist films as required by the Ministry. In Grierson's absence, the chief producer/director was Basil Wright, the seasoned documentary maker, who became advisor to the Ministry of Information and Head of the Crown Unit. All these units were based at Pinewood, which had been commandeered by the War Department and which now housed the Royal Mint, Lloyds of London and a sugar store. A studio and production area were allocated to the film units and were staffed by servicemen, many of whom had been technicians and craftsmen in the industry before the war. The output was huge and the Crown Unit quickly acquired a great reputation in the UK and overseas. Amongst the most memorable films from Crown during the war were *Target for Tonight, Western Approaches, Merchant Seamen, Coastal Command, Fires Were Started, The Silent Village, Listen to Britain, London Can Take it* and *Close Quarters*.

For Edward Williams, as for many of his young contemporaries, to be involved in documentary film-making was the height of ambition, with a glamour and excitement that far out-shone feature film-making. One of the producers, Paul Rotha, in his 1972 *Documentary Diary* noted that their method of film production had become world famous, commenting that no other country in the world had created this tradition of factual film-making. To his mind, a continuity of creative purpose and public service that was unique in the unstable history of motion pictures had been built up round the unit.

In a memo to Grierson in 1941, Wright indicated the pressure under which the unit was working and mentioned a new, non-musical role for Muir. He reported that the demand for more and more films was becoming intense. The job of the unit was not merely to meet the demand, but to identify gaps in the propaganda field and try to fill them. They were trying to get vital ideas across and to be long-term as well as short-term, whilst simultaneously fighting countless battles on issues of policy and coping with production problems. Rotha and Cavalcanti were 'helping to take the strain' at the British Film Council Films Committee. Wright told Grierson that Muir Mathieson was now with them at Film Centre (a body of producers and directors with headquarters in Soho) for a few months, commenting that Muir had a better film mind than most and would be valuable as a producer and even, to some extent, in making policy decisions.

The strain of overload was beginning to tell on them all and by 1942 Wright was becoming slightly disenchanted with Rotha, complaining to Grierson that his paranoia was becoming a bit more than normal. (Rotha remarked of Grierson that, had he remained in Britain during the war, 'he would have been driven mad, as were most of us, by the sheer incompetence and amateurishness of those at the top of official information and propaganda services'.)

The Forces units made short films of men in uniform and were divided broadly into Instruction, Education, Science or Civics. An enormous range of short films was made for the general public. Humphrey Jennings, artist and poet-film-maker, who had made several memorable pre-war GPO films (*The Story of the Wheel, The Birth of the Robot* and others) went on to make a magnificent, morale-boosting series for Crown Films during the war – *London Can Take It, Words for Battle, Listen to Britain, The Silent Village, A Diary for Timothy*. For Lindsay Anderson (*Sight and Sound*, 1953) 'They will last because they are true to their time, and because the depth of feeling in them can never fail to communicate itself. They will speak for us to posterity, saying: This is what it was like. This is what we were like, the best of us.'

Muir's close friend over many years was the brilliant Chief of Sound for Crown Films, Ken Cameron (younger brother of the distinguished journalist, James Cameron). The family had lived for a time at Wendover, but Ken remembered little of their life there and retained few personal memories of either parent, who both seem to have been somewhat detached. His mother died when he was nine. In an unpublished memoir, he recalls the anguish of being taken to see her after her death and the subsequent trauma of the break-up of the family. His aunt, a forceful and highly intelligent woman, came down from Scotland to try to mend matters, but without success. His father, a journalist, returned to Dundee to work for the *Sunday Post*, for whom he had been writing serial stories over the years. James ('at a very young age') was sent to the Manchester office of that same paper, to work as an office boy. As for Ken himself, 'My aunt took me, with my kitten, back to her home in Helensburgh on the Firth of Clyde. I lived with her, respected and adored her, until I watched her die nearly half a century later, in her ninety-ninth year.'

Throughout her life, Aunt Rita made great sacrifices on Ken's behalf, moving several times to provide a home for him in various circumstances. He was sent to one of Scotland's most prestigious public schools, Glasgow Academy, and went on to study electrical engineering at Glasgow University. In his first year there, he joined the students' section of the Film Society, under the chairmanship of Charles Oakley. Through Oakley, Ken met many of the leading film-makers of the time and came under the influence of the already-legendary John Grierson. 'It was from him that I caught the film bug, which, once in one's veins, is quite incurable.'

The electrical engineering course at Glasgow University consisted of a four-year 'sandwich' course – two terms of intensive university study each year, interspersed with a term of practical training as an apprentice to a suitable engineering firm. His increasing interest in cinema led him to persuade John Grierson to accept him as a summer trainee in the sound department of the GPO Film Unit – and then to persuade the university authorities that this was a valid training for his degree. Thus began what is arguably one of the most illustrious careers in the field of sound engineering.

After graduation, Ken Cameron was appointed second assistant to the Sound Department of the GPO Film Unit. At first his jobs were lowly – he was used more often as runner than technician; but fairly soon after his arrival, two senior men in the department left. To his surprise, he found himself in charge. At that time sound engineers were considered inferior and unimportant by more lofty technicians, who saw themselves, by contrast, as essential and creative; but all the time Ken was laying the foundations of what was then a relatively new science. Under his stewardship, that science would be honed and perfected through constant innovation and experiment. At last the importance of sound engineering was acknowledged throughout the industry.

Like Muir, Ken was called up at the beginning of the war, but was immediately placed in the Reserved category. Again, like Muir, he was sent to work for the unit on a series of government films, mostly directed by Cavalcanti, Humphrey Jennings and Harry Watt. Immediately after the Dunkirk disaster and Churchill's famously defiant address to the nation, the unit was asked to make a film illustrating the courage and determination of the British people – and to make it in record time. It was an exhilarating experience. The team worked day and night to produce *Britain at Bay*. According to Ken's account, the script was written and the voice-over read by J.B. Priestley within a matter of hours. Muir Mathieson booked an orchestra to record Richard Addinsell's score at Elstree the following morning. The film (directed by Cavalcanti, Jennings and Watt) was edited and the sound track mixed that afternoon. Ken wrote that it showed just what they could achieve together.

From the time of the transfer of the GPO unit (now the Crown Unit) to the Ministry of Information, Muir and Ken invariably worked together and became lifelong friends. Ken said that Muir taught him everything he was to know about music recording . . . 'One could not work with Muir without some of the skill and excitement and love of his job attaching to his colleagues.' There was also, of course, a bond of Scottishness between them, as well as shared interests and enjoyments – not least that of a dram at the end of the day.

At that time – though he married very happily later in life, after his beloved aunt's death – Ken was a cheerfully gruff bachelor, well liked and highly respected. Quite early on in his career, he had made a conscious decision to stand out from the crowd by some personal eccentricity. 'If one is different from everybody else in films, one is half-way there.' This he did with considerable success. Friends and colleagues still comment on his custom of wearing his Erracht Cameron kilt daily, everywhere and in all circumstances. If required to attend an evening function, he would appear, resplendent and magnificent, in full highland evening dress.

The renowned pianist Dame Myra Hess (who, it may be of mild interest to note, was Nigella Lawson's great aunt) had begun to organise lunchtime concerts in the National Gallery for the people of London. They responded with huge enthusiasm, queueing up cheerfully and filling the gallery to its full capacity and beyond. Ken helped to record one or two of them, and it occurred to him that lunchtime concerts for service personnel and film crews at Pinewood would provide relaxation and pleasure. He discussed the possibility with Dame Myra, who immediately offered to come down and give some recitals. Moiseiwitsch, Solomon and other soloists also came to perform. These concerts were warmly appreciated and always well attended. If a soloist was not available, Ken arranged a recorded concert.

At this time Muir was also providing concerts, but on a much greater scale than those at Pinewood. He toured the country, conducting with a gallery of major soloists; conducted opera at Sadler's Wells and the Old Vic, as well as arranging and conducting concerts for the BBC. He understood the overwhelming power of music to influence mood and emotion – at times inspiring, at others, perhaps, healing – 'wings to the mind', as Plato had called it. Muir knew the importance of his work and did not spare himself.

> There is one name that appears very frequently in British screen credits – the name of Muir Mathieson, the musical director. Note that name, please. Remember it. Honour it. Of all the people who have served the British cinema brilliantly in wartime, I should put this young, ardent little Scotsman very near the top of the list.
>
> Muir Mathieson is not only a solid conductor and a scholarly musician in his own right; not only has he arranged countless scores for films and conducted film orchestras, large and small; but his enthusiasm and engaging personality have cajoled one after another of the great composers into writing original music for the cinema. Vaughan Williams, Arthur Bliss, William Walton, William Alwyn, Richard Addinsell, and the Master of the King's Musick, Sir Arnold Bax; these people trust Muir Mathieson. He has musical integrity. He is one of their own kind. The film people trust him too. He is a swift and practical worker. He knows the screen. To him, the alliance of image and sound is something of a burning mission. He is an idealist – with all the solid caution of a Scot.
>
> – *C.A. Lejeune, the leading film critic of the day, in Nov. 1944*

Muir was also responsible for the music for the BBC's annual Christmas Day programme *Christmas Round the World*, which was broadcast in the afternoon, immediately before the King's address to the nation. Both programmes had a large and attentive audience: almost everyone listened eagerly, whether members of the forces gathered in the mess, or families sitting together round their firesides. Because so many countries and time variations were involved, Muir was needed by the BBC for most of Christmas Eve and Christmas Day, and was seldom at home for the family.

Despite this, it was evident that the happiness of his family was always uppermost in his mind; Muirne recalls:

> I remember the magic of Christmas – coming down to a beautifully trimmed tree that he and my mother had decorated after we had gone to bed, and to the presents he had made for us all. He had a small workshop at the back of the house and from that emanated, one Christmas after another, the most beautiful, imaginatively produced wooden toys. There was a fully fitted, three-storey dolls' house, complete to the last detail – even bread on the table – any little girl's dream: then a farm that folded away into a large box, complete with barns, roads, fences, and of course, the animals. One year there was a pedal car – perfectly constructed – which I was able to ride out on the open road; and finally a fully equipped puppet theatre with lighting grids, scenery, curtains and everything for a complete production of *Peter Pan*, which he and my mother produced on Christmas evening.

The constant travel, the rehearsals, the performances, his film work, the Crown Film Unit and even his duties as an air-raid warden added up to a gruelling existence during those wartime years. At the same time there was never a cessation, or even a temporary gap, in the spate of feature films requiring Muir's musical direction. In 1944, Sydney Box's *The Seventh Veil*, starring James Mason and Ann Todd, was in production. First screened in October 1945, the film portrayed a brilliant young pianist slowly being brought to recovery from depressive amnesia by being submerged in a psychiatrist's deep hypnotic trance. The score included new music by Ben Frankel, but also flashback scenes of the young pianist in concert: a valid reason this time for including excerpts from a Chopin prelude, the Grieg Piano Concerto and Beethoven's Pathetique Sonata. The Oscar-winning script and the individual portrayals were excellent. Muir conducted Eileen Joyce and the London Symphony Orchestra (LSO), which he described as 'the perfect film orchestra', in what were deemed to be magnificent performances. The film broke box office records in Britain and was unusually well received in America.

Blithe Spirit was filmed in 1945. The Noël Coward script was hilarious and the cast outstanding. Muir again brought Richard Addinsell in as composer. The tale was of a glamorous first wife who is accidentally called up from the dead by a highly eccentric medium (Margaret Rutherford). She is physically apparent to her husband (Rex Harrison), but remains invisible and inaudible to his rather dull second wife. Her feline attempts to undermine the new marriage, the husband's dilemma and the medium's earnest but clumsy mistakes in trying to rectify the call-up, all make for sparkling entertainment.

In the very week that the war came to an end in May 1945, Muir was working on the score for the film *Brief Encounter*. The original film script was Coward's, but was rewritten for the screen by the Cineguild sub-committee – director David Lean, producer Anthony Havelock-Allen and cameraman Ronald Neame. The story concerns two married people gradually falling in love with each other after an accidental meeting. At a script conference, Coward rather loftily described the character of the female lead and the prim and dreary routine of her life as he imagined it: 'She usually takes lunch at the Kardomah Cafe, goes to the library in the afternoon – and listens to Rachmaninov.'

The weekly meetings continue and as time goes on they are greatly tempted, but ultimately part without consummating the affair: he to work overseas, she to the warmth and security of her suburban home and unexciting husband. As he sits reading his paper and smoking his pipe, she mentally unburdens herself, relating the poignant story of her would-be lover, while music plays on the radiogram. As she ends her silent account, the dull-ish, predictable, husband looks at her over his newspaper, smiles and says simply, 'You've been a long way. Thank you for coming back to me.' This is an odd remark, considering that as far as he is concerned she has simply been shopping in town every Thursday afternoon. As the music and the film end, the audience comprehends that the story has not been about the thwarted, temporary, passion of two people at all: it is about the unspoken anguish of the loyal husband, who has instinctively known what was happening all the time.

Coward, as co-director, insisted that Rachmaninov's Second Piano Concerto should be the music she has chosen to play, providing a continuous undercurrent throughout the film. This contradicted Muir's dictum that music should be specially designed for each film, but Coward was adamant. There was temporary disagreement, but a compromise was reached. Muir conceded, provided that the concerto was not chopped up 'Hollywood style', to suit the film. Rachmaninov's emotional music was manifestly Coward rather than Mathieson, but Muir worked to arrange it, once again conducting Eileen Joyce's performance. The concerto could not, of course, be used in its entirety, but Muir ensured that it was played in the correct sequence, beginning with the eight opening piano chords and ending on the coda of the third movement over 'The End'.

> *Brief Encounter* was a very fine British film, homely and real, moving and effective, but I think it was a mistake to use the Rachmaninov Piano Concerto No 2 in this particular case. I like the Rachmaninov No 2 far too well to be able to follow a first-class film at the same time, which is largely unrelated to the music . . . As soon as the story begins to unfold we are continually distracted from the plot to listen to Eileen Joyce, with Muir Mathieson and the National Symphony Orchestra, in a brilliant rendering of a work which, despite many hearings, still requires my full attention. It cannot be done. Either you listen to Rachmaninov or Coward, but they have so little in common that you cannot listen to both'
>
> – John Huntley in *British Film Music*

Initially, the film was not a great box-office success. The main characters are unglamorous and the settings drab, but with the combination of Lean's direction, a sentimental script, the sympathetic acting of Celia Johnson and the romantic, yearning music, it became one of Britain's all-time favourite films, ranking alongside Hollywood's *Casablanca* – and securing the Second Concerto's permanent position at the top of classic charts.

Britain's film-makers ended the war on an appropriately triumphant note. They had made their own particular contribution to victory, had struggled manfully against impossible difficulties, scarcity of materials, shortage of stock – of everything imaginable. Like the population in general, their buildings had been bombed and they had suffered personal injury, as well as the loss of friends and colleagues in the blitz. In spite of it all, the output had been remarkable and moving. During those years British film-makers had found their feet and the public had responded. Now, with the long-awaited return to comfort and plenty, it seemed as if the industry was poised on the edge of a new and even more productive future.

By the end of the war, Crown had lost several of its most important producers. Alberto Cavalcanti and Harry Watt had left to work with Balcon at Ealing Studios. Their departure was followed by those of Alex Shaw, John Taylor and Jack Holmes. Furthermore, it was now apparent that the unit's occupation of Pinewood would soon end as post-war feature film-making returned to the studios.

Before Crown left Pinewood, a very important film was made. Towards the end of the war, Muir had had an inspiration. He had always had a particular mission in life – to open the doors of music to children and to return to them some of the delight that it had brought to his own life. Sir Denis Forman recalls the events. He had recently returned from war service and joined the Central Office of Information Films Department. The first time he met Muir was over a project to make a film to display the instruments of the orchestra to schoolchildren: showing what each instrument looked like, how

Muir Mathieson on crane directing the film *Instruments of the Orchestra*.
Malcolm Sargent is conducting the London Symphony Orchestra

it sounded and what its place was within the orchestra. It was hoped that Benjamin Britten would agree to write the music.

Sir Denis attributes the successful outcome of the project to Muir's vision and tenacity. 'This was a very unlikely venture on the part of everyone involved, as it was to be much more expensive than the normal schools productions. To start with we got support from Jacquetta Hawkes (who later married J.B. Priestley), a great friend of my wife, and then of mine. She was at the Ministry of Education. She lobbied and we lobbied and I should think it took us about a year until we actually got the film on the road. Muir was the most enthusiastic and active member of the quartet, which included Basil Wright. He approached Benjamin Britten and, after a great deal of discussion, got him to agree that he would compose it. After that we all worked away at it.'

Britten had felt unhappy and homesick in California. He longed to be back in Suffolk and returned to England in 1942, faced a Conscientious Objectors' Tribunal, and spent the remainder of the war producing a magnificent canon of work, including his opera *Peter Grimes*. In some circles he was already beginning to challenge Walton's position as Britain's greatest living composer.

The result of Crown Films' approaches, with the support of the Ministry of Education, was that the film entitled *Instruments of the Orchestra*, or, as Britten preferred to call it, *A Young Person's Guide to the Orchestra*, was finally released in 1946. Britten had delayed starting work on the project for a time, but in the end it took him only about a month to compose. It is quite likely, though, that his ideas for the work had been brewing for some time before that: Britten apparently liked to compose in his head, preferably during long journeys.

The theme was adapted from the hornpipe from *Abdelazar*, by Henry Purcell. After the introduction, the instruments are introduced as soloists, one by one. The piece ends with a loud, triumphant, coming-together of all the instruments in the magnificent fugue-like finale. In what was to be a new and exciting role for him, Muir directed the film himself, with Malcolm Sargent conducting the Liverpool Philharmonic Orchestra and narrating the script.

Ken Cameron and his colleague Ken Scrivener recorded the music. Scrivener recalls the day of the recording, which took place at Watford Town Hall. He and Muir were walking round, talking together, when they came across Benjamin Britten and the harpist Marie Goosens in a sound box. Marie was rehearsing her solo piece and she was very upset. In a few moments she was going to have to go into the main hall and record it for posterity:

> I think hers was the third or fourth instrument to play. She was having great difficulty over an awkward hand movement at bar 37. Muir immediately understood the problem and suggested that she should come in a moment or so before directed by the score. He said that it would not affect the performance, but would give her a split second longer to form her hand in the right shape for the next chord – after that it would be plain sailing, he said. Benjamin Britten agreed to this proposal and when she played for the recording she did as Muir had suggested. Her face lit up. Afterwards she thanked Benjamin warmly, though of course she knew that it was Muir who had arranged it. It was a lovely moment and I think Marie Goosens's harp solo was one of the finest passages in the entire piece.

A Young Person's Guide has been seen, and the music listened to, by generations of schoolchildren. For many, it has been their first introduction to 'classical' music. A second Ministry of Education film, *Steps of the Ballet*, followed in 1948. Possibly with echoes of his 1935 film *Wings of the Morning* in mind, Arthur Benjamin provided the score. Muir again directed this half-hour film, which explored the composition of music for a ballet performed on screen by Sadlers Wells, but it failed to match the impact of Britten's work.

Ken Scrivener had first met Muir through their mutual friendship with Ken Cameron. He remarked that he particularly remembered Muir's voice. He thought it very pleasant, with many sibilants, which made it very clear so that it cut through any background noise.

One day, in Wembley Town Hall, Muir was conducting a rather difficult piece of music. The hall was full of musicians tuning up, yet Muir was holding a detailed conversation with a player who must have been at least thirty or forty feet away from him. He was explaining how he wanted the attack on a particular chord to be changed. Scrivener thought how wonderful it was to have such a clear voice that it could carry over such a distance and in such circumstances.

Ken Scrivener had another recollection: 'On one occasion we were doing a recording session for a film – at Watford, as it happened. The composer was an inexperienced young chap and he was making an awful mess of fitting the music to the film. He looked at me in desperation, but then Muir said to him kindly 'We won't record this now. We will record it tomorrow, and you and I can spend this afternoon in the cutting room.' So Muir and this youngster went off into the cutting room and spent the entire afternoon there. When they came back they had obviously worked extremely hard – for four or five hours, probably. Now the music was lovely and it fitted well.

'I thought what an excellent thing it had been for this youngster that Muir had been able to straighten him out. The next day, at the end of the recording, the young man cheerfully accepted many handsome compliments on his work, without a word of acknowledgement to Muir. I stood up indignantly and said 'Hang on a minute!' but Muir shook his head. He had changed the music and he had saved the day, but he did not wish to take any credit for himself. I think that was typical of the man.'

Sir Denis Forman confirms Ken Scrivener's view. He worked closely at Crown with Muir in the early post-war years and speaks of him as 'a most talented and likeable guy . . . something of a backroom boy. He tended to do a lot of work for which other people took the credit . . . he was a wonderful arranger of music for films . . . perhaps his greatest talent was as an impresario and fixer.'

Work on major films was now returning to Pinewood, and Crown moved to Beaconsfield, where it continued to make important short films at the rate of seventy-five a year. Humphrey Jennings was again amongst the foremost directors of these films, whilst Muir and, later, John Hollingsworth, were the unit's musical directors. According to Ken Cameron's account, by now the atmosphere within Crown was rapidly deteriorating, due to interference by civil servants. Crown had been virtually autonomous throughout the war, but now officials constantly pestered and organised them, adding greatly to the cost of running the unit and to the mounting resentment of producers and directors. Wright resigned as producer in charge of the Crown Film Unit in 1945, complaining of overlapping and gross inefficiency. In a later article, he pleaded for international co-ordination in the documentary field, emphasising the urgent need for constant exchanges of personnel and for annual conferences. These, he said, could help to avoid the tendency for any one country to concentrate on selfish national propaganda.

To add to the gathering gloom, Humphrey Jennings was killed in 1950, after falling down a cliff-face while filming in Greece. He was forty-three. It was a grievous loss. Lord Attenborough has written of Jennings . . . If you want to see what life was like in the 1940s, what we put up with and what our motivations were, go and see one of his films . . . I was in such awe of this man and of the poignancy and economy with which he portrayed an atmosphere, a period, an incident, which reverberated either in one's eardrums or on one's retina . . . '

The Unit was finally disbanded by the government of the day 'as an economy measure' in 1952, but not without vehement protest in Parliament, in the press and in the country at large. A letter to *The Times* appeared, coincidentally, on the day of the Queen's Accession:

Letters / The Times
Thursday 7 February 1952
To the Editor

Sir, The Composers Guild of Great Britain most ardently supports the protests against the closing down of the Crown Film Unit. 'Crown', largely owing to the enlightened policy of its musical directors, Muir Mathieson and John

> Hollingsworth, was ever in the forefront of the battle for specially composed music by British composers of distinction or promise: it has not only given opportunity and encouragement to many a lesser known composer, but has also shown the world that our great ones have it in them to enhance the artistic value of films.
>
> Those of us who have had the privilege of working with and for 'Crown' cannot stand by and hear it condemned to death without petitioning against a sentence so discouraging to our colleagues at home and our prestige abroad.
>
> We are, Sir, your obedient servants,
> Ralph Vaughan Williams, President
> Guy Warrack, Chairman
> Composers' Guild of Great Britain, 7 Deanery Street, W1

The passing of Crown Films was a cruel blow to the many film-makers and technicians who had been involved with the unit. Muir was indignant and saddened on behalf of his colleagues, though he himself was relatively unaffected. By now he was based at Pinewood, having resumed work on feature films and in the concert hall. His friend and sometime protegée, John Hollingsworth, had succeeded him as Musical Director for Crown.

Ken Cameron was deeply affected by the demise of the unit, having worked exclusively for either the GPO unit or Crown for all his working life. In *All Squeak and No Bubble* he records that the axe fell upon them so swiftly that Beaconsfield was turned into a dismal wilderness, with mail left unsorted, files abandoned, racks of trims and spares hanging in the cutting room bins. Soon the whole place was stripped of furnishings and equipment. Papers were burned in huge bonfires. Ken personally rescued Vaughan Williams's partly burnt original score for *Coastal Command* from the flames. He found it unbelievable that civil servants could be so ruthless.

Out of the ashes of Crown Films, a new production company was born: Anvil Films. Ken Cameron and colleagues Ken Scrivener, Richard Warren and Ralph May combined to form a company to carry forward something of their work. This was a formidable combination. Ken Scrivener, who had worked closely and harmoniously with Ken Cameron for many years, was one of the most conscientious and talented re-recording engineers in the country. Richard Warren had been Crown's efficient and popular production manager. Ralph May – Crown's last producer – was highly experienced in the field of finance. The Treasury allowed five members of the sound department to remain for three months to complete outstanding work. From then on the team was on its own and the task was daunting. Money was needed to set the company up. Apparently, in those days overdrafts were forbidden, but a friendly financier known to Ralph May came to the rescue and Anvil came into faltering existence in July 1952. It was, in a sense, the great-grandchild of Empire Marketing Board Films of the mid-1920s, having passed through the intervening stages of GPO and Crown.

Many friends in the industry, though entirely sympathetic, were gloomy about the prospects for the fledgling company. In the beginning it seemed that these fears might be justified. At first Anvil was invited to produce slightly dreary training films (*Methods of Garment Assembly Layout* for the National Association of Hosiery Manufacturers was their first production). These offerings were followed by an interesting series of instructional films for the Admiralty and Army, and soon other institutions began to sponsor their own educational films. Despite this improvement in the outlook of the company, times were still hard for the four directors. They had mortgaged their homes to set it up, but for quite a long time there was no money to pay themselves an income. Moreover, as they could not afford to employ cleaning staff or maintenance people, they were forced to perform the most menial of tasks themselves.

By great good fortune, a government film unit known as Group Three, headed by John Grierson, took over Beaconsfield. Anvil was allowed to remain there, in return for providing Group Three's production needs at reduced rates. Group Three (makers of *The Brave Don't Cry*), was eventually dissolved, but once again Beaconsfield was taken over by friends – Peter Rogers, originator of the *Carry On* comedies, acquired the premises, happily permitting them to remain. Although their rent was increased and Anvil's fees to Peter Rogers's company reduced, they were once again saved.

In time, Peter Rogers moved to Pinewood. Beaconsfield became home to the newly-established Independent Artists. This entailed yet another hike in rent, but fortunately the new company involved Anvil in a new and massive production schedule. Ken recorded that by now they were 'able to face the world with an adequate staff, a good deal of new equipment and a reputation for fast, effective work which was not surpassed in the country.'

Unusually within the industry, the unit became universally respected for retaining its own first-class team of permanent staff technicians. Ken Cameron and Ken Scrivener became world-renowned for the excellence of their work. Their reputation grew rapidly, with all the major production companies soon vying for available time-slots for post-syncing and final recording there.

Muir frequently worked closely with the two Kens. In 1951, Anvil made a short film that would later lead to a fortunate consequence for Anvil. The film was in two parts – a recital of the outstanding musicians Dennis Brain and Denis Matthews performing Beethoven's Sonata Opus 17, combined with a lecture by Brain on the history of the horn.

Brain was arguably the greatest horn-player of his own or succeeding generations. He played the modern French horn, but he was also an expert on the development and history of the instrument, from the early hand horn, dating from about 1705, to the present day. He had a delightful sense of fun and once famously played a hunting call on a hosepipe, to demonstrate that 'on any tube containing a column of air a series of notes determined by nature can be produced'. Memories of Brain live on undiminished. He was tragically killed in a road accident in 1957, at the age of thirty-six. Denis Matthews was a magnificent pianist: the combination provided a celebration of the genius, both of composer and instrumentalists. The film attracted praise far beyond the expectations of its makers and was shown both in this country and widely overseas, through the British Council.

The original company of Anvil Films spawned several subsidiary companies. Muir was a director of at least two: Anvil-Realist Films, of which Basil Wright was a co-director, and Anvil Films (Scotland). All three companies worked constantly and closely with Anvil's sound department. Realist was one of the most respected names in the field of documentary production. Anvil Films (Scotland) had been born out of a proposal for a film to be made in the Cairngorm mountains, on behalf of the Children's Film Foundation. Films of Scotland were happy to part-sponsor the film and because of Anvil's reputation they were anxious for that company to make it. A problem had arisen, however. They stipulated that, if they were to finance the film, it must be made by a Scottish-based company. Ken sped northwards and, with the help of a friendly solicitor, formed the new company overnight. *The Kid from Canada* – scored by Cedric Thorpe Davie, under Muir's musical direction – was the successful result and the first of many Anvil (Scotland) productions.

In an issue of *Kinematograph Weekly* in 1962, ten years after the birth of Anvil, Muir wrote, 'I must have worked with Ken Cameron on some of my very first recordings. Things haven't changed much – though I'll admit there isn't so much string used nowadays to hold the machines together and not so many loose bits of wire hanging about. A session at Anvil still has an air of expectancy and urgency and, if Ken hasn't got out of (or into) his kilt on the wrong side, an air of excitement, which for musicians is a joy!'

In 1967, the Anvil lease at Beaconsfield expired. Space there had always been limited. Visiting acoustics experts had often scoffed at its size and limitations, but Ken Cameron remarked that somehow it had worked – rather, perhaps, Ken and his colleagues had enabled it to work. After a doleful period of contemplating the possibility of a bleak future, to their surprise they were able to take over the magnificent sound studio at Denham, with its enormous stage, theatres, sound block and refined equipment. Ken Scrivener now inhabited a newly-built re-recording theatre and another building was leased for the camera department. From tentative beginnings, a major company – referred to as 'the hub of an active group of production organisations' had emerged triumphant.

The demise of the Crown unit in 1952 did not mean the end of publicly-financed film making. The nationalisation of the railways (along with buses and waterways) in 1948, and the need to generate income, meant that it was essential to expand the use of the now publicly-owned system – people must be encouraged to travel throughout Britain on their own trains. Foreign holidays were beyond the dreams of most families and privately owned motor cars were the prerogative of a comparatively small section of the population. Most people used train or bus for whatever journeys they made. To stimulate general interest, it was decided to form a film company.

British Transport Films (BTF) was established in 1949, under the direction of the seasoned documentary maker Edgar Anstey as Producer in Charge, with Muir as Musical Director and Stewart McAllister as Editor in Chief. The unit's original headquarters were located at 25 Savile Row. The unit was set up, in part at least, to show the population – and potential visitors from overseas – what wonders were to be explored throughout Britain, from Thurso to Penzance, Scarborough to Llandudno. Of the seventy-two films made by BTF, however, travel films were only a small part of the output. Many of the films produced demonstrated day-to-day work and the many problems overcome by the skill and ingenuity of British Transport's staff at the time.

John Legard, a film editor who had been with the Crown Film unit from 1944 and who joined British Transport Films in 1951, especially remembers Muir's splendid handling of music recording sessions. 'First he would go through the whole score with the orchestra, just reading at sight, while the picture ran through the screen. Then he would rehearse each section – again with the picture on the screen – once for the music and secondly for the timing. If he was satisfied with both orchestral performance and timings, he would nod "OK, let's go for a take!"'

Between 1949 and 1982, when the unit was disbanded, British Transport Films produced films covering almost every part of the country. Each film was about twenty minutes long, beautifully made, with titles that still arouse a yearning to see both the films and the locations: *Journey into Spring, Between the Tides, North to the Dales, Blue Pullman, Snowdrift at Bleath Gill, West Country Journey.*

Travel films were only a small part of the BTF output. There were many more practical day-to-day films. *Snowdrift at Bleath Gill,* as the title implies, was about a goods train stuck in a snowdrift in the Yorkshire Dales. *Making Tracks* observed the work of re-laying several miles of railtrack on a busy mainline stretch, over one weekend. *Wild Wings,* a film about Peter Scott's bird sanctuary at Slimbridge, was awarded a Hollywood Oscar. John Taylor directed and the score was by Edward Williams.

After working with Muir for some time, Edward and he had parted company, at Muir's suggestion, so that Edward could develop his abilities as a composer. Muir was of the opinion that he should undertake academic study, but in the end Edward found his own way, composing scores for several dozen films. He remained ever grateful to Muir for giving him his first chance. He went on to write scores for twenty-seven of BTF's films – as John Legard has said, providing music of a remarkably wide range and variety, suiting the mood and background of each of the landscapes perfectly.

Although *Wild Wings* was the only Oscar-winner, the unit went on to win one hundred and eighty-five awards. Anvil was responsible for many of the soundtracks, which were recorded at Beaconsfield. A potential catastrophe was narrowly averted during a recording session for a film called *The England of Elizabeth*. Muir had learned that Ralph Vaughan Williams was taking a temporary break from major composition and had taken the opportunity to invite him to provide the film score – which Muir later rearranged as a concert suite under the title *Three Portraits from the England of Elizabeth*. On the day of the recording, Muir was ill with flu. John Hollingsworth took his place as conductor, though not without some difficulty. He found Vaughan Williams's work very difficult to read (his music manuscripts were notoriously untidy) 'so I just followed the contours at first'.

John Legard recalls that the eighty-five year old composer was sitting beside the conductor on the platform. Gradually – almost, it seemed, in slow motion – his chair began to slip backwards, until at last he was hanging over the edge of the platform, with his feet raised above his head. Everyone present was frozen with horror, but fortunately Edgar Anstey, standing nearby, managed to catch him in time to prevent a terrible calamity. (A similar accident, but with more serious consequences, had happened to Holst in 1923, when he fell backwards off the platform, hitting the back of his head. There was no serious injury (he suffered concussion), but the effects of the fall remained with the composer for several years)

Kenneth Jones, Professor of Music at the Royal College and founder of the Wimbledon Orchestra, wrote scores for fourteen of BTF's films. One of these was a 1959 film about construction of a Scottish Hydro-Board dam. This was sited in the hills above Killin, far from the railway or, indeed, any major roads. The theme was the way in which materials for the construction had been transported to the remote site. The film had a tight schedule for completion. Music would be all-important, but there had been no time to pre-prepare a sound track and the recording was to be made 'from cold'. By the appointed day, even Muir had not seen the score. Moreover,

Kenneth had been unable to attend the session. The orchestra having assembled, an unruffled Muir turned over the first page of the score, saying cheerfully 'Now let's see what he has given us!' and smoothly proceeded with the rehearsal and recording.

Another renowned musician to write scores for BTF was Elisabeth Lutyens. The first of these was for the 1954 film *The Heart of England*. For John Legard 'the music shone, with Elisabeth at her most lyrical – a fairly rare occurrence!' Ken Scrivener has a memory of a dinner party at the Savile Club (Muir was a member) after a recording session. He and his wife were present, with Ken Cameron, Muir and probably John Hollingsworth. Elisabeth Lutyens was the principal guest and she and Muir were seated together at the other end of the table. Suddenly, Elisabeth raised her voice and burst out, ' . . . but you don't want music. You want elastic!' Muir roared with laughter. 'You've struck it in one! That's what we do! You know what musical directors are. We are dressers. We dress up the film with the music, so it must be done correctly. We must make sure that the elastic on the knickers is tight enough, but not too tight, so that the whole thing is on a sound basis and won't let you down!'

Elisabeth Lutyens went on to score five more films. Others on Muir's list of composers for BTF included Arnold Bax, Doreen Carwithen, Edwin Astley, Herbert Chappell, John Greenwood, Clifton Parker, William Matthias and Cedric Thorpe Davie. Muir composed a number of scores for BTF himself – *Going Places* (a promotional film to be shown on board passenger liners arriving in England), *Sing of the Border*, *Journey Intercity* and *Operation London Bridge*. For this last he adopted the theme of the nursery rhyme *London Bridge is Falling Down* and played with the old melody, making intricate patterns, turning it sideways, upside down, inside out. That was to be Muir's final film and his final composition, written shortly before his death in 1975.

Chapter 7

Charlock in the Corn

During the war years the Mathieson family had been growing. In 1942, whilst still living at the Little House, Denham, a son, Niall, was born. The composer William Alwyn dedicated his *Suite of Scottish Dances* to Niall's arrival. A second daughter, Shuna, was born in 1944. The youngest of their four children, Fiona, was born in 1950. When Shuna was four months old, the family moved to The Marish, a large, rambling Tudor house close by. Hermione's parents were living with them at that time, and here there was plenty of room for everyone, though, as she recalls, perhaps not enough furniture.

The family stayed at The Marish for almost four years, but soon after the war they began to feel that the children should have more permanent roots. Hermione wanted to have something substantial to tackle, rather than the entertaining that took up so much of their lives and required resident staff.

Some of their friends were farming successfully, quite apart from their 'normal' businesses, and obviously enjoying it. It was quite a fashionable way of life at the time. Muir's agent Allan Grogan and his wife Winifred ran a farm in Sussex, and Grogan encouraged them, advising Muir that, in addition to its many pleasures, certain tax advantages were attached to farming, as losses could be written off against other income. Hermione's school-friend Bobbie and her husband, the industrialist Denis Ferranti, were farming in Cheshire.

Their way of life appealed to the Mathieson family and they

began to search for a suitable farm themselves, despite knowing nothing whatsoever about agriculture. (Hermione's father's family had been farmers in America, but that was of little help.)

It was a steep learning curve. In 1947 they found a beautiful, unmodernised, Tudor farmhouse and cottage in the Chiltern Hills – Shogmoor, with one hundred and thirty-seven acres of land. The only bath was in the scullery, with a copper boiler. There was single-phase electricity. Cows trampled into the yard and up to the kitchen door so, in order to have dry feet, it was necessary to use a plank to get to the gate. It was a daunting undertaking: but the orchard was in blossom and the uninterrupted view across fold after fold of hills to a distant western horizon was irresistible. They sold The Marish to John Mills and his wife, Mary Hayley Bell, and bought Shogmoor, lock stock and barrel.

This proved to be a mistake as the motley collection of milking cows went down at the first TB test. They built up a second herd with pedigree Guernseys, but had unfortunately kept one of the original cows and were soon in trouble again. They learned to farm by trial and error, studying books on the subject. Above all, they were lucky enough to have a very successful farmer and neighbour as friend and adviser. Jim Connell saved them from many other mistakes and pitfalls. When one of their fields turned yellow, they thought it was mustard. Jim roared with laughter and informed them that it was charlock in the corn, which must be sprayed urgently.

There is a theory that human beings have a subconscious longing to return to the environment in which they lived at the age of seven. It may be that for Muir the move to Shogmoor represented a return to the freedom and delight of his boyhood holidays at Kippen. The house was carefully and lovingly modernised and a beautiful garden created. Hermione remembers it as a very happy time. The children loved it. They had ponies and a donkey, and helped with the harvest. Muir and Hermione's eldest daughter, Muirne, commented, 'As children we were truly blessed. The love

Muirne and Shuna, with their parents and ponies

that my parents had for one another gave us the most incredibly happy, stable background. Through thick and thin, they were always there for each other.' Muir and Hermione ran the farm with the help of a foreman/herdsman, a tractor driver, a land girl initially (later a boy), and Ted, a wonderful old hedger and ditcher. Hermione did the bookwork, looked after the chickens and turkeys, dealt with salesmen and sold the corn.

Their lives had changed dramatically, but the new owners of the farmhouse in the Oxford countryside continued to welcome guests as warmly and unreservedly as ever. Old friends would visit. Musicians from abroad, including the legendary Max Steiner (composer – not with Muir – of such scores as *Gone With the Wind* and *Casablanca*) and Angelo Lavagnino, the Italian composer, who later worked with Muir on *The Wind Cannot Read* (1958) and *Hot Enough for June* (1968), came to stay.

By 1947, travel was once again possible and enjoyable. Muir worked in France, Germany, Italy, Romania and Czechoslovakia.

Hermione too looked forward to joining him for occasional visits to film festivals abroad.

In 1948, Dock was responsible for inviting Vaughan Williams to write the score for Michael Balcon's epic film *Scott of the Antarctic*, with John Mills playing the role of Scott. Initially, Dock and Michael had difficulty in persuading Williams to do it, but he ultimately agreed and produced a magnificent score, which he later developed to become his great Seventh Symphony, the *Sinfonia Antarctica*.

Dock's wife had developed Hodgkinson's Disease in 1947, shortly after the birth of their son, their second child. In 1952, as her health declined, Muir encouraged Dock and Eileen to come, with their family (a daughter, Alison, had been born just before Dock left for India, and Angus, now aged five) to come and live close to them in their home village of Freith. Despite the family sadness, Alison recalls the happiness and freedom shared by all the cousins as they were growing up.

Muir worked solidly at his music, either at the studio or in the converted barn. Just as his father, JG, had worked alone in a studio attached to his home, surrounded by all the paraphernalia of his art,

Muir and Dock in cheerful mood at Shogmoor

Muir as bricklayer. Building a sun trap round the lily pool at Shogmoor
(copyright of London Film Productions Ltd)

Muir's workroom was a private and peaceful domain, home to his piano, with scores and records piled up on the floor all around him. All the same, he took the farm very seriously and, according to John Huntley, would work out milk yields and cattle feed quantities between takes at Denham. He was very practical, interested in cars and their engines, fond of carpentry and of brick-laying. He personally designed and built a bull-pen for the farm.

Muirne's first grown-up party was to be held at Shogmoor and a day or two beforehand Muir enthusiastically removed a wall between two of the rooms, to provide a huge room for dancing. They had two horses and Muir loved to ride, and to walk, with the family over the steep rolling fields after lunch on Sundays. During harvest-time he would come home from a gruelling day's work, change into old clothes and drive the tractor or stack the shocks of corn onto the trailer. One night he came back from conducting a concert at the Royal Festival Hall to find that the cowman was struggling to deliver a calf. Still in evening dress, he had to lend a hand on the end of a rope – an experience that left him (and possibly the cow) feeling somewhat shaken. By the time they gave up

Muir in the farmyard at Shogmoor

farming (though not Shogmoor) fifteen years later, they had built up a herd of home-bred Jerseys.

Financial management was never an easy matter for Hermione or Muir. His mother's gene for thrift had obviously passed him by. Friends – John Hollingsworth, Dusty Buck and others close to them – were puzzled and a little dismayed on their behalf: by now Muir was earning a very handsome salary, but where was it all going? (With the expense of keeping the farm going and the children now at school at Sherborne and Rugby, intermittent penury is not so difficult to understand.) According to Hermione, Sir David Cunninghayme, a senior executive at London Films and Muirne's godfather, eventually persuaded them to try to save a little every week.

If Muir occasionally found it necessary to shout at colleagues and friends, he certainly never raised his voice to his family. Muirne again – 'He was firm with us and we respected him. If he said that an ice-cold swim in the sea off the north-west coast of Scotland was required before he would serve breakfast, then that was the way it was. Our friends, camping with us, were not so sure, but quickly found that those were the rules. He was a lateral thinker and considered every angle of a problem before making his judgement. He would often find the solution to a worry before I had even voiced it. 'I'll see you in my study!' became a family joke – we never did see him there, because the study moved around the house so often that we never knew where to find it. We were very close. He was a friend and confidant – one could talk to him about anything.'

'Talking about anything,' especially at meal times, was a family characteristic: Muir encouraged lively debate. Niall recalls endless discussions on any and every subject, from the Arts to Labour Relations. Shuna also remembers times when conversation was disconcertingly interrupted by a rhythmic tapping, as her father – quite unaware of what he was doing – tried out a musical phrase on the underside of the table.

Niall, Muir, Muirne and Hermione at home at Shogmoor

Muir's career had already been long and distinguished, yet he was not yet forty, with many active years ahead. He was very wrapped up in his family and in the farm, but he was still very much in demand as the leading musical director of his time. Had he but known it, though, the halcyon days were passing.

The hopes of post-war film-makers were to be dashed in the face of a harsh reality. The ending of the war did not bring an end to restrictions and shortages. Life in Britain was still difficult: clothes, fuel and food were rationed, and apart from the unparalled blessing of peace, existence was generally dreary and lacked a sense of purpose now that the great goal had been achieved. The Government, faced with a huge post-war debt, introduced new and stringent taxes all round. Although it viewed the film industry with a quizzical benevolence as a potential source of revenue, a tax was imposed that had an unexpectedly adverse effect on British film-making *vis a vis* Hollywood. Coincidentally, although audiences remained fairly loyal for a time, the public appetite for cinema-going was gradually diminishing. People were suffering from a post-war sense of *ennui* and their thirst for film-going was not helped by a series of rather poor films from British studios. Whatever the reason, the fact was that audiences and revenues were falling. British film-making began its descent into yet another trough.

All the same, many triumphs were still to come. One significant post-war success was David Lean's 1946 adaptation of *Great Expectations*. It was a great film, made by the usual Cineguild production team of Lean, Havelock-Allan and Ronald Neame. The film was awarded Oscars for Photography and Art Direction and earned nominations for Best Picture and Best Director. The experience was not particularly pleasant for Muir, however. Lean had asked for Walter Goehr to compose the score, as he had been personally recommended to him. According to Lean's biographer, Kevin Brownlow, Muir cordially disliked Goehr. In the event, Lean, as well as his musical director, found his score very disappointing and inadequate. Major changes and cuts were necessary and two other composers were hurriedly brought in to fill the gaps. To add insult to injury, Muir, who had worked hard on the arrangement and subsequent rearrangement, had expected to conduct the music as usual. At the last minute Goehr insisted on conducting it himself, at the same time making sure that he was awarded credits as composer and musical director.

Five years later, Lean directed another Dickens adaptation for Cineguild; *Oliver Twist* (released 1951). If it was less sparkling than *Expectations*, it was only marginally so, with Guinness again heading the cast as Fagin – with such panache that Jewish groups in America protested that it was an anti-semitic film. (It was not, as Guinness himself protested. He was merely playing a scoundrel to his utmost – and astonishing – ability and, as many pointed out, the character of Bill Sykes was much worse than that of Fagin.)

A preliminary music conference for Cineguild's *Take My Life* (1947) at Pinewood Studios. Left to right: Jack Harris (supervising editor) Fred Lewis (Music Adviser), William Alwyn (Composer), Muir Mathieson (Music director and Conductor), Ronald Neame (director) and Geoffrey Foote (Editor)

This time Muir's first suggestions of Walton or Bliss were rejected in favour of Sir Arnold Bax. Bax accepted with his usual shy reluctance, but David Lean gave extremely precise directions as to his requirements. Having accepted the challenge and viewed the film, Bax asked Muir to allow him to use piano music, to be performed off-camera by Harriet Cohen, for part of the score. Muir consulted Lean, who was not enamoured of piano music, but Muir assured him that it would work well. Bax and Muir worked closely together for the next two months to produce the finished score. This time Bax apparently quite enjoyed the experience, but he was never enamoured of film composition, complaining that it was unsatisfactory, since the music was frequently toned down in favour of 'quite unnecessary talk'.

So there were triumphs, yes . . . but some flops as well. The staggeringly expensive and loss-making *Caesar and Cleopatra,* screened in 1946, was a Rank production, directed by Pascal and supervised by the author – Shaw. The play on which the film was based was witty and dry, peppered with Shavian wisecracks – but, being Shaw, without the leavening of a love interest. Despite the title roles being played by the exquisitely beautiful Vivien Leigh and veteran Claude Rains, the film turned out to be a yawn as far as the public was concerned and they stayed away in droves. Georges Auric's not-very-distinguished score did not help matters.

The outstanding successes of that decade included Olivier's *Hamlet* in 1948, again magnificently scored by Walton, who wrote the music, including the funeral march, during the final illness of his long-term partner, Lady Wimborne. The film was premiered during the week of her death. The score required an orchestra of fifty. According to Muir, Walton, despite his tragic personal circumstances, was, as always, on hand during the recordings 'checking points with the orchestra, discussing improvements with Sir Laurence and taking a most active part in the music-making.'

Both John Huntley and Edward Williams were back from the war and had rejoined Muir as assistants – Huntley as technical assistant and in charge of publicity. Williams arrived in time to work on *Odd Man Out*. The director was Carol Reed. This was a magnificent film about a fatally wounded IRA fugitive moving round the dockyards in Belfast. The part was played by James Mason in what was probably the finest performance of his life, as he staggers through the night towards his death, bleeding, delirious and in agonizing pain. William Alwyn provided a wonderful score. Edward Williams is inclined to think that for once Muir overdid the music, though of all people Muir and Alwyn were agreed on the virtue of an absence of music. Very unusually, Mason played what would surely be the greatest and most memorable scene of his career with a live orchestra behind him. The score received many plaudits, as did the film.

William Alwyn was a poet as well as composer. He, with his wife Olive and their two sons, were close friends and frequent visitors to Shogmoor. William later married Doreen Carwithin, a young composer of whom Muir had a high opinion. Doreen herself composed the score for a number of films under the musical direction of Muir, or of his deputy director, John Hollingsworth. She commented that both Muir and John always discussed the score with her in great detail. 'You always saw a film in a little theatre and had a look at it. Would you like to do it? Sometimes you would and sometimes you were told that you were going to do it! Then you'd have a much more lengthy session, reel by reel, discussing where we'd put the music – where we'd start, where we'd stop, what the ideas should be and that bit should tie up with later on, when they climb a mountain or something' (*The Best Years of Film Music*). John Hollingsworth died, aged only forty, in 1963. Ken Cameron and his aunt were expecting him to join them for lunch that Christmas Day, but he did not come. He was found dead at his home the following day.

The brief but glamorous sixteen-year existence of Denham Studios ended in 1952. Rank, who had bought out the Pru's share in 1944, could no longer afford to maintain two studios with many unused stages. The buildings were converted on behalf of his new venture – producing photocopiers. Eventually most of the buildings (though not the sound studios) were demolished. Korda's stately pleasure dome had crumbled into dust.

Sir Alexander Korda, with whose life and films Muir had been associated all his working life, died in 1956. Despite his charm, his many successes, his high lifestyle, his powerful friends and his knighthood, Korda's life seems to have been strangely disappointing. Although he had left England for Hollywood so publicly in 1940, he had never really left at all, frequently braving the Atlantic crossing by plane or by sea. In 1942, whilst in London to receive his knighthood, Arthur Rank offered him an opportunity to stay on, as co-ordinator of the Rank Organisation's film programme. Korda was delighted and ready to accept, but the Prudential – Rank's financial backers – strongly disapproved of the appointment after their previous unhappy dealings with him and firmly put a spoke in the wheel. He returned to California in low spirits, but the following year MGM offered him a deal to part-manage the company's affairs in England. Perhaps this was a Louis B Mayer ploy to rid himself of this turbulent rival. The two men loathed each other – perhaps they were too alike. Korda settled back in some style in Claridges Hotel, but he was not content. His wings had been clipped and he was unhappily conscious that J Arthur Rank had overtaken him as Britain's leading film-maker. Moreover his marriage to Merle was in terminal decline.

Back in England, Korda made *Perfect Strangers* – which went well over budget as usual – with Deborah Kerr and Robert Donat, but in a re-run of what had happened with the Fox organisation in 1930, his attachment to MGM was brief. Korda preferred to be his own master and he parted from the company in 1945 with some ill-feeling, but with a sense of relief. With one bound he was free of Louis B and out of the shadow of J. Arthur Rank and could resume his favourite pastime of wheeling and dealing amongst the great and the good, this time on behalf of his own new company, Lion

Films. However, it seemed that Korda had lost his touch. He fell in love again (in his own way) a couple of times, introduced wide-screen Cinemascope to the British public, made a few films that flopped (including *Bonnie Prince Charlie,* with David Niven), lost some money (mostly other people's), married for a third time, and died. He had charmed his way through life, had more or less single-handedly established a viable film industry in Britain and re-invigorated it once or twice when it was ailing. But in many ways Korda was out-ranked (literally, as it happened, though not in his lifetime: Rank was elevated to the peerage in 1958).

More than anyone, J. Arthur Rank attempted to revitalise the British film industry founded by Korda. His contribution to, and support for, the wartime output had been outstanding. He had freed directors and producers to make their own decisions, had set up training schemes for technicians and founded a research scheme. He had provided a charm school to teach British stars to become more glossy and glamorous, to speak less affectedly and to become more acceptable to American audiences. At the end of the war, however, the Rank Organisation was in debt. In the 1950s, Rank went into profit for a while, but in the end he too would have to accept that film-making in England was financially disastrous.

Meantime, *Genevieve,* made at Pinewood in 1953, cheered everyone up. It was a sophisticated British comedy, financially backed by Rank. It proved to be immensely popular, but because of its quintessentially English style and sense of humour it was never thought likely to capture the hearts and minds of American audiences. It concerned two couples – friends – who race their vintage cars (one is a 1904 Darracq) home from the London-to-Brighton rally. The plot is simple, hilarious and whimsical.

The producer/director of the film, Henry Cornelius, apparently surprised Larry Adler by inviting him to write the score – his first. Adler recalls that a woman executive at Rank listened to him playing the piano one evening and engaged him in conversation. Cornelius telephoned the following morning. Adler, a brilliant chromatic harmonica player, performed classical music (Bach, Vaughan Williams, Gershwin) as soloist at major concerts, but he was not a formally trained musician. He played and composed by ear.

Muir may have viewed the prospect of working with an inexperienced score-writer with caution, but he was enthusiastic. Before the approach to Adler, he and Cornelius would have discussed possibilities for the score and decided that the vibrating music of the harmonica might well fit the bill, subtly reflecting the grinding and turning of the car wheels. (Moreover, as they were working on a tiny budget, the expense of employing an orchestra would be avoided). Larry Adler was asked to provide a 'catchy tune' for the film: a cheerful, rhythmic undercurrent as the cars 'raced' through the countryside.

What Adler provided (as he himself admits) was a chaotic jumble of ideas jotted on bits of paper. If Muir was slightly bemused, Cornelius was astonished, commenting that even Adler did not know the intended sequence of these crumpled offerings. Much work obviously lay ahead to achieve a usable score and fit it to film. Muir and Larry began a lengthy journey together. The final outcome was a triumph – infectious, light-hearted, as original in its choice of solo instrument as Anton Karas's zither had been in *The Third Man* of three years earlier (for which Muir's successor at London Films, Dr Hubert Clifford, was responsible).

Meantime, however, word had reached Hollywood of Adler's role. In the fevered cold-war atmosphere of the time, the infamous Un-American Activities Committee, aided by the FBI, was seeking to flush out communists, or anyone thought to have left-leaning views. Adler, along with many leading figures in the American entertainment business, had been blacklisted by a Committee vengefully intent on smashing the careers of its victims.

Adler had come to live in Britain, but the power of the Committee stretched far beyond the shores of America. The Rank Organisation was informed that if the film was to have any chance of American distribution, Adler must be axed without further ado. Cornelius, who had mortgaged his house to help to finance the film, nobly stood his ground, though he undoubtedly had a legal right to withdraw – at that stage, Adler admits, he had no written contract, only a verbal agreement. Though he wanted to finish the project, he had no desire to harm the film in doing so, advising Rank to advertise the film credits (which he referred to as 'the billings') as they saw fit. The cash-strapped British Rank Organisation, desperate to secure American distribution, was all too vulnerable to blackmail. Accordingly, in America, Muir Mathieson's name appeared on the credits as Musical Director: Adler's name was omitted, though of course everyone in the business knew the name of the composer perfectly well.

Contrary to initial expectations, *Genevieve* was enthusiastically received, both in America and world-wide, and went on to bring in excellent returns, in which Adler, who now had a contract for a percentage of the grosses, shared. He, Cornelius and the Rank Organisation were the main beneficiaries of what became a financial windfall. Adler records that he was able to educate his family on his share of the proceeds. The leading actors – Kenneth More, Dinah Sheridan, Kay Kendall and John Gregson – received a one-off fee of £2,500 each.

Genevieve was named Best British Film of 1953 and everyone rejoiced. But there was trouble on the horizon. In 1954, the score was nominated for an Oscar. The Certificate of Nomination read:

Academy of Motion Picture Arts and Sciences
Be it known that LARRY ADLER and MUIR MATHIESON
were nominated for an Academy Award for Outstanding
Achievement: Scoring of a Dramatic or Comedy Picture,
GENEVIEVE.
This Judgement being rendered with reference to motion
pictures first regularly exhibited in Los Angeles district in
year ending December 31st 1954

At this point the Un-American Activities Committee again intervened to insist that Larry Adler's name be omitted from the credits for the Oscar awards. Muir Mathieson's name went forward alone. In the event, the Oscar for Best Musical Score was awarded to Dimitri Tiomkin for *The High and The Mighty*. The writer Michael Freedland records that Adler later told him he was pleased to learn of this result. A few months later, greeting Muir at a charity function, Adler asked why he had allowed his name to go forward. Muir responded that his understanding was that he was being nominated for his work as Musical Director. 'I believed him,' added Adler, referring to Muir as 'a gentle Scotsman, a peer among his own kind'.

Adler went on to score three more films. In 1986, the Board of Governors of the Academy of Motion Pictures, Arts and Sciences retrospectively amended the list of credits to record Larry Adler's name as composer of the score of *Genevieve*.

The following year another 'English' film, *Hobson's Choice*, was made. David Lean directed. Laughton plays the owner of a somewhat dreary shoe-shop in the uninspiring setting of Salford in Victorian times. To add to the atmosphere of general gloom, the shopkeeper dominates his three (motherless) daughters. The two younger girls are flighty and absurd. To everyone's surprise, the eldest of the three – plain, already on the edge of spinsterhood, but feisty and determined – bullies her father's wimpish employee into marrying her. With some difficulty, she succeeds in inspiring in him a degree of manhood and business acumen, arranges her sisters' marriages, and finally turns the tables on her father. John Mills plays the nervous and bewildered new husband to perfection.

According to Kevin Brownlow, Muir chose Malcolm Arnold to score the film on account of 'his Rabelaisian sense of humour', because he was coincidentally the son of a shoe manufacturer and because they had always worked together very successfully. Arnold produced a splendidly evocative score just over a week after first viewing the roughcut. One memorable scene shows the inebriated

Hobson pausing to behold the moon's reflection in a series of puddles as he steps over them. The sight confuses him. This confusion is accompanied by a section of the score known as 'The Dance of the Puddles' – strange, artfully effective instrumental sounds that indicate his state of mind (and body). Arnold later remarked that the music had particularly appealed to the people in the north, where the film was set. Contrary to expectations, the film was well received in America and also won an award at the Berlin film festival that year.

Muir's cousin, Cedric Thorpe Davie – Grandpa Davies's third grandson – was by now a celebrated composer and academic. He founded the Department of Music at St Andrews University in 1945, where he was Master of Music and would become Professor (1973–78). He had studied at the Scottish National Academy of Music and then at both the Royal College of Music (under Vaughan Williams, where he won the Cobbett and Sullivan prizes for composition), and at the Royal Academy of Music. As a young man he studied composition with Kodaly in Budapest and with Sibelius in Finland. There were many similarities, as well as close friendship, between the cousins. Muir and he were almost the same age. Cedric was a fine composer, but also an excellent pianist and a good conductor. Like Muir, he loved Scottish Country Dancing and Scottish songs. He was completely without pomposity – a good-looking, jolly, friendly man with a wry sense of humour, very popular with students and the public alike.

Apart from his major symphonic and operatic works, Cedric scored over fifty films. In 1947, Muir invited him to score *The Brothers* for Sydney Box, *The Bad Lord Byron* in 1951 and others, including *Kidnapped*. One of the most memorable of these was the Walt Disney production, *Rob Roy – A Highland Rogue* (1954), starring Richard Todd in the leading role. Rob Roy MacGregor was a rogue and a cattle-thief. He was also a Jacobite leader and supporter, who brought a small army of his clan to fight against the imposition of William of Orange as king, at the battle of Killiecrankie in 1689.

Over the centuries Rob Roy has acquired an aura similar to that of England's Robin Hood in Scottish legend. As is usual with historical films, the facts were somewhat distorted. In an impossible scene, Rob (having been pardoned for his part in the rebellion) and his merry band march forth to visit the Hanoverian King George in the wake of a piper in full blast. At this point the cousins played an 'in' joke and probably celebrated it over a dram or two. Though perhaps few would have noticed, the music played by the piper as they marched into King George's palace was a Scottish comic song, *The Muckin' o' Geordie's Byre* – or, as the singer Andy Stewart mockingly translated it into English, *The Cleansing of George's Cowshed.*

The cousins were both awarded OBEs for their individual contributions to music – Cedric received his in 1955 and Muir in 1957.

1958 was the year of Hitchcock's brilliantly disturbing psychological thriller, *Vertigo*, a *film noir* starring James Stewart and Kim Novak, with a suitably spooky, spine-chilling score by Bernard Herrmann, Hitchcock's most trusted film composer, who would freeze a few more spines with his score for *Psycho* two years later. Muir was scheduled to record the music for *Vertigo* in Hollywood, but when the time came the American musicians were on strike and the recording sessions took place in Vienna. Though not at first a major box office success, the film began to attract large audiences and was in time acclaimed as Hitchcock's finest. Some have rated it one of the finest films of all time: a debatable claim, perhaps, but certainly in terms of tension and suspense it is a masterpiece of the 'thriller' genre.

Over the intervening forty years, tins containing reels of the deteriorating film had lain forgotten and neglected at the back of various storerooms in the studio. To the delight of Hitchcock fans, they came to light in 1995, and the dedicated team of Robert Harris and James Katz began an intricate two years' work, lovingly and laboriously restoring the film frame by frame. By a coincidental stroke of luck, Muir's original recording sessions were discovered elsewhere. The sound track (which had been nominated for an Oscar in 1959) was restored and reproduced in Dolby Digital. This updated version of *Vertigo* is now available to a new generation of DVD viewers.

In 1957, Lindsay Anderson, writing in *Declaration*, complained that English cinema was 'snobbish, anti-intelligent, emotionally inhibited, blind to the conditions and problems of the present, dedicated to an out-of-date, exhausted national ideal'. A list of 1950s films certainly indicates an enthusiasm for gaiety and amusement on the part of the British public: it includes *The Titfield Thunderbolt, The Belles of St Trinians, Carlton Browne at the FO, The Ladykillers,* as well as at least two of the Carry On films. Also on offer, however, were *The Bridge on the River Kwai, Richard III, Room at the Top* and *The Dam Busters*. The latter half of the decade was one of low unemployment, relative personal affluence and a rising standard of living for most. Despite underlying anxieties over the growth of nuclear weapons, the cold war and the beginning of the space race, people were generally comfortable and content. If, as Anderson's remarks may have hinted, they themselves were dedicated to an out-of-date, exhausted ideal, they were about to be stirred and shaken.

Chapter 8

Changes

The 1960s was, of course, a decade of profound change: a period of excitement, of experiment, of protest against injustice, and of tilting at the windmills of authority and convention. A new, iconoclastic generation had inherited the world. Music had also begun to change. Rock 'n' Roll in the late 1950s, the emergence of the Beatles in the early 1960s, the electric guitar and multi-track recording techniques, all combined to alter the musical landscape forever. Films and film-making changed too – and perhaps not before time. A fresh influx of brilliant directors (John Schlesinger, Lindsay Anderson himself, Ken Loach, Ken Russell, Tony Richardson and others), brought new dimensions, ideas, frankness, realism and greater urgency to the medium.

The tide of change was not confined to Britain. It surged through the studios in every country. In France, the *Nouvelle Vague* of Jean Luc Godard, Louis Malle, Truffaut and others had begun to roll inshore at the end of the 1950s, and swept on unimpeded throughout the next decade. Fellini, Pontecorvo and De Sica were at work in Italy; Ingmar Bergman in Sweden. In Hollywood, which had perhaps reached a peak in the fifties, led by John Ford, Billy Wilder, Cukor and Mankievitcz, the tide became unstoppable as the rigid studio system started to crumble and collapse and the old moguls began to fade and die.

At fifty, Muir was a relatively young man, but his post as Musical Director for Rank's Denham and Pinewood had come to an end with Rank's withdrawal. He was now freelancing, but his was perhaps no longer the name that first sprang to mind as young producers and directors studied new scripts and discussed their choice of Musical Director. At the end of the 1950s, the mystic film-maker Stanley Kubrick had begun a new trend (or reverted to a very old one), instituting a custom known as 'needledrop'. This meant choosing and cutting into a recording of existing music – classical or pop – rather than demanding a fresh score for each film. For Muir, this lack of originality, however careful the selection, must have been a painful development, though perhaps softened by the fact that he was semi-retired. Kubrick's epic *Spartacus* (2001) and *A Clockwork Orange* all made use of music composed in previous generations, though Wendy Carlos transcribed Beethoven's Ninth Symphony into an original electronic score for *Clockwork*. Other directors copied the trend for a time, though by no means all – Maurice Jarre's score for *Lawrence of Arabia*, Michel Legrande's for *Les Parapluis de Cherbourg* and the score for *The Godfather* are all examples of brilliant contemporary scores.

By now Muir and Hermione had given up farming. Their older children were already young adults. For almost the first time since leaving the Royal College – though over the years he had frequently conducted performances at Sadler's Wells – Muir now had the opportunity to devote himself to music in the concert hall. Apart from his remaining film work, he was much in demand and fitted in concerts in London at the Festival Hall, the Albert Hall, Manchester's Free Trade Hall, and in Glasgow, Birmingham, Liverpool, Edinburgh and Stirling.

One big new venture was the Harrow Schools' concerts. Muir was invited to devise a five-year plan for six concerts a year – three for juniors and three for seniors – to cover a large repertoire over the school life of a child. After much consultation, Muir produced the plan. The concerts, which would be free to the children, were to be held at the Granada Cinema in Harrow, which held three thousand people. A leading orchestra would perform each programme under

Hermione and Muir leaving for Prague Film Festival in 1947

Muir's baton. In addition, individual members of the orchestra would visit the schools to demonstrate their instruments.

Muir gave an enlightening commentary, discussing the music, the composer and the orchestration, during the concerts, which flourished for twenty-five years, under a series of Directors of Education for Harrow – Alfred Dodd, Warbie Knight and Reg Ball. Over the years, Muir received many letters of gratitude from people who had first developed a love of music through these concerts. Sadly, they came to an end when the Granada was no longer available and there was no other suitable building in Harrow.

Despite his protestations to Korda in 1933 that he could only write indifferent music, Muir proved himself wrong. Grampian Television, serving the north of Scotland from Dundee to the Shetland Islands, was established in 1961. Muir composed a rhapsodic score known as the Grampian Suite, the predominant theme of which, entitled *Lochlaggan* – a setting with variations on Hamish McCunn's *Land of the Mountain and the Flood* – opened the company's programmes each day. In the suite, McCunn's beautiful theme is encompassed and linked by original arrangements of well-known Scottish airs – gentle and tender strathspeys, wild and stirring reels, even a syncopated interlude. These were woven together in his intricately unfolding score – an affectionate evocation of the country of his childhood. Here a little nod in the direction of the Jacobite cause (which had already been hinted at in *Rob Roy*) might perhaps be detected: one of the themes hidden within the score is *Charlie is My Darling* – a song in praise of the Young Pretender, Prince Charles Edward Stuart. But who could be a member (even a detached one) of a Scottish clan without retaining a little bit of nostalgia for the dream that might have been and an affection, however unjustified, for 'The King over the Water'?

The admiration and success aroused by the Anvil educational film with Dennis Brain and Denis Matthews several years previously had not been forgotten. This memory resulted in an invitation to Anvil to film a series of lectures given to schoolchildren by Jimmy Blades, a well-known session percussionist and member of one of the country's leading orchestras. Three films were made – *Orchestral Percussion, Melodic Percussion* and *Timpani*. This time Muir directed the films himself. Ken Cameron was producer, Ken Scrivener the sound recordist. Although Muir had both directed and produced films previously, he was not first and foremost a film director and may have felt rather daunted initially. At his request, the already-seasoned young film editor Bob Keen joined the team. Muir and he worked closely together, both during the shoot and afterwards, during the edit.

The cameraman on all the films was Leslie Dear, who had joined Anvil in 1955 and who, apart from a break between 1966 and 1973, remained on the permanent staff until 1978. His recollection is of a very happy time – of Muir's unfailing courtesy and equanimity, and of his delight in the project, constantly turning up with books and illustrations he wanted to use or discuss with him. Ken Cameron remarked that Dear's imaginative camera set-ups greatly enhanced the images within the films: by using more than one camera, the audience was able to see the instruments and Jimmy's techniques in a way not previously seen in a lecture hall. Dear found that one of the additional, and hitherto unexpected, pleasures of these shoots lay in listening to a constant barrage of good-natured banter between Muir and Ken. Bob Keen recalls Muir's enthusiasm during filming and his excitement during the editing stages. It was quite a common occurrence for him to arrive at Keen's home – often on a Sunday morning – to discuss matters.

The three films worked well and their success led the Educational Foundation for Visual Aids to invite Muir and Anvil to make a further series of films displaying other musicians and their instruments, under the title *We Make Music*. In addition to directing the films, Muir was asked to write the scripts. This involved much research and a thorough study of the history of the chosen instruments. Each film presented an eminent musician talking about his instrument and explaining how its design had developed and evolved from earlier times. In the second part of the film the instrumentalist gave a solo performance to demonstrate technique.

It would be hard for Muir to have found finer musicians of the day for the enterprise. Amongst others, Yan Pascal Tortellier presented the cello, Ossian Ellis the harp, John Williams the guitar, Denis Matthews the piano, Jack Brymer the clarinet, Richard Adeney the flute, Simon Preston the organ – this last, released in two parts, was filmed at Westminster Abbey. Bob Keen recalls that 'shooting could not take place in the Abbey during the day, so we moved in after Evensong on two consecutive evenings. Naturally, most of our time was spent in the organ loft, but Muir organised some lovely panning shots of the interior of the Abbey. The results were most effective.'

Leslie Dear was cameraman on all the shoots, apart from one where Simon Preston presented the organ and another which was shot at Edinburgh Castle. This film was of Major General Frank Richardson and Lieutenant John Maclellan demonstrating the bagpipes. For most of the musicians, filming was a new experience

Rehearsal with Suffolk Youth Orchestra
(Free Press photograph)

and a refreshing change from concert hall work. Everyone enjoyed the project. Twenty-one films were made, culminating in a film displaying the work of the National Youth Orchestra, conducted by the Norwegian, Oivin Fjelstad.

Bob Keen edited sixteen of these films before being promoted to become Anvil's Editor in Chief, but he remained very much involved in the final five. Editing a film is an intensive process, requiring long hours and much patience and discussion (not to say argument), and is particularly exacting, with director and editor usually cooped up together for many hours in a small cutting room (nowadays known as an edit suite). Keen recalls that 'Muir threw himself heart and soul into the project, as I was to learn he did in anything in which he was involved.' Muir and Keen worked closely and harmoniously. Occasionally there would be disagreement. ('As we were shooting to a very strict time schedule, sometimes things became a little tense, but the Muir twinkle was always there.')

Hugh Osgood, on behalf of the Educational Foundation, was delighted, describing the completed series as a 'notable aesthetic experience' and the films continued to be shown to schoolchildren for many years. Indeed, Ken Cameron thought them so timeless that there was no reason why they should not continue to be shown indefinitely.

Muir's particular love of working with young people led to his eager acceptance when Arthur Veal, Director of Music for Nottingham Education Committee, approached him with the idea of conducting the Nottingham Youth Orchestra. Veal arranged a week's course for the children, enlisting the help of music teachers from across the county. Muir was in charge of training the orchestra for that week, insisting on tackling a serious classical programme, by way of a real challenge to them. He quickly established an easy rapport with the students, some of whom were quite young. All responded with enthusiasm. At the end of the week Muir conducted the final concert at the town hall. He loved this and in return the students idolized him. It became an annual date in Nottingham and the idea spread to education authorities up and down the country – Carlisle, Bury St Edmunds and others established their own training weeks and invited Muir to be in charge.

Dock, who shared Muir's enthusiasm for encouraging young people, was teaching violin and viola for Oxford County Youth Orchestra. Ealing Studios had closed in 1959. Dock's final comedy from that studio was Alexander Mackendrick's brilliantly grotesque *The Ladykillers*, starring Alex Guinness and Peter Sellers. Although he was director of music for one or two further films at Elstree, the company was breaking up. Whilst working full-time on films, Dock had rigorously maintained his daily routine of instrumental practice. Playing both violin and viola for practice and personal enjoyment was very important to him and because of this he was able to slip seamlessly into teaching again. For a few years he taught music in Hertfordshire and supplemented his income by playing in

Dock in
'Hungry Hill'

orchestras and at film music sessions. He appeared as a gypsy fiddler in the Two Cities film *Hungry Hill*.

This was an anxious and unhappy time for the family, as by now Dock's wife Eileen was terminally ill. Some time after her death, and having remarried, he returned to Oxfordshire. Here he founded the Youth Orchestra and set up the Saturday morning music school in Witney, Henley and Oxford, to which young people came from all over the area. Through Dock, Muir was invited to conduct the Youth Orchestra's annual concert at Oxford Town Hall. Later, he was asked to train the senior instrumentalists at the Saturday school there, while Dock took charge of the junior orchestra in Witney. This continued until the year of Muir's death in 1975, by which time he was teaching the children of some of his original students.

Both Muir and Dock (who died in 1985) were wonderful teachers, explaining everything simply and carefully to each student. Muir was particularly patient with the younger pupils, whilst Dock preferred teaching the slightly older groups. The brothers were as close to each other as they had been in childhood. Muir still tended to rush headlong at life, whilst Dock was content to take life unhurriedly. If Muir was in the throes of composing, he relied on Dock's opinion, discussing the work in detail with him as it progressed. Both could be short-tempered under stress – when working on an important project – and as a result there could

Muir and Dock
(copyright of the J. Arthur Rank Organisation Ltd)

sometimes be a certain amount of tension in the air at home. Their families learned to keep out of the way at such times. Dock's daughter, Alison, has remarked of her father, 'He was always fair, if a little strict. He was great at organising impromptu outings, and always encouraged me to do what I wanted.'

Muir, Dock and their families remained close to their parents in Scotland, visiting them – or being visited by them – frequently, until their deaths. The children were particularly fond of their grandfather, who was warm and approachable, taking a great interest in their lives and activities. Dock transformed his father's life by buying him a car to take him on sketching (and angling) expeditions round the countryside.

Although his involvement in feature films was beginning to wind down, there were still many major commissions for Muir. In 1960, he worked on a new version of *The Swiss Family Robinson,* starring John Mills and Dorothy McGuire. William Alwyn composed the music and the director was Ken Annakin. The young sound assistant, Harry Fairbairn, recalled his initial nervousness at being asked to work with Muir, having heard mixed reactions and anecdotes of their experiences from other people. Fairbairn sat next to Muir on the podium. His job was to rig the microphones and act as liaison between conductor, music mixer, projectionists and recording machine operator. He found Muir to be a real professional, very pleasant and easy to work with, remarking that anyone who worked alongside him would never forget it. One orchestral direction that remained in his memory was of Muir, seeking to underline emotion in a particular passage, instructing the string section to add 'Schmalzando – lots of schmalzando, gentlemen, please!'

In 1968, Muir was musical director for *Shalako*, a Sean Connery/Brigitte Bardot film set in 19th-century New Mexico. Edward Dmytryk was director, with music by Robert Farnon. For the recording session, Muir was positioned, as always, facing the large screen on which the film was run. The orchestra did not have this advantage: they faced Muir, with their backs to the screen. During the scene in which a topless Bardot emerges from a river, Muir noticed several musicians casting furtive glances over their shoulders in the hope of catching a glimpse of the action. At last, he threw down his baton in exasperation. 'Very well, gentlemen, why don't we all just stop and watch the film? Then perhaps we can get on with making music!'

Ken Scrivener remembers that in 1970 or '71 Muir wrote the music and spoke the commentary for two little films made for the Scottish Tourist Board. Scrivener was responsible for recording them both. The first film was called *Highlands and Islands* and he liked the music, but felt there were perhaps rather many references to Scottish melodies. The second piece, however, was entirely Muir's own composition, with no reference to original Scottish tunes. This piece, he thought, was very beautiful and he greatly

Muir's family about 1986.
Standing: Hermione, Niall, Shuna. Seated: Muirne, Fiona

regretted that such lovely, lyrical music would have such a limited audience.

Over the years, friendship with the Ferranti family had been close and deep-rooted. Bobbie and Hermione had lived near each other in Chelsea Park Gardens as children and attended the same school for a time. They married and had children at about the same time, and the families melded. There was much visiting and many holidays were spent together in France, Scotland, Ireland, or sailing in the Mediterranean. Bobbie Ferranti's recollection of Muir is of his excellent company and his appreciation of good food and wine: but there was much more than that. She remembers his thoughtfulness when her husband Denis's eyesight began to fail. The two men had shared an interest in cars, though Denis's knowledgeable eye for the finer points of the internal workings of their engines possibly escaped Muir. But now Muir would take the trouble to sift through motoring magazines regularly, picking out the articles most likely to interest his old friend, tape-recording and posting them on to him, to Denis's delight: his own early version of Talking Books.

Muir's cancer of the oesophagus was first diagnosed in 1970, when he was only fifty-nine. Initially he had non-invasive treatment, driving to Oxford for therapy every day before continuing to the studio for a full day's work. The illness lasted for five years. Meantime, Muir continued his work without interruption, composing and conducting the music for films, in the same way as he had done over the years. He continued his involvement in teaching young musicians, conducting one of the youth concerts in Oxford the day before he went to have an operation on his throat: an operation that he must have realised was never likely to be successful, though he remained outwardly optimistic. Afterwards he remained in intensive care for a week or two, but failed to recover consciousness. He died in the Radclyffe Hospital in early August 1975, leaving a gifted family of his own, a legacy of great film music and a new generation of music-makers.

John Huntley, who knew Muir as thoroughly as anyone, commented, 'He was completely devoid of the theatrical airs and graces so often beloved by some of our leading musical personalities: down to earth – forthright sincerity – that is the mark of true genius and ability in a man who knows his job and gets on with it.' Ken Cameron wept on hearing the news. Speaking at the Thanksgiving Service held in honour of Muir's life, his old friend Basil Wright concluded by saying, 'He was the dearest of friends'.

Where does a particular love and ability for music, dance, art, science, or literature originate: in the head, or in the heart, or in the genes, or in environment and upbringing? Who can tell? Perhaps Muir's passion for music went back as far as that first-mentioned Davie in Tillicoultry, five generations earlier – or perhaps it had begun somewhere in the many generations before him. Whatever its source, within the time and space of their own lives Muir, Dock and Cedric were able to use their gift to bring that same delight to very many others.

Analysis of Muir Mathieson's Musical Scores

Introduction

Presented here is an analysis of some of the film scores that Muir Mathieson worked on as Music Director or Conductor. The films were selected to provide as broad a cross section as possible of the types of movie with which he was associated. While Mathieson was celebrated among his peers for his ability to entice composers of art music like Vaughan Williams and Walton to write for the big screen it should not be overlooked that he was equally adept at extracting organised and effective scores from lesser luminaries such as Clifton Parker. Therefore, an analysis of Parker's score for *Western Approaches* (1944) is included alongside the work of the bigger guns on *49th Parallel* (1941) and *Hamlet* (1948).

On occasion in the 1940s British Cinema would pull out all the stops and create showpiece, 'quality' pictures that still have the power to overwhelm: David Lean's *Oliver Twist* (1948) is a case in point, and the extraordinary Laurence Olivier adaptation of *Henry V* (1944) seems to have been conceived not just to bring the Bard to the masses but to push the boundaries of what popular cinema was capable of showing. As landmark movies, these scores are drawn into the fold. *Henry V* also aspires to encapsulate and articulate some sense of Britain and Britishness, and, as this implies, with the Second World War affecting British cultural life so profoundly the importance of music in the creation of propaganda must not be overlooked. The films *In Which We Serve* (1942) and *Dangerous Moonlight* (1941) are examined in this respect. *Dangerous*

Moonlight also proves interesting in itself as a work that meditates upon the rôle of music and musicians in wartime. British cinema also boasted a strong tradition of feature length documentary production and Mathieson's work in this field is explored as well, through *Fires Were Started* (1943) and *Western Approaches* (1944). *Vertigo* (1958) was to an extent self-selecting because of the outstanding quality of its score, and Mathieson's remodelling of Rachmaninov for *Brief Encounter* (1945) is included not least because the music is clearly one of the reasons why this film is regarded with such enduring affection by so many.

As original scores are either hard to come by or impossible to find, all of the analysis has been done by ear. This presents a number of problems. Tonal centres and the notation of melodic material can be arrived at easily enough by simply playing along with the film using an accurately tuned piano, but confusion can arise in relation to enharmonics: is what we hear a C sharp or a D flat? In addition, some aspects of metre, tempo and dynamics can be hard to call without recourse to an *Urtext* and precise instrumentation is occasionally difficult to pick out, not least owing to issues of sound quality. It is hoped, however, that without begging too much latitude the essays here are not wildly inaccurate and that they will demonstrate that much good, constructive work can be done by ear alone.

Also, while the analyses are as extensive as possible, they are not absolutely exhaustive. If a specific cue is not discussed this is normally because doing so would have been either repetitious or clumsy because the cue itself was too slight to merit close discussion without breaking up the flow of the argument. The use of popular songs in these films is also addressed. Analysis of the musical systems of any of these movies must take into account such songs and other elements of 'found' music as the interplay between the original score and these other musical elements is often fertile.

As those approaching this book with an interest in film may not have a grounding in musicology, while those interested in music might not be up to speed with the jargon of film studies, a full glossary has been appended at the back of the book.

Film music is something of a poor cousin in both of these fields. Film analysts often elide discussion of the score owing to a perceived lack of technical facility, while musicologists have traditionally held film music in low esteem viewing the work of art music composers in this sphere as ephemeral at best and, at worst, an aspect of their careers that a scholarly veil needs to be tastefully drawn over. It is also certainly true that art music composers themselves have on occasion regarded working for the cinema as being less than edifying, and the goalless draw played out between Stravinsky and Hollywood tells an instructive tale. This doesn't, however, have to be the case and speaks as much of the cultural attitudes of the elite realm of classical music as it does of any problem inherent in cinema. One of Muir Mathieson's key achievements was the opening of a productive dialogue between high culture and popular culture worlds.

Moreover, during the study of these scores it was quickly discovered how tightly and impressively organised the music was. It is a mistake to assume that film scoring is somehow hack work with the music simply thrown together, that film scores are tatterdemalion collections of gestures and textures responding only to the unsubtle demands of the narrative as it thunders on. On the contrary, scores with which Mathieson was associated tend to be rigorously structured in their form and development. They often take a central thematic concern of the narrative, translate this into musical terms and work it through logically as the film progresses. There is little or nothing *ad hoc* about the music analysed here. In terms of its formal construction it is often as tightly organised as any sonata, especially given the additional need to keep to timings and hit accent points.

Something else that swiftly became apparent was just how much the music contributed to the impact of the films. The music in these films is of key importance in their construction and, as we shall see, this is something often acknowledged in opening and closing credit sequences. We will also note some of the many uses that music has in film. While its emotional impact is clearly one reason why the music is there, through the present analyses it will become clear that a good score fulfils many other functions.

Finally, it must be stressed that these analyses offer just one reading of the scores. As Elizabeth Wilson's *Shostakovich: A Life Remembered* (1994) demonstrates so well, meaning in music is wonderfully mutable. We will all hear different things, and should be grateful for this as it is precisely what makes the conjunction of music and the moving image such an interesting field of study.

In short, this music might not be 'pure' in the sense of its being abstract and Apollonian, but it's still for the most part tremendous music, certainly music that deserves a closer listen.

To close, I must thank my co-author Sheila Hetherington and all at Scottish Cultural Press for their patience during the lengthy gestation of these analyses. Ben Marsden proofed many of the pieces for me, though not all, and any errors that remain are entirely mine. I also need to acknowledge the support and encouragement of my colleagues within the Department of Film & Media Studies at the University of Stirling, in particular Peter Meech, Stephanie Marriott, John Izod and Jane Sillars. My academic mentors, who will be horrified at the lack of method and theory in this work, must also be thanked as key formative forces nevertheless: Mike Cormack and Simon Frith. I must also note my great debt to Otto Karolyi, whose inspirational teaching of Music at Stirling changed so many of his students' lives – I know because he changed mine.

Finally, on a more personal note, I need to thank my daughters Caitlin and Kathryn who all too often have been frustrated by my work commitments, and to offer my apologies to Steve who has had to listen to all sorts of music being played VERY LOUD at ALL HOURS for some nine years now.

– Mark Brownrigg

Dangerous Moonlight

(1941)

Director: Brian Desmond Hurst
Music: Richard Addinsell
Music Director: Muir Mathieson
Production Company: RKO, GB

Dangerous Moonlight is a film about music. It argues that music and musicians are a vital part of our lives, and that in times of extremity musicians remain hugely significant, perhaps more important than the contingent, if pressing, problems of the moment. The film asserts this by telling the story of a Polish composer-pianist, Stefan Radetzky (Anton Walbrook), who falls in love with a rich young American reporter, Carol Peters (Sally Gray), at the start of the Second World War. As Europe collapses under the weight of the German onslaught, the couple escape to New York where Stefan is fêted as a genius before returning to the fight against Carol's wishes, flying with the British against the Nazis. The film is constructed in flashback form, beginning and ending with Carol's attendance on Stefan at the psychiatric hospital in which he is an amnesiac convalescing following a plane crash. In between times their story is told, along with the story of the gestation of Stefan's masterpiece, his Warsaw Concerto.

Addinsell's score for *Dangerous Moonlight* is remarkable for the way in which it harnesses the art music tradition in terms of composition and performance, and in its further assertion that this music is a marker of civilisation and humanity that can be used as a cultural weapon in the fight against barbarism and tyranny. While many movies articulate the importance of popular music during wartime, from *The Glenn Miller Story* (1953) through to Terence Davies' *Distant Voices, Still Lives* (1988), *Dangerous Moonlight* argues that high culture art music should occupy a uniquely privileged position. With the exceptions of a brief burst of good-time, big band jazz motivated by a soirée in Carol's father's home and the use of the traditional Irish tune 'The Rose of Tralee' as a theme for Stefan's friend Mike during the airfield sequence towards the end of the movie, the music in the film is drawn exclusively from the Romantic idiom of the art music tradition.

The importance of the high culture musician in wartime is signalled explicitly early on as Stefan's doctor discusses both his problems and significance with a fellow specialist. It transpires that everyone bar Stefan recognises his value and uniqueness, from the Polish Air Force to his best friend, from his wife to his impresario; even New York taxi drivers are impressed by him. This is not simply because he is very good at what he does, but rather because his character operates on two distinct levels. He is on the one hand an atomised, if remarkable, individual in love with his wife and his music and on the other the embodiment of the spirit and tradition of his country, Poland, and, by extension, non-Nazi Europe. This dichotomy animates a key conflict that will impact profoundly on the narrative of the film.

The importance of music to Poland's self-image is articulated not only through its pilots' efforts to secure Stefan's safety. The opening bars of Chopin's A major Polonaise Op 40 No 1 are played on vibraphone and broadcast on the wireless in a loop as an index of Poland's resistance against the Nazis. The Polonaise is the national dance of Poland, and while Chopin wrote within the form in many moods here the feel is a heroic, affirmative one, assertive and stirringly melodic. This piece is reprised on full orchestra as Stefan flies to safety in Romania and witnesses his ruined homeland from the air, the music's usual affirmation muted, tempered in response to the all too evident beleaguered state of the country. Later, the same Polonaise is played tetchily by Stefan before he tells Carol of his decision to return to Europe to rejoin the war, a symbol not just of Poland's stoicism but of his personal defiance of Carol's wishes, an idea that reaches fruition when Stefan encores with the work following the triumph of his concerto's premiere. Here, the Chopin works simultaneously as a public statement of political defiance and as a private insult to Carol, reanimating the central dichotomy of his character outlined above. Carol storms out of the theatre only to be confronted by the performance continuing on the radio in her taxi cab: Stefan's will, like his talent, is inescapable, spilling over boundaries of performance space as well as of nation. Chopin, popularly construed as a nationalist-in-exile who grew up during a particularly nationalist period of Poland's history (Whittall 1987: 73), is thus evoked in the film as emblematic of his nation's spirit, temperamentally as well as culturally. In this frame, Stefan becomes a contemporary avatar of him.

Curiously, however, Chopin is not the musical model for Stefan's own compositions. The main influences here are clearly Tchaikovsky and Rachmaninov, composers indebted to Chopin's lyrical, emotional, virtuoso *oeuvre* but nonetheless significantly different in style and sound. In spite of their Russianness, Tchaikovsky and Rachmaninov work effectively as models for a hypothetical Polish composer like Stefan because they retain an exotic, Eastern European sound. Furthermore, they are both also immensely popular composers whose musical language can be readily appreciated by the filmgoing audience. After all, as a European composer working in the 1940s Stefan might just as easily be an atonalist following the serial lead of Schoenberg who, as a Jew in exile in Hollywood, would be a powerfully symbolic figure for the filmmakers to use, but this degree of authenticity would come with the danger of leaving the mainstream film audience behind. Familiar with and appreciative of the rhapsodic Tchaikovsky-

Rachmaninov style, the audience recognises and decodes correctly both the emotions inscribed in Stefan's music and the prowess of his performances. These are musical ideas the audience can instantly grasp, a language it can respond to and understand.

The Romantic Russian idiom chosen is also inherently, almost neurotically, a passionate and dramatic one with *bravura* melodies voiced *fortissimo* in three or four octaves or, alternatively, carried by a middle voice buttressed by chords and arpeggios on the left hand and decorated with florid ornamentation in the upper register. Passages of grand passion alternate with more introspective sections where the melody becomes lyrical and yearning, the arpeggio accompaniment soft and supportive. The drama and passion of this music could be seen to articulate well the turbulence and heightened emotion of wartime life and love, if not the melodramatic aspects of the narrative. On a further, more allusive, level both Tchaikovsky and Rachmaninov suffered from mental illness: in *Dangerous Moonlight* we first encounter Stefan in a traumatised state approaching catatonia, in what we take to be a psychiatric hospital.

Leading up to this, the opening title gets straight to the point. The piano, by extension the musical personality of Stefan, is the first instrument we hear, hammering out a series of grand chords in support of a *fortissimo* melody played in octaves that, thanks to its descending chromaticism, is as yearning as it is dramatic. A brass and timpani crescendo amplify its intensity. The key is F minor, a tonal centre that will be worked through during the cue's development to a resounding F major by the close of the credits, implying that the journey the film is to follow will be a hopeful one, an important consideration given the wartime production date and the movie's propagandistic rôle. The piano introduction over, the orchestra piles in *tutti* with the first voicing of one of the film's big tunes given over to violins, piano arpeggios ranging the length and breadth of the keyboard driving restlessly and passionately beneath. The importance of this theme (F-G-A-E-A,-B flat- C-D-F,-

G,-A,-G sharp . . .) to what follows is signalled by its entrance over the appearance of the title of the movie in the credit sequence. This is the tune Carol will later hum the first bars of in an effort to spark some sort of memory in Stefan, and it continues throughout the title sequence interrupted only by a martial waltz figure that hints at the wartime context of the action and at notions of romance (the waltz) becoming compromised by militarism (its martial rendition). As well as providing an element of musical contrast, this passage also provides a springboard for the effective restatement of the lyrical main theme over the cast credits.

The movie has opened like a piano concerto, and a hugely crowd-pleasing one at that featuring big tunes, dramatic accompaniment, an overt emotionalism and plenty of virtuoso fireworks from the soloist. None of this prepares us for the music that follows on directly from this grand effusion: we fade up on a pair of hands at the keyboard playing a series of seemingly random discords. This evolves into a fragmented passage of trills executed with impeccable rhythm but on the wrong notes, of erratic arpeggios landing on jarring finishing notes. Over this seemingly senseless, musically illogical backdrop Carol hums the first notes of the opening title's melody, notes that are lost amidst the random misfires of Stefan's musical synapses. This is the piano keyboard depicted as psychic seismograph, as a vivid expression of the dysfunction of the musician's mind. Melody and form are absent, replaced with the inconsequential and chaotic.

Heard differently, on the other hand, the discords struck by Stefan are actually quite pleasing to an ear attuned to Twentieth Century modernism, sounding almost Stravinskian, the wonky arpeggios prefiguring the work of Thelonius Monk. Clearly, though, we're meant to hear this music as disturbing, a reading reinforced by the dialogue between two doctors discussing Stefan's case. Here, the loss of Stefan's playing skills is conceptualised as not just tragic for the pianist, but for the world. His physicians determine to cure him for posterity as much as for his own peace of mind. As well as attempting to reassert musical order, Carol interjects the notes of the opening title theme to reassert herself in Stefan's life. We'll learn that he ascribed the tune to her during their honeymoon: 'This is your melody . . . You gave it to me.'

Then, a miracle occurs: the fragmentary sequence halts and we hear Stefan embark on a sudden, fully formed exposition of the chromatic introduction to the title sequence, coupled with a new theme that rises with a Mahlerian sense of spiritual ascent, building, optimistic. The Romantic idiom is heard to reassert itself over the discord of Twentieth Century art music. The pyrotechnics on the keyboard are such that the orchestra of the opening title is hardly missed or, indeed, noticed as it rejoins towards the end of the tracking shot in on Stefan at the keyboard.

As we see a double exposure of the pianist's rapt face in the present and the bomb-blasted streets of Warsaw in the past, the lush harmonies and Romantic melodies are gradually subsumed by a swell of discord overlaid with the sounds of shells exploding. Once more we have moved from musical order to musical chaos and an eerie organ discord hangs over the opening shot of the flashback. As Carol picks her way through the rubble, she hears Stefan's playing from off screen, a development of the ascending theme introduced in the hospital a moment before. Stefan's playing in the middle of a blitz seems no less miraculous than in the London hospital of the story's future. In a scene of Humphrey Jennings-like surrealism, Stefan is discovered playing a spotless grand in a formerly elegant room now lacking its exterior wall.

Music is conceptualised in many ways in this film, on occasion expressly in terms of sanity. In the scene that follows Stefan explains to Carol that he's playing the piano because it soothes his nerves. This marks the beginning of an important conversation, being the first time in the film where we hear Stefan playing and talking in a lucid state; it is also the first time he and Carol meet. While music's properties as an emollient are to be located on a Biblical scale through Stefan's citing of the story of David and King Saul, music is also linked to love as he suggests that Carol's voice is music, 'music as lovely as my own'. Their conversation reveals in addition that Stefan has played before all the crowned heads of Europe, indicating not just the magnitude of his talent but the high culture status of his music and its border-crossing, international appeal, a catholic aspect running directly counter to the nationalism associated with war. Music is also here characterised as an obsessive compulsion for Stefan, as it transpires that it is neither his piano nor his apartment that we are in. He simply noticed the instrument from outside and couldn't pass it by, climbing in through the bombed out window much as Hana does in Anthony Minghella's film of *The English Patient* (1995).

All the while the Romantic arpeggios and melodies bubble away under their dialogue, hinting at an emotional depth and powerful undertow belying the brittle nature of parts of their exchange. Indeed, his playing here, however melodic and harmonious, could also be seen as just as automatic as his distracted, fragmented ramblings at the hospital keyboard: his eyes pay almost no attention to his hands, he stares coolly ahead throughout. The playing is brought to an abrupt halt as Carol stumbles upon the central dichotomy of his character, forcing him into admitting that he's a pilot as well as a pianist, an admission offered in an anger foreshadowing their eventual separation for this very reason. Finally in this conversation the alchemical power of music is noted when Stefan reveals that the music he has been playing has come to him that very night, his mind transforming the blasted rubble and straightened circumstances of wartime into a fluid outpouring of noble and beautiful sound: the nucleus of his Warsaw Concerto. Music's magical expressive power is alluded to again later as Michael and Stefan pore over the score of his concerto on a train at the start of his tour. 'Funny looking things,' muses the former on the notes Stefan is scribbling down on manuscript paper. 'They say much more than I can in words,' is Stefan's response.

Stefan's Warsaw Concerto itself, a piece of music conceived by

Richard Addinsell not only to move and stir the audience but also to foreground the virtuoso's staggering technique, is, interestingly, never heard in full. Rather, we are offered glimpses of it, the filmmakers leaving it to us to fuse together the various snatches we hear of it in our minds. The lengthy scene of the performance of its third movement at Stefan's last American concert (sharing the bill pointedly with a Beethoven piano concerto: the Germans are also capable of *this*) is the closest we come to hearing an extended sequence from the work, and even here a series of dissolves imply ellipses in its progression.

While Stefan's composition is associated with Warsaw both within the film and in the wider world (Spike Milligan bemoans its wartime ubiquity in his autobiographical writings), the concerto is also linked to his relationship with Carol: 'This music is you and me, it's the story of the two of us…' Polish Stefan and New Yorker Carol, East and West, are therefore translated into symbols of a wider alliance and a physical conflict bigger than both of them. Not knowing the fate of their relationship in such turbulent times, Stefan doesn't know how to finish his concerto. They at once are subject to and personify world events. They are both individuals and embodiments of the larger idea of an anti-Nazi alliance of civilised humanity, their credentials as civilised beings asserted by the high culture sheen of the music.

As well as being portrayed as a gifted composer, Stefan is also a manifestation of the virtuoso figure, a mystical and Protean creature in Western music to which certain values are traditionally ascribed, most notably a hypnotic, quasi-sexual power over the audience and a disturbing sense of the diabolic. Paganini was among the first to cultivate a Faustian mystique (Schonberg 1997: 142), and while Stefan is no demon he is often shot in close up at the piano, his glowing eyes staring keenly out in much the same way as fellow Eastern European Bela Lugosi in *Dracula* (1931) eyeballs his victims. This comparison may not be as fanciful as it initially sounds if we remember the ambiguous manner in which Stefan repeatedly intones: 'It is not safe to be out in the night with the moonlight so bright.' His deadpan delivery voices the line as part invitation, part mystical threat. The sexual pull of Stefan's playing is more obvious, however, foreshadowing that of another Stefan in Max Ophuls' *Letter from an Unknown Woman* (1948). In this, Louis Jourdan plays a priapic concert pianist who lures Joan Fontaine into his arms only to seduce and abandon her. Music again is the bridge between the characters, the thing that excites Fontaine's fascination and draws her from her girlhood bed to a stairwell perch outside his apartment. Similarly, a mesmerised Carol is powerless to resist the draw of her Stefan and at the climax of the Warsaw flashback finds herself compelled to advance on the piano as if in a dream. Here, Stefan has the power of a snake charmer or a pied piper and Carol is bewitched. In this sense, Stefan is an embodiment of that other virtuoso, Liszt, that great 'orgasmatron of the concert platform' (Howitt 1995: 195), the prowess of whose playing could set corseted ladies fainting.

The lion's share of the music in the film is diegetic, with non-diegetic cues rare, mostly comprising orchestrations and variations on the Warsaw concerto, adding emotional gloss to Stefan's candlelit dinner with Carol and the young couple's subsequent ascent of the staircase in her family's 'shack' on the first night of their honeymoon. In contrast, non-diegetic music adds a spectral feel as the spare woodwind and lonely harp accompanies Carol's fruitless pursuit of Stefan to the same building following their separation. But for the most part the film plays out to a musical silence, foregrounding Stefan's music when it appears, marking it as important rather than just another element of an overwhelming saturation score. Climactic sections like Stefan's dramatic dogfight with the Nazis are left entirely unscored, the sound effects of plane engines, bullets and explosions rushing in to fill the sonic vacuum, a frequent device in war films. This sequence, featuring repeated extreme close-ups of his hands pushing controls, firing on the enemy, reveals him as a master pilot rather than master pianist:

Dangerous Moonlight's Music Director Muir Mathieson at the piano, an instrument which he had played since the age of five

there is no place for his music here, and his hands are clearly expert at things other than piano playing. Music and bullets are both key weapons in the fight against Germany.

Music is indeed explicitly conceptualised as a weapon in *Dangerous Moonlight*. Carol argues that Stefan is worth more to Poland's war effort behind the keyboard than he is in the cockpit of a plane; during the montage sequence of his American tour Stefan complains that he is a man fighting two wars at the same time, one with the Nazis, the other with his music. Towards the end of this sequence, the pleasing tones of a concert rendition of his work are interrupted visually by a series of crash-edited headlines signalling the collapse of Belgium and aurally with the interjection of sudden brassy discords disrupting the smooth and elegant flow of the music. His concerto reasserts itself by swelling dramatically as

Stefan recalls his pledge to return to Poland one day. The tension between Stefan's value for posterity and propaganda on one hand, and his abilities as a pilot on the other comes to a head during the couple's argument after the departure of Mike for England, where Carol contrasts the 'power and magic' in the hands that can write and play music such as his and the 'stupid patriotic notion' of risking these hands in battle. Her argument holds sway for a while, but not for long.

As Carol has feared, Stefan does indeed become a casualty of the conflict. The flashback structure of the movie comes full circle with the crashing of Stefan's plane into a Nazi bomber. Here amid the flames of the wreckage his face is superimposed, snapping back to consciousness. The notes of his music he's been playing come to an end and we track back to see Carol standing before his piano, her back to the camera as before. If the visual symmetry is satisfying, the musical symmetry is, too. The movie ends with a purely orchestral rendition of the main theme of the movie, safely in the F major tonality promised by the close of the opening title cue. In this shot, Stefan has left the keyboard to embrace Carol, and his music is permitted to finish in the most affirmative of fashions. Without the piano rippling through the non-diegetic strings, he appears to embrace his wife as a man rather than a genius.

Filmography

Distant Voices, Still Lives, Dir: Terence Davies, Mus: various (BFI/Film Four International), 1988

English Patient, The, Dir: Anthony Minghella, Mus: various (Miramax), 1995

Glenn Miller Story, The, Dir: Anthony Mann, Mus: various (U-I), 1953

Letter from an Unknown Woman, Dir: Max Ophuls, Mus: Daniele Amfitheatrof (Universal), 1948

49TH PARALLEL

(1941)

DIRECTOR: Michael Powell
MUSIC: Ralph Vaughan Williams
MUSIC DIRECTOR: Muir Mathieson
PRODUCTION COMPANY: Ministry of Information/Ortus Films, UK

As with Powell and Pressburger's home front drama *A Canterbury Tale* (1944) and the truly singular *A Matter of Life and Death* (1946), *49th Parallel* (1941) isn't only about the Second World War, but uses the conflict as a springboard launching the filmmakers into a meditation on matters less time-locked than the simple recounting of a narrative dealing with the present conflict. In its use of remote and authentic settings, it also returns to the maverick location shooting of Powell's extraordinary *The Edge of the World* (1937), whereby the director turned the process of filmmaking into an adventure unto itself. Telling the story of the flight of a wrecked U-boat crew across rural Canada, *49th Parallel* isn't just a propaganda piece, though this it most certainly is on one level. The film also uses the backdrop of the Second World War to work through more universal ideas of peace, humanity and civilisation. The political boundary signalled by the title is, pointedly, a peaceful one, undefended, and a chronic lack of humanity is what ultimately defeats the Nazi fugitives.

It's significant that Powell and Pressburger chose Ralph Vaughan Williams as their composer. Rather than opting, quite legitimately, for a snare-rattling, brass and woodwind-heavy war movie score, as Kubrick did in *Paths of Glory* (1957), they hired one of the foremost exponents of the English pastoral school, and it was the first time the composer had worked for the cinema. As we shall see, through the use of a pastoral model to suggest the good, and an inversion of this to depict evil, Vaughan Williams' music posits Canada as a rural idyll, an eternal Eden that can both endure the war and prevail over the forces of evil. The importance of the music in the film is signalled clearly in the opening credits as Powell's stellar cast are named: 'Leslie Howard, Laurence Olivier, Anton Walbrook . . . and the music of Ralph Vaughan Williams in *49th Parallel*'. It goes without saying, notwithstanding the endemic quirkiness of Powell and Pressburger title sequences, that this is a rare honour indeed for a film composer.

After such a build up, Vaughan Williams does not disappoint. He dignifies the opening title with a moving, hymn-style cue prefacing the noble, flowing melody that follows with the motif E flat-F-E flat'-C over a swelling series of E flat chords moving from major to dominant seventh. The music then moves from this to the score's home key of A flat for the melody proper, unison strings spinning out a longline melody over softly supportive brass. This tune returns often to the opening motif, but builds and grows around it before rising into a recapitulation a passionate octave higher as the title of the movie appears on screen. Formally, the music echoes the images it underscores. Powell's title sequence comprises of a single long, flowing aerial shot of a snowy mountain range; Vaughan Williams provides a melody as grand, leisurely and uplifting as the opening shot itself. The seamlessly organic feel of its evolution is aided by its constantly shifting meter, the composer frequently varying the basic 4:4 time with shorter and longer measures of 3:4, 5:4 and 6:4, emphasising the fluidity of the melodic line.

While the cue ends grandly with a loud A flat *tutti* complete with cymbal splashes, this sense of noble affirmation is instantly contrasted as an unseen narrator introduces us to the storyworld of the film, contextualising the 49th Parallel of the title. The aerial photography of the title sequence is followed with a track in, effectively from outer space, on a marked globe showing North America. For this Vaughan Williams provides some suitably Holstian invert pedals on high strings, with gnomic, questioning clarinets describing abstract motifs beneath. The uncertain harmonic feel of the music is pushed over into a definitive minor key as we dissolve to the first shot of the movie proper: a range of mountains photographed from a rapidly moving car, truck or train. The spareness of the bare fifths in the harmony briefly recalls Shostakovich before Vaughan Williams brings us back to a more pastoral feel using a Native American-sounding pentatonic figure on woodwind to back shots of fields of wheat sheaves at harvest time. A grand, major key fanfare then plays over another aerial shot, this time of a great metropolis far below which is then linked by a sequence of dissolves to the rural idyll of lakes and islands. Both of these brief snatches of music, for the sheaves and for the city, will be reprised and developed later in the film as the action moves to these locations. The cue is brought to a dramatic and harmonically unresolved *sforzando* ending as Powell's camera settles on the sea, the orchestra then gently revoicing the motif that opened the score over the E flat chords at the start of the title. Vaughan Williams, then, uses these opening musical statements to introduce material that will be returned to throughout the film and, through the closing recapitulation of motifs from the opening title, signals that his score will follow an organised, structured trajectory.

By way of contrast, the music then enters minor key, horror movie mode for the surfacing of the U-boat and its sinking of an allied vessel, insistent discords and gothic minor key fanfares sounding, lower brass settling on a menacing paraphrase of fragments of the German national anthem. Here the feel *does* become martial, with waspish brass and rumbling snare drums providing a brisk march. This is the distopian world of war and conflict that the film, through its evocation of the healing spirit of Canada's landscape, will attempt to lift us up out of, and the music sounds appropriately harsh, dissonant and ugly, effectively providing us with a binary opposite to the noble grandeur of both the music and the mountains of the opening title.

Other cues follow this that in terms of form are familiar to us from other war films discussed in this book: industrious, xylophonic scurrying for the transmission and reception of Morse code signals in various control centres, equally busy up-tempo hurrying cues for the pursuit of the U-boat and so on. The reversion to major key for these marks the Allies as good and the Germans as bad. With these passages, and the use of horror-style and martial sections, Vaughan Williams shows that he is not just writing orchestral music for this film, but, seemingly quite self-consciously, *film* music, informed by all the conventions this involves. He is also withholding melody from us, keeping us waiting for a return to the moving, lyrical music of the opening title.

Some sense of melody, and again of the major key, returns as Vaughan Williams moves into full-on pastoral mode for a montage sequence depicting the lives of the Inuit and white settlers around the Hudson Bay trading post, the woodwind chirping cheerfully over relaxed, and expansive strings and calling French horns. In true pastoral style, the woodwind section moves to the fore, a solo oboe combining with octaval piccolo for the rendition of a Puckish, folk-style tune, a bassoon adding its voice to the mix along with a solo horn then the clarinets. This, of course, is the very arrangement drawn on by Beethoven in his 'Pastoral' Sixth Symphony, with horns, woodwind and strings becoming conventionalised as markers of rusticity in programme music since then, the horns derived from hunting calls and the woodwind relating back to a shepherd's pipes. (Indeed, Vaughan Williams in turn offered a 'Pastoral' symphony of his own, his Third, in 1922, and revised it in 1955.) Through this music the land, and the people that live on it, the Inuit, the trappers and the traders, are typed good and wholesome. Not so the advancing German brigade, who are accompanied by music that is starkly contrasting in its sparseness: a descending, scalar three-note motif describing a minor third that is repeated over and over dropping down through the octaves of the strings.

If for Beethoven's 'Eroica', and for many composers since, the key of E flat major has been thought of as heroic, the minor third allotted the Germans comes in E flat minor, typing them harmonically as *not*-heroic. The use of such conventional associations of specific keys is apparent also in the C major of Laurence Oliver's preposterously 'French' Johnnie's song on squeeze box, a key that, as we shall see in *In Which We Serve*, is allied to light, simplicity and purity. These associations are pitted against and undercut by the German threat advancing on the unsuspecting men in the cabin.

The German take over and occupation of the trading post, a lengthy sequence culminating in their escape by hi-jacked pontoon plane, plays out to an extended musical silence, their flight returning us to images consonant with the aerial shots of the film's opening. When they crash land, they fall into a kind of Eden, a Canadian countryside quite different from the remote and desolate shores of Hudson Bay. Although the filmmakers could have used music to make either the escape or the plane crash even more exciting, it is only once the brigade stagger ashore and are confronted with their surroundings that Vaughan Williams strikes up the band once more: strings play a cue that modulates upwards through a series of minor modes, spiking on the discovery of the death of one of the soldiers. A French horn answers this moment, and it becomes clear that Vaughan Williams is scoring the Germans with a harmonically skewed distortion of the pastoral sound. As we've seen, strings and horns are staples of the pastoral, and we know already that the pastoral is typed good in this film. Here, strings and horns play darkly in a series of muted minor modes the crabbed modulations of which don't even offer the comfort of a stable tonal centre. In a sense, this music is the negative image of the wholesome pastoral positive found elsewhere in the movie.

We remain in the minor key as the soldiers begin to make their way across country, stalking pizzicato strings sounding over quietly drawn-out woodwind chords: the pastoral becomes a minor key march theme. Their arrival at a Hutterite prairie farm, however, brings a change back to a more pleasant, orthodox pastoral sound, a solo oboe dancing over a rustic droning fifth provided by French horns and clarinets. Young Anna's song as she works on the scarecrow blends the musical worlds of the diegetic and non-diegetic, a solo clarinet picking up on her tune effortlessly: this magical crossing of musical dramatic space accents the spellbinding nature of the moment. Musically, this is a brief glimpse of a pastoral idyll, and at this communal settlement one of the Germans, Vogel, will indeed be humanised (and pay for it with his life).

Reprising the Native American-style music heard at the start of the film over shots of sheaves of wheat, the harvesting sequence at the community returns to this pentatonic idea, voicing it in a busy, barn dance-ish 3:4 time. Then, as the community's leader, Peter (Anton Walbrook), surveys the plenty of the seemingly limitless grain fields, the solo oboe reappears over a flute pedal E, further pentatonic twists evoking a Debussyesque pastoral feel, a sense of musical utopia cut short by Lieutenant Hirth's myopically Nazi speech to the gathered community during the electrical storm. However, the lilting melody on oboe has yet to recapture the sense of breadth, emotional depth and grandeur promised by the opening title. Still we are kept waiting for a return to this.

Following the cynical execution of Vogel by his peers, the progress of the remaining three Germans is backed with a return to the minor key march that now Mickey Mouses the rhythm of the soldiers' footsteps, the beat timed precisely to land on the footfalls of the men. The arrangement is once more a distortion of the pastoral palette: dogged, stalking pizzicato strings, a glum bassoon describing a chromatic melody over minor key horn chords. Their arrival at Winnipeg, as with the previous harvest sequence, occasions a *da capo* to earlier in the score as we hear once more the bustling *tutti* first encountered over the aerial shot of the city during the film's opening montage. The continuation of the progress westwards to Vancouver reintroduces the grim march arrangement, which binds together the montage sequence of their journey. The relentless, plodding 4:4 eases a little as the group first begins to straggle then rests at the roadside, but their hijacking of a broken down motor car brings forth the deeper, darker elements of the orchestra in a threatening way, returning us to the minor key fanfares that introduced the U-boat back at the beginning of the film, an unresolved *sforzando* 'hard-out' cresting this cue, too, as the driver is hit with a spanner. The repetition of such thematic material, orchestral textures and formal devices helps unify Vaughan Williams' score and underlines that it isn't merely responding to the stimuli of the image track in an *ad hoc* way, but is constructed as a logical, premeditated and wholly coherent musical system.

If the scenes with the Inuit first ushered in the pastoral aspects of the score, a key set piece of the film occurs as the Germans are discovered among the crowd at a Plains Indian pageant. The sequence is ushered in in typical film fashion, with a pounding drum *ostinato* signifying the 'primitive' nature of the Native Americans and a melody on unison woodwind including a number of phrases with pentatonic inflections. As musical markers of American Indians in the movies these remain constant from *Stagecoach* (1939) on, even John Barry's score for the revisionist Western *Dances With Wolves* (1990) allotting menacing strokes of the bass drum to the Pawnee. As those thought of as being closest to the spirit of the North American land, it is ultimately, through a sequence of iconic extreme close ups, the Indians that stare out the Germans and spring them from their cover. The youngest of the three is taken, leaving just Lieutenant Hirth and one of his minions at large.

Muir Mathieson conducts the film score of *49th Parallel*
(Eric Portman on screen)

Their now panicked flight is no longer accompanied by the plodding march of their previous Westering, but with a percussive, motific cue twisting the dynamism and ebullience of Aaron Copland's music (an American model for the pastoral in music) into an anxiety-inducing tumult. Vaughan Williams finally drops the pace and settles on a slow and muted statement involving lower strings, horns, clarinet and bassoon, the sequence becoming more pastoral as it evolves, an expansive pedal on strings articulating the magnitude of the landscape the men begin moving through.

The Leslie Howard/Philip Armstrong Scott section is lent a surreal edge with the inclusion of banks of Debussyesque piano arpeggios that are eventually revealed to be emanating from the idealistic aesthete's wireless and labelled as decadent and degenerate by the Lieutenant along with books by Thomas Mann and the work of Magritte and Picasso. The conjunction of Impressionistic pianism on the soundtrack and images of Howard angling from a canoe on an impossibly calm lake provides a typically audacious Michael Powell moment, one that clearly marks the director's identification with this character. Modernist high culture here is allowed to stand up against the philistinism of the Nazis.

It is only following Hirth's eventual defeat that Vaughan Williams reintroduces the powerful melody from the opening title. We've been kept waiting for it for close to two hours, and once again it sounds in its affirmative A flat major, echoing the E flat-A flat chord change of the movie's introductory flourish by concluding with a powerful cadence from an E flat seventh back to A flat for good measure. With the Nazi unit vanquished, Canada can once more bask in the glow of this wonderful tune.

For *49th Parallel* Vaughan Williams provides a score that speaks at once in his own voice but works effectively and efficiently as film music. The choice of this composer with his innate feel for the pastoral was perfect for the project, bringing not just excellent music but an added kudos to Powell's production through Vaughan Williams' art music credentials (another reason for signalling the composer's contribution so clearly in the opening title). The score, as with all those midwifed by Mathieson, is very tightly organised indeed, a piece of work that is highly successful both technically and creatively.

Filmography

49th Parallel, Michael Powell (General Film Distributors/Ortus Films Ltd), UK, 1941

Canterbury Tale, A, Michael Powell/Emeric Pressburger (The Archers), UK, 1944

Dances With Wolves, Kevin Costner (TIG Production), US, 1990

Edge of the World, The, Michael Powell (Rock Studios), UK, 1937

In Which We Serve, Noël Coward (British Lion/Two Cities), UK, 1942

Matter of Life and Death, A, Michael Powell/Emeric Pressburger (The Archers), UK, 1946

Paths of Glory, Stanley Kubrick (Bryna Productions),US, 1957

Stagecoach, John Ford (Walter Wenger), US, 1939

IN WHICH WE SERVE

(1942)

DIRECTOR: Noël Coward (co-director David Lean)
MUSIC: Noël Coward
ORCHESTRAL CONDUCTOR: Muir Mathieson
PRODUCTION COMPANIES: Rank/Two Cities, UK

The score for *In Which We Serve* is just one part of Coward's signature contribution to this film, for which he won a special Academy Award. While Coward merely provided themes for the score that were subsequently structured and arranged by Mathieson, this is not unusual practise within the film industry then or indeed now. Charlie Chaplin scored *City Lights* (1931) with similar help from Alfred Newman; Danny Elfman (*Batman*, 1989, *Hulk*, 2003) works today in close partnership with orchestrator Steve Bartek.

Drama and dignity, fittingly, inform the construction of the opening title cue. A roll on timpani crowned with an exciting gong strike ushers in the full orchestra, whose introduction lifts us through an affirmative series of upward modulations before settling on a cheery C sharp major, frequent cymbal splashes adding a dash of epic grandeur. The music continues to undergo regular changes of key, though never straying from the major, and the melodic line is built around repeated rising motifs, each upward evolution building a sense of excitement and positivity. We then modulate up again to E major, and the cue moves into a dignified, Elgarian march on unison strings eventually joined by supportive brass chords hinting at solidity and determination, mettle through the metal. This title cue, then, tells the audience that it's in for excitement, affirmation and a story concerned with strength through dignity, an idea echoed by the noble, sculptural look of the credits themselves, suggestive of both eternity and solidity. By extension, these values can therefore be applied to the British nation as a whole.

The subject of key signatures in this film is not so steadfast, however, as it throws up a number of interesting problems. The keys of C sharp major and E major, apparently returned to frequently in the film, have been arrived at by comparing the music as it sounds today with the pitch of a contemporary, digital keyboard. There are, however, good reasons to question these findings. C sharp major is an odd key to write in, for three main reasons. Firstly, it is not a natural key in which to write for brass in what is, after all, a very brassy score. Secondly, even if we were to call it B flat major, as the flat keys are more comfortable for these players, it seems a complicated, fussy key to write in, rehearse and perform from under circumstances where, even more so than usual in the film world, speed must have been of the essence in the scoring process.

Thirdly, if we were to transpose the score down a semitone we'd arrive at the keys of C major and E flat major. C major has been associated with light and purity since Baroque times, and E flat is the heroic key of Beethoven's *Eroica*. It makes far more sense to score this patriotic flag waver in those keys, tonal centres with resonant associations widely known in the musical world. A slight cranking up of film speed, resulting in this rise in pitch, might be accounted for by technical reasons, with an error creeping in during the dubbing and editing of the original film, its transfer onto VHS/DVD or during television broadcast, where films are run at twenty five frames per second rather than their customary twenty four, again for technical reasons. On the other hand, Coward might have deliberately cast his score within tonalities purposefully a semitone out from such heroic keys in order to subliminally question or undermine the main, propagandistic thrust of the film. In the absence of a score, of any papers relating to it, or of anyone extant who was associated with the musical aspects of the film, the question must remain an intriguingly open one. References to notes and keys throughout appear as heard today, without any downward transposition.

From the opening title we move straight into another extensive music cue underscoring a montage sequence depicting the construction of the *Torrin*. Scurrying triplets on violas and cellos create a sense of urgency and industry, and a folk-style theme on strings and Puckish woodwind connects with both the working men and boys we see building the vessel and the innate Britishness of the enterprise. Again, the music modulates upwards at regular intervals, building excitement and imparting an affirmative tone. The ship is launched with a reprise of the introduction from the title cue, this time scored for an emphatic brass fanfare that will become associated with the vessel throughout the film, and a return to C sharp major. Further modulations and a development of the fanfare motif underscore the ship's sea trials.

The music here is behaving just as we'd expect film music to behave. It provides a sense continuity, binding together the essentially disjointed nature of the montage sequence, and features a couple of musical punctuation marks that embellish important moments in the unfolding narrative: a dramatic *sforzando* for the smashing of the champagne bottle at the launch and a grand swell on brass for an exciting whip pan showing the sea rushing by the speeding ship. The music also emphasises the drama and excitement of the images we're seeing, providing a dynamic backdrop for a dynamic sequence. As we catch our first glimpse of the *Torrin*'s crew, the music drops down in volume, but the revoicing of the ascending notes of the fanfare adds a Mahlerian nobility to their raising of the British ensign: music of quiet strength and dignity accompanies the first waving of the flag in this archetypal flag-waver. The music sneaks out unobtrusively before a militaristic snare drum *crescendo* and muted bugle call transport us to the world of the *Torrin* at war.

The musical opening of the film has been concerned with providing an up-beat and positive start to the picture, giving a sense of impending drama and excitement to the proceedings, and also with imparting a uniquely British flavour. Through the musical shorthand of the snare drum and bugle the score moves us quickly into the sphere of military action. All of this has been accomplished with the utmost directness and certainty: thus far, the score moves as happily and efficiently as the ships Captain Kinross (Noël Coward) likes to run.

On board ship, the opening naval battle is played out to musical silence, the sounds of conflict rushing in to fill the vacuum on the soundtrack, giving a sense of verisimilitude and immediacy to the scene. A similar device was used in the conflict sequences in *Dangerous Moonlight*. The orchestra comes rushing back in, however, upon Kinross' order to engage the German warship. We hear a fast-paced, *tutti* cue once more constructed around motifs featuring rising sequences of notes, modulating upwards. Now, however, the sound is tempered by a darker tone, a sense of danger that enters through a new-found chromaticism and turn towards a minor key feel for the first time. The immediate battle over and won, the happy continuation of the *Torrin*'s patrol is marked by a return to the major key fanfare figure, the hard-working efficiency of the crew hinted at by a return to the scurrying triplets of the opening montage sequence, for variety's sake given this time to upper strings and woodwind. An urgent 'hard out' accompanies the fateful spotting of the enemy aircraft squadron that will sink the ship, and again the conflict begins with musical silence.

Where before the orchestra returned to the fray upon Kinross's conclusive order, this time it re-enters as he is submerged in the rising sea water, a translucent harp *glissando* and gentle strings describing a Debussyesque pentatonic fragment (an apt reference to the sound world of 'La Mer') ushering in the first of the film's flashback sequences. This temporal transition is handled smoothly by the score, and while the earlier optimistic certainty of the music has gone, the pentatonic figure quickly adds form and direction to a cue that threatened to sound the first note of doubt in the music through its abstraction of tempo and the chromaticism of the *glissandi*, a contrast made plain by the harp returning at the end of the cue, this time playing in comparatively organised arpeggios. Over further Impressionistic string and harp figures, a muted, faintly militaristic trumpet sounds, introducing a lyrical, longline melody that is handed over to woodwind. The feel here is one of serenity, belying the peril of Kinross as he flashes back on taking command of the ship. While we've lost in terms of force and affirmation, this gentle music opens us up emotionally for the sentimental nature of the various flashbacks that follow. It also hints at the calm with which Kinross is dealing with the situation.

Kinross' memory of arriving at home and being greeted by his wife Alix (Celia Johnson) is scored for a chipper waltz, suggestive both of the romantic nature of their relationship and of happier times. Indeed, another waltz plays as Freda (Kay Walsh) falls asleep with her head on Shorty's (John Mills) shoulder after meeting him on board a train, returning again as they discuss their felicitous meeting in a café later where, fittingly, they arrange to go dancing the next evening. Waltzes become important to characters in this film: Alix recalls the effect of 'The Blue Danube' upon her after a honeymoon quarrel with Kinross, alleging it left her feeling 'pent up and emotional'.

A return to the Debussyesque soundworld swiftly brings us back to the present as Kinross surfaces and he and his fellow survivors swim for the life raft, before the same eases us into Walter Hardy's (Bernard Miles) flashback to domestic life before the *Torrin*'s commissioning. Variants of this Impressionistic passage act as the default springboard backwards and forwards through time throughout the film, the harp arpeggios an aural analogue of the rippling dissolves that effect the visual transitions. The rapid commissioning of the vessel itself is accompanied by a sprightly, up-beat cue making light of the hard work so clearly involved and once more unifying the disjointed strands of this montage sequence. The process is brought to a conclusion by a brief statement of the *Torrin*'s fanfare motif.

Two of the score's unifying strategies can be divined in the cue that accompanies the *Torrin* being towed home after suffering a hit in conflict. In the first instance we find a clear use of recurrent tonalities as the E major march sequence of the opening title returns. In contrast, Richard Attenborough's young deserter's shamed disembarkation at port is scored with a downbeat E minor. A second unifying device is the continual recurrence of the *Torrin*'s *leitmotif* (say, F sharp-G sharp-B-G natural-G sharp-A-B-C sharp, but the sequence is transposeable). Repetition of themes, motifs and keys holds the score together, enabling it to operate as a coherent musical system.

As well as the non-diegetic score, however, other music is heard coming from within the story world, or diegesis, of the film. The first passage of this we hear is of the maritime hymn 'Eternal Father, Strong to Save', an appropriate text that works on a number of levels, suggestive of a naval milieu and of the future narrative predicament of the shipwrecked sailors with its plea for help 'for those in peril on the sea'. In addition, the very act of hymn-singing itself imparts a religious sanction to the vessel and those who sail in her, and we also hear her crew singing in a harmony suggestive in turn of their well-ordered work practise. These men sing and fight as a cohesive unit, each contributing their own part to the whole; on an essential level, the individual voice is just one among many.

Meanwhile, the film also features communal singing of another kind. A solo harmonica and lone whistler engender a sing-song of 'If You Were the Only Girl in the World' on board a train carrying Shorty and Freda. It's the tune they fall in love to and an episode calling to mind Coward's famous remark on the potency of 'cheap' music. This melody will return on barrel organ for the arrival of Shorty's telegram home telling Freda and his mother he's safe after the sinking of the *Torrin*. In addition, the sing-along lends an air of community and togetherness to the disparate group of travellers. As with the hymn previously, diegetic, or source, music is used to bind people together.

Elsewhere, popular music is used not quite so benignly: cowardly Richard Attenborough gets a pianola rendition of 'Run Rabbit Run' for his penny in the pub, which promptly segues cruelly into a communal rendition of the same (with harmonica once more) back on the battered life raft. 'Roll Out the Barrel' then starts up to raise the spirits and cue Hardy into a reminiscence of its performance during a music hall outing with his wife Kath (Joyce Carey), Shorty and Freda. The use of recognisable popular songs would, at the time, have given a sense of contemporary verisimilitude to the film; today it locks the action indelibly into a specific time and a specific place: Britain in the Second World War.

Another, perhaps more dramatic, use of diegetic music occurs as a jolly march plays on military band over a long tracking shot revealing the shocked, reflective faces of the infantrymen deposited back home by the *Torrin*. Paradoxically, so powerful is the juxtaposition of sound and image that watching today it is hard to be sure of the intended effect: is it a comment on the futility of war, on the resilience of Britain's armed forces when under strain, or both?

The film ends with a muted voicing of the *Torrin* motif on noble French horn, evolving into the dignified march theme in E major, the strains of which swell for the closing dedication of the movie to the Royal Navy and a reprise of much of the score's thematic material for the closing credit crawl, which lifts us again through an upward modulation to a final, triumphant voicing of the ship's *leitmotif*.

Coward's music, as formalised by Mathieson and in conjunction with the film's use of source music, has several functions. In the first instance it does many of the things we expect film music to do: it unifies the movie through the use of recurrent themes, keys and *leitmotifs*; it smoothes potentially choppy edits, typically at the beginning and ending of flashbacks; it provides continuity during the film's montage sequences; it adds drama and excitement where they are needed, becoming more lyrical and expressive where the sentimental aspect of the narrative requires amplification. But, quite clearly, other things are going on, too. The music is an active agent in presenting the work of Britain's armed forces as noble and heroic, and the folk-style elements and Elgarian marches find a sense of musical Britishness foregrounded. Hymns and popular songs of the day are woven into the fabric of the film giving a sense of community, of time and of place.

Interestingly, in alluding to composers and musical styles from right across Europe, from Elgar and Debussy to the quasi-Mahlerian affirmation of the rising fanfares and motifs, from the use of waltz time with its similarly Viennese connotations to a cameo for Mendelssohn's 'Wedding March', the score also appears to seek to synthesise many aspects of the high culture, European musical tradition at the same time as asserting a sense of Britishness and British grit.

Fires Were Started

(1943)

Director: Humphrey Jennings
Music: William Alwyn
Musical Director: Muir Mathieson
Production Company: Crown Film Unit, UK

In 1943 Mathieson worked with composer William Alwyn to score Humphrey Jennings' poetic and morale-boosting documentary *Fires Were Started*, a work released through the Crown Film Unit ostensibly intended to honour the work of the Auxiliary Fire Service but also providing a showcase for Jennings' powerful and often surreal screen sense. Alwyn was a composer of 'pure' music, of sonatas, concertos and symphonies for concert performance, but would also become a particularly prolific composer for film. His, however, is not the only music featured in the movie. In effect, *Fires Were Started* synthesises music from a wide variety of traditions, Alwyn furnishing cues drawing on both the British art music idiom and the conventions of fiction film scoring while a rich vein of music emanating from the characters in the film itself incorporates strands relating to jazz, popular and folk music. Furthermore, if Jennings, as a surrealist, aims to transform our view of the world through the images he captures, Alwyn's music often works to transform our emotional and intellectual response to what we are shown.

The score begins in a suitably heroic mien with a solid, mid-tempo opening title featuring a recurring fanfare on horns, instruments which for Richard Strauss were 'always a yardstick of heroism'. Equally heroic is the image the music underscores, a sculpted frieze of firemen in action, their helmets evocative of Trojans', the sculptor's style suitably neo-classical. Juxtaposing these fanfares with a purposeful melody on unison violins, the cue wanders through a series of key centres before settling on an uplifting B major; as with *In Which We Serve* (1942) the general progression is a positive, upward one. Then, over a pulsing *tremolo* pedal B the fanfare is revoiced in B minor as the Blitz becomes a point of reference via a title card. Increasing the new sense of foreboding, we remain in minor mode as we see a shot of a burning line of fire, the horns sounding repeatedly over shots of a fire engine emerging from its station and racing through London. Cellos and basses continue the pulsing pedal motif and are joined at the opposite end of the pitch spectrum by an urgent piccolo *ostinato* reminiscent of a Morse code signal. Heroism and danger, then, are signalled at the very start of the score.

The music halts before the first dialogue scene begins, allowing the non-actors to perform in as unmediated a way as possible and creating a sense of naturalism. This is the first of many periods of musical silence in the film, a technique well understood by Mathieson, as shown in many of the score analyses in this book. When the music returns it ushers in determined, rhythmic strings to lend continuity to a montage sequence of the fire crew arriving for the start of their shift, showing the different parts of London they are drawn from: the docks, shops, terraced streets. The uniforms link the various men we see, but so does the music, which acts as an index for the nature of the fire fighters, its beat stoically regular and dependable, the pervading musical texture understated yet dignified.

The orchestra sneaks out as we hear the first music coming from within the diegesis of the film: a man stands on the stoop of a terraced house playing a lilting, childlike melody on recorder.

Alwyn's score leaves us in the same key as the recorder music, providing an effortless transition, and this also helps ease us into one of the film's first surreal moments, the innocence of the tune and the lightness of its ornamentation offering a profound contrast with the wartime street scenes the film has offered us up until now. It is to this music that the fire crew meet up at the fire station, the recorder, an instrument replete with Tudor associations, both crystallising and historicising their Englishness. A further comic moment featuring diegetic music soon occurs as two men peel potatoes by the station's rabbit hutches duetting on 'Oh, Sweet Mystery of Love and Life I've Found You'. This vocal performance is answered with a rendition of 'I Do Like to be Beside the Seaside' as the fire engine is polished.

Industrious major key strings then rejoin as we see scenes of office life inside the station and watch the men and women co-ordinating the fire service at work. The energy of the music ameliorates the sedentary nature of these desk jobs, imbuing the otherwise largely static images with life, and also makes light of the hard work and drudgery of the intercut footage of firemen training on, maintaining and swabbing down fire equipment outside. This cue profoundly affects the way we respond to everyday life at the station, transforming the mundane and routine into the vital and engaging. This alchemical process culminates in the cavalry-style bugle call that backs the announcement of lunch: 'Come and get it!' The sequence thus presses us to read all of its component shots as being as exciting as the occasional inserts depicting firemen ascending frighteningly tall telescopic ladders.

On the other hand, rhapsodic strings, almost pastoral in their rhythmic evocation of 'One Man Went to Mow', accompany Johnny and the new recruit Barrett's exploration of the dockland streets and warehouses of the station's catchment area, rising into the freedom of their upper register for some footage of sailboats flashing by on the river but becoming compromised by a shift into troublingly chromatic waters as we watch heavy artillery being loaded and unloaded from ships. The pastoral feel soon returns as the men's tour of the docklands progresses, the disjunction between image and music gently linking these grimy, industrial streets with the rural England of popular mythology. Finally, a note of foreboding is struck, as at the end of the opening title, with a shift to a minor tonality over a pedal note as we see a barrage balloon being launched into the air: there is a threat to this England.

The repetition of this musical device, first heard at the end of the opening title, serves to unify both score and film. In turn, it transpires that the ghosting of 'One Man Went To Mow' is no accident: in a later scene showing the fire crew preparing for their night duties Johnny and Barrett will perform this song for the company. In a touching and comic sequence, as each verse ascends numerically another member of the crew enters the room and joins in beside the piano, Barrett altering his accompaniment to suit the personality of each addition. The styles he chooses range from the plodding bass octaves of a classical etude for the crew's commanding sub-officer to the showy pyrotechnics of a honky-tonk bordello sound for the unit's spiv. Music is used, again as in *In Which We Serve*, to reinforce the social connections between characters, and this communal performance is brought to a halt by the distant song of an air raid siren. In response the men regroup to finish with a defiant eighth verse, climaxing with some howling falsetto work imitating the wail of this alarm.

Further instances of diegetic music being used to evoke a sense of community are provided by an accordion number as the men play snooker and darts while awaiting a call-out and by Barrett impressing his new comrades with an extempore piano medley straddling classical and jazz idioms, his music spilling over to underscore an impressive sequence of shots showing massive ships moving by and, in the next breath, a comic sequence depicting two firemen dancing clumsily together. Barrett's piano playing is crucial to his acceptance by and integration into his new unit. As the bombs start falling, the station staff begin a sing-song accompanied by accordion, waltzing with the office girl who enters the mess to give them their first call out of the night. During this sequence, Barrett joins in on piano and the fire station begins to sound more like a stereotypical East End pub than anything else. After a near miss during the bombing the piano strikes up, saloon-style as after a bar-room confrontation in a Western, to reinvigorate the spirits of the station and recommence the sing-song. During Heavy Unit One's journey to the fire at Trinidad Street, Johnny's singing vies with the ringing of the engine's bell and gives as good as it gets.

The extensive opening of this central fire fighting sequence plays out to another musical silence, Alwyn and Mathieson allowing the images to do the talking. The soundtrack is filled instead with the drone of planes, the shouts of the men, the sounds of explosions and falling bombs and the contrasting efficient and controlled conversations of those at their desks back at the various command centres. Alwyn's score only makes its entrance again as we approach the fire from a boat on the river, the orchestra entering *tutti* complete with aquatic harp arpeggios. This cue is motific rather than melodic in its construction, the repetition of its various short figures adding a sense of drama and urgency. It also announces a return to the chromatic sound world of the artillery sequence from Johnny and Barrett's previous visit to the docks. Alwyn creates tension not just through motific repetition and a move to chromaticism, but through the deployment of particularly angular musical ideas linking together notes that are either intervalically far apart or only tenuously related to each other harmonically. He also uses *tremolo* strings and pedal point to ramp up the tension. Moments where the firemen achieve minor victories, such as the return of their water supply following the rupture of a mains pipe, are punctuated with sudden swings to major key fanfares. In formal terms then, this cue moves very much as any action cue would in a thriller or action movie.

From here, as the operation is further complicated, musical silence returns until the orchestra elbows its way in again with a *sforzando* brass chord followed by a noisy *tutti* as the warehouse explodes, marking this as a climactic and important moment. The next entry, underscoring the silhouettes of firemen hosing down the inferno of the warehouse, uses a demonic *crescendo* on timpani and chromatic muted brass in another motific cue, this time emanating from the lower sections of the orchestra, the dynamics swelling and dropping in a highly effective way that mirrors the rising and falling of the billowing flames. As the fire fighters work to regain the upper hand they are bolstered by the appearance of a unison line for violins in their lower register and a chord progression that inexorably ascends. The tonality is still minor key, however, so victory is by no means assured. The strength, purpose and unity of the men is suggested by the introduction of martial-sounding snare drums that also contribute to the overall building of the sequence. This unity is then underlined by an antiphonal passage where unison strings play a line that is immediately echoed by similarly undivided brass. The cue then moves into a more affirmative major key and develops a dogged, march-like character that relents only for a more gentle and circumspect section accompanying a shot of the treatment of the brigade's sub-officer who was injured in the initial explosion. The cue is crowned by a series of climactic cymbal splashes and a grand fanfare on now open-voiced brass. In this section of the score Alwyn articulates the heroism of the fire fighters by overcoming a series of musical problems just as they overcome the physical problems set by the fire: he moves from tenebrous, motific, muted and chromatic music sounding from the lower regions of the orchestra through a gradual transition to an affirmative major key melody culminating in the shiny, trebly crash of cymbals and full-throated acclamation of unmuted brass and upper strings.

As victory over the conflagration is confirmed, a montage sequence depicting the smoking rubble and relieved fire fighters is accompanied by an affirmative fanfare on the noble horns heard during the opening title. This is answered with the sound of the all clear on a symphony of sirens from all around the city. However, as the men wearily pack up, a dark passage on lower strings and muted, divided violins, momentarily enlightened by a puckish melody on solo clarinet, indicates that all is not yet well. The dark sonority continues until a lone fireman discovers a battered helmet under a pile of rubble, whereupon side drums, snare off, sound funereally. With victory has come sacrifice. Nevertheless, as we see London starting the new day during a celebrated sequence of shots of members of the public pushing prams and walking past the smoking ruins, Alwyn reverts to a light, major key march suggesting the over-riding resolution and endurance of the city and

Muir conducts a recording session

its inhabitants despite this sadness, indicating through martial music that these people, like soldiers, are in the front line of the battle.

The film ends with an exhortation to the tired fire fighters to snap out of their subdued mood whereupon, after a narrative ellipsis, an upbeat bugle call sounds over shots of them burying their fallen comrade, *divisi* strings swelling emotively before being rejoined by the bugle, effectively transforming the funeral into an affirmation of life and hope. This bugle, we might recall, was first heard somewhat incongruously announcing lunch; here it returns in changed circumstances, the unorthodox becoming conventional.

If it is a common approach of British cinema during the war years to envision the various strata of society struggling together to overcome common adversity, then the diverse musical tapestry of *Fires Were Started* achieves a similar purpose through its happy unification of a variety of different musics, classical, popular, jazz and folk. As the high culture composer, Alwyn may sit on top of the heap but many of the film's most memorable musical moments are sourced, quite harmoniously, from elsewhere. Be that as it may, part of the power of Alwyn's score lies in its frequently transformative nature, its ability to raise the mundane and the routine to the level of the heroic, to work slowly but surely from darkness to light and to argue that through loss and suffering victory will come. Perhaps most extraordinary is his decision to score the run-down, urban docklands with what amounts, effectively, to a piece of pastoralia, thereby suggesting that these images of grime and workaday decay are simply another facet of a traditional and beloved England. Like the movie, this is music with a message.

Henry V

(1944)

Director: Laurence Olivier
Music: William Walton
Music Director/Conductor: Muir Mathieson
Production Companies: Two Cities Films, UK

As music director, Muir Mathieson worked on a number of different types of film with a number of different types of composer, from Noël Coward through to Ralph Vaughan Williams, but in every instance the finished score is a carefully considered work, not simply a piecemeal creation reacting haphazardly to the prompting of the narrative or the image track. These scores work as coherent musical systems. Sir William Walton's score for *Henry V* (1944) is by no means an exception to this.

In his *Henry V*, Laurence Olivier provides a reading of the play that successfully rides two horses with just the one behind: the work is at once a Shakespearean period picture and a cogent piece of morale-boosting wartime propaganda. In Olivier's conception, England's past and present are brought effortlessly together. Accordingly, Walton's score also pulls in two different temporal directions, with passages that are clearly pastiches of a variety of early music idioms alternating with those with a more contemporary flavour, in a melodic, harmonic or textural sense. Yoked to this is the alternation of pieces of music that might stand as 'pure' music in the concert sense (as some indeed do) with cues that are more conventionally filmic in nature, a departure in style for the composer.

Walton uses the opening minutes of *Henry V* to set his stall out, musically speaking. It begins with a handful of measures devoted to an upward swell of divided, muted strings, throbbing with *vibrato*, playing with an intoxicating mixture of tenderness and intensity, a sound that will be returned to for the moving 'Touch Her Soft Lips and Part', the cue that plays as Pistol leaves Mistress Quickly for the war and a movement included in the stand-alone concert suite Walton derived from his film score. This rising motif (G-A-C-E . . . G-A-C-G') will recur in various transformations and transpositions throughout the score. The throbbing strings are supplanted by a solo flute tracing Debussyesque arabesques that mirror the trajectory of the theatrical flyer blown by the wind that is the first image proper of the film. As the text of the bill becomes clear to us, Walton ushers in a buoyant fanfare on brass backed with exuberant percussion. Something about these bare fourths and fifths looks forward to the brass harmonies Miklos Rozsa would employ to suggest the archaic in a string of historical epics in the 1950s and '60s. In any case, the form of the fanfare acts in itself, here and throughout the film, as a marker of historical period as well as of grandeur, power and importance.

Walton continues with this epic mien over the fabulous miniature model shot showing Elizabethan London reflected in a calm and glassy Thames, a suitably theatrical drum roll sounding before motifs circulating through the lower regions of the orchestra are joined by Ravellian vocalising choir. Upper strings then woodwind join in, developing the material first sounded by the lower instruments, and the opening sunrise of 'Daphnis and Cloe' becomes a still keener point of reference. The whole is garnished by a return of the brass fanfares and the substantial prolongation of this climax. The sound is epic and grand, and the harmonic world of late Romanticism and Impressionism, until the final bars where the choir strike a bare fifth and the feel suddenly becomes less anachronistic, although a final shimmer on violins and woodwind as the Globe Theatre's flag is raised return us to Ravel. In these last moments, then, the score begins to waver between a more contemporary sound and music associated with the period of the film's setting. By the same token, the allusions to the Impressionistic style of Debussy and Ravel foreshadow the French aspirations of King Henry in the drama that follows.

Hot on the heels of this non-diegetic cue, music from within the world of the story quickly locates us historically as the theatre musicians strike up. A brief period of tuning up is quelled by a fanfare resounding on post horn, after which the musicians throw themselves into a brisk, tuneful pastiche of Elizabethan music: over a droning fifth on lower instruments, precise unison violins and upper woodwind play a cheerful modal melody, a side drum, snare off, beating out a regular dotted rhythm in accompaniment. Walton, then, moves effortlessly from the opening title of the film, written in the Impressionist manner of Ravel in 1912, into a pastiche of Elizabethan music from the sixteenth century. The change does not confound us with a crash edit between the two contrasting styles, however. We have been prepared for the move to period idiom by the interval of a fifth struck by the choir towards the end of the miniature shot, and the shift from non-diegetic to diegetic musical spheres also softens the transition.

As Chorus engenders us through his prologue to make our 'imaginary forces work', the orchestra joins anew with a reprise of the throbbing string swell and solo flute texture that began the score, only to be followed instantly, upon the conclusion of our narrator's exhortations, by the theatre band providing some more sprightly Elizabethiana. Thus we are prepared to divide our attention between two different time zones on the soundtrack, just as the action on the screen will move seamlessly between the Elizabethan 'present' of the play being performed in the Globe to a second time zone, that of the run up to Agincourt itself. The film, then, will time-shift visually as well as aurally. During these early, stage-bound scenes from the play, the theatre musicians provide a sonic glue between scenes, topping and tailing each to maintain dramatic flow during the scene changes, though on occasion there is an element of doubt as to whether we are actually listening to the non-diegetic orchestra with the burden of the music moving imperceptibly from the theatre pit to it. The brisk, two-part invention for strings during our introduction to the backstage area is a case in point. This straddles time periods through instrumentation (massed strings from the non-diegetic orchestra) and musical form (the two-part invention typed as a period form, if a little anachronistically given its Baroque associations). From here, a sequence of suitably warlike fanfare cues punctuates the scenes laying the ground for Henry's invasion of France, and the reappearance of Chorus occasions a return to the rising string motif that accompanied him before and, indeed, began the movie.

At this point the film begins to effect its magical transformation from stage-bound drama to full-blown period movie via a transition section featuring highly stylised backdrops and sets, such as that on Henry's ship, that give, for the first time in the movie since the opening miniature shot, a real sense of spatial depth. Our transportation to this maritime world is managed via a brief spot of Impressionistic sea music (the usual Debussyesque harp arpeggios and rippling woodwind). More archaistic aspects then become important to the score once more with the celebration of mass on board the King's ship at Southampton occasioning a diegetic liturgical call and response cue featuring a sung line for tenor solo in plainchant style that is answered by a full choir, equally modal and voiced in harmonically spare parallel fifths. Thus a sense of antiquity as well as spirituality is conveyed.

The excitement of the impending departure for France occasions a *tutti* flourish from the orchestra, up-tempo and brilliant in tone, that is then undercut as we dissolve to a tavern for the death of Falstaff. Lower strings slowly sound the recurring figure (F-E-F-C-D flat-C-D flat–A flat . . .) that will form the ground bass of the solemn cue that follows. Although the harmonic palette of this is neo-Romantic in hue, the form, as with the liturgical cue discussed above, is an archaic one, in this case that of the *passacaglia*: the music progresses, in 3:4 time, guided by a continually repeating bass figure as muted upper strings evolve a slowly changing accompaniment. The resulting cue is at once tender, yet poised, formal and grave, and Walton once more calls upon a musical form from a bye-gone era to help shape his contribution.

The sense of musical melancholy continues as Pistol and his friends take their leave of Mistress Quickly. Again, the cue is written in triple time, but here we are returned by the composer to the tender *vibrato* strings of the film's opening bars. 'Touch Her Soft Lips and Part' is a delicious blend of gently lilting rhythms, delicately muted *divisi* string sonorities and lush harmonies, concluding on a major seventh that seems the natural destination of the warm, colour chords that have preceded it. By the same token, however, the repetitive dotted rhythm of both the melody and its accompaniment impart an antique dance feel underlying the cue's Impressionistic use of harmony, a wilfully anachronistic blend of form and content again quite typical of Ravel (for example, 'Tombeau de Couperin').

We then return to the excitable sound world of the navy's departure for France, where bustling strings and rippling harps once more add zest to Chorus' evocation of the journey. Then, in an extraordinary moment of intertextuality, Walton chooses to introduce us to the French court via a direct quotation of the lyrical main theme of the 'Baïlèro' from Canteloube's evocative, folk-inspired 'Songs of the Auvergne'. So as not to overwhelm Chorus' voiceover, Walton eschews Canteloube's intoxicating orchestration in favour of a simple solo oboe over at first chromatic, then *tremolo* strings, a backing indicative of the French king's apprehension regarding the English challenge to his throne. The melodic allusion to Canteloube is enough to provide a sense of place (for those in the know!) before a modal melody on solo flute, backed with harp, reminds us of the historical as well as geographical location of the action through its nod to the somewhat notorious pastoral fascinations of the French nobility. Subsequent court scenes are often scored for variations of this arrangement (say, harp, guitar and a duet of modal flutes). As the King prepares for the arrival of the English heralds, the ideas of chromaticism and *tremolo* string effects are brought together once more in an anxiously scurrying cue scored for unison violins that is capped with an initially discordant fanfare at its close. As this flourish straightens itself out harmonically, it crosses over from being non-diegetic to diegetic in nature, using both the form and the bold, triadic harmonies of the fanfare to reassert a sense of period.

The first scenes of the promised English invasion are accompanied by music that owes more to the cinema for its formal properties than any pre-existing classical model. Cues written for action sequences in movies tend to be highly motific in form, rather than melodic. They also tend to be up-tempo, rhythmic pieces of writing. Frequently, the orchestra is used in a highly compartmentalised way, with brief, rhythmic ideas being passed from one section of the orchestra to another to give a sense of textural variety that would otherwise be negated by the lack of melody. Musical accents fall on foregrounded moments of physical action (punches, explosions, arrow impacts and so on), and frequent use is made of key modulation to escalate and deflate tension, upward movements intensifying events, downward modulations relaxing us.

This first combat scene finds Walton composing true to this model. A shot of a cannon being hauled ashore finds strings repeating an urgent, six-note motif that is followed swiftly by an upward modulation as the fighting suddenly spills onto the beach from behind some rocks, the brass answering the string motif with another of their own. As Henry declaims 'Once more unto the breach . . .' we hear a dizzying sequence of upward modulations in the rapid, motific writing before the music sneaks out to allow

Henry's oration to continue. As the combat element leaves the scene, so does the action music. This will be a cinematic musical form that Walton will return to, however, later in the score.

In contrast, our first meeting with Katherine is accompanied by a shimmering return to Canteloube's 'Baïlèro'. Here, the *tremolo* strings hint more, perhaps, at the trembling occasioned by ardour than fear: this is the first appearance of Henry's future queen. Wagnerian horns pompously announce the departure of the Dauphin from the castle before we are returned to the pastoral strings, harp and woodwind as Katherine reflectively walks the battlements before, tellingly, embarking upon an English lesson centred around naming parts of the body. The alternation between the Wagnerian brass and Impressionistic 'Baïlèro', repeated at the close of the scene as the Dauphin returns, effectively sets Katherine apart from her spiteful brother and, given the associations between Wagner's music and Nazi Germany, in the context of Olivier's propaganda piece types the Dauphin as evil. This fanfare, indeed, will become a *leitmotif* for the French as the film progresses.

The French king's resolution to confront and capture the advancing Henry is accompanied by a cheerful march for side drum, snare off, and piccolo duet, an instrumental combination that sounds authentic enough but lacks the bravura aspect of the Wagnerian fanfare that is reprised immediately as the Frenchman Mountjoy approaches Henry in the field with his taunting ultimatum, hinting at the monarch's frailty. Impressionism, however, returns to the score for the piece of night music Walton provides beneath Chorus' description of the French and English camps in the dark, an invert pedal on high violins floating over uncertain *tremolos* on lower strings and low woodwind chording, distant and spectral fanfares sounding the hours in the nocturnal encampments. Ultimately, as we discover Henry walking around the tents of his army, this night music gradually coalesces, through the introduction of a pacing *pizzicato* motif on basses and a resolution of the string *tremolo* from minor to major mode, into a reworking of the rising motif on *vibrato* strings that opened the score right back at the beginning of the film, this time given to woodwind backed by gathering string harmonies. After the free-floating formlessness of the music that precedes it, the concrete delineation of this motif (here B flat-C-D flat-A flat) sounds newly positive and hopeful. As if to underline this sense of reborn resolve, a diegetic bugle call sounds, strong and clear, derived from this motif and returning us to the historical period. If this revisiting of the score's opening motif provides a powerful sense of continuity in the score, a further instance of this is found as Henry overhears a priest performing mass using the antiphonal versicle-response-amen form first encountered when the navy prepared to embark for France. Here, its voicing is more muted and circumspect, contrasting with the ebullience of the previous occasion. This tying together of musical loose ends, so to speak, gives a profound sense that all has been leading up to this moment, to the battle of the day to follow.

That the odds are stacked heavily against the English is reflected in the music that accompanies the two armies' preparations for battle the following morning. A bright, shiny cue backs the confident French, strings recycling a three-note motif over slower brass chording connoting power and strength; when we dissolve to the English camp, the volume drops markedly and the same material is played in the minor key. Things sound ominous as the three-note motif descends by octaves through the string section, ending up with a muddy and uncertain *tremolo* sounding through minor chords on lower woodwind. After Henry's rousing St Crispin's day speech, however, the orchestra, like the troops, set to with renewed vigour, stealing the bustling, industrious, optimistic music of the French.

Indeed, Walton's music now sweeps in prominently over the montage sequence depicting the final preparations of each side. The feel is up-tempo and exciting, the interplay of fanfares and military marches interspersed with moments of humour. A knight in heavy armour being winched down onto his horse is not just visually amusing, but musically so, too: Walton uses the film music technique of Mickey Mousing, where the composer slavishly and literally follows the action on screen in the explicit manner of cartoon scoring. As the knight is lowered in successive stages, a woodwind figure plays in time with each drop; in addition, the direction of the figure, like that of the knight, is downwards. Traditional musical forms (fanfares, marches), then, are mixed with more filmic musical forms.

This side-stepping into the filmic is continued as the cue progresses, Walton once more writing in action sequence form, furnishing a series of up-tempo, rhythmic, motific passages delineated by changes in instrumentation and key modulation. The mounting of the tension is maintained by the continuous pounding of side drums beneath Henry's final parley with Mountjoy, maintaining the rhythmic drive and providing a change in musical texture from the brassy excitement of what went on before. The music for the battle proper is likewise highly cinematic in conception. *Marcato* basses play a dogged quaver *ostinato*, while motific fanfares sound on brass and woodwind.

When English bows are raised and the French horses move to a trot, Walton responds by modulating up, thereby increasing the tension, timpani and strings now offering a new and faster-sounding triplet pattern for the brass to sound above. As they move to a canter, Walton modulates up once more, and unison upper strings join the brass motifs, discords sounding on lower strings adding the spice of danger to the mounting excitement, snare drums providing a propulsive rhythm to the whole. As the charge hits a gallop, Walton truncates the brass and upper string motif and repeats it insistently, adding to the music's increasing sense of speed. A cut back to the waiting English archers occasions another upwards modulation, increasing the tension in spite of the image track's move from the dynamism of the charge to this entirely static image.

A tension-increasing pedal is held, brass and string rhythmic motifs sounding repetitively over it, as we see the archers, Henry poised to give the signal to fire, and the French charge heading towards sharp stakes of the English lines. This modulates up a semitone as we see the archers, then Henry once more, the pedal feel retained. The tension created by this is released along with the arrows as a sudden hard out marks a brief musical silence that foregrounds the sound of the arrows flying through the air. As they impact on the advancing French, the orchestra crashes back in with cymbals, drums and frantic brass now simply repeating a single chord over and over, completing the movement systematically shortening the motific lines the instruments have described since the start of the cue. As the first French attack is repulsed, new motifs on brass are passed on first to the woodwind, then to the strings, and the tonal centre continues to be moved higher and higher. The move to hand to hand combat occasions a passage of loud, *tutti* discords and fragmented motifs on woodwind, underlining the chaos of the scene, many landing in time with the blows.

The English attack on the French secreted in the forest is signalled by a long, low roll on timpani to which first motific brass, then strings, are added. The timpani roll, like the brief musical silence accompanying the release of the arrows, acts to cleanse the aural palate, to give us momentary breathing space before the next musical assault. Once this begins, the feel is again rhythmic and up-tempo, returning us to the charge motif first heard at the start of the conflict. Cymbal splashes resound as French soldiers drop on the English knights, their metal-on-metal sound an analogue for the sword blows that fall thick and fast. As the English prevail and continue their charge, another moment of musical silence allows Henry to be heard urging his troops on before the brass loudly voice a variant of the rising string motif that opened the movie: victory is surely at hand. Over a brass pedal, strings repeat an ever-shortening series of cycles of the charge motif as the French horsemen make a ragged retreat. This pattern of brief musical silence, or timpani pedal, followed by frantically escalating passages of rhythmic, motific writing reaches something of an acme during the nefarious French sacking of the camp and murder of the young pages sheltering there. We're brought back down from this high pitch of excitement via a sobering reprise of the night music heard earlier in the film: *tremolo* strings and spectral bugle calls. Be that as it may, Walton has scored the battle scene using precisely the same musical conventions as can be found in many action sequences ranging from those of the swashbuckling *Gunga Din* (1939) to the futuristic martial arts Jet Li vehicle *The One* (2002).

As the French ride up to offer their surrender, muted trumpets then *divisi* strings sound the motif that began the score: with the promise of victory the music threatens to become radiant. Shorn of their haughtiness and scorn, the French also lose their Wagnerian *leitmotif*: their herald appears unheralded. Further *divisi* strings usher in a victory hymn backed by an ecstatically swirling *tutti* orchestra; the melodic line is modal in construction, reaffirming a sense of historical period after the extensive passages of time-neutral action music Walton has used for the battle scenes. A triptych of liturgical cues is completed as Henry calls for, and gets, a *Non Nobis* in thanks to God for his overwhelming victory. This time the music starts off as polyphonic rather than being antiphonal in nature, with multiple voices gradually being added to strengthen each strand of the counterpoint until the whole male choir swells into a plainchant voiced in parallel fifths. This melody is then picked up by church bells as we dissolve to winter and a period-sounding chamber group plays, this time with female unison voices over. The smoothness of the musical transitions helps ease the visual and temporal transitions of the images and the narrative, and the archaic feel throughout reinforces the sense of period, as does the jocular bassoon that chuckles through Pistol's escape to England with a pig and a chicken.

A diegetic choir and non-diegetic orchestra greet the pageantry of Henry's entrance into Agincourt and here, interestingly, no period feel is attempted in either the choral or instrumental writing. Walton, rather, furnishes a cue in the neo-Romantic idiom, giving an unambivalent signal of happiness and rejoicing. As Burgundy bemoans at length the fallen state of the France, we are returned to the 'Baïlèro' theme, playing in its familiar orchestration of oboe and *tremolo* strings that are gradually joined by harp, brass and high woodwind. The diegetic choir vocalises once more as Henry is left alone with Katherine and proposes marriage. The music then halts, enabling the courtship scene to play out, replete as it is with resonance for a wartime audience with its talk of soldiers as kings and Henry's protective reluctance to part with a village of France. These messages ring out clearly without the aid of music.

When Henry and Kate kiss for the first time, the 'Baïlèro' reaches its apotheosis with the choir in the background intoning the melody

In 1944, Muir invited Walton to write the score for Olivier's *Henry V*. It was, as Olivier declared, an outstanding score, contributing enormously to the success of the film (Muir was the film's Music Director and Conductor)

Copyright of Baron Studios

in vocalise, backed with strings. The wedding pageant that concludes the film finds choir, *tutti* orchestra and orchestral bells joining together in celebration before the music shifts, smoothly, back to the Elizabethan chamber group in the Globe theatre as we are returned to the 'real' world at the film's close. Chorus' epilogue is backed with these musicians playing the opening motif of the score one last time, a melodic anachronism given on period-sounding instruments, bringing the musical past and present together effortlessly, and the film full circle.

Walton, then, constructs his score from a variety of sources. Like Olivier's production itself, he time-shifts by harnessing numerous musical forms and idioms, from the fanfare and the *passacaglia* though to the Wagnerian and the Impressionistic. He also furnishes music, particularly for action scenes, that finds its inspiration in more cinematic conventions. Like the play itself, Walton's score moves easily from the tender to the warlike, from moments of great excitement to those of more introspective reflection. Finally, the choice of Walton, a highly respected composer in the English tradition, adds a finishing gloss of art music to Oliver's high culture, yet deeply patriotic, project. As with the singling out of the musical contribution of Vaughan Williams in *49th Parallel* (1941), in the closing title of the film Olivier emphasises the contribution of Walton, Mathieson and the London Symphony Orchestra by placing their credit, unusually, at the very end, with Walton's final, climactic flourish playing under it.

Filmography

49th Parallel, Dir: Michael Powell, Mus: Ralph Vaughan Williams (Ortus Films Ltd), UK, 1941

Gunga Din, Dir: George Stevens, Mus: Alfred Newman (RKO), USA, 1939

Henry V, Dir: Laurence Olivier, Mus: Sir William Walton (Two Cities Films), UK, 1944

One, The, Dir: James Wong, Mus: Various (Columbia TriStar), USA, 2001

Western Approaches

(1944)

Director: Pat Jackson
Music: Clifton Parker
Music Director: Muir Mathieson
Production Company: Crown Film Unit, UK

Up until now we have largely been considering the use of music directed and conducted by Muir Mathieson in fiction films, but in the 1930s to 1940s British cinema was not only turning out this kind of feature but, under the auspices of the GPO/Crown Film Unit, producing a string of highly influential documentaries (Barnouw 1993: 93; 144). Straddling the worlds of fiction and factual film, a frequent documentary tactic of the time, *Western Approaches*, photographed in startling colour by the great Jack Cardiff and written and directed by Pat Jackson, was inspired by the experiences of British merchant seamen during the Second World War. Shot with a *verité* edge, it uses non-actors to re-enact the rescue of a group of stranded sailors whose ship has been torpedoed by a German U-boat.

While many Realist films shun the excessive use of non-diegetic music as an unwarranted intrusion of artifice into their carefully constructed sense of verisimilitude and immediacy, *Western Approaches* sticks with the union of music and moving image that had proved so effective in previous projects like *Night Mail* (1936). While Clifton Parker would prove to be no Benjamin Britten, his score nevertheless combines imagination with efficiency and remains an important part of our experience of the film.

His music opens in expansive mode, a *tutti* orchestra sounding grandly over shots of the overcast Northern Atlantic sky. The tonality is C major, associated, as we have seen, with purity and light. To begin with the pace is leisurely, the opening bars unfolding over a bass pedal C, the harp *glissandi* shimmering up and down and the fragmentary oboe *ostinato* limning a major third ushering us instantly into the maritime sound world of Debussy's 'La Mer'. A resolute melody then sounds on unison violins and noble French horns and the sense of space and grandeur is reinforced by a bar-long, modal drop down to B flat major in pedal and harmony before a return to C. While the cue then evolves to trace a complex harmonic pattern, shifting tonality freely from major to minor as it goes, it finally returns to the grand C of its opening, an insistent major *tutti* chord repeated pointedly and sturdily over the close of the credit crawl and preamble.

From here, via a swelling roll on timpani, we take an unexpected twist into a loud, *sforzando* discord as the first images of the angry sea flood the frame. The contrast generates an immediate sense of peril, trilling woodwind shrieking over a C/F sharp bass pedal: the tritone, the 'devil in music' banned as diabolically dangerous by the church in medieval times. In *Western Approaches* the result is to produce a passage wherein the harmony is as unstable as a ship at the mercy of the waves (presumably no pun is intended on the name Triton, Greek sea god and son of Poseidon). The brass blare *fortissimo* discords over more percussion rolls as the sea pitches and rolls before us and we catch our first glimpses of figures huddled on board a small lifeboat, the survivors of the wreck of the *Jason*. First the music and then the sailors' cries become lost as the roar of the wind and the water fills our ears. We have moved dramatically away from the leisurely C major melody of the opening bars of the movie, the new and fittingly unstable harmonic world of the tritone pedal succeeded by the awesome din of the elements.

Musical silence then descends on two quieter scenes, one at HQ where the lifeboat's position is plotted on a giant map and the next our introduction to the men in the lifeboat who recount the wreck of their ship and decide to head for the safety of Ireland. At this point a harmonica is produced and the crew launch into an uplifting rendition of 'It's a Long Way to Tipperary', the sense of distance implied by the title adding a dash of gallows humour. In parallel with *In Which We Serve*, and *Fires Were Started* the singing reinforces a sense of togetherness and community, of the dogged determination of the spirit in spite of adverse circumstances. The harmonies the men strike are warm and spontaneous: this is a crew that works well together, the parts they sing indicative of the varying and mutually supportive parts they play in the course of their everyday work. They are, quite literally, a harmonious company. This song leads naturally into a chorus of 'I'm Glad That Salvation is Free', a hymn with a fitting sentiment at once defiant and declamatory, yet hopeful and imploring of God to help them in their hour of need.

As they raise the mast and sail of the vessel to these lines, the orchestra re-enters with another modernistic discord on shrill, high woodwind that resolves into a B minor passage bridging a dissolve between an extreme long shot of the lifeboat and another of the New York skyline, which is in turn swiftly dwarfed by the leviathan form of a huge ship, the *Leander*, at dock. Over a steady, rhythmic accompaniment a montage sequence shows the boat being loaded with tanks and planes, rapid triplets on xylophone and snare drum adding a sense of industry to the bold, solid orchestral chording which has now completed a shift to a more hopeful major key.

When we move inside the vessel to the roundtable briefing planning the convoy's crossing back to Britain, a pattern in the score begins to become clear. When the participants in the film are speaking at any length the orchestra keeps quiet: here the movie maintains a naturalistic musical silence. As we have seen, this happened before on board the *Jason*'s lifeboat. As with there, the men at the briefing are allowed centre stage, their untrained speaking voices neither challenged nor compromised by the addition of a music track. Contrast this with the orchestra that shadows so much of Celia Johnson's interior monologue in *Brief Encounter* (1945). Parker and Mathieson save their score for action scenes and montage sequences where the music can enhance the drama and suture the potentially choppy and distracting editing respectively. We are therefore presented with a curious irony: the scenes where actuality footage is involved (montages of the *Leander* being loaded up, shots of naval exercises) are scored like a fiction film while staged and rehearsed footage, on the other hand, plays out to a documentary-style musical silence.

As if to confirm this, the shots of the convoy setting out for sea in the fog are accompanied by an invert pedal A flat on high strings and murky, low notes on harp, this latter a device used similarly by Max Steiner in arguably the first true film score of the sound era, *King Kong* (1933), as the ship there moves through the fog by Skull Island. Parker scores the departure from New York with a muted orchestral palette, the strings articulating an introspective, chromatic melody. There is no attempt to pastiche a Sousa march, for example, which would have sent the flotilla on its way in gung-ho style and entirely in keeping with the location. A sense of expectancy it thus set up, as if the boats are feeling their way out rather than striking out.

As they move further out to sea the pedal note falls to an A flat in the lower brass, the volume cranking up, adding a note of urgency. With the seas getting heavier we return to the harp *glissandi* of the opening title and upper strings trill an additional high pedal. An affirmative fanfare, once more like those of *In Which We Serve*, attempts to break through, but its rising progression is reversed, falling away in a sequence of downward notes couched in E minor. Again, when we move to watch conversations taking place on board the ships the music sneaks out and the scenes play out to musical silence.

From here we cut back to the men aboard the *Jason*'s lifeboat and, miraculously, they are still singing, providing aural continuity between this sequence and their last; visual continuity is provided by another shot of the mast and sail and a return to the same frame composition of the men on board. This time, however, the men seem not quite so quick to join in with the song as before. The harmonies, too, are not as disciplined. Musically, they are revealed as fraying a little at the edges, quite understandably. During the third song in the sequence, after a little goading their performance improves and their spirits are restored.

The eastward progress of the convoy is scored, again in Impressionistic style, for full orchestra, returning us to the leisurely pace of the opening title. Again, as the cue wears on, discords enter and the volume increases as the power of the sea is shown. A stunning sequence depicting sunset over the Atlantic is accompanied by the twin Debussyisms of harp and serpentine solo woodwind before Parker settles on a reprise of the expansive chords and strings of the film's beginning, underlining the vastness of the seascape.

A montage sequence of the convoy pressing on through a storm at sea follows, and is scored with a fairly conventional orchestral storm featuring rapid chromatic runs on flutes and piccolos, urgent brass, frantic harp *glissandi* and an overall reliance on motific rather than melodic writing. As at the film's opening, the music vies with the sounds of the wind and the water before it is eventually vanquished by these. The dominance of the storm sounds adds an urgency to the convoy's negotiations of the foul weather.

A parallel sequence at the heart of the film occasions the most complex cue in the score yet. The set piece begins with our introduction to the U-boat and its crew which is initially backed by musical silence; notwithstanding this, the high-pitched noise of the submarine's engines sounds like an unsettling, discordant tone cluster, holding a steady pedal whine. As it closes in on the unsuspecting lifeboat the U-boat is rendered menacing through more conventional means via a passage in B minor with the orchestra's lower *tessitura* dominant, if augmented by some gnomic, chromatic writing for upper woodwind. As we move above to its quarry the tone palette lightens, strings joining in a higher register mirroring not just our upwards progress from the ocean depths to the surface but investing the British sailors with a lighter, less menacing musical backdrop. The tension is maintained, however, with a metronomic octave *ostinato* on harp, the retention of the chromatic flavour and a building, upwards harmonic drift. As we move briefly back to the U-boat the tension is cranked up quickly via a simultaneous *crescendo* and *accelerando*.

The two strands of this parallel sequence, the lifeboat and the U-boat, are joined by a third as the music crests on a shot of the prow of a rescue vessel racing to the scene. From here the music loses a little of its insistence, becoming slower and quieter but no less chromatic, the harp *ostinato* replaced by another on violas, an eight note pattern that cycles on through downward modulations of a semitone at a time. Thus, the music subtly raises and lowers the tension in the scene. In addition, Parker's score is timed as impeccably as any feature film's: a return to the rescue vessel is accented musically once again; a brief close up of the *Jason*'s ship's boy's Saint Christopher's medal is marked by a major key chord, allowing hope and certainty to radiate from it; a move back to the U-boat is underscored with sudden, menacing chords on lower brass. The build to the climax of the sequence is achieved through the introduction of a booming timpani pedal, anxious, ascending figures on violins and an orchestral *ostinato* featuring another sudden escalation of tempo. The whole reaches an urgent climax, with a *rallentando* of the *ostinato* balancing the previous cranking up of the pace, the music ending on a 'hard out' as the rescuers are spotted by the lifeboat.

The sequence's music, then, has several functions, uniting the various strands of the parallel narrative and easing the potentially jarring cross-cutting, building and slackening tension, marking certain moments as significant and, ultimately, sculpting the dramatic climax of the sequence. After this moment musical silence descends again, as is customary in the film, allowing the men to discuss their next move in an extended dialogue scene.

The torpedoing of the rescue ship by the U-boat utilises a convention of fictional war movie scores: the silent attack. It is quite common for climactic battle sequences to be left, initially at least, unscored, thus allowing the sounds of battle to take over. The explosions, gunshots, cries and so on become fetishised in major combat scenes in war movies from *The Sands of Iwo Jima* (1945) through to *Saving Private Ryan* (1998), and rush in to dominate the soundtrack in the absence of music and sustained dialogue. A sense of immediacy is garnered by presenting important combat scenes without the mediating effect of a score behind them positioning the viewer in relation to the action and in effect sign-posting the progression of the sequence. Music after all is organised, structured and planned; the sounds of battle, in contrast, are chaotic, random and visceral. *Western Approaches* adopts this tactic at its first combat scene, the roar of the torpedo's impact and the howl of the ship's sirens to the fore in the mix, contrasting dramatically with the clinical, silent passage of the torpedoes through the water.

The retaliation sequence that follows is likewise musically silent, eventually the sounds of the machine guns, their bullets zipping through the air and ricocheting off metal provide all the accompaniment necessary. Here, there is no music to glue the various strands of the narrative together, the rescue vessel, the U-boat and the lifeboat, and the film moves from one to the next in a seemingly spontaneous way, a technique made all the more effective by its contrasting with the extensively scored parallel sequence that preceded it. The effect is to bring an extraordinary sense of actuality to bear on these scenes: one has the feeling that anything might happen. The decision to leave the music out here, and it must have been a conscious decision to allow one of the film's most dramatic reels to stand alone without the aid of scoring, pays off, in the context of the extensively backed surrounding sections, grandly.

When music returns it is to signal the British victory. The orchestra rejoins in sprightly, major key mode, strings and woodwind playing a folk-like melody over heraldic brass fanfares, characterising Britain as timeless and proud. As those on board the lifeboat are rescued by the larger ship, the melody from the opening title returns, this time affirmative and not compromised by any sense of discord. The rescue complete, we are returned to the C major of the opening bars of the score for a concluding flourish.

Without being an exceptional work, Parker's score is a tightly organised and effective one. As we've seen, for large sections it moves just like an orthodox fiction film score, shaping and grading the tension in scenes, providing continuity in terms of recurring thematic material, instrumental combinations and tonal centres. It smoothes the editing process and amplifies the emotional content and overall mood of the images it accompanies. It even echoes conventional war movie scores through its use of musical silence underlying key combat scenes. An interesting feature, however, is the paradox whereby the extensive, staged dialogue scenes are left unscored, like a documentary, while much of the actuality footage is backed with full orchestral accompaniment. What is in no doubt, however, is that the professionalism and logical organisation of the score, overseen as they were by Mathieson, contribute greatly to our experience of the film.

Filmography

Brief Encounter, David Lean (Eagle-Lion/Cineguild), UK, 1945

In Which We Serve, Noël Coward (Rank/Two Cities), UK, 1942

Night Mail, Basil Wright/Harry Watt (GPO Film Unit), UK, 1936

Sands of Iwo Jima, The, Allan Dwan (Republic), US, 1945

Saving Private Ryan, Steven Spielberg (Paramount/Amblin/Mutual), US, 1998

Western Approaches, Pat Jackson (The Crown Film Unit), UK, 1944

Brief Encounter

(1945)

Director: David Lean
Music: Sergei Rachmaninov
Music Director: Muir Mathieson
Production Companies: Cineguild/GCF/Rank, UK

Featuring a score constructed from what an artist might term 'found' materials, *Brief Encounter* (1945) presents an opportunity for us to discern where and when David Lean and Muir Mathieson have decided music is necessary as well as for what purpose. The movie is scored using a series of fragments drawn from Rachmaninov's Second Piano Concerto and assembled, collage-style and out of sequence, according to the needs of the film's narrative, radically altering the form of the original composition. The effect, however, is electrifying, presenting the music not so much out of context as framing it within a new one. While the film charts the story of two middle aged Britons struggling to contain their emotions, the effusive passion of Rachmaninov's music enunciates perfectly the feelings largely suppressed by the principal characters and serves as a marker of the extraordinary in a film conceived as a story of two ordinary people.

As the movie begins with a dramatic low angle shot of a somewhat Freudian steam engine powering through a provincial railway station at full tilt, a train whistle blows before being drowned out by the thrum of iron wheels on rails. These sounds are in turn subsumed by the opening broken piano chords of Rachmaninov's work, equally loud, equally dramatic. The mundane (an express train pointedly not stopping at a provincial station, progressing unhindered from one more important place to another) is translated into the epic visually through dynamic framing and aurally by being placed alongside the dramatic grandeur of Rachmaninov's opening. This tension between the ordinary and the extraordinary is one that animates much of what follows.

The music develops, the soloist giving way to unison strings playing a lyrical, longline melody over deep, urgent piano arpeggios. As this passage builds to a climax, another whistling express drowns out the music in turn as rail noise fills our ears once more and we cut to a shot of Albert the station guard (Stanley Holloway) checking his watch by its progress. Time will become important to the lovers in this film, and the flowing Rachmaninov, which can be thought of as a timeless work of art, is contrasted with the rigid regularity of a world rejoicing in the clockwork governance of the timetable. The figure of the guard is an important one in this context, for just as the Rachmaninov replaces the roar of the express, at the end of the title sequence Albert's cheery whistle will replace the sound of the train as the movie proper begins: musically we have moved from the formality of the concert hall to the informality of a cheerful whistle, from the extraordinary to the everyday.

This opening title cue fulfils many of the functions one would expect of it. It promises excitement and drama through its grandly chorded opening and the urgency of the subsequent melody and accompaniment. It also locates us firmly within the genre of romantic melodrama, the combination of piano and strings being a frequent one used to underscore narratives tracing affairs of the heart from Daniele Amfitheatrof's score for *Letter from an Unknown Woman* (1948) through to Michael Nyman's remarkable music for *The Piano* (1993). As we've seen, the use of Rachmaninov's music also flags up an important thematic concern that will run throughout the film with its juxtaposition of the prosaic and the poetic.

But this opening sequence does more even than this. After all, we move from the prosaic sound world of the opening sound effects and through the rarefied passage of hyper-emotional music before finishing up once more back in the world of rail noise. The heroine of the film, Laura (Celia Johnson), will experience just such a progression in the narrative that follows, finding herself plucked from the world of the everyday and dropped into a new world of romantic passion, only to be returned to the old order of her life at the close. Finally, the use of classical music (Eileen Joyce soloing with the National Symphony Orchestra, no less) marks the movie out as being of cultural quality and artistic merit, an important consideration given the remarkably frank and sympathetic portrayal of adultery that is to follow. Laura may speak of feeling 'cheap' after her botched assignation with Alec (Trevor Howard) in Steven's flat, but the music helps elevate the nature of her feelings and their relationship in a crucial way. The movie is not yet two minutes old and already the filmmakers have laid its heart bare.

From here the film progresses in musical silence for nearly six minutes. Throughout the dialogue scenes that follow in the station café the soundtrack is filled with the noises of railway life: squealing brakes, train whistles, guards' whistles, ringing bells, puffing engines and so on. These everyday sounds culminate in the crescendo of an approaching express whistle that will eventually return to mark Lean's magnificent canting of camera angle and Laura's destabilised flight from Dolly as the scene is reprised at the end of the movie. As a sound world these effects, musical as many of them are in a Cageian way, are the antithesis of the Romantic piano concerto they will vie with throughout the movie to come.

The first music cue of the film proper suggests that the Rachmaninov is closely allied with Laura's inner world and again exists in opposition to the external world around her. Dolly has accompanied her onto the train and chatters on maddeningly. The camera begins a slow track in on Laura, drawing us close to her, preparing us for her internal monologue which begins a moment after the music enters with a gently melancholy chromatic French horn figure and softly supportive woodwind. This music, then, is Laura's and matches her mood. It allows us entry into her mental and emotional world, providing information about her thoughts and feelings as rich and telling as the voiceover we hear. If Laura takes the audience into her confidence at this moment, the music eases this passage from outer world to inner psyche – another thematic idea keenly pursued by the film.

As Dolly snaps Laura out of her reminiscence the music ends abruptly: we break from her inner reflections and we break from the music. Reinforcing the relationship between the music and Laura's inner world, as she drifts off again, willing Dolly to shut up, the self-same French horn cue repeats. As Dolly's interminable gossip reasserts itself in the sound mix the music disappears yet again, this process recurring for Laura's longer reflection ending with the train's arrival at Ketchworth. This time we hear another, more extended passage scored for piano, strings and woodwind: as we move deeper into Laura's psyche and closer to the nub of what is troubling her the music responds commensurately by becoming more complex. The score is used initially, therefore, to demarcate Laura's internal thoughts and feelings amidst the banality of the outside world but it also reveals this inner world to be a resonant and complex emotional space.

The Rachmaninov makes its next entrance as a piece of diegetic music. Laura switches the wireless on in her living room as her husband, Fred, mulls over a crossword. The flowing lyricism of the music contrasts with the mundane ordering of words within Fred's grid and with Laura's sewing, and she arrives at the piano concerto out of choice, twiddling the knobs through a couple of bursts of big band music and a talk show before settling on the Third Programme. This is the most extended and foregrounded piece of music since the opening title, and it returns us to its melodic world. Our move to Laura's voiceover, however, is supported with a reprise of the French horn figure that was used before on the train, returning the concerto to its non-diegetic status, this time augmented with a development section extending the tune over expectant, *tremolo* strings. Again, we feel that we are moving closer to Laura and deeper into her mind as the music progresses.

If the music provides a bridge for us leading deep into Laura's thoughts, it also provides a bridge to the past as it continues under a complex series of dissolves moving us gradually from the living room in the present to the refreshment room at Milford station in the past as Alec walks into Laura's life, its tones sneaking out unobtrusively as we get our first look at him. It next returns again ushering in Laura's voiceover as she continues imagining talking Fred through her reminiscence after Alec has removed the fateful grit from her eye. As the flashback continues, jumping forward a week, the music again provides sonic glue to join the scenes together smoothly, helping elide the temporal shift in the narrative.

When we see Laura shopping in Boots the Chemist for the first time her voiceover is allowed to continue without the support of the music. Tellingly, she confines her descriptions now to the prosaic minutiae of her actions there: here we see Laura in her mundane world, buying toothbrushes and taking out library books, not reflecting on a grand passion. There is no place for Rachmaninov here; indeed the piano music we eventually hear comes from a barrel organ in the street playing 'Let the Great Big World Keep Turning', its tinny sound and popular melody contrasting with the rich, lush tones of the Rachmaninov in Laura's mind. Compounding this, we then have a comic interlude featuring the over-baked playing of an amateur piano trio as Laura and Alec enjoy their first impromptu lunch together; the bespectacled cellist is subsequently discovered moonlighting as a cinema organist as the couple go to the movies together. If this wurlitzer music, the barrel organ's and the trio's are typed as prosaic, equally unappealing is the musical hyperbole accompanying the trailers and adverts in the cinema: the beginning of Laura and Alec's relationship is deliberately surrounded with light music, music apparently lacking the high culture lustre and emotional depth of the Rachmaninov. The Rachmaninov returns, however, to mark the moment when Laura begins to fall consciously for Alec, as he discusses diseases of the lung in the station café. The return to the art music signals a significant shift in the nature of their relationship, the source of the sad travails that will follow from this moment. The Rachmaninov, then, is not only the music of Laura and a soundtrack for her affair, but a music of melancholy and trouble, of emotional suffering. The look of startled realisation on Laura's face as it enters here makes this abundantly clear.

From here the cue formalises another important use of music in the film: to make plain the true feelings lying beneath the surface actions and reactions of the characters. Laura and Alec fall in love at the same moment, and even although Alec's dialogue amounts to a catalogue of names of lung complaints the mounting piano and strings playing in the background lets us in on the emotional charge of what is truly passing between the couple. This conversation may have started as a polite enquiry about Alec's job, but the music makes plain that the ground has shifted between them. This time the music sneaks out not as Laura is interrupted in her dreaming, but as she makes a vain attempt to push Alec back down into being a mere acquaintance: he asks repeatedly to see her again and she demurs in a brittle, British fashion. This time she has choked off the flow of the feelings, and the music, between them. The everyday sounds of the station rush in to occupy the space left by the absence of the music.

But then, as Alec insists and Laura suddenly relents and consents to another meeting, the solo piano returns energetically, sounding chords, arpeggios and octaved melody, banking the notes higher and higher, joined ultimately by strings when she leaves the refreshment room to wave him goodbye as his train departs. Here the music mirrors the sudden bursting of hope and light into Laura's life, her mounting excitement, her abandonment to her feelings. When Alec's train is no longer visible her face falls and her voiceover begins to qualify and problematise her response to him; the music moves with her mood once more, the piano losing its strings, losing energy, becoming more reflective and circumspect, its bounding arpeggios becoming subdued then disappearing, its melody played in a quieter, more introspective way before fracturing into a series of scalar chromatic figures, all lyricism lost. The transition is hugely effective, right down to the dolorous, pacing orchestral chords that play as Laura walks off. As a feeling of danger sweeps over her, the music is subsumed by the hissing steam of her arriving train and she is broken out of her reverie.

Musical silence then accompanies the scenes that follow as Laura nurses her son, who has been knocked down by a car, and even confesses her meeting with Alec to an unconcerned Fred. This silence is somewhat unusual as both events could be read as dramatic ones: the injury of her child as if in punishment for her thoughts of infidelity; her confessing all to her husband. The absence of music, however, doesn't simply mark them as peripheral to the real action of the movie, Laura's developing relationship with Alec, for, as we shall see, key moments in the film will play out to a similar musical silence on the soundtrack. In effect, these unscored passages work to de-romanticise what Laura is doing; the music isn't there to carry us off to places we ought not to go and we witness these important moments without the mediation of music. Ultimately, perhaps, the Rachmaninov is there to be resisted, like intimacy itself.

The Rachmaninov next returns as she waits forlornly for Alec in the refreshment room (we have revisited the ladies' trio at lunch who now appear mirthless and sad without the boyish, fun-inducing catalyst of his presence). The Puckish woodwind create a sense of expectancy as she gives up her wait, however: we know a positive development is around the corner as the score has not sounded a melancholy note. Then, as Alec appears running up the slope of the subway, the piano underlines his progress with a dynamic upwards progression of notes that also suggests an upsurge in emotion from Laura as she sees him. The orchestra sounds *tutti* as she gets him onto his train and they make a date for the next Thursday. The sweeping urgency of the music, as with the sudden urgency of their feelings, has brushed aside all thoughts of a retreat from intimacy. We have been carried away by the music as they have been by their passion.

The music then acts again as a bridge through time, easing the transition to a week later and the couple's second visit to the cinema. Rachmaninov suffuses every frame of their outing to the boating pond, coming to a comic halt as Alec crashes their boat into a bridge. Then, as with Laura's confession to Fred, her and Alec's candid admission of being in love with one another in the boatkeeper's lodge plays out to musical silence, as does their first kiss in the station subway. It is only after they break from this clinch that the music comes in again, a *fortissimo, tutti* passage that acts as another bridge out of the flashback and back to the film's present. The concerto is once again diegetic, emanating from the wireless, and its ardour is remarked upon by Fred who asks for it to be turned down in a good-natured way. Then, as the piano rhapsodises over soft strings, Laura drifts back off into another flashback, the music acting as a bridge into the past once more.

As we discover Laura on the train home after her kiss with Alec, the score is up-beat and jolly, dancing quavers and semi-quavers on piano answered by light strings, amplifying the happiness she recounts in her voiceover. From nowhere, the music then segues into a waltz (not Rachmaninov) as she imagines herself and Alec dancing the night away and we hear the sounds of an orchestra tuning up at the opera, then of Italianate mandolins as she imagines floating with Alex in a gondola in Venice. At the close of this fantasy sequence the Rachmaninov returns only to be replaced by the sound of the train wheels on the track as Laura comes back to reality. Just as three alternative musics, the barrel organ, the trio, the film music, interrupted the flow of the Rachmaninov at the start of their relationship, this escape from reality of Laura's is also punctuated with three alternative musical styles. This symmetry helps unify the film, and momentarily clears the aural palate of the piano concerto. The passage also marks her flights of fancy as 'silly', which is how she describes them herself: the waltz, the tuning up and the mandolins lack the gravity of the Rachmaninov.

After Laura tells her first lie to Fred about her actions with Alec in town, piano arpeggios play, deep and foreboding as she regards herself in her dressing table mirror, and are answered by low woodwind and *agitato* cellos. If the music soared upwards when Alec ran towards her through the station subway, as she puts the phone down after filling a friend in on her deceit the music progresses downwards, suggesting a dampening of spirits, a descent into something darker, something troubling. Again, the music becomes a bridge leading forward to the next section of the flashback via a recap of the melancholy French horn motif that ushered in Laura's first reflections at the start of the movie, unifying the score once more. The subsequent montage sequence depicting their drive in the country is also held together by the score, a quite conventional function of film music. The tone of this cue is not as happy as it might be, however, not as sprightly as the Rachmaninov that hopped and skipped merrily earlier before her fantasy dreaming on the train. The music swells as they kiss on the bridge, acting as an index of their rising passions, before dying down again as they arrive back at Steven Lynn's flat and fading out as they return to the station. Their kiss here is played out not to a crescendo of the Rachmaninov but a swelling express train whistle, and we are returned momentarily to the Freudian imagery of the opening title as we see the express thunder through.

As Laura arrives back at Steven's flat, having decided to take Alec up on his implicit offer of consummating their relationship there, the music returns in an upward-banking, arpeggiated cue for piano and strings building tension and passion. If Laura's lie to Fred was accompanied by a descending passage, here we find her in the grip of an ascending one, an aural motion underlined by the visuals which show her climbing a flight of stairs, the camera booming up with her as she goes. The music cuts out abruptly as Alec opens the door to her. Again, an important watershed in their relationship plays out to musical silence. This time they kiss and are disturbed by Steven's return, and at no point does music enter here to enhance the emotive aspects of the scene or create suspense regarding their discovery. Later, they will agree to begin winding up their relationship to another musical silence.

The Rachmaninov comes crashing back in with a virtuoso passage for piano and full orchestra as we shift focus to Laura fleeing Steven's flat through a rainstorm. The storm of arpeggios and trills mirrors the storm of rain that in turn matches the storm of conflicting passions and emotions surging through Laura. Her aimless nocturnal wandering though Milford is accompanied by more circumspect piano apreggios, the urgency of the initial flight now past and the rainstorm spent. A melancholy feel is thereby allowed to inflect the score again, a mood continued in the cue underscoring their arranging of their final date and Alec's confession of his imminent emigration to South Africa. Here, limpid *pizzicato* strings accompany a lyrical piano melody as he puts her on the last train home. As the train pulls away the music modulates from major to minor, underlining the shift in mood, before carrying on as a bridge to the following week and their final day together as Laura's reminiscence draws to a close. Again their drive in the country is presented as a montage sequence backed with the Rachmaninov, which this time is allowed to continue through to their final return to the train station. It continues gently under their final conversation, the beauty of the melodic line and grace of instrumentation suggesting the beauty and nobility of the feelings they harbour for one another despite the self-professed 'vulgarity' of their situation. Dolly's annoying arrival, bringing the film full circle, occasions the music to drop out of the mix altogether. The everyday noises of the station fill the soundtrack as before, the music having left Laura's life.

The final cue returns us safely from Laura's flashback into her present, the final swelling bars of Rachmaninov, safely contained by the wireless now and no longer raging spontaneously in her head, concluding over a chaste embrace with her husband. The dream, like the concerto, is over.

In *Brief Encounter*, then, Lean and Mathieson use the 'found' music of Rachmaninov in a variety of ways, moulding the pre-existing material in such a deft and effective way that if one wasn't aware of the score's provenance one might easily assume it had been an original commission. The music is used not just to amplify the mood of a given scene but aims to offer a conduit into the inner world of the film's protagonist. It also smoothes temporal transitions in the film, not just during montage sequences but during ellipses in the flashback narrative. It locates the film firmly within the sound world of romantic melodrama through its use of piano, strings and lyrical, longline melody. Finally, for all the passion, both emotional and sexual, inherent within Rachmaninov's neo-Romantic idiom, the high culture, art music status of the score works to assure the audience that it is witnessing something more than an account of petty adultery, that the passions on display are as grand and rarefied as the music that engenders and accompanies them.

Filmography

Letter from an Unknown Woman, Max Ophuls (Universal), US, 1948

The Piano, Jane Campion (Entertainment/Ciby 2000), Australia, 1993

Hamlet

(1948)

Director: Laurence Olivier
Composer: William Walton
Music Director/Conductor: Muir Mathieson
Production Company: Rank, UK

If Walton's score for *Henry V* (1944) time-shifted between idioms past and present, his music for Laurence Olivier's riveting, horrific reading of *Hamlet* (1948) chooses to organise itself around a key thematic strand animating Shakespeare's play: doubt and equivocation as opposed to action and directness. Walton signals doubt where it appears in the text by creating music that is either subtly or highly chromatic in nature, while certainty and strength are connoted through the use of more straightforward diatonic harmony. Beyond the odd diegetic pageant, dance number or imperial fanfare little attempt is made through the music to reinforce a sense of historical period. The majority of the score is written in either the late Romantic or Modernist idiom, for reasons that become clear if we briefly pause to examine what is meant by these terms.

The Nineteenth Century Romantics had been concerned, amongst other things, with the expression of the internal thoughts and emotions of the individual and, thereby, produced music of an increasingly psychologically complex nature. As the century wore on, and particularly after the contribution of Wagner, their reliance on the melodic forms, harmonies and chord progressions of simple diatonic harmony (Doh-Re-Me-Fah-Sol-Lah-Te-Doh and all the conventions attending this) became less sure, and by the turn of the century composers had moved away from simple scales of just eight notes, predominantly to a chromatic style whereby all twelve tones encompassed by the octave became options for use. In the first part of the Twentieth Century, some Modernist composers threw the old rule book out altogether by adopting atonal methods, where each of the twelve tones was endowed with equal harmonic weight: there was no longer a Doh to anchor the scale in a conventional sense of harmony. By the time atonal music appeared its first exponents, Schoenberg, Berg and Webern, were readily associated with the Expressionist movement, an artistic approach revelling in the laying bare of the complexities of the anguished mind. But the intensely chromatic approach of Richard Strauss in florid, sexual psychodramas like 'Salome', 'Electra' and the supremely neurotic 'Josephs Legende', and the equally fraught work of the psychologically troubled Alexander Scriabin, seemed equally suited to the musical exploration of the mind. With their musical roots still embedded in a recognisable sense of harmony, albeit one often pushed to the limits, these composers and others like them used all twelve notes of the scale to shift tonality in an incredibly mutable and, psychologically, highly responsive way, allowing each chord to create its own evocative nuances in the context of the others around it. Note by note, the impressions created by the music could develop and change. One thing chromaticism gave composers was a key tool for working out in music what Freud had been working out in psychoanalysis: the darker aspects of the human unconscious. Indeed, several of Strauss' earlier operatic narratives were quite self-consciously psychoanalytic in nature.

What better musical styles than these, then, could Walton use to unlock the secrets of the Prince of Denmark's troubled mind? He chooses to underscore this psychodrama with a markedly chromatic score, spiced with occasional passages of extreme dissonance and atonality. After the iconic Rank gong, he signals his intent instantly, beginning his score with the gentle harmonic chaos of the orchestra tuning up. This at once connotes a theatrical milieu (just as the Globe's musicians were heard tuning up towards the beginning of *Henry V*), creates a sense of anticipation with its associations with the beginning of classical concerts and signals a complex use of harmony, the music seeming fragmented and random though held together by the keystone tuning tone of A.

After a flourish capped with a cymbal crash, the title proper begins on loud *tutti* orchestra. It might not be overstating things to label this cue funereal due to its minor key tonality, slow pace and dark, brooding nature. While the music is written in an unequivocal E minor, and the melodic lines are basically diatonic in nature, Walton does introduce some unusual chord progressions lifting us momentarily away from these keys into a more chromatic harmonic world and requires the woodwind and upper strings to play stormy, scurrying chromatic figures in answer to the more forthright pronouncements of the brass. Indeed, after the opening melodic statement a contrasting second section traces a chromatic descent by semitones that is reprised later in the cue before it comes to a close with chromatic strings playing over a low, solid pedal E minor chord as tenebrous as the image of Elsinore atop its cliff. A minor key tonality laced with moments of chromaticism introduces us to the dark and troubled world of the film.

If, as Olivier's opening voice-over announces, this is 'the tragedy of a man who could not make up his mind', the ensuing music accompanying Bernardo as he walks the battlements cannot make up its mind what key it is in: we hear a succession of rapid, rising-falling figures on cellos and basses that are entirely chromatic in nature, moving quickly through series of semitone intervals. In the darkness and fog the sentries are thrown into confusion just as the music displays, apparently, a matching harmonic uncertainty.

This, however, is as nothing compared to the extraordinary cue fashioned for the appearance of the ghost of Hamlet's father.

Conventional notions of harmony are abandoned altogether for a sudden burst of extreme discord so radical that at first one is not sure whether it is the orchestra that's playing or a sound effect we are hearing. The 'chord' swells in a sudden and terrifying *crescendo,* beginning with a rumble of timpani that's swiftly joined by a high-pitched, discordant tone cluster on violins and the dislocated chime of an orchestral bell. The volume increases as percussion and brass grow another dramatic discord, the noise ending suddenly leaving only the fragmented, heartbeat-like sounding of a drum. Even the implication of this is unclear: are we hearing heartbeats or laboured footsteps? Is it even the pounding of blood in the temples? It's a moment at once frightening and disorientating, a sudden intrusion of the harmonically chaotic into the world of the film. The ghost, the agent precipitating Hamlet's descent into doubt and uncertainty, appears to music with neither traditional harmonic logic nor order, and as the scene progresses Walton astonishes further. As Horatio speaks to the ghost, cellos bend and slide pitch in a series of seemingly random *glissandi* over multi-layered discords on brass and woodwind. While the music is no longer as close to being atonal as before, upper strings sweep in with furious chromatically scalar figures. These are orchestral effects one would expect to find emanating from the pen of Jerry Goldsmith in a horror film from the 1960s-70s; Roy Webb's score for the roughly contemporaneous and rightly celebrated *The Body Snatcher* (1945), in terms of both harmony and use of orchestral texture, seems pedestrian in comparison. Walton, like future generations of film composers, is harnessing the musical language of the avant-garde to convey the extremity of horror: fragmentation, atonality, tone clusters, pitch slides. It is a bold and effective move, and the music of these two spectral cues would not be out of place in a horror movie today. And, after all, key to the feel of Olivier's adaptation is, surely, the conception of the piece as horror film as much as tragedy: this is on one level at least a haunted house story.

As we begin to move down labyrinthine stairways into the heart of the castle, gentle strings play an abstract, descending passage not far removed from the introverted, chromatic string writing of Bartok. In comparison with what has gone before the impression created is a gentle one, but, through the use of chromaticism, the harmonic palette remains disturbing. This troubling statement reaches some sort of resolution as a more Impressionistic idea enters with a solo oboe playing a pastoral, Debussyesque melody: this will become Ophelia's theme, and it enters here as the camera settles on the archway that leads to her living quarters in the castle. As we are taken to the court of Claudius the transition from chromaticism to diatonic harmony is completed as a plain, bold fanfare sounds above the meeting chamber. Here there is no doubt, only strength and power, and as Olivier has taken us on an odyssey through the passageways and windows of the castle, so Walton has led us from complex chromaticism to simple triadic harmony via the stepping stone of Impressionism. The shining confidence of the fanfares that bristle around Claudius' entrances, proclamations and exits acts as a polar opposite to the swelling brass cacophony that underscored the appearance of the ghost of the man he murdered.

Indeed, as the camera booms down and in on Hamlet left alone in the court room, Claudius, Hamlet's mother and the courtiers having departed through the sheen of another trebly fanfare, we draw closer to the prince psychologically as well as spatially through a contrasting low, mellow chromatic descent on brooding cellos. The move closer to Hamlet occasions harmonic doubt to enter the score once more and as other string lines join in equally chromatic counterpoint the sound world reverts to that of Bartok for the first soliloquy. This is music that seems cerebral rather than emotional in its angularity, perfect for our first glimpse into the mind of the antihero, an ascetic musical response to a speech that problematises the corrupting forces of sensuality's 'incestuous sheets'.

Laertes' farewell to Ophelia brings us back to the pastoral, Impressionistic oboe and strings: Ophelia is yet to be complicated by the narrative. However, as Laertes asks that she keep in touch with him in France, she replies: 'Do you doubt that?' On mention of the concept of doubt the music halts, tellingly and abruptly. That Ophelia is destined to become a victim of Hamlet's doubt and indecision is indicated shortly after as Polonius forbids her to think more on the Prince. Here, the music that creeps in has already become chromatic, albeit more Wagnerian in its chromaticism than in the Bartokian style of Hamlet's soliloquy. Again the solo oboe has a key part to play, sounding a piquant, yearning figure over gently throbbing strings. Ophelia's pastoral idyll has been compromised already.

When Hamlet sends Horatio away, having been informed of the appearance of his father's ghost and becoming resolved to watch for it that night, his brief soliloquy is at first accompanied by deep, brooding lines on lone cellos and basses revolving around the progression F#-G-G#, a sequence of three semitone intervals by definition chromatic in nature. The repetition of this pattern speeds up and upper strings respond with the equally chromatic figure F-F#-D. Uncertain discords play gently on brass, violins continuing to worry away at their three-note motif, a clarinet effecting the transition between the darkened court room and the castle atop its rocks at night with a rising, chromatic scale that's backed by a soft-stick cymbal *crescendo* and answered by *forte* violins playing two chromatic lines in a disconcerting contrary motion, a harp picking out a dissonant chord in its upper register. From here, beneath the dialogue on top of the platform at midnight, the upper strings continue to play chilly-sounding chromatic lines in a quiet contrary motion, finishing off rocking gently back and forth on a *tremolo* rising and falling by semitones. While this deeply chromatic music introduces Hamlet's vigil, Claudius' carousing below is suddenly announced by the simple triadic harmonies of a fanfare and sprightly courtly dance: the contrast between these two worlds could not be made plainer by the composer.

In turn, this makes the nebulous, discordant cue announcing the reappearance of the ghost of Hamlet's father even more spine tingling. As before, clumping, heartbeat-like percussion starts up and a high pitched tone cluster on violins sounds long. Replacing the undulating cello *glissandi* we find, this time, pitch bends on echoed female voices, vocalising and wordless. The brass swell in a sudden, discordant blare as Hamlet recoils and the spirit appears, leaving only the heartbeat or footstep sound behind. The pitchlessness of this gesture, unlike, say, the repeated, tuned stroking of timpani, fails to ground even the end of the cue in a sense of conventional harmony.

As Hamlet follows the beckoning ghost, dark chords well up in the brass and the strings play skin-crawling chromatic lines around them, runs traversing from cellos to violins. Walton repeats the chords and the scurrying over and over, a gradual *crescendo* increasing the urgency of the cue until woodwind join in with the strings in their frantic chromaticism. Hamlet's confrontation with the spectre occasions a sudden return to the loud, discordant ghost music. From the carousing scene on, the three main idioms of the score, diatonic harmony (Claudius), chromaticism (Hamlet) and bruitistic atonality (the spectre), are laid side by side, their associations made plain.

The flashback to Claudius' poisoning of Hamlet's father in the orchard is scored for unsettling *tremolo* strings that move in semitone steps, their chromaticism drifting up and down, suggestive of the billowing of the fog surrounding Hamlet's vision. Again, contrary motion organises the chromatic lines, cellos moving up if violins move down. There is no melody here: all is instrumental texture, the mirror image contrary motion providing a fearful symmetry, the gentle swelling and falling of the *tremolo*'s dynamic seeming to shade, psychologically, every moment of the scene. As the vision ends, so does the cue. Here, the chromaticism has worked to give an unearthly feel, the contrary motion pulling towards and moving away from an unheard centre of musical gravity. The retreat of the spirit is scored for another chromatic sequence of brass chords, manic semitone runs on violins and upper woodwind and the return of the heartbeat percussion and loud brass discords: the ghost's and Hamlet's music are thus brought together in the same cue. The whole is capped with a macabre strike on gong as Hamlet collapses to the ground. As he and his friends swear an oath of secrecy, the discordant brass blast and heartbeat, which we can now identify as a *leitmotif* for the ghost, reappears as Hamlet hears his father's voice again.

The music bridge that takes us from here to Ophelia's soliloquy takes the form of another passage of vague, unsettling chromaticism, flutes moving in uneasy triplets over tremolo strings and a solo, mid-register trumpet repeating the semitone interval G-F#. As she speaks of Hamlet's approaching her, doublet unlaced, unison violins play a minor key melody beneath her words. This cue makes us aware of how so much of what we have heard before is *lacking* in melody, and also contrasts the melancholy of this theme with the pastoral oboe that played in happier days for Ophelia before. However, as she describes Hamlet's strange behaviour towards her the tune loses its accompaniment and becomes steadily more chromatic, less defined melodically, the violins moving into an uncomfortable upper *tessitura,* at one point providing a pitch slide that threatens to go beyond mere *portamento* into something more unsettling. As we return to the close up of Ophelia reflecting on this flashback, the full orchestra enters once more in the highly chromatic style of the music bridge from before, disconcerting now, bordering on discord. Clearly, Ophelia is being sucked into the same strange harmonic place that Hamlet occupies in the score. That in the film's next breath Polonius pronounces Hamlet mad seems to tie this music in with insanity.

As Polonius and Claudius set up Hamlet's meeting with Ophelia to test his mental state further, the pastoral oboe melody of before sounds as she walks forward through a poetic dissolve, although this time the string background is not as relaxed as when we first discovered her with Laertes, rather continuing with the melancholy feel behind the beginning of her previous soliloquy. The frailty of the oboe seems to underline the innocence of the white gown she wears. Building up to Hamlet's appearance, the violins rise, as they did in her dream, into an uncomfortably high register and finish on a harmonically unresolved fourth. At the scene's close, as the camera pulls away from Ophelia lying crying at the bottom of a huge staircase, dark chromatic strings enter once more and as the camera progresses through the shadowy passages of the castle this mood is developed further as lower woodwind join in, *tremolo* strings below. In a bravura piece of miniature model shooting, the camera begins a dizzying ascent through Elsinore up to the battlements, violins and upper woodwind providing the now customary fast chromatic runs of the 'castle' music.

This provides the prelude to the 'To be or not to be' soliloquy, which is entered into via a loud and stormy passage for full orchestra where the writing once more is chromatic, though now also tempestuous. Over a pedal F#, trombones intone a series of martial chords backed by snare drum, strings play a series of racing, upward chromatic runs in answer and the whole swells to a noisy climax ending with a vertiginous downward run on woodwind and strings backed with savage brass trills as the camera appears to penetrate the head of the Prince. The only break from the profoundly chromatic styling of this cue is a brief, tantalising Impressionistic interlude that occurs as the camera settles briefly on the heavens above the castle; all else is anxious, edgy in the extreme, indeed quite violent-sounding.

Gentler strings play as the monologue shifts to an internal one, returning us to the Bartokian sound world, violins playing a series of highly chromatic figures (F-F#-E, for example), the cello and bass accompaniment moving downwards by falling semitones. A sudden *sforzando* trill on full orchestra alarms us in the middle of this hypnotic progression ('To die, to sleep . . .'). It sounds as the screen is filled with an extreme close up of Hamlet's forehead, and gives us a vivid musical taste of the hysterical state of the mind within it. The harmonically uncertain interval of the semitone is key to this cue, and the very essence of chromaticism.

A sombre, abstract line for basses takes us from this scene to the next, where Polonius disturbs Hamlet in a darkened room, the old man preceded by a skeletal *glissando* on xylophone. With the company of players he ushers in the musical idiom changes to diatonic harmony as a diegetic dance tune plays, lightening the mood of Hamlet as well as the film. Chromaticism has left, momentarily, and Hamlet can welcome the players with genuine warmth. Once Hamlet has asked the lead player to insert some apposite new lines into 'The Murder of Gonzago', he experiences a sudden rush at having moved beyond thinking into action against Claudius for the first time: the music Walton provides moves from a happy period cue for the diegetic musicians, regarded with a somewhat melancholy detachment by the Prince, through into the non-diegetic orchestra where, after a brief chromatic passage, the music that breaks out is both positive and positively diatonic in nature as Hamlet is given a fanfare of his own. His equivocation temporarily over, the harmonic palette of the score straightens out accordingly and the film's music of power and strength is given over to him.

Hamlet's rehearsal of the play itself returns us to the orchestra tuning up that we heard at the start of the film. Claudius' entrance in turn returns the positivity of the fanfare to himself, no fewer than six buglers grandly announcing his arrival, the procession of the king and queen proceeding to the pomp of the theatre musicians' rendition of a florid, period-sounding piece. The dumbshow re-enactment of the murder in the orchard is accompanied, nominally, by these same on a variety of period aerophones and a lute, with some sparse string backing. This period feel is complicated a little by the intrusion of some anachronistic *sul ponticello tremolo* work on cello for the approach of the murderous 'Claudius', and after this the music crosses over to the non-diegetic orchestra where strings pick up a dark *tremolo* and the skeletal xylophone sounds again over

Claudius' recognition of the scene before him: Walton moves effortlessly into full-on chromatic mode once more. As the dumbshow continues, the music is briefly given back to the diegetic musicians before becoming chromatic and non-diegetic again for 'Claudius'' wooing of the widowed queen. The troubling of Claudius' mind, and that of the court around him, has seen Hamlet's music, the deeply chromatic, given to him. Just as Hamlet was allowed briefly to bask in the glory of a fanfare of his own, so Claudius tastes here the music that normally follows Hamlet around. Claudius' storming out of the play is given music as swirling and tempestuous as that leading up to 'To be or not to be…', and, for the time being, it seems as if Hamlet has conclusively turned the tables on his stepfather. Indeed, the whole is crowned by a wild song of celebration from Hamlet himself (cf. his criticism of Claudius' penchant for songs and wassailing earlier in the film).

As if to underline this sudden shift in Hamlet's character, his next soliloquy, in which he decides to meet his mother and 'talk daggers' at her, is not backed with music at all. The former chromatic tones of doubt and darkness are absent, and the result is that his musings seem resolved and concrete, rather than troubling and self-limitingly circular. Sadly, Hamlet is soon after returned to his equivocal state as he passes Claudius, who is praying unawares, and Hamlet vacillates over whether to dispatch the scoundrel right away. The music that brings him on screen, and that plays under his soliloquy here, is as brooding and chromatic as ever: he is back at square one as *tremolo* strings descend by semitones and solo woodwind trace and transpose a recurring, chromatic motif (F-F#-E) handing it on to the other sections of the orchestra as the speech progresses. Hamlet's epiphany has been a short-lived one and he now finds himself as circumscribed by doubt and questioning as ever; Claudius, meanwhile, now thrown into a state of turmoil whereby he questions his murderous actions, loses the harmonic simplicity of his fanfares and dance music and remains in the chromatic realm accordingly.

This music spills over into Hamlet's approach to his mother's chamber, increasing in urgency as he nears it then sneaking out as their scene together begins. At the peak of Hamlet's fury he hallucinates the appearance of his father's ghost. Although the spirit itself is initially unseen by us we're made aware of its presence in Hamlet's mind by the music alone: its *leitmotif* sounds with the heartbeat percussion, pitch-bending vocalisations, high string tone cluster and savage brass *crescendo*. When at last we hear his father's disembodied voice, alongside the heartbeat muted strings describe swarming *glissandi* over a soft brass discord. The spirit leaves the room to a series of *fortissimo* brass discords, but the understated *piano* of the *glissandi* heard moments before is as frightening an orchestral device, if not more so.

As Claudius demands Hamlet leave for England instantly, and Hamlet questions the meaning of the words father and mother, over *tremolo* strings and a harp that descends by semitone intervals, a solo oboe repeats the now familiar chromatic motif of three semitones, here B-A-B flat, which is then augmented by cellos to B flat-B natural-A-B flat. As Claudius reveals the murderous ambitions he has for Hamlet's journey in soliloquy, violins play anxious figures with a chromaticism that spreads to the full orchestra.

The beginning of Ophelia's mad scene is scored for a chromatically nightmarish reconfiguration of the pastoral cue that played when we met her first: the oboe sounds plaintive and vulnerable over a complex *tremolo* string background, a harp playing bewildering arpeggios beneath chromatic clarinet and flute lines. The disarray of Ophelia's hair visually communicates her mental torment, but the warping of her original orchestration communicates her distress just as effectively. However, her innocence is underlined by the minor key folk-like lament she sings to Claudius and Gertrude, then to Laertes on his arrival and after her passing out of floral tokens: it seems that she has now passed beyond the chromatic world of the rest of the score and, in her folly, has been returned to a more simple diatonic harmony, albeit that of a minor hue. We last hear her singing her lament as she floats off to her drowning, a minor key rendition of the pastoral oboe theme playing below, and as a heavenly yet chromatic celesta plays ethereal tinkling sounds, we are reminded of Hamlet's earlier description of Ophelia's beauty as 'celestial'. As if in response to the pathos of Ophelia's lamenting, the gravedigger making her grave sings a cheerful folk song as he goes about his work.

After Hamlet's return from England, Claudius is thrown into a state of fear: as well as holding a legitimate claim to the throne, Hamlet threatens all Claudius has secured for himself through the affection in which he is held by Gertrude and the People. This state of fear is revealed by the soundtrack as much as anything else: as Claudius and Laertes plot revenge on Hamlet, rather than playing the diatonic music of control and action the orchestra enter with the chromatic figure B-B flat-G-F#, which is stretched out into a *piano* discord; this motif, transposed and finished with an extended semitone trill on clarinet, is repeated throughout the scene. Claudius is well and truly unsettled. When Hamlet and Horatio appear above, unawares, a 3:4 cue accompanies them quietly, a waltz made strange by its context and the spiky, chromatic melody lines that are passed from oboe to strings. The cue gives a quiet dynamism to the two characters, and the lightness of its rhythm and texture serves to separate them from the darker music given to Claudius and Laertes without diluting the chromatic atmosphere. By this device, in spite of the deaths and murders trailing in Hamlet's wake our sympathy is aligned with him rather than the plotters below. The allotting of chromatic music to Claudius' scheming also enables Walton to draw a further contrast between the poison of the king's interior mind and the brashly diatonic fanfares and processional music that announce his public arrival in the throne room for the duel as Hamlet and Horatio finish their discussion.

The actioning of each stage of Claudius' plan is accompanied by diatonic music. Claudius explicitly calls on the directness and energy of the 'kettledrum' and the 'trumpet' as he puts his plot into action by introducing the duel, whereupon the timpani and bugles roar back into action again. The duel itself gets underway accompanied by massed snare drums in a cue that is purely rhythmic. Claudius dropping the poisoned pearl into Hamlet's wine goblet is announced by another brash fanfare. All music here speaks of directness and the accomplishment of aim. It is, then, ironic that as the poison is drunk (the final stage in Claudius' plan) the music that plays is again diatonic, a poised, mid-paced theme on court orchestra: only, contrary to expectation, it is Gertrude who has drunk it. Claudius' plan has developed a life of its own, and the music carries on implacably, almost mockingly, in the background, refusing to respond to what we know has happened. The same, however, grinds to a scandalised halt as Laertes, in a most ungentlemanly fashion, cuts (and poisons) Hamlet with his foil in the next break between bouts.

As Laertes is in turn pierced by Hamlet, and Gertrude collapses under the effects of poison, the orchestra re-enter, violins playing an urgent tremolo motif on G#-G natural, reasserting a chromatic feel that pervades the entire denouement. When Hamlet ultimately acts and kills Claudius, it is all too late: the principals of the drama are either dead or dying. There is no sudden lifting of the music into a diatonic major to remind us of the grand flourish that underscored Hamlet's epiphany after the arrival of the players earlier in the movie. Here, rather, the chromaticism loses its customary brooding quality and becomes savage, the chromatic intervals far apart (G-G#', more than an octave away) as well as neighbouring (the more conventional semitone drop G#-G). Timpani pound violently over *tremolo* cellos. When the music threatens to evolve into the resolution of a conventional diatonic minor as Hamlet and Laertes make a final peace, Walton promptly reins this in and adds further chromatic twists to the writing both in terms of top line and accompaniment. He ends his score with a return to the funereal march theme that he began it with as Hamlet's body is carried from the court and up through the castle, ending, after a discordant and cacophonous series of fortissimo chords, on a simple and final cadence to E minor. The recapitulation of this cue adds an element of fatalism to the proceedings: the end of the drama was inevitable from the beginning.

The cold, alienated chromatic style of much of this score is not one we would immediately associate with Walton's concert work. We should not, however, be surprised that he could pull music like this out of the hat, given the success he enjoyed with the protean multiplicity of musical styles deployed in 'Façade'. In *Hamlet* he uses diatonic, chromatic and on occasion even atonal music to profound dramatic effect, his complex orchestral textures contributing much to the unique atmosphere of Olivier's production. Once more, this is a score that is logically developed and that complements the thematic ideas behind the film as a whole. This music isn't just an afterthought brought in to intensify the action: it is conceived of as a key part of the film's argument.

Filmography

Body Snatcher, The, Dir: Robert Wise, Mus: Ray Webb (RKO), USA, 1945

Hamlet, Dir: Laurence Olivier, Mus: Sir William Walton (Rank/Two Cities), UK, 1948

Henry V, Dir: Laurence Olivier, Mus: Sir William Walton (Two Cities) UK, 1944

Oliver Twist

(1948)

Director: David Lean
Composer: Arnold Bax
Conductor: Muir Mathieson
Production Companies: Cineguild/J Arthur Rank, UK

Although not structured around a clear narrative-thematic idea as Walton's music for *Henry V* (1944) and *Hamlet* (1948) seems to be, the score provided by Arnold Bax, the King's Master of Musick, for David Lean's strikingly cinematic adaptation of *Oliver Twist* (1948) is no less rigorous in its organisation. Bax appears to opt to write his score around forms more familiar from classical music (first subject, second subject, development and recapitulation), from an awareness of narrative symmetry and the considered, complementary repetition of effects and textures. As we shall see, Lean, Bax and Mathieson made some novel and highly effective decisions as to where music should play, when the orchestra should stay silent, and what sort of music should sound. If during chase sequences the cues composed by Bax are entirely conventional in nature, on several other occasions the music behaves quite differently from what we might expect, and a particularly brave decision was taken to leave the film's climactic scenes entirely unscored.

The form of the opening title is an unusual one. Rather than going for a hyperbolic, brassy flourish (epic! exciting! unmissable!), followed by an equally florid passage of music designed to crank up dramatic expectations still further, Bax opts for a more circumspect approach using an A-B-A structure where after the first theme a second, contrasting one is heard before the initial idea returns. Equally formalised is the symmetry of the cue's beginning and ending on the same note, played the same way. The strings enter on the first strike of the Rank gong with a quiet, suspense-building pedal *tremolo* C#, ambivalently hinting at neither major nor minor key. When the brass enter we find ourselves in an understated F# major. Over a continuation of the string pedal, trumpets, playing well within themselves, describe the motif that will shape much of the cue that follows: C#-C#-F#-G#-B-C#-F#'-F#'-E . . . This figure will crop up throughout the film as a *leitmotif* for Oliver's true lineage, being associated in particular with the locket that proves his mother's identity. Following this, and its relatively warm harmonic backing, for the appearance of the title of the film Bax shifts to a two-part violin line, chromatic and, for now, colder sounding in its parallel progression (A#-A#-B-A#-A natural-A#-F#'-D . . .). This soon, however, evolves into a more lyrical section for *divisi* violins then strings as a whole before the brass recapitulate the opening motif, though this time giving it a minor key cast. This move to a darker sound is underlined by a pacing, downward *pizzicato* that finishes with a return to the soft *tremolo* that opened the cue, only this time we are denied a cadence of harmonic resolution to F#: the note played by the violins is once again the ambivalent C#. Bax, then, has used his opening title to enunciate two contrasting themes, one initially warm and affirmative, the other more troubled and yearning, and to take us from major key to minor key. There is indeed something quasi-symphonic in the way the character of the opening motif has, by the time of its recapitulation, become modified by the nature of the second subject. The whole is neatly bookended by a quiet string *tremolo* on C#, and the absence of a repeat of the opening cadence to F# at the close leaves us hanging: there's more to come. Adding to this impression is our sense that both composer and orchestra have yet to fully extend themselves as any overt drama has been eschewed, with both the beginning and end of the cue notable for their lack of dynamic intensity. Indeed, David Lean's credit appears in complete silence, and is marked as special by this device. The idea of musical silence will return at the film's climax.

There then follows the arrival of the storm and Oliver's mother's progression through it to the workhouse. Again, the writing remains understated. Bax keeps the orchestra silent until an extreme close up of a thorny briar, where he has violins, split into two parallel parts as in the colder passage from the opening title, describe a F-A flat-F *crescendo-diminuendo* progression with chilling *portamento* slides. Again, Bax, Lean and Mathieson might have chosen to have a *tutti* orchestra blaring and crashing like thunder and lightning, but have opted not to follow the path of tempestuous excess. The economy of this simple rising and falling figure is astonishing; the sounds of the storm itself, the thunder, the wind, the rain, a lantern swinging madly in the gale, are allowed to take precedence giving a sense of immediacy to the images, which are, after all, highly stylised with their canted angles, expressive use of lighting and the formalism of their controlled repetition and development. We'll need to wait until later in the film for Bax to provide some truly stormy music.

When we next hear music it is after Oliver's mother's death where lyrical strings play as the shutters are pulled back from the windows. As in the opening title, the progression has been from a spare, cold two-part string line (the F-A flat-F in the storm) to a warmer, more emotive passage. If the progress of the B section of the title cue is recalled here, so is material from the A: as Mrs Thingummy spots the locket around the dead girl's neck, the brass *leitmotif* plays once more following, as before, a pedal string *tremolo*. This time, however, the exchange has modulated up by a full tone to D#, a simple way of indicating, subliminally, that things have moved on by shifting the tonal centre.

After this recap of formal devices and musical material made

A discussion on the score of *Oliver Twist*
with composer Sir Arnold Bax during recording

familiar to us in the opening title, when the baby Oliver is taken down into the workhouse proper Bax introduces an important new element into his score: a solo piano sounds, backed with orchestra in the manner of a quasi-concerto or rhapsody. There remains an odd disjunction between this lyrical, Delius-like melodism with its warm, Impressionistic backing and the images we see of cold, dark brickwork and faintly hectoring religious slogans, even if the solo clarinet that plays under a title card confirming the birth of Oliver Twist into the domain of the Beadle and the Matron does bring a more lonely element to the mix. On the whole, the cue seems unusual within its context; it is only as the film progresses that the narrative logic underpinning its instrumentation becomes clear.

The dogged plodding of the cue accompanying Oliver being marched off to work at six o'clock on a snowy winter's morning seems more immediately apt, however, becoming spikily modernist as we see watery gruel being dished out to the boys. This is balanced by the quirkily comic energy of the music following Oliver's asking for more soup, noisy *tutti* chords percussively punctuating the montage of power figures looking aghast at the request. The musical silence preceding this effectively acts to build suspense during the run-up to this iconic moment, and the passage that follows showing the poster advertising Oliver's services as an apprentice maintains the grotesquely comic mood with its angularity and up-beat energy. A similar gloss is given to Oliver's arrival at his new employer's, the undertaker Sowerberry, which is scored for a quietly Stravinskian march.

Against this the sudden burst of *chinoiserie* following Oliver's discovery of his sleeping quarters in the coffin workshop stands out sharply in the curiosity of its invention: following a chromatic passage for subdued brass and strings, loud chords announce a momentary movement to a pentatonic sound world, and a xylophone clicks with a skeletal onomatopoeia. From here, Oliver's fear is communicated by more conventional means, with *tremolo* strings shaking and trembling for him, the use of macabre minor key fanfares and the dominance of chromaticism and motific writing, but the sudden burst of Orientalism is an unusual and, it must be said, effective device creating a powerful sense of 'otherness'. With the series of cues following on from Oliver's request for more we have moved steadily away from the longline melodies and warm harmonies of the Delius-like cue that introduced us to the workhouse. A certain grim humour is never far away, though, as the amusing use of the xylophone attests, and, underlining this, Bax finishes this cue with a cadence landing in precise time to Oliver blowing out his candle followed by a Puckishly Tchaikovskyian figure for nimble flutes.

These instruments return shortly after to usher in the music for

Oliver's first gig as a mute walking behind the cortege of a dead child. Again Bax surprises here, not furnishing a funereal cue or a death march but music that evolves from the introspection of the chromatic flutes that open it into a strangely sprightly passage reflecting not the ill-fortune of the child in the coffin but the momentary up-turn in prospects for Oliver following on behind it. Again Bax strikes a humorous note, Mickey Mousing Oliver's halting half-run, half-walk with alternately fast and slow figures and marking Noah's peeved kicking of a stone with a *pizzicato* cello pluck.

In contrast with this, the G minor cue underscoring the now ailing Mrs Thingummy's search for Oliver at Sowerberry's is backed with suitably sombre, muted strings and a mellow *cor anglais* that plays a soft melody (D-G-A-B flat-D-G'-F . . .) derived from the brass fanfare lineage *leitmotif* that opened the score. This is subsequently passed on to flute backed with the Delius-like strings we heard during our introduction to the workhouse. As the locket appears to re-enter the story through the persona of Mrs Thingummy, so a version of the fanfare reappears; as a character from Oliver's workhouse days pops up again, so we revert to the string writing we associate with that place. Here, Bax is both unifying his score through the recapitulation of musical ideas heard previously and subtly orientating the viewer to a conjunction of worlds within the narrative.

Similarly, Mrs Thingummy's death scene reprises the minor key variant of the fanfare motif which plays above gentle, *tremolo* strings that become progressively more chill as the scene wears on, finishing as Matron leaves the room declaring her 'stone dead' and having told nothing at all of what troubled her. If the circumspect nature of the writing here amplifies the subdued atmosphere of the scene, the rambunctious, up-tempo music underscoring Oliver's punch-up with Noah brings out the spirit and energy of that sequence; when the Beadle is sent for to discipline the boy he approaches Sowerberry's establishment to the same Stravinskian march figure as before, again providing continuity with Bax's score and pointing up a narrative repetition.

When Oliver runs away at dawn the following morning, Bax returns to the rhapsodic solo piano and orchestra we last heard as we were introduced properly to the world of the workhouse. When the music played then, it announced Oliver's entry into that world following his birth; with the music's return, Oliver is about to embark on another life, to be 'born again' into the community of thieves and scoundrels in thrall to Fagin, the questionable authority figure that will replace Bumble the Beadle. And just as a title card popped up to contextualise the images during that opening workhouse sequence, so another appears now telling us of Oliver's flight to the anonymity of London. Completing the symmetry, we see Oliver scampering away across the same moor we watched his mother fight her way across during the first frames of the movie.

In this first section of the film, then, Bax has kept a tight control of his musical resources. He has used the repetition of thematic, harmonic and textural devices to provide a sense of continuity and to point up echoes and symmetries within the narrative. He has surprised us with his choice of music on a number of occasions, but has worked more conventionally at other times. The formally tight construction of the opening title has been matched by a similar control of the music of this opening act.

The contrast of life in London is signalled from the off with the first diegetic music of the film, street musicians playing cheerfully amid the scrum of a teeming street. In London, music enters the ears of Oliver for the first time. The happy sound of the players forms just part of the vibrant soundscape of the city, swiftly being subsumed by a Babel of overlapping voices, bird and animal cries. When the Artful Dodger appears, apparently as Oliver's saviour, the music Bax supplies for their progress into the tenement squalor of the inner city speaks otherwise with its dark, threatening brass and breaks for rumbling, lowering percussion; dense, chromatic writing accompanies their ascent through a building to Fagin's eyrie. Suddenly, however, the music becomes diatonic and affirmative once more, opening out into a grand *tutti* as the lads emerge onto a walkway linking teetering housing blocks in the foreground of a staggering special effects shot of the rooftops leading to St Paul's. This dispelling of musical anxiety is sustained as Fagin sets about teaching Oliver how to pick pockets through an amusing dumbshow: a merry jig plays that begins by sounding quite English in disposition but becomes more exotic as it progresses, accentuating Fagin's ethnicity with a series of exotic melodic figures including a decidedly Spanish-sounding passage. It is interesting to note that despite the exaggerated Jewishness of Alec Guinness' characterisation of Fagin, Bax's score avoids any equivalently stereotypical *Klezmer* sound (solo violin, clarinet, Jewish scales). A grand *tutti* climax accompanies the Dodger's successful 'theft' of Fagin's valuables, the up-beat geniality of the music underlining Oliver's delight at the performance. Through the move from the dark chromaticism of the entry to the underworld to these more affirmative cues, it becomes clear that the music wasn't, as we might at first have assumed, simply providing a moral commentary on the action, but rather communicating to us Oliver's state of mind: the darkness of fear and anxiety giving way to awe and ultimately amusement.

The same music of amusement is quietly reprised as Fagin cuts bread for Oliver's breakfast the following morning and asks him to try to pick his pocket. It continues as we watch the Dodger at work for real, before shifting up a gear into a frantic hurry cue as the boys are chased through the streets by Mr Brownlow, who will prove to be Oliver's true saviour, together with assorted passers-by. The hurry cue emphasises the speed and drama of the chase through its *presto* tempo, its loud, exciting volume, the rapid movement of the semiquavers making up its repeating motifs and the increase and decrease of tension caused by their ascending or descending progression. The whole culminates in a *tutti, staccato* final chord timed to sound just as an oncoming fist knocks Oliver out; the ghost of this chord carries on delightfully over the subsequent black screen of Oliver's unconsciousness via the decay of a piano discord. Again, the effect is as darkly comic as it is dramatic. A similar hurry cue is heard later in the film for the Dodger's tailing of Nancy as she runs through the soaking streets featuring up-tempo, urgent, rhythmic and motific writing that ultimately drifts into intriguing, slow and chromatic woodwind lines as she makes her fateful rendezvous with Brownlow to pass on information about Oliver's whereabouts.

Oliver's next loss of consciousness, this time under interrogation at the police court, occasions the next cue: this time Bax provides an abstract, questioning figure on a bassoon playing in its upper *tessitura* that is answered by a vague-sounding clarinet before Oliver's collapse is shadowed by the tailing off of a *glissando* descent on solo cello, a muddy timbre used to evoke a fuzzy mind: as the boy falls, the note falls. The music accompanying Fagin and the boys' precipitant flight fearing betrayal by Oliver is in marked contrast: if the fainting cue had been a model of the indistinct and undefined, the rush of the gang is accompanied by a furious rush in the orchestra, including an explosive burst for the mustering of Sykes' dog. As with the chase cue, the music is fast and motific in construction, purposeful brass underpinning urgent chromatic runs on woodwind. Bax modulates up through a number of key changes, underlining the increasing tension of the frantic escape.

As we might expect by now, the dawn of a second new life for Oliver, this time within the household of the benevolent Mr Brownlow, is underscored with a return to the rhapsodic piano and strings of the introduction to the workhouse and the flight to London, both, similarly, birth/rebirth sequences. This time the piano plays quiet, radiant arpeggios over a gentle woodwind background before strings join in accompaniment, an expressive solo violin floating over all. As Oliver wakes up, the woodwind take up the piano's arpeggios over a harp and solo cello, and as he throws his arms impulsively and gratefully around the maid's neck the orchestra swells emotively to mark the moment: this is the first time we have seen the child being hugged since the death of his mother. Musically, Mr Brownlow's household is painted as a calm, beautiful place. Lyrical, longline melody is allowed to return to the score and the harmonic palette used by Bax here is lush, almost intoxicating. After the privations of the picture up until now, the opulence of the townhouse seems idyllic, almost extravagant, displaying a richness picked up on by the music.

Altogether darker are the cues that accompany the Matron's series of flashbacks to Mrs Thingummy's death. In the first segment, minor key *tremolo* strings are interlaced with a ghostly *piano* reminiscence of the locket/lineage *leitmotif* of the opening title as Sally tells her tale. In the second, as a scrap of paper falls from Sally's dead hand chromatic flutes play a descending motif over another string *tremolo*: all sounds seem expectant, the various *tremolos* building a sense of suspense. As well as creating a feeling of anticipation as to the *denouement* of the death scene, the music is also used to neatly demarcate the flashback scenes from the film's present: only the flashback sections are scored. The music thus fulfils a functional as well as an expressive rôle, facilitating easy reading of the narrative as it shifts rapidly back and forth in time.

We then return to Oliver at Mr Brownlow's, and the music sounds in complete contrast to that above: playful flutes and light *pizzicato* strings sound as the boy plays on a swing and is told by the maid that Mr Brownlow wants to see him. As she takes Oliver indoors, it becomes clear that in this brief cue the music is once more suggestive of his mental state: the playful music of the swing, complete with jocund bassoon, is replaced with a sudden string *tremolo* of trepidation as he nervously edges his way towards the library door. Bax again cues us in on the progression of feelings in the child. None of this prepares us, though, for the sudden welling of lush strings that announce Oliver's discovery of the portrait of his (unrecognised) mother: she is described as beautiful by them both and the music sounds commensurately beautiful with its warm harmonies and rich timbres. We may at this point be reminded of the similar burst of lush strings that played after her death while Mrs Thingummy opened the shutters of the sick room.

As Oliver is kidnapped by Sykes and Nancy, yet another new life threatens to open up for him. Once more, Bax announces this by bringing concerto-style piano into play. As Lean realises the episode, we see Brownlow playing chess awaiting the boy's return while Oliver is being dragged by Sykes to Fagin's new den. The music underscoring the scene in Brownlow's parlour returns us to the feel of the rebirth music: a piano plays soothingly over soft strings. When we cut to Oliver and Sykes, however, we're startled by sudden, dark brass sounding loudly over agitated cellos and basses, and we shift to the minor key. When the piano enters here it sounds loud and anxiously chromatic, and while the playing is no less virtuoso in style the poise and sophistication of the preceding piano passage has gone. The contrast between the boy's two possible futures could not be made clearer.

If during Sowerberry's funeral procession we were denied a suitably funereal cue, Bax furnishes something close to one for our return to Brownlow's house late on the first night of Oliver's disappearance. The pace is deathly slow, and sombre minor key strings play introspectively over dark woodwind chords. If this house occasioned a rebirth for Oliver, it now seems to be in mourning for his disappearance. This, of course, makes all the more shocking and vulgar the drunken singsong (dynamically led by a young Hattie Jacques) in the smoky inferno of the Three Cripples: again, the filmmakers use musical contrast as a powerful dramatic tool. This cue is as shameless and flagrant in its Bacchanalia as the funereal music that went before was sober and grave; again the difference between the two worlds of the narrative, of civilisation and squalor, hope and despair, is made plain.

The brief hope offered by the dawn that lightens the sky over London after Nancy is beaten by Sykes is greeted with a noble melody on French horn as we see the city waking up, but the optimistic glow of the horn is soon undercut by a dark, chromatic *tremolo* on strings as we are returned to the underworld alleys. Bax grows this into a tempestuous *tutti* climax for our discovery of Sykes and his realisation of what he has done to Nancy, who lies dead on the floor: this is the sort of swirling, elemental music Bax might have written for the storm scene that opened the movie. Instead, he uses it to illuminate a psychological storm in the mind of Sykes. We then move deeper into his thoughts as *crescendo-diminuendo* string *tremolos* and a modal oboe usher in his doubts: was Nancy guilty or had he been set up by Fagin? We see a series of shots of the room from his point of view, of Nancy's vanity table, of their empty bed, all coloured by this pulsing *tremolo*, the woodwind above it threatening to turn stormy once more. The strings seem to tremble as his dog does.

Having approached this close to the film's heart of darkness, from here the climactic scenes of the movie comprising Sykes' return to Fagin, the police chase of his dog, the storming of the gang's tenement, Sykes' attempted escape and the capture of Fagin, all play out to an extended – and extraordinary - period of musical silence. Lean has chosen to let the power of his images and the terse sparseness of his dialogue carry the burden of the drama on their own. Even Oliver's perilous scaling of the roof lacks musical backing, and the full horror of Sykes' final fall is felt without the orchestra needing to be heard. It is only once the drama is over and Oliver is reported to be safe that the music can begin again, with a series of affirmative fanfares giving way to a stately Elgarian march as Brownlow and his grandson walk home: all is well in this England once more.

The music that plays over the closing credits is initially a rapturous translation of the cold, chromatic second subject of the opening title, transformed into a cheerful major key *tutti*. This then gives way to a resounding rendition of the opening title's fanfare-like first subject, the lineage *leitmotif*, the cue ending with a hugely affirmative cadence to a pure C major chord, banishing entirely the harmonic ambivalence of the tremolo C# that opened the score and the complexity of the key centres adopted there.

As well as its concerns with contrast and formalism, Bax's score is a study in narrative symmetry. It goes straight to the heart of the deep structure of the story and takes this as its lead. Simple repetitions such as Bumble's two approaches to Sowerberry's are signalled using the same musical means; more subtle connections are made musically by the rhapsodic piano and orchestra that link the various birth/rebirth scenes. By the same token, passages of music that we might expect to find in one place in the film turn up, to great effect, in another: stormy music underscores not the opening storm scene but Sykes' torment and aberration, funereal music accompanies not a child's funeral but Oliver's failure to return home. The music of London, its street musicians and its gin palace drinking songs, is revealed to be both entertaining and morally reprehensible. And perhaps the bravest, and most effective, stroke of all is the decision to pull the plug on the music for the last reel of the picture. These bars of silence are as effective as any cue in the score.

Filmography

Henry V, Dir: Laurence Olivier, Mus: William Walton (Rank/Two Cities), UK, 1944

Hamlet, Dir: Laurence Olivier, Mus: William Walton (Rank/Two Cities), UK, 1948

Oliver Twist, Dir: David Lean, Mus: Arnold Bax (GFD/Cineguild), UK, 1948

Vertigo

(1958)

Director: Alfred Hitchcock
Composer: Bernard Herrmann
Conductor: Muir Mathieson
Production Company: Paramount, US

No survey of the contribution of Muir Mathieson to film music would be complete without an analysis of the score for *Vertigo* (1958), written by the great Bernard Herrmann, whose music forms such a vital part of our experience of 1950s-1960s Hitchcock movies like *The Trouble With Harry* (1955), *North By Northwest* (1959) and *Psycho* (1960). Herrmann's career was remarkable, his first film score being that for *Citizen Kane* (1941) and his last the memorable, nightmarish big-band phantasmagoria of Martin Scorsese's *Taxi Driver* (1976). As one of the great thriller scores, we should not be surprised to note that the score for *Vertigo* is both a summation of and a blueprint for the genre's musical style, with its reliance on chromatic, but firmly tonal, writing, its unsettling play with modulation, a tight rein on the deployment of melody favouring rather the use of obsessively repeating patterns and motifs. Herrmann also knows when to use music which is informed by a cerebral, technical ingenuity, and when to press all the big Romantic buttons and furnish cues of a more effusive, emotional nature.

The tightly structured symmetries underpinning the opening title seem to locate it as one of the more cerebral cues in the movie, perfect for a film as concerned with the hero's psychology as this. Harmonic uncertainty is announced from the off, the music seeming to open on the cusp of D minor and E flat minor, so chromatic is much of the writing. The opening motif, a descending triplet followed by an ascending triplet tracing the notes D-B flat-G flat-D'-G flat-B flat plays with this, the wedding of these two keys a semitone apart creating constant tonal ambiguity. Beneath this, the reverse of the triplet sequence is played out (D-G flat-B flat-D,-B flat-G flat), creating a precise, symmetrical feel, the repetition of both triplet figures creating musical palindromes that also reflect each other in a precise contrary motion. The interlocking triplet motif begins on upper strings, but woodwind also join, providing the quiet contrary response, before the motif as a whole passes on to celeste and harp. The odd, echoing tones of a vibraphone can also be heard, an instrument that will take on a special rôle as the score develops. Meanwhile, the brass punctuate the continually cycling pattern with loud D and C unison notes. The triplet motif is passed back and forth between louder strings and woodwind and quieter harp and celeste, the brass stabs becoming louder and more dissonant, eventually being augmented with a *vibrato* electric organ. The loudest and most dissonant brass chord sounds as the title of the movie appears on the screen.

Incredibly, more than a minute passes before a second idea emerges on trilling strings, their oscillations further complicating ideas of tonality. This ascending chromatic rise remains backed by the opening motif on harp and celeste, and eventually leads to a full-throated enunciation of this motif on violins with dense, less fragmented chording on brass. The swelling climaxes of this passage foreshadow the more romantic elements of the score. The triplets then lose a little of their chromatic feel, becoming more arpeggiated in nature. From here, the motif evolves quasi-melodically, but remains rhythmically constant, never breaking entirely free of the arpeggios into full-blown melody. After this motific development, the original interlocking triplets return, this time at a hypnotic faster tempo, again on harp and celeste, again with the brass stabs on D and C. As this faster section progresses, the triplets are passed from harp and celeste to strings and woodwind as before, now sounding like a precursor of the work of Philip Glass with the trance-like circularity of their repetition, until the tempo drops again and we return to the arpeggiated triplets on strings, once more backed with dense brass chording.

The original chromatic interlocking triplets return again, made urgent by another increase in tempo and their additional picking out by *pizzicato* violins, the whole resolving on a gong splash and low brass pedal on D, nearly three and a half minutes of tightly controlled musical development appearing at last to find a stable tonal centre. If melody can be thought of as the music of the heart, then this music is more like the music of the head, highly technical, almost abstract writing involving interlocking patterns and carefully plotted twists and turns.

The cue that follows, backing Scottie's rooftop chase, is likewise motifically constructed, shorn of melody, swarming strings and chromatic stepwise runs on oboes creating a cloud of notes that chromatic, ascending brass and bass clarinets lift higher, cranking up the tension still further. Just as the movie plunges straight into the excitement of a police chase, Herrmann gives us no room to draw breath heading straight into his hurry cue even before the final D of the opening title has ended. The tempo is fast, the tonality minor key and motific repetition is once more the structural device generating the cue. Having moved gradually and chromatically upwards from this D, as Scottie slips on the rooftop and breaks his fall by grasping desperately onto a gutter that partly gives under his weight, the tonal centre settles on D flat: through chromatic ascent Herrmann takes us as far from the opening D as he can, the interval of D-D flat' being in addition a highly discordant one.

The radicalism of this sort of interval is then harnessed explicitly as vertigo grips Scottie for the first time. Thanks to a simultaneous track and zoom, the ground appears to fall away beneath him;

meantime, the grounding of conventional harmony also falls away as Herrmann provides *fortissimo*, wildly discordant wide, chromatic leaps up and down – we could call these the 'vertigo' chords. The jumping and falling of the music fits neatly with the jump and possibly imminent fall of the hero. Just as the opening title finally settled on a low, dark D, so this cue ends, after its own manic motific repetition and stabbing brass chords, on a low, dark D flat.

As we fade up on Scottie bantering with Midge in her apartment some time later, Hitchcock's sudden change of dramatic register from the nightmarish to the comic is underlined musically as we shift from Herrmann's dark and ferocious sound world to the light touch and poise of some diegetic chamber music playing quietly in the background. This spools on unperturbed, even given its minor key, throughout their scene together until Scottie finally asks if it can be turned off as it itself is giving him vertigo. This request is a humorous one, but it also allows the romantic balm of music to be tellingly absent from their subsequent discussion of brassieres, Midge's love life and their own abortive three-week engagement some time in the past. The inability of these two characters, so well suited to one another, to connect romantically is just one of the many melancholy threads running through the film, and its signalling so early in the narrative might lead us to assume that by the end of the movie the two will be together.

This expectation is of course thwarted as the story progresses; that it is Scottie who asks for the music to be turned off presages his subsequent movement away from this 'wholesome' romantic possibility. This idea is developed further, musically, when Scottie faints after climbing Midge's kitchen steps as the discordant soundworld of his previous attack of vertigo is returned to with a stabbing brass chord followed by a ghostly organ *vibrato* discord and a descending chromatic figure on bass clarinet and lower brass; the horror of the film's opening is invoked just as he falls into Midge's arms: this is not the romantic music of a screen clinch, despite the embrace.

From here, music leaves the movie until Scottie has his first glimpse of Madeleine in Ernie's restaurant. *Vertigo* is, of course, not just a psychological thriller but a love story, albeit a dark and morbid one, and with the entrance of the leading lady Herrmann changes generic idiom from the abstract, intellectualised music of the psycho-thriller to the music of love and romance: soft strings swell in warm harmonies strongly reminiscent of the sound world of Wagner's 'Tristan and Isolde', another tale of doomed love and overwhelming, destructive passion. Madeleine's mellow theme (G-A flat-C-B flat-A flat-F-G-F…) sounds in start contrast with everything we have heard up until now. The motor, motific feel has gone, replaced with a lyrical effusion of longline melody; the strident violence of much of the music has been banished in favour of sweet harmony; the edgy urgency has been supplanted by a languorous rapture. While as the cue progresses the music remains deeply chromatic at heart, modulating through a supple series of key centres, it is not the angular chromaticism of the opening title, but the lush, intoxicating chromaticism of late Romanticism. Whatever key centres the music wanders through, however, they are all minor: there is a note of melancholy caution sounded at the very beginning of this romance. The music is at its most intense and yearning when the camera is closest first to Madeleine, then Scottie, winding down again as their physical proximity to each other, as well as the camera, wanes. It is as if this music, which begins as an index of Madeleine's beauty, is also expressive of Scottie's passion for her, being at its most intense when they are closest.

As we dissolve to Scottie tailing Madeleine for the first time, Herrmann begins a retreat from longline melody, a repeating, syncopated rhythm on clarinets providing the backbone for further string lines that, while they lack the freely evolving lyricism of Madeleine's theme, are derived from its ascending opening notes and are not yet entirely as motifically circumscribed as the string writing of the first two cues of the score. These short phrases still sound contained by the gently obsessive clarinet rhythm, though, which in a neat exchange is soon passed on to the strings themselves, woodwind taking over, in return, the melodic line above.

Hitchcock has now embarked on a long, slow section of the movie where not much happens other than Scottie driving along through San Francisco behind Madeleine's car. We need to be drawn in by the music here, not turned off, if the sequence is to work as intended, to bring us under the spell of the film just as Scottie will be brought under the spell of Madeleine. Herrmann keeps the feel of the music constant throughout, but slowly modulates key and changes instrumentation to provide a sense of forward movement and evolution. If the first part of the cue (woodwind underpinning strings) was written in B minor, the second (strings underpinning woodwind) moves up a semitone to C minor. The third section of the cue, in which the rôles of strings and woodwind are once more reversed when Madeleine pulls up in an alleyway behind a florist's, hikes the tonal centre up a further semitone to C# minor. Subtly, then, Herrmann is turning the tension up by gradually shifting key upwards. As Scottie gets out of the car, the syncopated rhythm sounds for the first time on *pizzicato* strings and we move up another semitone to D minor. This change in the texture of the accompaniment, while preserving the cue's structuring device of the repeating rhythm, happens precisely as Scottie gets out of the car for the first time and walks towards where he knows Madeleine is. Gently building intensity again, Herrmann next shortens the length of the sections of the cue. If the three sections leading up to the *pizzicato* had each been ten bars in duration (a two-bar introduction enunciating the rhythm in isolation by the backing instruments then eight bars of strings and woodwind playing together), when we move to the *pizzicato* passage the section lasts just two bars before the rhythm is taken over by clarinets, who in turn play it for two bars. In addition, at this point Herrmann subliminally alters the rhythm, inserting a beat's silence into its second bar. With an ear for musical symmetry matching that at work in the opening title, just as we hear three ten-bar sections, we are given three two-bar sections, the final given according to rotation to *pizzicato* strings.

Now, as Scottie moves inside the florist's, Herrmann changes the texture of the cue by abandoning the hypnotic rhythm of the pursuit in favour of two long woodwind chords that are answered by two long string chords: suspense is generated. After this, Scottie opens the door on an explosion of colour within the shop and as Madeleine is revealed, a monochrome figure with powdered skin and peroxide hair dressed in a grey suit who basks in the ardour of the shop's blooms, the strings take off into a heartfelt reprise of her theme. Scottie returns to his car closing two doors: as he does so, a harp sounds both times, the strings playing a sombre variant of Madeleine's theme. As she closes the back door of the florist in turn, the harp sounds again. If this all sounds very geometrical, almost schematic, that's because it is. The lulling rhythms, the standardisation of section lengths and the constant alternation between strings and woodwind act to hypnotise us: as Scottie falls further under Madeleine's spell, we too find ourselves drawn in by the trance-like repetitions. At the heart of this spell lies the vision of Madeleine in the flower shop, and here is where the music blossoms forth into Madeleine's theme, free and unencumbered by the syncopated rhythm.

The brief continuation of the pursuit finds the ghostly organ *vibrato* joining the strings and woodwind. We have moved to 3:4 time now, and the clarinets repeatedly play a dotted minim rhythm over which the strings complete their come down after the effusion of the florists by playing a series of descending motifs. Scottie has trailed Madeleine to a cemetery, and the idea of him falling further under her spell, descending, effectively, into an obsession, is caught by the diegetic church organ that sounds as he walks after her through the chapel: the instrument merely plays the same six-note motif (two crotchets, four quavers) in a series of nine methodical downward progressions, before ironing things out with a move to melodic resolution in the tenth bar. The closing cadence, when it comes, is to B flat minor (a traditionally dark key, cf. Chopin's *Funeral March* piano sonata). In this melancholy film, so far even the putatively diegetic music is cast in a minor key (cf. the chamber music in Midge's apartment).

As Scottie sees Madeleine in the graveyard, the violins play Madeleine's theme above long, discordant woodwind chords: its lush splendour in the restaurant and the flower shop has gone now, and here it sounds disturbingly bleak, the melody meandering elusively, out of kilter with its accompaniment. As we see Scottie's point of view of the gravestone of Carlotta Valdes, the object of Madeleine's pilgrimage, an orchestral bell tolls loudly, foreshadowing the bell sounds that will end the film, and a *sforzando* bass clarinet leers grotesquely out of the woodwind backing.

A short period of music silence then falls, clearing our aural palate before music next plays as Scottie follows Madeleine into the art gallery. Here, a new syncopated rhythm reappears, this time on harp as it and *piano* unison violins intone a pedal E flat softly, a pedal that will last the duration of the cue. With Carlotta Valdes fresh in our minds the rhythm sounds Latin American, like a *habanera*. It continues hypnotically over further woodwind chording, more relaxed now than the discords in the graveyard but still in the minor. As each element of the Madeleine/Carlotta enigma is shown us by Hitchcock (the matching posies, the matching hair swirls), a vibraphone sounds an E flat, a soft echo of the tolling of the bell that sounded so morbidly over Carlotta's grave. Once again strings take over the accompaniment from the woodwind, and it is only when we move back outside the gallery that the pedal E flat relents and a second, balancing period of musical silence is allowed to descend.

After this, the music again picks up in much the same manner as before, though this time in B minor providing harmonic variation after the unequivocal E flat of the gallery sequence. Madeleine is now entering the McKittrick Hotel and this time Carlotta's *habanera* rhythm is taken up by pulsing cellos and the other strings chord around it. This new, exotic rhythmic *ostinato* has now supplanted the previous *ostinato* of the pursuit: we have moved on, we have moved deeper into the mystery. Her appearance in the window of her room is marked by an F minor chord and the lustre of a vibraphone figure derived from the opening of Madeleine's theme. As Scottie enters the building we modulate down a semitone to B flat minor for a series of held brass chords, open brass alternating with muted brass. It is the first time we have heard from this section of the orchestra since Scottie's vertigo attack at Midge's, so dominant have the strings and woodwind been meantime. Indeed, the melancholy chord sequences played here are a *piano* restyling of the two-chord brass stabs heard as Scottie contracted acrophobia dangling from the guttering during the opening roof-top chase. Herrmann, therefore, chooses this moment to bring in the idea of vertigo again: with the spectral disappearance of Madeleine the ground of reason has fallen from beneath his feet. Muted brass play again as the concierge climbs the stairs to check out 'Miss Valdes''s room, mysteriously claiming she hasn't seen her enter the building. This time, they play a variant of Madeleine's theme in neat juxtaposition with the previous statement of the 'vertigo' chord *leitmotif*. As Scottie drives back to Madeleine's apartment block the strings come in once more with yet another variant of her theme, reinstating a dominant texture of the pursuit and underlining the sense of mystery surrounding her disappearance, the whole pursuit sequence finally closing inconclusively in harmonic terms: we're left hanging, denied a cadence to the tonic at the end.

So concludes an extraordinary fifteen minutes of filmmaking, backed with fifteen minutes, more or less, of extraordinary music. The economy of Herrmann's writing is remarkable, and the variation he is able to squeeze out of limited musical means, given the self-imposed restraints of the repeating rhythm, the worrying away at Madeleine's theme and the overwhelming reliance on strings and woodwind, is impressive. The first pursuit sequence has moved slowly in dramatic, visual and musical terms, but this pacing decision has drawn us ineluctably into the film. Like Scottie, we're now hooked. In the film up until now, six key musical ideas have been floated: the symmetrical triplets of the opening title, with their accompanying brass blares; the scurrying chromatic semiquavers of the chase sequence; the wild sounds of the 'vertigo' chords themselves; the contrast of Madeleine's lyrical theme; the hypnotic rhythm *ostinato* of the pursuit scene and its obsessive reworking of motifs derived from Madeleine's theme; and the *habanera* rhythm allotted to the spirit of Carlotta Valdes.

A brief cue bridges Midge's leaving of Scottie in the car after their trip to the Argosy Bookshop and Scottie reporting back to Gavin Elster. It opens with a melancholy reprise of the string arrangement that concluded the pursuit sequence but this time evolves into a restatement of the Latin rhythm so dominant elsewhere in that sequence. The Madeleine theme and the Carlotta rhythm bring us directly to Elster, the puppeteer of the scenario. The syncopated rhythm is restated as Scottie spies on Madeleine in the gallery again, this time voiced as a repeating E flat first on muted horns then on harp. Refreshing things, Herrmann abandons the old pursuit music as Scottie follows her car down to the bay, a new variant of the Madeleine theme playing on strings backed by woodwind figures, brass chording and a repeating quaver motif on harp. The cue is aquatically Debussyesque, alerting us immediately to the importance of water in the scene that follows (cf. the soundword of *La Mer*).

Madeleine dropping flower petals into the bay is underscored with gentle chords on clarinets and bass clarinet, a mellow vibraphone played with a soft beater glowing over them, its five-note motif (beginning E flat-F-G flat) evoking the Madeleine theme variant heard on strings and woodwind during the first pursuit sequence. Muted strings contribute to the feel of calm and repose in these shots, an atmosphere shattered as Madeleine suddenly throws

trilling motif that recalls the frantic chase semiquavers of the opening rooftop scene and Scottie dashing after Madeleine in the tower the first time. This provides a profound sense of our having come full circle once more. Ominous, low woodwind chords underscore the further revelations Scottie intuits about the relationship between Judy and Elster, but as Judy pleads her case, explaining that she couldn't leave Scottie after meeting him again, the four-note motif returns to build to the reintroduction of the love theme as they kiss one final time. The kiss, and Judy's life, are cut short by the shadowy appearance of a nun investigating the source of the voices she has overheard: as Judy falls screaming to her death we hear a similar loud, low chord to that which sounded when we saw Madeleine's body lying on the rooftop after her plunge from the tower. The nun then rings the bell in the tower, an action foreshadowed by the orchestral bell that tolled over the close up of Carlotta's gravestone, an idea perpetuated by the chiming tones of the vibraphone elsewhere in the score. Over this the brass intone the love theme one final time before closing on a *tutti* C#.

Herrmann's score for *Vertigo* plays as vital a part of our experience of the film as his music for *Psycho* plays in that film. If this is a film in which one wouldn't change a frame, it's also a score in which one wouldn't alter a note. Muir Mathieson must have been impressed by the exemplary tightness of Herrmann's organisation of his material when he saw the score for the first time. After all, he had been pushing film composers to work this way since the 1940s.

Filmography

Citizen Kane, Orson Welles (RKO), US, 1941
North by Northwest, Alfred Hitchcock (MGM), US, 1959
Psycho, Alfred Hitchcock (Universal), US, 1960
Taxi Driver, Martin Scorsese (Columbia), US, 1976
Trouble With Harry, The, Alfred Hitchcock (Paramount), US, 1955
Vertigo, Alfred Hitchcock (Paramount), US, 1958

Films in which Muir Mathieson is credited as . . .

Musical Director

1933 – The Private Life of Henry VIII (Assistant Musical Director)

1934 – Catherine the Great
The Private Life of Don Juan
The Scarlet Pimpernel

1935 – Moscow Nights
Sanders of the River
The Ghost Goes West

1936 – Things to Come
Rembrandt
Men are Not Gods
The Man Who Could Work Miracles
Forget Me Not

1937 – Wings of the Morning
The Green Cockatoo
Fire Over England
Dark Journey
Storm in a Teacup
Elephant Boy
Thunder in the City
Farewell Again
Under the Red Robe
Knight Without Armour
Action for Slander
The Return of the Scarlet Pimpernel
Victoria the Great
The Rat
Dinner at the Ritz
Paradise for Two

1938 – The Divorce of Lady X
South Riding
Vessel of Wrath
The Drum
The Challenge
Prison Without Bars
Sidewalks of London

1939 – Q Planes
The Four Feathers
The Spy in Black
Over the Moon
The Lion has Wings

1940 – Men of the Lightship
21 Days
Contraband
Conquest of the Air
On the Night of the Fire
Gaslight

1941 – The Thief of Baghdad
War Front
Christmas Under Fire
Freedom Radio
Old Bill and Son
Dangerous Moonlight
Love on the Dole
Pimpernel Smith
49th Parallel

1942 – Coastal Command
Penn of Pennsylvania
The First of the Few

1943 – Fires Were Started
Before the Raid
Tomorrow We Live
Desert Victory
The Gentle Sex
The Demi-Paradise

1944 – Western Approaches
The Tawny Pipit
On Approval
The Way Ahead
Henry V

1945 – 29 Acacia Avenue

1946 – A Defeated People
Men of Two Worlds

School for Secrets
The Woman in the Hall

1947 – The Upturned Glass
Take My Life
School for Danger
Master of Bankdam
The Mark of Cain
The Cumberland Story
Captain Boycott
Blanche Fury
The Man Within
The End of the River

1948 – Hamlet
The Weaker Sex
Vice Versa
Trouble in the Air
Penny and the Pownall Case
Mr Perrin and Mr Traill
It's Hard to be Good
Here Come the Huggetts
Easy Money
The Calendar
One Night With You
Song of Tomorrow
Escape
So Evil my Love

1949 – The History of Mr Polly
Helter Skelter
The Passionate Friends
~~Quarter~~
Cardboard Cavalier
Britannia Mews
Trottie True
The Blue Lagoon
Woman Hater
Diamond City
Madness of the Heart

1950 – Waterfront
They Were Not Divided
The Cure for Love
The Black Rose
The Wooden Horse
The Miniver Story
Prelude to Fame

1951 – Tom Brown's Schooldays
David
The Adventurers
Lady Godiva Rides Again
The House in the Square
Hallmark of Fame (for TV)

1952 – The Sound Barrier
The Crimson Pirate
Lady in the Fog
The Ringer

1953 – Star of India
The Malta Story
The Kidnappers
Genevieve
The Story of Gilbert and Sullivan
Single-handed
Melba
The Beggar's 0pera
The Master of Ballantrae
Sie Fanden Ein Heimat

1954 – The Sea Shall Not HaveThem
Rob Roy, the Highland Rogue
Hobson's Choice
Grand National Night
Beau Brummel
The Teckman Mystery
The Seekers
Value for Money

1955 – Geordie
Dance Little Lady
The Ship That Died of Shame
A Prize of Gold
I Am a Camera
Passage Home

1956 – Wicked As They Come
A Hill in Korea
High Flight
The Baby and the Battleship
Trapeze
Port Arrique
Smiley
Reach For The Sky
Zarak

1957 – Rockets Galore
Dangerous Exile
After the Ball
Fortune is a Woman
The Prince and the Showgirl
Manuela
The Truth About Women
The Smallest Show on Earth
Sea Wife
Windom'sWay

1958 – The Two-Headed Spy
Sea of Sand
Heart of a Child
The Man Inside

Harry Black
Intent to Kill
Tom Thumb

1959 – The Rough and the Smooth
Horrors of the Black Museum
The Headless Ghost
The Bandit of Zhobe

1960 – A Story of David
The Malpas Mystery
Sink the Bismarck
Once More With Feeling
Kidnapped
Circus of Horrors
Macbeth
The Hellions
The Greengage Summer

1962 – Life for Ruth
Waltz of the Toreadors
Crooks Anonymous
The Main Attraction
In Search of the Castaways
The Mind Benders
Becket
Woman of Straw
The Informers
The High Bright Sun
Calamity the Cow
Shalako
You Can't Win 'Em All

Muir . . . as Conductor

(In almost every case, Muir was also Musical Director for these films)

1937 – The Squeaker

1939 – Squadron

1940 – Men of the Lightship

1941 – Green Girdle

1942 – Coastal Command
Battle is Our Business
The Day Will Dawn
They Flew Alone
In Which We Serve

1943 – Close Quarters
The Flemish Farm
Escape to Danger
Yellow Canary
The Lamp Still Burns

1944 – Men of Rochdale
Hotel Reserve
This Happy Breed

1945 – Steam Conductor
A Diary for Timothy
Blithe Spirit
Great Day
I Live in Grosvenor Square
The True Glory
Perfect Strangers
Brief Encounter (listed as music adaptor)
Caesar and Cleopatra
The Rake's Progress

1946 – The Last Shot
Green for Danger
Journey Together
They Knew Mr Knight
I See a Dark Stranger
The Years Between
A Girl in a Million

1947 – The October Man
Dear Murderer
Daybreak
Odd Man Out
Hungry Hill

1948 – Hamlet
Sleeping Car to Trieste
Portrait from Life
Esther Waters
Daughter of Darkness
Oliver Twist
Miranda
London Belongs to Me
Broken Journey

1949 – Blue Scar
The Astonished Heart
Dear Mr Prohack
Adam and Evelyne
Christopher Columbus
The Chiltern Hundreds

1950 – Science in the Orchestra
Highly Dangerous
Family Portrait
Madeleine
The Rocking Horse Winner

State Secret
Treasure Island
The Golden Salamander
Trio
The Mudlark

1951 – The Magic Box
Journey into History
Home to Danger
The Galloping Major
Scrooge

1952 – The Stranger Left No Card
Ocean Terminal
The Long Memory
It Started in Paradise
Innocents in Paris
Gift Horse
The Happy Family
Home at Seven
Encore
The Faithful City
Robin Hood
Saturday Island
The Card
The Gentle Gunman
Venetian Bird

1953 – The Holly and the Ivy
The Million Pound Note
The Kidnappers
Forest Heritage
A Day to Remember
La Bergere et le Ramoneur
Curtain Up
The Net
Street Corner
Sea Devils
Four Sided Triangle
The Captain's Paradise
The Sword and the Rose
The Man Between
The Red Beret
The Conquest of Everest

1954 – Elizabethan Express
The Beachcomber
The Intruder
Our Girl Friday
Hell Below
Father Brown
The Belles of St Trinians
Doctor in the House
The Sleeping Tiger
The Black Knight
War in the Air
The Purple Plain
Svengali

1955 – On the Twelfth Day
Jumping for Joy
To Paris With Love
That Lady
Richard III
The Constant Husband
Above Us the Waves
The Deep Blue Sea
Doctor at Sea
The Cockleshell Heroes
Tomorrow's Man

1956 – The Spanish Gardener
Our Native Shore
The Long Night Haul
Jacqueline
The Green Man
Eyewitness
Checkpoint
The Man Who Never Was
Safari
The Black Tent

1957 – Night of the Demon
High Tide at Noon
The England of Elizabeth
Seven Waves Away
Doctor at Large
Fire Down Below
Interpol
Action of the Tiger
The Admirable Crichton
Sea Wife
Campbell's Kingdom

1958 – The Sheriff of Fractured Jaw
Passionate Summer
The Immortal Land
A Cry from the Street
A Tale of Two Cities
The Safecracker
I Accuse!
Gideon's Day
Another Time, Another Place
Vertigo
Indiscreet
The Revenge of Frankenstein
Rooney
A Night to Remember
Law and Disorder
No Time to Die
The Silent Enemy
The Horse's Mouth

The Wind Cannot Read

1959 – The Savage Innocents
North-West Frontier
Left, Right and Centre
Floods of Fear
The Thirty-nine Steps
Shake Hands with the Devil
Beyond This Place
The House of the Seven Hawks
Ferry to Hong Kong
Third Man on the Mountain
Il Terrore dei Barbari
Killers of Kilimanjaro
The Bridal Path

1960 – The Malpas Mystery
The Hellfire Club
Depth Charge
Blue Pullman
The Big Day
The Story of David
The Jazz Boat
The World of Suzie Wong
The Swiss Family Robinson
The Grass is Greener

1961 – Sink the Bismarck!
Konga
The Naked Edge
The Hellions
Echo
Gorgo
The Canadians
The Treasure of Monte Cristo
The Greengage Summer
The Housemasters

1962 – Satan Never Sleeps
Only Two Can Play
HMS Defiant
Night of the Eagle
Waltz of the Toreadors

1963 – Hide and Seek
The Mind Benders
Call Me Bwana
Sammy Going South
The Running Man

1964 – Devils of Darkness
Hot Enough for June
1965
Devils of Darkness
Lord Jim
Genghis Khan]

1966 – The Great Highway

Muir . . . as Composer

Grampian Suite, 1961

Additional music for Brief Encounter (uncredited)

Score for – Wild Wings
Call Me Bwana
Hide and Seek
Calamity the Cow
Mr Horatio's Nibbles
Anoop the Elephant
Crooks Anonymous
What a Carve-up
Circus of Horror
Highland Journey
Going Places
Sing of the Border
Journey Intercity
Operation London Bridge

Muir . . . as Film Director

A Young Person's Guide to the Orchestra

We Make Music: Series of 21 films for the Educational Foundation for Visual Aids

Appearances on Screen

The Story of Gilbert and Sullivan (as Sullivan)

The Magic Box (as Conductor)

A Girl in a Million (as Conductor)

The Seventh Veil (as Conductor)

Glossary of Technical Terms

The following glossary for many of the technical terms used in the analytical essays is intended as a ready reckoner and not as a substitute for a good subject-specific dictionary or reference work. Film studies jargon and musical terminology are both covered – organised in alphabetical order. Words in italics in the definitions are defined elsewhere in the glossary. Explanations have been kept as simple as possible in the hope of clarifying any issues the reader might have from Accelerando to Zoom.

' An *octave* higher. A' is and octave above the first A mentioned.

, An *octave* lower. A, is an octave below the first A mentioned.

*Sharp*.

Accelerando A quickening of pace.

Actuality Footage Shots of real-life events taken as they happen and not staged for the camera.

Aerophone An instrument which is blown, such as those in the *brass* and *woodwind* sections (although church organs and harmoniums are also, technically, aerophones as well).

Agitato Played in an agitated, restless or anxious way.

Antiphonal Writing A passage of music in which one group of performers 'respond' to a musical statement made by another either by echoing it or answering it with a statement of their own.

Arabesque An ornate *figure*.

Arpeggio The notes of a *chord* not sounded together, but in succession.

Ascending Sequence A passage of music where either the melodic line or its accompaniment climbs upwards in pitch.

Atonality The absence of an established *key* in a passage or composition. Compare *tonal music*. Atonal writing is often highly *discordant*, and is an avant-garde technique pioneered by Arnold Schoenberg (1874-1951) in the early twentieth century. It is an abiding and pleasing irony that this most rarefied and extraordinary of high culture musical techniques should find mass appreciation not in the concert hall but the cinema where it delights and moves fans of the horror film.

Aural Dissolve Music or sound from one scene is mixed with that from the next so that for a brief period the two can be heard simultaneously.

Bar A simple unit of musical organisation. If you count in a tune by saying '1, 2, 3, 4…' before launching into it, you have enunciated a bar as well as telling others how fast you'll be going and when you'll be starting.

Bare Interval The sounding of an *interval* of a *fourth* or larger without another note sounding between the upper and lower note.

Boom Shot The camera is placed on a crane or a long lever over a fulcrum and bodily lifted up or dropped down. The sensation is akin to becoming suddenly airborne or landing.

Brass A section of the orchestra made up of wind instruments such as trumpets, trombones, French horns, tubas and so on.

Bravura Either a difficult musical passage that requires formidable skill to play or a showy, virtuoso performance style.

Broken Chord A *chord* whose notes are

staggered, rather than sounded together.

Cadence The concluding *chord* sequence that brings a musical thought to a satisfying completion, if only temporarily. Cadences can be found at the end of melodies, where they can provide a sense of closure, but also at the end of melodic phrases, separating them.

Cageian Adjective derived from surname of composer John Cage (1912-1992), who heard music in sound. His most famous composition consists of four minutes and thirty three seconds of silence, inviting the audience to listen to the sound of themselves, the auditorium and its environs. He also pioneered aleatory music, music generated by, incorporating or being structured around random or chance elements.

Call and Response A musical form where a performer or a group of performers make(s) a musical statement which is then responded to by another performer/group. A priest singing a line and the choir or congregation singing another back is a simple form of call and response. (See *antiphonal writing*, *versicle*.)

Canted Angle Rather than being set up to show an entirely flat horizon as is usual, the camera is set up at an angle creating striking and dramatic pictorial effects through skewing the horizon to a diagonal.

Chord Most often three or more notes sounded together simultaneously, though sometimes two will do.

Chord Progression A sequence of *chords* that have been organised into a developing pattern.

Chromaticism The interpolation of notes normally foreign to the *home key* of the music. There are eight notes in a simple scale running from Doh-Doh, but chromatic music adds other notes in alongside the Doh-Re-Me . . . progression. Chromaticism can create a variety of impressions depending on how it is used. It can contribute to an angular or discordant musical style (Bela Bartok [1881-1945]) or be used to broaden the composer's palette and produce music of intoxicating lushness (Richard Strauss [1864-1949]).

Chromatic Harmonica A chromatic harmonica has all 12 notes of the chromatic scale available, allowing an instrumentalist to play in any key. A slide operated by a button provides a further range of notes.

Colour Chord A note that is added to a conventional *triad* producing a warmer, more complex sound. Added *seconds*, *fourths*, *sixths* and *major sevenths* make simple colour chords.

Contrary Motion A passage where two parts move in opposite directions, one up, one down.

Counterpoint The simultaneous sounding of two or more melodic lines. A canon or round, such as 'London's Burning' is a simple form of this, JS Bach's (1685-1750) 'Art of the Fugue' a complex one.

Crash Edit A jarring cut which disrupts, either intentionally or unintentionally, the smooth, seamless flow of shots preferred by mainstream cinema.

Crescendo Getting louder.

Crescendo-diminuendo A passage of music that gets louder then immediately quieter. The combination can happen once or be repeated, getting louder and quieter over and over in rapid succession.

Cross-cutting Typically, images from one location repeatedly cut into a sequence of images from another. Editing back and forth between shots of the heroine riding to the rescue and footage of the hero tied to the railway tracks constitutes cross-cutting.

Crotchet See *note*.

Cue A passage of music with a beginning and an end that are timed to start and finish at precise points. Most film scores are made up of a series of cues. Compare *saturation score*.

Da Capo A musical marking instructing the performer(s) to go back to the beginning and play the music through again (i.e. from the head of the score).

Descending Sequence A passage of music where either the melodic line or its accompaniment moves downwards in pitch.

Development The elaboration or reworking of musical material that has been heard before.

Diatonic Harmony A non-*chromatic* approach to harmony. Strictly speaking, diatonic music should be written using only the eight notes (Doh-Re-Me...) of the *major* or *minor* scale, but the term can be used more loosely to refer to a compositional style wherein these notes dominate any chromatic insertions.

Diegetic Music Music that emanates from within the world of the story, usually meaning that the characters can hear it. Music they listen to in the car, the orchestra tuning up at the opera they attend, songs they sing in the pub: all these are examples of music coming from within the diegesis of the movie. Compare *non-diegetic music*.

Diminuendo Getting quieter.

Discord A group of notes played together that do not sound pleasantly harmonious in the conventional sense. Discords can be harsh and abrasive or soft and gentle and ideas of discord have changed with time.

Dissolve The brief superimposition of two images so that they appear on screen momentarily together. A smoother editing transition than a cut, a dissolve often intimates either the passage of time or a movement forwards or backwards in time. A dissolve can be quick (a quarter of a second), or long (three seconds). Compare *double exposure*.

Dissonance Another word for *discord*.

Divisi Divided into many parts. It is customary for the violins in an orchestra to be organised into first, second and third violins; *divisi* string writing can call for these sections to be subdivided still further right down to individual desks or players. A *divisi* string sound is one of the hallmarks of the lush, Romantic style of movie scoring dominant in Hollywood in the 1930s-1940s.

Dotted Rhythm In musical notation, the addition of a dot after a note increases its value by half. Typically, this is compensated for by shortening another note or notes to make up for the extra time allotted the dotted note, thus enabling the music to keep time *bar* by *bar*.

Double Exposure Two images appear on screen at the same time for an extended period of time. Compare *dissolve*. More than two images on screen is referred to as multiple exposure.

Ellipsis In editing a shot transition that enables time to be dropped out. Rather than show the hero running up all twenty four stairs to evade his pursuers, it is enough for the editor to show him running up the first six before cutting to a shot from the top of the stairs showing him running up the last six. We neither notice the sleight of hand nor miss the dozen stairs elided by the editor and this speeds the sequence up considerably. Similarly, a narrative ellipsis moves the narrative forwards in time, as summed up by the intertitle: 'Seven months later...'.

Etude A piece written as a practising aid for a musician. Etudes typically foreground one specific technique, allowing the performer to concentrate on this aspect of her playing. Some composers, such as Frederic Chopin (1810-1849), have elevated the etude into an artform as absorbing as any other.

Extreme Close Up A small detail is framed by the camera and fills the screen. Extreme close ups are generally used sparingly as their intensity can become wearing after a while.

Extreme Long Shot The subject of the shot is very small and far away from the camera, and the frame composition is dominated by their environment. Extreme long shots are often used at the beginning and end of scenes in order to fix the location in the audience's mind, or whenever the filmmaker wants to recontextualise the action. Explosions are also typically filmed in extreme long shot endowing the pyrotechnics with a sense of scale.

Fifth The *interval* arrived at by climbing four *scalar* steps away from any given note e.g. C-G, D-A, E flat-B flat etc. It's called a fifth because the G is the fifth note of a *diatonic scale* beginning on C, as the A is of a scale beginning on D and so on.

Figure A short musical phrase.

Flat See *note*.

Form The underlying structure of a composition or a passage of music. *Pure music* is seldom entirely spontaneous, but rather organised according to a wide variety of different forms, sonata form, rondo form, theme and variations, fugal form and so on. Film music, while it can don these clothes from time to time, has formal concerns of its own. It is shaped not only by abstract notions of repetition, variation and contrast as with pure music but by where it is to begin and end, its need to respond one way or another to narrative stimuli and the need to produce accents, climaxes or other effects to mark specific moments within a scene. These concerns, and others like them, dictate the composer's choice of rhythm, *tempo*, *orchestration* and whether the music is *melodic*, *motific* or *textural*.

Formalism The composition of music privileging artistic technique over content. A pejorative term and a highly subjective notion.

Forte Loud.

Fortissimo Very loud.

Fourth The *interval* arrived at by climbing three *scalar* steps away from any given e.g. C-F, D-G, E flat-A flat etc. It's called a fourth because the F is the fourth note of a *diatonic scale* beginning on C, as the G is of a scale beginning on D and so on.

Fragmentation A trait of *modernist* music. A fragmented passage is one in which a series of seemingly random and unrelated musical events occur without the underlying structural logic provided by a constant *tempo*, a sense of melodic or harmonic evolution, or of underlying musical *form*. Whether loud or quiet, fragmented music can often be disturbing and chaotic and, like *atonality*, is consequently a stock element of horror music.

Glissando A nebulous effect that changes according to the instrument performing it. On piano a glissando is created when a finger is run rapidly over the keys in any direction. Similarly, a harp glissando is created when the player runs a finger or fingers rapidly across the strings. But on stringed instruments a glissando is created by sliding a finger up or down the string(s), bringing notes that fall outside the customary *tones* and *semitones* of the scale (microtones) into play. A trombonist can use her slide to create a glissando, while woodwind players can glissando from one note to another by increasing lip pressure.

Habanera A Cuban rhythm named after the island's capital Havana, most often realised as a *dotted crotchet* followed by a *quaver* and two more *crotchets*.

Hard Out A loud ending to a music cue, often unresolved harmonically, striving for a stridently dramatic effect. Compare *sneaking out* and see *harmonic resolution*.

Harmony 1) The structure, functions and relationships of *chords*: what notes make them up, what they are used for within a passage of music, how they sound together and how a composer can move from one to another in a musically coherent way. This is a hugely complex subject: American composer Walter Piston (1894-1976) wrote a book 592 pages long on the subject. In this sense harmony refers to *dissonant* chords as well as those that sound 'harmonious'. 2) A second melody or group of chords that support the main melodic line.

Harmonic Progression The sequential movement of *chords* within a passage of music. The smallest possible element of harmonic progression consists of two chords played one after another. Our experience of listening to music leads us to expect chord sequences to progress in certain familiar ways. Pop music often features a highly conventionalised sense of harmonic progression, Blues even more so. Composers of all kinds can surprise us by subverting these expectations. The typical goal of a harmonic progression is a sense of *harmonic resolution*.

Harmonic Resolution A satisfying feeling of completion in the music, sometimes only temporary, which seems to bring a *harmonic progression* to a close. Typically this is achieved through a *cadence* to the *tonic* chord of the key, C *major* if the piece is in C or C *minor* if it's in C minor. As with *harmonic progression*, it is an effect that listeners are entirely used to even if they are not sure how it happens.

High Angle The camera is placed above the eye level of the subject, looking down on him. Compare *low angle*.

Home Key The *key* a film score concludes in. This can be signalled at the beginning of the picture and worked back towards throughout the subsequent score. The return to the home key at the film's ending gives a suitable feeling of closure to the movie and, presumably, the composer a burst of job satisfaction. See *key* for more on the use of *tonal centres* in film scoring.

Hurry Cue A cue intended to add a sense of urgency and energy to an action sequence. Typically this is achieved by adopting a fast tempo, increasing the volume and writing *motifically* rather than *melodically*, using upward *modulations* to increase the tension and downward ones to slacken it off.

Impressionism A term used normally in connection with the works of Claude Debussy (1862-1918) and Maurice Ravel (1875-1937), two French composers concerned with tone colours, shifting musical textures and a sensual approach to melody, harmony, rhythm and orchestration. The term draws an analogy between their music and the techniques of Impressionist painters.

Index An indication of something. A puddle is an index of rain that has fallen recently.

Intercut Footage One sequence of images interpolated into another by the editor. Images of a house on fire can be intercut with others showing its owner working obliviously in an office. Compare *cross-cutting*.

Intertextuality A technique whereby one artwork makes a self-conscious reference to another.

Interval The distance in pitch between two notes.

Invert(ed) Pedal A high note which is sustained unchangingly either on its own or during a harmonic progression. Compare *pedal point/pedal note*.

Inversion A voicing of a *chord* where its root note is not at its base. A C major *triad* can be played simply as C-E-G. It would be said to be inverted if the chord was played as E-G-C', with the root note C on top of the pile an octave higher rather that forming its foundation. A further inversion of the same C major chord would be G-C'-E'.

Key The particular scale a composer has used as the basis for a composition. It is named after the *note* (A-B-C-D-E-F-G and the various *flats* and *sharps* of the *semitones* between them) that takes on the rôle of Doh in a Doh-Re-Me . . . *scalar* sequence. Compositions can move from one key to another at any point through *modulation* of key. From Baroque times certain keys have become associated with certain ideas. C *major* (a scale running from C to C on just the white keys of a piano) is allied with purity and light; the E flat major of Beethoven's 'Eroica' symphony has subsequently been associated with heroism because of this key's connection with military brass instruments; D *minor* can be conceptualised as demonic after the music Mozart composed for Don Giovanni's descent into hell; F# as very exotic because of distance from C. If some film scores have a *home key*, many others used the repeated return to specific keys as a structuring device. In his score for *Lord of the Rings: The Fellowship of the Ring* (2001), Howard Shore reverts to a demonic D minor every time the forces of Saruman and Sauron are shown; the music for the Shire is written in an altogether more wholesome C major.

Key Centre The scale at the heart of a passage of music. A stable key centre is one where there is little doubt as to what *key* the music is written in; an unstable key centre problematises this and is often associated with highly *chromatic* writing or a move to *atonality*.

Klezmer Music A traditional Jewish folk style, typically foregrounding solo violin and clarinet. John Williams alludes to this tradition allotting prominent parts to these instruments in his score for *Schindler's List* (1993).

Leitmotif A brief motif or musical figure that appears in the score whenever a specific character, place, thing or abstract idea appears or is alluded to on screen. Richard Wagner (1813-1883) formalised the technique in his 'Ring Cycle' of operas, using it as an important structural device unifying his grand conception. A leitmotif must sound appropriate for what it refers to: Darth Vader would look silly if he came on screen announced by a trilling piccolo. Leitmotifs can also be varied to suit the fortunes of the narrative elements they symbolise, sounding happy when things are going well and sad when they are not.

Longline Melody A lyrical, fully developed tune typically structured around a series of eight-bar phrases. Compare with *motif*.

Low Angle The camera is placed below the eye level of the subject of the shot, looking up at her. Compare with *high angle*.

Magnetic Tape Recording on to tape, an advance that allowed for easier editing and manipulation of sound, longer stretches of sound/music to be recorded and had the added advantage of improving overall fidelity to the original sound – the pops and crackles of earlier disc-based systems were eliminated.

Major Key One of the two predominant scales of western music, the other being the *minor*. Major key writing tends to sound happier than minor key music. 'Ode to Joy' by Beethoven (1770-1827) is an example of major key music, while the beginning of the 'Funeral March' by Frederic Chopin (1810-1849) is written in the darker world of a more sombre minor key.

Major Seventh A *colour chord* created by placing a *seventh* over a *major triad*. A C major seventh chord would be notated: C-E-G-B.

Major Third A note an *interval* of two whole *tones* away from another. E is a major third away from C, and is of crucial importance in establishing *major key tonality*. If the E was a *minor third*, just one and a half tones away from C, C *minor* rather than major would be strongly suggested.

Marcato A heavily accented, emphatic playing style.

Melodic Writing Writing in which the expression of melody is uppermost in the composer's mind. Compare with *motific writing* and *musical texture*.

Metre The underlying rhythm beneath a melody or *harmonic progression*. Two particularly common metres are three beats in the bar (3:4 time) and four beats in the bar (4:4 or 'common' time).

Mickey-Mousing A scoring technique whereby the composer slavishly mimics in sound what is happening on screen. If a character is rushing up a flight of stairs, the music races upwards in pitch; if a character throws himself off a cliff the music plunges down in pitch. As the name suggests, it was a technique favoured by composers working in cartoons, such as the great Scott Bradley who scored many of the most enduring 'Tom and Jerry' shorts: as Jerry Mouse blinks at the camera, a xylophone dinks in time with his eyelids. While often used pejoratively to decry the lack of imagination displayed by film composers, as Bradley's work suggests Mickey-Mousing can be an artform in and of itself and live action film composers often use the technique to great and subtle effect.

Mid-Tempo Medium paced music, neither markedly fast nor noticeably slow. Compare with *up-tempo*.

Minim See *note*.

Minor Key One of the two predominant scales of western music, the other being the *major*. Minor key writing tends to sound darker and more sombre than major key music. The beginning of Chopin's 'Funeral March' is an example of music written in a minor key while Beethoven's 'Ode to Joy' is written in a brighter, happier major key.

Minor Third A note an *interval* of one and a half *tones* away from another. E flat is a minor third away from C, and is of crucial importance in establishing *minor key tonality*. If the E flat was a *major third*, two full tones away from C, C *major* rather than minor would be strongly suggested.

Mix 1) The mixture of sonic elements on a soundtrack. Sometimes music is uppermost in the mix, at other times sound effects and dialogue are foregrounded. 2) The sense of sonic perspective in the musical element of a soundtrack. An instrument brought to the fore in the mix is one that sounds louder or closer to the microphone than the others; one dropping into the background of the mix sounds more quietly or from further away.

Modal Writing Writing using *scales* other than the conventional *major* and *minor*. Depending on which mode the composer selects, the sound created can suggest anything from antiquity to spirituality to a sense of the exotic.

Mode Another word for *scale*.

Modernism An avant-garde musical movement spearheaded by the likes of Igor Stravinsky (1882-1971) and Arnold Schoenberg (1874-1951) that challenged the 'givens' of conventional musical wisdom by favouring the free use of *dissonance*, the liberation of rhythm and writing for often unconventional ensembles. Tone clusters, pitch slides and fragmentation are all modernist techniques.

Modulation Changing *key*. An upward modulation shifts the *tonal centre* higher, a downward modulation moves it lower.

Montage Sequence A fragmentary series of images collapsing a lot of story time into a little screen time. The building of a ship may take many months, but can be suggested on screen in a few moments by quickly editing together a series of shots showing the various stages of the process from inception to completion and launch. Because montage sequences are by their very nature disjointed, a feeling of smoothness and continuity is given by using music beneath the images.

Motif A brief musical phrase or idea which will often recur.

Motific Writing A passage of music created by the manipulation of a motif or series of motifs. The motifs are typically repeated, *transposed* or *varied*. The creation of melody is not the prime concern of motific writing. Compare *melodic writing*.

Music Bridge Music from one scene that carries over into the next for a few moments, thereby smoothing a potentially jarring cut between the two. Equally, the bridge can run the other way with music from the second scene beginning a few moments before we leave the first. Sound, incidently, can be used in the same way, in which case it's termed a sound bridge.

Musical Silence The absence of music from parts of a film that have been left unscored by the composer.

Mute A device used to soften or change the usual sound of an instrument.

Narrative Repetition An event that occurs more than once in a story. The repetition often invites comparison between the occurrences.

Narrative Symmetry Deep echoes set up by the story. In *Jurassic Park* (1993), the humans start out controlling the dinosaurs, then the dinosaurs dominate the humans; the quasi-family unit of Alan, Ellie and the two children are balanced out by the group dynamic of the velociraptors that hunt them at the end. *E.T. The Extra-Terrestrial* (1982) begins with E.T. arriving on earth and leaves with him ascending into the heavens once more; Elliot's close bond with the creature is balanced out both by the antagonistic relationship the youngster has with his big brother and by E.T. standing in for Elliot's absent father.

Neo-Romanticism The dominant idiom of film scoring, where screen composers working in the twentieth (and now twenty-first) century harness the style and precepts of art music's Romanticism, a movement often associated with the nineteenth century.

Non-diegetic Music Music in a film that the audience can hear but the characters cannot. Most commonly this is the scored music provided by the composer, although pop music can serve just as well. Compare with *diegetic music*.

Note A single musical *tone* named according to its pitch using a letter of the alphabet between A and G. The note D flat is a *semitone* below D, while a D sharp is a semitone above D. Notes are also defined by their duration. A semibreve lasts a count of four; a minim a count of two; a crotchet a count of one; two quavers make a count of one beat; four semiquavers together make up a count of one beat. A triplet is a group of three notes performed in the time normally allotted to two. See also *dotted rhythm*.

Octave (Octaved, Octaval) The *interval* between the first and last notes of a *major* or *minor* scale. Notes which are an octave apart are called by the same letter. Encompassed within an octave are the eight notes of the *scale*. Octaval playing occurs when the same melody or accompanying pattern is heard at intervals an octave, or several octaves, apart.

Orchestration The choice of instrumentation for a passage of music. When allocating parts to instruments the composer must bear in mind the *timbre* of the instruments, their range in terms of pitch and what it is humanly possible to play on them. Then, how the parts written for these instruments sound in combination is of key importance.

Ornament An often fleeting and nimble embellishment of a melody.

Ostinato A pattern of notes or rhythms that repeats itself over and over.

Parallel Intervals (i.e. thirds, fourths, fifths) As a phrase or melody develops on one line, another shadows, or parallels, its movements above at the constant interval of a third, fourth fifth etc.

Parallel Sequence An editing technique whereby events happening in two or more distinct locations are cut together, creating a powerful sense of simultaneity. Often, the filmmakers are also prompting the audience to compare and contrast the elements. At the climax of *The Godfather* (1972), Francis Ford Coppola constructs a classic parallel sequence cutting together shots of Al Pacino attending a baptism and footage of a series of gangland executions as his rivals are bumped off one by one. Watching the sequence unfold, there is a strong sense that the events we are watching are happening at the same time; we infer that Al Pacino has a hand in both the baptism and the murders; and we might feel ourselves speculating about the dramatic double standards on show.

Passacaglia A series of *variations* on a theme sounding over a constant bass accompaniment. Often played at a leisurely pace.

Pastoral Music evoking a rural feel, typically foregrounding French horns, woodwind and strings. The device is used famously in the Beethoven symphony given that name (no.6).

Pedal Point/Pedal Note A low note which is sustained unchangingly during a harmonic progression. Compare *invert pedal*.

Pentatonic A scale made up from just five notes that span the octave. If you run your fingers up the black notes on a piano this is the scale you'll be tracing. It often has a markedly Oriental feel, although folk music traditions from all over the world build melodies from it. Hollywood composers traditionally score scenes featuring Native Americans using a pentatonic scale. Meanwhile, 'Amazing Grace', is also a pentatonic melody. Differences in orchestration, harmony and intonation help lock the pentatonic into one musical tradition or another.

Percussion A section of the orchestra comprising instruments that can be hit, scraped or shaken. Timpani, xylophone, tambourine, triangle and snare drum are percussion instruments. This section can be subdivided into tuned and untuned percussion; tuned instruments produce a note with a definite pitch while untuned ones are used for their rhythmic and *timbral* properties.

Piano 1) Quiet 2) A tuned *percussion* instrument.

Pianissimo Very quiet.

Pitch Bend The effect achieved by sliding around a note or playing a *glissando* on a string instrument. Pitch bends allow microtones (intervals of pitch between *tones* and *semitones*) to be heard, and the effect produced is often an eerie or scary one. Pitch bends are another technique from avant-garde music incorporated into the horror sound.

Pizzicato A musical marking asking string players to pluck their instruments rather than bow them.

Plainchant Also known as Gregorian chant, plainchant or plainsong refers to liturgical melodies sung by unison voices. The term originates in the thirteenth century when it had to be differentiated from the emerging *polyphonic* style, but the form predates this considerably.

Point of View Shot A shot in which the viewer experiences a powerful sense that s/he is seeing what the character sees as they see it. Conventionally, point of view shots are preceded by the character looking at something, then the editor cuts to what it is they are looking at. Other point of view devices include masked shots such as the classic binocular or telescope effect which instantly makes us feel we see what a character is seeing as they see it.

Polyphonic Music that is conceived around many independent parts sounding simultaneously. If *plainchant* comprises one unison melodic line, a composer of polyphonic music is concerned with weaving together many different vocal or instrumental lines all of which can be heard as melodic in their own right. The sky is the limit here, Thomas Tallis (c. 1505-1585) writing a remarkable piece, 'Spem in alium', for forty independent vocal parts.

Portamento An effect used in the performance of vocal or string music where a *note* is slid up or down to in a brief, continuous glide for (occasionally florid) expressive effect.

Presto Very fast.

Programme Music Music with a narrative purpose that seeks to describe a place, tell a story, characterise an individual etc.

Pure Music Music without a narrative programme.

Quaver See *note*.

Rallentando Becoming gradually slower.

Realist Film A loaded term in film studies. A realist film is one in which the filmmakers typically deal with a social problem in as direct and unstylised a way as possible. Often politicised individuals, realist filmmakers seek to use cinema as an instrument of social change rather than as an escapist diversion. Location shooting, non-professional actors, a slow editing pace, deep focus images, the avoidance of special effects and an unblinking approach to often grim subject matter are some of the hallmarks of a realist text. The rôle of music is often, though not always, downplayed: the British realist filmmaker Ken Loach speaks of cutting to music as a 'treat' he only rarely allows himself. What realism does not mean is that something looks realistic, i.e. the space ships in *Star Wars* (1977). They might look convincing, but *Star Wars* is not a realist film.

Recapitulation The return of musical elements heard before in a piece of music, sometimes subtly altered, which in a film score helps unify the music and in art music can create a sense of homecoming, completion and resolution.

Register (Lower, Upper) The range of different pitches an instrument can produce. The upper register comprises the *notes* to the top of this range, the lower those towards the bottom of it.

Reprise The repetition of material heard before.

Resolution See *harmonic resolution*.

Rhapsodic Music that is heroically free flowing in character.

Romanticism A term used to describe nineteenth-century music after Beethoven. During the Romantic era, art music became increasingly complex harmonically and rhythmically, composers became concerned with expressing a sense of their own individuality in music. Romantic music sought to articulate the inner world of the individual, or to tell a story (see *programme music*) in musical terms and also in many ways struggled against musical convention. It is not hard to see how Romantic music became the blueprint for film composers: it provided a ready-made library of musical effects depicting character and narrative events, audiences liked it and it talked up the cultural status of movies given the high culture associations of orchestral music. One other aspect of later Romantic music was a tendency towards the spectacular, an element not missed by movie producers.

Saturation Score Unlike a score made up of discrete *cues*, a saturation score begins with the opening title and hardly lets up again until the end of the movie. Many of John Williams' scores for Steven Spielberg and George Lucas and Danny Elfman's for Tim Burton are good examples.

Scalar Moving in stepwise motion, along the *notes* of a *diatonic scale*.

Scale A progression of notes in either an ascending or descending order.

Second The *interval* arrived at by climbing one *scalar* step away from any given note e.g. C-D, D-E, E flat-F etc. It's called a second because the D is the second note of a *diatonic scale* beginning on C, as the E is of a scale beginning on D and so on.

Segue Another word for *dissolve*.

Semibreve See *note*.

Semitone Half a *tone*. There are twelve semitones in an octave, and each key on the piano constitutes an individual semitone.

Semiquaver See *note*.

Serial Music After Schoenberg's experiments with *atonal* music, serial music was his effort to formalise the potential chaos of the new sound world. Rather than *notes* being allowed to sound in any random order, serial music sought to structure the effects of atonality by requiring the composer to formulate a tone row, a sequence of twelve notes which could then be used to generate music through being played the right way round, backwards, upside down, in *transposition* and so on.

Sforzando A sudden and surprisingly loud accent on one *note* or *chord*.

Sharp See *note*.

Simultaneous Track and Zoom A starling in-camera visual effect achieved by tracking the camera back and zooming the lens in on the subject at the same time, providing a eye-popping distortion of perspective.

Sneaking Out An expression neatly describing the phenomenon where, at the end of a cue, the music becomes quieter and quieter so that when it eventually stops the audience doesn't notice because they're not really listening to it any more. An unobtrusive way of ending a cue. Compare *hard out*.

Solo An instrument or a voice performing on its own, either with or without accompaniment.

Sonata Form A venerable musical form organising art music compositions ranging from the movements of symphonies and to those of chamber music. At its simplest, sonata form is tripartite in nature: the material, often two contrasting musical *subjects*, is presented in the Exposition; it is expanded on in the Development section; the initial material is then returned to in the Recapitulation. Sometimes a coda follows on behind, a brief section bringing the movement to a satisfying close. A plan of *key* changes is normally also followed by the composer allowing for harmonic contrast from section to section.

Source Music 1) Another term for *diegetic music*. 2) Music in a film drawn from sources other than the composer of the score, often pop music but equally hymn tunes, military music etc.

Spike The musical accenting, often dramatic, of a precise moment in a sequence.

Staccato Played in a crisp and detached fashion.

Strings The section of the orchestra comprising violins, violas, cellos and double basses. It is customary to exclude other stringed instruments such as piano, guitar and harp from this section.

Subject A theme, a melody, a musical idea.

Sul Ponticello An instruction asking string players to bow closer to the bridge than normal, producing a thin, spidery effect lacking the resonance we expect from these instruments.

Syncopation The characteristic rhythm of jazz, where the accent falls on parts of the bar not normally accented (e.g. on the second beat of the common 4:4 bar).

Tempo The speed at which the music is played.

Temporal Transition Any of a number of techniques the editor has of signalling movement forwards or backwards in story time.

Tessitura An instrument's range, as encompassed by its top and bottom notes.

Textural Writing, Texture Writing that is led neither by melody nor by a *motific* approach, but focuses instead on producing a *timbral* effect more concerned with the sound quality produced by certain instrumental or harmonic groupings.

Theme 1) Narrative: the underlying subject explored by the story. 2) Music: a melody.

Timbre The quality of sound tone displayed by a voice, instrument or combination of instruments.

Timbral Adjective derived from *timbre*.

Timing Film cues must begin and end at precise moments, and hit prearranged accent points in between. Part of the film composer's art is the development of the ability to be in the right musical place at the right time: the music must sound as if it is doing all of this effortlessly.

Title Sequence The part of the film, often but by no means always at the beginning and the end of the movie, where the names of those involved in the production appear on screen. The title sequence at the beginning is referred to as the opening title, and that at the end the closing title.

Tonal Centre The key that the music is in, or that it gravitates back towards if the composer has digressed harmonically. See *key centre*.

Tonal Music Music that is informed by the principles of either *diatonic harmony* or *chromaticism*. Compare *atonal music*.

Tonality The key that the music is in. See *key centre*.

Tone 1) An interval comprising two *semitones*. 2) A *note*. 3) The quality of sound or *timbre*.

Tone Cluster A group of *notes* close together in *scalar* terms that are sounded simultaneously and in a sustained manner.

Tonic The first note of the scale, the one that it's named after. C is the tonic of C major and minor.

Tracking Shot The camera is mounted on a carriage known as a dolly which is in turn placed on rails. The dolly is then pushed along the rails producing a smooth, linear movement of the camera. The camera can track in, out, forwards, backwards, left, right or in an arc around the subject.

Transpose To translate into another *key* without altering any of the *intervals* between the notes.

Tremolo The rapid, sustained reiteration of a single *note*, or the equally rapid alternation of two or more notes. Often used to indicate excitement, trepidation etc.

Triad A simple chord of three *notes*. In the key of C a major triad in the key can be notated C-E-G, a minor triad as C-E flat-G, a diminished triad as C-E flat-G flat and an augmented triad as C-E-G sharp. Triadic harmony produces a clear and unambiguous sense of *tonality*.

Trill An *ornament* consisting of the rapid alternation of adjacent *notes*. A trill can be fleeting or extended.

Triple Time Three beats in the *bar*; waltz time. See *metre*.

Triplet See *note*.

Tritone An *interval* comprising three full *tones*, highly unstable in *harmonic* terms and outlawed by the church in medieval times as the *diabolus in musica* (the devil in music). To this day a difficult interval to sing.

Tutti All of the performers of the orchestra, or a section of the orchestra, playing at the same time (i.e. tutti strings).

Two-part Invention A composition for two players/groups of players/melodic lines making use of the techniques of *counterpoint*.

Unison Two or more instruments, groups of instruments or singers playing or singing the same melodic line using either the same pitches or *parallel octaves*.

Up-tempo Fast.

Variation, Variant The modification of a theme or motif in such a way as to alter in noticeably.

Verité A documentary style of shooting typified by the shooting of *actuality* footage, often of the everyday world, on location using hand held cameras. The style is so distinctive that fiction film can use similar techniques, in particular hand held cameras, in an effort to attain a similar feeling of spontaneity and verisimilitude.

Versicle A short verse sung by a priest, choir or congregation.

Vibrato An expressive technique whereby the player or singer sounds or sings tiny and rapid fluctuations of pitch so a note is not played and sung purely, but inflected by these quick pitch changes. Not an unpleasant effect unless overdone.

Vocalise The singing of notes but not words: Aaah, Oooh, Mmmm etc.

Whip Pan The camera pans right or left quickly and suddenly, creating a blur of motion on the screen.

Woodwind The section of the orchestra comprising piccolos, flutes, clarinets, oboes, bassoons, cor anglais and so on.

Zoom The shrinking or magnification of the size of the subject within the frame by means of a specific lens. A zoom in makes what is shot grow bigger, a zoom out makes it grow smaller.

Bibliography

Adaire, Gilbert and Glen Riddick, *A Night at the Pictures: Ten Decades of British Film*, Columbia Books in association with the British Film Year Book, 1985

Aldred, John, 'Korda's Denham Studios' (internet), Association of Motion Picture Sound, Pinewood & Denham

Barnouw, Erik, *Documentary – A History of the Non-Fiction Film*, OUP, 1993

British Music, The Journal of the British Music Society, Vol. 15 (1993)

Brownlow, Kevin, *David Lean*, Richard Cohen Books, 1996

Bruce, David, *Scotland – The Movie*, Polygon, 1996

Cameron, Ken, *All Squeak and No Bubble* (unpublished autobiography: a copy of this book is held at the BFI)

Carpenter, Humphrey, *Benjamin Britten: A Biography*, Faber & Faber, 1992

Close-up, vol. v, no. 5, 1929

Coutts, Ben, *Bred in the Highlands*, Mercat Press, 1997

Cross, Brenda (ed.), *The Film 'Hamlet'*, Saturn Press, 1948

Donnelly, KJ, *Film Music – Critical Approaches*, Edinburgh University Press, 2001

Drazin, Charles, *Korda: The Definitive Biography*, Sidgwick & Jackson, 2002

Fisher, Hugh, *The Story of the Sadler's Wells Ballet*, Adam and Charles Black, 1954

Holloway, Ronald, *The Bulgarian Cinema*, Associated University Press, 1986

Howitt, Basil, *Love Lives of the Great Composers, Sound and Vision*, Toronto, Canada, 1995

Huntley, John, *British Film Music*, Skelton Robinson, 1947

Jackson, Gerald, *First Flute*, Dent, 1968

Kennedy, Michael, *Richard Strauss*, OUP, 1995

Korda, Michael, *Charmed Lives*, Allen Lane, 1979

Limbacher, James L, *Film Music*, The Scarecrow Press, 1974

Listener, *The,* 27 October 1960, article by Edmund Tracy

Low, Rachel, *Film Making in the 1930s*, George Allen & Unwin, 1985

Macdonald, Kevin, *Emeric Pressburger: The Life and Death of a Screenwriter*, Faber & Faber 1994

Macnab, Geoffrey, *J. Arthur Rank and the British Film Industry*, Routledge, 1993

Manvell, Roger (ed.) *The Penguin Film Review*, 1947

Manvell, Roger and John Huntley, *The Technique of Film Music,* Focal Press, 1954 (produced by committee of William Alwyn, Ken Cameron and Muir Mathieson)

Matchett, Dr Grace and Frank Spedding, *The Royal Scottish Academy of Music and Drama, The First 150 Years*, 1997

Murphy, Robert, *British Cinema and the Second World War*, Continuum, 2000

Noble, Peter (ed.), *The British Film Year Book, 1949-50*, The British Film Industry, 1950

Review, New York Times, 1929

Rotha, Paul, *Documentary Diary*, Hill & Wang, 1973

Rozsa, Miklos, *Double Life*, Allen Lane, Penguin Books, 1980

Ryan, Paul (ed.), *Never Apologise; The Collected Writings of Lindsay Anderson*, Plexus Publishing Ltd, 2004

Schoenberg, Harold C, *The Lives of the Great Composers*, third edition, Abacus, 1997

Stephen and Jones, *The British Labour Movement & Film*, Routledge & Paul, 1987

Swynnoe, Jan G, *The Best Years of British Film Music, 1936-1958*, Boydell Press, 2002

The Times, Letter to, 7 February 1952

Tonks, Paul, *Film Music*, Pocket Essential, 2001

Towers, Harry Alan and Leslie Mitchell, *The March of the Movies*, Saturn Press, 1948

Warrack, Guy, *The Royal College of Music: The First Eighty-Five Years*, 1970 (unpublished, a copy of the manuscript is in the RCM)

Wright, Basil, *The Long View*, Secker & Warburg, 1974

Whittall, Arnold, *Romantic Music – A Concise History*, Thames and Hudson, 1987

INDEX